Excavations at Cerro de Trincheras, Sonora, México

Volume I

edited by
Randall H. McGuire and Elisa Villalpando

compiled by
Stacy A. Tchorzynski
Félix Acuto
and
Amy Groleau

Arizona State Museum Archaeological Series 204

Arizona State Museum
The University of Arizona
Tucson, Arizona 85721-0026

Printed in the United States of America

ISBN (paper): 978-1-889747-89-7
Library of Congress Control Number: 2011937527

ARIZONA STATE MUSEUM ARCHAEOLOGICAL SERIES

General Editor: Richard C. Lange
Technical Editors: Laura Burghardt, Elizabeth May, Laura Eichelberger

The *Archaeological Series* of the Arizona State Museum, The University of Arizona, publishes the results of research in archaeology and related disciplines conducted in the Greater Southwest. Original, monograph-length manuscripts are considered for publication, provided they deal with appropriate subject matter. Information regarding procedures or manuscript submission and review is given under Research Publications on the Arizona State Museum website: *www.statemuseum.arizona.edu/research/pubs.* Information may be also obtained from the General Editor, *Archaeological Series*, Arizona State Museum, P.O. Box 210026, The University of Arizona, Tucson, Arizona, 85721-0026; Email: langer@email.arizona.edu. Electronic publications and previous volumes in the Arizona State Museum Library or available from the University of Arizona Press are listed on the website noted above.

The Arizona State Museum *Archaeological Series* is grateful to the many donors and supporters who continue to make this publication possible, particularly those who supported the 200th volume of the *Archaeological Series.*

Cover: Aerial photograph of Cerro de Trincheras (courtesy of Adriel Heisey).

Distributed by The University of Arizona Press, P.O. Box 210055, The University of Arizona, Tucson, Arizona, 85721-0055.

Contents

Volume I Contents

Volume II Contents

Figures

Volume I Figures

Figures, continued

Figures, continued

Figures, continued

Figures, continued

Figures, continued

Volume II Figures

Figures, continued

Figures, continued

Figures, continued

Figures, continued

Figures, continued

Tables

Volume I Tables

Tables, continued

Tables, continued

Volume II Tables

Tables, continued

Acknowledgments

The Cerro de Trincheras Excavation project was the work of many hands, many hearts and many minds. The project was a collaborative bi-national effort with researchers from numerous institutions in the United States and México. We undertook eight months of excavation at Cerro de Trincheras evenly divided between the springs of 1995 and 1996. Each season the project included a dozen or more archaeologists and 30 to 40 local people. We carried out our analyses at the Centro INAH Sonora, the Arizona State Museum (University of Arizona), and at Binghamton University. The writing, editing and production of this volume also involved persons at all three of these institutions. The National Science Foundation funded our research with grant SBR9320224 and four undergraduate training supplements. We thank John Yellen for all of his advice and help at the NSF.

Forty-five people worked on the excavation in the spring of 1995 (Figure 0.1). The archaeologists included Elisa Villalpando, Randall McGuire, Maria O'Donovan, John McGregor, Emiliano Gallaga, Eréndira Contreras, Mary F. Price, Janna Huey, Mike Rudler, Guadalupe Sánchez de Carpenter, Victoria Vargas, and Víctor Ortega (Figure 0.2). During that season archaeologists Jane Kelley, Lloyd Neff and Arthur MacWilliams spent several days in the field as volunteers on the project. A total of 30 local people assisted the project as cooks, laboratory assistants, and laborers, and are named in the list below. We would most especially thank our excellent cooks Hortensia Zavalza and María Teresa Anaya.

Martha Álvarez	Carlos Bejarano B.	Carlos Bejarano V.
Eugenio Bejarano	Fernando Bejarano	Martín Campillo
Ramón Cáñez	Rubén Cáñez	Rafael Celaya
Francisco Diaz	Rubén Espinoza	Noe Martínez García
Paola Gaxiola	Edgardo Martínez	Luis Carlos Martínez
Mercedes Martínez	Heriberto Murrieta	Juan Murrieta
Rafael Murrieta	Raúl Murrieta	Mauro Reyna
Arturo Salazar	Medardo Salazar	AntonioVingochea E.
AntonioVingochea M.	Heriberto Vingochea	Rafael Yescas
Ramón Yescas		

During the spring of 1996 forty-one people assisted the excavations (Figure 0.3). The archaeologists included Elisa Villalpando, Randall McGuire, Maria O'Donovan, John McGregor, Emiliano Gallaga, Eréndira Contreras, Júpiter Martinez, Víctor Ortega, Bridget Zavala, Gillian Newell, Debbie Landers, and Beth Bagwell (Figure 0.4). Archaeologists Gavin Archer and Victoria Vargas assisted us for a week as volunteers. A total of 28 local people assisted the project as cooks, laboratory assistants, and laborers, and are named below. For the second year in a row Hortensia Zavalza and María Teresa Anaya prepared us excellent meals.

Martha Álvarez	Carlos Bejarano B.	Erik Bejarano
Eugenio Bejarano	Frnando Bejarano	Fancisco Bejarano
Rafael Cáñez	Ramón Cáñez	Rafael Celaya
Darío Espinoza	Noe Martínez García	Paola Gaxiola

Figure 0.1. Archaeologists during the 1995 field season.

Figure 0.2. All project personnel, 1995.

Figure 0.3. Archaeologists during the 1996 field season.

Figure 0.4. All project personnel, 1996.

Edgardo Martínez
Mercedes Martínez
Heriberto Murrieta
Rafael Murrieta
Raúl Murrieta
Samuel Murrieta
Leonel Enrique Ochoa
Raúl Rivera
Medardo Salazar
Antonio Vingochea E.
Antonio Vingochea M.
Heriberto Vingochea
Rafael Yescas
Ramón Yescas

The people of Trincheras welcomed us to their community and aided our efforts in many ways. The Ayuntamiento of Trincheras arranged for us to house our lab in the then unused library building. The Presidente Municipal, Medardo Murrieta Reyna, and the Trincheras Cronista Rogelio León assisted us in many ways. Other members of the community who provided us with help included the medical doctors at the Centro de Salud.

The Arizona State Museum (ASM) supported us logistically providing us a postal address, equipment and a base in southern Arizona. We would like to thank Raymond H. Thompson who was director of the ASM at that time, and all of his staff for their help. Suzie and Paul Fish of ASM hosted members of the crew on several visits to Tucson, as did Michael and Annette Schiffer. Mike Jacobs assisted us in viewing ceramic type collections at the museum.

The Centro INAH Sonora in Hermosillo provided institutional support for the project. They provided lab space, computers, and curation of the projects artifacts. In the lab, Víctor Ortega, Emiliano Gallaga, Bridget Zavala, Dawn Greenwald, Penny Minturn, Lorrie Lincoln-Babb, Eréndira Contreras, and Victoria Vargas performed analyses. In addition to the many members of the Centro who worked in the field or did laboratory analysis, we must thank César Villalobos who managed our publication efforts in Hermosillo, and Carlos Licón for his volunteer help during field seasons.

The project contracted with Western Mapping Company (then GeoMap, Inc.) of Tucson, Arizona to do the project mapping. Western Mapping established a site grid and took the field maps, plans and drawings that the field archaeologists made and included them in an AutoCad map of the site. When we produced the final report, Western Mapping prepared maps reproduced in this report and included in the companion materials (http://www.statemuseum.arizona.edu/pubs/archseries/companion_materials.shtml). Jim Holmlund's and his staff's commitment to the project and to archaeological knowledge is evident in the maps of this report.

Binghamton University supported the project in various ways. Many of the faculty in the Department of Anthropology, including William Isbell, Peter Stahl, Mike Little, Charles Cobb and Albert Dekin, provided help to the project. The Public Archaeology Facility (PAF) under the directorship of Nina Versaggi assisted us with computer software. Jim Levandowski of PAF produced Golden Software Surfer maps. David Tuttle developed film, printed pictures and advised us on matters photographic. The staff of the Department of Anthropology, including Ann Pierce, Robin Barron, and Heidi Kenyon, aided us in too many ways to list. The Binghamton University office of grants and research helped us secure grants and manage our money. We would especially like to thank Stephen Gilje, Paul Parker, Lisa Gilroy, Carol Verhoeven and Joe Walker of this office.

The project consulted with the Tohono O'odham Nation concerning the project and the possible reburial of the inhumations that we found. Due to objections from the Consejo de Arqueología de INAH in México we were unable to accomplish the reburial (McGuire 2000, 2008). We do wish, however, to thank Joseph T. Joaquin, José Johnson, and Fernando Valentine of the Tohono O'odham Nation for working with us.

Many of our colleagues helped us with advice or by being sounding boards for our ideas. These individuals would include Ben Nelson, Charlie Miksicek, Gary Nabhan, Todd Bostwick, Jeff Eighmy, Mike Whalen, John Fountain, John Carpenter, and Alan Ferg. Our fieldwork and interpretations are better for their help. Penny Minturn and Lorrie Lincoln-Babb did preliminary analysis of inhumations from the site and Jim Watson followed up with further analysis. Adriel Heisey took aerial photographs of the site and surrounding area for the project.

Most of the chapters in this volume originated as undergraduate honor's theses, tesis de Licenciado, or Master's Theses. Two undergraduates at Binghamton University prepared honor's theses that did not become chapters in this report but that we did use in our analyses. Debra R. Langer (1997) did her thesis on "Site Formation Processes and Ceramics at Cerro de Trincheras." Tracy Erin Hanna (2003) prepared her undergraduate honor's thesis on "A Ceramic Analysis of Form and Function at Cerro de Trincheras."

The process of editing, organizing and formatting the final report took several years and required much work. Krista Feichtinger prepared many of the feature maps in this report. Ann Hull drafted most of the rest of the feature maps, profiles and figures in the report. Félix Acuto translated, assembled and organized our Spanish language report to the Consejo de Arqueología in México. Marina Weinberg aided the translation of abstracts. Amy Groleau, Susan DeLeonardo, Stephanie Bower put in many hours editing and organizing the report. E. Charles Adams and Richard Lange at the ASM managed the publication of this report in the Arizona State Museum Archaeological Series.

Randall McGuire edited and finalized the report during his sabbatical year (2007-2008). During this time he was a visiting researcher at the Crow Canyon Archaeological Center in Cortez, Colorado and at the Department of Anthropology, University of Arizona in Tucson Arizona. He would like to thank both institutions for their support.

This report would never have finally been published without the great effort, dedication and hard work of Stacy Tchorzynski. Stacy worked as a research assistant for two years assembling the manuscript, formatting contributions, scanning photos and doing all of the other tasks necessary to turn the work of over 20 authors into a coherent monograph.

Editor's Note:

Interested researchers should be alerted to the use of site numbers in these volumes. The numbers have been standardized in format, but not all have the attribution normally given to AZSITE numbers. Site records may be located in AZSITE (Arizona State Museum, University of Arizona) or in the Centro Regional del INAH office in Hermosillo, Sonora.

Chapter 1
Introduction

Randall H. McGuire. Binghamton University
Elisa Villalpando. Centro INAH Sonora

Prehispanic northwestern México, that area from the international frontier south to the southern borders of the Mexican states of Sonora and Chihuahua, has been an immense gray zone. Whether it was peripheral to the aboriginal history of the southwestern U.S. or not, it has been peripheral in the minds and theories of both Mexican and U.S. archaeologists (McGuire 2003; Phillips 1989; Whalen and Minnis 2001). Traditionally they explained cultural developments in northwest México in terms of one of two models. Either these developments are simply the southern fringes of the Hohokam, O'otam or Mogollon traditions of the U.S. Southwest (Haury 1976; Hinton 1955) or they result from the intrusion of Mesoamerican merchants or settlers from the south who set up major centers as trade and/or military outposts (Di Peso 1974, 1983; Noguera 1958). Later archaeologists recast these debates using models of World Systems that reached south into Mesoamerica (Weigand 1982; Whitecotton and Pailes 1986), or regional systems and peer polities developing in situ, based primarily on local ecological relationships (McGuire 1999; Minnis 1989; Whalen and Minnis 2001). At the core of all of these debates is the nature of socio-political organization at major northwestern Mexican centers such as Cerro de Trincheras, Trincheras, Sonora, México (Figure 1.1).

Cerro de Trincheras is the largest site in the Trincheras Tradition and the most visually impressive archaeological ruin in Sonora (Figure 1.2). It sits atop a large, isolated, volcanic hill on the south side of the modern town of Trincheras, Sonora. From this perch, the site commands the surrounding landscape and is visible at distances of over 40 km. The hill covers an area of over a kilometer square and rises over 150 m above the surrounding desert floor. The most obvious features at the site are the more than 900 terraces on the slopes of the prominence. Some of these run for 100 m or more, but most are between 15 and 30 m in length. They range in height from tens of centimeters at the base of the hill to more than 3 m high at the summit.

Research Design

Randall McGuire (Binghamton University) and Elisa Villalpando (Centro INAH Sonora) developed the Cerro de Trincheras Excavation project to consider propositions about the prehistoric socio-political organization of Cerro de Trincheras. This project was a bi-national, joint effort by the Centro INAH (Instituto Naciónal de Antropología e Historia) Sonora in Hermosillo, Sonora and Binghamton University in Binghamton, New York, and was supported by the National Science Foundation. The project addressed numerous site issues raised by previous investigators, including the timing of growth at the site, the size and permanence

Figure 1.1. General view of Cerro de Trincheras.

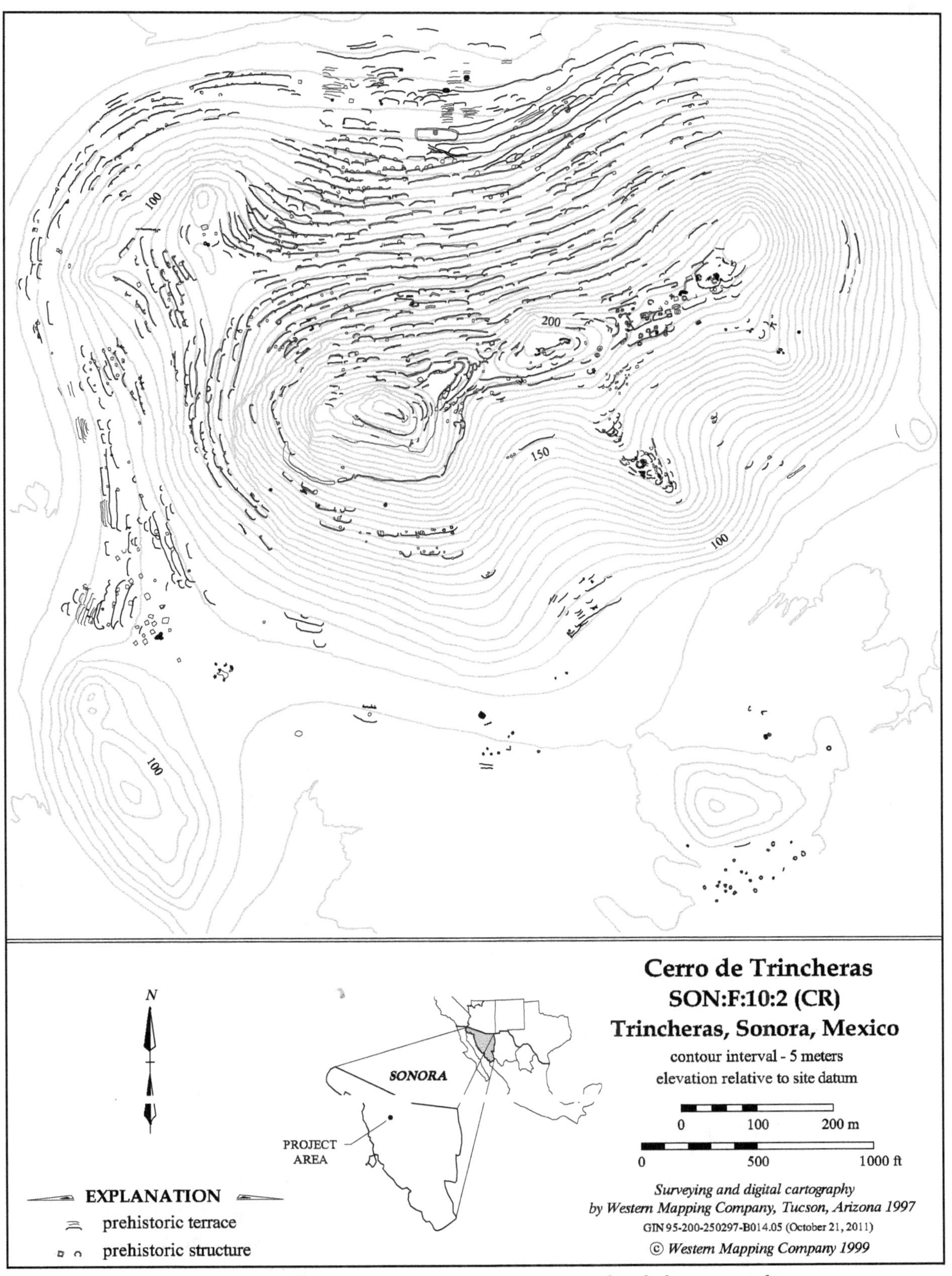

Figure 1.2. Map of Cerro de Trincheras. For a more detailed map, search on http://www.statemuseum.arizona.edu/pubs/archseries/companion_materials.shtml.

of human population, the nature of activities at the site, and the role of the site in a larger regional and inter-regional economic system. We obtained the data to address these questions through extensive excavations at Cerro de Trincheras in the springs of 1995 and 1996. During two four-month fieldwork seasons, we excavated 830 m^3 in 13 different areas both on terraces and around the base of the hill. We exposed 118 prehistoric features, including 15 houses, and recovered over 1,000,000 artifacts, including over 900,000 ceramic sherds. We also collected ethnobotanical samples to reveal prehistoric diets and radiocarbon samples to date the site. We processed 30 radiocarbon dates with 27 of the dates in the range of A.D. 1300 to 1450. This monograph summarizes our excavations, describes the data that we obtained, and draws conclusions concerning the timing of growth at the site, the size and permanence of human population, the nature of activities at the site, and the role of the site in a larger regional and inter-regional economic system.

Overall Theoretical Focus

At the end of the twentieth century, many archaeologists began to question the adequacy of archaeological reconstructions that treat regions as independent, self-contained systems. They noted that, to the extent that an aboriginal society had to interact with other regions in consumption and production, we must consider the larger system of relationships to account for its prehistory. This observation led many to apply some interpretation of Wallerstein's (1974, 1978, 1980) World Systems Theory to the study of ancient pasts both outside (Blanton et al. 1981; Blanton & Feinman 1984; Carmack adn González 2006; Ekholm & Friedman 1982; Kohl 1979; Smith and Berdan 2000) and inside the Southwest (Di Peso 1983; Plog et al. 1982; Plog 1983; Upham 1982; Weigand 1982; Whitecotton & Pailes 1986). Even individuals not advocating World Systems Theory proposed interpretations of prehistory which link the Southwest/Northwest as a whole (Cordell 1997; Cordell and Gumerman 1989; Le Blanc 1986; McGuire 1989) or question the separateness of the Southwest/Northwest from Mesoamerica (Braniff 2001; Mathien & McGuire 1986; McGuire et al. 1994; Weigand and Harbottle 1992). Acceptance of a Southwest/Northwestern prehistory that emphasizes interregional connections has not, however, been universal (Haas 1984; Minnis 1985; Reid 1985). Archaeologists working in Europe proposed the notion of Peer Polity interaction as an alternative to a World Systems approach (Renfrew 1986) and some North American archaeologists applied this idea to the prehistory of the Southwest/Northwest and northern México (Kanter 2004; Minnis 1989; Whalen and Minnis 2001; Wilcox 1999). The model of Peer Polity interaction emphasizes an intermediate scale of analysis between the local and the inter-regional. The stress is on interactions within a region and it is assumed that the interactions within the region are more important to cultural change than external relations.

The World Systems and Peer Polity models are not so much opposing theories as they are arguments for analysis at different scales. In this sense they are not inherently antithetical, but each theory does give primacy to a certain scale in accounting for cultural change. At the core of the debate are the questions about the origin and development of major centers. Did the growth of major centers in the Southwest/Northwest result from local factors, so that the exchange links between these centers are a consequence of their prominence as indigenous centers? Or, did long range political and economic relations provide the reason for the origin and growth of the centers?

The theory that guided our project was multi-scaler and asked how relations and interactions at different scales came together in specific cases to create the patterns and changes that we see (Lock and Molyneaux 2006; Marquardt 1992; Marquardt and Crumley 1987). As we change the scale of our analysis, we frame a different set of relations. The pattern in these relations will disappear at a different scale as a new pattern of unevenness appears. Social groups live and act in a world of varying scales and their positions vis-à-vis others change as their scale of reference changes. Our choice of scale, therefore, brackets an area for study allowing us to view a particular set of social relations, while denying us access to sets visible at other scales. This theory would suggest that the relations of scale might not be as simple as the oppositions in the theoretical debate suggest. It is, however, useful to start with the simple question and then try and develop more complex models from our attempts to answer it.

Cerro de Trincheras was one of the largest late prehispanic towns of Northwest México and a big place for any time period or region of the Southwest/Northwest. The *cerro* has more than four times the number of terraces than any other *cerro de trincheras* and is the only *cerro de trincheras* that could possibly be considered a major center. It is an appropriate place to address the broader question to wit: was the development of regional centers in Northwest México the result of colonial expansion by either Mesoamerican states or Southwestern U.S. polities, or was it the result of indigenous processes centered on the local community? Our results can be compared to ongoing research asking similar questions at the much larger center of Casas Grandes in Chihuahua (Douglas 1992; Minnis 1989; Minnis and Whalen 1992; Whalen and Minnis 2001). This will necessarily entail consideration of the theoretical issues raised by World Systems and Peer Polity theories of Southwest/Northwestern prehistory.

Research Problem

Thus, the larger question is: was the development of prehispanic regional centers in Northwest México the result of colonial expansion by either Mesoamerican states or Southwestern U.S. polities, or was it the result of indigenous processes centered on the local community? To answer this broad question we need to ask it at the major centers in Northwest México and then compare our results. Such comparison may not give us a simple answer, but instead indicate a variety of processes at different places and times.

Scholars have advanced numerous propositions to account for the appearance and development of the center at Cerro de Trincheras. Each of these propositions would answer the larger question in a different way. Two of these, the idea that the site was a refuge fort (McGee 1898), or that it was a massive terraced agricultural field (Huntington 1912), can be rejected based on recent research in southern Arizona and at the site (Downum 1993; Downum et al. 1994; O'Donovan 2002). It is now clear that the site was a terraced village. Four others remained open questions that we evaluated during this project.

One of the most common artifact types at the site is shell jewelry manufacture waste. The prevalence of this material has led to the proposition that Cerro de Trincheras was a trade outpost specializing in the manufacture and exchange of shell jewelry. The shell trade outpost hypothesis takes two forms: (1) that Cerro de Trincheras was a rude station, specializing in the production of shell jewelry, at the southern periphery of a Hohokam regional system (Brand 1935b, 1938; McGuire & Howard 1987; Robles 1973; Sauer & Brand 1931; Tower 1945; Woodward 1936) or (2) that Cerro de Trincheras was a fortified village established by Mesoamerican merchants to protect their shell industry (Di Peso 1983). In both of these hypotheses Cerro de Trincheras developed as a result of far flung economic relations and the colonial expansion of foreign cultures or polities.

Two other models base the foundation and growth of Cerro de Trincheras in local processes. The first model questions that the site was a major center and instead sees it as a rustic village of the desert branch of the Hohokam; that is, as a provincial adaptation of the Hohokam culture to the local environment (Haury 1976; Johnson 1960). The second model posits that Cerro de Trincheras was an indigenous center of a late prehistoric polity in the Río Magdalena drainage (Braniff 1985; McGuire and Villalpando 1989, 1993; O'Donovan 2002).

Research Objectives

To consider these propositions we will address numerous issues that were raised by previous investigators at Cerro de Trincheras. These include the timing of growth at the site, the size and permanence of human population, the nature of activities at the site, and the role of the site in a larger regional and inter-regional economic system.

Chronology

Chronology building remains an essential problem for research in northwestern Sonora. Archaeologists have only just begun to work out ceramic sequences and only a limited number of chronometric dates exist for archaeological sites in Sonora. Theories of the site as a trade outpost depend upon the site being coeval with the larger systems that it is supposed to be an outpost for. It is also important to date the development of the site. Trade outpost theories, such as the Mesoamerican merchant model (Di Peso 1983), imply the rapid construction of a pre-planned town as opposed to the gradual expansion of an indigenous settlement. Estimations of site size, population, and labor investments also depend upon good dating. In all of these estimates, we need to infer what features were or were not contemporary at the site.

Population

Much of the debate about Cerro de Trincheras centers on how many people lived there. Both the models of the site as a rustic village and as a Southwest/Northwestern shell trade outpost posited relatively small site populations. Conversely the Mesoamerican merchant model and the indigenous center model require large resident populations.

Activity Structure

Our 1991 mapping project suggests a complex activity structure at Cerro de Trincheras with temporal, functional, and social distinctions between each site loci (O'Donovan 2002). This complex activity structure is contrary to the expectations of the rustic village model and the shell trade outpost model. In these models the site would be limited in scope and complexity. It is consistent with the expectations of a Mesoamerican merchant model, with Mesoamerican elite resident in the site, and the indigenous center model. To test this inference of complexity we looked at four parameters: (1) subsistence, (2) craft production, (3) elite residence, and (4) ceremonial activity.

The nature of Trincheras Tradition subsistence practices is an area of considerable debate. Johnson (1960, 1963) argued in his statement of the rustic village model that the prehistoric people of the middle Magdalena Valley continued to primarily depend on gathered foods throughout the Formative Period. Shell trade outpost models for sites in the Papagueria have suggested that shell was exchanged for food (Marmaduke and Martynec

1993; McGuire and Howard 1987) suggesting a limited range of subsistence activities at these sites. Both of the other models, with large populations at the site, suggest intensive use of wild and domestic plants to support that population.

All models for Cerro de Trincheras recognize that there was intensive craft production of marine shell jewelry. The rustic village and indigenous center models see this production for local consumption and expect to see a range of other productive activities. The other two models argue that craft production was primarily or exclusively for export. A Mesoamerican merchant model would expect evidence for production of material with value in Mesoamerica, such as turquoise, in addition to shell. The shell trade outpost model would suggest a near exclusive emphasis on production of shell jewelry.

The models differ in their implications for the presence and nature of elites at the site. Both the rustic village and shell trade outpost models either deny the existence of elites or place them somewhere else to the north. The other two models both require the presence of elites, but in the indigenous center model they would be the same as the local people, while in the Mesoamerican merchant model they would be from the south.

The question of ceremonial activity is key. The presence of unique specialized ceremonial features and precincts would not fit the rustic village or shell trade outpost models. We would not expect major ceremonial features in a provincial village or in a village specialized to craft production for exchange. If Mesoamerican merchants established the site, we would expect to find evidence of Mesoamerican ritual, gods, and iconography on the hill.

Larger Economic Systems

To place Cerro de Trincheras in larger economic systems we must ask what was being traded in and out of the site, in what quantity, and where? Both the shell trade outpost theory and the Mesoamerican merchant model would suggest large amounts of external exchange. In the later case we might expect significant connections with other purported commercial centers such as Casas Grandes. In both the rustic village model and the indigenous center model, long distance exchange may be present, but should not be the driving force of the economy.

The Trincheras Tradition and *Cerros de Trincheras*

The name Trincheras refers to an archaeological tradition; several pottery types associated with that tradition (Trincheras Polychrome, Trincheras Purple-on-red, Trincheras Lisa); a specialized site type, *cerros de trincheras*; and to the site of Cerro de Trincheras. For clarity we refer to the site of Cerro de Trincheras in capitalized normal type, the site type, *cerros de trincheras*, in lower case italics, and the tradition by the word Trincheras.

The Trincheras Tradition (Figure 1.3) extends over the Sonoran Desert of northwestern Sonora. On the west, it stretches from the Gulf of California to just east of the Río San Miguel. The northern boundary of the tradition lies roughly on the international border and Trincheras remains extend as far south as Desemboque on the gulf coast. A coil and scrape produced reddish brownware with pronounced scraping marks on the interior characterizes this archaeological tradition (McGuire and Villalpando 1993:25-43). In some cases, prehispanic potters painted this brownware with purple paint to produce the types Trincheras Purple-on-red and Trincheras Purple-on-brown or added white or red paint to produce the types Nogales Polychrome and Altar Polychrome. The people making this

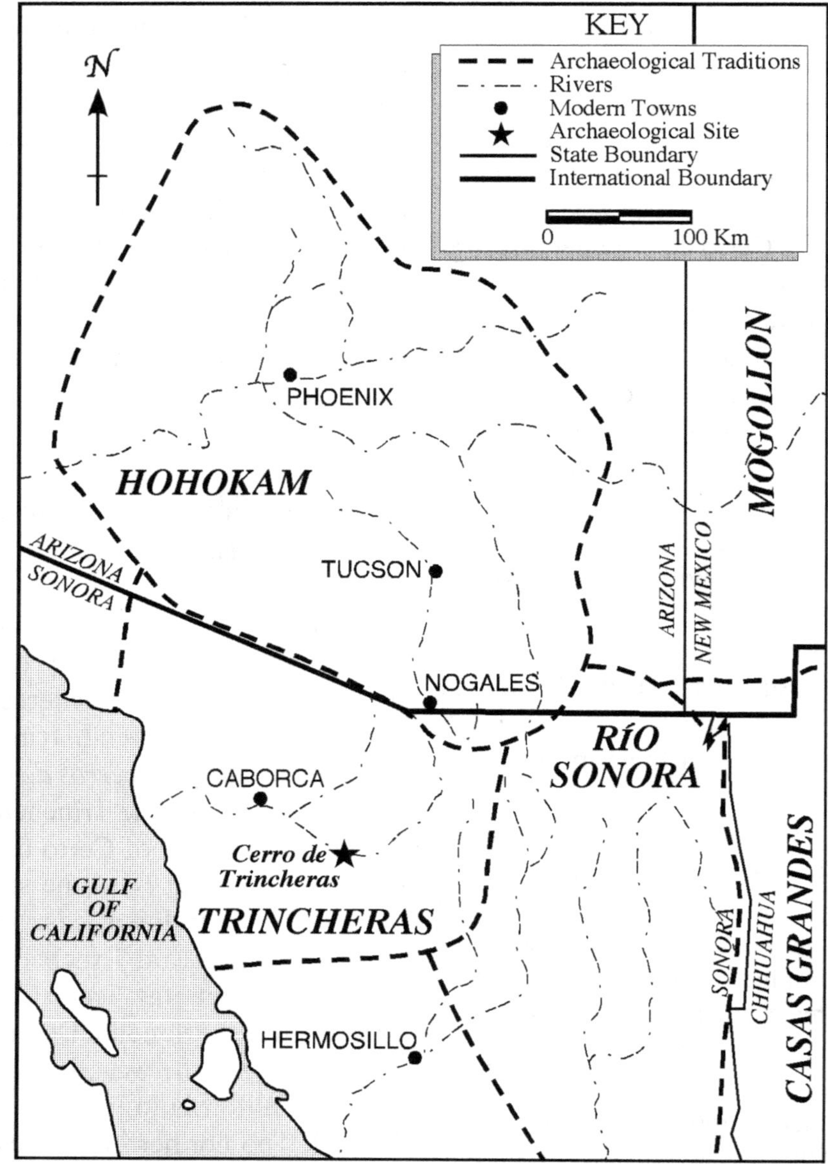

Figure 1.3. Map of the Trincheras tradition.

pottery practiced irrigation agriculture and grew corn, beans, and squash. They cremated their dead and buried them in urns. Settlements included pithouse villages on the valley floors and *cerros de trincheras* on the surrounding hills. The tradition made extensive use of marine shell to manufacture jewelry and large shell mounds with Trincheras pottery occur along the Sonoran Coast. What we do know about the Trincheras Tradition indicates a relatively complex prehistory with major shifts in adaptation, developments in social organization, changes in long-range interactions and a continuum to the historical period (Braniff 1992; McGuire and Villalpando 1993). A general lack of excavation and systematic survey data, however, means that archaeologists have a very poor understanding of the nature or chronology of cultural change in the Trincheras Tradition.

The lack of comparable data makes comparison of the Trincheras Tradition to the archaeological traditions of the southwestern U.S. difficult. The Trincheras Tradition most closely resembles the Hohokam Tradition of the Sonoran Desert in southern Arizona with its shallow pithouses (houses in pits), shell jewelry, irrigation agriculture, and cremation burial. Obvious differences from the Hohokam include dissimilar primary methods of ceramic production, different ritual artifact assemblages, no platform mounds or ballcourts among the Trincheras, distinct ritual features on Trincheras' *cerros de trincheras,* and different design styles on rock art, ceramics, and shell. With the notable exception of the site of Cerro de Trincheras, Trincheras Tradition settlements were consistently smaller and less built up than Hohokam settlements. The exact nature of the similarities and differences between the two traditions is a major theme in the analyses of Cerro de Trincheras materials presented here.

Cerros de trincheras occur on isolated dark volcanic hills or low peaks in the Basin and Range geological province of the Sonoran Desert of southern Arizona and Sonora, and in the Chihuahuan Desert of southern New México and Chihuahua (Fish and Fish 2007). They crosscut several archaeological traditions of the Southwest/Northwest including the Hohokam, Trincheras, Río Sonora, and Casas Grandes Traditions. In a broad sense, *cerros de trincheras* represent the northernmost extent of a continuum of hilltop sites that stretch at least as far south as Oaxaca, México (Kowalewski 2007; McGuire 1998; Nelson 2007). Prehispanic peoples constructed *cerros de trincheras* by covering desert prominences with dry laid cobble features that include terraces, round and square structures, walls and large unroofed enclosures often erroneously referred to as "corrals" (Fish et al. 2007). The first examples of such sites occur in the earliest agricultural phases of the region from approximately 3,000 to 2,000 BP (Hard and Roney 2007; Wallace et al. 2007). Suzanne Fish, Paul Fish, and Elisa Villalpando (2007:1) speak of a "Trincheras Phenomena" that spans three millennia. Cerro de Trincheras is the largest *cerros de trincheras* regardless of time and space.

Numerous propositions have been offered to explain why people choose to construct *cerros de trincheras*, and live on isolated volcanic hills (Fish et al. 2007). The most long standing and entrenched of these ideas is that these sites were defensive refuges (Manje 1954; McGee 1898; Sauer & Brand 1931; Wilcox 1979) and LeBlanc (1999:132-133) revived this idea in his arguments for a violent prehistory of the Southwest/Northwest. Other researchers have interpreted these sites as fortified villages placed on isolated hills for defense (Di Peso 1983; Hard & Roney 1998). Not everyone found the location of these sites on hilltops as convincing evidence for a defensive function. Huntington (1912) argued that these sites were terraced agricultural fields and some recent researchers also emphasized this use for the hills (Fish et al. 1984). In the Trincheras Tradition, many researchers linked these sites with the production of shell jewelry (Brand 1935b, 1938; Robles 1973; Sauer & Brand 1931; Tower 1945; Woodward 1936). Di Peso (1974) proposed that some *cerros de trincheras* in Chihuahua, México were signal stations. Finally, a number of analyses emphasized the use of terraces to create a sense of "monumentality" on these hills (Downum et al. 1994; Haury 1976; McGuire & Villalpando 2008; O'Donovan 1997, 2002). All excavations of *cerros de trincheras* encountered habitations (Downum 1986, 1993; Downum et al. 1994; Fraps 1936; Hard & Roney 1998; O'Donovan 1997). It is clear from these excavations that *cerros de trincheras* were multifunctional and that the various single function interpretations given for these sites are not necessarily mutually exclusive. Our research at Cerro de

Trincheras sought to reveal and explicate the complexity of activities, social organization, and meaning at the site.

Previous Research

Many people have seen Cerro de Trincheras, been impressed by it, and speculated about it, but very little archaeological work had been done at the site before our long-term efforts began in 1991. The modern border between the U.S. and México has no meaning for the events of prehistory. It has, however, had a profound effect on the nature and extent of archaeological research in the greater Southwest/Northwest (McGuire 2003; Villalobos 2004). While archaeologists intensively studied and classified the prehistory of Arizona they did much less work in Sonora. Up until the middle of the twentieth century Trincheras Tradition sites were primarily known from superficial examinations by travelers, geographers, and archaeologists. Regional, but still very broad scale, archaeological surveys (some with subsurface testing) began in the 1970s. It was only in the last two decades of the twentieth century that archaeologists undertook intensive surveys and excavations in the tradition. César Villalobos (2004) provided the most detailed and insightful history of archaeological research in Sonora.

Traveler's Reports

The Spanish captain Juan Mateo Manje (1954) published the first report of Cerro de Trincheras in the late seventeenth century. Manje coined the name Cerro de Trincheras for the site and interpreted it as a fort. Literally translated in modern Spanish, the name means "hill of trenches." This translation is nonsensical because terraces, not trenches, cover the hill. However, in late seventeenth century Spanish, the term trincheras also referred to fortifications (Covarrubias 1943). Thus, the more accurate translation would be Fortified Hill.

In the late nineteenth and early twentieth centuries, Anglo travelers in Sonora reported the existence of large hills covered by terraces, walls and rooms, what we now call *cerros de trincheras* (Hamilton 1883:35; Schumacher 1881). As largest of these, Cerro de Trincheras received the most attention (Carmony & Brown 1983; Lumholtz 1912; McGee 1895, 1896, 1898). All of these travelers interpreted Cerro de Trincheras and the other sites of this type as fortifications.

Geographers and Archaeologists

In 1910, Ellsworth Huntington (1912, 1914) visited *cerros de trincheras* in the Magdalena Valley, including Cerro de Trincheras. He provided the first detailed and accurate description of the site (Figure 1.4). Huntington interpreted the hills as terraced agricultural fields to fit his arguments for environmental determinism. He noted that agriculture would not be possible on these terraces given the modern climate. In a decidedly circular argument, he concluded that the environment must have been moister when the site was occupied, to allow the cultivation of grapes on the terraces.

In the 1930s, researchers carried out more systematic large-scale surveys and defined three archaeological traditions in Sonora and Chihuahua. Frank Midvale visited the Trincheras area and the Altar Valley as part of his survey of the Papagueria for the Gila Pueblo, but Sonora received only brief mention in the final report (Gladwin and Gladwin 1929:1113). Two geographers, Carl O. Sauer and Donald Brand (1931), conducted an extensive survey in northern Sonora to gather data on *cerros de trincheras.* They used this data to refute Huntington's theories of environmental determinism. They coined the term Trincheras Tradition for those prehistoric sites contain-

Figure 1.4. Ellsworth Huntington 1910 photograph of Cerro de Trincheras. Image Number 8236. Courtesy of the Ellsworth Huntington Papers, Manuscripts and Archives, Yale University Library.

ing primarily Purple-on-red pottery. In a later article, Brand (1935a) defined three cultural complexes in northern Sonora and Chihuahua (Chihuahuan Casa Grandes, Río Sonoran, and Trincheras) and two pottery types for the Trincheras Tradition (Trincheras Purple-on-red, T. Polychrome). Arthur Woodward (1936) visited the site of La Playa, several kilometers north of Cerro de Trincheras, in 1935 and identified a distinctive Trincheras shell jewelry industry at that site. Gordon Ekholm (1939, 1940, 1947) conducted a wide-ranging survey of Sonora and northern Sinaloa. Other studies of *cerros de trincheras* were carried out in the Papagueria (Fraps 1936; Hoover 1941; Ives 1936). Also during the 1930s and 1940s Emil Haury and J.D. Harrington recorded sites in the Trincheras area.

Archaeological research from the 1940s to the late 1960s primarily sought to relate the Trincheras Tradition to the Hohokam of southern Arizona. Edward Danson's (1946) survey of the Santa Cruz River Valley dipped into the Trincheras Tradition area and Julian Hayden (1956) conducted a survey along the central coast of Sonora. During the excavation of the Paloparado site in southern Arizona, Charles Di Peso sent Thomas Hinton (1955) to do a survey of the Altar Valley. Di Peso (1956) used this data to include the Trincheras Tradition in his O'otam culture. In the late 1950's, A.E. Johnson (1960, 1963) conducted limited excavations at the site of La Playa and two *cerros de trincheras* adjacent to that site. Haury (1976) used this research to argue that the Trincheras Tradition was an environmentally derived variation of the Hohokam culture. William Wasley (1968; see also Bowen 1976a, 2002) conducted an extensive survey in Sonora to find evidence of Hohokam migrations. The survey focused on the western Trincheras area and included the excavation of a canal (Bowen 1976a: 267). Thomas Bowen (1972) used data from Wasley's survey and some later trips to the region to prepare a summary of the Trincheras Tradition. In the 1950s, Eduardo Noguera conducted a far ranging archaeological survey of Sonora for the INAH. He later published the first archaeological summary for the state (Noguera 1958).

Systematic Archaeology in Sonora

In the mid1970s Di Peso (1974) presented his monumental report on the site of Casas Grandes in Chihuahua. His bold theory that Casas Grandes was an outpost of Mesoamerican pochteca led archaeologists to rethink the prehistory of northwest México. He later proposed that pochteca also built Cerro de Trincheras (Di Peso 1983).

The most important development for Trincheras archaeology was the establishment in the 1970s of the Centro Regional de Sonora de INAH in Hermosillo (Braniff and Felger 1976). In its first decade, the Centro recorded scattered sites in the region, published a compendium of known archaeological sites in Sonora (Braniff 1982; Braniff & Quijada 1978), and conducted survey and excavations in Trincheras sites near Caborca (Braniff 1985). The Centro also established site files for Sonora using a site numbering system based on the system used at the Arizona State Museum. All of the site numbers given in this report are Centro Regional de Sonora site numbers and the site records are kept at the centro in Hermosillo. The site numbers may or may not be in AZSITE.

Beatrice Braniff's (1985) dissertation summarizes the initial work INAH did in northern Sonora with special emphasis on sites in the Río San Miguel and Cerro Calera, west of Caborca. In this work, Braniff suggested that scholars should understand cultural change in northwest Sonora, including the development of Cerro de Trincheras, as part of local processes, and not as peripheral to processes in other regions.

A variety of other projects in Sonora during the 1980s also produced information relevant to studies at Cerro de Trincheras. In 1983, Richard Carrico (1983) completed a study of petroglyphs at Cerro Calera and in the following years the French archaeological mission to México published research on the same site and on a petroglyph site in the Sierra El Alamo to the west (Ballereau 1984, 1988, 1989). The French archaeological mission to México completed an archaeological and ethnohistorical project at Quitovac, northwest of Caborca in the early 1980s (Rodriguez-Loubet and Sanchez 1990). This project became very controversial with conflicts between the French and the local Tohono O'odham. These disputes resulted in the only repatriation of human remains to an indigenous group in the history of Mexican archaeology (McGuire 2000; Villalobos 2004). INAH sponsored a 1986 conference on archaeological shell from the Gulf of California (Alvarez and Cassiano 1988; Bowen 1988; Villalpando 1988).

In the 1980s, the Arizona State Museum (ASM) carried out a long term and innovative study of two *cerros de trincheras*, in southern Arizona, Los Morteros and Cerro Prieto. This work cast doubt on interpretations of *cerros de trincheras* as simply refuge forts or terraced agricultural fields (Downum 1986, 1993; Fish et al. 1984). The ASM studies were the most extensive and intensive to date, with detailed mapping and excavation at each of these sites. These studies confirmed Fraps' (1936) earlier observation that the largest *cerros de trincheras* sites were villages (Fish et al. 1984). ASM archaeologists excavated four pithouses and a masonry room on terraces. These were fair sized villages with anywhere from 77 to 232 structures present. They recovered agave fibers and corn pollen from flotation and pollen analyses of terrace and house structure fills. This led the archaeologists to suggest that the sites' occupants grew these crops on some terraces associated with the villages.

Randall H. McGuire and Elisa Villalpando initiated their research with two surveys in the Trincheras region. During the summer of 1984 we conducted an extensive automotive survey of the Magdalena, Rio Concepción, and the Altar River drainages to decide on a smaller region for intensive research. A total of 18 known sites were relocated and 12 new sites recorded (McGuire 1985). We followed up this preliminary work with a systematic sample survey of the lower half of the Altar Valley in the spring of 1988. The survey recorded a total of 98 sites ranging in age from the Early Archaic to early twentieth century Tohono O'odham. Over half of the sites recorded dated to the late prehispanic period and we located nine *cerro de trincheras* (McGuire and Villalpando 1993; Rubenstein 1993).

The Cerro de Trincheras Mapping Project

In the fall of 1991, Elisa Villalpando and Randall McGuire (McGuire et al. 1993) conducted a surface survey and mapping project at the site of Cerro de Trincheras. Marie O'Donovan (1997, 2002) analyzed and wrote up the results of this research for her dissertation at Binghamton University. The project contracted with Geo-Map Inc. of Tucson Arizona (now known as Western Mapping) to produce a photometric contour map of the site. Survey crews then systematically walked over the entire site to locate all features visible on the ground surface, even amorphous rock piles and isolated rock alignments. The crews measured and mapped each feature, and then plotted it on aerial photographs (Figure 1.5). In Tucson, Western Mapping transferred the features from the aerial photographs to the contour map. The crews made detailed maps of several prominent features with a theodolite and EDM (Electronic Distance Meter). They also examined looter's

Figure 1.5. Ruth Rubenstein mapping a terrace in 1991.

holes to get estimations of soil depth and site condition.

We used dog-leash collections to make systematic and controlled surface collections from each terrace and feature. We recovered more than 23,000 artifacts in these collections. These materials included ground stone, chipped lithics, ceramics, large quantities of marine shell, and a handful of stone beads, including two of turquoise. Artifact density ranged from one or two artifacts per square meter to over 200 artifacts per square meter on different parts of the site, with an overall average artifact density of ten artifacts per square meter. Our analyses of the artifacts indicate a variety of activities, including food preparation, burial of the dead, shell working, pottery making, and stone tool production, which archaeologists normally associate with a habitation site that is a village or a town. We found few sherds of Trincheras Lisa 1, Trincheras Lisa 2, Trincheras Purple-on-red, Altar Polychrome, and Nogales Polychrome (n = 42) that date between A.D. 800 and 1300. The vast majority of the ceramics were plainwares (Trincheras Lisa 3 and Lisa Tardía) and imported polychromes (n = 20,306) that date from A.D. 1300 to 1450 (McGuire and Villalpando 1993, O'Donovan 2002).

A variety of features cover Cerro de Trincheras. The most obvious of these are terraces with over 900 examples (Figure 1.6). Approximately 50 of these terraces are narrow and defined by a single row of rock. Based on similar features in Arizona we think that these may be for raising agave. O'Donovan (2002:38-39) interpreted the vast majority of the terraces (420 to 600) as platforms for habitations. She based this inference on their artifact content, size, the presence of midden fill, and their resemblance to excavated habitation terraces in Arizona (Downum 1993; Fraps 1936). Other features included walls (n = 7),

Figure 1.6. Terraces on the hill's north face. Excavations in La Cancha and Area B6 at the base of the photograph (photograph courtesy of Adriel Heisey).

trails (n = 2 as well as many fragments), rectangular dry laid cobble rooms (n = 57), circular dry laid cobble structures (approximately 271), La Cancha, a large rectangular feature at the base of the north slope of the hill, and El Caracol, a spiral enclosure with dry laid masonry walls on top of the hill.

The Cerro de Trincheras mapping project provided us with both the information necessary to plan a major excavation and an overview of the site that allowed us to generalize from our excavated areas to the entire site. Because of this project we knew the number and distribution of terraces and other features, and the relationship of these to artifact distributions so we could design a well-informed sampling plan for excavation. O'Donovan's (2002) analysis gave us basic information on terrace characteristics and fill conditions so that we could make reasonable level of effort excavation decisions.

Research Since 1996

In 1998, Suzanne and Paul Fish (1999, 2007) conducted the Cerro de Trincheras Settlement and Land Use Survey Project. This was an intensive full coverage survey of approximately 75 km^2 around the site of Cerro de Trincheras. The survey recorded more than 240 sites in this area dating from the Archaic to Historical periods. Among these sites were 16 *cerros de trincheras,* each of which they mapped in detail. The survey crews conducted controlled and grab bag artifact sampling on each site, including the *cerros de trincheras.* The results of this project allow us to place our analysis of Cerro de Trincheras in a local settlement context.

Programa INAH-PROCEDE in Sonora conducted surveys from 1996 to 2000 as a result of changes in *ejido* land ownership. The Centro INAH crew recorded Trincheras Tradition sites including five *cerros de trincheras* near the towns of Magdalena, Imuris and Sasabe (Martínez & Villalpando 2000).

The La Playa project is an ongoing effort sponsored by INAH and CONAYCT and is directed by John Carpenter, Guadalupe Sanchez, and Elisa Villalpando. The project is investigating the Archaic and Trincheras Tradition site of La Playa, which is located to the north of Cerro de Trincheras. The project produced a detailed map of this immense site and conducted excavations in the Archaic, early agriculture, and Trincheras components of the site. The Trincheras occupation of La Playa spans all of the Early Ceramic Phase in the area and appears to have ended by the time the site of Cerro de Trincheras was built (Carpenter et al. 1999).

Culture History

Bowen (1972, 1976a) suggested the first chronology for the Trincheras Tradition based primarily on data collected in Wasley's (1968; see also Bowen 2002) 1960s survey. He divided the region into four zones: (1) fluvial--the Altar, Concepción, Magdalena and San Miguel River Valleys; (2) coastal; (3) the mouth of the Concepción River; and (4) interior which encompasses all areas not in 1 to 3. He partitioned the prehistoric occupation of these zones into four numbered phases, starting with an Archaic Phase 1, which is essentially equivalent to the Cochise. More recent projects have focused on developing phase sequences for specific river valleys and basins.

The Trinchereños produced painted pottery only in Bowen's Phase 2 and 3. His Phase 2 (AD 200?-800) is marked by the appearance of Trincheras Purple-on-red pottery. He argues that these sites essentially resemble San Pedro Cochise sites with the addition of pottery. They occur most frequently in the coast and interior zones. Phase 3 (AD 800-1300) sites yield Trincheras Purple-on-brown and Trincheras Polychrome and include large villages such as La Playa in the fluvial zone. Production of shell jewelry begins during Phase 3 and the Trincheras Tradition appears to be interacting with the Hohokam.

Phase 4 (AD 1300-1450) sites occur principally in the fluvial areas. Bowen (1976a:275-276) proposed that the *cerros de trincheras* were constructed during this time and that the local production of painted pottery ceased in this phase. Intrusive ceramics include Salt Red, Gila Polychrome, Tucson Polychrome, and some Chihuahuan polychromes. Another characteristic of this period is urn cremation. Cerro de Trincheras is the largest known site in northwest Sonora during Phase 4 (AD 1300-1450) with the next largest *cerros de trincheras* being less than a quarter the size of Cerro de

Trincheras. Bowen and Hinton suggested that the Trincheras artifact pattern ends in Phase 3 to be replaced by an O'otam artifact pattern but these results are not consistent with the radiocarbon dates derived by Braniff (1985), which suggest the Trincheras pattern continues until the fifteenth century. It is also not consistent with our research at Cerro de Trincheras. It now appears that the cultural history of the Altar Valley is different in the late prehistoric period from the rest of northwest Sonora and that Braniff's chronology works outside the valley.

Bowen (1976a:277) defined no protohistoric phase, but Hinton (1955) located protohistoric sites in the Altar Valley containing a distinctive ceramic series, including Oquitoa Plain, Oquitoa Red-on-brown, and Altar Red. Carrico (1983) noted these same pottery types at Cerro Calera and both authors link them to protohistoric Pimans. Hinton (1955) advocated a cultural continuum from the Trincheras Tradition to the historically known O'odham populations of the region.

Villalpando and Carpenter's (Carpenter et al. 1999, 2005) research in the site of La Playa suggests a much more complicated Trincheras Phase 1 than hypothesized by Bowen. Archaeologists in southern Arizona found that the transition from the Archaic to an agricultural, ceramic making, village living Formative Period did not occur in a single event of diffusion, but rather over a long period of transition. They labeled this long period of transition the Early Agricultural Period (Silva 2005) dating from 4000 to 2000 BP. The earliest *cerros de trincheras* found in Chihuahua and southern Arizona date to this period. The largest component at the site of La Playa dates to this Early Agricultural Period and greatly resembles contemporary assemblages from southern Arizona. We have not yet definitively identified any *cerros de trincheras* in the Magdalena drainage to this period, but based on surface evidence Fish and Fish (1999) believe that one such site across the river from Cerro de Trincheras may date to the Early Agricultural Period.

Our work in the Altar valley supported the broad outlines of Bowen's chronology for the ceramic Phases 2 and 3. Bowen's Phase 4 does not exist in the Altar Valley and we instead find a Hohokam Classic Period Papaguerian artifact assemblage (McGuire and Villalpando 1993). We proposed a six phase ceramic sequence for the Altar valley: (1) Atil, (2) Altar, (3) Realito, (4) Santa Teresa, (5) Oquitoa, and (6) Papago. The first two of these phases are prehistoric and correspond to Bowen's Phases 2 and 3. The Santa Teresa spans the Protohistoric to early Spanish periods and the Oquitoa and Papago are historical. These results confirmed Hinton's (1955) argument for a continuum from late prehispanic to Tohono O'odham occupations of the valley. The lack of intrusive dated pottery makes the temporal placement of the three prehispanic phases (Atil, Altar, and Realito) difficult. Salado polychromes occur in Realito Phase sites suggesting a fourteenth and fifteenth century date. A distinctively Trincheras artifact assemblage exists in the Atil and Altar Phases with coil and scrape manufactured Purple-on-red and plainware pottery, and a distinct milling complex. *Cerros de Trincheras* may appear in the Atil Phase. They are certainly present in the Altar Phase and are also built in the Realito Phase. In the Realito Phase of the Altar Valley and subsequent phases, however, the material culture assemblage shifts from a Trincheras Tradition to an assemblage like that in the Papagueria of southern Arizona.

In the Río Magdalena, Fish and Fish (1999, 2007) defined a tentative phase sequence that corresponds well with Bowen's Phases 2 to 4. An initial ceramic interval includes distinctive plainwares and corresponds to Bowen's Phase 2 and the Altar valley Atil Phase. The subsequent Early Ceramic Phase equates with Bowen's Phase 3 and the

Altar Phase of the Altar Valley. Local production of painted pottery had virtually ceased by the Cerros Phase (AD 1300-1450) occupation of the Cerro de Trincheras. The Cerros Phase corresponds in time with Bowen's Phase 4 and the Realito Phase, but the Trincheras ceramic tradition continues in the Cerros Phase of the Magdalena Valley and is not replaced by Papaguerian wares, as is the case in the Altar Valley. There is only slight evidence for the occupation of the middle Magdalena Valley during the Protohistoric period corresponding to the Santa Teresa Phase in the Altar valley. Archaeologists found a few hundred sherds of the type Whetstone Plain that characterizes this phase in survey and on Cerro de Trincheras a single archaeomagnetic date from La Playa dates to this period and a handful of burials we excavated at Cerro de Trincheras may date to the Protohistoric. When Manje (1954) first visited the region in the late seventeenth century the middle Magdalena was not occupied.

Cerro de Trincheras

The site of Cerro de Trincheras lies in the Magdalena River drainage of northern Sonora (Figure 1.7). The Magdalena and Altar River Valleys were the two most heavily populated areas in northwestern Sonora at the Spanish entrada in the 1680s (Spicer 1962). This was also the case prehistorically as the major sites of the Trincheras Tradition cluster in these valleys (Bowen 1972; Braniff 1985; Sauer and Brand 1931; Wasley 1968).

Environment

The Magdalena River Valley is in the Basin-

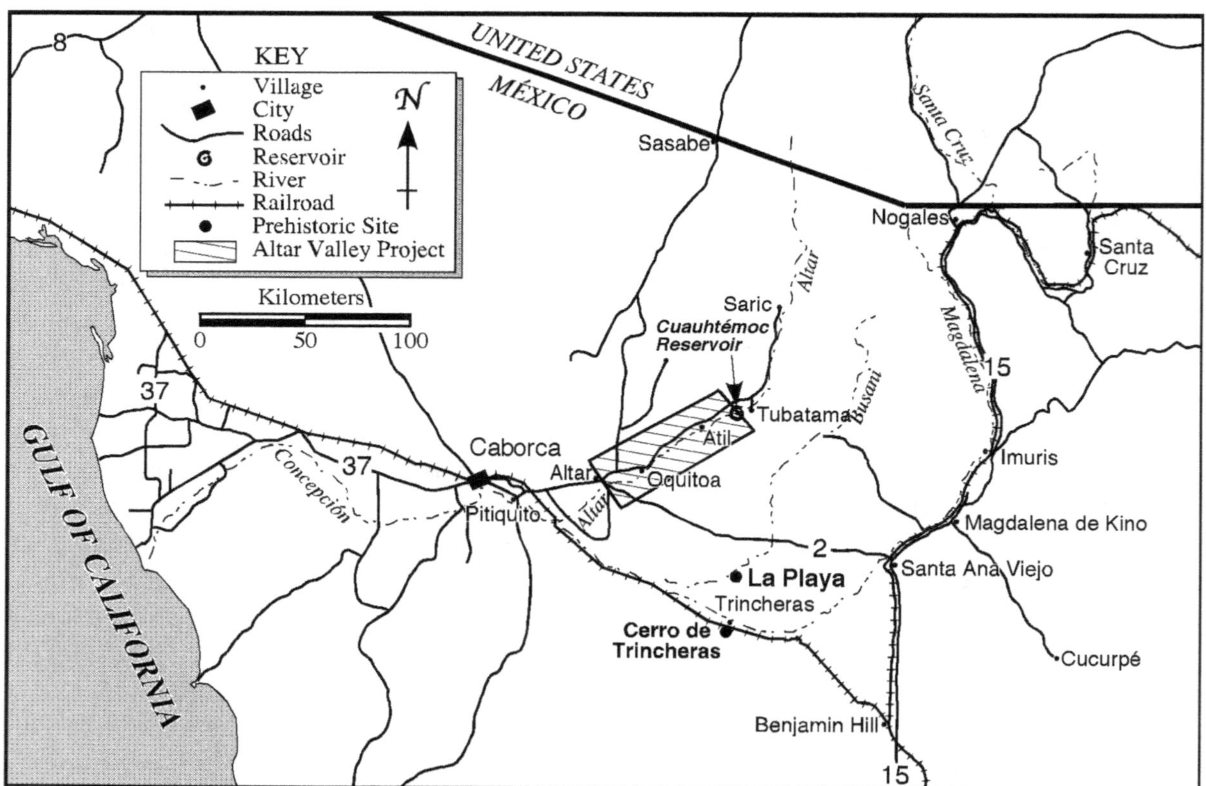

Figure 1.7. Local map of Cerro de Trincheras.

and-Range topographic province and in the Sonoran Desert (Phillips and Comus 2000). The river rises in the mountains south of Nogales, Sonora and flows west to meet the Altar River southeast of Caborca forming the Río de la Concepción, which flows west to the Gulf of California. From its source, the river flows in a relatively narrow floodplain flanked by low hills and terraces. The river passes into a broad basin with a very wide floodplain just above the modern town of Trincheras. A modern dam closes off the river just before the floodplain opens up and diverts the river flow for irrigation. Today the river is a deeply cut arroyo and dry most of the year. Before water pumping and arroyo cutting began in the late nineteenth century (Lumholtz 1912), the river was permanent, wide and shallow with marshes common along their courses. When Manje (1954) passed through the valley in the late seventeenth century the river carried water from its source to Trincheras. Here the river broadened into a large, shallow marsh, or *cienega*, and then to the west of the site it disappeared to flow under the desert sands. From this point to the sea, the river would surface when it encountered volcanic dykes beneath the ground, flow for some distance, and then duck under the sands again.

The Río Magdalena is probably the most important environmental variable affecting settlement at Cerro de Trincheras. The cerro forms an igneous intrusion into the channel of the river forcing water near the surface and with a higher water table creates a cienega. This igneous feature also creates a natural place to head irrigation canals.

Precipitation comes to the region primarily in the form of summer cloudbursts with lesser amounts of rain falling in extensive winter fronts. Today annual precipitation for the town of Trincheras fluctuates between 200 to 300 mm (8 to 11 in) (INEGI 2007). Both rainfall and temperature depend on elevation, with higher elevation increasing rainfall and decreasing temperature. Thus, as you move to the coast the average precipitation drops to less than 100 mm (4 in) a year. Temperatures between the months of June and September routinely exceed 40° C (104° F). In the winter, freezing temperatures can occur at night, but do not last through the day. Nowhere in the region does sufficient rain fall to support corn, bean, or squash agriculture without the use of irrigation or devices to concentrate and channel runoff.

The pattern of rainfall and temperature has a pronounced effect on the vegetation of the area. With the exception of the highest mountains, the entire area is part of the Sonoran Desert. The Magdalena River (Figure 1.8) rises in the Arizona Uplands subdivision of the Sonora Desert and Cerro de Trincheras lies in the region where this subdivision transitions into the Lower Colorado River Valley subdivision (Dimmitt 2000). Creosote and cholla *(Opuntia* sp.*)* cover the flat plains, which are cut by shallow arroyos filled with ironwood (*Olneya tesota*), mesquite (*Prosopis),* and acacia (*Acacia constricta* and *A. greggii*). Several species of columnar cactus including saguaro (*Carnegiea gigantea)*, cardón *(Pachycereus pringlei)*, senita *(Lophocereus schottii)*, and organ pipe *(Stenocereus turberi)* thrive on the lower slopes of the mountains (the bajada) along with palo verde (*Cercidium microphyllum*), acacia, and other cacti. These species also cover the isolated volcanic hills such as Cerro de Trincheras. In the floodplains of the rivers, remnant riparian plant communities include ironwood and mesquite with introduced tamarisk *(Tamarix)* trees.

The Site of Cerro de Trincheras

During the 1991 field season, we named a number of the physiographic features of the hill to facilitate talking about locations (Figure 1.9).

Figure 1.8. View of the environment around Cerro de Trincheras with Río Magdalena in the foreground.

On the southern side of Cerro de Trincheras are three smaller remnant volcanic hills. The largest of these to the southwest of the cerro, we named the "Cerrito del Oeste." The smallest of these directly to the south of the cerro we called the "Cerrito del Sur" and the easternmost hill we labeled "Cerrito del Este." Three distinct peaks top the crest of Cerro de Trincheras. Turkey vultures perch on the largest and tallest of these peaks at the western end of the crest and their roost inspired us to call this peak "El Pico del Zopilotes." We labeled the next peak to the east "El Pico del Medio" and the furthest eastern peak "El Pico Este." Two saddles separate these peaks, "La Abra Oeste" on the west and "La Abra Este" on the east. A lower peak lies at the northwest end of the cerro and it is connected to El Pico de Zopilotes by a large saddle. We named this peak "El Cerrito de la Virgen" after the painted image of the Virgin Mary on its north face and the large saddle "La Explanada." To the south-southwest of the crest, two ridges run down the south slope of the hill. The westernmost of these we labeled "El Borde Sur" and the westernmost "El Borde Sureste."

O'Donovan (2002) used the 1991 map of the site and artifact collections to make some preliminary inferences about the activity structure of the site. She defined five areas that may be functionally and/or temporally distinct from each other (Figure 1.10). Our map of Cerro de Trincheras and the measurements that we took on all visible features provide a tentative basis for estimates of site population and labor investment (McGuire et al. 2002). We estimate that the population of the site would have been in excess of 1,000 people and that the labor investment to build it was comparable to a Chaco great house of 600 to 700 rooms. These estimates are very crude because we can only make educated guesses at some of the parameters used to make them, such as: how many terraces were habitation terraces, how many houses existed per terrace, what is the construction history of the site, and how many

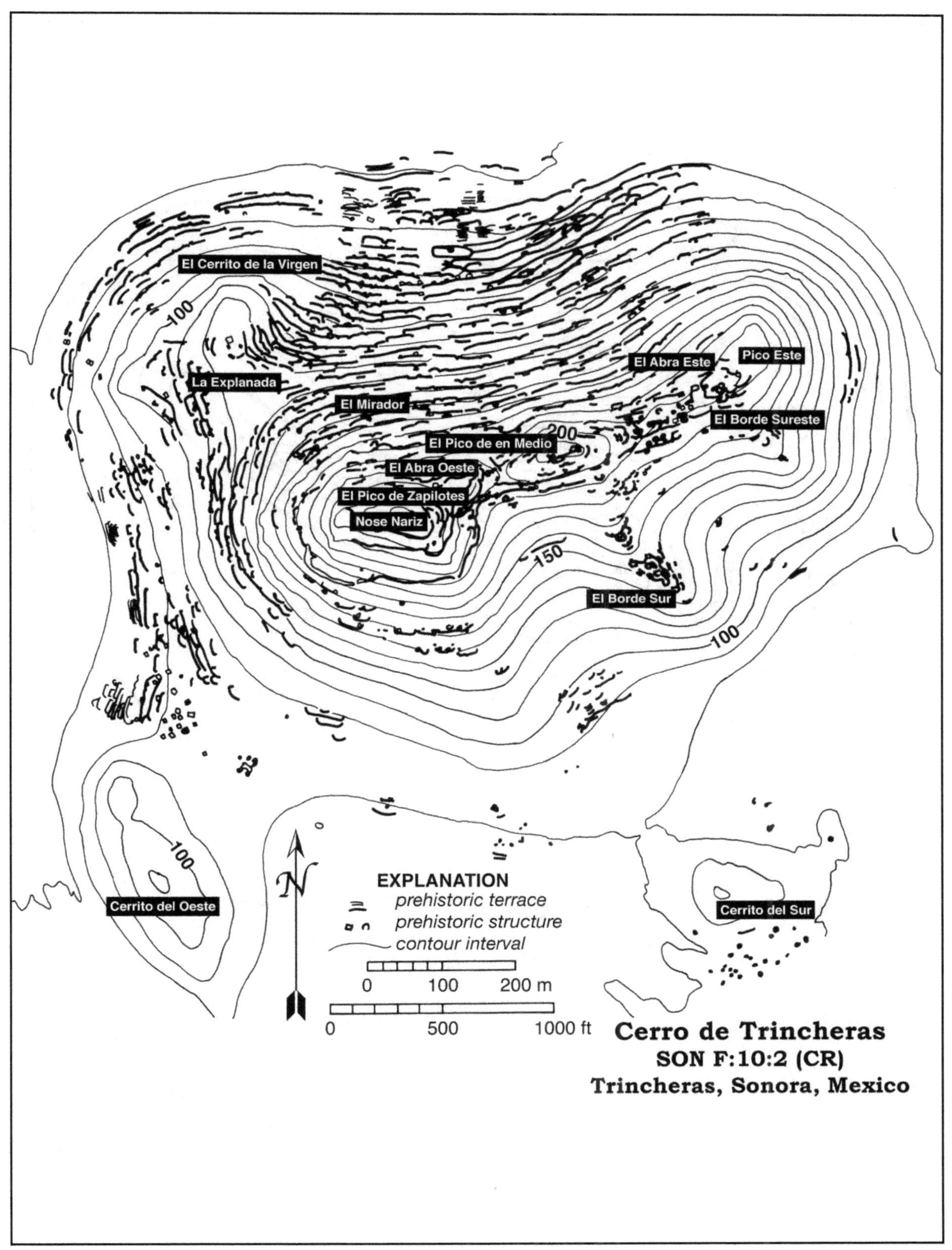

Figure 1.9. Map of site with place names.

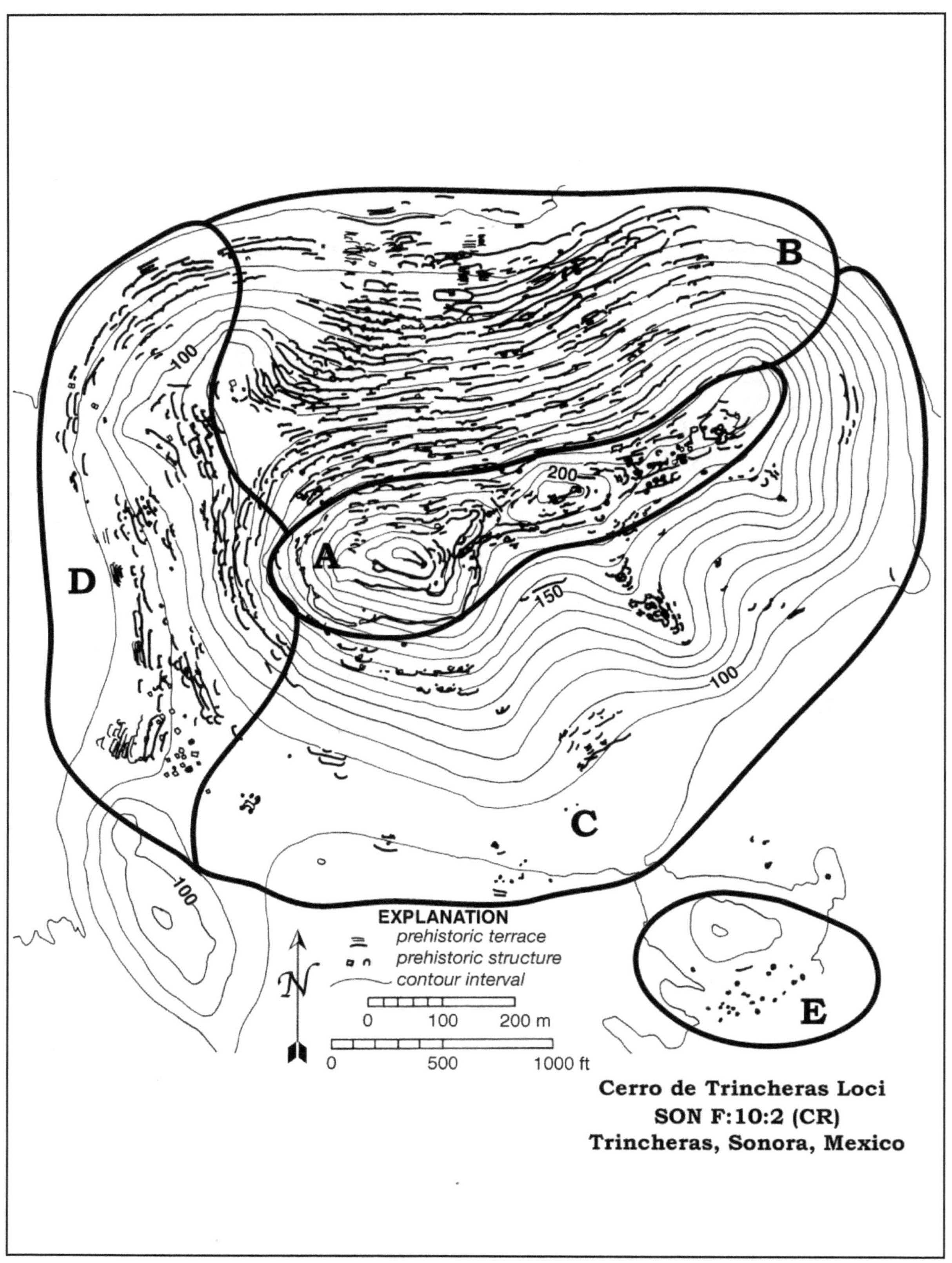

Figure 1.10. Map of Cerro de Trincheras showing loci.

houses were occupied at any one time. Our excavations sought to answer these questions, and others, to refine these estimates.

Area A is the crest of the cerro. The features on the crest include a variety of circular structures, El Caracol, and various walls and compounds. The sites' occupants terraced El Pico de Zopilotes with massive walls to reshape it into something resembling a stepped pyramid (Haury 1976; O'Donovan 2002). They filled each of these massive terraces (or steps) with rock and placed no soil in them. The only architectural features at the top of the peak are two walls that meet to form a "V" facing to the east-southeast. Terraces, square structures, and circular structures cover both of the saddles and the other two lower peaks on the crest. One of the most distinctive architectural features of the site, El Caracol, lies on the east side of El Pico del Medio in the Abra Este. Terraces on the crest and along the side of the crest, like those on the summit, were filled with stone and have no soil in them. A series of terraces and walls connect around the edge of the crest and run to cliffs on the west and north sides of El Pico de Zopilotes to form a continuous barrier that separates Area A from the rest of the site. The 1991 survey found a markedly lower artifact density in Area A than the rest of the site and no evidence of shell manufacture. Soils in Area A have a natural reddish color in contrast with the more midden like grayish soils of the north (Area B) and west (Area D) slopes of the hill. O'Donovan (2002) inferred that Area A was the ritual/administrative center for the community of Cerro de Trincheras.

Area B is the north face of the hill and includes El Cerrito de la Virgen and the east face of La Explanada. Area B contains the majority of the terraces and other features at the site. O'Donovan (2002) interpreted most of these terraces to be residential. The Trinchereños filled these terraces with cobbles topped with 10 cm to 50 cm of soil. The higher terraces are the largest and the most elaborately constructed. One group of three terraces on a prominent rock outcrop stands out from the rest and we labeled this group "El Mirador" because the whole of Area B is visible from these terraces. The mid-level terraces directly below La Explanada all contained large amounts of shell debitage, raw shell, and shell ornaments broken in manufacture. They also had the highest artifact densities on the site. O'Donovan interpreted this area as a precinct of shell workers. The lowest terraces are the least substantial and had the sparsest distribution of artifacts. Towards the bottom of Area B is a large, rectangular feature built on a terrace. We called this feature "La Cancha." Below La Cancha are many narrow terraces that O'Donovan (2002) interpreted as agave fields.

Area C is the south side of the hill. This area has a markedly lower density of architectural features and artifacts than the other loci. Area C includes two complexes of circular structures and walls on the ridges (El Borde Sur and El Borde Sureste) running down the south slope of the hill. The 1991 data suggests these are residential terraces (O'Donovan 2002). Elsewhere on the south slope we found a scattering of what appears to be residential terraces and at least one trail system leading up the southeast slope of the hill.

Area D appears to be a residential quarter with agricultural terraces below it (O'Donovan 2002). It lies on the southwest slope of the cerro below La Explanada and between El Cerrito del Oeste and El Cerrito de la Virgen. We found most of the square rooms in this area. The 1991 survey did not establish if this area is functionally, temporally, or just spatially different than Area B.

Area E is around El Cerrito del Sur directly to the south of the main cerro. There is a Cerros Phase pithouse village to the south of the small hill and there is a badly potted cremation cemetery to the north of the hill. Scattered petroglyphs cover the hill. Based on the 1991 survey, we defined Area E as part of the site of Cerro de Trincheras and we excavated it as such in 1995. The Fish and Fish (1999, 2007) survey of the Middle Magdalena River found many similar Cerros Phase pithouse hamlets scattered on either side of the river near Cerro de Trincheras. Area E appears to be the closest of these hamlets to Cerro de Trincheras and more properly regarded as a separate site and not a locus of Cerro de Trincheras.

Site Formation Processes

Cerro de Trincheras is composed of a medium grayish rhyolite that weathers to a dark gray. Cobbles of this rhyolite litter the surface of the hill and there is very little naturally occurring soil on the crest or slopes of the hill. The Trinchereños used these cobbles to build the architectural features on the hill. They constructed terraces by first building a wall on the slope and then filling most of the space behind the wall with cobbles. In most cases, they then applied a layer of soil obtained from below the hill on top of these cobbles. In some cases, the fill of the terraces consisted of domestic trash, ash, and cobbles. In all cases, the vast bulk of the terrace fill by volume is rhyolite cobbles. Where soil deposits exist they are fine silt about the consistency of talcum powder and usually only 10 to 50 cm in depth. Naturally deposited soil from humic deposition, wind erosion, or water erosion is negligible on the terraces. In a heavy rain, the rock filled terraces absorb the water and the terracing itself mitigates runoff so that there is little or no evidence of water erosion displacing artifacts and deposits on the hill. In this regard, it is noteworthy that the densest concentrations of artifacts occur in the mid-level terraces of Area B, and not in the lowest terraces, as we would expect if significant erosion of deposits had occurred. The fineness of the soil, the shallowness of the deposits, and the high permeability of the rock filled terraces produce conditions of extremely poor artifact preservation. The only organic materials that we recovered were animal and human bone and these were generally in only fair to poor condition. Architectural features such as jacal houses, hearths, and prepared floors were also poorly preserved. Preservation was considerably better in Area E, the small pithouse hamlet to the south of the cerro. Here deposits were deeper and the soil more compact.

Cultural formation processes have had a profound impact on the site. These include economic use of the hill, impacts emanating from the town of Trincheras, and the construction of the railway through the region in the 1940s. Various efforts by the townspeople and INAH have mitigated these impacts.

In the middle of the nineteenth century, the village of San Rafael del Alamito was established on the north side of the Magdalena River, about a kilometer and a half from Cerro de Trincheras. When Huntington (1912) visited the site in 1910, people still lived in San Rafael, but one family built a rancho off the northwest tip of the site, below the Cerrito de la Virgin. At least one of the houses from that rancho still stands today. According to the local history, the inhabitants of San Rafael abandoned their town soon after Huntington's visit because of a flood and established the modern village of Trincheras. Here they continued to raise cattle and grow wheat in the floodplain of the river. After World War II, the coming of the railroad greatly increased the population of the community and converted it from a Norteño farming community to a railroad town.

Cerro de Trincheras is a remnant volcanic feature directly south of the Magdalena River and the modern town of Trincheras (Figure 1.11). A railroad line passes east to west along the north face of the hill. The modern community of Trincheras lies on the north side of the railway about a kilometer south of the

Magdalena River. Irrigated agricultural fields lie on each side of the Magdalena River for a distance of a kilometer or more. The area of Cerro de Trincheras was never farmed, but has been extensively used for cattle grazing. The Ejido de Trincheras y San Rafael owns the land area of the site. Mexican Route 2 lies about 22 kilometers north of Trincheras and until 2005 only a gravel road connected Trincheras to Route 2. In 2006, Mexican route 2 was converted into a four-lane toll road between Santa Ana and Altar, Sonora. The libramiento or free route from Santa Ana to Altar now follows the Magdalena River to Trincheras and then cuts north to Route 2.

The major economic use of the hill for two centuries or more has been to graze cattle. Due to the shallowness of the deposits on the site, the trampling from cattle has had a significant impact on the artifact assemblage. One striking thing about the ceramic assemblage is that the vast majority of potsherds are quite small, averaging only 5 cm^2. Debra Langer (1997) did an analysis of the ceramics to determine why they were so tiny. She found post-depositional trampling by cattle had caused most of the breakage leading to such small sherds. Trampling impacted lithics and shell much less because these materials are considerably harder and less brittle than ceramics. The only other obvious economic use of the site was a prospect hole on the top of El Pico Este in Area A and a road built up the east end of the hill, probably for this prospecting. In 1990, INAH constructed a 2 m high chain link fence around Cerro de Trincheras, primarily to keep cattle out of the site. The fence was initially only marginally effective because *ejidatarios* would simply open the gate to let their cattle into the site. After the year 2000, the municipal government of Trincheras put locks on the gates to prevent stock from entering the site. People can still easily enter the site by crawling under the fence at several points.

Figure 1.11. Cerro de Trincheras looking south with Area B excavations showing as lighter terraces (photograph courtesy of Adriel Heisey).

Workers began construction on *The Ferrocarril Sonora-Baja California* (The Sonora to Baja California Railroad) in 1937 at Mexicali Baja California del Norte, and they finally completed the line at Benjamín Hill, Sonora in 1947. In order to obtain stone to build up the railroad bed and to construct bridges for the track, workmen stripped cobbles off of the volcanic hills along the route. They would start at the top of a hill and push the cobbles down to the base where they would load them into trucks. This process left the hills with alternating vertical strips of dark cobbles and reddish exposed desert soil. The workmen laid the railroad track along the north face of Cerro de Trincheras barely clipping the northeast tip of the hill. They pushed the cobbles down from almost all of the volcanic hills around the hill including the Cerritos del Este and Sur y Oeste directly south of Cerros de Trincheras. They left oblong piles of stone strewn between the Cerrito del Oeste and the Cerrito del Sur. This stone collecting may also have destroyed gridded gardens that Huntington (1914:69) described as being at the south base of the hill. Construction workers stripped stone from numerous *cerros de trincheras* on the north side of the river and virtually destroyed the *cerro de trincheras* on the Trincheritas (O'Donovan 2002:33-34). This small volcanic hill lies in the town of Trincheras and about a half kilometer northeast of Cerro de Trincheras. They brought in a bulldozer to strip rock from the northeast edge of Cerro de Trincheras. The bulldozer passed through La Cancha puncturing the northern and southern walls of the feature. Our excavations located imprints of the bulldozer's tracks in the surface of the feature (Figure 1.12). According to local informants, the Municipal President of Trincheras protested these actions to the engineers building the railroad and the workers stopped removing cobbles from the hill. The damage to the site resulting from these activities is largely restricted to the lower slopes on the northeast edge of the hill.

Elderly informants told us in 1995 and 1996 that in their youth Cerro de Trincheras was covered with metates, manos and even an occasional whole or partial ceramic vessel. Over the years, these materials disappeared as people collected them and brought them to their homes. We were also told that a couple would come down from California every year and buy any artifacts that the local people might have to sell. When we first started visiting Trincheras in the mid-1980s locals routinely offered us stone axes, metates, and manos for sale. We did not encounter such offers when we returned in 1991.

There is little evidence of pot hunting on the hill itself, but looters dug up nearby cremation cemeteries. Our 1991 survey found fewer than 20 looter's holes on the terraces (O'Donovan 2002:34). We located a cremation cemetery south of Cerro de Trincheras and north of the Cerrito del Sur. This cemetery was extensively pot hunted, and according to local informants yielded large numbers of polychrome vessels. People living on the southern edge of the town of Trincheras (the north side of the site) also reported to us that they occasionally found cremation urns while excavating for tree plantings or construction purposes. There is a growing awareness in the community of the damage that looting does to archaeological sites. In March of 2007, the municipal president of Trincheras presented to the Centro INAH Sonora nine ceramic cremation urns that a family dug up while constructing a septic system on the southern edge of the town of Trincheras (Figure 1.13).

The people of Trincheras visit Cerro de Trincheras often. It is a place of adventure for children's play and where teenagers go to escape the scrutiny of adults in the community. Individuals regularly light candles at the shrine to the Virgin Mary painted on the north face of the Cerrito de la Virgin. On the Day of the

Figure 1.12. Bulldozer tracks from the 1940s on the floor of La Cancha.

Figure 1.13. Ceramic vessels found during construction of a septic system.

Virgin (December 12), a procession winds its way from the town church through the community to the shrine. When we did our first survey of the area in 1985 this shrine was not present, but it had appeared by 1988. Of the many features on the crest of the hill (Area A), one is composed of stacked rock in the form of a Roman numeral five just below the Pico Este. We learned during our excavations that a fifth grade class from the Trincheras elementary school had constructed this "V" while on a field trip to the site about thirty years ago (O'Donovan 2002:34). More recently with the establishment of cell phone service in the town of Trincheras, the cerro has become a lookout point for drug smuggling. Drug smugglers pay individuals to sit on the hill with cell phones and watch for Mexican Army patrols in the surrounding area. When a drug plane comes in, the pilot calls the lookout to check for patrols before landing in the surrounding desert. On the hill, we find snack wrappers, drink cups, and cell phone cards where the lookouts sit.

In 2007, the INAH made money available to develop Cerro de Trincheras for tourism. As we finish this monograph these developments are underway. They include the construction of a visitor's center on the north side of the railroad tracks and an interpretive trail from the base of the site to El Caracol in the Abra Este. In 2008, preparations for the visitor's center revealed over 130 urn cremations. At the time of this writing, these cremations have not been fully analyzed and, therefore, were not included in this report.

Stratigraphy

The stratigraphic profiles from all of the areas we excavated on the hill (that is all but Area E) revealed a consistent set of stratigraphic relationships. The Trinchereños generally built terrace walls on bedrock. They then filled in behind the walls with cobbles. Sometime this fill included trash and in other cases it did not. Above El Mirador, the fill of the terraces is only cobbles, but below El Mirador, they topped the cobble fill with very fine silt obtained from below the hill. Some of this silt filtered down between the cobbles and the rest of it formed a level of soil 10 cm to 30 cm on top of the cobbles. The people lived on this level of silt, built jacals and ramadas on it, and carried out the activities of daily life. In some cases, they packed the surface into a hard level or *apisonado,* but in most cases they did not. In none of the terraces did we find evidence of earlier terraces inside later ones or multiple use surfaces.

Once we returned to the laboratory, we systematically classified every layer we had defined in the field to a typology based on the stratigraphic profiles and our interpretation of the formation processes that had created that layer. Terrace fill (*relleno de terasa*) was those levels that the Trinchereños had laid down behind the terrace walls to create the flat terrace surface. We assumed that the artifacts and ecofacts (primarily ash and charcoal) that we found in these levels are in secondary context (Schiffer 1987), meaning that they do not reflect activities on the terrace we found them, but rather were produced from activities in other areas of the site and then transported to the terrace as trash. We used artifacts from these deposits to make general inferences about activities at the site and to date the construction of terraces. Occupation levels included those levels above the terrace fill, and artifacts and ecofacts from *apisonados.* We assumed that these levels represented primary, or in some cases, defacto contexts, which is where artifacts and ecofacts were deposited at their place of use. We used these levels, and only these levels, to make inferences about the distribution of artifacts and activities on specific terraces. Feature fill referred to soil, artifacts, and ecofacts we removed from within features. Usually these deposits were quite shallow (5-10 cm) and we used them to interpret the dating and use of features. Occupation levels and feature fill accounted for 625 m^3 or 75 percent of the total volume excavated.

Field Methods

We conducted excavations at the site of Cerro de Trincheras, from February 5, 1995 to April 29, 1995. Randall McGuire and Elisa Villalpando directed the fieldwork. The project employed ten archaeologists from both United States, and Mexican institutions (John McGregor, Maria O'Donovan, Mary F. Price, Janna Huey, and Mike Rudler of Binghamton University, Maria Guadalupe Sanchez de Carpenter of the University of Arizona, Victoria Vargas of Arizona State University, and Eréndira Conteras Barragán, Emiliano Gallaga Murrieta and Victor Ortega Leon of the Centro INAH Sonora). During the course of the excavation the project employed up to 28 people from the local community of Trincheras as cooks, field laborers, and laboratory help. In the field, the usual ratio of archaeologists to laborers was less than 1 to 4.

We returned for a second season of excavations at the site of Cerro de Trincheras from February 11, 1996 to May 4, 1996. Randall McGuire and Elisa Villalpando again directed the fieldwork. The project employed ten archaeologists from both United States and Mexican institutions (John McGregor, Maria O'Donovan, Bridget Gaitan, Gillian Newell, and Debbie Langer of Binghamton University, Beth Bagwell of the University of New México, and Eréndira Conteras Barragán, Emiliano Gallaga Murrieta, Júpiter Martínez Ramírez, and Victor Ortega Leon of the Centro INAH Sonora). During the course of the excavation the project employed up to 29 people from the local community of Trincheras as cooks, field laborers, and laboratory help. In the field, the ratio of archaeologists to laborers was 1 to 4 or less.

Both years we contracted with Western Mapping (then known as Geo-Map) of Tucson, Arizona to prepare an overall map of the site and maps of individual loci. This company had done the mapping for the 1991 mapping project. They added the data from the two years of excavation to the AutoCAD map that they had prepared for that project. These AutoCAD files are archived at Western Mapping, Binghamton University, and at the Centro INAH Sonora, in Hermosillo, Sonora.

Crews

Excavation crews worked in different loci on the site and usually did not have contact with each other during the day, therefore, each crew functioned as an independent team. Teams consisted of two archaeologists and crewmembers from Trincheras. The number of laborers varied depending upon the tasks at hand. One of the archaeologists on the crew served as crew chief and the second was primarily responsible for record keeping. The archaeologists shared responsibility for making decisions about the excavation and for the interpretation of their area.

Provenience Control

The site of Cerro de Trincheras covers an area of more than 100 ha, and the differences in elevation across the site are extreme, over 150 m. We therefore did not try to maintain a single grid or elevation datum over the entire site. Instead we established a grid and elevation datum in each area. We used a two level designation with a capital letter and a number to designate each area (grid). At the highest level, we used the loci defined by the Cerro de Trincheras Mapping Project designated by capital letters A, B, C, D, and E (O'Donovan 2002). Within these very large loci we designated each new datum by a number, 1, 2, 3, creating smaller 'areas' (e.g., Area B1). During the project we defined and excavated 13 areas (A1, B1 to B11, D, and E). At the end of the project, Western Mapping of Tucson mapped in the datums and grids for each area, and added them to the site map. We used the same procedures to establish grids in each area. On flat areas, (A1, D and E) we ran the base line from true north to true south. On the steep slopes of Area B, we placed the base line along the long axis of the terraces.

The volcanic hill that Cerro de Trincheras sits on has strong magnetic properties. These properties are strong enough to pull a compass needle away from magnetic north. The extent of this effect varied at different points on the hill. We therefore used surveying instruments and the overall site grid established by Western Mapping to determine true north when needed.

Grid unit sizes also varied between the level and sloped loci. The basic unit of provenience control on the terraces in Areas A and B were a 1 m square. In Areas E and D, which are off the hill and where excavations were more extensive, we used 2 m squares. We designated each square by the letter and number of the area and the grid coordinates of the northeast corner in the following format A1:N100/E100. In every grid, we set the elevation datum at 100 m so that we did not have to work with positive and negative elevations, with the result that all elevations were taken below datum.

We numbered features continuously across the entire site. In Spanish, we referred to features as *construcciones,* and therefore, field feature numbers always had the prefix C. Each feature received a unique number regardless of what it was. The only exceptions to this were subfeatures within larger features, such as a hearth in a pithouse or a group of postholes from a ramada. In this case, the larger feature received a number, and the smaller features were numbered as sub-features. For example, a pithouse would receive a feature number C10, and a hearth in the pithouse would be numbered C10.1 and a posthole C10.2. Bridget Zavala analyzed the features from the site. She classified and renumbered the features by type (Chapter 2 and Table 1.1).

General Excavation Procedures

The project directors chose excavation areas using the feature types and loci defined in the mapping project (O'Donovan 2002). By taking a sample of different feature types, we were able to infer different activity units, and by sampling within and between loci we were able to discuss the distribution and chronology of these units across the site. This procedure allowed us to estimate parameters such as the number of houses per residential terrace etc. necessary for making inferences about population and labor investment. Such a broad based sample gave us chronometric dates from all portions of the site, and information on activity structure from across the site.

During the 1995 excavation season we focused our work on Areas B, D, and E. In Area B we worked in a section that the 1991 survey had determined contained large amounts of shell (Areas B1, B2, B3, and B4). During the 1996 excavation season we focused our work on Areas A and B. Area A is the crest of the hill where there are numerous unique features that may be ritual or administrative in character. We excavated the most prominent of these features, the Caracol (Area A1). Our work in area B sought to gain a larger sample from what had been the primary habitation area of the site (Areas B6, B7, B8, B9, B10, and B11). We also excavated a portion of the most prominent feature in Area B, La Cancha (B5).

The physical remains, topography, and

Table 1.1. Feature Field Numbers and Final Feature Designations

Feature category/ Categoría del elemento	Feature number/ Número de elemento	Field feature number/ Número de elemento de campo	Locus/ Area
Pithouse	6	#	E
Rock Arrangement/Configuración de piedras	4	1	D
Pithouse	2	4	E
Hearth/Fogón	12	4.1	E
Circular Stone Structure/Estructura Circular de Piedra	2	7	A1
La Cancha	"La Cancha"	8, 8.3, 8.4	B5
El Caracol	"El Caracol"	9, 9.1	A1
Burial/Entierro	1	11	E
Hearth/Fogón	1	12	E
Pit/Hoyo	10	13	E
Hearth/Fogón	5	14	E
Jacal	7	15	B1
Jacal	1	16	B1
Platform/Plataforma	3	19	B4
Jacal	2	20	B2
Pit/Hoyo	14	21	B2
Circular Stone Structure/Estructura Circular de Piedra	17	22	B3
Ancillary Terrace/ Terraza Anciliaria	1	23	B3
Access Feature/Elemento de Acceso: Escalones	2	24	B3
Pit/Hoyo	1	25	E
Hearth/Fogón	3	26	E
Hearth/Fogón	4	27	E
Pit/Hoyo	2	28	E
Pit/Hoyo	3	29	E
Pit/Hoyo	4	30	E
Pit/Hoyo	5	31	E
Pithouse	1	32	E
Puddling Pit/Pozo de mezcla	2	33	E
Midden/Basurero	1	34	E
Pithouse	7	35.2	E
Pithouse	8	35.3	E
Pithouse	9	35.4	E
Rock Arrangement/Configuración de piedras	5	36	D
Hearth/Fogón	17	36.1	D
Pit/Hoyo	19	37	D
Burial/Entierro	11	38	D
Pit/Hoyo	20	39	D
Burial/Entierro	3	40	B2
Quadrangular Stone Structure/Estructura cuadrangular de piedra	3	41	D
Pit/Hoyo	3	42	D
Pit/Hoyo	21	43	D
Pit/Hoyo	22	44	D
Pit/Hoyo	23	45	D
Pit/Hoyo	9	47	E
Pit/Hoyo	6	51	E
Hearth/Fogón	6	52	E

Table 1.1. Feature Field Numbers and Final Feature Designations, cont'd

Feature category/ Categoría del elemento	Feature number/ Número de elemento	Field feature number/ Número de elemento de campo	Locus/ Area
Possible House Floor/Piso Posible de casa	1	54	E
Rock Arrangement/Configuración de piedras	1	55	E
Pit/Hoyo	12	55.1	E
Possible Ramada/ramada Posible	1	57	E
Quadrangular Stone Structure/Estructura cuadrangular de piedra	4	58	D
El Caracolito	"El Caracolito"	59	D
"Petrograbados"	1	69	B3
Pit/Hoyo	15	70	B4
Hearth/Fogón	14	71	B4
Pit/Hoyo	11	72	E
Occupational Surface/Superficie Ocupacional	2	73	E
Hearth/Fogón	13	73.1	E
Pit/Hoyo	13	73.2	E
Hearth/Fogón	10	74	E
Occupational Surface/Superficie Ocupacional	3	75	E
Burial/Entierro	2	76	E
Hearth/Fogón	8	77	E
Hearth/Fogón	9	78	E
Rock Arrangement/Configuración de piedras	2	79A	E
Access Feature/Elemento de Acceso: Escalones	1	79B	B4
Rock Arrangement/Configuración de piedras	3	80	E
Pit/Hoyo	7	81	E
Occupational Surface/Superficie Ocupacional	1	82	E
Hearth/Fogón	7	83	E
Midden/Basurero	2	84	E
Pit/Hoyo	8	85	E
Hearth/Fogón	11	86	E
Pithouse	3	87	E
Hearth/Fogón	2	88	E
Pit/Hoyo	16	89M	B4
Jacal	3	89	B4
Burial/Entierro	4	90	B4
Pithouse	4	91, 50	E
Pithouse	5	92A, 49	E
Jacal	4	92B	B6
Puddling Pit/Pozo de mezcla	1	92. 1A	E
Hearth/Fogón	15	92.1B	B6
Pit/Hoyo	17	92.2B	B6
Burial/Entierro	5	93	B6
Circular Stone Structure/Estructura Circular de Piedra	18	94	B6
Quadrangular Stone Structure/Estructura cuadrangular de piedra	1	95	B6
Platform/Plataforma	1	96	B6
Circular Stone Structure/Estructura Circular de Piedra	19	97	B6
Platform/Plataforma	2	98	B6
Circular Stone Structure/Estructura Circular de Piedra	20	99	B6
Occupational Surface/Superficie Ocupacional	4	100	B6

Table 1.1. Feature Field Numbers and Final Feature Designations, cont'd

Feature category/ Categoría del elemento	Feature number/ Número de elemento	Field feature number/ Número de elemento de campo	Locus/ Area
Burial/Entierro	6	101	B6
Burial/Entierro	7	102	B6
Burial/Entierro	8	104	B6
Pit/Hoyo	18	105	B11
Burial/Entierro	10	107	B11
Rock Arrangement/Configuración de piedras	6	108	B11
Jacal	5	115	B7
Hearth/Fogón	16	116	B7
Access Feature:Ramp/Elemento de Acceso: Rampa	2	117	B8
Quadrangular Stone Structure/Estructura cuadrangular de piedra	2	118	B9
Jacal	6	119	B9
Burial/Entierro	9	120	B9
Circular Stone Structure/Estructura Circular de Piedra	3	121	A1
Circular Stone Structure/Estructura Circular de Piedra	4	122	A1
Circular Stone Structure/Estructura Circular de Piedra	5	123	A1
Circular Stone Structure/Estructura Circular de Piedra	6	124	A1
Circular Stone Structure/Estructura Circular de Piedra	7	125	A1
Circular Stone Structure/Estructura Circular de Piedra	8	126	A1
Circular Stone Structure/Estructura Circular de Piedra	9	127	A1
Circular Stone Structure/Estructura Circular de Piedra	10	128	A1
Circular Stone Structure/Estructura Circular de Piedra	11	129	A1
Circular Stone Structure/Estructura Circular de Piedra	12	130	A1
Access Feature: Ramp/Elemento de Acceso: Rampa	1	131	A1
Circular Stone Structure/Estructura Circular de Piedra	13	132	A1
Circular Stone Structure/Estructura Circular de Piedra	14	133	A1
Circular Stone Structure/Estructura Circular de Piedra	15	134	A1
Circular Stone Structure/Estructura Circular de Piedra	16	135	A1
Circular Stone Structure/Estructura Circular de Piedra	21	136	A1
Circular Stone Structure/Estructura Circular de Piedra	22	137	A1
Circular Stone Structure/Estructura Circular de Piedra	23	138	A1
Circular Stone Structure/Estructura Circular de Piedra	1	139	A1
Circular Stone Structure/Estructura Circular de Piedra	24	140	A1

soil conditions vary enough between features and loci that a single excavation method could not be used over the entire site. Some general procedures were, however, followed in all areas. All excavations were done by hand. Stratigraphic profiles were drawn whenever appropriate and in as much as is possible artifacts were collected by natural and cultural levels. With the exception of exploratory trenching, all fill was passed through either 1/4-inch or .5 cm mesh screens to maximize artifact recovery. When field crews encountered buried features they excavated, collected, mapped, and photographed them in their entirety. We plotted all excavations and features on the site map generated by the mapping project.

The completeness and condition of archaeological materials at the site was disappointing. Archaeological deposits at Cerro de Trincheras tended to be very shallow, usually not more than 10 cm to 20 cm in depth and composed of fine silt. This meant that the preservation of materials was generally quite poor. Organic materials were only present if charred, and the preservation of bone, both animal and human, was generally poor. Features also had not survived in good condition. Houses, both surface jacales, and pithouses, usually showed evidence of lots of disturbance and poor preservation. Artifacts also have suffered damage as a consequence of the shallow deposits. For example, potsherds tended to be quite small from trampling by cows (Langer 1997). A second consequence of the shallow deposits is that looters have removed an unknown, but clearly large, amount of material from the surface of the site.

In Areas D and E the initial problem was how to discover buried features. Area D contains most of the square rooms at the cerro and Area E was a pithouse hamlet near Cerro de Trincheras. We dug a set of trenches regularly spaced at 10 m intervals across each locus to identify buried houses and then we excavated a sample of the houses and other features. Crews dug additional trenches and stripped between trenches to define courtyard patterns similar to those archaeologists have observed in Hohokam sites. Crews devoted about half of their effort in these areas to the discovery of features with the second half used to dig features.

We began the excavation of each terrace in loci A and B by digging a stratigraphic trench along the short axis of the terrace. From these trenches, we could discern the construction sequence of the terrace and identify layers deposited during and after the occupation of the terrace. In these loci, trenching did not work as an effective way to discover features. The prehistoric inhabitants had filled the terraces with pebbles and cobbles and then topped them with a thin layer of very fine silt. The occupational deposits in these terraces varied in depth from 10 cm to 20 cm. Numerous attempts to discover features through trenching in Areas B1 and B2 proved to be ineffective. With this failure we switched to stripping each terrace in 1 m units with whiskbrooms and trowels (Figure 1.14). This procedure proved effective in locating features and in recovering artifacts from occupational layers.

The research design for this project did not call for the excavation of burials. To the south of the hill, we located a prehistoric cremation cemetery that was coeval with the site, but we did not do excavations in this area. Numerous individuals who lived on the south side of the modern town of Trincheras reported to us that they had found urn cremations while digging in their yards. Despite our efforts to avoid burials we did encounter a total of ten inhumations and one cremation during our excavations. We excavated each of the inhumations in their entirety, then collected, recorded, and photographed them.

General Recording Procedures

The project developed a series of forms to track the flow of materials, and to record data. These included special forms to record all features (Forma de Construccion), special samples such as pollen, flotation, radiocarbon (Forma de Muestra), photographs (Forma Fotografías), and excavation units by level (Forma de Unidad).

Crews separated materials in the field into four categories: sherds, ceramics, shell, and small objects. They bagged each of these materials separately, and gave every bag a unique bag number that they recorded on the field form. When the field crew brought the materials to the laboratory, the laboratory crew recorded the bag numbers on a laboratory form. We used this form to track the material through the laboratory processing, and then through analysis. After analysis we boxed the materials by their category and bag number. Archaeologists point provenienced, mapped, and bagged separately any unusual or temporally diagnostic artifacts and all artifacts in contact with a structure floor. They placed objects that appeared fragile, or small objects that had been point provenienced into a plastic vial and then put the vial in a bag.

Each archaeologist kept a field journal in either English or Spanish (or both). Each day's entry began on a fresh page with the day's date and the recorder's name in the top left hand corner of the page. The journals summarize the days work including: which laborers worked on the crew that day, where excavations were done, what excavation strategy was used, how much excavation was done, and what features were excavated. They used graph paper in the notebooks to draw and label the units that had been excavated each day. A reader can leaf through the graph pages and see the progress of excavation from day to day and identify the location and shape of all units. The archaeologists discussed what excavation strategies they followed that day and why. They noted general soil conditions, such as, color, rocks, roots, and animal disturbances. They reflected on any types of problems they had encountered during the day and described notable finds that the crews made during that day. The project directors encouraged the archaeologists in the field to speculate in their comments about what was going on in their area, how it may relate to the rest of the site, or any other ideas they might have about the site.

During the 1995 field season, John McGregor and Randall McGuire were the survey and mapping crew for the project. They did all surveying, general mapping, profiles, and feature maps. They used a theolodite and EDM to establish base lines, datum and grids. In 1996, McGregor took over all surveying duties. He and Beth Bagwell conducted most of the feature mapping at the site in order to guarantee consistency in the finished products. During the 1995 field season, the surveyors

Figure 1.14. Hand excavation with trowels and whiskbrooms in Area B8.

mapped terrace and feature walls as units and used a standard rock pattern to fill the walls on the map. During the 1996 field season, the mapping crew drew in every rock visible in a plan view of the excavated walls. Western Mapping included the maps from both years into the AutoCAD map file for the site.

Archaeologists did all photography using film cameras. Each crew had a 35 mm camera loaded with black and white film. The archaeologists took photographs to illustrate the progress of the excavation, to show crews at work, and to record features. They listed every photograph taken on the photo record. The first photograph on each role of film was an identification card with the date, crew initials, the roll number for the film, and SON:F:10:2 (CR). Record shots always included a mugboard with SON:F:10:2 (CR), the area, the feature number, and the date. The archaeologists took multiple exposures for record shots and photographed each feature from multiple directions. In addition, Randall McGuire took photographs with a 35 mm camera loaded with color slide film and a Pentax 67 medium format (6 mm by 7 mm) camera loaded with black and white film. He also made record shots of almost all features with these two cameras. In addition, he shot 35 mm slides of the site and of the fieldwork.

During the 1996 field season, we hosted Adriel Heisey who used an ultra-light airplane to take photographs of the region (Figure 1.15). Adriel Heisey is an internationally known photographer who does art photography from the air. *National Geographic* has done an article on his photography, including a cover, and he has staged exhibits at many museums including the Arizona State Museum, the Albuquerque Museum of Art and History, the National Museum of Natural History, the University of Colorado Museum of Natural History, the National Museum of the Marine Corps, the

Figure 1.15. Adriel Heisey and Randall McGuire in Heisey's ultra-light plane photographing Cerro de Trincheras (photograph courtesy of Adriel Heisey).

Anasazi Heritage Center, and the Museo de Sonora. He published two books that include photographs from his visit with us and of Cerro de Trincheras (Heisey 2000, 2004). In addition to his art photography, he also took black and white photographs and Randall McGuire took color slides for our research use.

Dating Samples

We collected radiocarbon and archaeomagnetic samples in the field. The field archaeologists collected the radiocarbon samples and Randall McGuire collected the archaeomagnetic samples from burned in situ features. We submitted 20 radiocarbon samples to the Beta Analytical Laboratory in Miami, Florida for analysis and we received excellent results on these samples. We sent eight archaeomagnetic samples from the 1995 excavation to the Colorado State University archaeomagnetic laboratory in Fort Collins, Colorado. None of the archaeomagnetic samples produced viable data because of the magnetic characteristics of the hill. For this reason, we did not take archaeomagnetic samples in 1996. In 2008, the Centro INAH Sonora submitted bone from ten of the inhumations from Cerros de Trincheras to the University of Arizona radiocarbon laboratory for Accelerator Mass Spectrometry (AMS) dating. Nine of these ten samples yielded dates. We present the results and interpretation of the radiocarbon dates in the concluding chapter of this report.

We collected radiocarbon samples only from features. Under no circumstances did archaeologists take radiocarbon samples from a screen. We gave priority to collecting burned annual material (reeds, matting, seeds, twigs, etc.) from good contexts in order to avoid the "old wood" problem in desert conditions (Schiffer 1982). Unfortunately we encountered very few situations that fit these criteria. Whenever possible we collected multiple samples from a single context. We collected large lumps of charcoal for species identification. The archaeologists point-provenienced all radiocarbon samples. Because the field crews encountered very few identifiable burned annual materials, we ended up running most of our radiocarbon dates on seeds (primarily corn) derived from flotation samples.

Biological Materials

The project collected three types of biological samples, which included pollen, animal bone, and flotation. We developed collection techniques in cooperation with the three specialists, who then analyzed the materials. The three consultants for environmental and subsistence analyses, who included Dr. Peter Stahl for faunal analysis, Dr. Charles Miksicek for flotation, and Dr. Suzanne Fish for pollen analysis, visited the field project in late March of 1995. At this time, excavations had progressed to the point that consultants could inspect the full range of project proveniences and advise on further sampling strategies. The specialists also reviewed laboratory processing, storage, and plans for later shipment of samples. Charles Miksicek trained laboratory personnel in the processing of flotation samples so that the recovery of charred remains could be undertaken in the field laboratory.

The field visit enabled joint reconnaissance of the Cerro de Trincheras environment with shared observations and impressions. Consultants familiarized themselves with the major biotic communities of current basin settings, directing special attention to the culturally modified conditions of agriculture. They collected comparative reference materials for faunal and botanical analyses.

We collected pollen samples from fresh exposures, whether from profiles or surfaces, in order to avoid contamination by modern airborne pollen. Before excavation began, we took several modern samples from locations at the bottom, middle, and top of the hill. In burials, we took samples at the head, feet, and in the pelvic cavity. We took pollen washes on intact ceramic vessels and metates from primary contexts. Although terraces usually contained other features, we sampled them in their own right as artificial constructions and, in some cases, as potential agricultural features. We took these samples from the stratigraphic profile of each terrace.

The field crews collected animal bone during the course of our general excavations. Whether located in the screens or in situ we bagged bone separately from all other artifacts. The archaeologist kept and submitted for analysis all bones that they encountered.

We standardized flotation samples at approximately 4 liters per sample. In practice, archaeologists filled one-gallon size Ziploc bags with enough dirt so that they could still be comfortably closed. We identified the best places to sample as the floors and roof fall areas of burned structures, hearths, or any thermal features like roasting pits, and any kind of stratified trash with visible ash, charcoal, bone, or shell. Basically we collected anywhere we saw a lot of charcoal flecks. Laboratory workers extracted both the light and heavy flotation fractions in the field by floating the samples in buckets. The sandy nature of the soil made the use of a flotation machine or chemical additives unnecessary. A project archaeologist examined the heavy float fraction under a magnifying glass in the field laboratory and set aside any bone in the samples for zooarchaeological analysis (Figure 1.16).

Laboratory Methods

We set up a field laboratory in the town of Trincheras and we conducted the preliminary cleaning, sorting, and analyses there. At the end of the field season, we returned all ceramics, chipped lithics, ground stone, and shell to the Centro INAH Sonora in Hermosillo for further analyses and curation. Certain samples (palynology, flotation, faunal, and chronometric dating) were removed to the United States for analysis and then returned to México. By 1999, all of the materials from the excavations had been analyzed, returned to México, and curated at the Centro INAH Sonora in Hermosillo. The analysts present the methods used in each analysis in their respective chapters.

We created a relational database for field and laboratory data using the Paradox database management program. The master database table, called "units," contained data for each excavation unit recorded in the field, including the interpretation of that unit in terms of the stratigraphic typology. Each unit was defined by its provience information (Area, grid coordinates, feature, and stratigraphic level). Each material type (ceramics, lithics, ground stone, shell, animal bone, etc) had its own slave table. The provenience information for each item or group (bag) of items in the slave table related or linked the slave table to the master table.

Contributions of Research

The results of the Cerro de Trincheras Excavation Project contributes to archaeological research on several levels. It significantly increases our understanding of aboriginal history, the dynamics of large-scale cultural change in the Southwest/Northwest, and the applicability of World Systems and Peer Polity models to prehistoric cultural change.

Ours was the first large-scale excavation project ever carried out in northwestern Sonora. As such, it supplies hard data to test many speculations previous researchers have made about the timing of growth at Cerro de Trincheras, the size and permanence of the human population, the nature of activities at the site, and the role of the site in a larger regional and inter-regional economic system. The project provides a base for further research in the region. Conclusions drawn from survey data were weak because not enough excavations have been done for us to interpret the character of features and sites from surface indications. Now that we know what excavated residential terraces, houses, and ceremonial structures look like on the surface, we can make reconstructions of sites based on survey data.

Each of the hypotheses considered here have a different implication for our broader explanations of cultural change in the Southwest/Northwest. If the site was either a rustic village or a shell trade outpost, then the peripheral nature of northwest Sonora to developments in the Southwest/Northwest is affirmed. If the site were the entrepot of Mesoamerican merchants, then it would have been a key center that shaped developments to the north and south. Finally, as an indigenous center, Cerro de Trincheras, would have to be included in explanations of Southwest/Northwestern prehistory and the interpretations of prehistoric regional systems as a place comparable to other late prehistoric towns.

The most basic question at stake in our research is a theoretical one: given the levels of development we see in the prehistoric Southwest/Northwest, is prehistoric cultural change

Figure 1.16. Paul Fish, Emiliano Gallaga and Suzanne Fish processing flotation samples in the field laboratory.

best explained in terms of long-range economic relations or local ecologies? World Systems theorists argue that systems of long-range exchange can drive or shape local developments in the late prehistoric Southwest/Northwest. Advocates of Peer Polity models argue that economies and technologies at this level of development are too weak for long-range exchange to be a driving force in their development. This opposition is ultimately too simple; however, by examining it in specific cases like Cerro de Trincheras, we can gain a richer understanding of the complexities involved in the opposition and build new theories. These theories will assist our attempts to explain cultural change in other places and times where we see levels of cultural development like those in the Southwest/Northwest.

Organization of this Monograph

Many hands contributed to the excavation of Cerro de Trincheras, including archaeologists, field laborers, laboratory workers, and cooks. This monograph is the collected work of 21 different authors from various institutions in the United States and México. From its inception, this project has been bilingual and individuals have kept notes and written documents in their native tongue, whether it be English or Spanish. This monograph is also bilingual with chapters in English and Spanish, although the majority of the monograph is in English. The Centro INAH Sonora has published a summary version of this monograph entirely in Spanish (Villalpando and McGuire 2009). Needless to say, all 21 authors of this monograph have not agreed on all interpretations and no "project" interpretation has been forced on them. In the concluding chapter, we will evaluate, summarize, and even disagree with the various interpretations in the monograph.

We organized the monograph in 23 chapters, including an introduction (Chapter 1) and a conclusion (Chapter 23). Chapter 2 presents a typology of features for Cerro de Trincheras and compares them to Hohokam features. Individual feature descriptions are included in subsequent chapters that describe each Area or excavation area. Seven chapters present the analysis of the artifactual material that we recovered from the excavation. These chapters include discussions of ceramics, lithics, ground stone, shell, spindle whorls and miscellaneous artifacts, beads, and culturally modified bone. Discussions of the archaeobiology of the site follow in three chapters on botany, fauna, and inhumations from the site. We describe the Areas that we excavated in 1995 and 1996 in ten chapters. We conclude the volume with a chapter that returns to the issues raised in our research design and synthesizes the results of the project. Companion materials to this report including a detailed map and all of the data bases we used in our analyses can be found by searching http://www.statemuseum.arizona.edu/pubs/archseries/companion_materials.shtml.

Chapter 2

Building Trincheras: An Analysis of Architectural Features at Cerro De Trincheras

Bridget G. Zavala. Universidad Juárez del Estado de Durango

Construcciones

Este capítulo analiza los 124 yacimientos registrados y excavados en Cerro de Trincheras durante las temporadas de trabajo de campo de 1995 y 1996. Las yacimientos incluídos: terrazas, estucturas circulares de piedra, estructuras cuadrangulares de piedra, casas semi-subterráneas, jacales, fosas, basureros, plataformas, ramadas, cimientos grabados, arreglos de roca, superficies de ocupación, carreteras de acceso, entierros y tres estructuras especializadas, La Cancha, El Caracol y El Caracolito. Zavala estudia las construcciones por tipo, concluyendo con la definición de cinco diseños arquitectónicos prinicpales que puden representar el uso diferenciado del espacio sobre y alrededor del cerro. Finalmente, la autora compara estos diseños con casos etnográficos y etnohistóricos del noroeste de México para entender el simbolismo monumental del cerro en comparasión con las construcciones efímeras usadas en la vida cotidiana.

Field crews recorded and excavated 124 features at Cerro de Trincheras during the 1995 and 1996 field seasons. This chapter presents the results of the excavation of the features by feature type. First, I present a brief summary of the distribution of the features by excavation area. Second, I describe the four terrace categories defined by the Cerro de Trincheras Mapping Project. Next, I define each of the general feature types found at the site: circular stone structure, quadrangular stone structure, pithouse, jacal, pit, midden, platform, ramada, bedrock engraving, rock arrangement, occupational surface, access feature, and burial. Each feature type description includes summary data from each feature excavated. In the final section of this chapter, I offer a summary and discussion of the data presented herein.

The crew excavated 10 different terraces (B1-4 and B6-11), La Cancha (the court) (B5), the top of the hill (A1), an area on the western side of the hill near the base (D) and an area off the cerro on the southern side (E). Table 2.1 shows the distribution of feature types by excavation area with the exception of the three specialized features (La Cancha, El Caracol, and El Caracolita). The majority of the features were located in excavation Area E (n = 50). The archaeologists also found the largest variation among features in Area E. Area A1 contains 21 features. Twenty of these are circular stone structures. The Caracol, which means "the snail," is also located in A1. The crew recorded 14 features in excavation Area B6, which is a few meters south of La Cancha, which means "the court." The team described twelve features in Area D, the majority of which were pits. The investigators recorded a total of 24 features in the remainder of the excavation areas, all of which were on the terraces.

Descriptions of Terraces by Type

The terraces are unarguably the most striking architectural features at the site (Figure 2.1). The labor investment in the construction of the terraces was massive. The crew recorded 880 terraces during the Cerro de Trincheras Mapping Project. During the excavation of the site 12 more terraces were recorded. These features are what make the site type *cerros de trincheras* unique. A feature description of the site would be incomplete without a brief description of types of terraces present on the site. Archaeologists defined three distinct terrace types were at the site: (1) terraces, (2) terraces with walls (Figure 2.2), and (3) narrow terraces. Additionally, a complementary terrace type was identified and called an ancillary terrace. Investigators established distinctions between the types on the basis of wall construction and dimensions.

Terraces

The terrace type was defined as those terraces that did not appear to have well built walls. Terraces were constructed using dry-laid masonry of irregular unshaped cobbles to create a berm like barrier, which served as the terrace limit. The space between the natural slope of the hill and the terrace wall was then filled with cobbles and trash in order to create a flat surface. The terraces measured from 10 to 100 m in length (O'Donovan 1997:101), from 1.5 to 5 m in width, and from .30 to 1.5 m in height.

Terraces With Walls

O'Donovan (1997) found that the terraces with walls are the largest terraces at the site. Builders constructed them using dry-laid masonry to form terrace walls. The terrace walls were core and veneer masonry. In this method terrace walls were built by constructing two parallel coursed walls and then by filling the gap between these walls with cobbles. The builder then filled the terrace with cobbles covered with a thin layer of soil to create a flat surface. The walls "were almost exclusively used to block access or sight, into the higher portions of the site" (O'Donovan 1997:105). Wall fall associated with these structures suggests that they once stood higher than they do today. Recorders found terraces with walls mostly in the higher elevations and on steeper slopes. According to O'Donovan (1997:102), the slope of the hill is such that it necessitates a greater investment in terrace wall construction to support the weight of the fill necessary to create a flat surface. This is the case both in terms of height and of wall thickness. The terraces range from 10 to 100 m in length, 1.5 to 5 m in width, and 1.5 to 3 m in height on the down-slope side.

Narrow Terraces

Narrow terraces are the most insubstantial of the typology. Builders constructed narrow terraces by laying down a course of irregular cobbles. The Mapping Project found the narrow terraces in clusters at lower elevations of the site. The narrow terraces measure on average 10.07 m in length, 1.95 m in width, and .38 m in height. Due to their small size and clustering, it is believed that these probably were single-function terraces (O'Donovan 1997:103).

Ancillary Terraces

Additionally, excavators identified another terrace type, ancillary terraces, which occur on some, but not all, terraces with walls. The down-slope faces of ancillary terraces look like sloping piles of cobbles and they do not have flat faced walls. Ancillary terraces range from

Figure 2.1. Terraces on the north face of the hill.

Figure 2.2. Terrace with wall.

7 to 11 m in length and 2 to 3 m in width. Up to 20 of these features were recorded in the higher parts of the hill (O'Donovan 1997:104).

Descriptions of Features by Type

The varieties of features on Cerro de Trincheras are vestiges of a once dynamic village. I have established 13 general categories for features at the site. In the section that follows, I define each feature type and describe the features that the crew excavated during our field seasons.

Stone Structures

Stone structures came in two configurations: circular and quadrangular. The inhabitants of Cerro de Trincheras built stone structures with dry-laid masonry using unshaped locally acquired andesite cobbles. These stone walls provided a base for a perishable superstructure. Three wall types were used in the stone structures. Some structures combined these wall types. Type 1, are stone foundations constructed of dry-laid or piled unshaped irregular cobbles that form a wall. Most walls of the stone structures were built with Type 1 walls. Type 2 walls are single coursed rock alignments along the perimeter of the structure that serve as a base for a perishable superstructure. Type 3 walls are terrace walls incorporated into the perimeter of the structure. On average, the walls of stone structures stand 1 m in height and they are typically .5 m in width. In most cases these walls showed signs of some collapse at the time of excavation. In the section that follows, I will elaborate on each of the stone structure types and characterize those excavated during the 1995 and 1996 field seasons.

Figure 2.3. Circular Stone Structure 18.

Circular Stone Structures

Circular stone structures (Figure 2.3) are defined as round to oval structures constructed of unshaped irregular sized andesite cobbles arranged in such a way as to provide low walls upon which a perishable superstructure was constructed. For all circular stone structures either stone foundations or terrace walls marked the perimeter of the structure. All excavated circular stone structures had unprepared floors. In a few cases excavators detected multiple use surfaces. The entries, when present, were built from a few flat laying cobbles, a break in the wall, or a section of the perimeter wall standing much shorter than the rest. The team recorded 271 of these structures during the Cerro de Trincheras Mapping Project (O'Donovan 1997:105), making circular stone structures the most numerous features on the hill after the terraces themselves. Circular stone structures appear to have functioned as domestic structures.

The crew excavated 25 circular stone structures in 1995 and 1996 (Table 2.2). They located one of these features inside the specialized feature, La Cancha. The circular stone structures we excavated range from 1.9 to 6.2 m in length and from 1.5 to 5.6 m in width.

Field crews had difficulty discerning the floors of the circular stone structures. Excavators identified the floors of the structures by a slight texture or color change. In a few cases, the builders used a layer of small cobbles and soil to create a level floor surface. In the case of Circular Stone Structure 17, a horizontal distribution of artifacts defined the floor. Archaeologists detected at least two unprepared occupational surfaces in Circular Stone Structure 18. The original floor level was constructed by utilizing small cobbles and soil to level off the caliche slope upon which the terrace sat. Field crews identified two hard-packed dirt floors in Circular Stone Structure 19. Builders constructed the floor of Circular Stone Structure 20 upon a level of small rocks and soil .35 m deep.

Builders used large irregular, unshaped cobbles at the bases of the walls and arranged smaller rocks around them to roughly build up the sidewalls. The stone portion of the walls appeared to serve as a base for the remainder of the wall, which is presumed to have been built of perishable material. No obvious postholes or roof supports were found on these stone walls suggesting that lightweight building materials, such as brush and daub, must have been used for the remainder of the walls. The height of the walls ranged from .2 to 1.1 m and from .2 to 1.6 m in width.

Excavators found entryways in 80 percent of the circular stone structures. Circular Stone Structures 18 and 19 had sloped ramp entries. Circular Stone Structure 20 did not show signs of having a clearly marked entrance. The size of the entrances ranged from .80 to 1.70 m.

Recorders did not detect any intramural sub-features in any of the excavated circular stone structures. Circular Stone Structure 4 did have a small ash lens in the center of its occupational surface suggesting a fire pit, yet no formal hearths were found in association with these structures.

Except in Area A1, excavators found a high density of artifacts inside structures of this feature type. Table 2.3 summarizes artifact distribution by circular stone structure. Plain ceramics and lithics were commonly recovered in these features. Outside of Area A1, an average of 2,833 pieces of plain ceramics and 527 lithics were recovered from the interior of circular stone structures. Interestingly, despite the low density of shell in most, Circular Stone Structures 18, 19, and 22 all have more than 35 pieces each. Circular stone structures in Area A1 yielded markedly less material (an average of 380 plain ceramics and 97 lithics per circular stone structure).

Quadrangular Stone Structures

Quadrangular stone structures (Figure 2.4) are roughly rectangular in shape. These structures are much larger than the circular stone structures. The mapping project recorded 57 quadrangular stone structures at Cerro de Trincheras. The builders used unshaped locally acquired andesite cobbles. The occupants piled the cobbles without mortar to build substantial foundations along a four sided perimeter. All three wall types: stone foundations, stone wall alignments, and terrace walls were used for walls in quadrangular stone structures. Morphology, distribution, and contents suggest these structures were used for habitation.

We excavated four quadrangular stone structures (Table 2.4), one each in excavation Areas B9 and B6, and two in Area D. The stone foundation walls of the quadrangular stone structures ranged from .3 to 1 m in height. It is assumed that the remainder of the stone foundation walls of the quadrangular stone structures was constructed of perishable material using the short stone walls as a base. Quadrangular Stone Structure 1 had stone foundations and terrace walls for walls. Quadrangular Stone Structure 1 shared its northern wall with Circular Stone Structure 18. T576's wall served as the back wall of Quadrangular Stone Structure. Since the stones from the wall T576 and Quadrangular Stone Structure 1 did not interlock, it suggested that Quadrangular Stone Structure 1 was built after the construction of T576. Quadrangular Stone Structure 2 used stone foundations and stone wall alignments. The northern and eastern walls were definable by alignments of small to medium sized cobbles standing at a maximum of .30 m. In the case of the northern wall this was constructed directly above the back wall of T280. Judging by the amount of wall fall present at the time of exca-

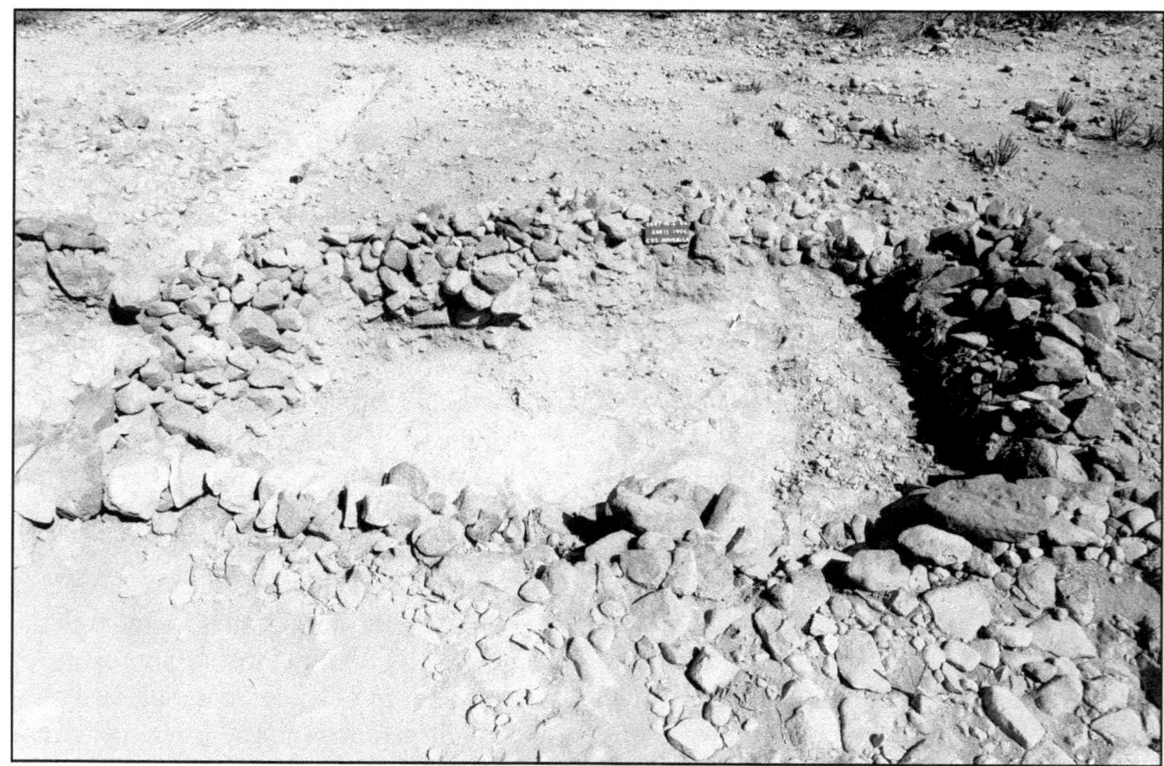

Figure 2.4. Quadrangular stone structure.

vation, the excavators noted that the walls of Quadrangular Stone Structures 3 and 4 were not well preserved.

The use surfaces of quadrangular stone structures were difficult to discern. The floors of Quadrangular Stone Structure 1 were not clearly definable. Several changes in color and consistency suggested multiple unprepared occupational surfaces. Quadrangular Stone Structure 1 surface was built upon a level of terrace fill that was built up higher than the remainder of the terrace surface. The crew did not locate an occupational surface for Quadrangular Stone Structure 2. The use surface of Quadrangular Stone Structure 3 was only indicated by a level of small rocks. Quadrangular Stone Structure 4 had a floor also defined by small rocks. Presumably, the rock floor of Quadrangular Stone Structures 3 and 4 was covered with layer of soil to create a flat surface.

Entrances to quadrangular stone structures were indicated by breaks in the perimeter of the structures. The archaeologists located the entryway to Quadrangular Stone Structure 1 at the North East corner measuring 1.15 m wide. The entrance of Quadrangular Stone Structure 2 was not found due to frequent breaks in the alignments that make up Type 2 walls. Presumably the entrance faced east because excavators found no breaks in the remainder of the Quadrangular Stone Structure 2. Excavators defined two entrances for Quadrangular Stone Structure 3. The entrance to the Southeast had a 4 m long rock alignment parallel to the western wall that formed a hallway into the feature. The northeastern entrance leads to T9 above the structure.

The crew found little evidence for the nature of roofing of the quadrangular stone structures. No postholes or any other subfeatures that could have served as roof support or wall support were identified. This suggests the superstructures were made of perishable material. No hearths, or any other intramural sub-features were identified during the excavation of the quadrangular stone structures.

The excavators recovered a high quantity of artifacts from the interior of quadrangular stone structures. Table 2.5 summarizes the counts for each material type by quadrangular stone structure. Shell, plain ceramics, and lithics were commonly found in these structures, suggesting a variety of domestic activities were carried out inside.

Pithouses

The pithouses at Cerro de Trincheras conform to the basic understanding of the term house-in-pit. Haury (1976:71) defines houses in pits as structures built in depressions where jacal side walls rise to meet the roof. True pithouses used the edges of pits as side walls. Trincheras pithouses have ramped entries into pithouse depressions no deeper than a few centimeters. Trincheras pithouses probably served as habitation structures.

The archaeologists identified nine pithouses at Cerro de Trincheras, all in Area E. Excavators defined Pithouses 6, 7, 8, and 9 by ramp entries, but their corresponding pithouse floors did not survive. Table 2.6 summarizes descriptive statistics on the pithouses excavated. The pithouses range from 2.57 m to 4.35 m in length and 2.25 m to 3.50 m in width, which suggests that the pithouses were round in shape. The floors of the pithouses were not uniform. The builders dug the pithouses into native caliche that they manipulated in order to create a flat occupational surface. The outcropping caliche resembled a burned, adobe plastered, surface in some areas. Pithouse 4 has a portion in its northeast corner that appears to have been burned.

Access into pithouses was provided by ramped entries, which were constructed of heavily burned caliche, creating a step on one end and a ramp on the other. Recorders did not detect entries into Pithouses 2 and 3.

The excavators recorded no postholes for roof support. The crew reported rock rings along the perimeter on a level above the pit-house use surfaces. These rock rings probably helped support the walls of the structure. The absence of substantial roof support suggests that the roofs of these structures were constructed of light perishable materials.

A hearth was located in Pithouse 2. Its boundaries were determined by edges of burnt caliche lined with a few rocks that cut into feature fill. Its southernmost edges showed signs of being especially burned. This hearth was filled with ash, as well as a small quantity of ceramic and lithic material. Crews found a possible hearth in the northeastern corner of Pithouse 4. This possible hearth consisted of a small oval area of burned caliche with a slight ridge only a few centimeters high.

Excavators found relatively little material inside the pithouses (Table 2.7). The plainware ceramics (<1000 except for Pithouse 1) and lithics (<200) make up the largest material type recorded for the pithouses. Because the exact perimeters of Pithouses 6 through 9 were never determined, artifacts could not be confidently assigned to these houses. The crew found only three shell artifacts from inside the pithouses.

Jacal Structures

The term jacal refers to wattle-and-daub houses. These could have been constructed of brush, sticks, and ocotillo often covered with mixture of mud. Upon excavation, jacales appeared as medium and small irregular cobbles arranged along a generally oval perimeter. These rocks formed part of the structure walls by providing wall support or were simply cleared from the space jacales were built in. We use the term jacal with the understanding that all of our structures (including our stone and pithouse structures) could technically be termed jacal structures because their superstructures were wattle-and-daub. Yet, we reserve the use of the term jacal for those structures that exhibit the aforementioned rock arrangement as a wall base and that lack an excavated depression.

The crew identified seven jacal structures during the excavation of Cerro de Trincheras. Table 2.8 presents descriptive statistics for the jacales excavated. Two jacales were found in Area B1, one in B2, one in B4, one in B6, one in B7 and one in B9. The jacal structures range from 2.26 m to 6.5 m in length, 1.60 m to 5.13 m in width, and .05 m to .30 m in depth.

The archaeologists had difficulties with defining the floors of the jacal structures. Very slight discontinuous changes in texture and concentrations of artifacts were observed in several of these structures and were recorded as possible use surfaces. In the case of Jacal 4, builders used native caliche as part of the original floor surface, while they created the remainder by placing small rocks and soil to create a flat surface. These structures appear to have multiple occupational levels that do not manifest themselves evenly throughout the extent of the jacales.

The crew had difficulty finding the exact location and nature of entrances into the jacal structures due to the lack of contiguous wall alignments. No entrances were located in Jacales 1, 2, 3, 5, and 7. Entrances were noted in two of the jacal structures. They did locate a possible entrance on the northwest extreme of Jacal 4. This entrance was defined by a gap in the alignments that constituted the walls of the structure. The entrance into Jacal 6 was identified as a gap in wall supporting cobbles on the northeast side of the jacal.

The excavators found evidence for roofing in Jacales 3 and 4. Seven postholes were found in association with Jacal 3. Four of the seven postholes were deep and well defined. Jacal 3 also yielded several fragments of daub, some of which showed ocotillo impressions. Crews collected several fragments of burned daub as well as one with well-defined ocotillo impressions from within Jacal 4. The remainder of the jacal structures showed no traces of roofing.

Excavators only recorded one hearth inside a jacal structure. A small hearth (.30 m diameter) was found in association with Jacal 4. The walls of the hearth showed evidence of burning. The hearth was filled with ash and small charcoal flecks.

The archaeologists found buried ceramic jars associated with jacales. Pit 17 was a pit with a ceramic vessel in it directly outside the entrance of Jacal 4 on the eastern end of the structure. The excavators located another buried ceramic vessel beneath the interior occupational surface of Jacal 2. Charcoal flecks, a number of ceramic fragments, and small rocks were found inside this long necked vessel.

The crew recovered a high quantity of domestic material from the interior of jacales. More than 3,000 plainware ceramics and 200 lithics were recovered from each of the jacales excavated. Vargas analyzed a total of 272 pieces of shell from jacales. The excavators collected more than 26,000 plainware ceramic pieces from Jacal 5 alone. Jacal 5 (Figure 2.5), located in B7, had more than 51 percent (n = 138) of the total shell found in the jacales. Table 2.9 shows the distribution of material by jacal.

Platforms

The crew defined three platforms during the excavation of Cerro de Trincheras (Figure 2.6 and Table 2.10). I distinguish platforms from terraces on the basis of construction strategy. Platforms do not have walls to delimit them.

Figure 2.5. Jacal 5.

Figure 2.6. Platform 2.

These platforms are generally limited by an alignment of medium sized cobbles at their extremes. Furthermore, platforms are built on the fronts of terraces. Piled rocks were used to create a level surface higher than the terrace surfaces upon which it was built. Rocks and soil were used in order to create a level surface higher than the original terrace. These surfaces were used as open air work areas.

The platforms varied greatly in size. The largest, Platform 1, measured 11.50 m in length and 6.60 m in width with a maximum thickness of .49 m. Platform 2 measured 9.83 m by 7.67 m with a maximum thickness of .15 m. The dimensions of Platform 3 were 9.83 m by 7.67 m with a maximum thickness of .15 m.

The floors of the platforms were built by creating a level surface of small rocks covered by soil. Crews detected these surfaces as a change in texture along a horizontal plane. The occupational surfaces of Platform 1 and 2 were some of the most well defined surfaces on the entire site with hard-packed surfaces with archaeological material laying on them. The workers found a high number of artifacts lying flat on the surface of Platform 1. Several sherd concentrations (representing approximately five vessels) were recovered from the surface of Platform 2. The excavators did not locate an occupational surface for Platform 3. Platforms 1 and 2 were built adjacent to T576. Platform 1 was built up against and has access into Circular Stone Structure 18. Circular Stone Structure 19 was built on the western extreme of Platform 2 and was connected to it by a small ramp. Circular Stone Structure 20 was constructed onto the north wall of Platform 2.

The boundaries of these platforms were discernable as alignments of rocks higher than the level of the terrace upon which it was constructed. This difference in height manifested itself as a sort of step. There is no evidence to suggest that these platforms were ever walled or roofed structures. Additionally, no sub-features were found in association with Platforms 1 and 3. A burial was found within the fill of Platform 2.

We found high quantities of artifactual material on the surfaces of platforms. On average, 11,943 plainware ceramics were collected from each of the platforms. The excavators recovered an average of 2,088 lithics, 34 stone tools, and seven ground stone tools from each platform. The artifactual material further suggests that these platforms served as extramural work areas.

Occupational Surfaces

The feature type Occupational Surface refers to areas characterized by a hard-packed unprepared surface or a concentration of material along a horizontal level. The crew recorded four occupational surfaces (Table 2.11), three in Area E and one in Area B6. Each occupational surface is described in the section that follows. Artifacts collected in association with the occupational surface are reported in Table 2.12.

Occupational Surface 1, in Area E, extended 5 m by 5 m. Recorders defined Occupational Surface 1 by a concentration of ground stone, lithic, and ceramic (all plainware) artifacts, the highest concentration of which was located on its northwest extreme. The crew did not excavate this feature.

Occupational Surface 2, in Area E, extended approximately 1 m by 2 m. Recorders describe it as a hard-packed surface with several flat-lying artifacts upon it. This surface was .18 m thick. A zoomorphic shell pendant, a shell bead, and some small burned animal bones were recovered from beneath this surface. This surface overlaid Hearth 8; therefore, the burned bone might be associated with it. No shell was found in association with Occupational Surface 2.

The archaeologists found Occupational Surface 3 in Area E. Excavators described Occupational Surface 4 as a hard-packed surface with flat laying artifacts on it. Occupational Surface 3 overlays Hearth 3. Vargas only recorded two pieces of shell on this occupational surface. The crew recorded Occupational Surface 4 in Area B6 as a concentration of artifacts, a hearth, a small rock platform, and two rows of stones that could represent the bases of two parallel walls. The hearth was roughly rectangular in shape with rock and adobe sides. The hearth has a maximum width of .23 m and a maximum depth of .16 m. It was filled with gray soil, charcoal and ash. The small rock platform was made of roughly flat stones arranged on the terrace surface. Two parallel rows of rocks set in adobe were located southwest of the hearth. It is possible, yet inconclusive, that these rows of rocks may have served as foundations for walls of a perishable material. Artifacts were clustered in two areas to the southeast and to the northwest of the hearth. These clusters contained large fragments of ceramic vessels and manos. A fragment of a metate was also located on this surface.

Access Features

The large number of terraces on the slopes Cerro de Trincheras necessitated access features to lead from one terrace or area to another. In some cases terraces walls exceed 3 m in height. In cases like these, ramps were required to get from lower to upper terraces. We identified two forms of access features at the site: ramps and stairs. One ramp was located in A1, another in B8. The crew recorded two sets of stairs, one in B4 and the other in B8. Artifacts collected in association with the access features are reported in Table 2.13.

Ramps

The site's occupants built ramps using the same method of construction for the terraces. They piled rubble fill to create a uniform sloping surface that connected one terrace surface to another. They then covered the rocks with soil in order to create a smooth surface.

The excavators recorded Ramp 1 in Area A1. Ramp 1 was built along the south wall of T716 (N 85-90, E 276-280) leading to El Caracol. This ramp served as the southern access point to the plaza of Area A1. It is 3.70 m long and 1.70 m wide with a maximum depth of .71 m and was constructed directly on bedrock.

Ramp 2 (Figure 2.7) is located in Area B8 (N 97-100, E 276-283) as part of El Mirador. Ramp 2 connects T280 with T278. It is located on the center of the posterior of T280. This ramp is 7 m long by 3 m wide. It has a southwest-northwest orientation. On its northern extreme it is bounded by the west back wall of T280, which measures .21 m to .67 m wide measured from the interior of the ramp, and 1.93 m from the exterior of the ramp. The ramp is limited to the south by the main wall of T277. From T280 the ramp rises narrowly, but widens as it approaches T278. We collected very little artifactual material from the ramps. The majority of material collected was plainware ceramics and lithics.

Figure 2.7. Ramp 2.

Stairs

We recorded two sets of stairs during the excavation. The stairs consist of rock alignments with fill behind them placed along bedrock slope. These stairs provide access from one terrace to another. Very little material was collected from these features.

Stairs 1 (N 106-108, E 120-123) in Area B4 connects T329 with T330. These stairs are approximately 2.5 m wide and consist of three steps. It is located in the NE corner of T329 providing the eastern boundary of the terrace. This feature was recorded, but not excavated.

Stairs 2 were located as access between T330 and T313 (N 106-109, E 120-124) in Area B3. These stairs are not very well preserved. They measured 3 m by 2.5 m. These appear as rock alignments over bedrock filled with rock and soil to create a flat surface. These stairs are located to the east of Ancillary Terrace 1.

Pit Features

The excavators found pit features to be the most numerous feature category at the site (n = 43). Pit features were found in excavation Areas B2, B4, B6, B7, B11, D, and E (Table 2.14). At Cerro de Trincheras, pits probably facilitated a variety of different activities. In the field this general pit category was divided into three broad categories: pits, hearths, and puddling pits. The section that follows describes the pits and attempts to further categorize them into broad types on the basis of their contents and morphology. Table 2.15 summarizes the distribution of artifacts for pits.

Pits were defined as depressions without evidence of burned walls. The crew recorded 24 pits at the site. After analysis, the category pit was further broken down on the basis of shape and contents. Consequently, I have defined nine pit types: multipurpose pits, caliche lined pits, trash filled pits, storage and processing pits, roasting pits, ash pits, and undifferentiated pits. To standardize the typology, I have employed the criteria used in the Pueblo Grande Project by Mitchell and Merewether (1994:85-105) in Phoenix, Arizona to classify the pits found at Trincheras. The section that follows represents a descriptive summary of these pit types.

Multipurpose Pits

The multipurpose pits were depressions of variable size and shape that show evidence of at least two of the following activities: storage, processing, food preparation, construction, or trash deposit. Archaeologists excavated four multipurpose pits at the site. All four of these pits occurred in excavation Area E. Two of the multipurpose pits were oval (Pit 1 and Pit 2). Pit 3 had an irregular shape and Pit 5 was round. The dimensions of multipurpose pits ranged from .44 m to 2.40 m in length and .50 m to 2.05 m in width. The multi functional pits range from .20 m to .94 m in depth. The average depth of the multi functional pits is .42 m. Only one of these multi functional pits (Pit 2) had stratified deposits. In Pit 2, the excavators found a more recent level of trash deposits and an older level of ash and charcoal separated by a level of water laid deposits.

Caliche Lined Pits

The crew recorded two caliche lined pits: Pits 4 and 12. The type was defined solely on the presence of a caliche lining on the perimeter of these features. The fill of these caliche lined pits differed. Pit 4 was filled with general cultural material, while Pit 12 was filled a mixture of fire-cracked rocks, ash, charcoal, and a small number of artifacts. Both caliche lined pits were situated in excavation Area E. Pit 4 was round with a diameter of .80 m. Pit 12 was oval (.70 m by .45 m). They had an average depth of .13 m. These features did not contain stratified deposits.

Trash Filled Pits

The trash filled pit was a depression with well defined walls and filled with trash. I differentiate this classification from that of a midden on the basis that the remains were found inside a depression. Pit 15, located in excavation area B4, was the only trash filled pit recorded. It is round and measures 2 m in diameter with a maximum depth of .43 m. It was filled with variety of material including ash, ceramics, and rocks. Excavators did not find stratified deposits in its interior.

Storage and Processing Pits

Mitchell and Merewether (1994:85-105) defined storage and processing pits as those depressions that show clear evidence for storage and/or processing. Pit 17, the only feature of this nature at the site, was an oval depression measuring .71 m in length and .56 m in width. This depression contained a small undecorated vessel and its rim was placed so as to appear flush with the living surface of the terrace it was built upon. This feature was located adjacent to Jacal 14 and most probably served as an associated storage feature.

Roasting Pits

Archaeologists identified two features as roasting pits. Roasting pits were recognized as depressions with some or all of the following: ash and charcoal in the fill, in situ burning, and fire cracked rock in the fill. The deposits were not stratified in any of the roasting pits. Pit 14 (Figure 2.8) was recorded in excavation Area B2, while Pit 24 was located in Area D. Pit 14 was round and measured 1.32 m long, 1.12 m wide, and .45 m deep. Contrastingly, Pit 24 was irregular in plan view and measured 3.44 m long, .70 m wide, and .12 m deep.

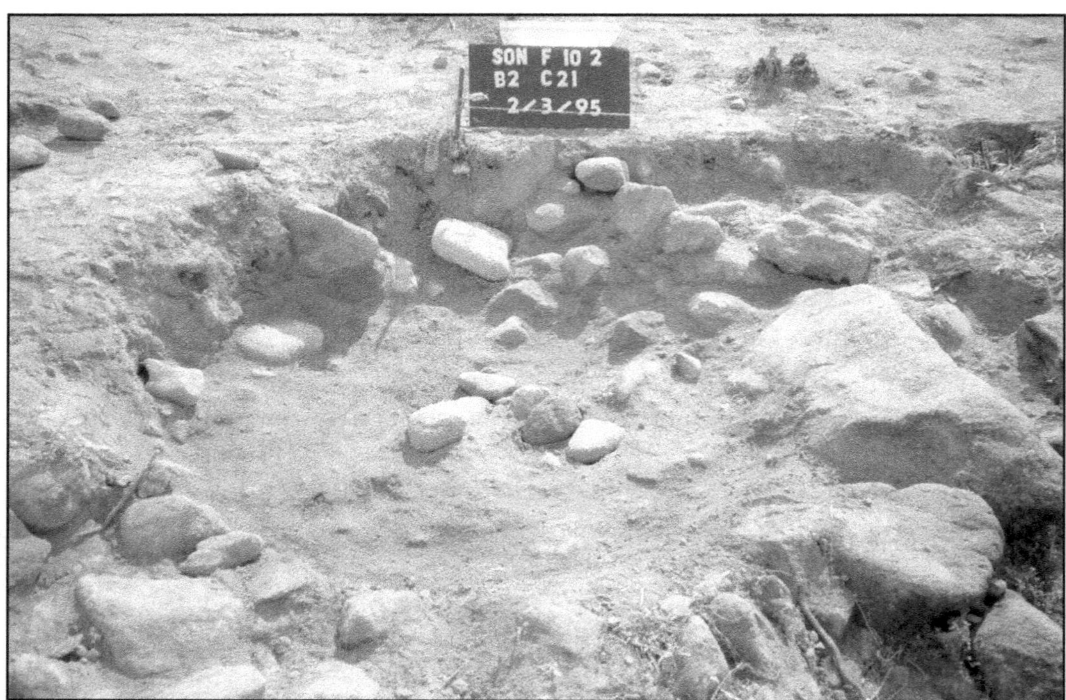

Figure 2.8. Pit 14: Roasting Pit.

Ash Pits

Recorders identified six features as ash pits. These features were defined as depressions primarily filled with ash, as well as small amounts of charcoal, in the absence of evidence of burned walls. The lack of evidence for in situ burning indicated that these pits were not the location of the primary processing activities, which produced the ash. Therefore, it is most probable that they served as receptacles for discarding ash. The ash pits were irregular in plan.

Pit 16 was round and Pit 8 was oval. All but one of these pits was located in Area E. Pit 16 was recorded in Area B4. The ash pits ranged from .10 m to .38 m in depth, .95 m to .50 m in length, and .42 m to .86 m in width. The crew did not find any ash pits with stratified deposits.

Undifferentiated Pits

The majority of the pits recorded could not be classified because they did not have clear evidence of a function. Undifferentiated pits were found to be unprepared. Eight of these were found throughout the site. Five were recorded in Area D, one in Area B11, and two in Area E. They were found with rectangular (n = 1), circular (n = 3), and oval (n = 4) plan views. None of their contents were stratified. The undifferentiated pits ranged from .20 m to .76 m in depth, .50 m to 1.58 m in length, and .40 m to 1.43 m in width.

Puddling Pits

Puddling pits were defined as depressions with caliche lined sides and bottoms and caliche in feature fill. Two circular caliche puddling pits were recorded at the site (Table 2.16). Excavators found both of these features in Area E. Puddling pits are differentiated from caliche-lined pits by the presence of caliche plaster in its interior. These pits were presumably used for the mixing of caliche and soil for construction purposes. No lithics, stone tools, ground stone, bone, or shell were collected from these structures (Table 2.17). Caliche puddling pits had an average depth of .11 m and the average diameter was .43 m. Pudding Pit 1 is associated with Pithouse 5. Pudding Pit 2 is nearby and probably associated with Pithouse 1.

Hearths

The crew defined hearths as those depressions whose walls showed evidence of in situ burning. Excavators recorded 17 hearths at the site. Hearths were located in excavation Areas B4, B6, B7, D, and E. All but two of the hearths recorded at the site were prepared. The depressions ranged from .08 m to .63 m in depth, .33 m to 1.30 m in length, and from .22 m to 1.10 m in width. The average dimensions of the hearths were .61 m long, .50 m wide, and .20 m deep. Table 2.18 summarizes descriptive statistics for the hearths we excavated. The hearths are generally round (n = 11) to oval (n = 5), with the exception of Hearth 5, which wass a curved semi-circle, and Hearth 6, which recorders categorized as irregular in plan view. The fill of these structures varied considerably including ash and charcoal, general cultural fill, and rocks. None of the hearths had stratified deposits.

Pits in Structures

Excavators recorded seven general pit features inside structures. These included ash pits, storage pits, puddling pits, and hearths. A brief description of each pit type identified inside structure at the site follows.

We located a storage and processing pit inside Jacal 2. As in the case of Pit 17, the pit in Jacal 2 was a small (.40 m in diameter and

.27 m deep) pit that contained a small ceramic vessel. This long necked pot was buried in terrace fill so as to have the rim of the pot flush with the occupational surface of Jacal 2. Charcoal flecks and ceramic fragments were found in its interior.

Puddling Pit 1 was recorded at the northwestern extreme of Pithouse 5. This caliche-lined pit had a diameter of .46 m and was .10 m deep. It is possible that this pudding pit was used for construction and renovation activities associated with Pithouse 5.

Archaeologists recorded five unprepared hearths inside structures at Cerro de Trincheras. Two were found in pithouses, two in jacal structures, and one inside a rock arrangement. Pithouse 2 included Hearth 12 (.71 m by .78 m, .23 m deep) in its southwestern corner. Hearth 12 was oval. We detected a possible hearth inside Pithouse 4. Excavators recorded an oval depression (.50 by .30 m) with evidence of burning. Because this sub-feature was not excavated we can only guess at its function. Jacal 4 included in its northern end a small (.30 m in diameter) irregular unprepared hearth (Hearth 15). Hearth 16 was located inside Jacal 5, and was an oval unprepared depression with evidence of in situ burning. Hearth 16 measured .63 m by 1 m with a maximum depth of .80 m. The crew also recorded Hearth 17 inside Rock Arrangement 5. Hearth 17 had a diameter of .50 m and is .32 m deep.

Middens

Middens are refuse deposits. The crew recorded two middens at Cerro de Trincheras. Both middens were located in Area E. Trincheras middens are visible from the surface as mound shaped concentrations of refuse materials. Artifacts collected in association with the middens are reported in Table 2.19.

Midden 1 (N 104-116, E 132-141) is a large oval concentration of refuse material deposited over three small pits. The deposits were stratified with sterile soil between them, which indicates multiple dumping episodes. Midden 1 measures 12 m long by 7.3 m wide by .52 m deep.

Midden 2 (N 127-132, E 114-120) is a small mound-like concentration of refuse. The crew did not excavate this feature in its entirety so the midden's exact shape could not be determined. This feature appears to have served some special use. The excavators estimated the dimensions of Midden 2 to extend 8 m by 4 m with an approximate depth of .50 m. All artifact classes were represented in this refuse deposit including a large quantity of organic material.

Ramadas

A ramada is a small area with a roof of branches, brush, and mud that is not walled. Posts support the roof of the ramada. The crew recorded one possible ramada in Area E of the site (Possible Ramada 1, Figure 2.9). The ramada was defined on the basis of a posthole located at N 124.76 E 120.60 and a beam impression burned into natural caliche. The beam impression was located directly northeast of the posthole. The posthole measures .39 m by .42 m and is .13 m deep. Recorders did not find a defined floor or associated sub-features. Excavators recovered only a few small lithics and one piece of shell from Ramada 1.

Petrograbados

Petrograbados refers to engravings carved deep in large rocks or bedrock (Figure 2.10). These occurred throughout the hill, but were not recorded systematically. The carving is deeper than a petroglyph, though no function could be confidently ascertained. The crew recorded one bedrock engraving in Area B3 (Bedrock Engraving 1 N 109 E 100). The grooves in the

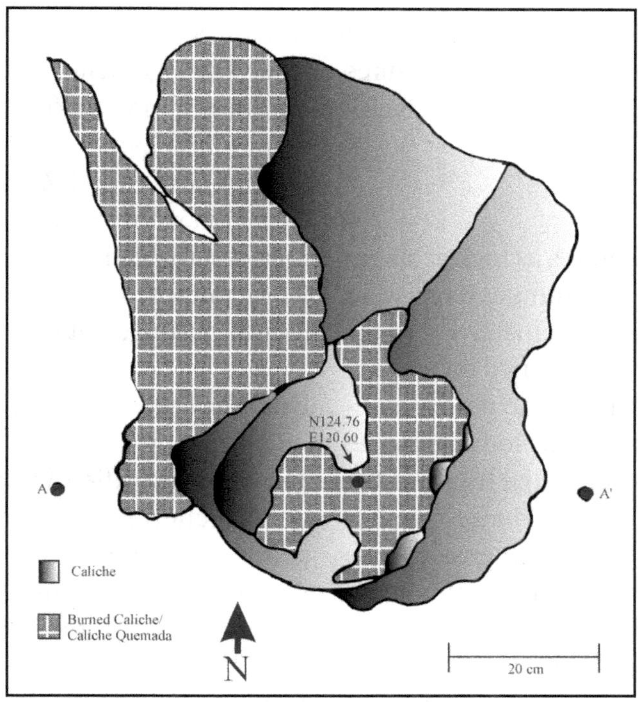

Figure 2.9. Map of possible Ramada 1.

Figure 2.10. Petrograbado 1.

bedrock are thick and linear. The engraving forms a half spiral design. The design measures 2 m by 1.3 m and is visible from the surface.

Rock Arrangements

The crew recorded six features as rock arrangements (Table 2.20). Rock arrangements were defined as a single course cluster of rocks arranged in a pattern to a delimited area along a single level. Rock arrangements are constructed of irregular unshaped local andesite cobbles. The rocks that define the limits of the rock arrangements tend to be large (greater than 30 cm). The rock arrangements can be divided into three different kinds: an alignment of cobbles, linear alignment of rock clusters, and rock piles. Three rock arrangements were recorded in Area E, two in Area D, and one in Area B11. They ranged from 2 m to 6 m in length; 1.5 m to 6 m in width, with an average width of 3.06 m; and from .05 m to .58 m in depth.

Rock Arrangements 1, 2, and 6 are aligned clusters large (greater than 30 cm) irregular andesite cobbles. Rock Arrangements 1 and 6 are circular, while Rock Arrangement 2 has an irregular shape in plan view. Rock Arrangement 1 included a caliche lined pit (Pit 12) on its eastern side. The excavation of Rock Arrangement 2 revealed a portion of adobe plaster from the entry ramp of Pithouse 7. Rock Arrangement 6 was constructed against the terrace wall for T553.

Rock Arrangement 3 was a linear alignment of three rock clusters. The crew found an ash filled pit in two of the clusters. The ash pit on the west side of Rock Arrangement 3 had a diameter of .80 m and was .36 m deep. The ash filled pit on the eastern end had a diameter of .92 m and a depth of .36 m. No pit numbers were assigned to these pits.

Rock Arrangements 4 and 5 were piles of irregular unshaped andesite cobbles of varied sizes. Rock Arrangement 4 was circular, while Rock Arrangement 5 was roughly rectangular. We located no sub-features in Rock Arrangement 5. Excavators recorded Hearth 17 at the northeastern end of Rock Arrangement 5. This arrangement of piled rock was the largest of the rock arrangements and probably served a different purpose than the rest of the rock arrangements excavated at Cerro de Trincheras.

Burials

The crew identified 11 burial features at Cerro de Trincheras. Two types of burials were defined: cremations and inhumations. Excavators only identified one cremation burial. The remaining ten burials found at the site were all inhumations. In the section that follows, I briefly summarize the burial features. Elisa Villalpando discusses the burials in greater detail in Chapter 12 (this volume).

Cremations

We recorded one cremation, Burial 1 (N 99.60-99.80, E 133.40- 133.60), in Area E. The cremation area was not included in the research locus. Excavators described Burial 1 as a small fragment (.13 by .10) of cranium lying upside down under a small reconstructible vessel. Excavators believe this to be the skull of a young subadult due to the small size. The cranial fragment was the only bone located. The excavated portion of the cremation measures .13 m by .10 m, and it is unknown what the remainder of this feature looks like.

Inhumations

Archaeologists recorded ten inhumations at the site. Three locations of inhumations were recorded at the site: pit burials, burials in terrace fill, and burials covered in rocks from a structure or terrace wall.

Excavators located Burial 2 (N 122.30-122.90, E 141.25-141.70) in Area E. This was likely an infant buried in a small, oval, caliche-lined pit (.55 m by .44 m, .08 m deep). The remains were placed extended in the small pit and covered with firecracked rock and charcoal. Most of the firecracked rock and charcoal were concentrated over the skull.

The crew located Burial 3 (N 104-105, E 89-90) in Area B2. Burial 3 was a semi-flexed primary inhumation, interpreted as an adult male. This individual was placed in a semi rectangular pit dug into terrace fill. The body was oriented approximately northwest-southwest and was placed on its back with its knees bent to the left side. The left arm was extended, and the bottom of the right arm was found resting on the sternum and neck. Recorders noted that the individual's lower vertebrae appeared to have been fused together, which could indicate pathology. A shell pendant, a green stone bead, and a plain ceramic fragment were recovered as part of this burial.

Archeologists located Burial 4 (N 105, E 115.68-116) in Area B4. Recorders described Burial 4 as the secondary inhumation of a subadult. The bones were not articulated. Skeletal elements recovered included the cranium, arm bones, two vertebrae, two ribs, and a femur. No defined burial pit was recorded. The remains extend over an area .40 m^2. Excavators did not recover any artifacts clearly associated with this burial.

The crew excavated Burial 5 (N 114-115, E 216-217) in Area B6. Burial 5 was the extended primary inhumation of an adult male running approximately east-west. The individual was located inside and over the occupational surface of Quadrangular Stone Structure 1. Recorders believe that this inhumation was most likely post-occupational in relation to Quadrangular Stone Structure 1. The individual was deposited under a layer of rocks and soil. No femoral or cranial fragments were recovered.

Excavators located Burial 6 (N 121-122, E 238-239) in Area B6. Burial 6 was the multiple primary inhumation of two subadults. Archaeologists located Burial 6 inside Circular Stone Structure 20. The individuals were located next to each other running approximately east-west, their crania at opposite ends. The individual on the northern side is better preserved than the other, and was positioned on its left side, knees bent, with the arms resting on the chest. The other individual was more deteriorated. Only the cranium and ribs were clearly identifiable. The head was probably lying towards the west with the body extended on the right side. Some disturbance was evident in the lack of articulation of some bones. These individuals were probably buried simultaneously. Excavators noted that this burial was deposited above the occupational surface of Circular Stone Structure 20 and was therefore most likely post-occupational. No associated artifacts were recorded.

The crew described Burial 7 as the primary flexed inhumation of a subadult. Burial 7 (N 118.35-118.83, E 237.96-238.08) was located in excavation Area B6. The individual was located in the fill of Platform 2. Burial 7 runs north-south with the head toward the southern extreme and the body positioned on the left side in fetal position. Three artifacts were found in association with this burial: a natural rock that the individual appeared to be holding, and two pieces of ground stone, one found under the lumbar column and the other over the lower abdomen.

Archaeologists located Burial 8 (N 113-114, E 212-214) inside Circular Stone Structure 18 in excavation Area B6. Burial 8 was the semi-flexed inhumation of a male adult in poor condition. This inhumation runs east-west with the cranium towards the east. The body was laid on its back presumably with the knees bent though no leg bones were recovered. A rodent burrow that runs through the middle of this burial disturbed many bones. Some remains were also located under the terrace wall that serves as the back wall of Circular Stone Structure 18. Rocks from the walls of this construction were utilized to cover the remains.

Excavators located Burial 9 (N 295-297, E 425-427) in Area B9 under wall fall from the ramp that lead from T277 to T276. Burial 9 was the semi-flexed primary inhumation of a subadult male. This individual was very well preserved. The body was positioned on its back with knees bent towards the left side. All elements were recovered except for the cranium and the patellae. Recorders posit the possible absence of these parts due to exposure. The orientation of Burial 9 was east-west with the head to the west. Burial 9 was deposited in a small oval pit whose limits were difficult to define. One ceramic sherd was located within the pelvis.

Burial 10 (N 104-106, E 305-306) was the primary semi-flexed inhumation of a infant 18 to 24 months old found in the terrace fill of Area B11. The positioning of this individual was not clearly defined. The cranium appeared to be oriented to the west with the frontal side facing south. Bones of the torso were oriented east-west. The lower extremities appear to have been disturbed after inhumation.

Burial 11 (N 95-95.80, E 64.60-65.50) was the semi-flexed primary inhumation of an individual of unknown age or sex. Burial 11 was located directly adjacent to Pit 20 in Area D. The individual was lying on its back with the knees bent and the arms straight at the sides. The remains were badly disturbed by a rodent burrow that passed through the middle of the inhumation. Two artifacts were recovered in association with Burial 11: a Conus ring was found where the right hand would have been and a plain ceramic fragment. The burial pit was shallow, not well defined, and interspaced with many large rocks.

Specialized Features

Three features recorded on the site seem to differentiate themselves from the others. Two of these, La Cancha and El Caracol are so striking that earlier explorers and researchers who visited the site described them. We defined a third feature during the excavation of Cerro de Trincheras, El Caracolito, which appears to have served a different purpose than the rest of the features on the site.

La Cancha

La Cancha is located almost at the base of the north side of the hill. This is by far the most visible feature at the site (Figure 2.11). This feature is very long and wide in comparison to the terraces on the hill. It measures approximately 15 m by 57 m. It is defined by two major walls that serve as its northern and southern extremes. These walls then curve inwards at the western and eastern ends of the feature. The walls were constructed with dry-laid masonry of irregular unshaped cobbles measuring up to 2.5 m in thickness and .5 m in height. All evidence seems to suggest that this feature was not roofed.

La Cancha has a circular stone structure in its interior, which is situated against the middle of the northern wall. It was recorded as a sub-feature of La Cancha. Its walls were constructed in much the same manner as the remainder of the circular stone structures. This circular stone structure has a diameter of 2.7 m. The entrance was identified by a single rock placed lengthwise. The walls at the southern end were quite deteriorated at the time of excavation. Three apparent occupational levels were defined in the interior of this feature.

El Caracol

The Caracol is the feature that has garnered the

Figure 2.11. La Cancha.

most attention from visitors and researchers alike. El Caracol (Figure 2.12) is one of the largest structures at Cerro de Trincheras (12.50 m by 8 m, .13 m deep) and is located at the top of the cerro in Area A1(N 95-104, E 266-280). This structure receives its name from the spiral shape of its walls resembling the cross section of a snail shell. The builders constructed the walls of the Caracol by piling large rocks on the outside and small and medium rocks along the inside of the walls. They laid the walls with irregular unshaped cobbles using no mortar. On average, the walls stand 1.6 m high. Recorders found the entrance to the Caracol at its southwest corner. The single wall begins at the southwest corner, outlines the perimeter and cuts into the interior of the structure forming almost a complete circle.

The archaeologists recorded El Caracol A, a circular rock structure (3.2 m by 2.8 m, .5 m deep) as a sub-feature of the Caracol. This rock arrangement was built against the southern wall of the Caracol. Recorders did not find a floor inside the structure.

El Caracolito

Archaeologists recorded a third specialized feature in Area D, El Caracolito, which means "the little snail shell," (Figure 2.13). El Caracolito (N 115-121.80, E 68.50- 74.30) measures 7 m by 6 m and is .40 m deep. The walls of the structure resemble a cross section of snail shell in plan view. The walls were constructed using irregular unshaped cobbles and dry masonry. The spiral effect is realized by a wall on the interior that runs east-west. In addition to its unusual form, this structure appears to have served a specialized function, because of the amount of decorated ceramics, worked ceramics, and shell (n = 510) recovered from the interior of this structure. Over one fourth

Figure 2.12. Aerial photograph of El Caracol (photograph courtesy of Adriel Heisey).

Figure 2.13. El Caracolito.

of the total shell found in structures at the site was found in El Caracolito.

This section has outlined basic definitions for the 13 feature types and three specialized features located at Cerro de Trincheras. The description of each feature category includes a definition and a description of the features we excavated. The description of each feature addressed morphology, contents, and to some extent function. This architectural classification is intended as a baseline for future research and comparison.

Reconstructing Cerro de Trincheras Features

An overview of the features at Cerro de Trincheras would be incomplete without a discussion of the site at the time it was built. In this chapter, I tackle this issue two ways. First, I examine the organization of features on the site. In this section, I conduct a spatial analysis to look at the distributions of features at the site and their associations. Second, I look for possible configurations of the superstructures of structures at Cerro de Trincheras. In this section, I consult the ethnographic and ethnohistoric record of Northwest México for structures that are similar to those the crew excavated at the site.

Organization of Features at Cerro de Trincheras

The site of Cerro de Trincheras is impressive not only for its size, but also because of its layout. The terraces at the site are not identical. The features, including the terraces, were not built in a haphazard manner. This suggests that the population of Cerro de Trincheras deliberately organized the space they lived in. The first step in a discussion of site structure is to consider the spatial distribution of features at a site. This section considers the distribution of feature types at Cerro de Trincheras.

The excavators recorded the largest number of features in Area E (n = 49). Area E's features were also the most varied. One ramada, two burials, two middens, three occupational surfaces, three rock arrangements, nine pithouses, twenty-eight pits, and one possible house floor were recorded in this area. The recorders found the only pithouses in Area E. The pithouses seem to indicate a possible courtyard group similar to those located in Snaketown (Doyel 1987). The arrangement seems to indicate a common work area (see Wilcox et al. 1981 for Hohokam courtyard groupings at Snaketown). The excavators also recorded the largest number of pit features in this area. Two caliche-lined pits, two pudding pits, four multi-purpose pits, five ash filled pits, thirteen hearths, and two pit features that could not be classified were found in this area. The number, variety, and nature of features found in Area E further suggest that it was a major locus of domestic activity.

The archaeologists recorded 22 features in Area A1. Almost all of the features in Area A1 are circular stone structures with the exception of one access feature and El Caracol. Because this excavation area is located at the top of the cerro, it is interesting that almost all the structures are of the same type. The artifact density of the circular stone structures in A1 is much lower than the circular stone structures in other areas. For example, the average number of ceramics in circular stone structures in A1 is 366, while in other areas the average is 2833. Furthermore, the proximity to El Caracol and the fact that this is the only segment of Cerro de Trincheras that affords some real privacy from the rest of the site, presents the possibility that these features were associated with the specialized function of El Caracol.

The crest of the hill has a distinct pattern marked by many circular stone structures, the presence of El Caracol, and a low density of artifactual material. This pattern, in combination with its private location, seems to suggest a ritual or ceremonial use of the features in this area. Further support can be gained from O'Donovan's (1997:197) spatial analysis of the organization and construction of terraces at the crest. She found that these terraces were used "to augment natural features, to create certain images, enclose areas and provide vantage points" (O'Donovan 1997:197).

Excavation Areas B1, B2, B3, B4, and B7 are very similar in structure. Each of these terraces has habitation structures, either a jacal or a circular stone structure, usually in combination with pit features. These excavation areas are clustered on the western end halfway up the north face of the hill. The crew recorded a total of 17 features total in these areas. Investigators identified two sets of stairs, connecting one terrace to another, in this section of the site. Archaeologists located a series of postholes in B7, an ancillary terrace in B3, and a platform in B4. These features were all open-air structures on which a variety of activities could have been conducted. The inhabitants built one circular stone structure, one platform, and three jacales on this part of the hill. Four different kinds of pits were located on these terraces: a trash-filled pit, a roasting pit, and two hearths. The high concentration of domestic material and the variety of associated features suggests that these terraces lent themselves to small scale day to day domestic activities.

The archaeologists who excavated Area B6 characterize it as a complex unit on which many different activities were conducted. Area B6 consists of two long terraces only a few meters south of La Cancha. The structure of B6 appears to be a larger scale version of B1 through B4 and B7. These areas combine habitation structures with open air spaces, in which a variety of activities were conducted. The crew recorded 14 features in this area, four of which were burials. Archaeologists identified three circular stone structures, one quadrangular stone structure, and one jacal. The excavators located a hearth and a storage pit in association with the jacal. The recorders also identified two platforms and an occupational surface, both dense in artifacts in Area B6.

McGuire and Villalpando named excavation Areas B8, B9, and B10 El Mirador. El Mirador is located high on the north face of the site and includes the terraces with the highest terrace walls. The crew recorded an ancillary terrace on the back of B8 with a ramp leading to B9, the terrace above. Excavators located two habitation features on B9, a jacal and a quadrangular stone structure. A burial was also located on the east side of B9. No features were located on the uppermost terrace of B10. McGuire and Villalpando have suggested that El Mirador was the home of the site's ruling household (McGuire and Villalpando 1998:4).

Excavators discovered four features in excavation Area B11. B11 is located on the eastern end of the north face of the cerro. The archaeologists recorded one circular stone structure, one rock arrangement, one pit, and one burial in this area. The configuration of B11 is distinct to that of the habitation areas on the west side of the north face of Cerro de Trincheras. B11 does not have the same combination of open-air living spaces and habitation structures.

The crew recorded twelve features in Area D. Most of the features in Area D are pits (n = 7). Archaeologists excavated two quadrangular stone structures and El Caracolito in this segment of the site. Two rock arrangements and a burial were also located in this area, which seems to be characterized by the pits that are concentrated in it. One pit was identified as a roasting pit and another as a hearth. The remaining pits are alike, but I was not able to classify them.

Summary of Site Feature Distribution

The site feature distribution indicates five main architectural patterns that may be the result of the differential use of space on the hill. Area E represents a complex unit of multiple features centered on habitation in pithouses and processing in the various pits found in the area. B1, B2, B3, B4, B6, and B7 can be characterized by a particular residential pattern that combines open air structures (i.e., platforms, ramadas, and occupational surfaces) with jacales or stone structures. The small number of features in El Mirador and their configuration suggests that this section operated as a specialized unit. A1, at the crest of the hill, is characterized by circular stone structures and El Caracol. The lack of domestic sub-features seems to indicate distinct specialized use of the features in this area. Area D is differentiated because of all the pits that occur in combination with rock arrangements and quadrangular stone structures. The differences in combinations and densities of features reflect differences in the use and organization of these spaces on the hill.

Looking for Superstructures in the Ethnographic and Ethnohistoric Record

The perishable nature of the superstructures of pithouses, jacales, armadas, and stone structures at Cerro de Trincheras requires investigators to look beyond the archaeological record for answers. I consulted ethnohistoric accounts by explorers of Sonora and Sinaloa and ethnographic reports by anthropologists studying the people of northern México and southern Arizona. These sources suggest a variety of structure configurations that, when applied to the feature data at Cerro de Trincheras, provide a clearer picture of the site.

The fact that the archaeologists did not recover the superstructure of any of the habitation features is not surprising. Hot temperatures characterize the Sonoran Desert through most of the year. Populations of hot, dry environments must consider four factors when building: 1) temperature, 2) humidity, 3) rate of air movement, and 4) radiation from walls, floors, ceilings, and other surrounding surfaces (Saini 1973). Two basic solutions to the heat exist. One solution is to build very thick walls, which will provide a cool interior by absorbing the sun's radiation. The second choice is to build walls that are permeable, allowing the cooling wind to sweep through the interior of these structures (McGuire 1998:personal communication). At Cerro de Trincheras, they chose the latter as evidenced by the impermanence exhibited in habitation structures.

As with archaeological research, ethnographic and ethnohistoric records of northern México are limited. In this analysis I include studies of the Upper Pima (O'Odham and Papago), Pima Bajo (O'Odham), Opata (Joylraua), Yaqui (Yoreme), Seri (Konkáak), Tepehuan (Odami), and Huichol. Unfortunately, few scholars provide detailed descriptions of the houses in which people lived. Nevertheless, I believe the accounts provide sufficient information to show how the structures at Cerro de Trincheras might have looked.

It is not my aim to simply project the ethnographic and ethnohistoric records of Northern México into the past at Cerro de Trincheras. Instead, I look for structure designs described in these records that would result in similar material patterns. Ethnoarchaeology can be useful when it "can establish uniformitarian relationships between behavior and its material patterning that can be taken to the archaeological record with confidence" (Arnold 1998:8). In the section that follows I will describe the material patterning for stone structures, jacales, pithouses, and ramadas recovered at the site and supplement these with the ethnographic and ethnohistoric descriptions of similar structures in northern México.

Stone Structures

Explorers and scholars of northwestern México have described the stone dwellings of several groups in the region (Beals 1973 [1932]; Grimes and Hinton 1969; Lumholtz 1904; Spicer 1969; among others). Spicer classifies dwellings in the southern highland and central and southern lowlands of northwest México as "oval mud and stone houses with peaked thatched roofs" (1969:778). Other investigators report stone houses for the Huichol, Tepehuan, and Ópatas. The stone dwellings of these groups share basic construction strategies with those at Cerro de Trincheras and therefore provide possible analogs for the roofing techniques of these structures.

Stone Houses in the Ethnographic and Ethnohistoric Record

Anthropologists and explorers have reported that the Huichol, Tepehuan, and Ópata had stone houses. Hrdlička reports that the Ópatas remember building stone foundations or walls to their habitations in previous generations (1904:59). Among the Huichol, Lumholtz describes single room round stone houses with flat, palm roofs and very low entrances (Lumholtz 1902: 2: 27). Later accounts describe the stone houses of the Huichol with thatched palm or grass roofs (Grimes and Hinton 1969:797).

The houses of the Tepehuanes in the 1970s are described as 3 m by 4 m stone houses with posts at the corners to support a brush roof. These are built over a platform that sometimes measures 10 m to 20 m (Riley 1969:817). Mason (1971:221) describes Tepehuan houses as constructed of field stone with thatched roofs, "the roofs are thatched with grass supported on posts, poles, and sticks, and the walls generally of stones, and extending to the eves, and the interstices."

Stone Structures at Cerro de Trincheras

At Cerro de Trincheras, stone structures appear as circular, oval or rectangular rooms made with dry-laid masonry of irregular unshaped locally acquired andesite cobbles of varying sizes. The circular rooms measure on average 3.9 m by 3.4 m. The quadrangular stone structures measure on average 5.34 by 4.44. The walls measure on average .60 m high and .60 wide at the time of excavation. Some of the wall thickness measured includes some wall collapse. No postholes were found in association with these structures.

The ethnographic and ethnohistoric accounts suggest that thatched flat roofs of grass or brush are possible configurations for the roofing of stone structures. Given the lack of postholes in the stone structures it is most likely that the superstructure was not very substantial. Lumholtz description of single room round stone houses with flat, palm roofs with very low entrances (Lumholtz 1902: 2: 27) seems to be consistent with the archaeological evidence at the site.

Jacales and Pithouses

The word jacal in Spanish refers to a hut. Jacales are usually wattle-and-daub structures and are very common in northern México. Amsden describes the ubiquitous Sonoran jacal: "Stones have no place in their construction. Between the corner poles thin shoots, as of ocotillo or cane are driven into the ground. Withes are interwoven to form an open frame and straw or some other mat of vegetation is tied onto the frame to compete the wall. Clay is tamped on the outside against the base of the structure so that water dripping from the roof is carried away instead of soaking in about the imbedded sticks. Enterprising natives also add a gutter about the hut" (Sauer and Brand 1931:115). I have included brush structures and mat structures in my discussion of jacales as well. Brush structures have walls that are constructed of brush (Hinton 1969; Hrdlička 1904; Russell 1975; Pennington 1980; Spicer 1969). Mat structures are characterized by mats tied to poles that serve as walls (Hrdlička 1904:58, Pennington 1980:336). These structures are similar to wattle-and-daub structures, but do not always include mud or clay as a building material. The wattle-and-daub, brush, and mat superstructures would leave a similar pattern in the archaeological record.

Pithouses are jacal structures built in depressions. The pithouses at Cerro de Trincheras conform to the definition of houses-in-pits, where pit sides are not used as structure walls (Haury 1976:58). The depth of the depressions can vary greatly. No specific references to houses-in-pits were located in the ethnographic and ethnohistoric record, yet it is probable that some of the jacal structures described in the section that follows were built in depressions or the depressions were formed by the regular activity of wetting and sweeping the house floor. The apparent shift to above ground structures about the time of European contact can also be used to explain the absence of these semi-subterranean structures from the literature of the Sonoran Desert. Yet, the construction strategies for the superstructure of jacales can be used to look for possible designs for the perishable superstructure of pithouses at Cerro de Trincheras.

Jacales in the Ethnographic and Ethnohistoric Record

Investigators commonly report dwellings built of wattle-and-daub, brush or mats in Northern México. The Ópata (Hinton 1969:881; Spicer 1954:50), Pima Bajo (Cabeza de Vaca 1944:63; Hinton 1969:881; Pennington 1980:334), Papago (Hinton 1969:881), Huichol (Grimes and Hinton 1969:797), and Yaqui (Hrdlička 1904:63; Spicer 1954: 2, 1969:836), built wattle-and-daub jacales. The

Seri (Hinton 1969:881; Hrdlička 1904:63; Russell 1975:155; Spicer 1969:790) used brush structures. Early explorers in Sonora and scholars describe houses made of mats (Hrdlička 1904:58) in the region. In the section that follows I summarize the descriptions of these types of dwellings gathered from the literature of the region.

The Ópata built wattle-and-daub jacales (Hinton 1959:17). The Ópata houses were described by the Diego de Alcaraz party of the Coronado expedition in the mid-1500s and later related by Father Mariano Cuevas as 600 mud houses with flat roofs (Sauer 1934:42). These were described as "plaited cane walls, sometimes heavily coated with mud, and a roof composed of layers of cane resting on a few mesquite rafters, with earth piled on top of the cane" (Sauer 1934:42). Spicer further states that these structures are often accompanied by ramadas that consist of a roof supported on "crotched mesquite posts" (1954:50). The jacales are less common and mostly replaced by the adobe houses (Hinton 1959:17).

Anthropologists and explorers also report jacal structures for the Pima Bajo, Papago, and the Huichol. Hinton describes Onova Pima structures as adobe or wattle-and-daub dwellings (1969:881). Cabeza de Vaca describes the people of the village of Corazones as living in buhíos (1944:63). Pennington interpreted this to refer to a simple Indian hut (1980:334). The same kind of dwelling was also described for the Huichol (Grimes and Hinton 1969:797).

The Yaqui also used wattle-and-daub dwellings. Spicer (1969:836) describes the Yaqui structures as dirt covered flat roofs over rectangular cane and mud wattle structures. Hrdlička (1904:63) describes the Yaqui jacal as "a fair-sized quadrilateral structure of poles and reeds, or of adobe reeds or brush, with a flat or more commonly, slightly sloping roof of grass and mud."

The Pima *ki* is also a wattle-and-daub structure but is constructed in more substantial way than the other jacales included in this section. Russell (1975:154) does a very thorough job of describing the construction strategy of the Pima *ki*:

> The central supporting framework is usually entirely of cottonwood, though other timber is sometimes used. The lighter framework is of willow on which is laid arrowwood, cattail reeds, wheat straw, cornstalks or similar material that supports the outer layer of earth.
>
> The roof is supported by four crotched posts set in the ground three or four meters apart, with two heavy beams in crotches. Lighter cross poles are laid on the last, completing the central framework. Light willow poles are set half a meter in the ground around the periphery of the circle, their tops are bent in to lap over the central roof poles, and horizontal stays are lashed to them with willow bark. The frame is then ready for the covering of brush or straw. Although earth is heaped upon the roof to a depth of 15 cm or 20 cm it does not render it entirely waterproof. When finished the ki is very strong and capable of withstanding heavy gales or supporting the weight of the people who may gather on the roof during festivals.

These structures are also described near Snaketown. This feature type is taken to provide the model of construction for the pithouses at Snaketown (Gladwin et al. 1938:60).

Investigators also report brush houses in ethnographic and ethnohistoric accounts. Ségesser in 1737 writes about the Tericopa Pima, "their houses were constructed in the shape of beehives with small entrances he had to crawl through on all fours when he visited the sick... If an Indian wanted to change the location of his hut, then eight or ten Indians just picked it up and moved it" (Pennington 1980:336). These structures were constructed by fastening petates (mats) to a frame of poles that could be moved. Hrdlička (1904:58) also makes reference to early accounts that state, "early explorers saw only dwellings made from brush and poles and palm leaves or mats (petates), and such may be seen among the Sonora natives today." These structures would leave ephemeral traces in the archaeological record.

Another housing configuration described in the literature of northern México and southern Arizona is the brush house. Among the Seri, Krober describes costal Sonoran houses as ocotillo framed, tunnel shaped, and brush covered (Spicer 1969:790). Hinton (1969:881) describes the temporary fishing and gathering camps of the Seri on the coast as "traditional brush wind breaks." Hrdlička (1904:63) describes similar structures for the Yaqui, "In the country districts I have come across an occasional, probably temporary, hut made in the same manner [as wattle-and-daub jacales], but entirely of brush and with but a few supporting poles." A brush structure is also described for the Pima Bajo, but these are A-framed structures (Pennington 1980:337):

> They are used today as summer sleeping quarters and to shield articles from rain. Two fork shaped poles, each about eight feet long, are put upright in the ground and a ridge pole is put between them, held in place by the forks. Side poles are affixed to them ridgepole about one foot apart to form an A-frame. They are tied to the ridgepole with fiber cordage or leather thongs. Any kind of straw or brush may be used or the cover... The cover material is laid on the pole frame and held down by slender saplings anchored transversely to the frame.

Jacales and Pithouses at Cerro de Trincheras

The jacales at Cerro de Trincheras are defined by an irregular non-contiguous alignment of rock along an elliptical perimeter. The interior of these structures was cleared of large rocks. The material remains of these structures are consistent with the protohistoric Pima sites recorded in the Santa Cruz, San Pedro, and Sonoita Creek Valleys of southern Arizona. "The locations where structures once existed are delineated today by elongated stone rings that measure approximately 6 ft by 12 ft. Rock sizes of 4 in to 6 in are typical and spacing between rocks is consistent in the structures of all three valleys (Seymour 1993:3)."

These ephemeral structures could have been built in almost all of the configurations I present from the ethnographic and ethnohistoric record. The description of the Pima *ki* seems to be the least likely configuration for the jacal structures at Cerro de Trincheras. A structure able to maintain the weight of several people during festivals would most likely require quite a bit of soil as part of its construction material and substantial roof support. Since the jacales at Cerro de Trincheras do not have that much fill, it is more likely that they took another less substantial form. Also the Pima *ki* is built with many thick posts along its perimeter. These posts would most likely leave a pattern in the archaeological record. The excavators found no such posthole pattern at Cerro de Trincheras.

Most wattle-and-daub structures are similar to each other differing only by building material. Any of these wattle-and-daub dwellings could have left a pattern such as the one archaeologists found for jacales at the site. The same can also be said for the brush and mat walled structures. Ségesser's description of mat walled structures as moveable (Pennington 1980:336) presents certain possibilities for the interpretation of jacal features at Cerro de

Trincheras. Movable structures would leave subtle traces in the archaeological record such as is the case at Cerro de Trincheras.

Pithouses at Cerro de Trincheras are also quite difficult to define. Pithouses were defined by the presence of one or more of the following: a slight depression which averaged .38 m dug into native caliche; caliche manipulated to create a flat occupational surface; and ramp entries. The pithouses measured on average 3.46 m by 3.21 m. No postholes were associated with these features; however, medium sized rocks were identified above the pithouse use surface. These rocks were probably used to weigh down roofing material. As with the jacales, the absence of postholes seems to suggest a less substantial building method than the Pima ki. The superstructure could have been built of brush, mats, or wattle-and-daub in any of the configurations present in the ethnographic and ethnohistoric literature.

Ramadas

Researchers of northern México often mention ramadas as architectural types present in the Sonoran Desert. These structures provide open-air shelter from the sun. Ramadas are roofs constructed of various materials, supported by poles.

Ramadas in the Ethnographic and Ethnohistoric Record

According to Pennington (1980:337), the Pima Bajo built armadas that were constructed by "[f]our posts usually with forked tops...placed upright on the ground. Beams are anchored to the post tops with leather thongs or with vines, and brush is added to a frame of saplings arranged across the beams" (Pennington 1980:337). Russell (1975:156) describes the use of the ramada among the Pima:

> The roof furnishes a convenient place for drying squashes, melons, fruit, and in the old days cotton, where the dogs and poultry can not disturb them. Under its shade the olla of drinking water is set in a crotched post or is suspended from above by a maguey fiber net. Here two parallel ropes may be hung and a cloth folded back and forth upon itself across them, thus forming an impromptu hammock in which to swing the baby. Here the metate and mortar are usually seen, and here the women sit and weave baskets or preform such other labors as may be done at home. It is the living room throughout the year around, and now that the fear of Apaches has gone it is becoming the sleeping place as well.

Little evidence of ramadas would survive in the archaeological record.

Ramadas at Cerro de Trincheras

The ramada is rather common in the Sonoran Desert; nevertheless, the excavators recorded only two possible ramadas. The archaeologists defined the possible ramada on the basis of a posthole and a beam impression burnt into caliche. It is possible that more ramadas were present at the site and left no remains. I base this on an experiment conducted by the crew that sought to build a ramada without digging the posts into the ground. The crew built the ramada by making a roof of ocotillo and palm and fastening it to poles of palo verde. The poles were supported by large cobbles from the hill. All construction materials were locally acquired. The ramada stood up quite well until cows grazing at the site ate it.

Summary of Possible Superstructure

The ethnographic and ethnohistoric literature provides a range of possible configurations for the features the crew excavated at Cerro de Trincheras. The stone structures were probably covered by a flat thatched roof. The roof could have been constructed of a variety of lightweight materials, including grass and brush. The jacales and pithouses were most likely walled by brush and ocotillo.

A Comparison of Trincheras and Hohokam Architecture

American archaeologists have traditionally viewed Trincheras from a Hohokam perspective, making interpretations without basic baseline research in the region. The data recovered from the excavation of Cerro de Trincheras makes a more thorough comparison between the Hohokam and Trincheras possible. In this chapter, I apply the data of the architectural features at Trincheras and compare these to the archaeological types previously established in the Hohokam area.

Hohokam Overview

The Hohokam is a major subdivision of the Northwest/Southwest culture area. The Hohokam reside in the Sonoran Desert in southern Arizona and northern Sonora. Generally, the Hohokam built their villages along major rivers in the region. Investigators have interpreted the Phoenix Basin, along the Salt and Gila Rivers, as the core area for the Hohokam (McGuire 1992:4). Scholars have interpreted the remainder of Hohokam area as peripheral. Hohokam researchers include the Tucson Basin and the Papaguería as Hohokam peripheries. Archeologists have noted that each of the Hohokam peripheries has its own developmental sequence and material pattern, yet participated in variable ways in the Hohokam system (Doyel 1977; Fish and Fish 1977).

The early part of the twentieth century saw the birth of Hohokam. Investigators derived the chronological sequence for the Hohokam primarily from excavations at the site of Snaketown (Gladwin et al. 1938; Haury 1976; Wilcox et al. 1981). Since then, many investigators have revised the Hohokam chronology (Plog 1980; Schiffer 1987; among others). Although the problems in Hohokam chronology are far from resolved, Dean (1991) has championed a chronology based on the radiocarbon and archaeomagnetic dates recovered by large-scale contract archaeology projects, and the tree-ring sequence recently established for the Tucson Basin. Table 2.21 shows Dean's chronology and several phase sequences for the Hohokam.

Researchers developed a general phase sequence from the excavation of Snaketown. Archaeologists call the earliest Hohokam period the Pioneer period (ca. A.D. 300 to A.D. 825). The development of agriculture, cremation burial, ceramics, and a transition to a sedentary lifestyle characterize the Pioneer period (Doyel 1987:7). During the Colonial period (ca. A.D. 825 to A.D. 1025) the Hohokam moved into peripheral areas, and sites became larger and more common. The Colonial period Hohokam centered many of their sites on communal architectural structures, such as ball courts and platform mounds. During this period, the Hohokam builders expanded, narrowed, and deepened irrigation canals. Cremation was the preferred method of burial. There was a sharp change in ceremonial architecture and ornate craft production industries develop during the Sedentary period (ca. A.D. 1025 to A.D. 1175). Although cremation burial was the most prevalent, extended burials became more common (Doyel 1987:7).

Researchers have documented major changes for the Hohokam during the Classic period. During this final phase of the Hohokam chronology, irrigation systems were expanded, above ground structures were used instead of houses in pits, ceramic styles changed, and there was a shift to inhumation as the preferred burial method (Doyel 1987:7). Classic period Hohokam was contemporaneous with the occupation of Cerro de Trincheras.

The past three decades have seen a real explosion in Hohokam research. Cultural resource management (CRM) firms have conducted the most recent work due to the rapid development of southern Arizona. The massive data has allowed investigators to document incredible variability within the Hohokam world. Despite the influx of new information, research conducted at Snaketown still informs much archaeological work today (Doyel 1987:10). Hohokam archaeologists still use the basic architectural categories Haury established at Snaketown (Martynec 1993).

Comparison of Trincheras to Traditional Hohokam Architectural Types

Sayles (1938) established the first Hohokam architectural typologies following the excavation of Snaketown. He identified a trend in Hohokam architecture from large square structures in the earliest period, to rectangular structures of similar dimensions, to rectangular and elliptical dwellings with formal sub-features (e.g., step entries). Later Haury (1976:44-77) refined Sayles' house typology based on his excavations at Snaketown in the 1960s. Haury created the architectural typology employed throughout most of the Hohokam area today (1976:45-77). In the section that follows, I summarize the residential architectural trends reflected in Haury's typologies and compare these types to the habitation architectural types present at Cerro de Trincheras.

Hohokam Architecture in the Pioneer Period

The Pioneer period witnessed a wide range of architectural variability. Haury defined seven house types for this period based on his excavations at Snaketown (1976:68). The Hohokam built Pithouses during the earliest part of the Pioneer period that were large (10 m to 15 m in diameter) and square with rounded corners. The builders constructed houses in pits by digging a shallow pit to caliche. Floors were prepared with a mixture of caliche and clay about 3 cm thick. Floor area for P-4 houses averaged 51 m^2. These houses had two sloping entries. Four large posts supported the roof (postholes were one m deep) as well a several smaller interior posts. The prehispanic inhabitants constructed the walls with 10 cm to 15 cm in diameter posts every 20 cm to 50 cm. P-4 houses included two clay-lined hearths inside.

The Hohokam built six other kinds of houses and a smaller version of the P-4 house during the Pioneer period. The P-3 were square in plan, built on native soil, a slight floor edge groove with post walls along the groove, when present. Four main posts supported the roof set almost at the corners of the structure. Entries were parallel sided with no step. The floor area averaged 22 m^2. The Hohokam constructed P-2 houses in the same manner as the P-3 houses, but they were rectangular in plan view. The roof of P-2 houses was supported by a roof of posts one meter from the edge of the structure. P-1 houses were rectangular in plan view with rounded edges. Floors were prepared with a mixture of caliche and red clay. P-1 houses had one parallel sided entry. The Hohokam constructed the walls with mesquite posts 10 cm in diameter set 25 cm apart, which the builders later covered with brush and a layer of clay. They generally aligned the interior roof supports in three rows parallel to the long axis of the structure. A hearth was found midway between the center of the structure and the edge. The floor area averaged 11 m^2.

Haury defined two smaller house types for the Pioneer period. P-6 houses were small rectangular structures (with a floor area of 6.2 m^2) with a well-prepared floor and no hearth. The P-6 structures had a pronounced floor groove to "engage the butt ends of inner reed lining" (Haury 1976:68) and outside posts. P-5 structures were the same as the P-6 structure without a hearth and with an end entry instead of a side entry. The P-5 structures had an average floor area of 8 m^2.

P-7 houses are the only true pithouses used by the Hohokam. The P-7 house uses the edges of the pit as side walls for the structure. A P-7 house is square with rounded corners and a prepared floor of a caliche and clay mixture. Pit sides rose .05 m high and were rounded toward the top. Several roof supports were placed inside the house, but no wall postholes were found along its perimeter. The P-7 house had a side entry with no step. The floor area for these structures averaged 25 m^2.

Hohokam Architecture during the Colonial Period

The Colonial period was a period marked by Hohokam expansion, but there was little change in styles of domestic architecture. The Hohokam builders made only slight modifications to pervious architectural styles. Haury defined three house types for the Colonial period (1976:65). The C-1 house is similar to a P-1 house, with a well defined posthole pattern along its perimeter, no internal roof supports, and no groove along its edge. The C-2 houses are rectangular with a floor of a caliche and clay mixture and an average floor area of 20 m^2. The C-2 house type has a parallel sided entrance near the mid point of the longer wall. Archaeologists often found steps at the entrance. C-2 entrances outside Snaketown have been found with stone risers at entrances. Internal posts supported the roof parallel to near the edges of the house. The Hohokam constructed the walls with a line of mesquite posts along the perimeter 10 cm in diameter and 25 cm to 50 cm apart, filled with reeds and brush, and capped with a layer of clay. A well made hearth is normally situated near the entry. The C-3 house type is rectangular, but shorter than the C-2 house. C-2 house floors were either prepared with a mixture of soil or built on native soil. Hearths were prepared clay-lined basins near the entry. C-3 houses are smaller and more formalized versions of the larger Pioneer period house types.

Hohokam Architecture during the Sedentary Period

Archaeologists studying the Hohokam have noted major changes in ceremonial architecture during the Sedentary period. Ball courts and platform mounds became more common. Nevertheless, changes in domestic architecture were slight. Haury defined five house types for the Sedentary period. S-1 houses were elongated with rounded corners. The floors were prepared with a clay-caliche mixture with an average thickness of .05 m to .15 m. Floor edges sometimes had small grooves or lips. The average floor area for S-1 structures was 20 m^2 to 25 m^2. Entries were positioned halfway along the long side of the structure. These were typically bulbous shaped. The Hohokam constructed several different types of step including, a step of a caliche flooring mixture with a molded sill at the top, a slab of mica schist, or stacks of small logs. Interior roof support was highly variable for this house type and lacked an obvious pattern. In a few cases no evidence for internal roof support was found. The builders constructed side walls in the same manner as C-1 houses, with a series of mesquite posts along the perimeter. They fastened a reed and brush covering onto the posts, and covered it with clay. Clay-lined hearths with an average depth of .25 m were situated near the entry. Trivets used in cooking were often found in S-1 structures. The S-2 house was larger than the S-1 structures and was square with rounded corners and marginally convex sides. The floor area for S-2 houses averaged 42 m^2. Entries to S-2 dwellings were typically short and parallel sided. The roof was flat and supported by the four major posts with auxiliary posts near the edges of the floor to support the side wall posts. The Hohokam built side walls similar to those in S-1 structures. The builders always placed hearths near the entry. Haury defined S-3 houses as big versions of S-1 structures. The floor areas for S-3 houses averaged 52 m^2. Due to its large size, three rows of roof supporting posts were placed in the interior. Sedentary period Hohokam built parallel sided entries with occasional stone risers.

Haury defined the S-4 type as a small, elliptical structure built in a pit .06 m below ground surface. The floors were prepared with a mixture of clay and caliche and had an average area of 8 m^2. The Hohokam sometimes built entrances with a large step. Clay lined hearths were placed near entries. Three aligned postholes were found in S-4 structures. The Hohokam built the side walls of a caliche and clay mixture puddled .15 m thick and rising to a maximum height of .65 m.

Haury gave the designation of S-5 to structures that were rectangular with square corners and adobe walls 10 cm thick. At the time of excavation only .10 m of the walls was preserved. Haury inferred that these walls sloped upwards to "support horizontal stringers" (1976: 62). The S-5 structures had an average floor area of 7 m^2. Hearths varied from burned areas on the floor to formal clay-lined hearths. Investigators have interpreted this house type as the source for the construction methods later employed in domestic architecture during the Classic period (Haury 1976: 63).

Hohokam Architecture during the Classic Period

The Hohokam changed many aspects of their way of life during the Classic period. The Hohokam area saw a major territorial reduction during the Classic period (Gummerman and Haury 1979: 86). Major changes in domestic architecture echoed the vast changes in the Classic period. The classic period Hohokam employed new methods of walls construction that included solid clay walls and post reinforced adobe walls (Gummerman and Haury 1979:86). Though the Hohokam continued to build houses in pits, the clay walled and post reinforced structures built above ground became more common. The above ground structures were often contiguous rooms and in the late part of the phase develop into multi-storied structures.

The Hohokam abandoned Snaketown before the Classic period, so Haury looked at a nearby Classic period site to elaborate his architectural typology for the period (1976). Classic period houses were built on desert surface or below with house floors of prepared clay. Classic period structures were rectangular with squared corners and an average floor area of 15 m^2. Walls vertical, built of puddled adobe with an average thickness of .25 m. Typically, the builders internally reinforced the walls with a series of regularly spaced posts 10 to 15 cm in diameter. Entries did not include passages as in earlier Hohokam house forms. Internal roof supports were variable or not detected. Hearths were centrally placed and clay lined. Haury defined two house types unique to the period Cl-1 and Cl-2 (1976). Cl-1 houses stood alone while Cl-2 houses were contiguous sets of rooms. Compound walls also characterize this period. The Hohokam often built Classic period structures on top of clay capped mounds that stood two meters or more in height (Gummerman and Haury 1979: 87). The multi-storied structures or "great houses" become more common toward the latter part of the Classic period. The great houses were often enclosed in rectangular compound walls.

Hohokam Outside the Core

Hohokam building strategies change through space as well as through time. The regions outside the Hohokam core exhibit quite a bit of variation. Yet, one factor is unmistakable, though architectural styles might vary, they still share a basic Hohokam pattern. For that reason, architectural typologies that were created for the Phoenix basin are still applied at Hohokam sites outside the core. In this section, I touch on the architecture of the Tucson Basin and Papaguería in contrast with that of Trincheras.

The Tucson Basin refers to the region surrounding the Santa Cruz River in Arizona. The Tucson Basin extends from the Tortolita to the Santa Rita Mountains. The Hohokam appears in this area during the Sweetwater phase and their population in this area climaxes during the Rillito phase (Doelle 1985: 15). Generally, Hohokam architecture looks much like the architecture of the Phoenix Basin. Though variation is visible when it comes to shape and size, Tucson Basin domestic structures are similar to those in the Phoenix Basin. Even structures built on Cerros de Trincheras share a basic Hohokam pattern.

Structures excavated at Linda Vista Hill, Fortified Hill and Cerro Prieto, cerro de trincheras sites look much more like traditional Hohokam houses than those we have excavated at Cerro de Trincheras. At all three sites investigators excavated structures that from the surface resemble Cerro de Trincheras' stone structure. The archaeologists after excavation described these structures as "masonry outlined pithouses" (Downum 1993: 67 and 1986; S. Fish et al. 1984; Greenleaf 1975). Downum describes Feature 4 at Cerro Prieto as a dwelling with a prepared floor, an entryway, and numerous domestic artifacts. In structures at all three sites excavators report post holes for roofing support in the interior of these structures. These pithouses seem to be a variation on traditional Hohokam house plan.

The Papaguería is the lesser know branch of the Hohokam. Papaguerían Hohokam lived in an area bounded by the Gila Valley to the north, the Santa Cruz River Valley to the east, the Colorado River valley in the west, and Caborca, Sonora, México to the South. The Papaguería is devoid of permanent streams. The material pattern of the Hohokam in the Papaguería led Haury (1976) to develop his Desert Branch of the Hohokam. Very few excavations have been conducted in the Papaguería. Archaeologists that have excavated in this area have uncovered architectural patterns though not identical to the Phoenix Basin, still resemble it in many ways (Withers 1973; Rosenthal et al. 1978; Marmaduke and Martynec 1993).

The Hohokam of the Papaguería built pithouses that were generally rectangular in plan view with rounded corners (Withers 1973; Rosenthal et al. 1978; Marmaduke and Martynec 1993). Though forms and post hole placement was less formalized, they still fall within general pattern for the Hohokam. Floors of Papaguerian houses were generally plastered. Hearth placement, as in other Hohokam house was typically near the door. Entries were either parallel sided or bulbous. A few informal feature types have been observed at Papaguerian sites (Martynec 1993: 119). Though Martynec refers to these structures as "ephemeral," they had prepared floors, and in some cases hearths and posts for roofing. These structures still appear much more formal and permanent than Trincheras features.

Is Trincheras Architecture Like Hohokam?

The Hohokam had a variety architectural styles that changed greatly through time. Despite the variation, some serious differences are apparent when we compare the domestic architecture of the Hohokam with that of Cerro de Trincheras. The contrast results from differences in basic construction strategies. Hohokam builders constructed more formalized and substantial structures.

The Hohokam builders built houses in several forms; yet, they all share some basic construction elements that are not present at Cerro de Trincheras. They typically prepared a floor with a mixture of clay and caliche. No preparation of this sort was used for any of the habitation structures at Cerro de Trincheras. The lack of preparation made floors difficult to identify. Though several patterns for roof supports were identified for the Hohokam, at Cerro de Trincheras no interior roof supports were located in pithouses, jacales, or stone structures. Hearths were identified in almost all Hohokam structure types. Generally, Hohokam hearths were prepared with a well fired clay lining. Hearths are rare in Trincheras structures; of the 65 jacales, pithouses and structures only 13 percent of these had hearths. All the hearths located in the interior of Trincheras residential structures were unprepared. No wall posts were identified along the perimeter of any of the jacales or pithouses at Cerro de Trincheras. Almost all Hohokam house types had a pattern of post holes along their perimeter. The entries of the pithouses at Cerro de Trincheras are usually indicated by ramps. Entries into Hohokam dwellings vary in form and construction material. Floor area of Hohokam domestic structures is highly variable. Table 2.21 summarizes average floor area for Hohokam house types and Cerro de Trincheras structures. The typical Hohokam dwelling house was more formally prepared and a more substantial superstructure than those our crew excavated at Cerro de Trincheras.

If Not Like Hohokam Then What is Trincheras Architecture Like?

The large body of information generated by the growth of cultural resource management has allowed Hohokam researchers to revisit long standing debates of Hohokam origins. New data has strengthened arguments that see the Hohokam as an indigenous development with antecedents in the San Pedro Cochise (Wilcox 1979). San Pedro Cochise origins have also been assumed for the Trincheras people. In this section I examine similarities between San Pedro Cochise and Trincheras architecture.

Hohokam researchers addressing this question have grappled with the apparent dissimilarity between the earliest Hohokam architecture and the San Pedro Cochise (Cable and Doyel 1987: 57). Differences in architecture surround the formal nature, and large size of houses built in the Vahki phase. Recent contract work has allowed Hohokam researchers to postulate an earlier phase for the Hohokam: the Red Mountain phase of the Pioneer period in the Phoenix Basin and Cienega phase in the Tucson Basin. During the Red Mountain period architecture can be described as small square houses with rounded corners (Cable and Doyel 1987: 59). Red Mountain houses have wall trenches, plastered floors and no evident pattern for roof supports. The Red Mountain phase allows Hohokam researchers to bridge the material gap between the San Pedro Cochise and the Pioneer period Hohokam. Researchers have also looked to the Cienega phase (ca. 800 B.C. to A.D. 150) found along the Santa Cruz floodplain to remedy the material gap leading to the Hohokam (Mabry 1997: 1). Gregory (1997:2) has described the architecture for the Cienega phase as circular pit structures, three to four meters in diameter, with a series of evenly spaced post holes along their perimeter. Floors were not prepared and no formal entries were found. More recently, archaeologists have discussed the Cienaga and San Pedro phases as early agricultural communities (Silva 2005). These more recent studies have also found circular pit structures.

In contrast to differences between the San Pedro Cochise and the Hohokam, Trincheras architecture shares certain similarities with San Pedro Cochise. The houses of the San Pedro Cochise have been described as oval or circular structures with informal hearth areas and no evidence of structural support (Cable and Doyel 1987: 58; Sayles 1945: 3-4, 1938: 125-129). Cable and Doyel have characterized these dwellings as giving the "overall impression ... of impermanence and only seasonal habitation" (Cable and Doyel 1987: 58). These structures sound very much like the jacal and pithouse structures excavated at Cerro de Trincheras.

Summary and Discussion

Trincheras research has traditionally been undertaken under the shadow of a Hohokam framework. Past interpretations that understood the Trincheras Tradition as a member or an outsider of the Hohokam system have been undertaken in the absence of fundamental baseline research. The Cerro de Trincheras Research Project has produced the kind of data necessary to take comparisons beyond the level of ceramic distributions.

Haury established an architectural classification for the Hohokam. Haury defined 16 different house types built between the Pioneer period and the Classic period. The Hohokam houses typically have plastered floors, in the pre-classic walls are generally built of posts covered with brush and reeds covered by a clay layer, in the Classic period walls were constructed of puddled adobe walls, formal hearths were placed near entries during the pre-Classic and centrally located during the Classic period, in most Hohokam house types roofs were supported by a pattern of large interior posts resulting in either flat or gabled roofs, entries were parallel sided or bulbous in the pre-classic while no passages were used during the Classic period. Sizes, shapes and configurations of entries of Hohokam house types were highly variable.

Generally, Hohokam houses are more formal and more substantial than domestic architecture at Cerro de Trincheras. The floors of Cerro de Trincheras were very difficult to detect in most cases while Hohokam house floor were typically prepared. The side-walls of both pithouses and jacal structures at Trincheras show no evidence for posts, puddled adobe walls, or post reinforced adobe walls set along the perimeter while almost all Hohokam house types exhibit evidence of a substantial wall construction. Post supports for roofing were usually found in the majority of Hohokam house types, no internal roof supports were found in stone structures, jacales, and pithouses at Cerro de Trincheras. Hearths in Hohokam dwellings are generally prepared with a clay lining and placed near the entries, while Trincheras hearths in structures are rare, very informal and unprepared. The typical Trincheras dwelling is much more ephemeral and less formalized than Hohokam houses.

The ephemeral nature of Trincheras domestic architecture is similar to that of early agricultural communities and the proto historic Pima. In both cases houses are typically, round to oval in plan with informal hearths and no evidence for structural support. Additionally, both housing strategies leave the impression of evanescence. Both the early agriculture and the Early Pima settlements have been described as rancheriá style. These settlements are dispersed and involve little planning. This is certainly not the case at Cerro de Trincheras. The sites internal organization is very complex. Further research needs to done in order sort out the architectural similarities and the organizational differences.

The study of features at Cerro de Trincheras seems to reveal a basic paradox between the monumentality of the site as a whole, and the apparent informality and impermanence of features on the site. The visual impact of Cerro de Trincheras has lasted more than 500 years. The inhabitants of Cerro de Trincheras invested more effort building a message of monumental scale visible from surrounding areas than in the local constructions used in day-to-day life.

Tables for Chapter 2

Table 2.1. Feature Type Description by Area

Feature type/ Tipo de elemento	A1	B1	B2	B3	B4	B6	B7	B8	B9	B10	B11	D	E	Total
Access feature/ Elemento de acceso	1	0	0	1	1	0	0	1	0	0	0	0	0	4
Ancillary terrace/ Balcon de terraza	0	0	0	1	0	0	0	0	0	0	0	0	0	1
Burials/ Entierros	0	0	1	0	1	4	0	0	1	0	1	1	2	11
Circular stone struct./ Estru. cir. de piedra	20	0	0	1	0	3	0	0	0	0	1	0	0	25
Pits/ Hoyos	0	0	1	0	3	2	1	0	0	0	1	6	28	42
Jacal	0	2	1	0	1	1	1	0	1	0	0	0	0	7
Midden/ Basurero	0	0	0	0	0	0	0	0	0	0	0	0	2	2
Occupational surface/ Superfice ocupacional	0	0	0	0	0	1	0	0	0	0	0	0	3	4
Petrograbado	0	0	0	1	0	0	0	0	0	0	0	0	0	1
Pithouse/ Casa semi-subterranea	0	0	0	0	0	0	0	0	0	0	0	0	9	9
Platform/ Plataforma	0	0	0	0	1	2	0	0	0	0	0	0	0	3
Possible Ramada	0	0	0	0	0	0	0	0	0	0	0	0	1	1
Quadrangular stone struc./ Estru. cuad. Piedra	0	0	0	0	0	1	0	0	1	0	0	2	0	4
Possible house floor/ Piso de casa poss.	0	0	0	0	0	0	0	0	0	0	0	0	2	1
Rock arrangement/ Config. de piedras	0	0	0	0	0	0	0	0	0	0	1	2	3	6
Total features per area/ Total de elementos por area	21	2	3	3	7	14	2	1	3	0	4	11	50	121

Table 2.2. Descriptive Statistics for Circular Stone Structures										
		Provenience/ Procedencia				Wall				
Number/ Número	Area/ Área	North - Norte	East/ Este	Length/ Largo (m)	Width/ Ancho (m)	Height/ Altura (m)	Width/ Ancho (m)	Floor/ Piso	Entry/ Entrada	Orientation/ Orientación
1	A1	74-80	252-257	4.35	2.30	0.85	0.50		Yes/Sí	SW
2	A1	107-113	289-297	3.30	3.37	0.85	-		Yes/Sí	S
3	A1	95-100	244-250	3.90	3.30	0.85	1.15		Yes/Sí	N
4	A1	100-105	244-250	4.10	4.00	0.55	1.03		Yes/Sí	N
5	A1	108-113	249-253	3.80	2.40	0.55	0.93		Yes/Sí	W
6	A1	112-116	242-246	3.20	2.80	0.50	0.60		Yes/Sí	NE
7	A1	118-124	242-248	4.80	4.40	0.80	0.83		Yes/Sí	NE
8	A1	116-121	248-252	4.00	3.70	0.60	0.75		Yes/Sí	NE
9	A1	108-112	254-258	2.90	2.60	0.45	0.60		Yes/Sí	NW
10	A1	95-100	295-300	3.70	3.40	0.58	0.60		Yes/Sí	N
11	A1	111-115	261-265	3.50	2.70	0.48	0.70		Yes/Sí	N
12	A1	115-120	266-271	4.10	3.20	0.95	0.75		Yes/Sí	NW
13	A1	95-100	295-300	3.30	3.00	0.45	0.55		No	-
14	A1	79-85	296-303	6.20	5.60	0.50	0.40		No	-
15	A1	88-93	290-295	3.20	2.60	0.40	0.70		Yes/Sí	S
16	A1	75-80	275-280	4.20	4.00	0.58	0.40		Yes/Sí	SW
17	B3	107-109	107-110	3.80	3.20	-			No	-
18	B6	113-117	211-216	3.25	4.50	-			Yes/Sí	N
19	B6	113-119	230-236	5.50	3.50	0.80	-		Yes/Sí	N
20	B6	121-125	236-240	3.25	3.21	0.70	-		No	-
21	A1	93-97	280-286	3.70	3.00	0.55	0.30		Yes/Sí	W
22	A1	68-74	268-276	6.20	5.20	-	-		Yes/Sí	NE
23	A1	73-79	266-270	4.50	4.10	0.40	1.50		Yes/Sí	S
24	A1	64-69	278-284	2.80	2.60	-	-		Yes/Sí	NW
25	B11	108-109	324-325	1.90	1.50	-	-		No	-
Average Dimensions/ Promedio de dimensiones				3.90	3.37	0.66	1.12			

Table 2.3. Distribution of Material by Circular Stone Structure

Circular stone structure/ Estructura circular de piedra	Area/Área	Plain ceramics/ Cerámica Lisa	Decorated ceramics/ Cerámica decorada	Lithics/ Lítica	Stone tools/ Herramientas de piedra	Ground stone/ Lítica pulida	Bone/ Hueso	Shell/ Concha
1	A1	365	0	5	0	0	5	1
2	A1	860	0	197	1	2	0	0
3	A1	0	0	10	0	0	0	0
4	A1	206	0	124	1	0	132	9
5	A1	507	0	68	0	0	7	1
6	A1	0	0	5	0	0	0	0
7	A1	207	0	58	2	0	0	1
8	A1	552	0	102	1	1	4	6
9	A1	8	0	19	0	0	0	0
10	A1	60	0	8	0	0	0	0
11	A1	39	0	10	0	0	0	0
12	A1	17	0	6	0	1	0	1
13	A1	4	0	4	0	0	0	0
14	A1	106	0	3	2	4	0	0
15	A1	270	0	233	0	1	2	2
16	A1	42	0	9	0	1	0	0
17	B3	1436	0	110	0	4	54	2
18	B6	5093	9	1241	15	9	32	46
19	B6	4876	16	862	18	7	13	46
20	B6	2187	0	304	10	3	21	12
21	A1	51	0	0	0	0	0	0
22	A1	3836	0	799	5	3	13	39
23	A1	5	0	141	1	0	0	0
24	A1	462	0	129	0	1	4	2
25	B11	575	0	118	0	0	4	0
Total		21764	25	4565	56	37	291	168

Table 2.4. Descriptive Statistics for Quadrangular Stone Structures

Quadrangular stone structure/ Estruct. cuadr. de piedra.	Area/ Área	Provenience/ Procedencia N	E	Length/ Altura (m)	Width/ Ancho (m)	Wall Height/ Altura de Muro (m)	Entry	Orientation
1	B6	111- 117	214 -222	6.5	5.18	0.7	Yes/Sí	NE
2	B9	297-300	407- 412	4	4	1	No	--
3	D	89-98	54- 62	7	3.45	0.3	Yes/Sí (2)	NE-SE
4	D	43-53	111-119	3.85	5.13	--	No	--
Average dimensions for QSS/ Promedio de medidas de las estructuras cuad. de piedra				5.34	4.44	0.67		

Table 2.5. Distribution of Material by Quadrangular Stone Structure

Quadrangular stone structure/ Estructura cuadrangular de piedra	Area/ Área	Plain ceramics/ Cerámica Lisa	Decorated ceramics/ Cerámica decorada	Lithics/ Lítica	Stone tools/ Herramientas de piedra	Ground stone/ Lítica pulida	Bone/ Hueso	Shell/ Concha
1	B6	8701	5	2226	22	12	185	109
2	B9	6167	0	314	0	1	8	12
3	D	6129	13	532	7	4	68	80
4	D	1732	0	492	6	4	14	59
Total		22729	18	3564	35	21	275	260

Table 2.6. Descriptive Statistics for Pithouses

Pithouse	Area/ Área	Provenience/ Procedencia N	E	Length/ Largo (m)	Width/ Ancho (m)	Floor/ Piso	Hearth Diam./Depth/ Diám. Profund. (m)	(m)	Entry Ramps/ Rampa de Entrada	Orientation/ Orientación
1	E	124-128	130-133	3.4	3.1	Yes/Sí	--	--	Yes/Sí	NW
2	E	125-131	84-89	4.25	4	Yes/Sí	0.78	0.23	N	NE
3	E	128-130	118-122	2.57	2.25	Yes/Sí	--	--	N	--
4	E	121-123	126-130	4.35	3.5	Yes/Sí	--	--	Yes/Sí	--
5	E	119-123	133-136	2.75	--	Yes/Sí	--	--	Yes/Sí	--
6*	E	129	139	--	--	No	--	---	Yes/Sí	--
7*	E	122	115	--	--	No	--	--	Yes/Sí	N
8*	E	124	114	--	--	No	--	--	Yes/Sí	N
9*	E	124	111	--	--	No	--	--	Yes/Sí	--

*Pithouses 6 through 9 were defined on basis of ramps identified/
Definimos los [Pithouses] 6 hasta 9 seguido las rampas identificadas

Table 2.7. Distribution of Material by Pithouse

Pithouse	Area/ Área	Plain ceramics/ Cerámica Lisa	Decorated ceramics/ Cerámica decorada	Lithics/ Lítica	Stone tools/ Herramientas de piedra	Ground stone/ Lítica pulida	Bone/ Hueso	Shell/ Concha
1	E	1122	0	198	1	3	76	0
2	E	422	0	183	5	2	1	2
3	E	263	0	164	0	2	43	1
4	E	27	0	16	0	3	0	0
5	E	1	0	1	0	0	0	0
6	E	0	0	0	0	0	0	0
7	E	0	0	0	0	0	0	0
8	E	0	0	0	0	0	0	0
9	E	0	0	0	0	0	0	0
Total		1835	0	562	6	21	120	3

Table 2.8. Descriptive Statistics for Jacal Structures

Jacal	Area	Provenience/ Procedencia N	E	Length/ Largo (m)	Width/ Ancho (m)	Depth/ Profundidad (m)	Orientation/ Orientación
1	B1	104-106	71-73	3.8	2.9	1.15	
2	B2	105-109	102-106	4.00	4.00	0.50	
3	B4	103-107	110-116	6.50	4.50	0.98	
4	B6	104-110	219-224	6.00	5.00	0.37	NE
5	B7	98-101	290-294	4.30	3.00	0.70	
6	B9	297-300	413-416	2.46	2.20	0.26	NE
7	B1	98-100	83-85	2.3	1.6	0.30	
Average dimensions/ Promedio de medidas				4.19	3.31	0.61	

Table 2.9. Distribution of Material by Jacal

Jacal	Area/ Área	Plain ceramics/ Cerámica Lisa	Decorated ceramics/ Cerámica decorada	Lithics/ Lítica	Stone Tools/ Herramientas de piedra	Ground stone/ Lítica pulida	Bone/ Hueso	Shell/ Concha
1	B1	6672	7	662	6	1	7	17
2	B2	7445	0	890	16	8	166	34
3	B4	2669	10	228	13	10	16	16
4	B6	5920	7	1196	15	1	9	22
5	B7	26476	24	2561	26	14	37	138
6	B9	9778	5	632	1	2	22	25
7	B1	3811	9	266	0	7	5	20
Total		62771	62	6435	77	43	262	272

Table 2.10. Distribution of Material by Platform

Platform/ Plataforma	Area	Plain ceramics/ Cerámica Lisa	Decorated ceramics/ Cerámica decorada	Lithics/ Lítica	Stone tools/ Herramientas de piedra	Ground stone/ Lítica pulida	Bone/ Hueso	Shell/ Concha
1	B6	14290	9	3154	40	3	27	49
2	B6	15012	1	2568	51	16	41	86
3	B4	6526	10	541	11	2	75	40
Total		35828	20	6263	102	21	143	175

Table 2.11. Descriptive Statistics for Occupational Surfaces

Occupational surface/ Superfice ocupacional	Area/Área	North/Norte	East/Este	Length/Largo (m)	Width/Ancho (m)
1	E	102-109	111-118.00	7.00	7.00
2	E	120-124	118-122.50	4.00	4.00
3	E	120-122	108-112.00	4.00	2.00
4	B6	105-109	227-232.00	4.50	3.35
Average dimensions of Occupational surfaces/ Promedio de medidas de Superfices ocupacionales				4.88	4.09

Table 2.12. Distribution of Material by Occupational Surface

Occupational surface/ Superfice ocupacional	Area/ Área	Plain ceramics/ Cerámica Lisa	Decorated ceramics/ Cerámica decorada	Lithics/ Lítica	Stone tools/ Herramientas de piedra	Ground stone/ Lítica pulida	Bone/ Hueso	Shell/ Concha
1	E	106	0	64	3	2	0	0
2	E	32	1	42	0	0	19	0
3	E	191	0	175	0	0	22	2
4	B6	3366	0	792	9	6	0	2
Total		3695	1	1073	12	8	41	4

Table 2.13. Distribution of Material by Access Feature

Access feature/ Elemento de acceso	Area	Plain ceramics/ Cerámica Lisa	Decorated ceramics/ Cerámica decorada	Lithics/ Lítica	Stone tools/ Herramientas de piedra	Ground stone/ Lítica pulida	Bone/ Hueso	Shell/ Concha
Ramp 1/ Rampa 1	A1	134	0	20	0	0	0	0
Ramp 2/ Rampa 2	B8	963	0	61	0	0	0	3
Stairs 1/ Escaleras 1	B4	0	2	0	0	0	2	0
Stairs 2/ Escaleras 2	B3	784	2	123	2	0	0	0
Total		1881	4	204	2	0	2	3

Table 2.14. Pit Data

Pit number/ Número de hoyo	Area/ Área	North/ Norte	East/ Este	Type/ Tipo	Depth/ Profúndidad (m)	Length (diam.)/ Largo (m)	Width/ Ancho (m)	Plan view/ Plano	Fill/ Relleno	Stratified deposits/ Depositos estratigrafi-cados
1	E	127.00-129.00	151.00-154.00	Multipurpose pit/ Hoyo de uso multiple	0.34	1.40	2.05	Oval/ Ovalado	Varied/ Varios	no
2	E	106.00-111.00	148.50-151.00	Multipurpose pit/ Hoyo de uso multiple	0.94	2.40	1.70	Oval/ Ovalado	Ash & carbon/ carbon ceniza	yes/ sí
3	E	126.00-128.00	154.50-156.00	Multipurpose pit/ Hoyo de uso multiple	0.20	1.72	1.31	Irregular/ Iregular	Varied/ Varios	no
4	E	126.10-127.00	151.00-152.00	Caliche lined pit/ Hoyo const. de caliche	0.12	0.80	0.76	Round/ Circular	Gen. Cult./ Rell. Cult	no
5	E	126.20-127.00	153.00-154.00	Multipurpose pit/ Hoyo de uso multiple	0.20	0.44	0.50	Round/ Circular	Varied/ Varios	no
6	E	119.00-119.80	114.60-115.40	Ash pit/ Hoyo de ceniza	0.14	0.76	0.58	Irregular/ Iregular	Ash & carbon/ carbon ceniza	no
7	E	128.00-128.90	144.17-145.10	Ash pit/ Hoyo de ceniza	0.13	0.95	0.86	Irregular/ Iregular	Ash & carbon/ carbon ceniza	no
8	E	124.20-125.00	128.60-129.40	Ash pit/ Hoyo de ceniza	0.15	0.67	0.57	Oval/ Ovalado	Ash & carbon/ carbon ceniza	no
9	E	109.25-109.95	128.15-128.65	Ash pit/ Hoyo de ceniza	0.10	0.54	0.42	Irregular/ Iregular	Ash & carbon/ carbon ceniza	no

Table 2.14. Pit Data, cont'd

Pit #/ Numero de Hoyo	Area/ Loci	North/ Norte	East/ Este	Type/ Tipo	Depth/ Profundidad (m)	Length (diam.)/ Largo (m)	Width/ Ancho (m)	Plan view/ Plano	Fill/ Relleno	Stratified deposits/ Depositos estratigrafi-cados
10	E	128.50-129.30	139.50-139.95	Ash pit/ Hoyo de ceniza	0.12	0.50	0.43	Irregular/ Iregular	Ash & carbon/ carbon ceniza	no
11	E	125.15-127.00	119.25-120.75	Unknown/ Tipo no identificado	0.25	1.58	1.43	Round/ Circular	Varied/ Varios	no
12	E	119.00-119.80	106.05-106.60	Caliche lined pit/ Hoyo const. de caliche	0.14	0.70	0.45	Oval/ Ovalado	Varied/ Varios	no
13	E	123.60-124.20	118.70-119.80	Unknown/ Tipo no identificado	0.20	1.24	0.64	Oval/ Ovalado	Varied/ Varios	no
14	B2	107.00-108.00	90.00-91.00	Roasting Pit/ Hoyo para hornear	0.45	1.32	1.12	Round/ Circular	Gen. Cult./ Rell. Cult	no
15	B4	106.20-108.30	98.30-100.10	Trash filled pit/ Hoyo lleno de basura	0.20	2.00	2.00	Round/ Circular	Varied/ Varios	no
16	B4	106.30-106.50	114.00-114.90	Ash pit/ Hoyo de ceniza	0.38	0.90	0.70	Round/ Circular	Gen. Cult./ Rell. Gen. Cult	no
17	B6	107.00-108.00	223.00-224.00	Storage & processing/ Hoyo proces.y almacenamiento	0.23	0.71	0.56	Oval/ Ovalado	Varied/ Varios	yes/ sí

Table 2.14. Pit Data, cont'd

Pit #/ Numero de Hoyo	Area/ Loci	North/ Norte	East/ Este	Type/ Tipo	Depth/	Length (diam.)/ Largo	Width/ Ancho (m)	Plan view/ Plano	Fill/ Relleno	Stratified deposits/ Depositos estratigrafi-cados
18	B11	109.00-110.00	321.00-322.00	Unknown/ Tipo no identificado	0.41	0.93	0.61		Varied/ Varios	no
19	D	86.60-87.10	70.05-70.54	Unknown/ Tipo no identificado	0.40	0.50	0.40	Oval/ Ovalado	Gen. Cult./ Rell. Gen. Cult	no
20	D	94.70-95.70	68.60-69.40	Unknown/ Tipo no identificado	0.30	1.00	0.80	Oval/ Ovalado	Gen. Cult./ Rell. Gen. Cult	no
21	D	86.80-87.30	68.50-70.00	Unknown/ Tipo no identificado	0.22	0.50	0.50	Round/ Circular	Gen. Cult./ Rell. Gen. Cult	no
22	D	87.45-88.20	69.69-70.35	Unknown/ Tipo no identificado	0.20	0.82	0.43	Oval/ Ovalado	Gen. Cult./ Rell. Gen. Cult	no
23	D	89.00-89.50	70.01-70.69	Unknown/ Tipo no identificado	0.76	0.50	0.50	Round/ Circular	Gen. Cult./ Rell. Gen. Cult	no
24	D	73.00-77.00	132.90-133.00	Roasting Pit/ Hoyo para hornear	0.12	3.44	0.70	Irregular/ Iregular	Rock filled/ Piedras	no

Table 2.15. Distribution of Material by Pit

Pit/ Hoyo	Area/ Área	Plain ceramics/ Cerámica Lisa	Decorated ceramics/ Cerámica decorada	Lithics/ Lítica	Stone tools/ Herramientas de piedra	Ground stone/ Lítica pulida	Bone/ Hueso	Shell/ Concha
Pit 1-Multipurpose/ Hoyo 1–Multiuso	E	651	0	92	0	1	7	1
Pit 2-Multipurpose/ Hoyo 2–Multiuso	E	1628	2	217	0	0	30	3
Pit 3-Multipurpose/ Hoyo 3–Multiuso	E	396	0	55	0	1	11	1
Pit 4-Caliche Lined/ Hoyo 4-Forrado de Caliche	E	56	2	2	0	0	9	1
Pit 5-Multipurpose Hoyo 5–Multiuso	E	7	0	7	0	0	0	0
Pit 6-Ash filled/ Hoyo 6-Lleno de Ceniza	E	62	0	32	0	0	1	2
Pit 7-Ash filled/ Hoyo 7-Lleno de Ceniza	E	6	0	1	0	1	0	0
Pit 8-Ash filled/ Hoyo 8-Lleno de Ceniza	E	132	0	2	0	0	3	2
Pit 9-Ash filled/ Hoyo 9-Lleno de Ceniza	E	0	0	0	0	0	0	0
Pit 10-Ash filled/ Hoyo 10-Lleno de Ceniza	E	107	0	39	0	0	26	10
Pit 11-Unknown/ Hoyo 11/Desconocido	E	192	1	116	0	0	12	8
Pit 12-Caliche Lined/ Hoyo 12-Forrado de Caliche	E	0	0	4	0	0	1	0
Pit 13-Unknown/ Hoyo 13-Desconocido	E	3	1	8	0	0	9	1
Pit 14-Roasting/ Hoyo 14-Asadero	B2	757	1	126	1	4	1	16
Pit 15-Trash Filled/ Hoyo 15-Lleno de Basura	B4	919	4	96	0	0	12	1
Pit 16-Ash filled/ Hoyo 16-Lleno de Ceniza	B4	64	0	1	0	0	0	0
Pit 17-Storage and Processing/ Hoyo 17-Depósito Tratamiento	B6	19	0	7	0	1	1	0
Pit 18-Unknown/ Hoyo 18-Desconocido	B11	0	0	13	0	0	0	0
Pit 19-Unknown/ Hoyo 19-Desconocido	D	6	1	0	0	0	6	1
Pit 20-Unknown/ Hoyo 20-Desconocido	D	0	0	0	0	1	13	4
Pit 21-Unknown/ Hoyo 21-Desconocido	D	12	0	1	0	0	0	0
Pit 22-Unknown/ Hoyo 22-Desconocido	D	75	0	0	1	0	3	2
Pit 23-Unknown/ Hoyo 23-Desconocido	D	0	0	0	0	0	0	0
Pit 24-Roasting/ Hoyo 24-Asadero	D	99	0	12	0	0	0	1
Total		5191	12	831	2	9	145	54

Table 2.16. Descriptive Statistics for Puddling Pits

Puddling pit/ Número de hoyo	Area/ Área	North/ Norte	East/ Este	Depth/ Profundidad (m)	Diameter/ Diámetro (m)	Plan view/ Plano	Stratified deposits/ Yacimientos estratificados
1	E	121.95-122.80	134.85-135.35	0.10	0.46	Circular	No
2	E	124.90-125.40	127.40-127.90	0.12	0.40	Circular	No
Average dimensions of puddling pits/ Promedio de medidas de hoyos de mezcla				0.11	0.83		

Table 2.17. Distribution of Material by Puddling Pit

Puddling pit/ Pozo de mezcla	Area/ Área	Plain ceramics/ Cerámica Lisa	Decorated ceramics/ Cerámica decorada	Lithics/ Lítica	Stone tools/ Herramientas de piedra	Ground stone/ Lítica pulida	Bone/ Hueso	Shell/ Concha
1	E	23	0	0	0	0	0	0
2	E	0	0	0	0	0	0	0
Total		23	0	0	0	0	0	0

Table 2.18. Descriptive Statistics for Hearths

Hearth No./ Número de fogón	Area/ Área	North/ Norte	East/ Este	Type/Tipo	Depth/ Profundidad (m)	Length (diam.)/ Largo (m)	Width/ Ancho (m)	Plan/ Plano	Fill/ Relleno
1	E	128.75-129.05	123.60-124.00	Unprepared/No preparado	0.15	0.33	0.22	Round/ Círcular	Ash & charcoal/ Carbón y ceniza
2	E	130.45-131.20	106.30-107.15	Prepared/Preparado	0.22	0.70	0.80	Round/ Círcular	Ash & charcoal/ Carbón y ceniza
3	E	127.14-127.70	152.90-153.60	Unprepared/No preparado	0.12	0.50	0.45	Oval/ Ovalado	Varied/ Variado
4	E	128.20-128.90	151.35-152.00	Prepared/Preparado	0.09	0.64	0.50	Round/ Círcular	Varied/ Variado
5	E	128.22-129.30	126.80-127.55	Unprepared/No preparado	0.15	0.55	0.40	Curved/ Curvado	Gen. Cult./ Rell. Cult. Gen.
6	E	126.00-126.80	122.00-122.70	Unprepared/No preparado	0.10	0.70	0.24	Irregular/ Iregular	Ash & charcoal/ Carbón y ceniza
7	E	121.00-122.50	119.00-120.20	Unprepared/No preparado	0.14	1.30	1.10	Oval/ Ovalado	Ash & charcoal/ Carbón y ceniza
8	E	120.65-121.35	109.15-109.85	Unprepared/No preparado	0.12	0.64	0.60	Round/ Círcular	Gen. Cult./ Rell. Cult. Gen.
9	E	120.62-121.12	?	Unprepared/No preparado	0.11	0.62	0.48	Round/ Círcular	Ash & charcoal/ Carbón y ceniza
10	E	123.40-123.96	108.80-109.35	Unprepared/No preparado	0.08	0.48	0.47	Round/ Círcular	Ash & charcoal/ Carbón y ceniza
11	E	103.15-103.90	135.00-135.70	Unprepared/No preparado	0.13	0.54	0.47	Round/ Círcular	Ash & charcoal/ Carbón y ceniza
12	E	128.20-129.06	86.14-86.94	Unprepared/No preparado	0.23	0.78	0.71	Round/ Círcular	Gen. Cult./ Rell. Cult. Gen.
13	E	120.00-121.00	122.00-123.00	Unprepared/No preparado	0.14	0.43	0.40	Round/ Círcular	Gen. Cult./ Rell. Cult. Gen.
14	B4	107.15-107.60	96.15-96.62	Unprepared/No preparado	0.12	0.40	0.30	Oval/ Ovalado	Ash & charcoal/ Carbón y ceniza
15	B6	107.51-107.81	220.71-221.00	Unprepared/No preparado	0.30	0.30	0.30	Round/ Círcular	Ash & charcoal/ Carbón y ceniza
16	B7	98.28-98.96	289.91-290.90	Unprepared/No preparado	0.63	1.00	0.80	Oval/ Ovalado	Ash & charcoal/ Carbón y ceniza
17	D	60.30-60.86	130.10-130.85	Unprepared/No preparado	0.50	0.50	0.22	Oval/ Ovalado	Rocks/ Piedras
Averages for hearth dimensions: Promedios de medidas de los fogones:					0.20	0.61	0.50		

Table 2.19. Distribution of Material by Midden

Midden/ Basurero	Area/ Área	Plain ceramics/ Cerámica Lisa	Decorated ceramics/ Cerámica decorada	Lithics/ Lítica	Stone tools/ Herramientas de piedra	Ground stone/ Lítica pulida	Bone/ Heuso	Shell/ Concha
1	E	5820	7	981	11	3	78	6
2	E	749	0	279	4	7	1	5
Total		6569	7	1260	15	10	79	11

Table 2.20. Descriptive Statistics for Rock Arrangements

Rock arrangement/ Configuración de piedras	Area/ Área	North/ Norte	East/ Este	Shape/ Forma	Length/ Largo (m)	Width/ Ancho (m)	Depth/ Profundidad (m)	Subfeatures/ Subelementos
1	E	119.00-121.00	103.20-106.60	Circular/ Círcular	3.40	3.00	0.05	Pit 12/ Hoyo 12
2	E	120.25-122.00	114.25-114.70	Irregular	2.40	1.60	0.15	Assoc. pithouse 7/
3	E	127.80-129.20	148.17-149.60	Aligned clusters/ Conjuntos alineados	2.00	1.50	0.46	Two pits/ Dos hoyos
4	D	63.00-69.00	139.00-145.00	Circular/ Círcular	6.00	6.00	0.43	None/ No
5	D	58.70-62.00	125.00-129.85	Rectangular	6.00	4.00	0.58	Hearth 17/ Fogón 17
6	B11	106.40-108.56	316.26-319.12	Circular/ Círcular	2.26	2.28	0.22	None/ No
Average dimensions for rock arrangements/ Promedio de medidas de configuraciones de piedras					3.78	3.06	0.32	

Table 2.21. Average Floor Area for Hohokam and Trincheras Domestic Structures

Hohokam house type/tipo de casa	Average floor area/Promedio de área del suelo (Haury 1976) (m^2)	Cerro de Trincheras structure type/tipo de estructura	Average floor area/Promedio de área del suelo (m^2)
P-6	6.2		
S-5	7.0		
S-4	8.0		
P-1	11.0		
C-1	11.0	Pithouse	11.0
Cl-1	15.0	Circular Stone Structure/ Estructura de Piedra Círcular	12.0
Cl-2	15.0		
C-2	20.0	Jacal	18.0
S-1	23.0		
P-2	22.0		
P-3	22.0		
P-7	25.0	Quadrangular Stone Structure/ Estructura de Piedra Cuadrilátera	24.0
S-2	42.0		
P-4	51.0		
S-3	52.0		
C-3	Unknown/ Desconocido		

Chapter 3

Tepalcates Trinchereños: The Ceramic Analysis from Cerro de Trincheras

Emiliano Gallaga Murrieta. Centro INAH Sonora

Cerámica

Este capítulo trata el conjunto de cerámica recuperado en Cerro de Trincheras durante las temporadas de trabajo de campo de 1995 y 1996. El equipo de campo recuperó más de 1,000,000 de fragmentos de un peso mayor a tres toneladas métricas y representativo de 24 tipos cerámicos cuya gran mayoría fueron cerámicas lisas. Los analistas no identificaron el tipo Hohokam. El tipo de cerámica lisa comparte las mismas características físicas que las cerámicas del resto de la región de Trincheras. La producción de cerámica se focalizó en cubrir las necesidades mínimas para la gente de Trincheras tales como almacenaje, preparación y consumo y Gallaga observa que como resultado, los Trinchereños no vieron la necesidad de decorar vasijas y desarrollaron un estilo local de decoración. Los análisis cerámicos y petrográficos muestran que los Trinchereños mayormente manufacturaron sus propias cerámicas, sino directamente en el sitio, en sus proximidades o inclusive en sitios más pequeños alrededor de Cerro de Trincheras.

Ceramic analysis helps archaeologists understand several aspects of a site, including the nature of activity areas, the utilization of natural resources, the routes of exchange and trade, and the sociopolitical structure. In northwest México, few investigations have included a thorough analysis of ceramic material. With respect to plainware ceramics, Braniff (1992:394) noted that they had not yet undergone systematic analysis, consequently, "we had to create and define new types and reuse old [types]" (McGuire and Villalpando 1993:26). This ceramic analysis was principally based on the ceramic typology established for the nearby Altar Valley (McGuire and Villalpando 1993). In the absence of a local ceramic typology, Altar researchers developed a classification system based on the type-variety method. A similar system was employed for the Cerro de Trincheras site. Prior to the analysis, we hypothesized that plainware ceramics were of local manufacture because the types found were similar to those recovered in the Altar Valley (McGuire and Villalpando 1993). Conversely, we suspected that decorated material was produced elsewhere, except for some local types belonging to the Trincheras Tradition. Existing typologies were used for the non-local polychrome ceramic analysis, like those employed by Bowen (1972, 1976a, 1976b), Braniff (1992), Di Peso (1956), Di Peso et al. (1974), Hinton (1955), and Jácome (1986).

The ceramics analyzed here were gathered during two field seasons at Cerro de Trincheras in the springs of 1995 and 1996. Workers excavated more than 1.5 percent of the site's nearly 100-hectare surface area. Excavations were distributed to get a representative sample of occupants' behavior across the site (Gallaga 1997; McGuire and Villalpando 1995). Among other archaeological materials, we recovered more than one million sherds (n = 1,044,262) with an approximate weight of 3.3 metric tons (3,361,177 k).

Ceramic analysis consisted of gathering data on the following variables: ceramic type, form, rim numbers, and number of burned sherds. For each of these categories we recorded the count and weight of sherds by provenience unit. Ceramic types were drawn from existing typologies; new types were not found. In general, we identified ten ceramic forms: bowl, jar, seed jar or tecomate, plate, comal, miniatures, partial bowl, partial jar, handle, and unknown. Miniatures, partial bowls, partial jars, and handles were recovered in small numbers and the remaining six categories: bowl, jar, seed jar or tecomate, plate, comal, and unknown, dominated the assemblage. We made interior and exterior drawings of all rims from each form found among the several ceramic types identified during analysis. Main attributes of the different ceramic types received special attention: manufacture, paste (color, presence of charcoal, texture, resistance, hardness, and temper), characteristics of the exterior and interior surfaces, presence of slip, thickness, rim type, form, and geographical distribution (Gallaga 1997).

Pots Anybody?

Ceramic analysis distinguished 24 distinct ceramic types distributed among the six dominant forms. Unfortunately, due to small sherd size (roughly .5 cm² on average) we could not determine form for the majority of the sherds that we classified as unknown. The majority of these were body sherds, making it difficult to determine vessel form (Gallaga 1997).

We divided the 24 ceramic types into two main groups: 1) plainware ceramics (n = 1,042,846 sherds, representing 99.86 percent of the total sample and six ceramic types) and 2) decorated ceramics (n = 1,416 sherds, representing .14 percent of the total sample and 18 ceramic types) (Gallaga 1997).

Plainware Ceramics

We identified six plainware ceramic types: Trincheras Lisa 3 (plain 3), Trincheras Lisa 3A (plain 3A), Lisa Tardía (late plain), Roja Tardía (late red), Whetstone Lisa (plain), and Colorado Buffware. The type descriptions for Trincheras Lisa 3 and 3A follow below. McGuire and Villalpando (1993) present type descriptions for Lisa Tardía, Roja Tardía, and Whetstone Lisa. Waters (1982) provides type descriptions for Colorado Buffware. These ceramic types were distributed homogeneously throughout the site.

Analysis resulted in the following percentages and absolute totals per plainware ceramic type among the total 1,042,846 plainware sherds: Trincheras Lisa 3 (64.04 percent or 668,777 sherds), Trincheras Tardía (34.66 percent or 361,893 sherds), Trincheras Lisa 3A (.99 percent or 10,300 sherds), Roja Tardía (.05 percent or 508 sherds), Whetstone Lisa (.07 percent or 716 sherds), and possible Colorado Buffware (.0005 percent or 6 sherds).

McGuire and Villalpando (1993) failed to identify the type Trincheras Lisa 3 in their 1988 Altar Valley survey. In their report, they identified Trincheras Lisa 3 as Lisa Delgado. It was only with the research at Cerro de Trincheras that we were able to identify this type as a continuation and final type of the Trincheras Plainware Tradition.

Type Description- Trincheras Lisa 3

Archaeologists of the Altar Valley project tentatively identified three variants of the plainware type Trincheras Lisa: Lisa 1, Lisa 1A, and Lisa 2. They also encountered 454 sherds of a type that they provisionally labeled as Thin Plain or Lisa Delgada (McGuire and Villalpando 1993:31). The paste and color of these sherds looked like Trincheras Lisa sherds and they were manufactured using the coil and scrape technique. They differed from Lisa 1 and Lisa 2 because they were markedly thinner and harder than these two types. Lisa Delgada made up less than 3 percent of the Altar Valley assemblage and occurred primarily in association with the dominant late-prehispanic plainware type of Lisa Tardía. McGuire and Villalpando were unsure how to relate the sherds that they labeled Lisa Delgada to the other ceramic types in the valley. At Cerro de Trincheras, sherds of this type made up the majority of recovered ceramics. The assemblage includes 668,777 sherds of this type (64 percent of the assemblage by count and 63 percent of the assemblage by weight). We defined this type as Trincheras Lisa 3 and identified one subvariant, Trincheras Lisa 3A, in keeping with the identification of variants begun in the Altar Valley project.

Trincheras Lisa 3

Synonyms: Thin Plain (McGuire and Villalpando 1993:31), Trincheras Lisa (Jácome 1986:51), Proveedora Liso, 1.1.2 exterior alisado e interior escobillado (Braniff 1985:384).

Manufacture: Coil-and-scrape, scraping marks commonly occur on jar interiors, rarely on exteriors and bowls.

Paste: Coarse with 30 percent non-plastic inclusions. Color: Varies from grey to black (5YR 4/1-5YR 2.5/1) to shades of brown (5YR 4/6-5YR 3/1). Carbon Streak: Rarely present. Texture: Finer than other local plainwares (Lisa 1, Lisa 2, and Lisa Tardía) but markedly courser than Chiuahuan polychromes. Hardness: Ca. 3 moh. Fracture: Irregular. Temper: Fine sand with lots of quartz and occasional fine gold mica, size range from .25 mm to .8 mm, averaging .5 mm.

Surface Features: Exterior: Well polished, usually not eroded, temper rarely visible. Color: Light to dark brown and occasionally greyish (7.5YR 5/4, 5YR 5/3-5YR 2.5/1).

Interior: Vast majority of sherds exhibit scraping marks, scraping marks are distinct hard lines, occasionally finger impressions are present. Color: (5YR 6/4, 7.5 YR 6/2-7.5YR N3/0).

Slip: None

Thickness: .25 cm to .8 cm with an average of .6 cm.

Rims: Jars generally have curved necks with recurved rounded rims, but some examples exhibit straight necks with straight rims. Bowls have curved and straight sides with rounded rims. Plates are straight with composite rims and seed jars (tecomates) have rounded or pinched rims.

Forms: We could not identify form for the vast majority of sherds recovered (99 percent of Lisa 3, n = 663,119). Of the 1 percent of sherds (n = 5,655) we could identify to form, 76 percent (n = 4,289) were jars, 17 percent (n = 973) were bowls, 6 percent (n = 350) were seed jars, and less than 1 percent (n = 43) were plates. Jar rim diameters varied from 12 cm to 20 cm with an average of 17.1 cm. Bowl rim diameters varied from 12 cm to 18 cm with an average of 15.1 cm. Seed jar rim diameters were from 12 cm to 14 cm with an average of 12.5 cm. Plates varied in diameter from 14 cm to 24 cm with an average of 20 cm.

Comments: Trincheras Lisa 3 is the thinnest, most polished, and hardest of the Trincheras Lisa series. It is less reddish and browner than these earlier variants. Lisa Tardía is also brown, hard, and polished, but it is thicker than Trincheras Lisa 3. Lisa Tardía was made using the paddle and anvil technique, thus it exhibits anvil marks on the interior with no scraping marks. We did not encounter any Trincheras Lisa 3 sherds exhibiting red lines or decorations. McGuire and Villalpando (1993:28, 31) recovered 206 sherds of Thin Plain with red decorations on them in the Altar Valley.

Type Description- Trincheras Lisa 3A

Trincheras Lisa 3A sherds exhibit the same general characteristics of Trincheras Lisa 3 sherds including distinct scraping marks. They also bear anvil marks or finger impressions that suggest that they were produced using a combination of the paddle-and-anvil and coil-and-scrape techniques. Sherds of this type comprised approximately 1 percent (n = 10,300) of the site total. We were only able to identify slightly more than 1 percent (n = 132) of these to form. The vast majority of these (93 percent or n = 123) were jar sherds with a small proportion of bowls (.5 percent or n = 6) and a few seed jars (.25 percent, n = 3).

Decorated Ceramics

Only 1,416 sherds belong to the decorated ceramic category. Together, decorated ceramics represent .1357 percent of the total recovered sherds, corresponding to a weight of 5.769 kg, or .1716 percent of the total weight recovered at the site after two field seasons. The distribution of this material at the site was not homogeneous in terms of ceramic type and quantity, but almost all areas seem to have had access to this material (Gallaga 2004a).

For better distribution and analysis of the sample, the decorated material was divided into five subgroups each containing several ceramic types from a specific archaeological tradition. The five groups are: 1) locally produced decorated ceramics from the Trincheras tradition, 2) non-local polychromes from the Chihuahua tradition, 3) non-local polychromes from southern Arizona, 4) non-local decorated ceramics from the Rio Sonora Traditions, and 5) unknown polychrome ceramics.

Locally Produced Decorated Ceramics from the Trincheras Tradition

One hundred and fifty-seven sherds were identified, representing 11.09 percent of the decorated ceramics total, weighing 689 grams (or 11.8 percent of the total weight). The ceramic type distribution consisted of: Trincheras Purple-on-red (Trincheras P/R) (2.4 percent of decorated ceramics or n = 34), Trincheras Purple-on-brown (Trincheras P/B) (4.09 percent of decorated ceramics or n = 58), Nogales Polychrome (.21 percent of decorated ceramics or n = 3), and Trincheras Purple-on-red or brown (4.37 percent of decorated ceramics or n = 62).

Non-local Polychrome Ceramics from the Chihuahuan Tradition

This subgroup was the largest of the decorated ceramics with 824 identified sherds representing 58.19 percent of the decorated ceramics total and weighing 2,768 g (or 47.38 percent of the total weight of decorated ceramics). Although numerous Chihuahuan ceramic types appear in the assemblage, sherd counts and weights suggest that the Cerro de Trincheras people obtained relatively few pots from Chihuahua. The ceramic type distribution consisted of: Ramos Polychrome (36.86 percent of decorated ceramics or n = 522), Babicora Polychrome (9.95 percent of decorated ceramics or n = 141) Carretas Polychrome (9.25 percent of decorated ceramics or n = 131), Corralitos Polychrome (.07 percent of decorated ceramics or n = 1), Huerigos Polychrome (.21 percent of decorated ceramics or n = 3), Madera Black on-red (Madera B/R) (1.69 percent of decorated ceramics or n = 24), and Playas Red (.14 percent of decorated ceramics or n = 2).

Non-local Polychrome Ceramics from the U.S. Southwest

This group was the second best represented with 365 identified sherds of different types representing 25.78 percent of the decorated ceramics total and weighing 1,891 kg (or 32.36 percent of the total weight of decorated ceramics). The following types were identified: Babocomari Polychrome (2.33 percent of decorated ceramics or n = 33), Gila Polychrome (1.27 percent of decorated ceramics or n = 18), Santa Cruz Polychrome (21.32 percent of decorated ceramics or n = 302), and Tonto Polychrome (.84 percent of decorated ceramics or n = 12).

Non-local Decorated Ceramics from the Río Sonora Tradition

Initially, the incised and punctuated sherds were placed into the Chihuahua group. In terms of the ceramic physical characteristics, they share the same attributes as the materials that Braniff (1992) describes for the Río Sonora and Di Peso et al. (1974) identifies for Paquimé. These attributes consist of finish, forms, decoration patterns, and similarity in the marks made by incision or punctuation. Upon realizing that these sherds originated from the Río Sonora area and not from the Chihuahua region, as previously thought, they were moved to their own subgroup (Gallaga 2004b; Arthur MacWilliams, personal communication 2002; Pailes 1972). In total, 36 sherds of this type were identified, representing 2.54 percent of the decorated ceramics total and weighing 174 g (or 2.98 percent of the total weight of decorated ceramics). The following types were identified: Incised ware (1.83 percent of decorated ceramics or n = 26), and Punctuated ware (.70 percent of decorated ceramics or n = 10).

Unknown Polychrome Ceramics

This subgroup accommodated all unidentified specimens. It is comprised of 34 sherds representing 2.4 percent of the decorated ceramics total and weighing 320 g (or 5.48 percent of the total weight of decorated ceramics).

Vessel Forms

One objective of the ceramic analysis was the identification of Trinchereños form assemblages. Unfortunately, due to the small size of the sherds and because most of them were vessel body sherds, vessel form was only identified for 1.98 percent of the entire sample. That 1.98 percent, however, gives us some idea of what vessel forms the Trinchereños used. The distribution was as follows: bowls (1.44 percent of the assemblage or n = 15,058), jars (.47 percent of the assemblage or n = 4,904), seed jars or tecomates (.06 percent of the assemblage or n = 579), plates (.01 percent of the assemblage or n = 137), comales (.001 percent of the assemblage or n = 3), miniatures (.001 percent of the assemblage or n = 2), and unknown (98.02 percent of the assemblage or n = 1,023,578). Only one handle was recovered from the site. We identified this handle as belonging to the Lisa Tardía type and it represented .001 percent of the total ceramic sample.

It seems likely that the majority of the unidentified sherds were bowls and the remaining minority were jars. The identification of three comales sherds is important because it illustrates the consumption of corn in the shape of tortillas. The distribution of the forms throughout the site in the different excavated areas appears to be homogenous. However, more research and analysis regarding vessel size and form per area is needed for the possible identification of areas used for specific purposes such as storage, cooking, or festivities.

Discussion

In the past, researchers identified Trincheras plainware as variants of the brown paste ceramics from the Papaguería, such as Sells Plain, Sells Red, Vamori R/B, Topawa R/B, Tanque Verde R/B, Papago Plain, Red Papago, and Papago B/R (Ezell 1954:16; Hinton 1955:9). More recently, McGuire and Villalpando (1993:43) argued that for northwestern Sonora they can identify two large local ceramic traditions: the Trincheras and the Seri traditions. Potters from both of these traditions produced their vessels by hand using the coil and scrape technique as opposed to the paddle and anvil technique, which distinguished Papaguerian ceramics from southern Arizona. The Trincheras tradition consists of Trincheras Lisa (all variants), Trincheras P/R, Trincheras P/B, Altar Polychrome, and Nogales Polychrome. Tiburon Lisa, Historic Seri, and Modern Seri compose the Seri tradition. No Seri ceramic types were found at Cerro de Trincheras. Consequently, the ceramic material recovered at Cerro de Trincheras is related to the Trincheras ceramic tradition.

Comparing the characteristics of the plainware ceramics of Cerro de Trincheras with the ceramic material recovered from the nearby Altar Valley provides a glimpse into what type of local interactions may have taken place at the site. Generally, the sherds of the Altar Valley contain ground rock as temper, although they lack mica, and the paste is reddish in color. The plainware of Cerro de Trincheras is darker in paste and, on the whole, the Trinchereños used mica and sand as temper (Gallaga 1997; McGuire and Villalpando 1993, 1995; McGuire et al. 1999).

Another marked difference is the types recovered in each valley. In the Altar Valley project, researchers identified four variants of Trincheras Lisa: Trincheras Lisa 1, Lisa 1A, Lisa 2, Lisa 3. In addition, they found paddle and anvil produced brownware ceramics that they called Lisa Tardía (see McGuire and Villalpando 1993 for ceramic type description). They recovered very few Lisa 3 sherds in that project and large numbers of Tardía sherds. Lisa Tardía is most likely the local variant of Sells Plain and its presence in the Altar Valley indicates a shift in the ceramic production of the area from the Trincheras Tradition to a Papaguerian Hohokam Tradition. This may also reflect a movement of Papaguerian people from the north that displaced the Trincheras people to the south (Hinton 1955; McGuire and Villalpando 1993). Of the four Trincheras types, we found only Trincheras Lisa 3, Trincheras and Lisa 3A (a local variant between Lisa 3 and Tardía) at Cerro de Trincheras. The assemblage also included Lisa Tardía. Lisa 3 accounted for approximately two thirds of the sample and Lisa Tardía made up about one third of the sample. Proceeding on the assumption that Lisa Tardía was a local Altar Valley type and that Trincheras Lisa 3 originated from Cerro de Trincheras, the above would suggest a trade connection between these two valleys. Here too, further research is needed to confirm this hypothesis.

The analysis of the plainware ceramics illustrates that Cerro de Trincheras and its inhabitants belonged to a local Trincheras ceramic tradition and that their production was restricted in consumption. Although the Magdalena and Boquillas rivers, which are located near the site, offer good natural clay deposits, no major clay source has been located in the area that demonstrates cultural activity. However, we have been able to establish that the composition of the sherds exhibits mineralogical characteristics common to the area, such as the presence of quartz and mica.

In chronological terms, Trincheras P/R, Trincheras P/B, Lisa 1, and Lisa 2 date between A.D. 700 and 1300. Of these types, we only found the first two at the site and not in great quantities (2.40 percent, n = 34 and 4.09 percent, n = 58, respectively). The ceramic types Lisa 3, Lisa Tardía, and possibly Lisa 3A, date from A.D. 1300 to 1500, to which almost all of the plainware ceramics identified at the site belong (McGuire and Villalpando 1995). Of the proto-historic ceramic types identified for the Altar Valley—Oquitoa Liso, Papago Lisa, and Whetstone Lisa- only the latter type was discovered at Cerro de Trincheras and in small quantities (McGuire and Villalpando 1993:25-43). The earlier sherds may reflect limited use of the hill by populations living in the valley below during the period from A.D. 700 to 1300. The hill enjoyed its greatest occupation and use between A.D. 1300 and 1450. The site was abandoned by A.D. 1500, but apparently used occasionally during the Protohistoric period (Gallaga 1997; McGuire and Villalpando 1995; McGuire et al. 1999). This chronology is consistent with the rest of the archaeological evidence, including the radiocarbon dates.

In spite of the generally small size of the sherds, we were able to reconstruct two vessels (Figures 3.1 and 3.2). Both were large Trincheras Lisa 3 jars. One had a long neck, more than 10 cm high, and a capacity of 35 liters to 40 liters. The other is smaller, with a short neck and a capacity of 15 liters to 20 liters.

In addition to these two reconstructed vessels, we have eight Trincheras Lisa 3 jars that a local family in Trincheras found in 2007, while excavating a new septic system in their backyard. These were cremation vessels from a cremation cemetery (Figures 3.3-3.10). They also found a Chihuahuan (Villa Ahumada Polychrome) jar (Figure 3.9). It is not clear if these vessels came from one or multiple cremations.

In respect to the imported polychrome ceramics, it is important to take note of their low percentage (.14 percent) in relation to the entire sample. This evidence indicates that the Trincherenos had limited contact with areas

Figure 3.1. Partial Trincheras Lisa 3 Jar.

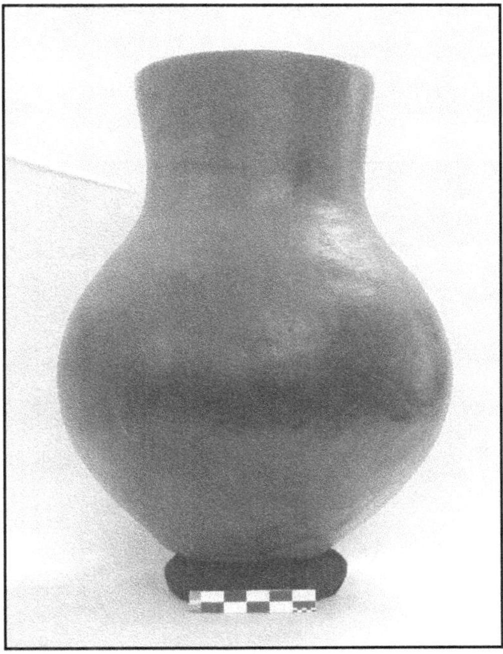

Figure 3.2. Reconstructed Trincheras Lisa 3 Jar.

beyond the Trincheras tradition, or at least not to the degree that past researchers have suggested. Numerous researchers (Brand 1935; Di Peso et al. 1974; Haury 1976; Robles 1973; Woodward 1936) depicted Cerro de Trincheras as a trade outpost or as a cultural branch of northern cultures, such as the Hohokam, Mogollon, and eastern Chihuahuan, or part of a Mesoamerican pochteca system. Based upon the ceramics, it seems probable that a pot of non-local origin arrived at the site only once a year on average. This represents a limited economy of regional prestige or of interregional exchange, instead of a well-established system of regional interaction over large distances. This is also confirmed by our shell analysis. Victoria Vargas found that the bulk of the worked shell material was likewise used to satisfy local consumption, more than macro-regional demand (Gallaga 1997, 2004a; McGuire et al. 1999; Vargas Chapter 6, this volume).

Figure 3.3. Trincheras Lisa 3 cremation jar.

Figure 3.5. Trincheras Lisa 3 cremation jar.

Figure 3.4. Trincheras Lisa 3 cremation jar.

Figure 3.6. Trincheras Lisa 3 cremation jar.

Further analysis indicates that the internal distribution of polychrome ceramics and shell demonstrates that apparently all sectors of the site had access to these materials. The result of the distribution analysis is interpreted to mean that the site did not have a sector of specialists or an elite class controlling the acquisition and distribution of such materials. Instead, the inhabitants of Cerro de Trincheras apparently enjoyed similar opportunities to acquire and distribute these materials (Gallaga 1997, 2004a; Vargas Chapter 6, this volume).

An interesting question emerges from the polychrome ceramic analysis. Geographically the site lies only 130 km from the Hohokam region of southern Arizona, 100 km from the Río Sonora area of eastern Sonora, and 300 km from Paquimé in Chihuahua, but the ceramic evidence indicates little or no contact with the Hohokam, slight contact with the Río Sonora and only modest interaction with Chihuahua. The lack of evidence of trade not only characterizes the ceramics recovered at Cerro de Trincheras, but also applies to cultural attributes such as adobe structures, ball games, figurines, copper, macaws, and pallets, among others. Ceramic findings and analysis confirm that macro-regional contact was indeed selected and limited. The textured and incised wares from the Río Sonora tradition are another illustrative example of this selective interaction with non-local cultural patterns. The sole presence of those types in the site indicates that the Trincheras community was acquainted with this type of decoration on vessels, but for some reason or another chose not to imitate or adopt the style. Moreover, this fashion apparently never enjoyed sufficient acceptance to acquire pottery with this style in great numbers.

Like the plainware ceramic chronological analysis, the identified polychrome types reveal a similar pattern further confirming the estimated life span of the site. The Trincheras P/R, Trincheras P/B types are dated between A.D. 700 and 1300. Textured and Incised wares were manufactured between A.D. 1000 and 1400, while the wares from the Chihuahua tradition are dated between A.D. 1218 and 1271 through A.D. 1390 to 1444. The U.S. Southwest wares fall between A.D. 1250/1300 and A.D. 1400/1450 (Dean and Ravesloot 1993; Gallaga 1997; McGuire and Villalpando 1993, 1995; McGuire et al. 1999). This pattern suggests that the site had some early intermittent occupation before A.D. 1300 and enjoyed its peak between A.D. 1300 and 1450, but before the prehispanic community of Cerro de Trincheras suffered its abandonment by A.D. 1450. The site was sporadically visited during Protohistoric period (Gallaga 1997; McGuire and Villalpando 1995; McGuire et al. 1999).

Petrographic Analysis

In addition to the usual, traditional ceramic analysis, the analysis of 102 petrographic samples was performed. Fifty-five samples from Cerro de Trincheras were compared with 47 ceramic samples from ten archaeological sites all, except one, in Chihuahua, located in the northeast portion of Sonora (Gallaga 1997). Those sites are La Morita (SON:G:3:4 [CR]), Derrumbadero II (SON:G:3:7 [CR]), Fronteras (SON H:2:1), Ojo de Agua (SON:H:2:2 [CR]), Cúcuta (SON:H:2:3 [CR]), San José Baviácora (SON:K:4:24 [CR]), El Jaicota (SON:L:3:8 [CR]), Peñasco del Pastor (SON:L:3:10 [CR]), La Presa (SON:L:3:11 [CR]), and Río San Pedro, Chihuahua.

From all the possible chemical analyses, I chose to undertake petrographic analysis because of its feasibility in México, it being relatively less expensive, and the presence of the laboratory of the regional institute of the Geological Institute of the Universidad Nacional Autonoma de México in Hermosillo. The laboratory provided the petrographic micro-

Figure 3.7. Trincheras Lisa 3 cremation jar.

Figure 3.8. Trincheras Lisa 3 cremation jar.

Figure 3.9. Villa Ahumada Polychrome cremation jar.

Figure 3.10. Trincheras Lisa 3 cremation jar.

scopes and the facilities necessary to make the thin sections. The analysis was performed in 1997.

Few petrographic analyses have been performed on ceramic material from northwest México that have been published. Previous to this analysis, only one was undertaken in Sonora, but with little profound archaeological analysis (Braniff 1992:3) and currently one is under way for the La Playa site by the Universidad de las Americas in Puebla from which a *licenciatura* thesis is expected soon. More work has been done in Chihuahua where some researchers have chemically analyzed Ramos Polychrome with X-ray fluorescence and performed some petrographic analysis of local wares (Woosley and Olinger 1993). Unfortunately, no other studies existed for the research area that could give me comparative samples.

Objectives

Due to the lack of comparative material, the petrographic analysis primarily was aimed at characterizing the pastes and tempers of various ceramic types found at Cerro de Trincheras. This analysis can thus hopefully serve as the basis for future work in the area and to start characterizing sand samples from the drainages in the area. In addition, the local samples were compared with non-local samples in order to determine their affinities and possible relationships, especially with those non-local polychrome ceramic types, such as Ramos and Carretas Polychrome (Gallaga 1997).

In general, when one does a compositional analysis of pastes, one considers the results obtained as a characterization of the sources and the preferences or behavior of the potter (Abbott 1994, 2000). Hence, the clay may come from one place while the temper materials may originate from another. The product of this mixture is clay ready for manufacturing pots. Normally, there are two types of temper materials present. The first occurs naturally in the clay generally in small proportions (less than 2 microns) due to formation processes or in the form of sand. Potters add the second type of temper to improve the elasticity of the clay. These temper materials can vary. They could be sand, rock fragments, organic and volcanic ash, organic material, crushed shell, sherd fragments, micas, or quartz.

According to ethnographic analogies (P. Rice 1987) a clay source can vary from place to place depending on the distance between them, ease of access, different characteristics of the natural tempers (types, origin, color, quality, plasticity, and texture), and most importantly, a potter's preference. Temper is an additional element that depends on the potter and may reflect one's experience with the clay. This is what may be recognized as a potter's tradition and is passed down over the generations (Zedeño 1994). To recognize a cultural tradition, tempers may be better suited to identify a potters' community (McGuire 1994; P. Rice 1987; Zedeño 1994).

Description of Samples

For this investigation, two ceramic traditions were selected for the petrographic analysis: the Chihuahua region and the Trincheras region. Each has distinct physical characteristics, but they are contemporaneous in time. Commonly, high quality kaolin clays with few temper additions characterize Chihuahuan polychrome ceramics. Trincheras ceramics contain low quality clay and moderate amounts of temper, principally sand and mica. In addition, for the purpose of comparison, petrographic analysis was performed on two ceramic types from the American Southwest: Whetstone Lisa and Santa Cruz Polychrome.

One hundred and two samples from both

plainware and polychrome ceramics were analyzed, coming not only from the site of Cerro de Trincheras, but also from ten other sites in Sonora. Of the 102 samples, 55 originated from Cerro de Trincheras (SON:F:10:2 [CR]). Having completed the 102 thin sections, the samples were analyzed using a system of counting points. I used a petrographic microscope Olympus BX50 with a special lens of 10 magnifications at intervals of 1 mm, an adaptable slide/platina for petrographic samples, and a point counter of eight variables of the brand Clay Adams. In this order, 13 distinct temper materials were identified: sand, quartz (monocrystal and polycrystal), plagioclase, microcline, myrmekite (potassium feldspar), muscovite, biotite (mica), pyroxenes, rock fragment, hornblend, heavy minerals, epidote, and unidentified.

Petrographic Results

Results will be divided between plainware and polychrome ceramic samples and by ceramic types within each category. It is important to mention that the analysis of the results of the petrographic samples is based solely on the composition of the ceramic pastes and not in relation to clay sources sampled from the Trincheras Valley, in the case of plainware, and clay sources from the geographical areas of the non-local polychrome ceramic tradition. The clay characterization of the Trincheras Valley is a work in progress and these results must be contrasted against further research.

Plainware Ceramic Types

Trincheras Lisa 3

The data indicate that the percentage of clay, 40-50 percent, is almost similar to that of quartz, 35 to 45 percent, while the other elements do not exceed 5 percent. This relationship (clay-quartz) indicates that the clay was not of good quality and that potters needed to add a high amount of sand as main temper to make it plastic. Other materials, such as micas (biotite and muscovite), were added as temper as well.

Trincheras Lisa 3A

The pattern of this type is similar to the previous one; it exhibits low quality clay and a high amount of sand (quartz) as main temper. Feldspars (pyroxenes) are also used, but as a second temper addition. It is possible that the combination of quartz and feldspars represents a different clay-sand source than the rest of the previously described samples.

Lisa Tardía

This type contains the same association between quartz and clay as the Trinheras Lisa types with slightly more mica (biotite and muscovite) and feldspars (pyroxenes and plagioclase). Again, the clay is of low quality and sand is the main temper, followed by mica and feldspars.

Roja Tardía

In this type, clay exhibits a higher presence, 45 to 58 percent, while quartz is at a lower percentage, 30 to 43 percent. The clay is of a somewhat higher quality than the previously described types. Nonetheless, the sample illustrates that the potter still added sand to work the clay. In addition, rock fragments and pyroxenes were added as temper materials. The clay source or the process of preparation for this type could differ from the above-mentioned ceramic types.

Whetstone Lisa

This type is similar to the previous type, the one difference being that pyroxenes and micas function as main temper materials. This type is not local, however, so its production and clay source must be outside the Trincheras Valley.

The analysis of the local plainware types serves to contrast information against the locally produced polychrome ceramics, in this case Trincheras Purple-on-brown and Purple-on-red.

Trincheras Purple-on-brown

Between 45 percent and almost 60 percent of the sample accounts for clay, while quartz remains at a lower lever with 25 to 35 percent. This ratio occurs more naturally and signifies that the clay is of better quality than those of the plainware ceramic types. With sand already present as non-elastic material, only rock fragments were added as temper or very little sand was added.

Trincheras Purple-on-red

Patterned similar to the preceding type, the data reveal a natural ratio of clay to sand (quartz). Therefore, we speak again of the clay being of better quality, in which only rock fragments and some mica (biotite and muscovite) were added as tempers.

From these preliminary results, some ideas can be developed. The clay worked into Trincheras Lisa pottery, with its three varieties, originates from a source with similar characteristics. It is clay of low quality or plasticity to which the potter needs to add sand as main temper, as well as mica and feldspars. It is also possible that the sand source used contained those materials already. These observations are not surprising since the Magdalena River renders these materials very accessible.

The remaining types, Roja Tardía, Whetstone Lisa, Trincheras P/B, and P/R, originated from a source of better quality, revealing mostly the addition of rock fragments and micas as tempers. This could mean a different clay source(s) and/or a different ceramic tradition. Taking into account the factor of time, Trincheras P/B and P/R appeared between A.D. 700 and 1300. Trincheras Lisa (3, and 3A), Lisa Tardía and Roja Tardía were associated with Cerro de Trincheras between A.D. 1300 and 1450. Whetstone Lisa dates between A.D. 1450 and 1600. On this basis, we can conclude that the polychrome Trincheras ceramics represent a ceramic tradition distinct from the plainware tradition, which is characterized by the quality of clay and the different types of tempers used. Similarly, Whetstone Lisa belongs to a ceramic tradition distinct from the locally produced ceramic types. Hence, it is highly possible that there is no direct or local relationship between the polychrome and the plainware Trincheras ceramics as was previously thought (Gallaga 1997; McGuire and Villalpando 1995; McGuire et al. 1999).

Polychrome Ceramics

Ramos Polychrome from Cerro de Trincheras

Clay occurs in 60 to 73 percent, while quartz remains at a low level between 15 and 33 percent. This is indicative of high quality clay with a significant low percentage of quartz occurring naturally. Only rock fragments are added as temper. It is important to point out that three of the samples (EG-32, 99, and 100) have very similar levels of quartz and rock fragments, suggesting that more rock fragments are added. Probably those vessels were made in different location. Data shows that the clays used in the manufacture of these vessels are consistent with those made in the Chihuahua region. The three previously mentioned samples show a different picture, suggesting that they were manufactured with different clay source but in the regional area.

Babicora Polychrome from Cerro de Trincheras

This type had high levels of clay between 58 and 68 percent, but was relatively inferior compared to the high kaolin contents of the Ramos

Polychrome. Quartz amounted to between 10 and 20 percent and the rock fragments accounted for 5 and 12 percent. This tight ratio indicates that ceramists were adding mostly the latter as temper materials. Worthy of mention is that they also included some heavy minerals as temper. This ceramic tradition is different from the previous type, but is highly possible that is been manufactured in the same regional area as Ramos Polychrome.

Carretas Polychrome from Cerro de Trincheras

The analysis illustrates that this ceramic type had a similar pattern as the previous type: high quality clay with naturally included quartz to which ceramists added rock fragments and heavy minerals as tempers. From the five samples, two (EG-38 and 41) did not conform to this pattern and had a higher level of quartz than rock fragments, probably indicating that the quartz was added, as well small quantities of rock fragments, as temper or that both were temper materials, showing a preference for sands. Either way, it seems that they used a different clay source or were manufactured in different location. Of the heavy minerals, a greater majority as hematite was identified. It seems likely that the color of the ceramics results from the presence of that mineral.

Santa Cruz Polychrome from Cerro de Trincheras

This type exhibits between 45 and 60 percent clay and between 23 and 35 percent quartz, indicating a high presence of quartz, probably added. Further, potters included a great number of tempers; the most notorious were the rock fragments, heavy minerals, feldspars, and mica. These results are similar to those Santa Cruz Polychrome samples analyzed petrographically from Snaketown, Arizona (Gladwin et al. 1938), which confirm its cultural affiliation.

The latter results from the Cerro de Trincheras samples were compared with those samples from similar polychrome ceramics types from other sites. In the particular case of the Santa Cruz Polychrome type, no sherds of this type were found in the rest of the ten-site sample that was used for this portion of the analysis.

Ramos Polychrome from Various Sites

The samples fail to form a clear pattern, but instead present different percentages. In general, 60 to 72 percent of the sample corresponds to clay, indicative of high-quality clay. The presence of quartz varies between 18 and 28 percent of the sample. In the samples with a higher percentage of quartz, this material was probably added. For those with a lower percentage, quartz was naturally there. In respect to the other materials, rock fragments vary the most in percentage ranging from 3 to 28 percent. Curiously, the samples with higher percentage of rock fragments correspond to samples with less quartz. The preceding indicates that the Ramos Polychrome vessels were not manufactured in the same location but in various places or using different clay sources. For example, the samples made from the site of La Morita SON:G:3:4 (CR) had the lowest amount of quartz, but the higher amount of rock fragments from the whole Ramos samples, while the samples from the site of San José Bavíacora SON:K:4:24 (CR) were completely the opposite, high amount of quartz and low amount of rock fragments.

Babicora Polychrome from various sites

Unfortunately, only ceramic material from three sites were represented or sampled. The material of the three sites (Ojo de Agua, Bavíacora, and Cerro de Trincheras) demonstrated similar compositions, with the exception of quartz being present, but in lower amounts, in the Cerro de Trincheras samples. Overall, the material consists of between 62 to 64 percent clay, 24 to 26 percent quartz, 8 percent rock fragments, 5 percent heavy minerals, and the rest distributed between micas and feldspars. These results indicate high-quality clay with normal amounts of quartz (sand). Of the quartz, one part could have occurred naturally and the other might have been added as tempers together with rock fragments and heavy minerals. The results show that the Babicora ceramic types had similar compositions and could have been manufactured if not in the same place, at least in the same cultural region. However, it is also possible that the ceramic material that arrived at Cerro de Trincheras originated in the Babicora area, though not from the same place as the previous two samples.

Carretas Polychrome from various sites

The majority of samples group together in a general pattern. Clay counts for 56 to 64 percent of the sample, quartz for 17 to 24 percent, rock fragments for 7 to 14 percent, heavy minerals for 5 to 7 percent, and the rest is distributed between micas and feldspars. From this, it is very possible that most of the sherds of this type were manufactured in the same area. Therefore, they reflect a homogenous ceramic tradition.

From the preceding results, I conclude that the samples of polychrome ceramics from the Paquimé region are similar to those described by Braniff (1992). In addition, it is highly possible that the sherds recovered in different Sonoran sites originated in that region and were not made locally. Although the sample used was limited to three sites and consisted of analyzing relatively few samples, the Babicora Polychrome ceramic tradition appears to have been manufactured in a very close area with similar clay composition or/and ceramic tradition. The analysis of Ramos Polychrome sherds, on the other hand, illustrates that there was not one, homogenous clay source from where the potters drew their clay. Because of minor variation, it seems likely that several sources were tapped. Clay composition analysis of possible sources used for the production of Ramos Polychrome ceramics in the Paquimé Valley is needed to verify this. The distinct percentages of clay components and presence of natural and added materials illustrate different cultural ways of preparing clay or different clay sources. In respect to Carretas Polychrome, the samples present a general pattern in the preparation of clay, suggesting that the pots are produced within the same clay source or in a very closely related area. To confirm these findings further, more research is needed in Sonora, as well as in Chihuahua.

Conclusions

The results of the ceramic analysis of all the ceramic material recovered during the Cerro de Trincheras excavation project has been presented here. More than one million sherds weighing more than three and a half tons represent the largest quantity of ceramic material recovered in any site in Sonora at the time of publication of this report. Between plainware and decorated sherds, considering both local and non-local types, 24 ceramic types were identified. From the ceramic and petrographic analyses we learned that the Trinchereños living at Cerro de Trincheras manufactured their own ceramics, if not directly at the site, at least in its proximity, or perhaps at the small sites around Cerro de Trincheras. No ceramic ovens or ceramic workshop areas were discovered and, consequently, none were studied at the site. Though ceramic ovens may yet be found, we speculate that instead vessels were cooked in open-air ovens due to the different tones of color that the pieces exhibit. Open-air ovens rarely leave evidence behind unless they were located at the same place over a long period of time, broken pieces of pottery are found nearby, and the area has been preserved through special circumstances.

Overall, the local production of plainware ceramics shares the same physical characteristics as the ceramics tradition of the rest of the Trincheras region. This ceramic production was focused on meeting the minimal needs for the Trincheras people, such as storage, preparation, and consumption of food. Perhaps because of such everyday uses, the people did not see the need to decorate them and develop a local decorated style. This pattern of behavior was also recognized in the lithic material. The most rudimentary alterations were made to meet only the minimal needs without further elaboration. The incised and punctuated wares are a good example of not being overly concerned with decoration. Archaeologically, those types were not found to occur in great abundance at the site. However, their presence shows that the Trinchereños knew of them, but chose not to produce similar types locally or regionally. Apparently, developing a local ceramic decoration did not occupy the Trinchereños mind.

On the other side, the decorated pottery found at the site was of non-local manufacture, but did not appear in great quantities either. The local decorated types, Trincheras P/B and Trincheras P/R, were no longer manufactured by the time of Cerro de Trincheras and Trinchereños did not seem eager to reproduce them. As a matter of fact, they did not reproduce any other ceramic decoration of any type.

The analysis of quantities and distances of the non-local ceramic material originating from the U.S. Southwest, the Río Sonora tradition, and the Paquimé area enabled us to conclude that in the specific case of Cerro de Trincheras the site's range of interaction might have been smaller than a 100 km radius. This distance would allow the inhabitants of the site to acquire some of these goods only once in a while, without having cultural macro-regional interactions with their manufactures. The ceramic analysis illustrated that probably no more than one non-local decorated vessel entered Cerro de Trincheras per year (Gallaga 1997).

In an area where little research has been undertaken, particularly focused on archaeological materials, these results are a major advancement in the understanding of prehispanic life in the area. Nonetheless, there is still a lack of investigation and further research is desperately needed to fill in the gaps and to clarify and expand on the ideas presented here.

Chapter 4
Lítica

César Villalobos. Centro INAH Sonora

Lithics

This chapter discusses the Cerro de Trincheras lithic assemblage recovered during the 1995 and 1996 field seasons. This flaked stone assemblage represented an expedient technology with few formal tools, very little evidence of use, and was dominated by debitage flakes. Tools recovered relate to cutting, scraping, pounding, and drilling. The Trinchereños made the vast majority of these artifacts from locally available basalts and rhyolites. Formalized tools included projectile points, bifaces, choppers, scrapers and drills. Investigations recovered only 32 projectile points: 21 small triangular points typical of ceramic periods in southern Arizona, 11 Archaic points including both Cienega Points and San Pedro Points, and a single biface that appears Clovis in age.

En el presente trabajo se encuentra la información del análisis y clasificación del material lítico tallado procedente de las dos temporadas de excavación del proyecto Cerro de Trincheras. Estos materiales arqueológicos son de suma importancia, ya que en ellos se encuentra reflejada parte de la vida cotidiana de la gente que habitó este sitio. Gran parte de las actividades que se desarrollaron dentro de comunidades sedentarias como ésta, requirieron necesariamente de herramientas para uso doméstico o trabajo especializado. En este sentido la piedra es la materia prima más accesible y que posee la gran diversidad de características físicas que le permiten ser la opción más versatil y adaptable para su utilización como herramienta. Es por ello que los antiguos habitantes del cerro aprovecharon las bondades de esta materia prima como uno de los recursos más abundantes, la qual les permitio una mayor y mejor apropiación del medio natural para su desarrollo y supervivencia.

Sistema de Clasificación

El material lítico tallado del Cerro de Trincheras se caracteriza por una falta de uniformidad estandarizada en la manufactura de las herramientas, así como el uso de una tecnología sencilla donde bastaban algunas extracciones por percusión directa para adecuar un canto rodado, o un subproducto de lasqueo para hacer de ellas una herramienta lo suficientemente funcional para llevar a cabo las actividades propias de la vida diaria. Por otro lado, la utilización de cantos rodados sin ninguna modificación para su uso, nos habla del pensamiento práctico de estos habitantes del cerro, ya que lo importante pareciera ser el resultado de la actividad y no lo sofisticado de las herramientas. En contraste con lo antes expuesto, tenemos herramientas formales con combinación de las técnicas de manufactura de percusión y presión, algunas con gran calidad de acabado. Fueron precisamente estas características las que nos llevaron a definir el sistema de clasificación tecno-funcional como el más adecuado para su aplicación en este material lítico, así como la definición de los atributos diagnósticos más pertinentes que nos permitieran observar objetivamente las cualidades de éstos artefactos como elementos culturales producto de la actividad humana.

Estos atributos permiten observar y registrar la información relacionada con la vida misma de cada artefacto, desde la obtención de la materia prima en que fué elaborado, su manufactura, uso o función y el abandono del mismo. Para el control y sistematización de esta información se utilizó una base de datos que permitió organizar el análisis en 4 bloques principales: Información general de excavación, Información morfológica general de los artefactos, Información tecnológica y de manufactura, e información funcional de las herramientas.

Información general de excavación. Este primer bloque está conformado como su nombre lo indica por la información procedente de campo, la cual permite ubicar los materiales tanto espacial como estratigráficamente, asi como su relación inmediata con construcciones o elementos relevantes. Estos datos básicos son: número de bolsa designado en campo, procedencia o área de excavación, ubicación espacial, nivel y construcciones.

Información morfológica general de los artefactos. Contiene además de los datos convencionales de cantidad, tamaño, espesor y peso de los artefactos, su clasificación por categoría, su estado de conservación, tipo de materia prima, y presencia de córtex.

Información tecnológica y de manufactura. En este tercer bloque se incluyen los rasgos tecnológicos y las características culturales que han modificado al artefacto, como lo son: grado de manufactura, cicatrices previas y modificación por retoque, dentro de éste último la ubicación y tipo del mismo.

Información funcional de las herramientas. Este último bloque está enfocado a la observación macroscópica de huellas de uso que pudieran indicarnos la función genérica que desarrollaron las herramientas. Así tenemos: función o funciones genéricas, ubicación de huella de uso, reciclaje y posible causa de abandono.

Con base a estos bloques de información se conformó el banco de datos para el análisis de los materiales líticos. A continuación describiremos cada uno de los rasgos analíticos utilizados y sus características.

Categorías

Estas han sido definidas con base en dos criterios, uno a partir del grado de manufactura alcanzado y su evidencia de uso, y otro, donde los mismos rasgos tecnológicos y funcionales, que son inherentes a su morfología le han dado arbitrariamente su nombre.

Lascas sin huella de uso aparente (DT)

Es todo aquel material lítico residual producto de la elaboración de otros artefactos líticos, o resultante de la actividad propia de producir lascas para uso o aprovechamiento posterior; sin embargo, en los dos casos se le denomina lascas sin huella de uso aparente por no presentar ninguna modificación o alteración por manufactura ni por uso.

Nódulos con huella de uso (NDHU)

Son todos aquellos nódulos que presentan huella de uso, pero que no tienen ninguna alteración o modificación de manufactura.

Nódulos retocados (NDR)

Representa grupo de artefactos bien diferenciado. Son aquellos nódulos -en su mayoría de gran tamaño- que han sido retocados únicamente en uno de sus extremos. Este retoque puede ser unifacial o bifacial, dejando el resto del nódulo sin alteración.

Fragmentos de nódulo (FND)

Aquí hemos reunido a aquellos artefactos que son el resultado de una sola aplicación de percusión directa, o sea, que por medio de un solo golpe se tuvo como resultado fragmentos mediales o casi mediales del nódulo. Dentro de este grupo encontramos algunos con huella de uso y otro que además presentan retoque.

Lascas con huella de uso (LSHU)

Son aquellas lascas producto de la elaboración de otros artefactos, o resultados de su producción, y que sin tener ninguna modificación de manufactura presentan huellas de haber sido utilizadas como herramientas.

Lascas retocadas (LSR)

Estas lascas son las que presentan modificaciones de manufactura posteriores a su extracción. Pueden o no tener huellas de uso.

Lascas de adelgazamiento (LSADZ)

En este grupo encontramos lascas planas muy pequeñas, producidas durante el proceso de reducción de un artefacto por medio de presión directa; en la mayoría de los casos se trata de subproducto de la manufactura de puntas de proyectil o bifaciales cuyo acabado se realiza por este medio.

Núcleos (NC)

Aquí hemos reunido a todos aquellos artefactos que resultan del proceso de extracción de lascas; pueden presentar algún tipo de retoque y huellas de uso.

Unifaciales (UNIF) y Bifaciales (BIF)

Dentro de este grupo se encuentran los artefactos que han sido reducidos mediante lasqueo. A esta acción de manufactura se le ha denominado adelgazamiento, y puede ser efectuada mediante percusión directa o presión. Como su nombre lo indica los unifaciales tienen el retoque en una sola de sus caras, ya sea dorsal o ventral, mientras que el bifacial posee el retoque en ambos lados. Pueden o no tener huellas de uso.

Puntas de Proyectil (PP)

Dentro de este grupo tenemos artefactos bien definidos, los cuales se encuentran manufacturados mediante retoque por presión, ya sea unifacial o bifacial. También puede presentarse con simple retoque marginal, pero conservando la morfología propia de esta categoría.

Perforadores (PF)

Son aquellos artefactos retocados o no, que morfológicamente respondan a esta función, y que presenten huella de uso de rotación total o parcial en el área de trabajo.

Grabadores (GB)

Dentro de este grupo se encuentran las herramientas que presentan en el área de trabajo el filo o ángulo necesario para efectuar incisiones, así como la huella de uso producida por esta actividad.

Artefactos reciclados (AR)

Son herramientas manufacturadas exprofo para un uso, y que posteriormente por algún motivo son desechadas y recicladas con otra función.

Conservación

Este apartado especifica el grado de conservación del artefacto a partir de su definición como categoría, y puede encontrarse completo o fragmentado. En el caso de las lascas, se considera: fragmento proximal, cuando puede apreciarse el punto de impacto y bulbo de percusión o una parte de este; fragmento distal, cuando puede apreciarse claramente el tipo de terminación de su extracción, y fragmento medial cuando no puede apreciarse ninguna de las dos características antes mencionadas.

Materia Prima

Aquí se incluye el tipo de roca en la cual se encuentra manufacturado el artefacto. Las materias primas que fueron identificadas son las siguientes: andesita, basalto fino, basalto medio, diorita, granodiorita, ígnea de textura fina, ígnea de textura gruesa, riolita, latita, cuarzo, sílex, y obsidiana. En el caso de las rocas igneas fue evidente que la categoría debería dividirse debido al tamaño del grano, pues de esta forma, se atendía una caracteristica que podria ser significativa en la interpretación de los resultados.

Córtex

La presencia de córtex fue considerada importante, en la medida en que podemos observar el grado de aprovechamiento de la materia prima dependiendo de su frecuencia y cantidad. En este análisis se manejaron cinco rangos: Ausencia de cortex, 1 por ciento al 33 por ciento de presencia de cortex, 34 por ciento al 66 por ciento de presencia de cortex, 67 por ciento al 99 por ciento de presencia de córtex, y 100 por ciento de presencia de córtex.

Tamaño

Para el tamaño de los artefactos al igual que en el caso del córtex, se unificaron criterios, manejándose lo siguientes rangos: menos de 3 cm, 3 cm a 6 cm, 6 cm a 9 cm, 9 cm a 12 cm, 12 cm a 15 cm, y más de 15 cm.

Peso y Espesor

En el primer caso, se utilizó como unidad de peso los gramos, y en el segundo el milímetro como unidad de medida del máximo espesor.

Grado de Manufactura

Aquí tratamos de definir a partir de sus características tecnológicas, el momento de su proceso de manufactura en el cual una herramienta fue abandonada. De esta manera tendremos: artefactos en proceso de manufactura, artefactos terminados, artefactos sin ninguna modificación posterior a su extracción, y por último, grado de manufactura indefinido en el caso de no poder determinarlo.

Cicatrices Previas

En este rasgo se anota el número de cicatrices que presenta cada artefacto previo a su definición como categoría. Modificación por retoque. Definimos como retoque, a toda aquella modificación por medio de lasqueo de percusión o presión, que se efectúa a un artefacto con la finalidad de adecuarlo para algún tipo de función. Manejamos tres clases de retoque: unifacial y bifacial.

Ubicación y Tipo de Retoque

Se ubica en el artefacto el área o las áreas retocadas, las cuales pueden ser lateral, bilateral, proximal, distal y total, especificando en cada caso si se trata de un retoque marginal o invasivo, y de la misma manera se observa si éste es continuo, discontinuo o denticulado.

Modificado por Huella de Uso

A partir de este momento se concluyen los atributos de manufactura y se inician los rasgos funcionales, el objetivo de éste bloque es identificar si los artefactos analizados presentan huellas de uso que permitan establecer que fueron utilizadas como herramientas. Dentro de este grupo manejamos dos posibilidades: las herramientas que fueron para un solo uso y que llamaremos unifuncionales, y las que fueron utilizadas para varias actividades y que denominaremos como multifuncionales.

Función Genérica

Dentro de este rasgo registramos las huellas macroscópicas que pueden ser observadas en los artefactos. Estas huellas se han determinado con base en patrones básicos que persisten en las herramientas al ser usadas. De esta manera se les ha designado una función genérica, que no es otra cosa que la acción misma que está efectuando la herramienta, actuando como sujeto activo sobre otro objeto o materia prima pasiva. Dentro de estas funciones genéricas tenemos la acción de raspar, cortar, machacar, perforar, afilar, desbastar, además de abrasión, percusión, incisión, desgaste, corte por percusión y corte por desgaste.

Ubicación de Huella de Uso

Para inferir la forma en que una herramienta fue utilizada, es necesario observar y registrar el lugar donde se encuentran ubicadas las huellas de uso, ya que igual que en el caso del retoque, puede presentarse en uno o varios sitios dependiendo de la vida útil del artefacto. De esta manera podemos ubicar en cada uno los siguientes puntos: lateral, bilateral, proximal, distal, marginal total, dorsal, ventral, irregular y generalizado irregular.

Reciclaje o Rejuvenecimiento

Llamamos reciclaje o rejuvenecimiento a la posibilidad que tienen los artefactos de alargar su vida útil, en el primer caso, la herramienta cambia de función o uso y en el segundo caso solo se le dá el mantenimiento adecuado para continuar la actividad que venía desarrollando.

Abandono

El abandono de una herramienta nos puede dar información acerca de la explotación, calidad de materia prima, habilidad en la manufactura y uso, entre otras cosas. Aquí se pretende conocer la probable razón de por qué fué desechado un artefacto, o en su defecto, el potencial de "vida útil" que pudiera tener al momento de su abandono. Dentro de las posibilidades encontramos: artefactos desechados por defecto de materia prima, es decir cuando la materia prima presenta problemas de calidad que imposibilita su manufactura o uso adecuado, esto es intrusiones o problemas de fractura. Otra posibilidad son los artefactos desechados en proceso de manufactura, sucede cuando al momento de estar elaborando un artefacto se provocan errores que impiden continuar la manufactura. Artefactos desechados por fractura, como su nombre lo indica sucede cuando una herramienta se rompe usualmente durante su uso. Artefactos desechados por agotamiento, es cuando puede observarse en un artefacto la intensiva utilización del mismo, lo cual imposibilita materialmente continuar con su función. Por último se considera la categoria de indefinido, cuando no puede precisarse el motivo del abandono.

Notas

Este último apartado contiene todas aquellas observaciones o singularidades que poseen los artefactos, y que no se encuentran tomadas en cuenta en los atributos seleccionados previamente.

Análisis de los Materiales

Materia Prima

Como resultado del análisis de los materiales fue posible observar que las materias primas más abundantes dentro de los artefactos líticos tallados son el basalto medio y el basalto fino, los cuales reúnen el 63.29 por ciento de la totalidad de los artefactos y un peso de 56.61 por ciento del volumen total. Le sigue en abundancia la diorita con 19.09 por ciento y en menor cantidad aunque significativa la andesita con 7.52 por ciento y la latita con 4.18 por ciento. En el caso del sílex también lo consideramos importante ya que si bien su presencia es de 3 por ciento, es en esta materia prima en la que encontramos herramientas formales. Con una presencia más reducida tenemos el resto de materias primas presentes, por orden de cantidad tenemos: ígneas de textura gruesa con 1.03 por ciento, cuarzo .78 por ciento, granodiorita .76 por ciento, riolita .62 por ciento, ígneas de textura fina .22 por ciento y obsidiana con .03 por ciento (Figura 4.1).

En cuanto a la relación de materia prima y categorias, tenemos que aparentemente no hay una preferencia bien diferenciada, dado que en las materias primas de mayor abundancia como los basaltos y diorita existen casi todas las categorias; en la andesita, latita y sílex, hay menos cantidad de material y variedad. Las siguientes materias primas, que son ígneas de textura fina y gruesa, cuarzo, granodiorita, riolita y obsidiana, decrecen tanto en frecuencias como en categorias.

Por otro lado, la gran cantidad que existe de lascas que no presentan huella de uso

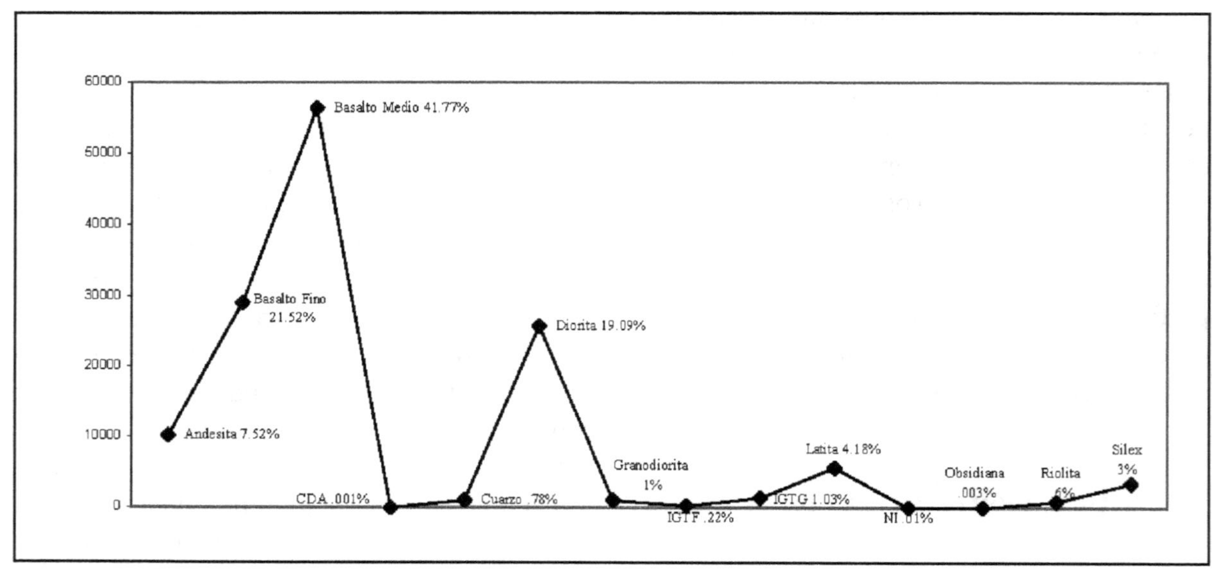

Figura 4.1. Presencia de materia prima en el total de la muestra analizada (muestra 135046).

aparente ni retoque, resulta un buen ejemplo del panorama general de aprovechamiento y explotación de la materia prima utilizada en el Cerro de Trincheras. Por sus características homogéneas y volumen total, este material se clasificó agrupándolo por materia prima, cantidad y peso. Asi tenemos que un gran volumen se encuentra en el basalto medio, el basalto fino y la diorita, y en menor cantidad tenemos la andesita, la latita y el sílex, le siguen la ígnea de textura gruesa, el cuarzo, la granodiorita y la riolita, ya en menor cantidad la ígnea de textura fina, y como escasa, la obsidiana.

Sin llegar a ser muy relevantes, se puede notar ciertas inclinaciones en cuanto a materias primas y algunas categorías. El grupo de las lascas, por ser el más abundante, presenta mayor incidencia de materias primas, y resulta lógico si vemos a este grupo como un subproducto de otras manufacturas o como resultado de la acción misma de producir lascas. Aquí se encuentran presentes casi la totalidad de las materias primas excepto ígnea de textura gruesa y obsidiana, las cuales son escasas en general. Por tanto las herramientas formales y las lascas en todas sus variantes, podemos encontrarlas en casi todas las materias primas y su frecuencia se encuentra relacionada con la proporción de material total. En cuanto a las lascas de adelgazamiento, su presencia es muy escasa, sólo tenemos 1 en andesita, 3 en sílex, y 2 en cuarzo, y el peso total de ellas no excede de 70 mg.

Las materias primas constantes siguen siendo el basalto fino, basalto medio, diorita, andesita y latita. Las pequeñas diferencias se encuentran en ciertas variantes, por ejemplo, con respecto al grupo de nódulos encontramos algunos en ígnea de textura fina y ocasionalmente en cuarzo y riolita. En los núcleos las materias primas ocasionales son granodiorita y riolita, y en cuanto a las herramientas formales, la mayor cantidad se encuentra en basalto fino y el resto se presenta dentro del mismo patrón, sólo que aquí es más significativa la presencia de herramientas formales en cuarzo, riolita, e ígnea de textura fina.

Dentro de los basaltos, que son la materia prima más abundante, podemos observar que consecuentemente tenemos el mayor número de categorías; sin embargo si bien el basalto medio es más abundante que el fino, es en este último donde se encuentra más variedad de herramientas.

Con respecto al sílex, aunque como ya se mencionó con anterioridad no es muy abundante, si es importante mencionar que es en esta materia prima donde se encuentra la tercera parte de la totalidad de puntas de proyectil, siendo las restantes de basalto fino, cuarzo, riolita, latita, ígnea de textura fina, andesita, y obsidiana.

La obsidiana como ya se mencionó, es escasa, y sólo tenemos 3 lascas sin huella de uso aparente y 1 punta de proyectil.

Uso y Función

Con respecto al uso y función, podemos observar que la mayoría de las herramientas corresponden a lo que podría denominarse como tecnología de uso inmediato; esto es, herramientas no formales que son el resultado del aprovechamiento del desecho de talla para su uso en las diferentes actividades de la vida diaria. Estas herramientas llamadas no formales, varían en tamaños y materia prima. Tenemos desde lascas con huellas de uso de dos a tres centímetros hasta nódulos de más de quince centímetros. En cuanto a su función pueden presentarse unifuncionales y multifuncionales, pero en ambos casos las huellas que presentan nos muestran una vida de uso muy corta (Figura 4.2 y 4.3).

En las herramientas se puede observar que el mayor índice de frecuencia se encuentra en las lascas con huella de uso. Tomando en cuenta su abundancia y la facilidad para su uso y desecho, es claro que las lascas cubrían parte de las necesidades básicas de uso sin grandes modificaciones, esto es más evidente si comparamos los totales de 421 lascas con huella de uso y 55 lascas retocadas.

Con respecto a los nódulos, es interesante observar la gran cantidad y variedad existente de materias primas, ya que tienen un papel importante por su uso como herramientas. Este caso sucede a la inversa de las lascas, ya que aquí es más numeroso el grupo de nódulos retocados que aquellos que fueron usados sin ningún tipo de modificación. Los núcleos van unidos al grupo de nódulos, debido a que la mayoría de ellos son la continuación de esta recolección de cantos rodados, modificados por una serie de extracciones, que les da su carácter de núcleos. En el uso y función de estos núcleos, es interesante observar la optimización del material, ya que la mayor parte de ellos presentan huellas de haber sido reutilizados como herramientas posteriormente a su función de productores de lascas.

Después de hablar de la adquisición, aprovechamiento y apropiación de la materia prima para su uso como industria y manufactura, a continuación presento algunas consideraciones sobre cada una de las categorías en nuestro material arqueológico.

Nódulos con Huella de Uso

La función que debieron haber tenido básicamente es la de percutores, ya que tanto unifuncionales como multifuncionales, presentan claras huellas de haber sido utilizados para golpear. Así pues, tenemos un 60 por ciento de nódulos con huella de uso unifuncionales, los cuales presentan exclusivamente huellas de

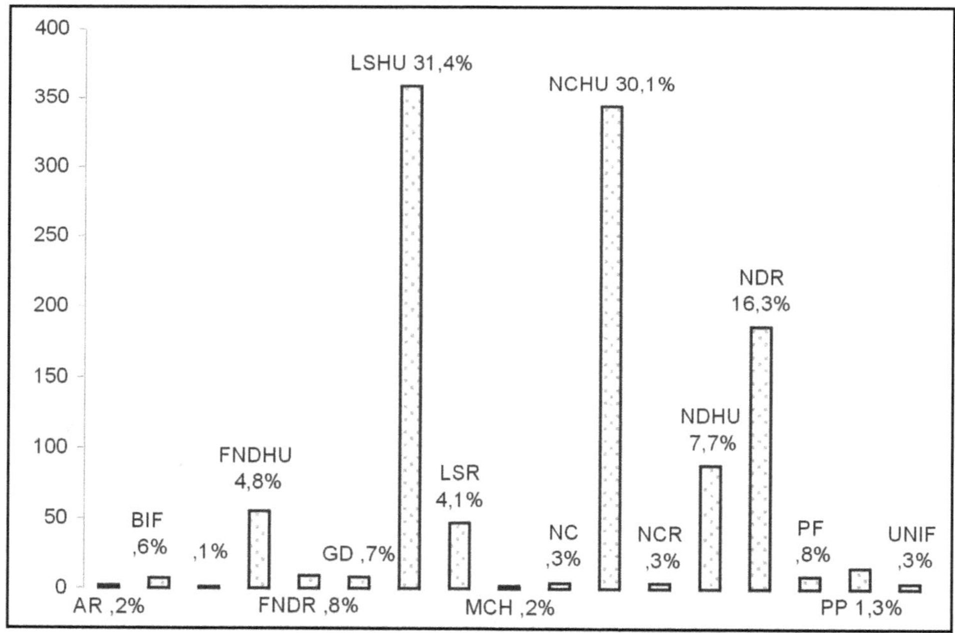

Figura 4.2. Tipo de herramientas (AR = artifactos reutilizados, BIF = bifaciales, FNCHU = fragmentos de núcleos con huella de uso, FNDHU = fragmentos de nódulos con huella de uso, FNDR = fragmentos de nódulos retocadas, GD = grabadores, LSHU = lascas con huellas de uso, LSR = lascas retocadas, MCH = machacador, NC = núcleos, NCHU = núcleos con huellas de uso, NCR = núcleos retocados, NDHU = nódulos con huellas de uso, NDR = nódulos retocados, PF = perforadores, PP = punto de proyectil, UNIF = unifaciales). Muestra 1144.

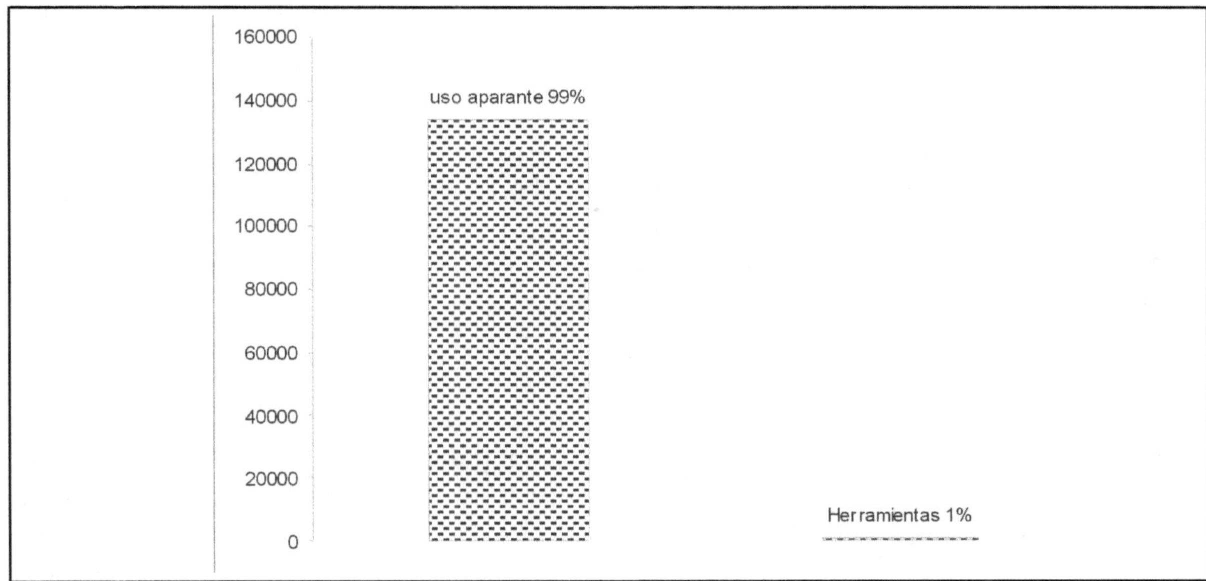

Figura 4.3. Herramientas y desecho de talla (muestra 135046).

percusión, y del 40 por ciento restante de nódulos multifuncionales, más de la mitad, además de percusión, presentan también evidencias de corte por desgaste, corte, abrasión, desgaste y raspado, aunque siempre en menor grado de frecuencia e intensidad.

Fragmentos de Nódulo

Como se describieron en su oportunidad, son aquellos fragmentos mediales o casi mediales de nódulo que fueron extraídos como resultado de la aplicación de un solo golpe de percusión directa. Estos fragmentos presentan huellas de uso que los caracterizan como herramientas. Cabe mencionar que al igual que en los nódulos con huella de uso, pasa algo similar en cuanto a función, ya que tenemos que en la mayoría presentan evidencia de uso como percutores. Sin embargo en los artefactos unifuncionales podemos observar otro tipo de huellas que no son únicamente las producidas por la acción de golpear. Tenemos dentro de las herramientas unifuncionales un 59 por ciento con huella de percusión, un 23 por ciento de raspado, 12 por ciento de corte, 6 por ciento de corte por desgaste y un 4 por ciento de desgaste. En las multifuncionales tenemos la presencia de diferentes tipos de huellas de uso, éstas son en orden de frecuencia: percusión, raspado, corte, desgaste y desbaste.

Nódulos Retocados

Podemos observar que presentan trabajo de retoque en la mayoría de los casos contínuo. Se obtiene por percusión directa formando un área de trabajo de menos de 90 grados, pudiendo ser unifacial o bifacial, y dejando el resto del nódulo sin alteración. Son de gran tamaño y esta misma característica es parte de su personalidad como herramientas, ya que el peso combinado con el “filo” del área de trabajo, provee de un buen utensilio de corte por percusión. Como en la mayoría de las herramientas tiene también caracter multifuncional, ya que presentan huellas de percusión en la parte no retocada, y en algunos otros casos, huellas de corte por desgaste y raspado; cabe mencionar que también tenemos algunos nódulos retocados sin huellas de uso aparente.

Fragmentos de Nódulo Retocados

Aunque son menos en comparación con las tres categorias anteriores, nos muestran de nuevo la tendencia que existe de utilizarlos como percutores; sin embargo, el retoque que presentan es la adecuación de un área de trabajo que permite mediante un retoque contínuo la obtención del filo necesario para realizar actividades de corte y raspado.

Lascas con Huella de Uso

Tenemos una gran parte de lascas utilizadas como herramientas y es por ello que se encuentran en toda clase de materias primas, diferentes tamaños y para usos muy variados. Son artefactos en su mayoría poco usados, y aunque puede presentarse en ellos funciones múltiples, el tiempo de vida útil como en la mayoría de los materiales líticos identificados en el Cerro de Trincheras, es aparentemente corto. Dentro de esta colección de lascas con huellas de uso encontramos que un 82 por ciento son unifuncionales y resalta entre ellas una gran incidencia de raspado. Le siguen en menor cantidad corte, desbaste y percusión, y de manera escasa perforación y desgaste. El 17 por ciento restante son herramientas multifuncionales, en las que a pesar de ser menor su cantidad, aparece en ellas una gran variedad de usos. Podríamos decir que exceptuando machacar, perforar y corte por percusión indirecta, en estas lascas aparece toda la gama de usos que se pudieron detectar y en una infinidad de combinaciones, ya que no siguen un patrón establecido.

Lascas Retocadas

Podemos mencionar que son escasas, con retoque en la mayoría de los casos poco elaborado. Generalmente se prepara unifacialmente algún extremo de la misma para adaptarla a alguna función o simplemente para aprovechar o reavivar algún filo. Un 40 por ciento no presenta huella de uso aparente, y del 60 por ciento restante la mayoría tiene huellas de raspado y en menor cantidad corte y percusión; también las hay multifuncionales sin patrón establecido, con combinaciones de corte por desgaste, desbaste, percusión, raspado, corte y perforación.

Núcleos

Como ya se mencionó anteriormente, no presentan regularidad en sus extracciones y son multidireccionales. Por tanto, no existe un patrón preestablecido morfológicamente, y aparentemente se están llevando a cabo las extracciones dependiendo de la decisión y habilidad de la mano del artesano y de las necesidades inmediatas de uso que pudieran presentar, ya que el objetivo principal de los núcleos no es solamente la utilización de su subproducto como herramientas, sino del aprovechamiento de todo el proceso. Esto es fácil de observar ya que la mayoria de los núcleos presentan huellas de uso por haber sido utilizados también como herramientas. Es posible que hayan aprovechado su tamaño y aristas cortantes para diferentes actividades como: corte, corte por desgaste, corte por percusión, raspado y naturalmente percusión. Es importante mencionar que el aprovechamiento como herramientas de los núcleos es significativo, ya que sólo tenemos tres casos de núcleos sin huella de uso, de los cuales dos presentan retoque y sólo uno carece de cualquier tipo de modificación. Retomando los núcleos con retoque, cabe mencionar que es mínima su presencia; podemos señalar que dicho retoque es unifacial invasivo y coincide con el área donde presenta huella de uso, por lo que podemos darnos cuenta que el mismo tenía la clara intensión de reavivar un filo para efectuar más eficientemente la función de corte por percusión, huella que puede observarse en el área de trabajo.

Herramientas Formales

En contraste con estas herramientas de aparente poca complejidad, contamos también con la presencia de herramientas que podríamos catalogar como formales o especializadas: grabadores y perforadores, unifaciales, bifaciales y puntas de proyectil. Es evidente que si comparamos la proporción numérica de éstas con el resto de los materiales tendremos un porcentaje muy bajo, sin embargo estos artefactos presentan una característica que los define entre los demás, y es el trabajo mucho más elaborado por medio de retoque de presión con un mejor control técnico de su manufactura. Es interesante poder observar el tratamiento tan diferente realizado en la manufactura de las herramientas domésticas o de uso cotidiano.

Grabadores

Son aquellos que presentan un área de trabajo ya sea preparada o simplemente aprovechada con un ángulo necesario para efectuar incisiones. En cuanto a la materia prima no existe aparentemente preferencia ya que aparecen en todas las materias identificadas. Los grabadores que tenemos en Cerro de Trincheras se presentan con y sin retoque. Los que no tienen retoque son lascas sin ningún tipo de preparación, en las cuales se aprovechó el filo presentando en esta área de trabajo huellas de uso de incisión. Otas herramientas están modificadas por retoque unifacial tanto unilateral como bilateral, casi todos presentan retoques marginales aunque también los hay invasivos. En la mayoría de estas herramientas el retoque es contínuo aunque también hay casos que presentan denticulado.

Perforadores

Se presentan en varias materias primas que incluyen desde basalto fino y medio, cuarzo, diorita, ígnea de textura fina y sílex. Tenemos dos clases de perforadores, los primeros no presentan retoque o modificación, se trata nuevamente del aprovechamiento de la morfología de algunos fragmentos de materia prima para ejecutar la función de perforar. En el segundo caso tenemos los retocados presentando modificaciones desde muy sencillas hasta muy sofisticadas. En la muestra analizada tenemos dos artefactos (uno de cuarzo y otro de sílex) con retoque unifacial; ambos bilaterales, uno marginal, otro invasivo. Un tercer caso es el de un perforador de diorita con retoque bifacial total invasivo. Este útimo parece ser que se fracturó durante el proceso de manufactura, el resto están terminados. En cuanto a su tamaño tenemos que varían entre los 3 y 6 cm. Dentro de los sofisticados tenemos a los que hemos denominado perforadores tipo Hohokam, y que presentan un trabajo fino y delicado a base de retoque bifacial invasivo cubriente, que les dan una apariencia muy elaborada; tenemos tres de ellos manufacturados en basalto fino, sílex y obsidiana. Con respecto a su función todo parece indicar que estas herramientas fueron especializadas y unifuncionales ya que aparentemente sólo se pueden observar las huellas de uso de rotación en el área de trabajo. En cuanto a su desecho, la mayoría de los casos presentan fractura en la parte distal, lo cual pudo ocurrir durante su uso.

Unifaciales

Estas herramientas se presentaron en andesita, basalto medio, diorita y latita. Su tamaño varía entre los 6 y 9 centímetros, todos presentan restos de córtex; uno de ellos (basalto medio) contiene más cantidad de córtex (un 60 por ciento aproximadamente), el resto es menor y oscilan ente un 20 y 30 por ciento. En cuanto al retoque de presión, dos no cuentan con este tipo de retoque, y su manufactura se interrumpe en el proceso de adelgazamiento por percusión.

Las dos restantes presentan retoque unifacial bilateral invasivo, siendo éste contínuo y discontínuo respectivamente. En tres de ellos se pudo obsevar claramente huellas de uso, y la función genérica que se determinó fue la de raspado, corte y en un solo caso, percusión.

Bifaciales

Aparentemente el tamaño de ellos varía entre los seis y nueve centímetros, mientras quela materia prima en la que fueron manufacturados es basalto fino, diorita, sílex y andesita. La mayoria de ellos no cuenta con córtex el cual fue desprendido en su proceso de adelgazamiento por percusión, sin embargo algunos tadavía cuentan con córtex, debido a que fueron desechados dentro del proceso de manufactura. En este caso se encuentran tres de ellos; en cuatro más es muy evidente que llegaron al final de su proceso de manufactura ya que además del adelgazamiento de percusión presentan retoque bifacial de presión bilateral invasivo o total invasivo. En cuanto a la función la mayoría no presentó huellas de uso aparente, excepto uno en el cual se puede observar huellas de raspado bilateral y distal. Dentro de este grupo destaca la presencia de dos bifaciales. El primero es un bifacial ovoide en basalto fino, probablemente de período de agricultores tempranos. El segundo es un bifacial con lasqueo cubriente muy fino posiblemente un cuchillo Clovis que presenta forma de laurel con base lateral pulida y aparentemente fue expuesto al calor antes de ser lasqueado.

Puntas de Proyectil

En cuanto a las puntas de proyectil, contamos con 43 artefactos. Dentro de este grupo, algunas se han considerado no diagnósticas debido a que se encuentran fragmentadas. Tenemos otras que han sido posible ubicarlas tipológicamente como las puntas de proyectil tipo San Pedro elaboradas en basalto fino, riolita y andesita; puntas de proyectil tipo Ciénega (y su variante aserrado) en basalto fino y sílex; puntas de proyectil triangulares de muescas laterales, ubicadas en el período cerámico contemporáneas al momento Hohokam, manufacturadas en sílex y latita; y por ultimo, puntas de proyectil de período cerámico, las cuales se caracterizan por su pequeño tamaño y poca elaboración. La materia prima en que se encuentran elaboradas es muy variada y comprende basalto fino, andesita, riolita, sílex, latita, cuarzo etc.

Artefactos Reutilizados

Dentro de la categoria de artefactos reutilizados, se encuetran dos herramientas fragmentadas. La primera es un percutor sobre un fragmento de hacha pulida en basalto medio, con un peso de 605 g y un tamaño de 9 cm, unifuncional con huella de uso de percusión generalizada e irregular sobre toda la herramienta. La segunda es también un percutor, pero esta vez sobre un fragmento de mano de metate en basalto fino, tiene un peso de 260 g y un tamaño de 9 cm, también es unifuncional y presenta huellas de uso de pecusión en sus áreas distal y proximal.

Áreas de Excavación

Después de la descripción detallada de los materiales líticos desde un punto de vista particular, pasaremos a ver el panorama general de estos materiales arqueológicos dentro del contexto de cada una de las áreas de excavación. Iniciando con materias primas, podemos observar la presencia -en frecuencia y volumen- de las diferentes materias primas dentro de cada área (Tabla 4.1).

Se puede observar que en cada una de las áreas se presentan todas las materias primas y se mantiene aproximadamente la misma

Tabla 4.1. Presencia de Materias Primas por Areas de Excavación

	Basalto fino	Basalto medio	Diorita	Andesita	Latita	Silex	Ignea de textura gruesa	Cuarzo	Grano-diorita	Riolita	Ignea de textura fina	Obsidiana	Materia prima no identificada
A1	2 444	4 580	2 116	344	421	501	28	105	24	45	15	1	
B						1		1					
B1	3 217	8 081	3 386	2 050	476	416	124	128	125	108	19		2
B2	2 190	5 207	2 673	3 195	371	300	20	108	51	115	22	1	
B3	1 587	1 009	1 070	16	302	108	149	18	18	84	39		
B4	2 080	1 908	1 479	829	339	155	124	21	26	52	46	1	1
B5	1 446	1 901	1 331	220	240	259	209	107	60	61	30		
B6	6 341	13 480	6 024	421	639	546	384	250	101	157	35	1	1
B7	2 172	5 885	1 832	123	207	203	52	71	23	52	9		
B8	1 148	3 386	1 141	66	134	144	7	12	2	7			
B9	547	1 544	492	24	71	37	1	4	1	2			
B10	255	661	312	11	27	26	1	3	4		1		
B11	1 519	3 842	1 699	49	218	408	72	112	7	27	6		
D	1 555	1 281	680	512	383	170	115	62	52	43	27		1
E	2 566	3 662	1 546	2 301	1 812	104	100	59	532	81	46		3

proporción de frecuencia de los materiales, dependiendo de la extensión del área de excavación. Tenemos la mayor concentración de materiales en los basaltos, diorita, andesita, latita y sílex, bajando su proporción en ígnea de textura gruesa, cuarzo, granodiorita, riolita e ígnea de textura fina y quedando en último lugar la obsidiana. Las ausencias se pueden mencionar de la siguiente manera, no tenemos riolita en el área B10, la ígnea de textura fina no aparece en B8 y B9. En cambio la obsidiana sólo la encontramos con un artefacto cada una en A1, B2, B4 y B6 (Tabla 4.2).

El área de excavación donde se encontró la concentración más alta de lascas sin huella de uso aparente es el área B6; le sigue como segundo bloque B1, B2, E, A1 y B7 con más de 10,000 artefactos; y por útimo con menos de 10,000 tenemos las áreas B11, B4, B8, B5, D, B3, B9 y B10.

En cuanto a herramientas también es el área B6 la que presenta mayor densidad. Esto es importante ya que esta área tiene características especiales por ser un área habitacional con elementos importantes y una estratigrafía compleja. Tenemos un segundo bloque con más de 100 herramientas, en B1, B2, B7 y E; el tercer bloque de 50 a 100 herramientas en B4, B3, A1, B5 y D; y el resto de las áreas va decreciendo en menos de 50, como en B8, B11 y B9. Por último tenemos a B10 con menos de 10 herramientas (Figura 4.4).

El grupo de lascas se encuentra presente en todas las áreas de excavación, la cantidad más significativa es de 101 lascas con huella de uso y 6 retocadas en el área B6, el resto se mantiene más o menos homogénea, excepto B8 y B9 en donde la presencia de lascas se reduce a 2 con huella de uso en cada área, y B10 en la cual no contamos con ningún tipo de lascas modificadas. El grupo de los nódulos también se encuentra distribuida a todo lo largo de las áreas, siendo el B10 donde se tiene la menor frecuencia. El grupo de núcleos se presenta también interesante, siendo los núcleos con huella de uso los más abundantes, aunque en B9 y B10 vuelve a bajar el número; en cuanto a los núcleos retocados sólo tenemos uno en el área B1, tres en B2 y uno más en B3, ya que en general la presencia de ellos es escasa. Con respecto a las herramientas formales, las puntas de proyectil son la categoria constante en todas las áreas de excavación aún con diferencias de densidad: B8 y B1 tienen seis puntas cada una y A1, B2 y B7 le siguen con cinco, el resto varía entre tres y una por área. Solo tenemos tres perforadores en el área D, dos en B3, y un solo en B1,B2, B6 y B7. Los grabadores aparencen cuatro en B3, dos en B6 y uno en A1, B1,B7 y E. Tampoco los unifaciales y bifaciales son muy abundantes. En unifaciales tenemos dos en B1, uno en D, y uno mas en E; los bifaciales son tres en E, dos en B6 y B2, y uno en B3 y B4. Por último en cuanto a artefactos reutilizados solo tenemos dos, uno en B1 y otro en B2 (Tabla 4.3).

Pasando a la función que debieron desempeñar las herramientas, las huellas de uso que se pudieron detectar fueron: raspar, cortar, percutir, perforar, incisión, afilar, desbastar, corte por percusión, corte por desgaste, y corte por percusión indirecta. La presencia de una o varias huellas de uso en las herramientas es lo que la define como unifuncional o multifuncional. En las descripciones se podrán encontrar en el caso de las herramientas multifuncionales, las funciones de varias huellas de uso; el orden en el cual se encuentran corresponden a la importancia en cantidad y calidad de las mismas en la herramienta.

Nos encontramos que sin duda las herramientas unifuncionales son las más abundantes con 984 artefactos; las multifuncionales son 234, lo cual es una cantidad considerablemente más baja que las unifuncionales. También queremos mencionar 118 herramientas que presentan modificaciones por retoque, unas veces sólo por percusión, otras veces de presión, y que sin

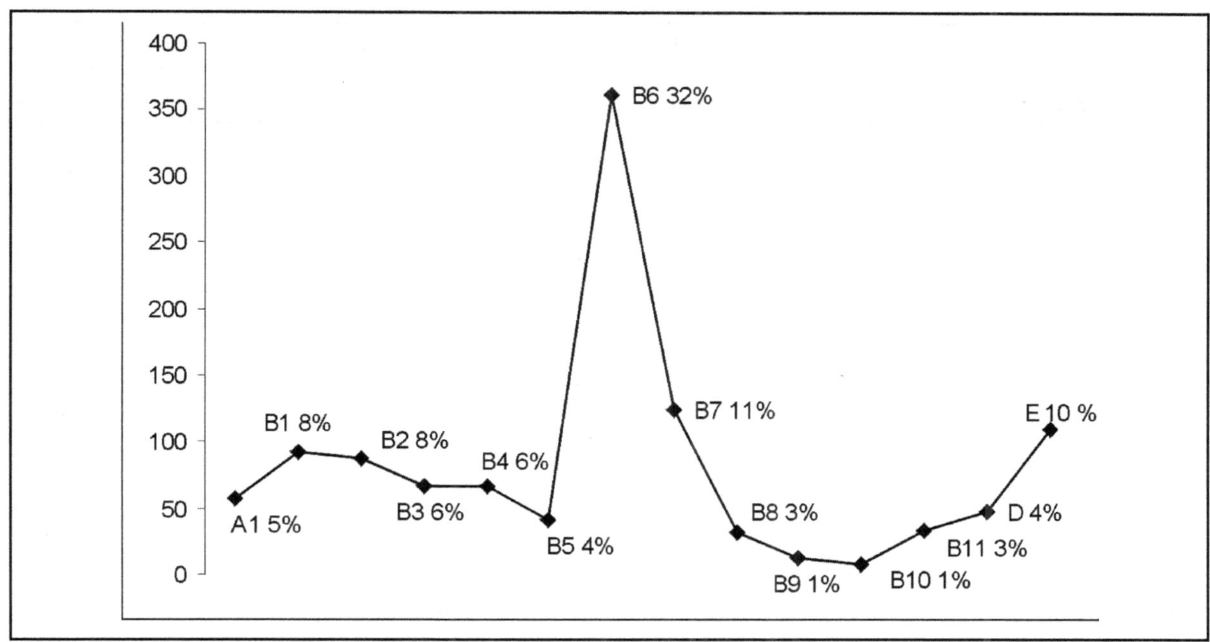

Figura 4.4. Herramientas por areas de excavación (muestra 1144).

embargo no presentan huellas de uso aparente, con lo cual no queremos decir que no hayan sido usadas. Es posible que el uso haya sido muy poco o que la acción de trabajo no haya dejado una huella clara que se pueda percibir a simple vista o con ayuda de una lupa.

Como se puede observar, las herramientas unifuncionales son más abundantes, y el área B6 cuenta con 328 y el B7 con 107, siendo las que reúnen la mayor cantidad de ellas, le siguen con más de cincuenta herramientas B2, E, B1, B3, B4, B5 y A1, y con menos de treinta tenemos las áreas D, B11, B8, B9, y B10.

En las multifuncionales baja en general toda la frecuencia, la B10 no presenta ninguna herramienta multifuncional y la B9 sólo cuenta con una. En las áreas A1, B3, B5, B8, B11 y D se tienen menos de diez herramientas, mientras que el resto oscilan entre 18 y 33. Sin embargo el área B6 de nuevo tiene la mayor concentración de artefactos, en este caso 70 herramientas multifuncionales.

En las herramientas que no presentan huella de uso aparente tenemos B2 con 17 artefactos, B1 con 16, B6 con 15, y E con 13. Le siguen D y B8 con 10 cada uno, y el resto tienen menos de 7 artefactos sin huella de uso aparente (Figura 4.5, Tabla 4.4 y 4.5).

Tenemos que la huella de uso más abundante es la de percusión con 497 artefactos Le sigue el raspado con 294 y el corte con 117; el resto no son tan numerosos ya que tenemos 22 de corte por desgaste, 15 de desbaste, 10 de incisión, 8 de perforado y 6 de corte por percusión. Con menor frecuencia tenemos 5 de desgaste, 4 de abrasión y 2 de corte por percusión indirecto.

La percusión como huella de uso más frecuente en las herramientas unifuncionales es también una de las más abundantes en las áreas de excavación. Así tenemos que el área B6 es en la que se presenta la mayor frecuencia con 220, de ahí baja considerablemente a 37 en B7, 33 en B5 y 30 en E. Después va decreciendo poco a poco entre los 14 y 26 herramientas en las áreas A1, B1, B2, B3, B4, B8, B11, D, y E siendo los mas escasos B9 y B10.

En el caso de la huella de uso de raspado, en B6 es también el más frecuente con 71, le sigue B7 con 48 y B2 con 36, el resto mantiene

Tabla 4.2. Frecuencia de Materiales: Herramientas y Lascas sin Huella de Uso Aparente

Áreas de excavación	Herramientas	Lascas sin huella de uso aparente
A1	66	10 558
B	2	
B1	115	18 017
B2	134	14 117
B3	71	4 329
B4	82	6 979
B5	65	5 799
B6	416	27 964
B7	132	10 477
B8	38	6 009
B9	14	2 709
B10	9	1 292
B11	36	7 923
D	52	4 829
E	110	12 702
Total	1342	133703

Tabla 4.3. Frecuencia de Función en Herramientas

Herramientas	Cantidad
Multifuncionales	234
Unifuncionales	984
Sin huella de uso aparente	118

Tabla 4.4. Frecuencia de Huellas de Uso en Herramientas Unifuncionales

Función	Herramientas unifaciales
Percusión	497
Raspado	294
Corte	117
Abrasión	4
Desbaste	15
Incisión	10
Desgaste	5
Perforado	8
Corte por desgaste	22
Corte por percusión	6
Corte por percusión indirecto	2

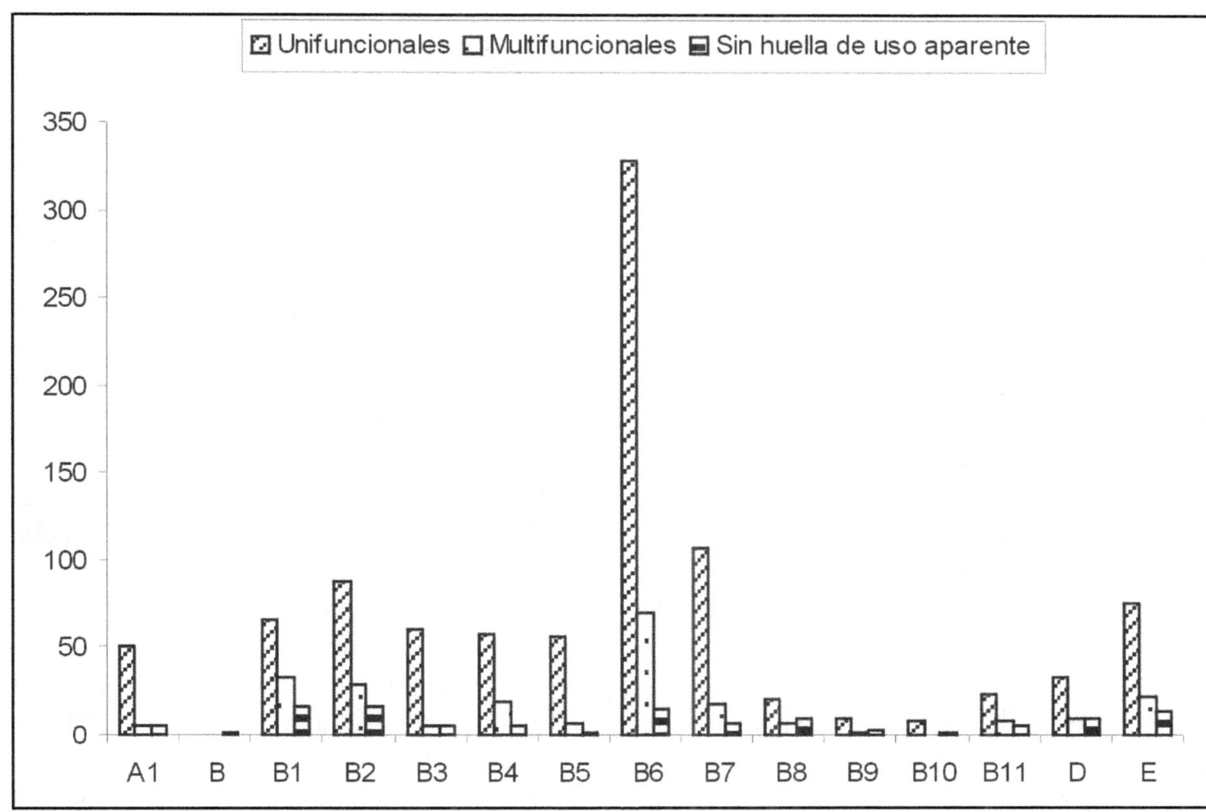

Figura 4.5. Frecuencia de herramientas unifuncionales, multifuncionales y sin huella de uso aparente.

Tabla 4.5. Frecuencias de Uso en Herramientas Unifuncionales por Areas de Excavación

Función	A1	B1	B 2	B3	B4	B5	B6	B7	B8	B9	B10	B11	D	E
Percusión	24	23	25	16	26	33	220	37	18	7	7	17	14	30
Raspado	19	21	36	22	24	15	71	48	1	1		5	7	24
Corte	3	16	20	3	4	3	21	13		2	1	1	7	13
Abrasión			1				2		1					
Desbaste	1					3	5	6						
Incisión	1	1		4			2	1						1
Desgaste		2						1	1					1
Perforado			1	2		1	1						3	
Corte por desgaste	3	2	3	1	3	1	6						1	3
Corte por percusión			2	1									1	2
Corte por percusión indirecto	1							1						

una constante entre los 5 y 24, sólo B8 y B9 presentan una herramienta y B10 no cuenta con ninguna.

El corte es menos frecuente que las dos huellas de uso anteriores. En este caso B6 con 21 artefactos y B2 con 20 son las frecuencias más altas; le siguen B1 con 16, y B7 y E con 13 cada uno, el resto oscilan entre 1 y 4 herramientas, excepto B8 en la cual no hay evidencia de corte. La distribución del resto de las huella de uso, en las diferentes áreas de excavación es más escasa y la frecuencia oscila de 1 a 5 artefactos en aproximadamente un 50 por ciento de las áreas.

La frecuencia de las huellas de uso en las herramientas multifuncionales, tiene un comportamiento diferente a las unifuncionales. En estas últimas la huella de uso es una unidad, mientras que en las multifuncionales cada diferente huella puede contarse tantas veces como aparezca en una herramienta. De esta manera se ha contabilizado la cantidad de veces que cada huella de uso se encuentra en las 234 herramientas multifuncionales con las que contamos.

Las huellas de uso más abundantes siguen siendo las de percusión con 155 frecuencias; le siguen el corte con 146 y el raspado con 122. De ahí continúa el desgaste con 79, corte por desgaste con 36, y desbaste con 18, y para finalizar abrasión con 8, corte por percusión 6, machacado con 4, afilar con 3, y perforar con 1 (Tabla 4.6).

La percusión vuelve a tener un papel primordial, y se presenta como la huella de uso más importante en el área B6 con cincuenta y cuatro frecuencias; le siguen veinticinco en B1, diecisiete en B2, trece en B4 y doce en E. El resto son menores de diez frecuencias y el B10 no cuenta con la presencia de esta huella de uso. El corte, raspado y desgaste, tienen más o menos la misma presencia que la percusión, pero proporcionalmente en menor cantidad, la única diferencia estriba en que en B9 al igual que la B10 no presentan las huellas de uso de corte, raspado y desgaste. El resto de huellas son escasas y sólo en la B6 se presentan otros tipos de huellas: una de abrasión, seis de desbaste, dos de afilar, y doce de corte por desgaste. Por último, señalaremos que además

Tabla 4.6. Frecuencia de Huellas de Uso en Herramientas Multifuncionales por Area

	A1	B1	B2	B3	B4	B5	B6	B7	B8	B9	B10	B11	D	E
Percusión	4	25	17	3	13	3	54	9	5	1		3	7	12
Corte	3	27	19	5	14	1	36	7	2			7	8	18
Raspado	3	14	12	2	9	5	44	9	6			4	3	12
Desgaste	2	13	4	3	7	2	24	6	3			4	3	8
Machacar			2											2
Abrasión	1		4				1			1				1
Desbaste	1					4	6	7	1					
Afilar							2					1		
Perforar				1										
Incisión		1												
Corte por desgaste	1	1	2	3	5		12	1	2			3	1	6
Corte por percusión		1	5											

de la dispersión y escasa frecuencia de huellas de uso en estas herramientas multifuncionales, B9 sólo presenta una evidencia de percusión y una de abrasión, y B10 no presenta ninguna herramienta multifuncional.

Si comparamos la información de frecuencias de herramientas unifuncionales y multifuncionales, podemos darnos cuenta de que hay cierto incremento de evidencia de desgaste de manera generalizada, y particularmente en el área E se ve también incrementada con huellas de uso de abrasión, machacado y desgaste, pero pierde otras como corte por percusión.

Por último tenemos aquellas herramientas que permiten mediante una tipología diagnóstica tener un panorama aproximado de su momento cronológico: me refiero básicamente a las puntas de proyectil, aunque también contamos con algunos unifaciales y bifaciales. Dentro del análisis también encontramos artefactos que no pudieron ser clasificados tipológicamente debido a que su estado de conservación (Tabla 4.7).

Descripción del Material por Áreas de Excavación

A continuación se procederá a llevar a cabo una descripción de los materiales arqueológicos recuperados en cada una de las áreas de excavación.

Área A1 (Plaza del Caracol)

En esta área de excavación se recuperaron 10,624 artefactos, los cuales tuvieron un peso de 55,638.3 g. De éstos 10,561 fueron artefactos sin huella de uso aparente con un peso de 40,824 g y sólo obtuvimos 63 herramientas con 14,814.3 g de peso. En los artefactos sin huella de uso aparente, tenemos presentes todas las materias primas, siendo las más frecuentes el basalto medio con 4,570 artefactos (16,973.6 g), el basalto fino con 2,430 (9,257.9 g) y la diorita con 2,098 (9,030.1 g); le siguen el sílex con 499 (923.9 g), la latita con 413 (2,471.8 g), la andesita con 336 (814.7 g), y el cuarzo con 104 (277.7 g); y como escasa la riolita con 44 (278 g), ígnea de textura gruesa con 28 (127.5 g), granodiorita con 24 (618.2 g), ígneas de textura fina con 14 (50.4 g), y obsidiana con 1 (.2 g). Dentro de este grupo tenemos como algo especial tres casos de lascas de adelgazamiento en sílex, las tres muy pequeñas y sin presentar ninguna modificación ni alteración posterior a su extracción (Figura 4.6).

Realizando una disección de estos materiales y excluyendo los tres materiales presentes en todo el sitio, los valores de los materiales restantes permite un nivel de análisis a otra escala. En realidad los resultados se mantienen, lo único que cambia es la expresión gráfica y su visualización en términos porcentuales, digamos, en sentido coloquial, que se hace un zoom. Resulta que en este sentido los valores más altos son para la andesita (23.18 por ciento), la latita (28.37 por ciento) y el sílex (33.76 por ciento).

El Caracol (C9)

Los materiales asociados a esta estructura corresponden en términos generales a los registrados en esta área, sin embargo, llama la atención la presencia al interior de la estructura de dos materias primas en particular, la latita y el sílex. Es decir, estas dos materias primas aparecen concentradas al interior de esta estructura en su calidad de desecho de talla. Cabe mencionar así mismo que hay un fragmento de punta de proyectil de latita, las demás materias primas existentes en la Plaza del Caracol se diluyen en toda el área.

Tabla 4.7. Herramientas con Tipología Diagnóstica

A1	2 puntas de proyectil de periodo cerámico.
	1 punta de proyectil triangular de muescas laterales tipo Hohokam.
B	1 punta de proyectil periodo cerámico.
B1	1 perforador o taladro tipo Hohokam.
	1 punta de proyectil periodo cerámico.
	1 punta de proyectil tipo San Pedro.
B2	1 perforador o taladro tipo Hohokam.
	2 puntas de proyectil, por su tamaño posiblemente periodo cerámico.
	1 punta de proyectil tipo san pedro.
	1 punta de proyectil triangular de muescas laterales tipo Hohokam.
B3	1 punta de proyectil tipo Ciénega.
B4	1 bifacial, posiblemente arcaico temprano.
	1 punta de proyectil de periodo cerámico.
B5	1 punta de proyectil triangular de muescas laterales tipo Hohokam.
B6	1 bifacial posible cuchillo Clovis en forma de laurel.
B7	1 punta de proyectil de periodo de agricultores tempranos.
	1 punta de proyectil de periodo arcaico temprano o medio.
	1 punta de proyectil tipo Ciénega.
	1 punta de proyectil tipo Ciénega aserrada.
B8	1 punta de proyectil periodo arcaico medio.
	3 puntas de proyectil de periodo cerámico.
	2 punta de proyectil triangular de muescas laterales tipo Hohokam.
B9	1 punta de proyectil de periodo cerámico.
	1 punta de proyectil tipo san pedro.
B10	1 punta de proyectil de periodo cerámico (temprano).
B11	1 perforador o taladro tipo Hohokam.
D	1 punta de proyectil de periodo cerámico.
	1 punta de proyectil tipo san pedro.
E	1 bifacial ovoide de periodo de agricultores tempranos.
	1 punta de proyectil, posiblemente Cortaro de periodo arcaico medio.
	1 punta de proyectil tipo san pedro.

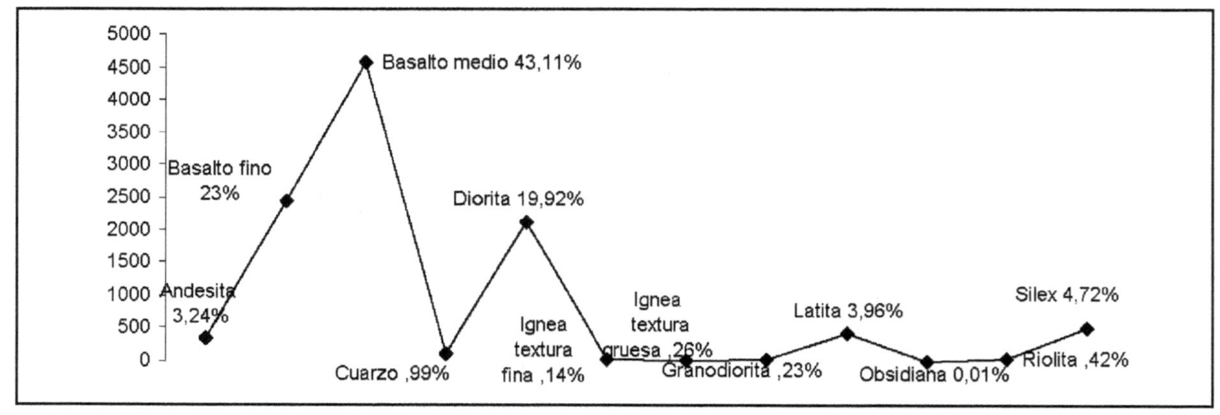

Figura 4.6. Materia prima en la Plaza del Caracol (muestra 10624).

El Caracol (C9.1)

Al igual que la anterior, los materiales asociados a esta estructura corresponden en términos generales a los registrados en esta area. Sin embargo, llama la atención la presencia al interior de la estructura de dos materias primas en particular, la latita y el sílex, o sea la mayor cantidad de estas materias primas aparecen concentradas al interior de esta estructura en su calidad de desecho de talla, las demás materias primas existentes en la Plaza del Caracol se distribuyen homogéneamente en toda el área.

Estructura Circular de Piedra 22

Esta estructura es la que presenta el segundo lugar en desechos registrados. En A1 presenta 804 fragmentos de los cuales el 94 por ciento corresponden a los basaltos y diorita. De igual forma si eliminamos estos, la representación de los materiales nos indica nuevamente la alta presencia de desechos de talla tanto de latita (38 por ciento) como de sílex (34 por ciento). Es decir, nuevamente el comportamiento vuelve a ser similar como en las estructuras anteriormente descritas.

Herramientas

Respecto a las herramientas en esta área podemos decir que del total de todo el sitio corresponde a la Plaza del Caracol tan solo el 5 por ciento (58 herramientas) entre las que predominan las lascas con huella de uso (37.97 por ciento). Le siguen los nódulos con huellas de uso (25.86 por ciento), nódulos retocados (18.97 por ciento), lascas retocadas (6.90 por ciento), nódulos con huellas de uso (5.17 por ciento), fragmentos de nódulos retocados (3.45 por ciento) y grabador (1.72 por ciento) (Figura 4.7).

En el grupo de las herramientas no contamos con todas las materias primas; aquí tenemos: en diorita 18 artefactos (7,085.2 g), 14 en basalto fino (2,376.1 g), 10 en basalto medio (1,427.1 g) 8 en andesita (552.8 g), y latita (3,365.2 g) respectivamente; como mate-

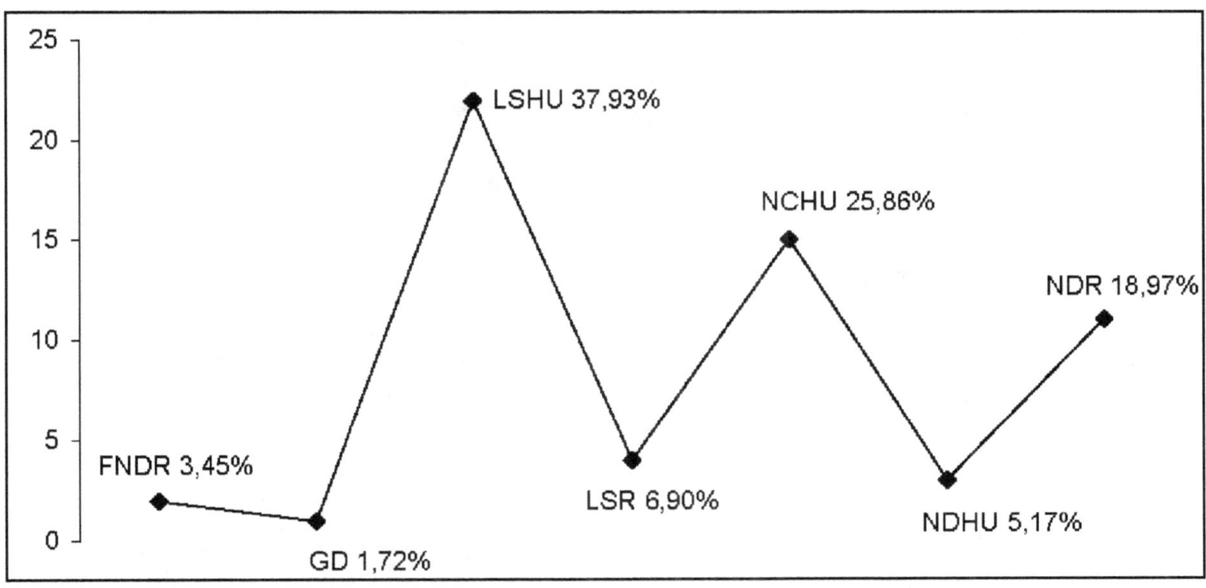

Figura 4.7. Frecuencia de herramientas en A1 (muestra 58).

ria prima escasa tenemos 2 en sílex (3.5 g), y sólo 1 herramienta en riolita (1.6 g), 1 en ígnea de textura fina (2.1 g), y 1 cuarzo (.7 g). Por lo que respecta a las herramientas formalizadas tenemos las siguientes:

Punta de proyectil (Figura 4.8).

Numero de bolsa: 21,505; Ubicación: Área A1 N100 E245. Largo: 2 cm; Espesor: 5 mm. Descripción general: fragmento medial de punta de proyectil manufacturada en riolita con retoque bifacial bilateral invasivo continuo.

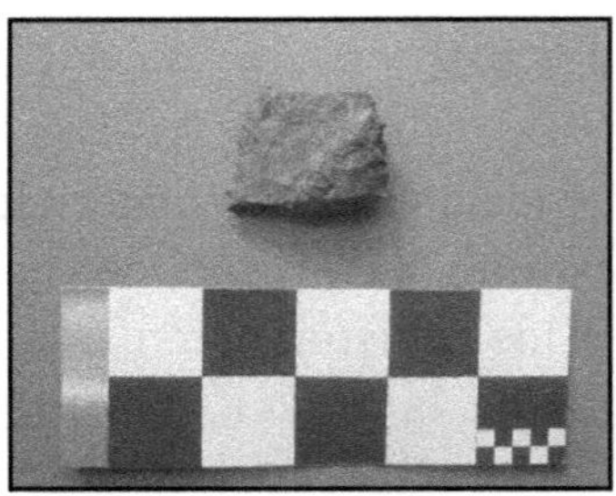

Figura 4.8. Punta de proyectil 21505.

Punta de proyectil (Figura 4.9).

Numero de bolsa: 25,032; Ubicación: Área A1 N89 E258. Largo: 2 cm; Espesor: 3 mm. Descripción general: punta de proyectil completa de periodo cerámico, manufacturada en cuarzo, con retoque bifacial bilateral invasivo continuo. Se encuentra despuntada.

Figura 4.9. Punta de proyectil 25032.

Punta de proyectil (Figura 4.10).

Numero de bolsa: 27,642; Ubicación: Área A1 N94 E267. Largo: 2 cm; Espesor: 3 mm. Descripción general: punta de proyectil completa manufacturada en de sílex, triangular de muescas laterales de posible filiación Hohokam, con retoque bifacial bilateral invasivo continuo.

Figura 4.10. Punta de proyectil 27642.

Punta de proyectil (Figura 4.11).

Numero de bolsa: 29,008; Ubicación: Área A1 N98 E271. Largo: 2 cm; Espesor: 3 mm. Descripción general: punta de proyectil completa de periodo cerámico, manufacturada en latita con retoque bifacial bilateral invasivo continuo.

Figura 4.11. Punta de proyectil 29008.

Punta de proyectil (Figura 4.12).

Numero de bolsa: 30,947; Ubicación: Área A1 (fuera de retícula). Largo: 2 cm; Espesor: 6

mm. Descripción general: fragmento distal de punta de proyectil manufacturada en roca ígnea de textura fina con retoque bifacial bilateral invasivo continuo.

Grabador (Figura 4.13).

Numero de bolsa: 25,128; Ubicación: Área A1 N93 E275. Largo: 6 cm; Espesor: 6 mm. Descripción general: grabador completo de diorita, presenta retoque unifacial lateral invasivo contínuo; unifuncional, con huella de uso en la parte distal aparentemente para hacer incisiones.

En esta área ha sido difícil la interpretación debido a varias cosas. En primer lugar no hay abundantes evidencias para realizar inferencias significativas; además, se argumenta que se trata de un espacio restringido pero se registró una buena cantidad de metates y manos de metate, además de cerámica roja tardía. Al parecer estos materiales podrían indicar desfase temporal respecto a la principal ocupación (1300-1450 d.C.), pues se ha propuesto que estos materiales corresponden con las fases finales de ocupación del cerro, es decir, entre 1450-1500 d.C.

La Plaza del Caracol se ha interpretado como un área especial en la que aparentemente no se desarrollaron actividades domésticas y/o de producción especializada. El área comprendida como Plaza está nivelada y a su vez delimitada por una serie de terrazas en sus flancos. La presencia de metates y manos de metates no corresponde con áreas de actividad específicas, por lo que estos materiales bien podrían representar una reutilización de estos espacios. Ahora bien, el hallazgo de pequeños desechos de lítica tallada tanto de sílex como de latita al interior de El Caracol (C9), El Caracol (C9.1) y en la estructura circular de piedra (C137), presentan una interrogante de sumo interés, ¿estos materiales representan una actividad ritual en el apogeo del sitio, o también son espacios reutilizados posteriormente?

Figura 4.12. Punta de proyectil 30947.

Figura 4.13. Grabador 25128.

La única evidencia sólida, en términos de comparación regional, que tenemos para argumentar algo al respecto es la presencia de una punta de proyectil (bolsa #27,642) cuya morfología está asociada a las fases Gila/ Civano (1300-1450) y a las fases III y IV de la cronología Pueblo (1000-1450 d.C.) (Sliva 1997). Se trata de una punta de proyectil triangular en sílex con muescas laterales. Según la cronología del sudoeste norteamericano esta forma es común a la temporalidad que corresponde con el apogeo del Cerro de Trincheras (1300-1450 d.C.). Con este argumento no podemos asegurar si el desecho de talla se trata de una actividad ritual, y pese a que esta punta se encuentra fuera de estas estructuras, cabe destacar que una de las mayores concentraciones de desecho de talla de sílex en esta área es la detectada al interior de El Caracol. A decir verdad una de las mayores concentraciones de sílex en todo el sitio se encuentra precisamente en La Plaza del Caracol (15 por ciento del total) únicamente por debajo del área B6 (16 por ciento del total), la que por sus propias características es la que mayor cantidad de materiales presente en todo el sitio, o sea, la alta presencia de este material en A1 debe tomarse con sumo cuidado.

Área B1. Bienes Terminados en Concha

Área en la que fue detectada una importante concentración de adornos en concha en varias etapas de su proceso de manufactura, así mismo los materiales muestran evidencia de que también sirvió como habitación. Es un área en la que se detectaron una gran cantidad de artefactos, y para nuestro interés se supone que hay evidencia de la producción de artefactos en piedra.

Dentro de esta área de excavación se encontraron un total de 18,132 artefactos los cuales dieron un peso de 143,167.2 g. De este gran total 18,017 artefactos con 120,721.5 g no presentaron huellas de uso aparentes, y sólo fueron 93 artefactos los clasificados como herramientas, las cuales tuvieron un peso de 22,445.7 g.

De acuerdo a la presencia de materia prima, respecto al total del sitio, tenemos los siguientes: andesita 11.31 por ciento, basalto fino 17.74 por ciento, basalto medio 44.57 por ciento, cuarzo .71 por ciento, diorita 18.67 por ciento, granodiorita .69 por ciento, ígnea textura fina .10 por ciento, ígnea textura gruesa .68 por ciento, latita 2.63 por ciento, no identificada .01 por ciento, riolita .60 por ciento y sílex 2.29 por ciento (Figura 4.14).

Una cosa que es de sumo interés es el comportamiento anómalo de la presencia de la andesita. En B1 es el segundo porcentaje más alto de andesita en todo el sitio (20 por ciento) solamente superado por área B2 (31 por ciento); llama la atención que el segundo valor más alto para esta materia prima es en el área E (23 por ciento). En las restantes áreas los porcentajes de estos materiales son realmente

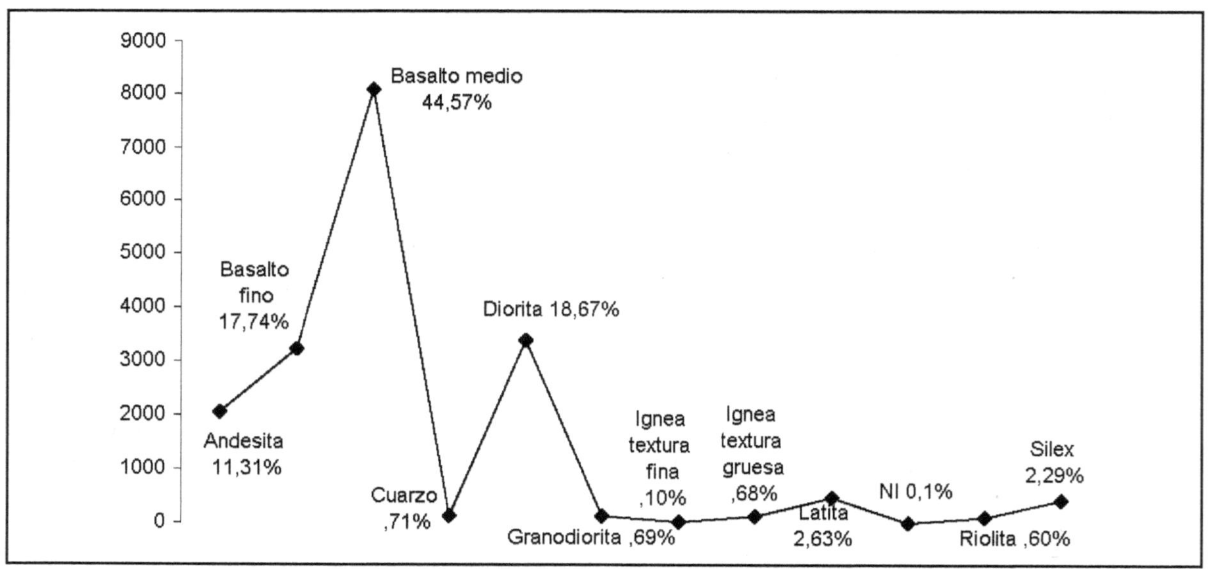

Figura 4.14. Frecuencia de materia prima en B1 (muestra 18132).

bajos. Es decir, estas tres áreas plantean una diferencia respecto a las demás, pero ¿qué significa esta presencia de andesita en áreas asociadas a la manufactura de concha (B1 y B2)? ¿Qué tipo de herramientas y qué tipo de huellas de uso se presentan en esta área? ¿Existe alguna relación entre la alta presencia de andesita y el trabajo de concha?

Respecto a la presencia de esta materia prima su distribución en las diferentes herramientas es la siguiente. De un total de 21 artefactos registrados se cuenta con 1 fragmento de nódulo con huellas de uso (4.76 por ciento), 16 lascas con huella de uso (76.19 por ciento), 2 nódulos con huellas de uso (9.52 por ciento), 1 nódulo con huellas de uso (4.76 por ciento) y 1 nódulo retocado (4.76 por ciento). Sin embargo no hay una concentración de estas herramientas en un sector en particular al interior de B1 (Figura 4.15).

Respecto a las herramientas generales en esta área podemos decir que del total de todo el sitio corresponde a esta área con 8 por ciento (93 herramientas), entre las que predominan las lascas con huella de uso (33.33 por ciento), le siguen los nódulos con huellas de uso (22.58 por ciento), nódulos retocados (10.75 por ciento), fragmentos de nódulo con huellas de uso (8.60 por ciento), nódulos con huellas de uso (7.53 por ciento), puntas de proyectil (6.45 por ciento), lascas retocadas (5.38 por ciento), unifaciales (2.15 por ciento) y de artefactos

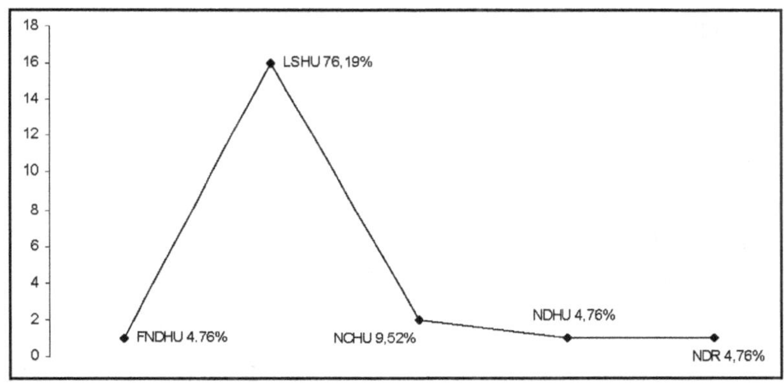

Figura 4.15. Herramientas en andesita en B1 (muestra 21).

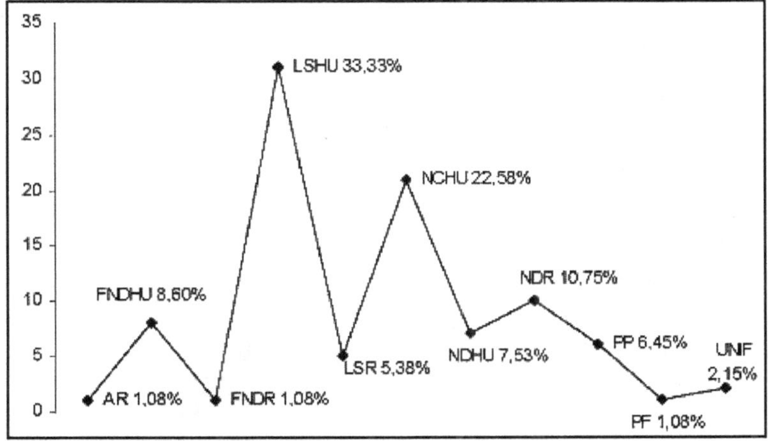

Figura 4.16. Frecuencia de herramientas en B1 (muestra 93).

reutilizados, fragmentos de nódulos retocados y perforadores (1.8 por ciento cada uno) (Figura 4.16).

Por lo que respecta a las herramientas formalizadas y/o con un mayor grado de estandarización tecnológica tenemos las siguientes:

Punta de proyectil (Figura 4.17).

Numero de bolsa: 10,136; Ubicación: Área B1 N108 E87. Largo: 3 cm; Espesor: 4 mm. Descripción general: fragmento medial de punta de proyectil en basalto fino aparentemente en proceso de elaboración, presenta retoque lateral invasivo discontinuo y posiblemente podríamos decir que es un fragmento de preforma de punta de proyectil.

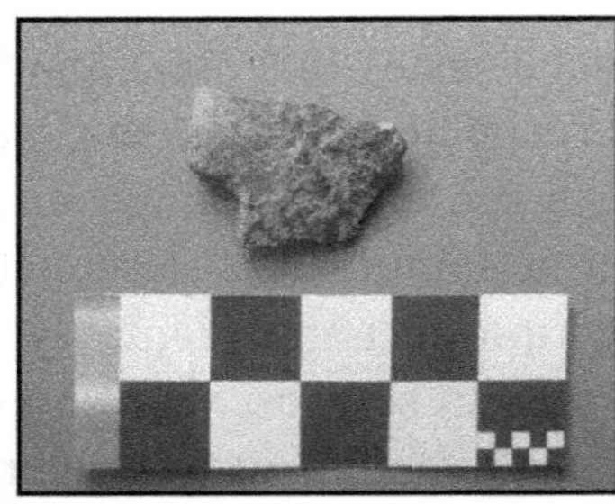

Figura 4.17. Punta de proyectil 10136.

Punta de proyectil (Figura 4.18).

Numero de bolsa: 10,143; Ubicación: Área B1 N110 E89. Largo: 2 cm; Espesor 3 mm; Descripción general: Punta de proyectil completa de período cerámico, manufacturada en cuarzo, con retoque bifacial total invasivo continuo. Del tipo de puntas pequeñas asociadas a los períodos cerámico tardío.

Figura 4.18. Punta de proyectil 10143.

Punta de proyectil (Figura 4.19).

Numero de bolsa: 13,655; Ubicación: Área B1 N106 E88. Largo: 3 cm; Espesor: 10 mm. Descripción general: punta de proyectil completa de materia prima no identificada aparentemente en proceso de elaboración, presenta retoque total marginal discontinuo, es posible que haya sido desechada durante su manufactura por defectos de la materia prima, además se encuentra muy erosionada. Probablemente se trata más bien de una punta votiva y no utilitaria.

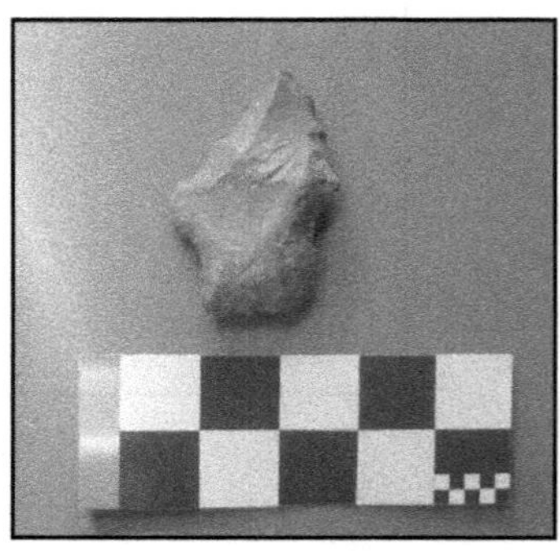

Figura 4.19. Punta de proyectil 13655.

Punta de proyectil (Figura 4.20).

Numero de bolsa: 15,275; Ubicación: Área B1 N100 E77. Largo: 3 cm; Espesor: 5 mm.

Figura 4.20. Punta de proyectil 15275.

Descripción general: fragmento medial de punta de proyectil manufacturada en sílex con retoque bifacial total marginal continuo, aparentemente en proceso de elaboración, posiblemente abandonada durante su proceso de manufactura.

Punta de proyectil (Figura 4.21).

Numero de bolsa: 16,223 Ubicación: Área B1 N105 E67. Largo: 6 cm; Espesor: 6 mm. Descripción general: manufacturada en basalto fino, con retoque bifacial total invasivo continúo. Punta asociada a los tipos San Pedro, según su morfología se ubica del 1200 al 600 a.C. (Sliva 1997).

Punta de proyectil (Figura 4.22).

Numero de bolsa: 16,828; Ubicación: Área B1 N105 E72. Largo: 3 cm; Ancho: Espesor: 4 mm. Descripción general: fragmento proximal de punta de proyectil de posible filiación Hohokam manufacturada en sílex con retoque bifacial bilateral invasivo continuo. Podría tratarse de un taladro; su retoque y la forma se parecen más a éste y no a una punta de proyectil.

Grabador.

Numero de bolsa: 10,817; Ubicación: Área B1 N109 E92. Largo: 6 cm; Espesor: 16 mm. Descripción general: grabador completo en latita, presenta retoque unifacial lateral invasivo continuo; unifuncional, con huella de uso en la parte distal aparentemente para hacer incisiones.

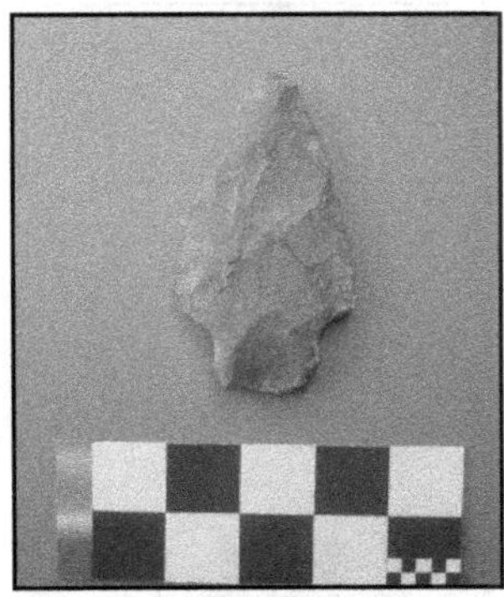

Figura 4.21. Punta de proyectil 16223.

Perforador (Figura 4.23).

Numero de bolsa: 12,580 Ubicación: Área B1 N102 E81. Largo: 6 cm; Espesor: 6 mm. Descripción general: fragmento medial de perforador de basalto fino, sin modificación por retoque, y por el tipo de fractura no se puede observar la huella de uso.

Herramientas No Formales

Nódulo Retocado.

Numero de bolsa: 13,012; Ubicación: Área B1 N96 E81. Descripción general: artefacto unifucional completo sobre nódulo de diorita, presenta retoque unifacial distal invasivo continuo. No se observan huellas de uso aparentes.

Figura 4.22. Punta de proyectil 16828.

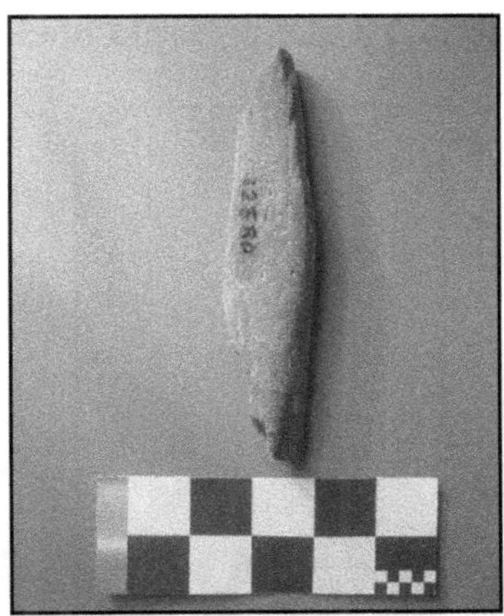

Figura 4.23. Perforador 12580.

Nódulo retocado.

Numero de bolsa: 13,739; Ubicación: Área B1 N102 E82. Descripción general: artefacto multifuncional completo sobre nódulo de diorita, presenta retoque unifacial distal invasivo continuo. Se observan huellas de uso de raspado y percusión ubicadas en la parte distal y lateral.

Núcleo con huella de uso.

Numero de bolsa: 13,739; Ubicación: Área B1 N99 E87. Descripción general: núcleo completo sobre nódulo de diorita con 60 por ciento de cortex, presenta huellas de uso de percusión ubicadas de manera generalizado e irregular.

Núcleo retocado (Figura 4.24).

Numero de bolsa: 12,575; Ubicación: Área B1 N100 E81. Largo: 8 cm. Descripción general: núcleo retocado completo sobre nódulo de basalto fino con 60 por ciento de cortex, presenta retoque unifacial bilateral invasivo continuo. No se observan huellas de uso aparentes.

Lasca con huella de uso (Figura 4.25).

Numero de bolsa: 13,267; Ubicación: Área B1 N100 E87. Largo: 7 cm. Descripción general: lasca secundaria completa de basalto fino con restos de cortex en la parte distal; artefacto multifuncional ya que presenta huellas de uso de raspado y desbaste doble ubicados en las secciones bilateral y distal.

Lasca retocada con huella de uso.

Numero de bolsa: 16,145; Ubicación: Área B1 N103 E70. Descripción general: lasca completa primaria circular de nódulo de basalto fino, presenta retoque unifacial distal marginal continuo. Se observan huella uso de raspado ubicados en el área distal.

Artefacto reutilizado.

Numero de bolsa: 16,179; Ubicación: Área B1 N105 E69. Descripción general: fragmento medial de hacha pulida de basalto medio, presenta huellas uso de percusión generalizado irregular.

Lasca con huella de uso.

Numero de bolsa: 16,762; Ubicación: Área B1 N107 E67. Largo: 7 cm. Descripción general: lasca terciaria completa de basalto fino, artefacto multifuncional ya que presenta huellas de uso de raspado y desbaste ubicados en las secciones bilateral y distal.

De esta área se obtuvieron 4 fechamientos por medio de radiocarbono, el rango temporal en el que se encuentra abarca del 1205 al 1455 d.C. Uno de los elementos diagnósticos que se registró sobre el apisonado del jacal 16, al parecer sin saqueos, es una punta de proyectil

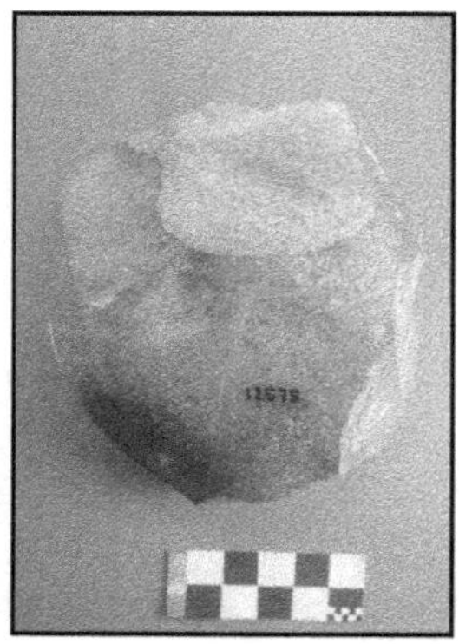

Figura 4.24. Núcleo retocado 12575.

Figura 4.25. Núcleo retocado 13267.

(#16828). Si este contexto del apisonado está intacto y la punta de proyectil corresponde a lo que marcan los fechamientos tendríamos un rango temporal confiable para esta forma de puntas en el cerro de Trincheras.

Asimismo en esta área se concentran un fragmento y una punta completa asociadas a períodos tempranos (puntas San Pedro). Evidentemente esos hallazgos se ubican en contextos funcionales correspondientes a períodos cerámicos tardíos. La interrogante vuelve a ser la misma que en otras áreas, la presencia indudable de este tipo de material sólo puede ser respondida en términos de reutilización de los materiales, ya sea como coleccionismo prehispánico o reutilización funcional de estos artefactos.

El conjunto de B1 representa un serio potencial para identificar y definir las relaciones entre las herramientas líticas y su probable vinculación en el proceso productivo de la concha; es evidente que se trata de un área especializada. Por lo tanto queremos proponer que las herramientas no formales detectadas en esta área pueden ser vistas como artefactos utilizados en las distintas cadenas productivas del trabajo de concha. Si bien no podemos argumentar una relación directa entre el tipo de artefacto en concha y el tipo y/o tipos de herramientas utilizadas en su elaboración, mostramos por ahora, las características morfológicas de las herramientas registradas en estos contextos fechados entre 1205 al 1455 d.C. Obviamente esta relación no excluye que dichas herramientas pudiesen haber sido usadas en otras actividades ya sea de forma paralela y/o excluyente al trabajo de concha.

Área B2. Bienes Terminados en Concha

En ésta área de excavación fueron recuperados un total de 14,251 artefactos que dieron un peso de 136,877.7 g, de los cuales 14,117 fueron lascas sin huella de uso aparente con un peso de 105,472.9 g. La distribución de acuerdo a su materia prima es la siguiente: andesita 22.42 por ciento, basalto fino 15.37 por ciento, basalto medio 36.54 por ciento, cuarzo .75 por ciento, diorita 18.76 por ciento, granodiorita .36 por ciento, ígnea textura fina .15 por ciento, ígnea textura gruesa .14 por ciento, latita 2.60 por ciento, riolita .81 por ciento, sílex 2.10 por ciento y obsidiana .01 por ciento (Figura 4.26).

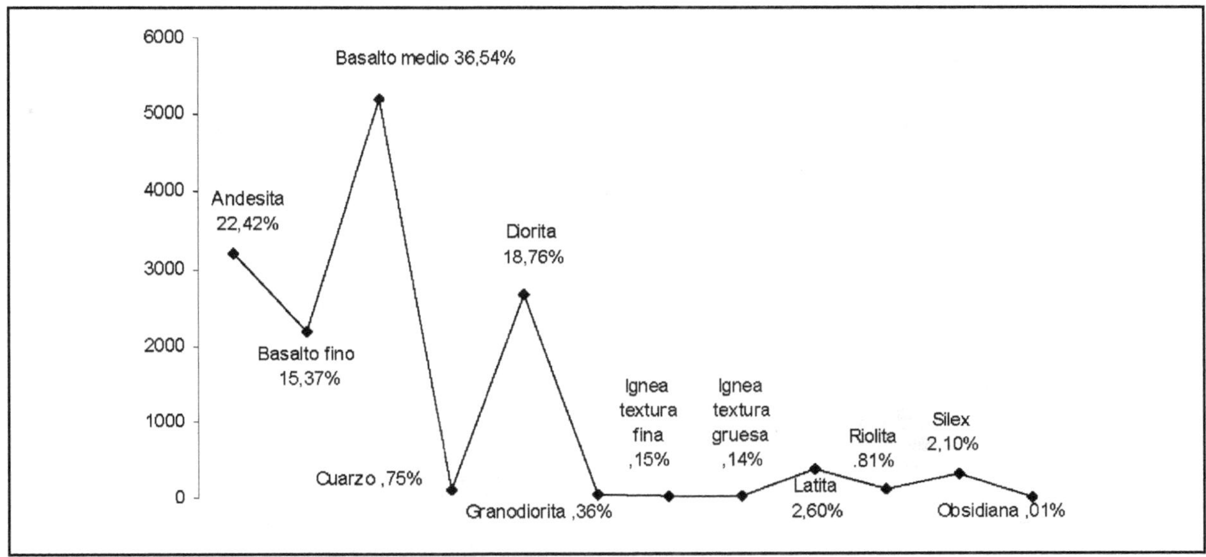

Figura 4.26. Frecuencia de materia prima en B2 (muestra 14251).

Al igual que en el área B1, resalta la presencia en altas cantidades porcentuales de andesita, como ya mencioné atrás, el porcentaje más alto de andesita en un área es precisamente en B2 (31 por ciento).

Herramientas

De un total de 39 artefactos detectados en andesita 18 son lascas con huellas de uso (46.15 por ciento), 3 lascas retocadas (.69 por ciento), 9 núcleos con huellas de uso (23.06 por ciento), 8 nódulos con huellas de uso (20.51 por ciento) y 1 nódulo retocado (2.56 por ciento) (Figura 4.27).

Respecto a las herramientas generales en esta área podemos decir que del total de todo el sitio corresponde a esta área con 8 por ciento (87 herramientas) entre las que predominan las lascas con huella de uso (33.33 por ciento); le siguen los núcleos con huellas de uso (18.39 por ciento), nódulos con huellas de uso (18.39 por ciento), lascas retocadas (9.20 por ciento), nódulos retocados (6.90 por ciento), puntas de proyectil (3.45 por ciento), núcleos retocados (3.45, bifaciales (2.30 por ciento) y artefactos reutilizados, machacador, fragmento de nódulo con huellas de uso y perforador (1.15 por ciento cada uno) (Figura 4.28).

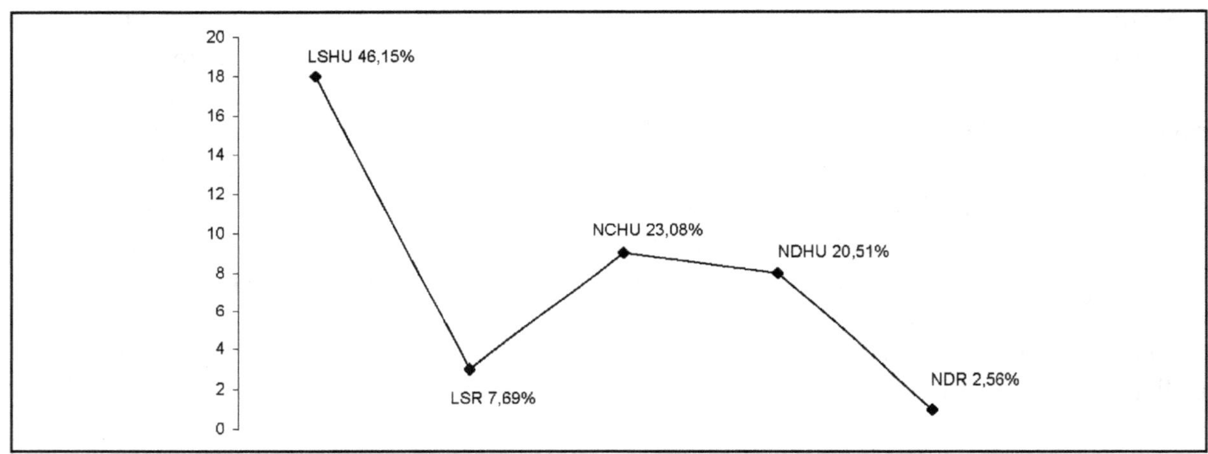

Figura 4.27. Herramientas de andesita en B2 (muestra 39).

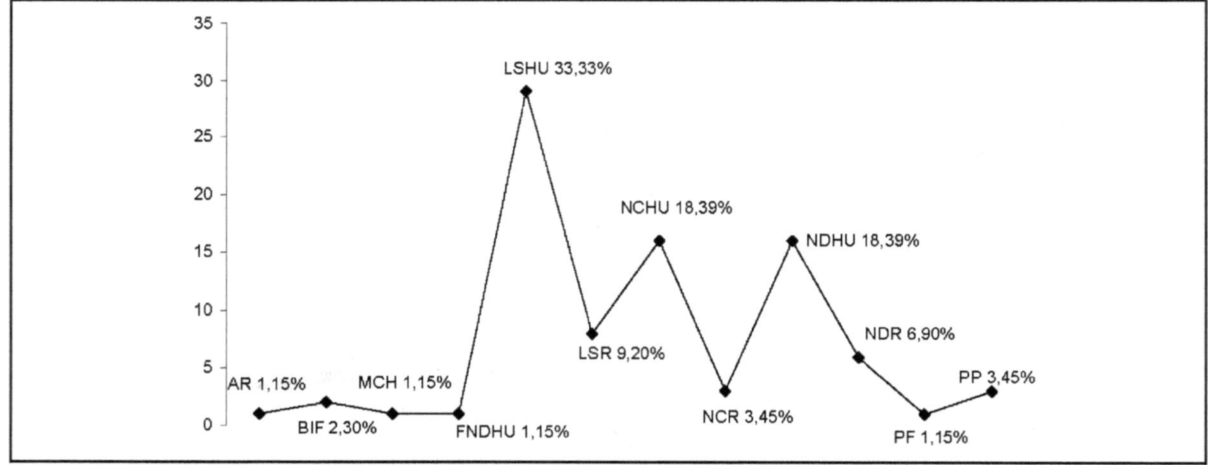

Figura 4.28. Frecuencia de herramientas en B2 (muestra 87).

Por lo que respecta a las herramientas formalizadas y/o con un mayor grado de estandarización tecnológica tenemos las siguientes:

Punta de proyectil (Figura 4.29).

Numero de bolsa: 10,530; Ubicación: Área B2 N104 E102. Largo: 3 cm; Espesor: 4 mm. Descripción general: fragmento proximal de punta de proyectil de posible filiación Hohokam, manufacturado en obsidiana, con retoque bifacial total invasivo, presenta márgenes aserrados, y es probable que haya sido abandonado por fractura.

Figura 4.29. Punta de proyectil 10530.

Punta de proyectil (Figura 4.30).

Numero de bolsa: 11,798; Ubicación: Área B2 N110 E103. Largo: 2 cm; Espesor: 7 mm. Descripción general: punta de proyectil completa manufacturada en sílex, de forma triangular con muescas laterales presenta retoque bifacial lateral invasivo continuo. Esta punta es muy parecida a la forma a las que Sliva (1997) llama Sedentarias las cuales pueden ser del período Sedentario Temprano (950-1150).

Figura 4.30. Punta de proyectil 11798.

Punta de proyectil (Figura 4.31).

Numero de bolsa: 12,058a; Ubicación: Área B2 N109 E106. Largo: 3 cm; Espesor: 3 mm. Descripción general: fragmento distal de punta de proyectil de basalto fino aparentemente en proceso de elaboración. Presenta retoque bilateral marginal continuo y es probable que dada la forma natural de la lasca su intención fuera aprovechar la misma para manufacturar el artefacto. Imposible identificar su tipo, pero por el tamaño y la materia prima parece que se trata de puntas del período cerámico.

Figura 4.31. Punta de proyectil 12058.

Punta de proyectil (Figura 4.32).

Numero de bolsa: 12,058b; Ubicación: Área B2 N109 E106. Largo: 2 cm; Espesor: 7 mm.

Descripción general: fragmento distal de punta de proyectil manufacturada en sílex, presenta retoque bifacial total invasivo continuo. Imposible identificar su tipo, pero por el tamaño y la materia prima parece que se trata de puntas del período cerámico.

Punta de proyectil.

Numero de bolsa: 12,742; Ubicación: Área B2 N97 E93. Largo: 6 cm; Espesor: 7 mm. Descripción general: punta de proyectil tipo San Pedro completa manufacturada en riolita.

Bifacial.

Numero de bolsa: 10,554; Ubicación: Área B2 N104 E92. Largo: 6 cm; Ancho: Espesor: 17 mm. Descripción general: bifacial completo manufacturado en sílex, con retoque bifacial total invasivo discontinuo; unifuncional con huella de uso aparente de raspado en las partes distal y bilateral.

Bifacial (Figura 4.33).

Numero de bolsa: 9,263; Ubicación: Área B2 N105 E94. Largo: 2 cm; Espesor: 6 mm. Descripción general: fragmento medial de bifacial manufacturado en sílex, presenta retoque bifacial total invasivo continuo. (Aunque cabe la posibilidad de que sea un fragmento de punta de proyectil).

Perforador (Figura 4.34).

Numero de bolsa: 12,484 Ubicación: Área B2 N97 E84. Largo: 6 cm; Espesor: 9 mm. Descripción general: perforador completo de basalto fino, sin modificación por retoque; unifuncional con huella de uso en la parte distal.

Herramientas No Formales

Fragmento de nódulo retocado.

Numero de bolsa: 12,920; Ubicación: Área B2 N98 E97. Descripción general: fragmento de nódulo completo de basalto fino, presenta retoque unifacial distal invasivo continuo. No se observan huellas de uso aparentes.

Núcleo retocado.

Numero de bolsa: 10,684; Ubicación: Área B2 N106 E102. Descripción general: núcleo retocado completo sobre nódulo de diorita con 60 por ciento de cortex; presenta retoque unifacial distal invasivo continuo. Se observan huellas de uso de percusión y de corte por percusión en sus partes distal y bilateral.

Figura 4.32. Punta de proyectil 12742.

Figura 4.33. Bifacial 9263.

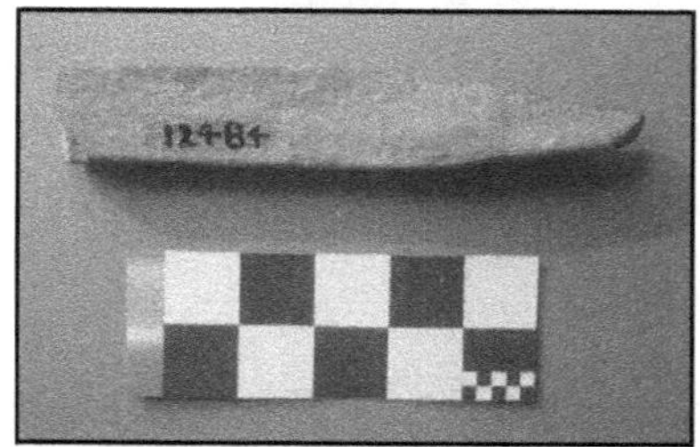

Figura 4.34. Perforador 12484.

Lasca retocada.

Numero de bolsa: 12,915; Ubicación: Área B2 N100 E94. Descripción general: lasca completa primaria circular de nódulo de basalto fino; presenta retoque bifacial distal bimarginal discontinuo. No se observan huellas uso aparente.

Artefacto reutilizado (Figura 4.35).

Numero de bolsa: 9,086 Ubicación: Área B2 N98 E97. Largo máximo: 6 cm. Descripción general: presenta huellas uso de percusión irregular. Fragmento de hacha de ¾ reutilizado.

Respecto a la andesita, como ya mencionábamos arriba, esta área presenta el valor más alto de todo el sitio en esta materia prima, sin embargo, la pregunta vuelve a ser la misma, ¿qué relación guarda este material con el trabajo de concha? De hecho, ¿existe relación entre la andesita y la manufactura de concha? Si existe o no relación entre ellos por ahora también será a nivel hipotético debido a que la deposición del material es por áreas generales. Un futuro análisis de las huellas de uso a nivel microscópico podría correlacionar estas variables (o sea el tipo de desgaste que deja la concha).

Figura 4.35. Artefacto reutilizado 9086.

Área B3. Área Habitacional con Producción Especializada en Concha

Esta área fue de producción especializada de objetos de concha combinada con actividades domésticas y habitacionales, representadas principalmente por estructuras circulares de piedra.

En esta área de excavación se obtuvo un total de 4,400 artefactos con un peso de 49,953 g de éstos, 4,329 fueron lascas sin huella de uso aparente, con un peso de 40,197.1 g. En cuanto a herramientas sólo se presentaron 67 piezas con un peso total de 9,755.9 g.

La distribución de acuerdo a su materia prima es la siguiente: andesita .36 por ciento, basalto fino 36.07 por ciento, basalto medio 22.93 por ciento, cuarzo .41 por ciento, diorita 24.32 por ciento, granodiorita .41 por ciento, ígnea textura fina .89 por ciento, ígnea textura gruesa 3.39 por ciento, latita 6.86 por ciento, riolita 1.91 por ciento y sílex 2.45 por ciento (Figura 4.36).

Herramientas

Respecto a las herramientas los porcentajes son los siguientes lascas con huellas de uso (41.79 por ciento), nódulo con huellas de uso (17.91 por ciento), lascas retocadas (13.43 por ciento), núcleos con huellas de uso (7.46 por ciento), grabadores (5.97 por ciento), nódulos retocados (4.48 por ciento), perforadores (2.99 por ciento), bifaciales, puntas de proyectil y fragmentos de nódulo con huellas de uso (1.49 por ciento cada uno) (Figura 4.37).

Por lo que respecta a las herramientas formalizadas y/o con un mayor grado de estandarización tecnológica tenemos las siguientes:

Punta de proyectil (Figura 4.38).

Numero de bolsa: 7,406; Ubicación: Área B3 N103 E129. Largo: 3 cm; Espesor: 8 mm.

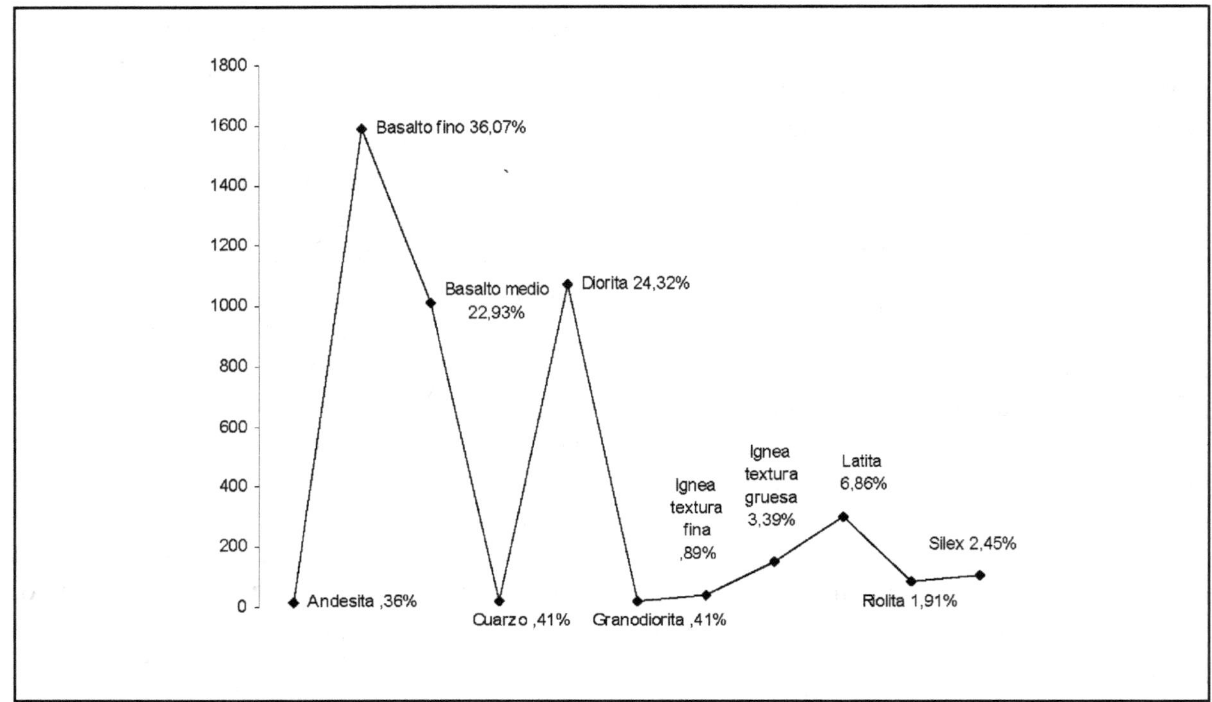

Figura 4.36. Frecuencia de materia prima en B3 (muestra 4400).

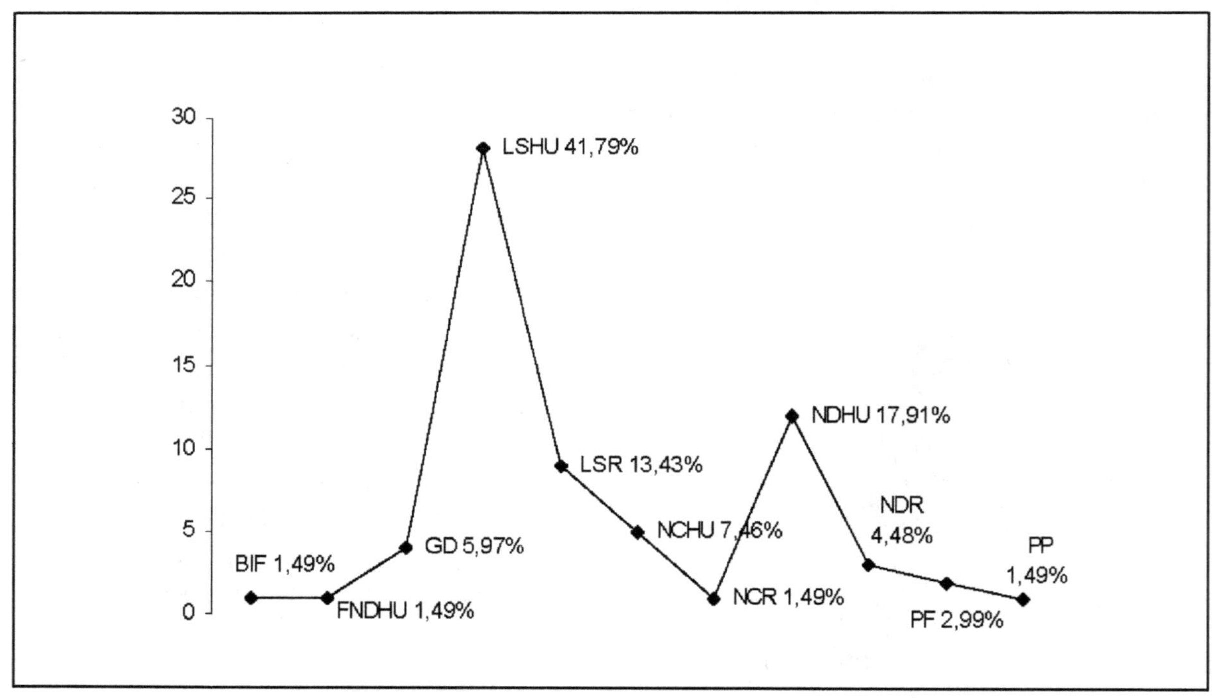

Figura 4.37. Frecuencia de herramientas en B3 (muestra 67).

Descripción general: punta de proyectil tipo Ciénega manufacturada en basalto fino; presenta fractura en su extremo distal, por lo que es probable que haya sido desechada por esta razón.

Figura 4.38. Punta de proyectil 7406.

Bifacial (Figura 4.39).

Numero de bolsa: 7,458; Ubicación: Área B3 N105 E124. Largo: 3 cm; Espesor: 5 mm. Descripción general: bifacial fragmentado en andesita, probablemente en proceso de elaboración; presenta retoque bifacial bilateral invasivo continuo. Podría ser una preforma de perforador.

Figura 4.39. Bifacial 7458.

Grabador (Figura 4.40).

Numero de bolsa: 6,673; Ubicación: Área B3 N108 E106. Largo: 3 cm; Espesor: 9 mm. Descripción general: grabador completo en basalto medio; presenta retoque unifacial bilateral marginal continuo. Unifuncional, con huella de uso en la parte distal aparentemente para hacer incisiones.

Figura 4.40. Grabador 6673.

Grabador.

Numero de bolsa: 7,094; Ubicación: Área B3 N104 E131. Largo: 2 cm; Espesor: 6 mm. Descripción general: grabador completo en andesita; presenta retoque unifacial lateral marginal denticulado. Unifuncional, con huella de uso en la parte distal aparentemente para hacer incisiones.

Grabador (Figura 4.41).

Numero de bolsa: 7,099; Ubicación: Área B3 N104 E131. Largo: 3 cm; Espesor: 6 mm. Descripción general: grabador completo en riolita; presenta retoque unifacial bilateral marginal continuo. Unifuncional, con huella de uso en la parte distal aparentemente para hacer incisiones.

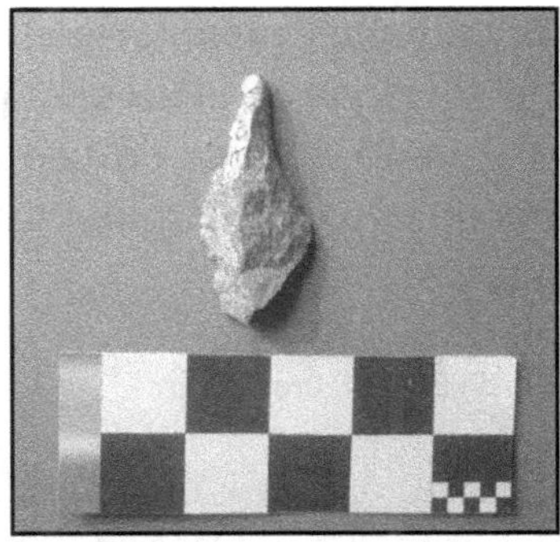

Figura 4.41. Grabador 7099.

Grabador (Figura 4.42).

Numero de bolsa: 7,140; Ubicación: Área B3 N108 E119. Largo: 3 cm; Espesor: 10 mm. Descripción general: grabador completo en basalto medio; presenta retoque unifacial lateral marginal denticulado. Unifuncional, con huella de uso en la parte distal aparentemente para hacer incisiones.

Figura 4.42. Grabador 7140.

Perforador (Figura 4.43).

Numero de bolsa: 7,142; Ubicación: Área B1 N102 E131. Largo: 3 cm; Espesor: 7 mm. Descripción general: perforador fragmentado manufacturado en sílex; presenta retoque unifacial bilateral marginal continuo; unifuncional con huella de uso en la parte distal.

Figura 4.43. Perforador 7142.

Perforador (Figura 4.44).

Numero de bolsa: 6,538; Ubicación: Área B3 N103 E110. Largo: 3 cm; Espesor: 8 mm. Descripción general: perforador completo manufacturado en basalto fino; sin modificación por retoque. Unifuncional con huella de uso en la parte distal.

Figura 4.44. Perforador 6538.

Herramientas No Formales

Fragmento de nódulo con huella de uso.
Numero de bolsa: 7,175 Ubicación: Área B3 N107 E120. Descripción general: artefacto multifuncional completo sobre fragmento de nódulo de andesita, sin modificaciones de manufactura aparentes; presenta huellas de uso de percusión ubicadas en la sección proximal y lateral, así como huellas de uso de corte por desgaste en la parte marginal total de su extremo distal.

Lasca con huella de uso (Figura 4.45).

Numero de bolsa: 6,548; Ubicación: Área B3 N104 E110. Largo: 3 cm. Descripción general: fragmento medial de lasca terciaria de latita;

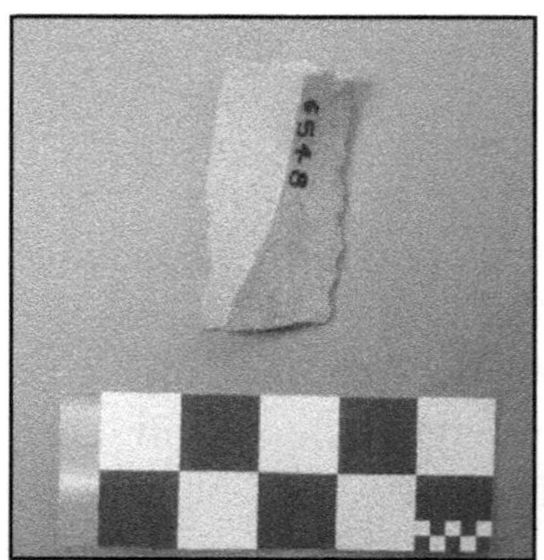

Figura 4.45. Lasca con huella de uso 6548.

presenta huellas de uso de corte y raspado ubicados en el área bilateral.

Cabe destacar que en esta área se registraron 4 grabadores representando un alto índice porcentual (50 por ciento del total) así mismo de los 9 perforadores totals; en el sitio 2 de ellos se encuentran también en B3. Si sumamos tanto los perforadores como los grabadores y un bifacial que más parece perforador, tenemos 6 instrumentos puntiagudos cuya función podría haber estado relacionada con el trabajo de la concha.

Área B4. Área Habitacional con Producción Especializada en Concha

Esta área fue de producción especializada de objetos de concha combinada con actividades domésticas y habitacionales, representadas principalmente por estructuras circulares de piedra. Dentro de esta área se obtuvieron 7,061 artefactos, los cuales dieron un peso de 72,865.7 g de este gran total tenemos que 6,979 de ellos fueron lascas sin huella de uso aparente con un peso de 52,118.6 g, y el resto fueron 67 herramientas con un peso de 20,747.1 g. La distribución de acuerdo a su materia prima es la siguiente: andesita 11.74 por ciento, basalto fino 29.46 por ciento, basalto medio 27.02 por ciento, cuarzo .30 por ciento, diorita 20.95 por ciento, granodiorita .37 por ciento, ígnea textura fina .65 por ciento, ígnea textura gruesa 1.76 por ciento, latita 4.80 por ciento, riolita .74 por ciento, sílex 2.20 por ciento, obsidiana .01 por ciento y no identificado .01 por ciento (Figura 4.46).

Herramientas

Respecto a las herramientas detectadas en esta área 67 en total (6 por ciento del total) los porcentajes son los siguientes: núcleos con huellas de uso (28.36 por ciento), lascas con huellas de uso (25.37 por ciento), nódulos

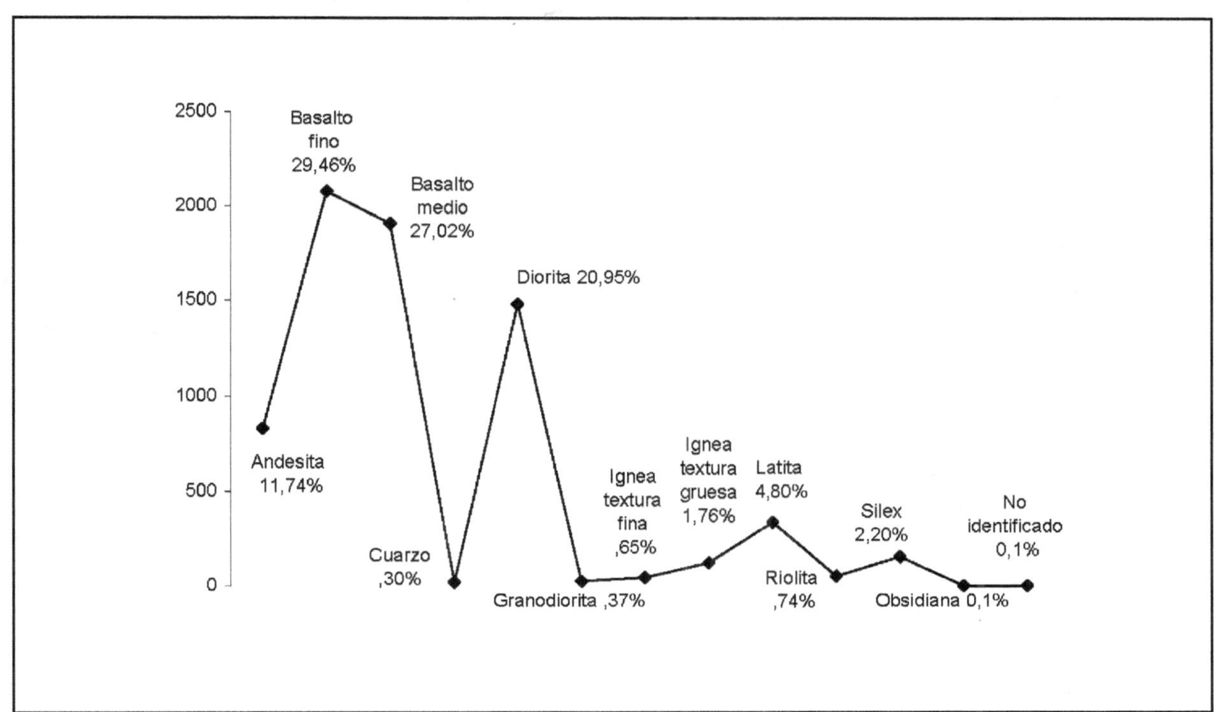

Figura 4.46. Frecuencia de materia prima en B4 (muestra 7061).

con huellas de uso (16.42 por ciento), nódulos retocados y lascas retocadas (10.45 por ciento cada una), fragmentos de nódulo con huellas de uso y núcleos (2.99 por ciento) y fragmentos de núcleo con huellas de uso y puntas de proyectil (1.99 por ciento cada uno) (Figura 4.47).

Por lo que respecta a las herramientas formalizadas y/o con un mayor grado de estandarización tecnológica tenemos las siguientes:

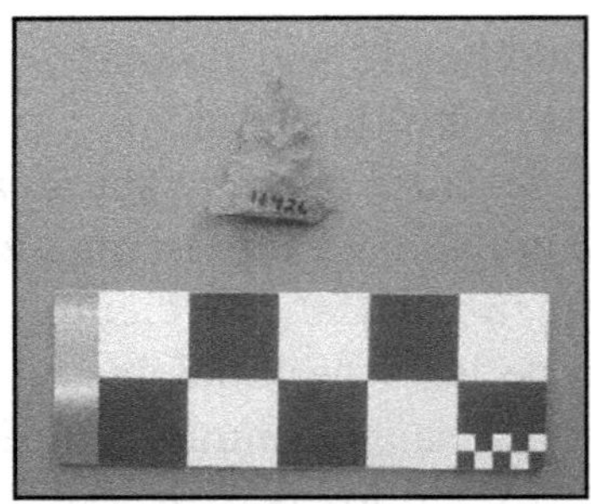

Figura 4.48. Punta de proyectil 16426.

Punta de proyectil (Figura 4.48).

Numero de bolsa: 16,426 Ubicación: Área B4 N106 E120. Largo: 2 cm; Espesor: 4 mm. Descripción general: punta de proyectil del período cerámico manufacturada en sílex con retoque bifacial total invasive. Por la fractura que presenta es posible que su abandono se haya debido a esa razón.

Figura 4.49. Bifacial 7716.

Bifacial.

(Figura 4.49). Numero de bolsa: 7,716; Ubicación: Área B4 N104 E122. Largo: 6 cm; Espesor: 7 mm. Descripción general: fragmento distal de bifacial probablemente

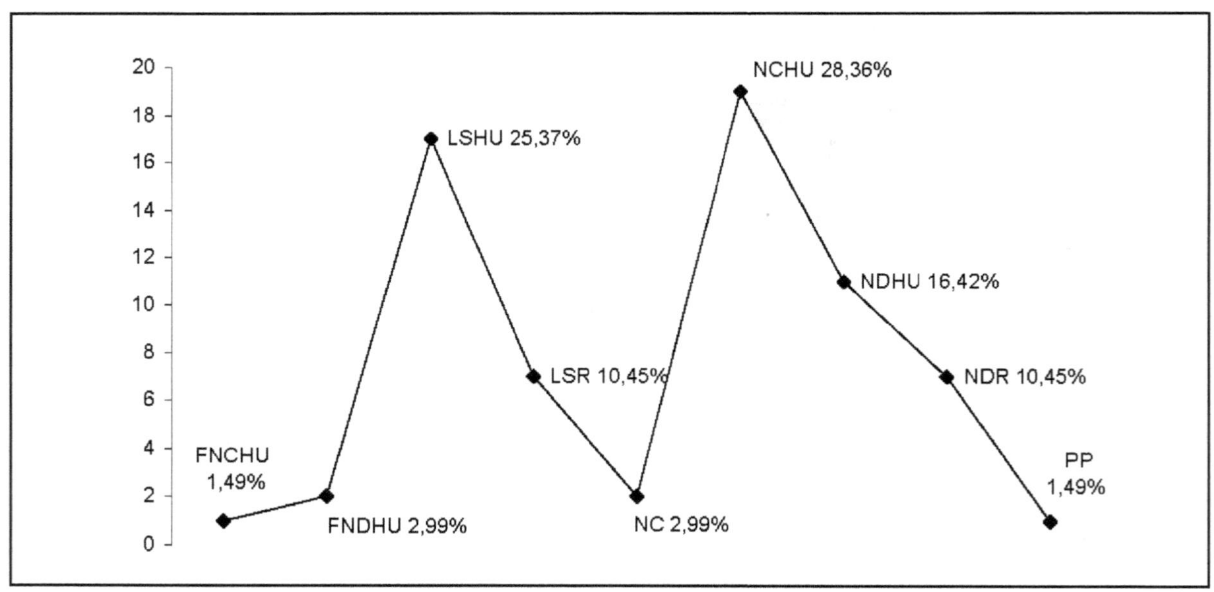

Figura 4.47. Frecuencia de herramientas en B4 (muestra 67).

Arcaico. Está manufacturado en basalto fino; presenta retoque bifacial bilateral invasivo discontinuo, y es posible que haya sido desechado por fractura.

Herramientas No Formales

Nódulo con huella de uso.

Numero de bolsa: 8,579; Ubicación: Área B4 N108 E106. Descripción general: artefacto unifuncional completo sobre nódulo de basalto fino, sin modificaciones de manufactura aparentes; presenta huellas de uso de percusión ubicadas en su sección lateral. No se observa reciclaje.

Fragmento de nódulo con huella de uso.

Numero de bolsa: 16,518; Ubicación: Área B4 N107 E119. Descripción general: artefacto unifuncional completo sobre fragmento de nódulo de basalto fino, sin modificaciones de manufactura aparentes; presenta huellas de uso de raspado ubicadas en la sección distal.

Núcleo.

Numero de bolsa: 8,311; Ubicación: Área B4 N108 E95. Descripción general: núcleo completo sobre nódulo de riolita, sin agotar con un 30 por ciento de cortex. No presenta ninguna alteración ajena, ni por retoque ni por modificación de huellas de uso.

Núcleo retocado.

Numero de bolsa: 7,933; Ubicación: Área B4 N105 E123. Descripción general: núcleo retocado completo sobre nódulo de diorita con 60 por ciento de cortex; presenta retoque unifacial distal invasivo continuo. No presenta huellas de uso aparente.

Lasca con huella de uso.

Numero de bolsa: 7,848; Ubicación: Área B4 N106 E90. Descripción general: lasca completa primaria de nódulo de basalto fino; presenta huellas de uso de corte y raspado ubicados en el área bilateral.

Área B5. La Cancha

Esta área presenta particularidades respecto al resto de las áreas del sitio ya que al parecer B5 se trató de una estructura de carácter cívico/ público sin evidencias de actividad habitacional. En lo referente a las materias primas encontradas tenemos los siguientes resultados. En esta área se recuperaron 5,864 artefactos líticos en total, con un peso de 45,929 g. De éstos, 5,799 fueron lascas sin huella de uso aparente con un peso de 28,171.5 g y 65 artefactos con huellas de uso que les dan carácter de herramientas, con un peso de 17,757.5 g. De acuerdo a la presencia de materia prima tenemos los siguientes: andesita 3.75 por ciento, basalto fino 24.66 por ciento, basalto medio 32.42 por ciento, cuarzo 1.82 por ciento, diorita 22.70 por ciento, granodiorita 1.02 por ciento, ígnea textura fina .51 por ciento, ígnea textura gruesa 3.56 por ciento, latita 4.09 por ciento, obsidiana 0 por ciento, riolita 1.04 por ciento y sílex 4.42 por ciento (Figura 4.50).

Nuevamente realizando la exclusión de las materias primas predominantes en todo el sitio, el resto se presenta de la siguiente manera. Los materiales predominantes son sílex (21.84 por ciento), latita (20.24 por ciento), andesita (18.55 por ciento) ígnea textura gruesa (17.62 por ciento); le sigue el cuarzo (9.02 por ciento), riolita (5.14 por ciento, granodiorita (5.06 por ciento) y finalmente la ígnea textura fina (2.53 por ciento). Estos materiales representan las características en esta estructura al interior.

Nos permitimos así mismo realizar el análisis de los materiales registrados al inte-

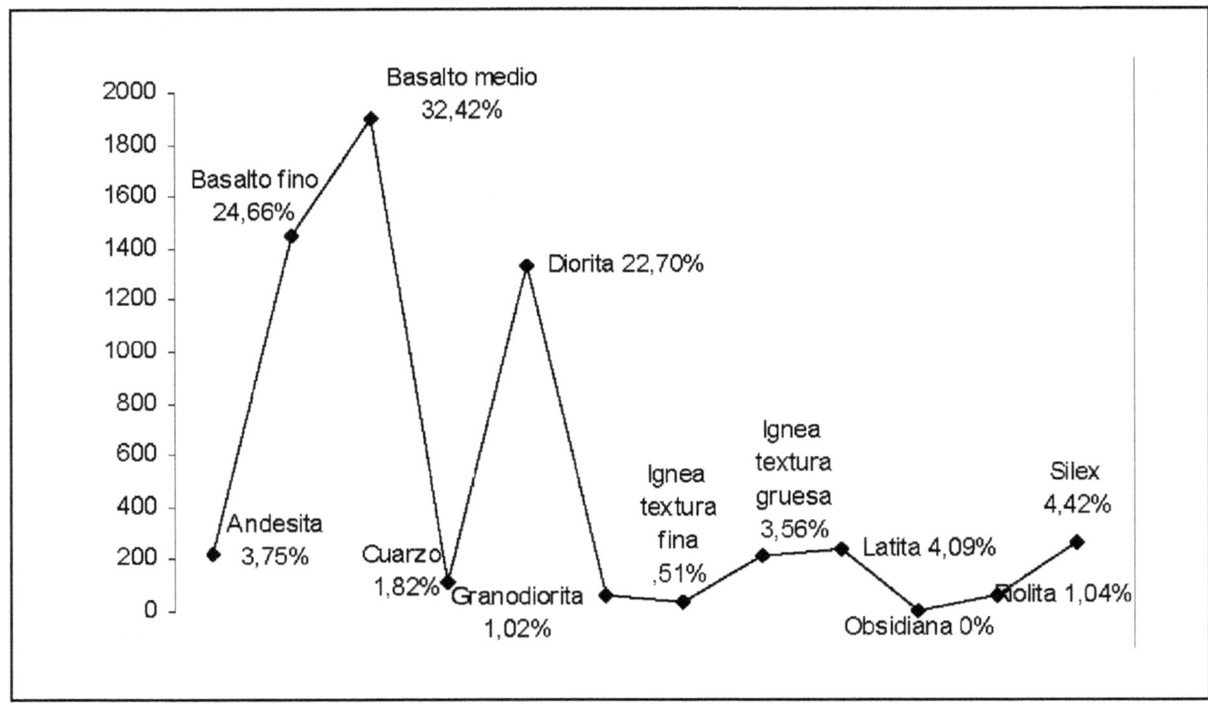

Figura 4.50. Frecuencia de materia prima en B5 (muestra 5864).

rior de la construcción 8.4 la cual se localiza en la parte central de La Cancha. Los resultados indican exactamente lo expresado en las gráficas de arriba; por ello, omito ponerlas nuevamente. Una mínima diferencia es que al interior de esta estructura se presenta un alto porcentaje de ígnea textura gruesa (32.99 por ciento), pero no es indicativa de nada pues es puro desecho de talla, evidentemente siendo parte del desbaste de las rocas. No hay ningún tipo de herramientas al interior de ésta.

Herramientas

En B5 La Cancha se registró el 4 por ciento de herramientas en el sitio, es decir, 42 piezas. Dentro de ellas las más numerosas fueron los nódulos con huellas de uso siendo más de la mitad del total de herramientas para esta área (58.38 por ciento); el valor más alto que le siguen son las lascas con huellas de uso (28.57 por ciento) (Figura 4.51).

Por lo que respecta a las herramientas formalizadas y/o con un mayor grado de estandarización tecnológica tenemos las siguientes:

Punta de proyectil (Figura 4.52).

Numero de bolsa: 24,765; Ubicación: Área B5 N105 E227. Largo: 2 cm; Espesor 3 mm. Descripción general: punta de proyectil triangular de muescas laterales en sílex. Está elaborada sobre una lasca y aparentemente fue desechada dentro del proceso de manufactura.

Un dato que no debe pasar por alto es también la presencia de un buen número de nódulos con huellas de uso (52.38 por ciento) o sea 22 artefactos. Por las huellas de uso que presenta la mayoría de ellos, nos permite inferir que fueron utilizados como instrumentos de percussion. Sin embargo, al no estar asociados con otro tipo de materiales, nuestra conclusión preliminar es que se trata de evidencias de derrumbe.

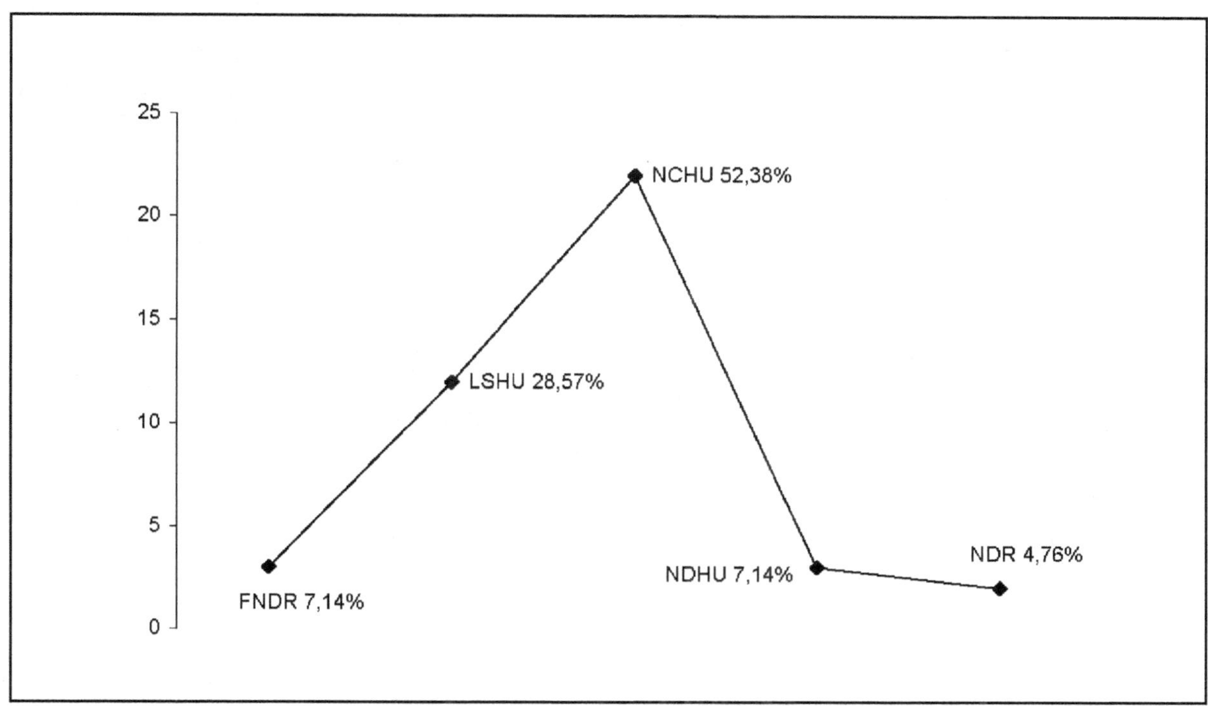

Figura 4.51. Frecuencia de herramientas en B5 (muestra 42).

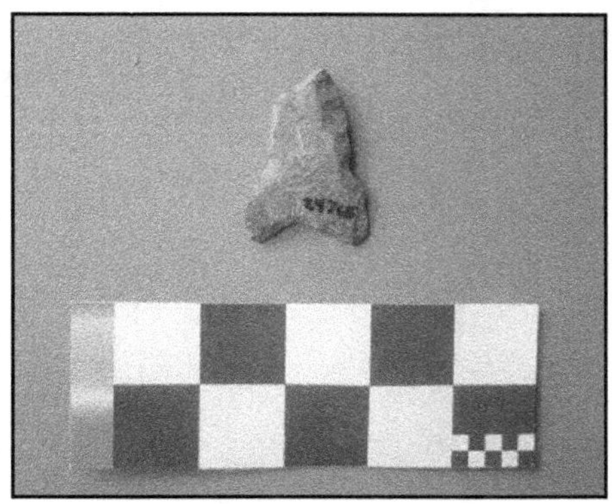

Figura 4.52. Punta de proyectil 24765.

Una interrogante interesante presenta esta area. Debido a que no hay evidencia de actividades habitacionales y/o de otra índole que pudiesen dejar algún tipo de restos materiales, y debido también a que su apisonado fue preparado con una tipo de tierra distinto, se podría suponer que todos los materiales recolectados son de arrastre. En efecto, los materiales registrados se encuentran homogéneamente distribuidos en toda el área, y aún, en la única estructura al interior de La Cancha (C8.4) tampoco presenta una agrupación de materiales específicos. Por su ubicación en la parte baja del área B y por sus propias características argumentamos que este espacio fue el principal receptor del derrumbe proveniente de otras areas. Así mismo, cabe destacar que los materiales comunes en todo el sitio también se encuentran presentes aquí; hay alta presencia de basaltos y de diorita los cuales, como ya argumentamos fueron parte del desbaste de las rocas para construir los muros correspondientes. El único artefacto diagnóstico que detectamos en La Cancha es una punta de proyectil cuya manufactura es tan irregular que sólo nos permite relacionarla con las puntas con muescas laterales que ya hemos descrito en A1. Sin embargo, debe considerarse que es tan solo un elemento aislado del que no podemos desprender otra serie de argumentaciones más que su simple descripción en esta área.

Área B6. Bienes Terminados en Concha con Arquitectura Especializada

Lo que podemos observar en el Área B6 es que se trata de un área donde el uso del espacio se ha especializado, las habitaciones son sólidas y presentan accesos controlados, no existe actividad habitacional de una unidad familiar y consideramos que se debe tratar de un área donde se controla la manufactura de la concha.

Así mismo está área es la que mayor densidad de materiales presenta (#28380) siendo el 21 por ciento de los registrados, o sea casi una cuarta parte del total recuperado. Como ya observamos, la distribución de materiales por materia prima corresponde a las mismas características de otros sectores. En esta área de excavación fue en la que se encontró mayor densidad de material lítico tallado ya que se obtuvo un total de 28,380 artefactos con un peso de 367,396.2 g. De ellos, 27,967 fueron lascas sin huella de uso aparente con un peso de 261,966 g y 362 herramientas con 105,430.2 g de peso. En términos generales el material en esta área presenta un comportamiento homogéneo de acuerdo a la presencia de materia prima como a continuación se expone: andesita 1.48 por ciento, basalto fino 22.34 por ciento, basalto medio 47.50 por ciento, cuarzo .88 por ciento, diorita 21.23 por ciento, granodiorita .36 por ciento, ígnea textura fina.12 por ciento, ígnea textura gruesa 1.35 por ciento, latita 2.25 por ciento, obsidiana.01 por ciento, riolita .55 por ciento, sílex 1.92 por ciento y no identificada .01 por ciento (Figura 4.53).

Realizando una disección de estos materiales y excluyendo los tres materiales presentes en todo el sitio, los valores de los materiales restantes permiten un nivel de análisis a otra escala. En realidad los resultados se mantienen y lo único que cambia es la expresión gráfica y su visualización en términos porcentuales. En este sentido los valores más altos son para la andesita (16.61 por ciento), la latita (25.21 por ciento) y el sílex (21.54 por ciento).

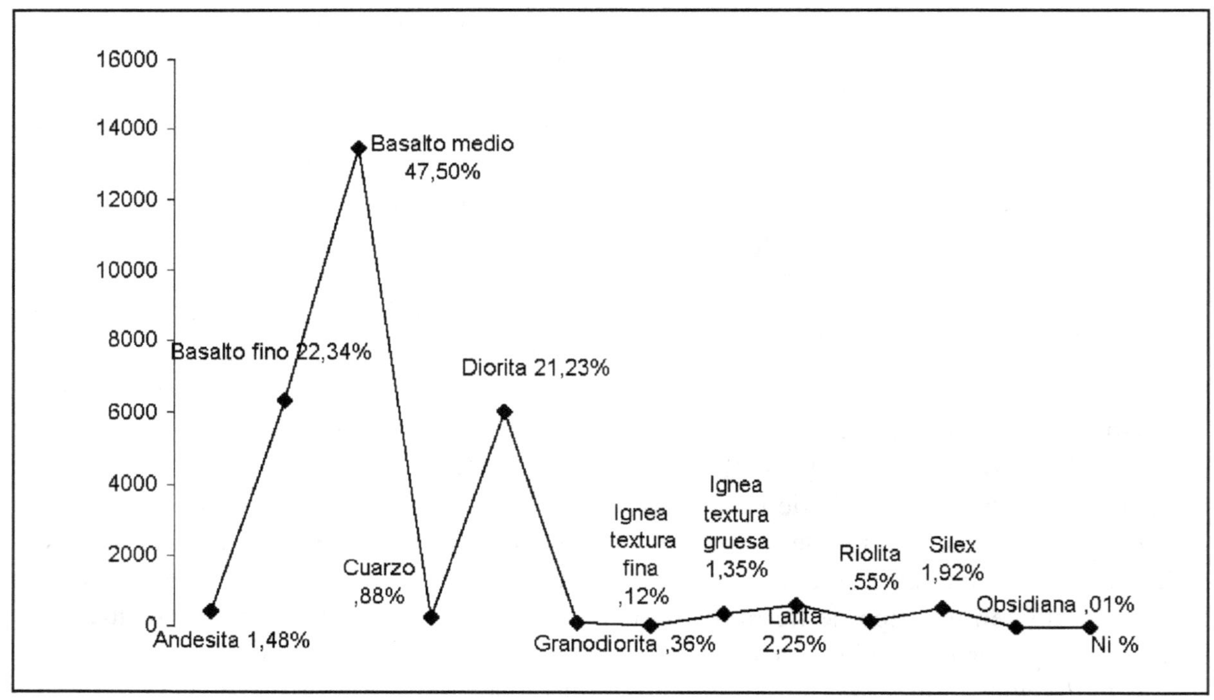

Figura 4.53. Frecuencia de materia prima en B6 (muestra 28380).

Herramientas

En B6 se registraron la mayor cantidad de herramientas en todo el sitio representado, el 32 por ciento es decir, 362 piezas. Dentro de ellas las más numerosas fueron los nódulos con huellas de uso siendo casi la mitad del total de herramientas para esta área (41.44); los dos valores más altos que le siguen a esta son las lascas con huellas de uso (24.31 por ciento), los nódulos retocados (20.99 por ciento) (Figura 4.54).

En cuanto a herramientas formales tenemos muy pocas si las comparamos con la gran cantidad de herramientas de tecnología de uso inmediato; a continuación las describimos:

Punta de proyectil (Figura 4.55).

Numero de bolsa: 29,807; Ubicación: Área B6 N108 E229. Largo: 3 cm. Descripción general: fragmento medial de punta de proyectil manufacturada en cuarzo con retoque bifacial bilateral invasivo continuo.

Punta de proyectil (Figura 4.56).

Numero de bolsa: 31,624; Ubicación: Área B6 N119 E242. Largo: 3 cm; Espesor: 5 mm. Descripción general: fragmento de posible punta de proyectil sobre lasca de sílex aparentemente en proceso de elaboración, no presenta retoque.

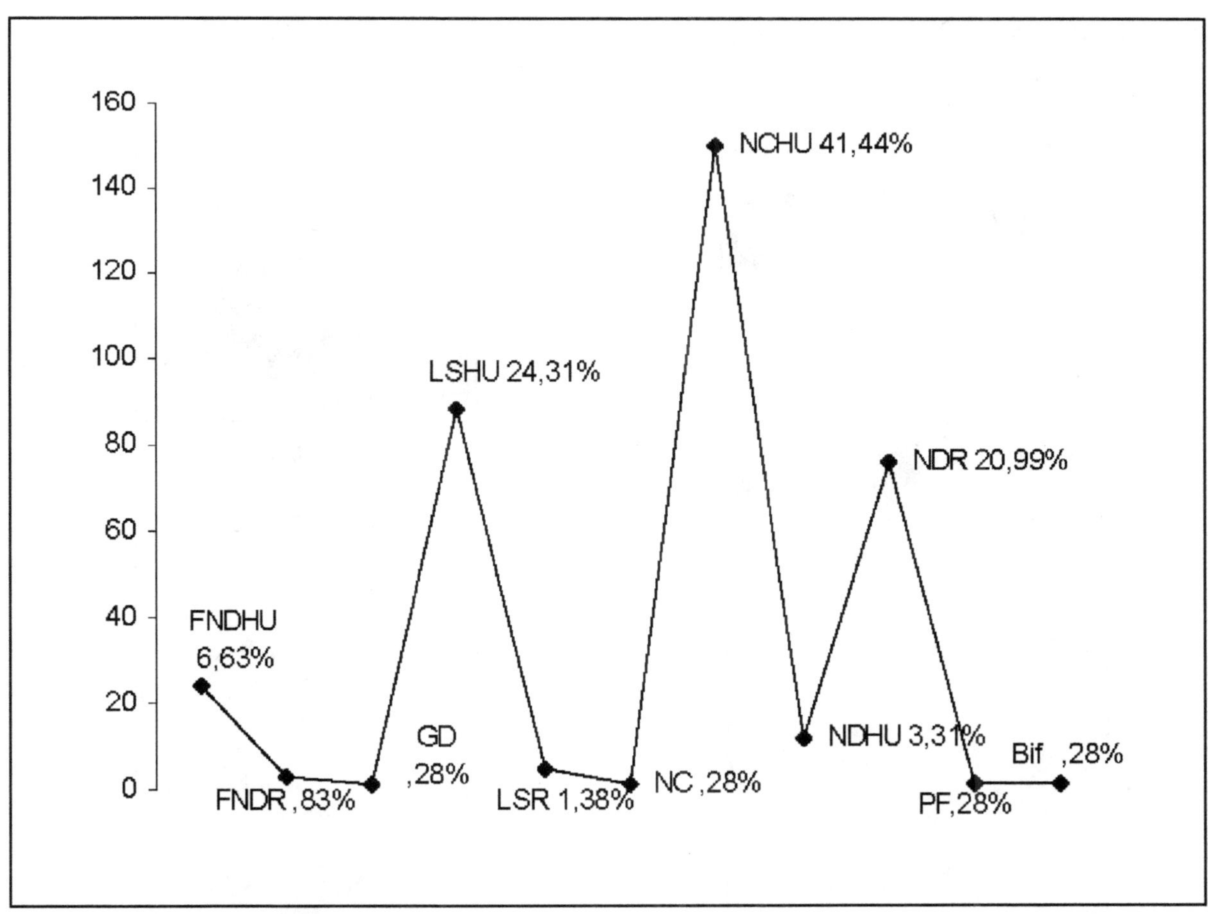

Figura 4.54. Frecuencia de herramientas en B6 (muestra 362).

Bifacial.

Numero de bolsa: 31,609; Ubicación: Área B6 N115 E233. Largo: 9 cm; Espesor 28 mm. Descripción general: bifacial completo manufacturado en diorita, presenta retoque bifacial total invasivo continuo.

Grabador.

Numero de bolsa: 22,567; Ubicación: Área B6 N108 E225. Largo: 6 cm; Espesor: 6 mm. Descripción general: grabador completo en diorite. No presenta ningún tipo de retoque; unifuncional, con huella de uso en la parte distal aparentemente para hacer incisiones.

Bifacial (Figura 4.57).

Numero de bolsa: 22,771; Ubicación: Área B6 N105 E218. Largo: 6 cm; Espesor: 4 mm. Descripción general: bifacial paleoindio manufacturado en sílex con retoque bifacial bilateral invasivo continuo. Probablemente se trata de un cuchillo Clovis en forma de laurel, de base lateral pulida, con un buen trabajo de adelgazamiento; es posible que haya estado expuesto a calor antes de ser lasqueado.

Grabador (Figura 4.58).

Numero de bolsa: 22,826; Ubicación: Área B6 N110 E217. Largo: 6 cm; Espesor: 11 mm. Descripción general: grabador completo en basalto fino. No presenta ningún tipo de retoque; unifuncional, con huella de uso en la parte distal aparentemente para hacer incisiones.

Figura 4.55. Punta de proyectil 29807.

Figura 4.56. Punta de proyectil 31624.

Figura 4.57. Bifacial 22771.

Figura 4.58. Grabador 22826.

Perforador.

Numero de bolsa: 22,965; Ubicación: Área B6 N118 E214. Largo: 3 cm; Espesor: 6 mm. Descripción general: perforador fragmentado manufacturado en diorite. Presenta retoque bifacial bilateral total invasivo continuo; unifuncional con huella de uso en la parte distal.

Herramientas No Formales

Nódulo con huella de uso.

Numero de bolsa: 20,869; Ubicación: Área B6 N106 E220. Descripción general: artefacto unifuncional completo sobre nódulo de latita, sin modificaciones de manufactura aparentes. Presenta huellas de uso de percusión ubicadas en las secciones distal, proximal y lateral. No se observa reciclaje.

Nódulo retocado (Figura 4.59).

Numero de bolsa: 20,664 Ubicación: Área B6 N106 E219. Descripción general: artefacto multifuncional completo sobre nódulo de materia prima no identificada, presenta retoque unifacial distal invasivo continuo. Se observan huellas de uso de raspado y percusión ubicadas en la parte distal y proximal.

Núcleo con huella de uso.

Numero de bolsa: 28,563; Ubicación: Área B6 N117 E211. Descripción general: núcleo completo de diorita sin presencia de cortex. Presenta huellas de uso de percusión ubicadas de manera generalizado e irregular.

Lasca con huella de uso (Figura 4.60).

Numero de bolsa: 31,328; Ubicación: Área B6 N116 E243. Descripción general: lasca completa secundaria circular de nódulo de basalto medio. Artefacto multifuncional ya que presenta huellas de uso de percusión, corte por desgaste y raspado ubicados en el área marginal total.

Área B7

Área habitacional de mucha intensidad. Mayor cantidad de cerámica decorada y la mayor cantidad de artefactos terminados de concha como anillos, brazaletes y cuentas. Dentro de esta área de excavación se recuperaron 10,609 artefactos en total con un peso de 77,965.2 g. De ellos, 10,477 fueron lascas sin huella de uso aparente con un peso de 54,048.5 g y como herramientas tuvimos 124 con 23,916.7 g de peso. La distribución de acuerdo a su materia prima es la siguiente: andesita 1.16 por ciento, basalto fino 20.47 por ciento, basalto medio

Figura 4.59. Nódulo con huella de uso 20664.

Figura 4.60. Lasca con huella de uso 31328.

55.28 por ciento, cuarzo .67 por ciento, diorita 17.27 por ciento, granodiorita .22 por ciento, ígnea textura fina .08 por ciento, ígnea textura gruesa .49 por ciento, latita 1.95 por ciento, riolita .49 por ciento y sílex 1.91 por ciento (Figura 4.61).

Antes de continuar me gustaría exponer los resultados del análisis de Jacal 5.

De acuerdo a las herramientas la presencia es la siguiente: lascas con huellas de uso (61.54 por ciento), fragmentos de nódulo con huellas de uso (11.54 por ciento), núcleo con huellas de uso (11.54 por ciento), nódulo retocado (7.69 por ciento), fragmento de nódulo retocado (3.85 por ciento) y grabador (3.85 por ciento) (Figura 4.62).

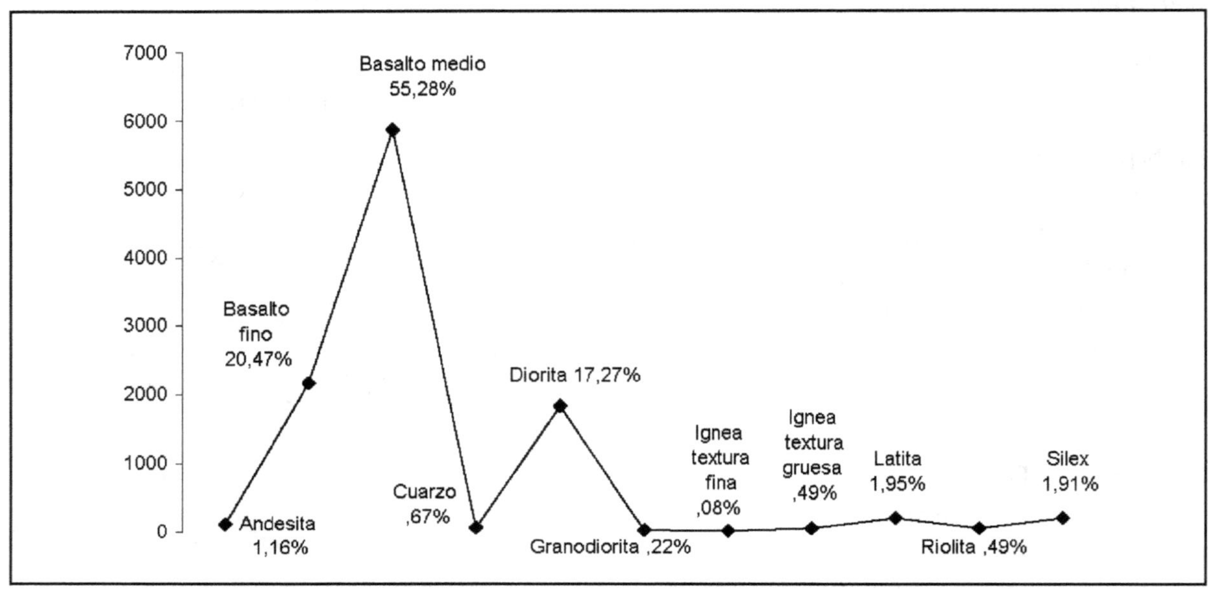

Figura 4.61. Frecuencia de materia prima en B7 (muestra 10609).

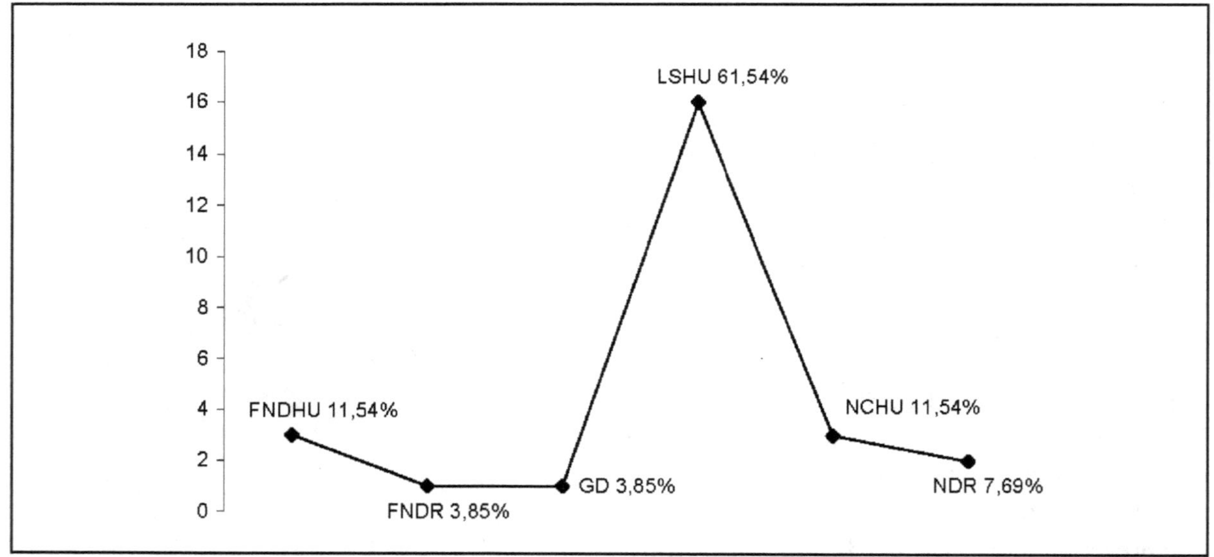

Figura 4.62. Herramientas al interior de Jacal 5 (muestra 26).

Herramientas

Respecto a las herramientas los porcentajes son los siguientes: lascas con huellas de uso (54.84 por ciento), núcleo con huellas de uso (17.74 por ciento), nódulos retocados (14.52 por ciento), fragmentos de nódulos con huellas de uso (5.65 por ciento), nódulos con huellas de uso (4.03 por ciento), fragmentos de nódulos retocados (1.61 por ciento), grabador y puntas de proyectil (.81 por ciento cada uno) (Figura 4.63).

Por lo que respecta a las herramientas formalizadas y/o con un mayor grado de estandarización tecnológica, tenemos las siguientes:

Punta de proyectil (Figura 4.64).

Numero de bolsa: 21,109; Ubicación: Área B7 N102 E290. Largo: 6 cm; Espesor: 5 mm.

Descripción general: punta de proyectil completa manufacturada en riolita, probablemente del arcaico tardío; presenta retoque bifacial bilateral invasivo continuo.

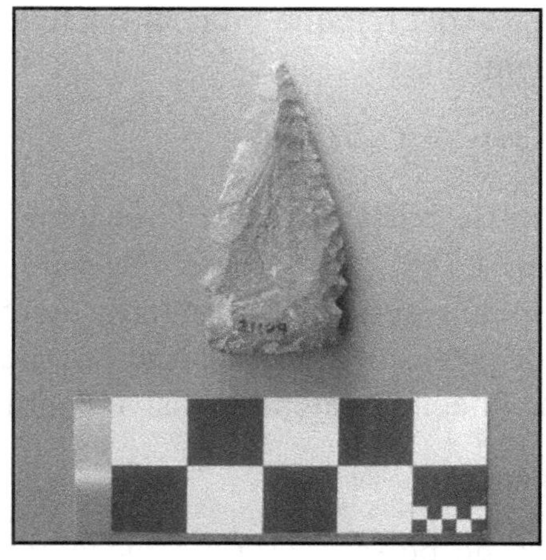

Figura 4.64. Punta de proyectil 21109.

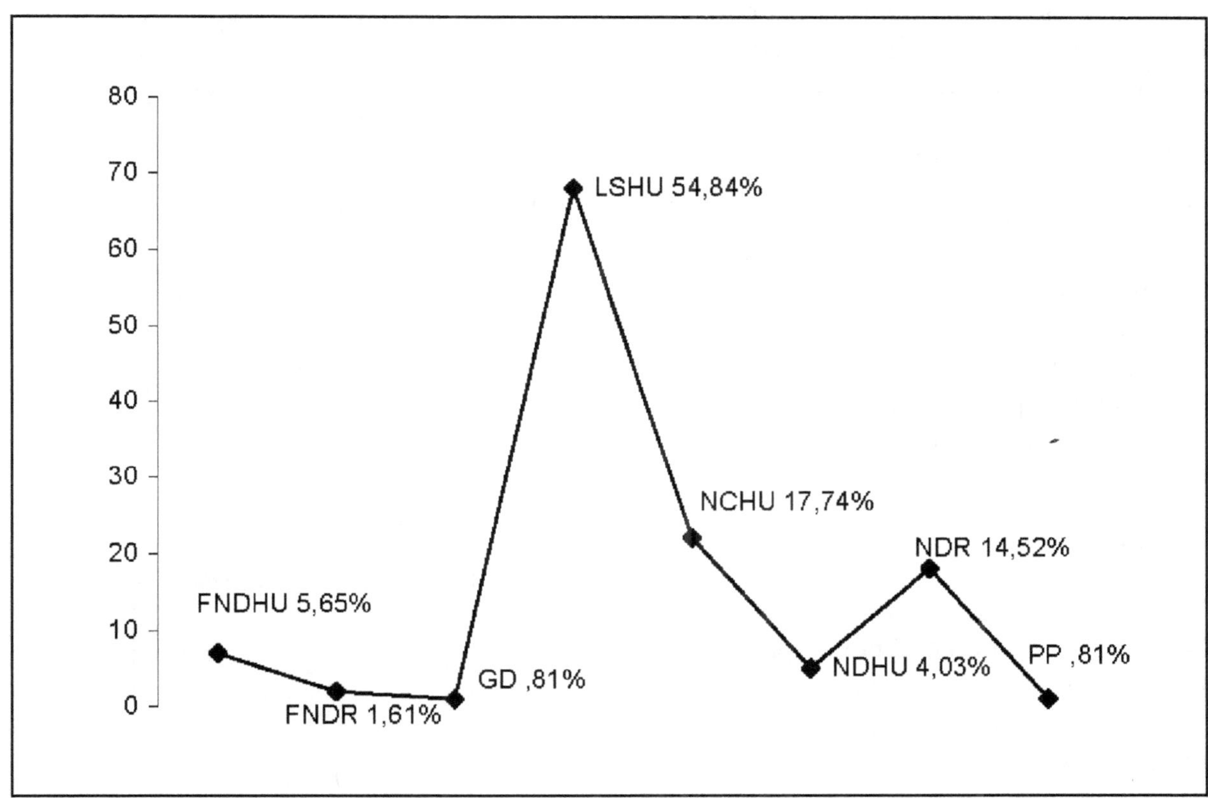

Figura 4.63. Frecuencia de herramientas en B7 (muestra 124).

Punta de proyectil (Figura 4.65).

Numero de bolsa: 21,479; Ubicación: Área B7 N99 E294. Largo: 6 cm; Espesor 5 mm. Descripción general: punta de proyectil tipo Ciénega aserrada, sin base, manufacturada en sílex; presenta retoque bifacial bilateral marginal denticulado.

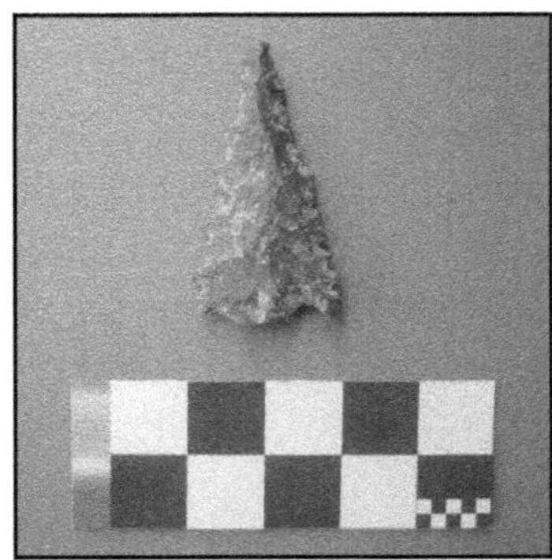

Figura 4.65. Punta de proyectil 21479.

Punta de proyectil (Figura 4.66).

Numero de bolsa: 23,152; Ubicación: Área B7 N107 E288. Largo: 3 cm; Espesor: 5 mm. Descripción general: fragmento medial de punta de proyectil manufacturada en sílex con retoque bifacial bilateral invasivo continuo.

Figura 4.66. Punta de proyectil 23152.

Punta de proyectil (Figura 4.67).

Numero de bolsa: 23,272; Ubicación: Área B7 N105 E291. Largo: 6 cm; Espesor: 6 mm. Descripción general: punta de proyectil completa tipo Ciénega manufacturada en basalto fino; presenta retoque bifacial bilateral invasivo continuo, se encuentra despuntada.

Figura 4.67. Punta de proyectil 23272.

Punta de proyectil (Figura 4.68).

Numero de bolsa: 23,492; Ubicación: Área B7 N104 E306. Largo: 3 cm; Espesor: 8mm. Descripción general: fragmento distal de punta de proyectil posiblemente del Arcaico (temprano o medio), manufacturada en sílex; presenta retoque bifacial bilateral invasivo continuo, y aparentemente un intento de rejuvenecimiento.

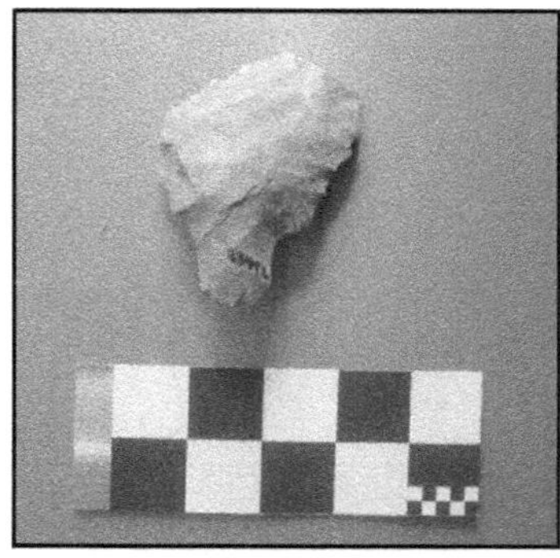

Figura 4.68. Punta de proyectil 23492.

Grabador.

Numero de bolsa: 23,112; Ubicación: Área B7 N102 E296. Largo: 2 cm; Espesor: 4 mm. Descripción general: grabador fragmentado en sílex; presenta retoque unifacial bilateral marginal continuo, posiblemente en proceso de elaboración. Unifuncional, con huella de uso en la parte distal aparentemente para hacer incisiones.

Perforador.

Numero de bolsa: 21,121; Ubicación: Área B7 N106 E287. Largo: 2 cm; Espesor: 4 mm. Descripción general: fragmento proximal de perforador manufacturado en cuarzo; presenta retoque unifacial bilateral invasivo continuo. No presenta huella de uso aparente, y es probable que se encuentre en proceso de manufactura.

Herramientas No Formales

Nódulo retocado.

Numero de bolsa: 27,091; Ubicación: Área B7 N103 E281. Descripción general: artefacto unifucional completo sobre nódulo de basalto medio; presenta retoque bifacial distal marginal continuo. No se observan huellas de uso aparentes.

Fragmento de nódulo con huella de uso.

Numero de bolsa: 23,046; Ubicación: Área B7 N104 E283. Descripción general: artefacto unifuncional completo sobre fragmento de nódulo de diorita, sin modificaciones de manufactura aparentes; presenta huellas de uso de raspado ubicadas en su extremo distal.

Lasca retocada con huella de uso.

Numero de bolsa: 21,102; Ubicación: Área B7 N101 E290. Descripción general: lasca completa primaria circular de nódulo de basalto fino, presenta retoque unifacial proximal invadiente continuo. Se observan huella uso de raspado ubicados en el área marginal parcial.

Si bien esta área se caracterizó por tener la mayor densidad de materiales arqueológicos, es realmente interesante que la deposición de materiales líticos no refleje esta constante, es decir, de acuerdo a los porcentajes de presencia de lítica, esta área presenta apenas el 8 por ciento del total. Es importante mencionar así mismo que B7 es el segundo índice más alto; el primero lo ocupa el área B6 cuyo porcentaje alcanza el 21 por ciento del total de materiales registrados. Lo anterior también se refleja en la proporción de las herramientas. Es decir, B6 es en donde se encuentra la mayor cantidad siendo B7 uno de los porcentajes bajos en todo el sitio (11 por ciento).

Áreas B8, B9 y B10. El Mirador

Debemos recordar que si bien esta área la componen 3 sectores diferentes (B8, B9 y B10), su agrupación como El Mirador, obedece a su posición y a sus características generales. Sin embargo, también hemos de mencionar que pese que en esta área se registró como un conjunto, la presencia de materiales al interior de cada una de estas áreas es distinta. De un total de 10,071 fragmentos, es B8 la que mayor cantidad de lítica tallada presenta (60 por ciento); le sigue B9 (27 por ciento) y finalmente B10 (13 por ciento). El peso total de las tres áreas alcanza 79,289.2 g.

El material en esta área presenta un comportamiento homogéneo de acuerdo a la presencia de materia prima; tenemos los siguientes: andesita 1 por ciento, basalto fino 19.36 por ciento, basalto medio 55.52 por ciento, cuarzo .19 por ciento, diorita 19.31 por ciento, granodiorita .07 por ciento, ígnea textura fina .01 por ciento, ígnea textura gruesa .09 por ciento, latita 2.30 por ciento, obsidiana 0 por ciento, riolita .09 por ciento y sílex 2.06 por ciento (Figura 4.69).

Realizando una disección de estos materiales y excluyendo los tres materiales presentes en todo el sitio, los valores de los materiales restantes permiten un nivel de análisis a otra escala. En realidad los resultados se mantienen, lo único que cambia es la expresión gráfica y su visualización en términos porcentuales. En este

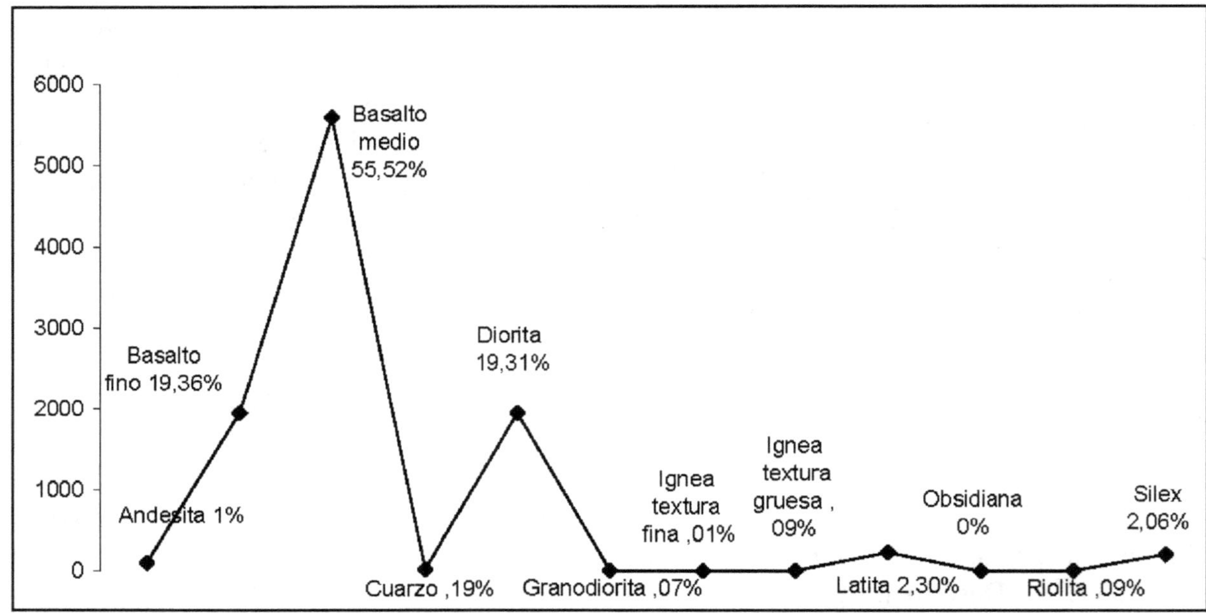

Figura 4.69. Frecuencia de materia prima en El Mirador (muestra 10071).

sentido los valores más altos son para la latita (39.66 por ciento), el sílex (35.38 por ciento) y la andesita (17.26 por ciento).

Herramientas

En El Mirador se registró uno de los porcentajes más bajos de herramientas por área (considerando que se reúnen B8, B9 y B10), el 5 por ciento de herramientas en el sitio, es decir, 52 piezas.

En B8 la distribución es la siguiente: nódulos retocados (53.43 por ciento), nódulos con huella de uso (25 por ciento), fragmentos de nódulo con huella de uso, nódulos con huella de uso y lascas con huellas de uso (6.25 por ciento cada uno), y finalmente fragmentos de nódulo retocado (3.13 por ciento).

Por lo que respecta a las herramientas formalizadas y/o con un mayor grado de estandarización tecnológica tenemos las siguientes:

Punta de proyectil (Figura 4.70).

Numero de bolsa: 28,075; Ubicación: B8 N105 E291. Largo: 6 cm; Espesor: 6 mm. Descripción general: punta de proyectil del Arcaico medio en basalto medio. Por su forma, tamaño y técnica de manufactura indudablemente se trata de una forma asociada al período arcaico, por el momento aún no ha sido identificada con algún tipo en especifico.

Figura 4.70. Punta de proyectil 28075.

Punta de proyectil (Figura 4.71).

Numero de bolsa: 30,017; Ubicación: B8 N98 E292. Largo: 2 cm; Espesor: 6 mm. Descripción general: punta de proyectil de período

Figura 4.71. Punta de proyectil 30017.

cerámico manufacturada en cuarzo; aparentemente fue desechada dentro del proceso de manufactura.

Punta de proyectil (Figura 4.72).

Numero de bolsa: 30,008; Ubicación: B8 N103 E295. Largo: 2 cm; Espesor: 3 mm. Descripción general: punta de proyectil triangular de muescas laterales manufacturada en latita, posiblemente fue desechada dentro del proceso de manufactura.

Punta de proyectil (Figura 4.73).

Numero de bolsa: 27,456; Ubicación: B8 N101 E288, Largo: 3 cm; Espesor: 3 mm. Descripción general: punta de proyectil de muescas laterales en latita. Punta cuya morfología es parecida a la *Classic flanged* (1050-1150 d.C.) (Sliva 1997). Es una de las puntas cuya morfología es perfectamente discernible. Sin duda asociada a periodos cerámicos.

Punta de proyectil (Figura 4.74).

Numero de bolsa: 28,189; Ubicación: B8 N104 E297. Largo: 2 cm; Espesor: 3 mm. Descripción general: punta de proyectil sobre lasca de riolita del período ceramic; aparentemente se encontraba en proceso de manufactura.

Punta de proyectil (Figura 4.75).

Numero de bolsa: 28,245; Ubicación: B8 N102 E284. Largo: 2 cm; Espesor: 2 mm.

Figura 4.72. Punta de proyectil 30008.

Figura 4.73. Punta de proyectil 27456.

Figura 4.74. Punta de proyectil 28189.

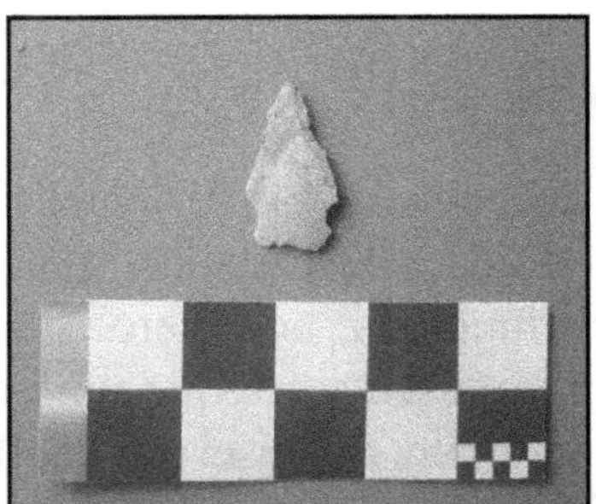

Figura 4.75. Punta de proyectil 28245.

Descripción general: punta de proyectil de período cerámico manufacturada en sílex; aparentemente no se encuentra terminada y parece estar desechada dentro del proceso de manufactura.

Punta de proyectil (Figura 4.76).

Numero de bolsa: 32,098; Ubicación: B9 N298 E416. Largo: 6 cm; Espesor: 7 mm. Descripción general: extremo proximal de punta de proyectil San Pedro de basalto fino; según su morfología se ubica del 1200 al 600 aC. (Sliva 1997).

Figura 4.76. Punta de proyectil 32098.

Punta de proyectil (Figura 4.77).

Numero de bolsa: 30,197; Ubicación: B9 N297 E418. Largo: 2 cm; Espesor: 6 mm. Descripción general: extremo proximal de punta de proyectil en sílex, en proceso. Podría traerse también de un taladro y no precisamente de una punta.

Figura 4.77. Punta de proyectil 30197.

Punta de proyectil (Figura 4.78).

Numero de bolsa: 32,358; Ubicación: B10 N406 E512. Largo: 3 cm; Espesor: 6 mm. Descripción general: punta de proyectil de período cerámico posiblemente temprano manufacturado en ígnea de textura fina. Nota: Morfología similar a una de las variantes de las puntas Ciénega. Según Sliva (1997), su rango temporal es de 400 a.C. al 550 d.C.

Figura 4.78. Punta de proyectil 32358.

Herramientas No Formales

Nódulo retocado.

Numero de bolsa: 27,370; Ubicación: Área B8 N104 E281. Descripción general: artefacto multifuncional completo sobre nódulo de andesita, presenta retoque unifacial distal invasivo continuo. Se observan huellas de uso de raspado, corte por desgaste y percusión ubicadas en las secciones distal y bilateral.

Núcleo con huella de uso (Figura 4.79).

Numero de bolsa: 28,493; Ubicación: Área B8 N99 E287. Descripción general: núcleo completo sobre nódulo de basalto fino con escasa evidencia de cortex; presenta huellas de uso de corte por desgaste y raspado ubicada en la parte marginal total.

De las 9 puntas de proyectil detectadas en

esta área, 4 están completas y su morfología es distinguible con cierta certidumbre; las cinco restantes son puntas en proceso de manufactura. De las 4 completas tres de ellas corresponden al período Arcaico y una solamente al período Cerámico. Las cinco restantes, pese a que se encuentran en proceso, podemos decir que se trata de puntas correspondientes a los períodos cerámicos tardíos. Lo que ahora no podemos contester, que permanece como interrogante, es la presencia de puntas de proyectil del Arcaico; en contextos fechados posteriores a 1300 d.C. Probablemente se trate de una especie de coleccionismo durante la época prehispánica. En términos generales se propone que las tres áreas que componen El Mirador tienen funciones diferentes: B8 se considera como un área administrativa con la presencia de pipas y de cerámica decorada foránea; B9 parece ser un área habitacional debido a al presencia de un jacal; y finalmente B10, debido a la baja presencia de materiales, se interpretó como una plataforma para actividades no domésticas. Uno de los problemas que se presentó a este nivel de análisis es que no existe una correspondencia del material lítico con estas hipótesis, es decir, la distribución de la materia prima se comporta de forma completamente homogénea. La distribución tanto al interior de las terrazas como al interior del jacal, es prácticamente la misma, por lo que habría que buscar otras variables y no sólo uno de ellos como lo es la materia prima.

Figura 4.79. Núcleo con Huella de uso 28493.

Área B11. Área habitacional

En el área B11 tuvimos un total de 7,959 artefactos con un peso de 68,160.6 g. El material analizado para esta área equivale al 6 por ciento del total registrado. De acuerdo a la presencia de materia prima tenemos lo siguiente, andesita .62 por ciento, basalto fino 19.09 por ciento, basalto medio 48.27 por ciento, cuarzo 1.41 por ciento, diorita 21.35 por ciento, granodiorita .09 por ciento, ígnea textura fina .08 por ciento, ígnea textura gruesa .90 por ciento, latita 2.74 por ciento, riolita .34 por ciento y sílex 5.13 por ciento (Figura 4.80).

Herramientas

Respecto a las herramientas en esta área podemos decir que del total del sitio, a B11 corresponde tan solo el 3 por ciento (34 piezas). Entre estas herramientas predominan los núcleos con huella de uso (35.29 por ciento), lascas con huellas de uso (23.53 por ciento), nódulos retocados (20.59 por ciento), fragmentos de nódulos con huellas de uso (8.82 por ciento), nódulos con huellas de uso (5.88 por ciento), lascas retocadas (2.94 por ciento) y puntas de proyectil (2.94 por ciento) (Figura 4.81).

Por lo que respecta a las herramientas formalizadas y/o con un mayor grado de estandarización tecnológica, tenemos las siguientes:

Punta de proyectil (Figura 4.82).

Numero de bolsa: 33,035; Ubicación: Área

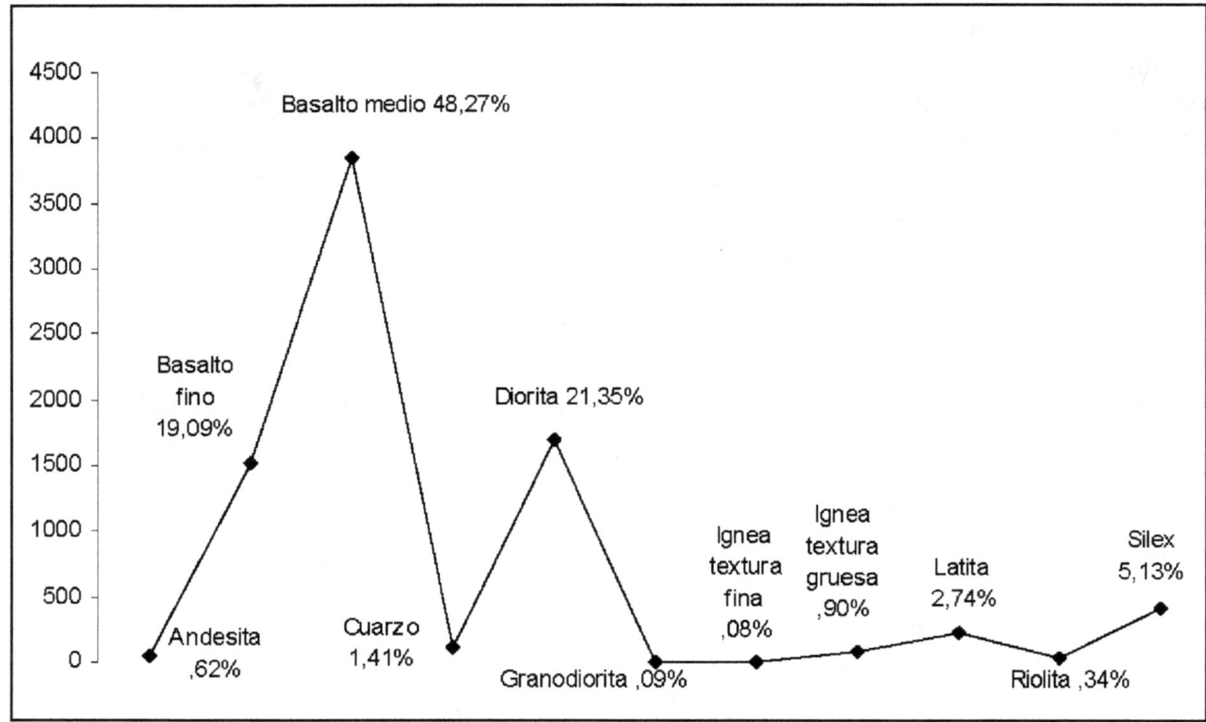

Figura 4.80. Frecuencia de materia prima en B11 (muestra 7959).

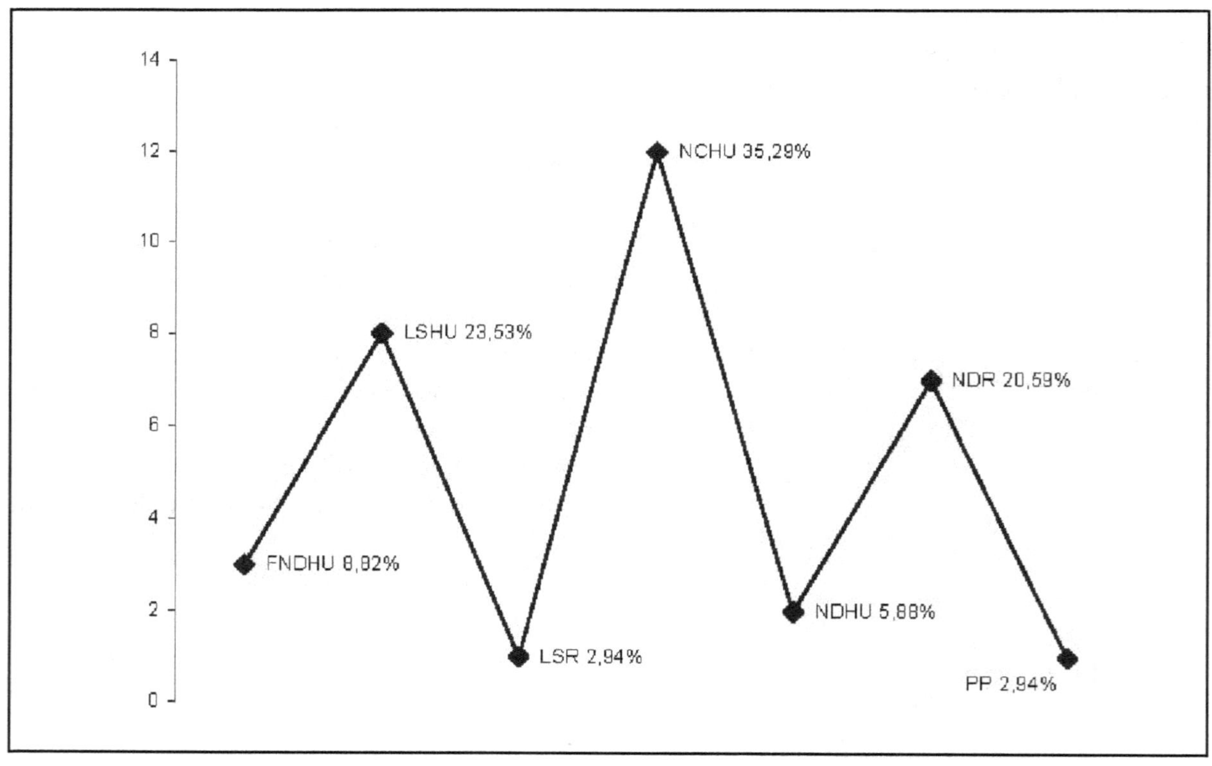

Figura 4.81. Frecuencia de herramientas en B11 (muestra 34).

B11 N107 E319. Largo: 2 cm; Espesor: 4 mm. Descripción general: punta de proyectil completa manufacturada en basalto fino. Presenta retoque bifacial bilateral invasivo continuo. Se encuentra despuntada y posiblemente fue desechada durante su proceso de elaboración.

Perforador (Figura 4.83).

Numero de bolsa: 33,275; Ubicación: Área B11 N106 E323. Largo: 2 cm; Espesor: 4 mm. Descripción general: perforador similar a los tipo Hohokam en basalto fino.

Área D

En esta área de excavación se obtuvieron 4,881 artefactos con un peso de 47,585 g. La distribución de los materiales líticos de acuerdo a su materia prima es la siguiente: andesita 10.49 por ciento, basalto fino 31.86 por ciento, basalto medio 24.26 por ciento, cuarzo 1.27 por ciento, diorita 13.93 por ciento, granodiorita 1.07 por ciento, ígnea textura fina .55 por ciento, ígnea textura gruesa 2.36 por ciento, latita 7.85 por ciento, riolita .88 por ciento, sílex 3.48 por ciento y No identificada .02 por ciento (Figura 4.84).

Figura 4.82. Punta de proyectil 33035.

Figura 4.83. Perforador 33275.

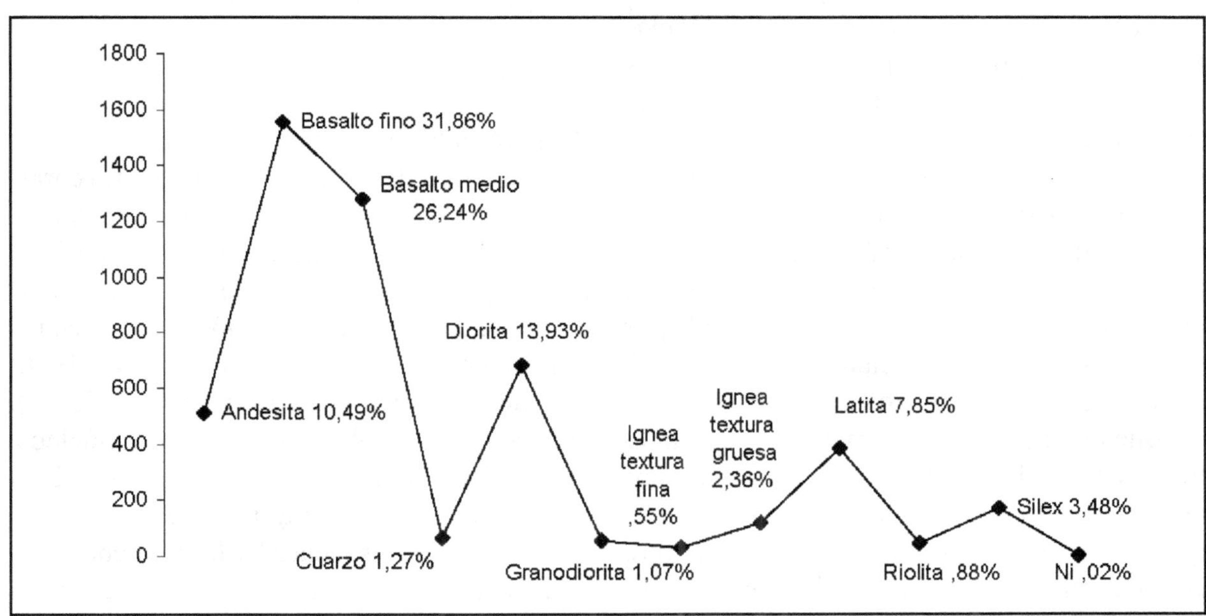

Figura 4.84. Frecuencia de materia prima en D (muestra 4881).

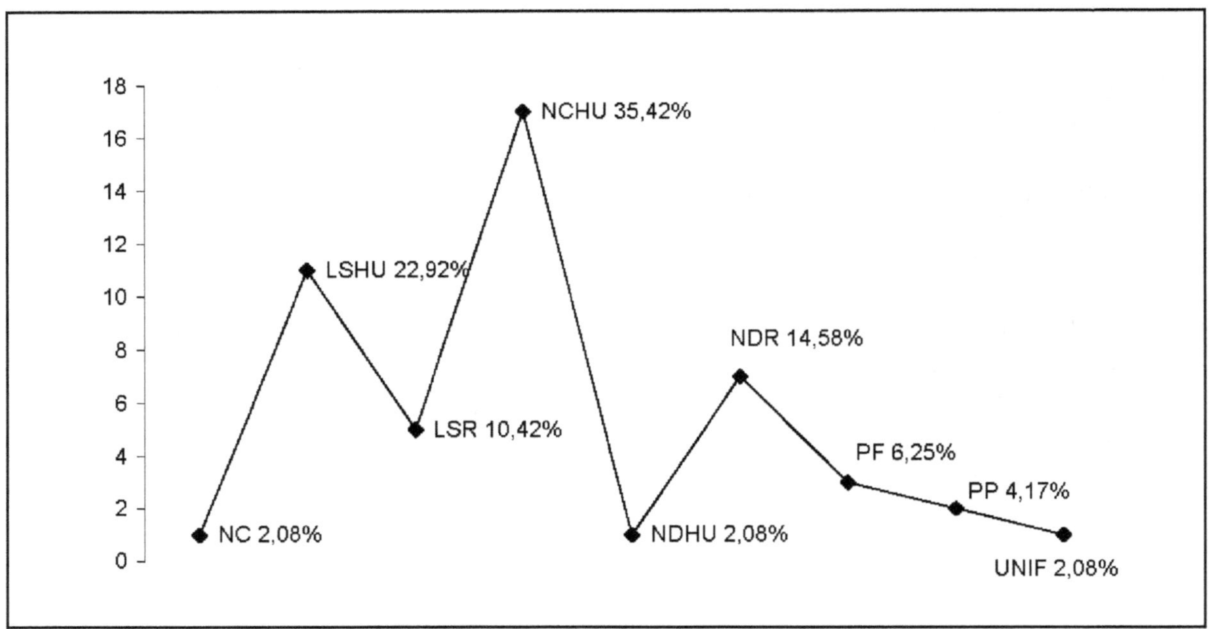

Figura 4.85. Frecuencia de herramientas en D (muestra 48).

El Caracolito

Esta estructura destaca por su forma ya que parece la sección de un caracol visto en corte, además en ellos se recuperó una alta cantidad de concha, especialmente del género *Conus.*

Las materias prima de las herramientas líticas se comportan como en otras áreas, es decir, con altos índices de basaltos y de diorita; sin embargo, si quitamos estos valores, la representación gráfica nos indica lo siguiente: andesita (15.79 por ciento), cuarzo (4.42 por ciento), granodiorita (5.47 por ciento), ígnea textura fina (4.42 por ciento), ígnea textura gruesa (10.74 por ciento), latita (45.68 por ciento), riolita (1.05 por ciento) y sílex (12.42 por ciento). Dentro de estos índices cabe destacar que uno de los valores más altos, quitando los basaltos y la diorita, es la latita (45.68 por ciento). Esto es un valor anómalo debido a que en la mayoría de las áreas la latita siempre es un valor menor al sílex. Al interior de El Caracolito se encuentran 21 herramientas distribuidas en las siguientes categorías: núcleos con huellas de uso (38.10 por ciento), lascas con huellas de uso (23.81 por ciento), lascas retocadas (14.29 por ciento), nódulos retocados (9.52 por ciento), nódulos con huellas de uso (4.76 por ciento), perforador (4.76 por ciento) y unifaciales (4.76 por ciento).

Herramientas

Respecto a las herramientas generales, en esta área podemos decir que del total del sitio corresponde a ésta un 4 por ciento (48 herramientas), entre las que predominan los núcleos con huella de uso (35.42 por ciento), lascas con huellas de uso (22.92 por ciento), nódulos retocados (14.58 por ciento), lascas con retoque (10.42 por ciento), perforadores (6.25 por ciento), puntas de proyectil (4.17 por ciento), núcleos, unifaciales y nódulos con huellas de uso (2.98 por ciento cada uno) (Figura 4.85).

Por lo que respecta a las herramientas formalizadas y/o con un mayor grado de estandarización tecnológica, tenemos las siguientes:

Punta de proyectil (Figura 4.86).

Numero de bolsa: 13,220; Ubicación: Área D N94 E62. Largo: 2 cm; Espesor: 4 mm. Descripción general: punta de proyectil completa de período cerámico manufacturada en sílex; presenta retoque bifacial total invasivo continuo.

Figura 4.86. Punta de proyectil 13220.

Perforador.

Numero de bolsa: 11,137; Ubicación: Área D N110 E80. Largo: 6 cm; Espesor: 15 mm. Descripción general: perforador completo manufacturado en materia prima no identificada, sin modificación por retoque; unifuncional con huella de uso en la parte distal.

Figura 4.87. Punta de proyectil 15022.

Punta de proyectil (Figura 4.87).

Numero de bolsa: 15,022; Ubicación: Área D N96 E80. Largo: 6 cm; Espesor: 8 mm. Descripción general: punta de proyectil completa tipo San Pedro manufacturada en riolita; presenta retoque bifacial total invasivo continuo.

Figura 4.88. Punta de proyectil 16963.

Punta de proyectil (Figura 4.88).

Numero de bolsa: 16,963; Ubicación: Área D N49 E113. Largo: 3 cm; Espesor: 9 mm. Descripción general: fragmento medial de punta de proyectil manufacturada en basalto fino; presenta retoque bifacial bilateral marginal continuo y aparentemente fue desechada dentro de su proceso de elaboración.

Perforador (Figura 4.89).

Numero de bolsa: 14,007; Ubicación: Área D N92 E64. Largo: 6 cm; Espesor: 6 mm. Descripción general: perforador fragmentado manufacturado en ígnea de textura fina; no presenta ninguna modificación por retoque. Unifuncional con huella de uso en la parte distal.

Figura 4.89. Perforador 14007.

Perforador.

Numero de bolsa: 15,896; Ubicación: Área D N121 E72. Largo: 6 cm; Espesor: 10 mm. Descripción general: perforador fragmentado manufacturado en basalto medio; no presenta ninguna modificación por retoque. Unifuncional con huella de uso en la parte distal.

Herramientas No Formales

Lasca con huella de uso (Figura 4.90).

Numero de bolsa: 16,762; Ubicación: Área D N119 E68. Descripción general: fragmento proximal de lasca terciaria de basalto fino; presenta huellas de uso de raspado ubicadas en la sección bilateral.

Unifacial.

Numero de bolsa: 16,605; Ubicación: Área D N118 E70. Largo: 9 cm; Espesor: 32 mm. Descripción general: unifacial completo, manufacturado en latita; presenta trabajo de descortezamiento unifacial bilateral invasivo irregular. Es probable que haya sido desechado dentro de su proceso de elaboración o que el lasqueo de descortezamiento sólo haya sido para preparar filos adecuados como área de trabajo, ya que presenta huella de uso de raspado ubicadas en área bilateral.

El área D es un espacio sumamente interesante, por dos cosas: presentar un área de alta concentración de concha del tipo *Conus* y por la presencia de tres áreas en actividades exclusivamente de uso habitacional (Terrazas 3, 9 y 11).

Área E

Esta área se ubica hacia el sur del cerro principal y del cerrito sur, por ello es un área sobre el piso del desierto y no presenta terrazas. En términos cualitativos esta área es diferente a las analizadas previamente.

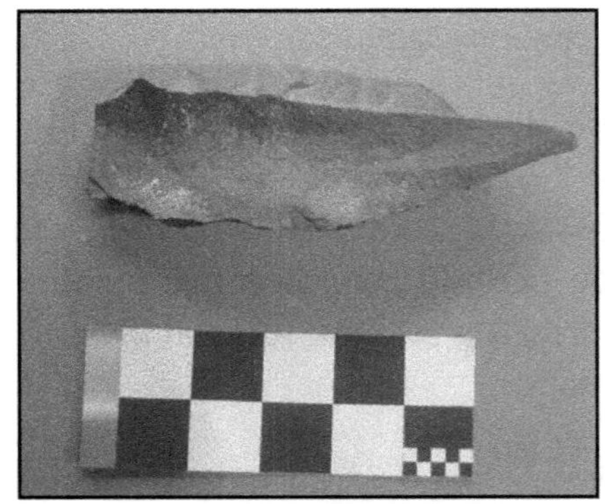

Figura 4.90. Lasca con Huella de uso 16762.

En ésta área de excavación se obtuvieron un total de 12,812 artefactos con un peso de 175,397.7 g. De acuerdo a su materia prima tenemos los porcentajes siguientes: andesita 17.96 por ciento, basalto fino 20.03 por ciento, basalto medio 28.58 por ciento, cuarzo .46 por ciento, diorita 12.07 por ciento, granodiorita 4.15 por ciento, ígnea textura fina .36 por ciento, ígnea textura gruesa .78 por ciento, latita 14.14 por ciento, riolita .63 por ciento, sílex .81 por ciento y no identificada .02 por ciento (Figura 4.91).

La materia prima se comporta como en otras áreas, es decir, con altos índices de basaltos y de diorita; sin embargo, si quitamos estos valores, la representación gráfica nos indica lo siguiente: andesita (45.67 por ciento), cuarzo (1.17 por ciento), granodiorita (10.56 por ciento), ígnea textura fina (.91 por ciento), ígnea textura gruesa (1.98 por ciento), latita (35.97 por ciento), riolita (1.61 por ciento), sílex (2.06 por ciento) y no identificada (.06 por ciento).

Herramientas

Respecto a las herramientas generales en esta área podemos decir que del total del sitio corresponde a esta área un 10 por ciento (110 herramientas) entre las que predominan lascas con huellas de uso (41 por ciento), núcleos con huella de uso (28.18 por ciento), nódulos retocados (13.64 por ciento), nódulos con huellas de uso (10 por ciento), lascas retocadas y bifaciales (2.73 por ciento cada una), fragmentos de nódulo con huellas de uso (1.82 por ciento) y unifaciales, puntas de proyectil y machacador (.91 por ciento cada uno) (Figura 4.92).

Por lo que respecta a las herramientas formalizadas y/o con un mayor grado de estandarización tecnológica tenemos las siguientes:

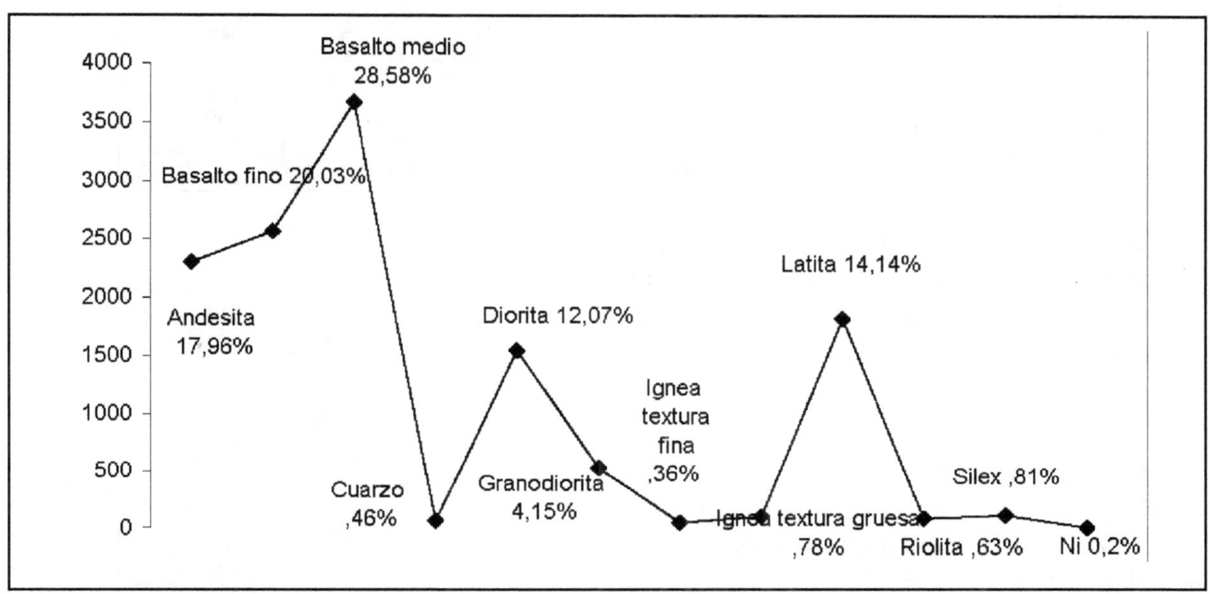

Figura 4.91. Frecuencia de materia prima en E (muestra 12812).

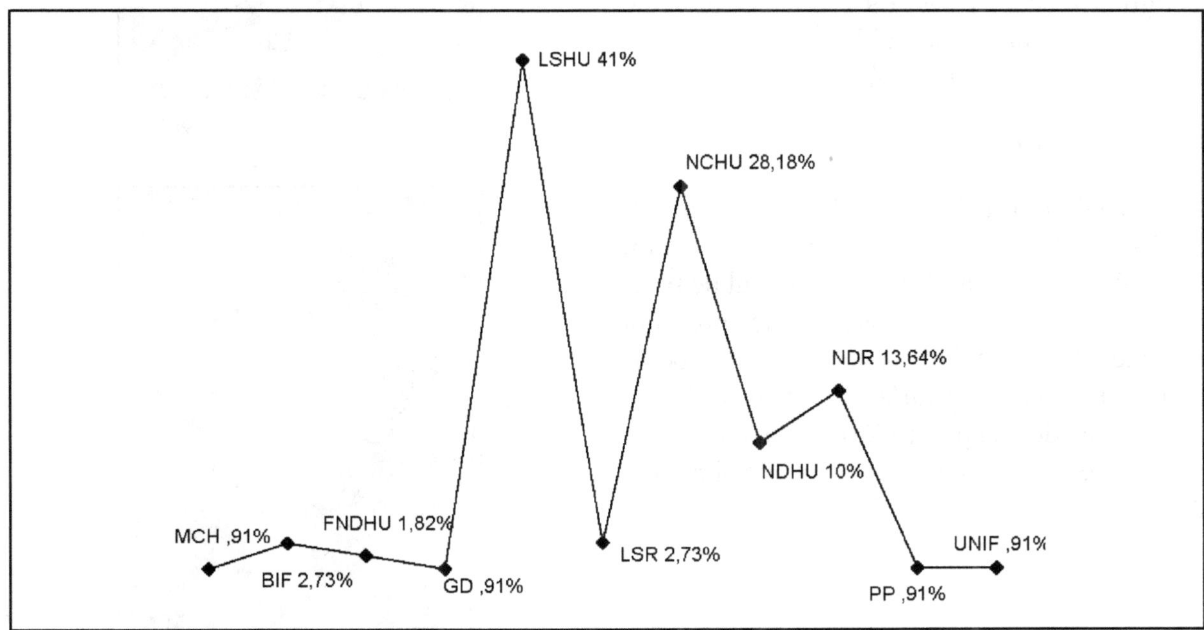

Figura 4.92. Frecuencia de herramientas en E.

Punta de proyectil (Figura 4.93).

Numero de bolsa: 14,357; Ubicación: Área E N114 E140. Largo: 6 cm; Espesor: 9 mm. Descripción general: punta de proyectil completa tipo San Pedro manufacturada en andesita; presenta retoque bifacial lateral invasivo continuo.

Figura 4.93. Punta de proyectil 14357.

Bifacial.

Numero de bolsa: 9,604; Ubicación: Área E N130 E128. Largo: 9 cm; Espesor: 33 mm. Descripción general: bifacial completo manufacturado en basalto fino, con retoque unifacial bilateral y distal marginal continuo, aparentemente desechado durante su proceso de elaboración.

Bifacial (Figura 4.94).

Numero de bolsa: 11,907; Ubicación: Área E N109 E140. Largo: 6 cm; Espesor: 6 mm. Descripción general: bifacial ovoide completo posiblemente de periodo de agricultores tempranos; presentan retoque bifacial ocasional lateral invasivo y retoque unifacial lateral marginal discontinuos. Es probable que éste retoque no se haya concluido y sea también un caso de proceso de manufactura.

Figura 4.94. Bifacial 11907.

Bifacial (Figura 4.95).

Numero de bolsa: 11,955; Ubicación: Área E N124 E110. Largo: 6 cm; Espesor: 10 mm. Descripción general: fragmento distal de bifacial manufacturado en basalto fino, presenta retoque bifacial total invasivo contínuo. A pesar de no tener la base, podría caber la posibilidad que se trate de una punta Cortaro dada la forma y acabado de la misma, cuyo período abarca el Arcaico tardío (Sliva 1997).

Figura 4.95. Bifacial 11955.

Unifacial (Figura 4.96).

Numero de bolsa: 13,067; Ubicación: Área E N130 E114. Largo: 9 cm; Espesor: 33 mm.

Descripción general: unifacial completo de andesita con retoque unifacial bilateral invasivo continuo, sin huella de uso aparente; es probable que haya sido desechado durante su elaboración.

Figura 4.96. Unifacial 13067.

Grabador (Figura 4.97).

Numero de bolsa: 9,616; Ubicación: Área E N130 E130. Largo: 3 cm; Espesor: 9 mm. Descripción general: grabador completo en diorita, presenta retoque unifacial lateral marginal continuo; unifuncional, con huella de uso en la parte distal aparentemente para hacer incisiones.

Herramientas No Formales

Lasca con huella de uso (Figura 4.98).

Numero de bolsa: 13,628; Ubicación: Área E N126 E126. Largo: 4 cm. Descripción general: fragmento de lasca secundaria de basalto medio; presenta huellas de uso en ambos lados.

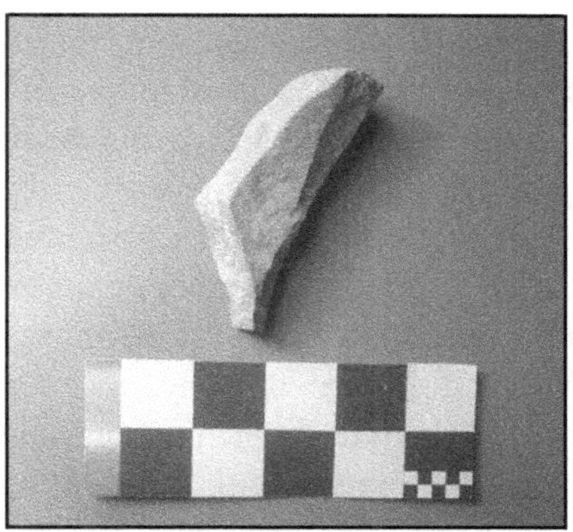

Figura 4.97. Grabador 9 616.

Conclusiones

Las conclusiones finales que aquí se plantean son un panorama general de las posibilidades de estudio de acuerdo a la metodología utilizada en el presene análisis. Con respecto a la materia prima en la que se encuentran elaborados los artefactos líticos tallados, creemos que se trata de una explotación local ya que los habitantes de este sitio bien pudieron haber tenido acceso a algunas áreas cercanas para proveerse de materia prima para su aprovechamiento.

El Cerro de Trincheras se encuentra situado dentro de una unidad geológica de suelos del cuaternario originados de rocas sedimentarias y volcánico sedimentarias. Al noreste del sitio, a tres kilómetros aproximadamente, se localiza una cadena de cerros con

Figura 4.98. Lasca con Huella de uso 13628.

rocas extrusivas ácidas de origen terciario, y al noreste una región de roca ígnea intrusiva intermedia del mesozoico. Otro medio de adquisición de materia prima es la recolección de cantos rodados, siendo probable que ésta se hubiera llevado principalmente en las márgenes del rio Magdalena, donde hasta la fecha puede observarse gran variedad de cantos en basalto, diorita, latita, andesita y cuarzo. Estos evidentemente tuvieron que ser una de las formas más accesibles de adquirir diferentes materias primas, en las que debieron de reconocer características físicas como tipo de fractura, dureza y resistencia, que reunieran los requisitos para desarrollar determinado tipo de actividad. Las materias primas más abundantes dentro de los materiales estudiados son basalto medio, basalto fino y diorita; le siguen andesita, latita y sílex y en menor frecuencia, ígnea de textura gruesa, cuarzo, granodiorita y riolita. Mas escasa tenemos a la ígnea de textura fina, y como ocacional tenemos la obsidiana.

Aparentemente no hay una especialización entre la materia prima y las categorías en general. Podemos encontrar todos los artefactos en todas las materias primas, solo difiere en el grado de frecuencia, dependiendo de la densidad de material arqueológico de cada área de excavación.

En las categorías tenemos dos grupos diferenciados, los cuales dependen de la materia prima en que se encuentran manufacturados. El primero es el conjunto de nódulos de los cuales se derivan aquellos que sin modificación alguna sirvieron como herramientas, los nódulos retocados, los fragmentos de nódulos ya sea con retoque o no, y los núcleos derivados de la acción de lasquear estos nódulos, así como el subproducto de ellos; las lascas ya sea modificadas por uso, por retoque o sin huella de uso aparente.

El segundo grupo es el concerniente al trabajo de adelgazamiento. Aquí contamos con pocos artefactos si se compara con el primer grupo que es tan numeroso (el de los nodulos); sin embargo se vuelven a encontrar las mismas materias primas del grupo anterior, pero proporcionalmente en menor cantidad. En esta industria de adelgazamiento encontramos artefactos con buena calidad en su acabado y un excelente control de la técnica de presión: los que son artefactos con una temporalidad temprana y que pudieron ser recolectados, almacenados y/o y reutilizados tardíamente. Tenemos también herramientas con un trabajo de adelgazamiento poco cuidadoso, y algunos más que sólo adecuaron con poco trabajo pequeñas lascas que pudieran semejar objetos como puntas de proyectil, perforadores, grabadores, etc.

Tenemos herramientas muy elaboradas como puntas de proyectil, bifaciales y perforadores, y otras poco elaboradas como algunos unifaciales, bifaciales y puntas de proyectil; tambien aquellas en las que sólo se aprovechó la morfología de la materia prima para la función a desarrollar como algunos perforadores o punzones y grabadores.

En cuanto a función, podemos ver que las herramientas más abundantes son las unifuncionales, mostrando claramente la función que desarrollaron. La huella de uso nos habla de especialización, o de una vida de uso muy corta por contar con otros artefactos para suplir fácilmente los ya usados. Las huellas de uso más frecuentes son percusión, raspado y corte, y aunque ninguna herramienta presenta un desgaste significativo que nos muestre agotamiento o constante uso, estas huellas están relacionadas con actividades de procesamiento de alimentos o implementos domésticos para la subsistencia diaria.

No hay evidencia en el material lítico analizado de Cerro de Trincheras que nos indique que estas herramientas sufrieron un uso intensivo, ya que raramente tenemos herramientas agotadas por uso. Casi su totalidad es posible que hayan sido desecho de talla tomado y utilizado como herramienta para posteriormente ser desechado y ocasionalmente vuelto a tomar para su reutilización.

En cuanto a la densidad de materiales en las áreas de excavación, guardando la distancia necesaria con respecto a las diferencias de extensión excavada, el área que se distingue por la abundancia de artefactos líticos tallados, así como por su variedad en materias primas, categorías y huellas de uso es el área de excavación B6, seguida por las áreas B1, B2, E y B7. En cuanto a las áreas A1 y B5, presentan aproximadamente la misma frecuencia de herramientas que es más baja que las áreas de excavación antes mencionadas. En cuanto a las lascas sin huella de uso aparente, el área A1 duplica visiblemente a B5. Las áreas B3 y B4, se mantienen dentro del promedio de frecuencias de materiales sin huella de uso aparente, pero la presencia de herramientas es más alta que otros con la misma cantidad de lascas sin huella de uso. En D, B8 y B11 tenemos una presencia moderada tanto de herramientas como de lascas sin huella de uso aparente, sin embargo las áreas que presentan menos densidad de material son B9 y B10.

Así pues, nos encontramos básicamente con una industria lítica productora de lascas de tamaño regular y que varían en su mayoría entre 3 y 9 cm aproximadamente. No tenemos macrolascas, por lo que es de pensarse que la mayoría proceden de nódulos producto de recolección de cantos rodados que tampoco exceden los 15 cm de diámetro. Como se ha podido observar en los nódulos y núcleos recuperados de las excavaciones, la técnica de manufactura utilizada para su extracción es a base de percusión directa, con grandes bulbos y conos de fuerza bien marcados; los núcleos encontrados nos indican que no hay un patrón establecido en las extracciones, pues las cicatrices que presentan son irregulares y multidireccionales. En cuanto al desecho de talla de manufacturas más especializadas, solo contamos con unas cuantas pequeñas lascas de presión de menos de un centímetro, producto de adelgazamiento.

En conclusión, podemos decir que la lítica tallada de Cerro de Trincheras presenta al igual que en otros sitios de comunidades sedentarias del noroeste de México y suroeste de los Estados Unidos, rasgos similares tecno-funcionales. Estudios llevados a cabo en la Universidad de Arizona han llamado a este tipo de tecnología "Expedient Technology" (Kaldahl 1995:13-17) cuya traducción aproximada sería "Tecnología de uso inmediato." Se caracteriza por la escasa presencia de herramientas formales y el incremento de uso de lascas producto de desecho de talla como herramientas. De esta misma manera, en el sitio Cerro de Trincheras pudimos observar una considerable producción de lascas, dentro de las cuales gran cantidad de ellas no presentan huellas de uso aparente; sin embargo, es posible ver lascas y materia prima de recolección utilizadas como herramientas cuya función posiblemente fue de uso cotidiano. Estos en su gran mayoria no presentan ningún tipo de modificación por retoque, o en su caso, éste es mínimo o apenas lo necesario para hacerlo funcional. Dentro de este grupo tenemos lascas y nódulos retocados, siendo éstos últimos los más cercanos a herramientas formales por presentar un área de trabajo manufacturada lo bastante funcional para efectuar corte por percusión. Por útimo, con respecto a lo que podríamos considerar como herramientas formales con una manufactura preestablecida convencionalmente, a pesar de ser escasa, podemos contar en nuestra colección con algunos unifaciales, bifaciales, grabadores, perforadores y puntas de proyectil con manufactura de adelgazamiento de percusión y de presión, siendo algunas de ellas de gran calidad.

Chapter 5
Ground Stone

Dawn Greenwald. DMG Four Corners Research, Inc.

Lítica Pulida

Este capítulo discute el conjunto de instrumentos de piedra pulida recuperado en Cerro de Trincheras durante las temporadas de trabajo de campo de 1995 y 1996. El arreglo de piedras pulidas incluía manos, metates, piedras de pulido, enderezadores de flechas, paletas, morteros, mano de mortero, hachas, un maza, azadas, bolas de piedra, un cuenco, pendiente, punzones, un exprimidor, una plomada, un anillo de piedra y preformas. Los Trinchereños hicieron la mayoría de estos artefactos de andesitaencontrado en el cerro. Este capitulo establece breves comparasiones con los intrumentos de piedra pulida Hohokam.

Methods

The ground stone analytical system was composed of 14 variables: morphological type, material type, artifact plan shape, profile (for manos and handstones), artifact condition, grinding-surface texture, number of grinding surfaces, production investment, production technique, evidence of multiple use or recycling, adhesions or residues, use wear, weight, and complete dimension measurements. Other attributes, such as heat alteration, and details of production or use were noted when applicable. Many morphological categories were traditional types, such as polishing stone, three-quarter-grooved axe, and mortar. Most of the mano and metate types were developed from previous survey results in combination with data that emerged during excavations. Material types were identified both macroscopically and microscopically using a 30x binocular microscope, when necessary, so that the most precise identification could be made. Artifacts were weighed to the nearest tenth of a gram on a triple-beam balance scale (< 2999.9 g). Large artifacts (≥ 3000.0 g) were either not weighed or were weighed on a bathroom scale. Measurements were made using a metric tape.

Milling stones and other grinding tools were assessed for grinding-surface texture (fine, medium, or coarse), since prehistoric tool users artificially roughened tool surfaces to achieve a desired texture. Texture classification was based on the material grain size as well as any surface pecking. Fine-grained texture was indicated by a smooth surface, medium-grain was an irregular surface or one with a slightly rough texture, and a coarse-grained surface was one that had pecks or vesicles that were > 2 mm in diameter or that had a rough texture.

Description of latitudinal profiles of manos and handstones (i.e., biplanar, plano-convex, etc.) permitted comparison of grinding patterns among tool types. Profiles also suggested the intensity of food grinding, as did the number of grinding surfaces.

All ground stone artifacts were assessed for production investment and manufacturing techniques. Production investment is the amount of shaping each artifact had undergone. For example, a "minimally altered" metate had been pecked only on the grinding surface. A "shaped" metate had been flaked and/or pecked on less than half of its entire form, including edges, ends, and faces. A "well-shaped" metate had been flaked and/or pecked on half or more than half of its form; one with evidence of production over all or nearly all of its form was "completely shaped." These categories represent the amount of energy invested in the manufacturing process and can indicate whether the energy investment correlates with artifact type, function, or other factors. Production techniques, such as flaking, pecking, and grinding were recorded for each artifact as well, since different horizontal and vertical forces also represent varying degrees of energy investment.

Multiple wear, adhesions, and use wear were determined by detailed observation of artifact surface area. Each artifact was scanned under a low-power microscope to detect traces of wear, discoloration, or residue.

Artifact Descriptions

Most artifacts were typical Southwestern U.S. forms. However, there were some forms, such as the portable grinding slicks, metates delgados, and concave mutates, that are rarely found north of the border. Typical ground stone artifacts included manos, metates, polishing stones, grooved abraders, palettes, mortars, pestles, axes, a maul, hoes, balls, a bowl, pendants, awls, a reamer, and a ring/donut. Table 5.1 lists all of the ground stone tools by the area they were found in. In addition to these tools, the sample also included numerous objects that local people had picked up off the hill but that cannot be located to Area and are therefore not shown on Table 5.1. Table 5.2 lists only the ground stone tools found in occupation levels as opposed to terrace fill and/or as construction material in walls.

The majority of ground stone (71.2 percent) was made of the local andesite or a grade of the same material that can be seen outcropping on the hill. The second most common material type (8.8 percent) was an indeterminate igneous that probably was also locally derived. Other materials represented 5.0 percent or less of the assemblage (Table 5.1). The igneous materials are postulated to have been available within a 20-kilometer radius from the site (McGuire et al. 1993:49). Most of the other materials were probably available from the streambed of the Magdelena River. Currently, metamorphics, various igneous types, including large vesicular cobbles, quartzites, and possibly sedimentary types can be found along the Magdelena. The origin of the schist and steatite is currently unknown.

Manos

Manos were categorized according to two major attributes: 1) whether they were shaped or unshaped, and 2) tool form. The shaped vs. unshaped criteria was based on whether there was evidence of manufacturing, such as grinding, flaking, or pecking, that modified the natural contours of the tool form. Repeated tool forms included loaf, square, oval, and irregular. Manos fell into two basic types: loaf manos and irregular manos. Loaf manos were long, loaf-shaped hand grinders that were often completely shaped, with coarse-textured use surfaces. Irregular manos were shorter, irregularly shaped hand grinders with little-to-no production modification and fine-textured use surfaces. Manos that did not fit either category were categorized as "Other Mano." These specimens included a wide range of production investment values and a variety of shapes. Fifty-two out of 320 manos were too fragmentary to determine type.

Loaf Manos

Loaf manos (Figure 5.1) were usually subrectangular to elongated ovals in plan view and plano-convex or bi-convex in profile, and they usually were wider in the center than at the ends. They represented the largest category of manos (n = 124), although only 20.2 percent were complete specimens. The majority was made of local light gray andesite and rhyolite (n = 96.0 percent), some of the finer-grained varieties outcropping on the cerro. Coarser-grained and slightly vesicular grades of the same material types, gray and light purple, occurred in the assemblage, but they were not noted on the cerro itself. The coarser grades made up 48.4 percent of the loaf mano materials, compared with 1.7 percent of the irregular manos, and were probably selected for the tools that required the coarser-textured surfaces, such as the loaf manos. The majority of loaf manos were coarse-textured (85.5 percent). Wear patterns on loaf manos included polish (87.1 percent), bidirectional striations (58.1 percent), and multidirectional striations were exhibited on 5.6 percent. Most specimens had two opposing use surfaces (67.7 percent), one use surface was found on 14.5 percent, and six manos (4.8 percent) had three use surfaces (two on one side and one on the opposite side); the rest (12.9 percent) were indeterminate.

Irregular Manos

Irregular manos (n = 117) were usually bi-convex in cross-section and were made of the

Figure 5.1. Loaf mano.

local, softer, andesite/rhyolite from the cerro (59.0 percent). The material from the cerro weathers irregularly, more so than the coarser varieties, so that there may have been some error in evaluating the extent of production modification on some of the irregular manos. In general, however, most appeared to have been either unmodified or minimally modified (57.3 percent). Grinding surfaces were usually fine-grained (85.5 percent), and condition was usually complete (62.4 percent). Wear patterns consisted of bidirectional striations (67.5 percent), polish (22.2 percent), multidirectional striations (5.1 percent), and abraded facets (.9 percent). Similar frequencies of irregular manos had one vs. two use surfaces (34.2 percent vs. 41.0 percent, respectively); one had three use surfaces, and the rest (23.9 percent) were indeterminate.

Other Manos

Twenty-seven manos (88.9 percent of them complete) did not conform to either loaf or irregular types. Almost half (48.1 percent) were oval, followed by rectangular/subrectangular (37.0 percent), round (7.4 percent), irregular (3.7 percent), and indeterminate shape (3.7 percent). Most were bi-convex (55.6 percent) or plano-convex (29.6 percent) in profile, and there were similar frequencies of those that were unmodified (25.9 percent) as those that were well shaped (33.3 percent) and completely shaped (18.5 percent). The coarse-grained variety of local andesite/rhyolite was used for other manos (22.2 percent), but not to the extent as the finer-grained variety (33.3 percent). Fine-textured grinding surfaces dominated (59.3 percent), and use wear patterns included bidirectional striations (70.4 percent), polish (44.4 percent), multidirectional striations (11.1 percent), and trough wear (abrasion and polish found on the ends of manos from continual contact with the walls of metates) (3.7 percent). The majority of other manos had two opposing use surfaces (66.7 percent), followed by one use surface (25.9 percent), and an indeterminate number (7.4 percent).

Metates

Five different metate types were recognized during the analysis process: slab, concave, basin, metate delgados, and portable grinding slick. Types were based on form and use wear pattern. Slab metates had flat grinding surfaces with various grinding use-wear patterns; concave metates were crescent-shaped in form and grinding surface; basin metates had round or oval, basin-shaped grinding surfaces; metates delgados were narrow, elongated forms with flat surfaces; and portable grinding slicks had flat grinding surfaces that were often tilted at an angle to the ground surface, with small, centrally placed, intensively ground use areas. A total of 202 metates were analyzed in the laboratory. Two concave metates were analyzed in the field, in Area A1, and a sample of 21 bedrock grinding slicks were analyzed in the field.

Slab Metates

Slab metates, or lapstones, had flat grinding surfaces. Thirty-six, or 55.4 percent, out of 65 slab metates, were complete. Initially, slab metates were divided into two types based on the extent of grinding wear, but since there was no difference in other attributes these two subtypes were later combined into one category. Slab metates were relatively small netherstones, with mean dimensions of 14.5 x 14.4 x 7.0 cm (length x width x thickness). There was little-to-no energy invested into their manufacture, so that the slab metate form was wide ranging and included irregular (23.1 percent), oval (13.8 percent), rectangular (10.8 percent), triangular (4.6 percent), round (3.1 percent), square (1.5

percent), diamond (1.5 percent), and indeterminate (41.5 percent). Most of the specimens were of the local fine-grained rhyolite/andesite (72.3 percent) and had fine-grained grinding surfaces (84.6 percent). Use wear occurred on the entire surface (38.5 percent) or on only a portion of the surface (61.5 percent) and consisted of both bidirectional (53.8 percent) and multidirectional (9.2 percent) striations, abrasive wear (75.4 percent), and polish (43.1 percent).

Concave Metates

Concave metates (Figure 5.2) were rarely found in complete form. Out of 36 analyzed in the laboratory, none were complete, and out of two specimens analyzed in the field, one was complete and appeared to have been minimally used. Unlike slab metates, concave metates were very specialized forms. They were the only metate that usually had a coarse-textured grinding surface, and they always had some modification, often appearing to be well- or completely shaped. Although the larger specimens, such as the complete metate, had flat grinding surfaces, most of the concave metates were well-worn and had concave use surfaces, apparently produced by long use of the tool. Thus, the data suggest that the concave metate gained its distinctive grinding surface over time, and the longer it was used the greater potential for tool breakage.

Concave metates were usually made of the local coarse-grained rhyolite/andesite (61.1 percent). Edges along the use surface were slightly rounded by pecking and flaking, with the use area, edges, and ends pecked and flaked to form flattened, approximately 90° surfaces. Unlike other metates, the most frequent wear attribute was polish (72.2 percent), and bidirectional striations were noted on 50.0 percent of the specimens. Based on the wear patterns, these metates were used in concert with long manos so that the ends of the manos matched or were longer than the edges of the metate. As the metate became well-worn, the mano would have developed an almost crescent shaped longitudinal convex use surface similar to the metate grinding area, with a much gentler slope and shorter wall than trough metates. Therefore, most of the vertical force was applied in the center of the mano, rather than on the ends. As with some trough metates, concave metates had two open ends where the mano (and meal) could slide back-and-forth in and out of the metate surface. The single complete specimen, from Area A1 near the Caracol, was approximately subrectangular-to-square in plan view and measured 55.0 cm in length, 50.3 cm in width, and 34.0 cm in thickness. It was only slightly ground within an area of about 30.0 cm x 34.0 cm.

Figure 5.2. Concave metate.

Basin Metate

One complete basin metate was recovered from Jacal 2, Area B2. It was an approximately triangular-shaped boulder, measuring 36.0 x 29.1 x 9.0 cm, of local fine-grained rhyolite/andesite. The boulder had not been shaped, but the central use area had been used for grinding. Abrasion and multidirectional striations were visible within a 14.0 x 14.0-cm area, and the depth of the basin varied between 1.4 cm and 1.6 cm.

Metate Delgado

A single metate delgado was found in Area B1. It appeared to be completely shaped, although it was only a fragment, of local coarse-grained rhyolite/andesite (vesicular). It had a broken length of 17.0 cm, a width of 9.8 cm, and a thickness of 5.0 cm. It exhibited bidirectional straie running longitudinally, and portions of the outer edges in the center of the metate were polished from contact with a mano. Both surfaces appeared to have been used.

Portable Grinding Slicks

Twenty-two metates were categorized as portable grinding slicks. These were generally unmodified irregular boulders of fine-grained local rhyolite/andesite with anywhere from a 5° to a 45° slant (16° mean) of the flat use surface to the modern ground surface. The use wear was often similar to wear found on bedrock grinding slicks, in which there was intensive grinding over a narrow area, probably the width of a small mano or handstone. The mean dimensions of a portable grinding slick were 20.5 x 16.2 x 8.3 cm. Many of the specimens exhibited grinding over much of the small metate surface with the most intensive grinding in the center, and sometimes the grinding was so intensive as to cause a slight concavity in the center. Depths ranged from flat to slightly concave (0-.9 cm). Mean dimensions of intensive, centralized use areas were 16.7 x 11.3 cm, and .2 cm in depth. Grinding-surface texture was usually fine-grained (90.9 percent), and the only wear attributes that were exhibited were bi-directional striations (54.5 percent) and polish (36.4 percent).

Bedrock Grinding Slicks

I analyzed a sample of 21 bedrock-grinding slicks (Figures 5.3 and 5.4) on the Explanada at the base of the Cerrito de La Virgen. Many slicks were found clustered so that an average of 2.6 grinding slicks occurred on the same or neighboring boulders. Within the sample there were single occurrences of slicks, as well as clusters of two, three, four, and seven slicks. Grinding patterns on the slicks indicated the orientation of the grinding and sometimes the grinder. Grinding orientation was usually either north-south or east-west, although variations such as northwest-southeast and northeast-southwest occurred as well. The size of grinding areas varied widely, with a length range of 8 cm to 36 cm and a width range of 7 cm to 18 cm. Mean dimensions were 20.5 x 11.7 cm, the approximate size of a portable grinding slick, although somewhat narrower. Six slicks had flat surfaces, although most had flat-to-slightly concave surfaces. The mean depth was 1.0 cm, with a range of .0 cm to 3.4 cm. Most slicks had slanted grinding surfaces (from the modern ground surface), with a mean slant of 13°. Bidirectional striations and polish were exhibited on less than half of the sample; usually abrasion was the only indication of grinding.

Polishing Stones

Polishing stones made up a small percentage of the ground stone assemblage (1.0 percent). These large pebbles had smooth surfaces with polish and often multidirectional striations as evidence of their prehistoric use. Many analysts believe that polishing stones provide indirect evidence of ceramic manufacture, based on ethnographic analogy and archaeological associations (Colton 1952; Geib and Callahan 1988; Sullivan 1988). They were used during ceramic vessel manufacture to smooth the plastic clay prior to firing. Nine of the 12 polishing stones were complete tools, with mean dimensions of 3.0 x 3.1 x 1.6 cm and a mean weight of 43.9 g. They were usually oval or round fine-grained pebbles of a variety of material types, includ-

FIgure 5.3. Bedrock grinding slick.

Figure 5.4. Bedrock grinding slick.

Figure 5.5. Reamers.

ing igneous NFS (not further specified) (25.0 percent), fine-grained basalt (16.7 percent), quartzite (16.7 percent), quartz (8.3 percent), and indeterminate (33.3 percent). One-half of the specimens exhibited use wear on two opposing surfaces, and the rest were used on a single surface. One polishing stone, from Area B3 (Bag 6746), had green streaks on one surface that appeared to be from a mineral source; however, there was no evidence of clay adhering to any surfaces.

Abraders and Reamers

Abraders consisted of handheld tools that were grooved and/or flattened/faceted by repeated grinding for the purpose of shaping or straightening other tools or objects. The tool user moved the abrader in short, repeated motions, either back-and-forth or at various angles, to achieve the desired abrasive or shaping effect on the target object. Shaft straighteners and whetstones are forms of abraders. Reamers (Figure 5.5) are also handheld tools, but they are used in a rotary fashion for enlarging or tapering holes in objects. Resultant use wear on reamers is rounding and rotary striations around the entire or partial circumference of a tool. Some of the abraders and reamers recovered from the cerro were probably used during the manufacture of shell products.

Out of 11 abraders, eight were grooved, one was faceted, and two were both grooved and faceted. The faceted specimen came from Area B2 (Bag 12925). It was a relatively small, truncated cylindrical stone of local rhyolite with longitudinal facets and smaller facets that beveled portions of the ends. The grooved abraders usually consisted of one or more U-shaped grooves, and two of the abraders had grooves that were flat-bottomed with sloping sides. Grooves ranged in width between .5 and 5.6 cm and ranged in depth between .1 and 1.0 cm, with a mean width of 1.9 cm and a mean depth of .4 cm. Six abraders were complete, with mean dimensions of 6.1 x 4.9 x 2.9 cm and a mean weight of 297.9 g. Abraders were made from sandstone (54.5 percent), local rhyolite (18.2 percent), sedimentary NFS (9.1 percent), igneous NFS (9.1 percent), and schist (9.1 percent). They exhibited a variety of shapes (rectangular, oval, round, irregular, and oblong) and were used as is, without production modification, or they were manufactured to varying degrees.

Four out of ten reamers were complete. Of those four, one was a cobble with no production modification, and three were shaped with varying degrees of production investment. Shapes included oblong (30.0 percent), cylindrical (10.0 percent), conical (10.0 percent), irregular (10.0 percent), and indeterminate (40.0 percent). Reamers had fine-grained surface textures and were composed of rhyolite (50.0 percent), igneous NFS (30.0 percent), and quartzite (20.0 percent) materials. Two reamers had been used for other purposes. One specimen, from Area D (Bag 15030) had extensive hammering/battering wear on the ends, and the other reamer, from Area B6 (Bag 31964) was used for grinding as well as reaming.

Palettes

Two artifacts were categorized as palettes — small, usually tabular slabs used for mixing paint pigments. Both palettes were relatively small, subrectangular in shape, with planar, fine-grained, and slightly undulating surfaces. One found in an occupation level of Area D, measuring 15.0 x 13.0 x 4.9 cm, was made of rhyolite and was less than half shaped by edge-flaking. Its entire surface was covered with the remnants of a pink pigment solution, probably hematite and water. The crew found the second palette in an occupation level of Area B1. It exhibited no use wear and had no adherents to its surface, but it resembled the first palette in relative size (8.8 x 5.8 x .9 cm) and surface attributes. It was made of micaceous schist and was completely shaped by grinding on the surfaces, edges, and ends. This artifact may have been newly manufactured by the toolmaker. These palettes resemble Hohokam palettes in their size, but are not nearly as elaborated or decorated as Hohokam examples. Hohokam palettes routine occur associated with censors (McGuire 1992). In contrast, archaeologists recovered no censors from Cerro de Trincheras.

Portable Mortars

The excavators recovered five portable mortars from five different areas (B1, B6, B7, D, and E). Only one mortar was complete (Area B6, Bag 31977). It was a small slab of local rhyolite, measuring 21.2 x 12.0 x 4.0 cm (1004.2 g), with two mortar holes, one of which was worn through the opposite surface. Although most of the mortars were incomplete, there appeared to be a wide variety of hole depths, ranging from 1.8 cm to 24.0 cm. Material type was restricted to local rhyolite/andesite, with both coarse- and fine-grained use surface textures. One specimen, from Area E (Bag 14336), had a small amount of indeterminate yellow substance adhering to the upper interior of the orifice. Mortars are food-processing tools, used to crush and mix seeds, pods, herbs, and other plants/parts. The Hohokam to the north historically favored mortars for grinding mesquite beans, which produces a sticky substance that is best contained in a small receptacle during the grinding process (Bell and Castetter 1937).

Bedrock Mortar

I recorded a single bedrock mortar in the field while sampling the bedrock grinding slicks on the Explanada at the base of the Cerrito de La Virgen (Figure 5.6). It was located in the southeast corner of an exposed masonry room. The center of the mortar was approximately 82 cm north of the south wall and 70 cm west of the east wall. It was ground 28 cm deep within the local fine-grained rhyolite bedrock. It measured 22 cm in diameter at the surface orifice and approximately 5 cm in diameter at the bottom.

Pestles

Pestles are the companion grinders to mortars. They are elongated stones that are held in one or both hands to pound and grind substances within the mortar. The crews found eight pestles from seven different areas (one each from B1, B2, B4, B6, B7, E and two from D). They were all made of igneous material, most of which was fine- or coarse-grained local rhyolite (62.5 percent and 25.0 percent, respectively). Six of the eight pestles were in complete condition, and five of these were well shaped or completely shaped tools. Four pestles had been used as manos prior to or during their use life as pestles. Mean dimensions for pestles were 12.8 x 8, 3 x 6.9 cm, with a mean weight of 1227.3 g.

Figure 5.6. Bedrock mortar.

Handled Pounder

I have described one artifact as a handled pounder for lack of comparable tools in the literature. The archaeologists found this tool on the surface of Area D. It had a large oval head (approximately 8.0 x 4.0 cm) on one end and a narrow handle at the opposite end. Approximately 8.5 cm from either end was a shaped shoulder that separated the use end and handled end. The artifact was pecked all over to shape, and all but the ends were ground to a polish, similar to the polish on axes. The large end exhibited light pounding wear.

Hafted Tools

Hafted tools included 2 mauls, 6 axes, and 8 indeterminate forms (maul or axe). Both mauls were complete, greater than three-quarter-grooved, and were well shaped or completely shaped. One maul from Area B2 exhibited use wear and the other from Area B6 did not. The worn maul may have been a recycled axe, due to the angle of the longer end. It measured 9.0 x 5.8 x 3.8 cm and had a groove width of 2.5 cm. The second maul was made of crumbly local rhyolite/andesite and narrow; therefore, it did not appear to be appropriate for heavy-duty tasks. It measured 12.3 x .9 x .6 cm and the groove was approximately 1.0 cm wide.

Five three-quarter-grooved axes (one each from B2, B6, B7, and B11) and one notched axe (B2) represented the axes. All of the axes were in complete condition. Of the three-quarter-grooved specimens, four were made of greenstone (Figure 5.7) and one was made of local rhyolite. They were all well-shaped or completely shaped; only two exhibited use

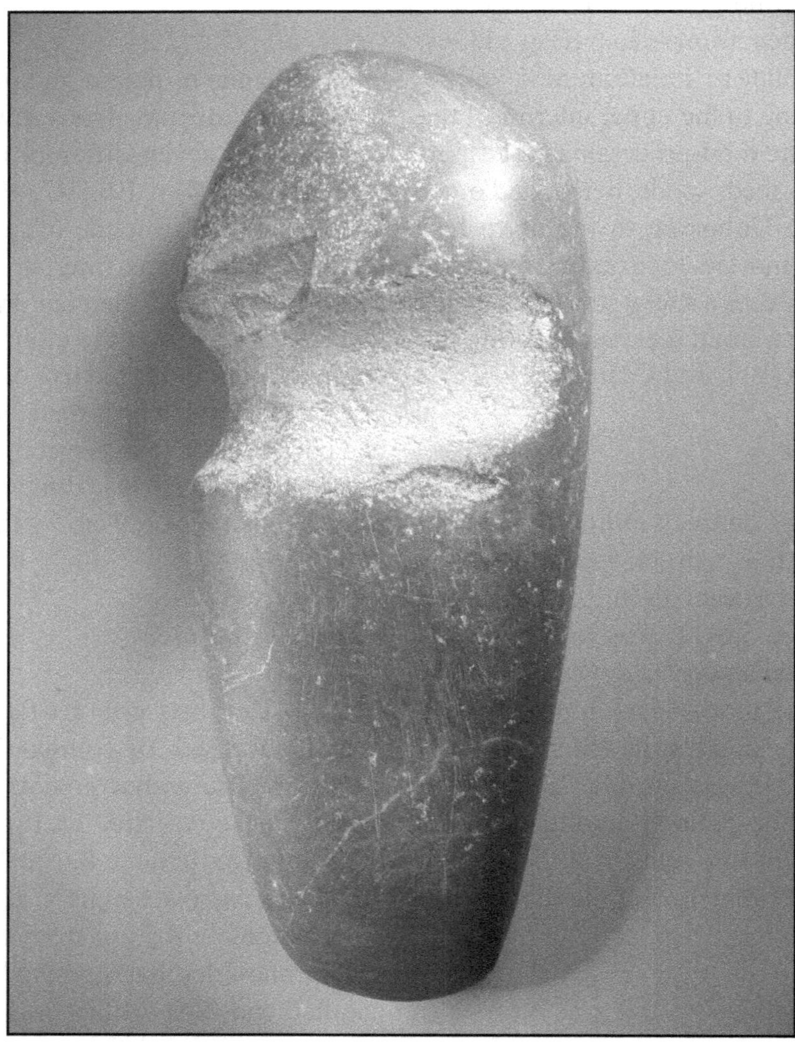

Figure 5.7. Three-quarter-grooved axe.

wear. Mean measurements for the three-quarter-grooved axes were 15.4 x 7.0 x 5.4 cm, and the mean weight was 995.8 g. One of the axes may have been a toy (Area B2, Bag 10617). It was small (8.0 x 4.0 x 3.0 cm), and the material was too soft to be effective as a real tool. Only the bit area was ground, and it had a shallow groove that was approximately .8-cm wide. Groove width on the other four axes ranged between 2.5 and 5.0 cm, and groove depth varied between .4 and .9 cm. The notched axe found in Area B7 was probably a child's toy. It measured 5.0 x 2.6 x .5 cm and was shaped from a flattened cobble of fine-grained basalt. The Trinchereños had made it by beveling the bit end and flaking and incising the notches.

Eight other tools had hafts, but they were too fragmentary to determine if they were axes or mauls. They were made of fine-grained and coarse-grained local rhyolite (12.5 percent and 50.0 percent, respectively), quartzite (25.0 percent), and greenstone (12.5 percent).

Stone Balls

Three complete stone balls (Figure 5.8) were found in Areas B1 and B7. They were all of similar size, not completely spherical, and the two balls from Area B1 may not have been finished artifacts. One of the stone balls from Area B1 measured 6.7 x 6.5 x 6.2 cm. It was flaked and pecked to shape from local rhyolite, with many facets around the circumference indicating that it was still in rough form and had not been rounded out. The second stone ball from Area B1 was made of igneous NFS material and measured 7.8 x 7.5 x 7.3 cm. It had two flat, cortical areas remaining on the surface, with the rest of the ball pecked and ground. The third ball, from Area B7, was fine-grained basalt pecked to an approximate sphere (7.1 x 6.9 x 6.1 cm). It exhibited battering wear that appeared to be from rolling.

Pendants

Five stone pendants came from three different areas, one each from Areas A and B4 and three from B1. All of them were broken at the drilled holes. Material types included igneous NFS (40.0 percent), schist (20.0 percent), rhyolite (20.0 percent), and a fine-grained, red sedimentary material, possibly argillite (20.0 percent). The schist pendant was subrectangular, but the other pendant shapes were too fragmentary to determine.

Stone Disk with Cross

We found one unusual ground stone artifact in Area B1 (Bag 10820). The Trinchereños shaped a piece pink non-local stone into a rough disk and carved a cross on it. They left the back of the stone unmodified. The disk is approximately 10 cm in diameter (Figure 5.9).

Architectural Stone

The Trinchereños modified a slab metate, from Area B3 (Bag 7363), to use it as architectural stone after it had been used as a slab metate. It was shaped by pecking and flaking into a long tabular slab with a notch at one end. Similar notched stones were used as braces to hold floor beams in the Hohokam, Prescott, and Mogollon prehistoric culture regions to the north. The unnotched end was secured into the subfloor of a domestic structure, and the notched end was upright and aligned with other notched stones to hold poles or beams for floor construction. The notched stone, made of the local rhyolite/andesite, measured 42.0 cm in length, 18.1 cm in width, and 7.0 cm in thickness. Metate use wear was most intensive by the notched end, with a slightly concave use surface approximately .5 cm in depth.

Figure 5.8. Stone ball.

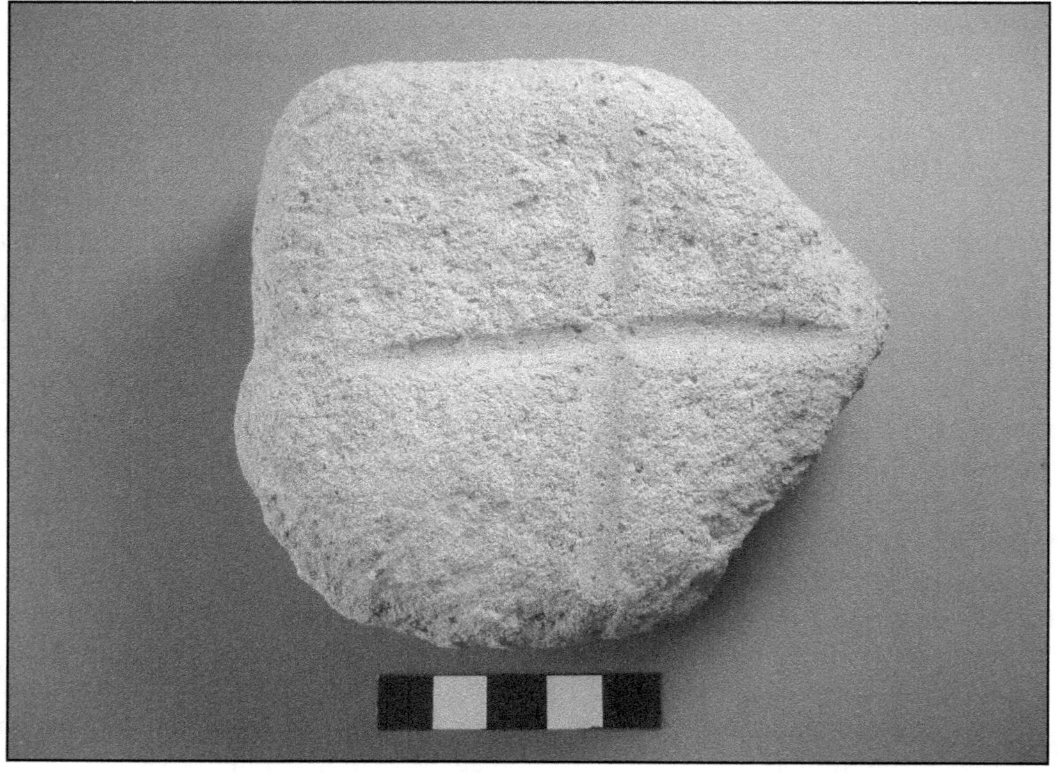

Figure 5.9. Stone disk with cross.

Stone Vessel

Excavators found a partial stone vessel Area D (Bag 13216). It appeared to have broken during the manufacturing process. It was still blocky in form, made of local rhyolite/andesite, with a broken length of 6.5 cm, a width of 7.0 cm, and a thickness of 5.5 cm. It had a small, shallow bowl pecked into the top (4.0-cm diameter and 2.7-cm depth). Although no use wear was evident within the bowl, there was slight abrasive wear on the base.

Stone Ring/Donut

Crews recovered a partial stone ring or donut-shaped stone from Area B2 (Bag 9077). It was broken approximately in half, with a diameter of 8.8 cm. The stone ring was made of vesicular basalt. It was completely modified by pecking and grinding, and it had a biconical perforation drilled into the center. The drilled surfaces were planar and exhibited evidence of burning. No use wear was noted. Functional interpretations for these artifacts have included a game element (Haury 1976:290-291), corn shellers (Haury 1976:291), and digging stick weights (Rodgers 1987:163).

Plummet

A single plummet made of local andesite was found in Area B1. It was wide and approximately subrectangular in plan view and narrow and tapering in profile. The artifact measured 3.2 x 2.4 x 1.3 cm and was completely pecked and ground to shape. A narrow groove encircled the artifact at one end. No use wear was apparent on any of the surfaces. These artifacts have also been referred to as "medicine stones" (Haury 1976:292; Sayles 1937:102) and "Acylinders" (Kamp 1995). Their function, although unknown, has been hypothesized. Rodgers (1987:162) has suggested that they were used as plumb bobs or weights to measure "some unknown kind of perpendicularity." Bruder and Gasser (1983:120) have referred to them as "phallus stones," their designation as medicine stones implies some ceremonial function. Most recently, Kamp (1995) has convincingly associated them with the scraping of ceramic vessels in the Sinagua prehistoric culture area to the north.

Tool Blanks

Out of four tool blanks that were recovered, two were mano blanks from Area B7, one was a possible metate blank from Area B6, and one from Area B8 was a blank for a hafted tool such as an axe or maul. The mano blanks were complete and made of the local rhyolite, with fine-grained surfaces. One was shaped by pecking and measured 31.0 x 14.5 x 10.0 cm; the other was shaped by flaking and measured 14.4 x 4.8 x 3.7 cm. The broken metate blank, made of coarse local material, was probably a concave metate. It had a coarse-grained surface and was shaped by pecking and flaking. The fourth blank was a greenstone cobble that was pecked and ground. One end was broken and then it was used for hammering/battering.

Other Stone

Other ground stone included hand grinders that could not be identified to type (i.e., polishing stone, mano, or abrader) (n = 12), netherstones that could not be identified to type (i.e., metates, palettes, or anvils) (n = 32), shaped artifacts that could not be identified to form (n = 23), and finished artifacts that had unusual forms or use wear (n = 14). During the excavation phase of work, some of the crew thought they recognized an artifact form that had been placed into the shaped, but not identified, category. These were small, well-ground, flat rectangular stones that had been broken on both ends, with incomplete lengths that ranged from 1.8 cm to 5.1 cm, and widths of approximately 1 cm. Six or seven of these artifacts were recovered from Areas B1, B2, B3, B4, and B7. They were interpreted as triggers for deadfall traps, animal traps in which a weight falls on the animal to kill or disable it. Some of these artifacts were battered along their length. Other types of artifacts that were recognized included awls or possible awls (n = 7) (Areas B1, B2, B3, B6, B11, and D), chopping tools that were also used as manos (n = 2) (Areas B4 and E), wall/floor polishers (n = 3) (Areas B3, B7, and E), a scraping tool (Area B7), a step (as in step and riser) (Area B3), a cogged stone (Area D), a phallic (Area B7), a possible spindle whorl fragment (Area B2), and possible pendant blanks (n = 2) (Areas B2 and E).

A small cuboid crystal of dark reddish-brown/black was recovered from Area B1. It was not modified and may have eroded from raw materials used at this location or was a prehistoric manuport. Three unmodified sandstone objects also may have been imported onto the site: a small, naturally flat slab that measured 4.8 x 4.5 x 3.1 cm; a naturally irregular spherical "marble" that was approximately 2 cm in diameter; and a flat, irregular cobble (9.6 x 4.1 cm) with a natural handle attached on one side.

Indeterminate Ground Stone

Eighty-three artifacts were too fragmentary to determine type or form. They were recovered from every locus and included many different material types.

Conclusions

The ground stone from Cerro de Trincheras easily fits in the range of ground stone types normally found in the prehispanic Southwest/Northwest but with some distinctions. The Trincheras Tradition and the Hohokam Tradition shared residence in the Sonoran Desert and the ground stone assemblages of both traditions are functionally similar. This is most apparent with the portable and bedrock mortars and pestles common to both traditions that were probably primarily used to process mesquite seeds. We also see parallels in ground stone axes to cut wood, stone hoes for cultivation, grooved abraders and polishing stones to finish pottery. The Hohokam were desert agriculturalists and their ground stone included trough metates and loaf manos for processing significant quantities of corn. The Trinchereños also had large metates with loaf manos but their concave metates and metates delgados are stylistically distinct from Hohokam trough metates. The Trinchereños' ground stone for working shell included reamers similar to those found among the Hohokam and portable grinding slicks that do not commonly appear north of the border. Overall the Cerro de Trincheras ground stone indicates an intensive agricultural adaptation to the Sonora Desert with stylistic distinctions from the Hohokam.

Tables for Chapter 5

Table 5.1. Ground Stone Tool Types by Area Including All Levels

	Area													
Morphological type	A1	B1	B2	B3	B4	B5	B6	B7	B8	B9	B10	B11	D	E	Total
Abrader/shaft straightener		2	1	1			5	1				1			11
Active grinder NFS							1		1				1		3
Architectural slab				1											1
Axe, 3/4-grooved			1				1	1				1			4
Axe, notched								1							1
Blank NFS							1		1						2
Haftable tool	1		1				4	1						1	8
Handled pounder													1		1
Indeterminate ground stone	4	7	9	3	7	1	12	12	1	2	1	5	8	9	81
Indeterminate netherstone	3	2	7				4	6	1	4	1	1		3	32
Lapstone	2	6	3	1	1		5	1		1		1	1	3	25
Mano blank								2							2
Mano, indeterminate	3	3	9	2	2	2	9	3	3	1		1	4	9	51
Mano, irregular	13	20	5	5	6	1	19	20	5	3	1	2	8	7	115
Mano, loaf (shaped)	11	16	15	6	10	3	14	11	3	3	3	2	8	10	115
Mano, one-hand shaped	2	3	1	1	3		4	3	3			1		5	26
Maul, 3/4-grooved			1				1								2
Metate boulder	1							1							2
Metate, basin			1												1
Metate, concave	10	5	3		1	1	5	2	1	3	1		1	2	35
Metate, indeterminate	4	20	18	4	5	1	5	7		1			3	5	73
Metate, slab	4	6	3	2	3	1	5	4	1				4	6	39
Metates delgados		1													1
Mineral, not used		1													1
Ornament, pendant		3			1				1						5
Other active grinder			4	1	2								1	1	9

Table 5.1. Ground Stone Tool Types by Area Including All Levels, cont'd

	Area														
Morphological type	A1	B1	B2	B3	B4	B5	B6	B7	B8	B9	B10	B11	D	E	Total
Other stone			1	3	3		1	2					2	2	14
Palette		1											1		2
Pestle		1	1		1		1	1					2	1	8
Plummet		1													1
Polishing stone		1	5	3		1	1	1							12
Portable grinding slick	1	3	1		2		9	2		1			2		21
Portable mortar		1					1	1					1	1	5
Reamer	2					1	1	4	1				1		10
Stone ball		2						1							3
Stone bowl/vessel													1		1
Stone ring (donut)			1												1
Stone, unworked				1	1		1								3
Stone, worked		4	5	2	1		3	3				1	1	3	23
Total	61	109	96	36	49	12	113	91	22	19	7	16	51	68	750

Table 5.2. Ground Stone Tool Types by Area: Occupation Levels Only

	Area														
Morphological type	A1	B1	B2	B3	B4	B5	B6	B7	B8	B9	B10	B11	D	E	Total
Mano, one-hand shaped	1	1						2	3			1		3	11
Mano, loaf (shaped)	9	9	9	1	4	3	7	9	3	2	3		5	4	68
Mano, irregular	9	9	1	2	1		8	15	5	1	1	2	4	3	61
Active grinder NFS									1						1
Mano, indeterminate	1	1		2	1	2	2	2	3			1	3	8	26
Other active grinder			3											1	4
Polishing stone		1	3	1		1		1							7
Abrader/shaft straightener		2					3	1				1			7
Metate, slab	4	5	1		1	1		3	1				1	1	18
Metate, concave	10	1			1	1	3	2	1	2	1			1	23
Metate, indeterminate	4	6	3	1	1	1	5	2						2	25
Portable grinding slick	1				1		3	1							6
Lapstone	1	2			1		1	1		1		1	1	2	11
Palette		1													1
Indeterminate netherstone	3	1	2				2	5	1	1	1	1		3	20
Architectural slab				1											1
Portable mortar		1											1		2
Pestle		1						1						1	3
Maul, 3/4-grooved							1								1
Axe, 3/4-grooved							1	1				1			3
Haftable tool	1		1					1						1	4
Stone ball		1						1							2
Ornament, pendant		1			1				1						3
Mineral, not used		1													1
Stone, worked		2	2				2					1	1	2	10
Stone, unworked				1											1

Table 5.2. Ground Stone Tool Types by Area: Occupation Levels Only, cont'd

	Area														
Morphological type	A1	B1	B2	B3	B4	B5	B6	B7	B8	B9	B10	B11	D	E	Total
Other stone				2				1						2	5
Reamer	1					1		3	1				1		7
Stone ring (donut)			1												1
Mano blank								1							1
Blank NFS							1		1						2
Metate boulder	1							1							2
Indeterminate ground stone	3	4	2	1	3	1	2	9	1	1	1	4	4	2	38
Total	49	50	28	12	15	11	41	63	22	8	7	13	21	36	376

Chapter 6

Marine Shell Artifacts

Victoria D. Vargas. Archaeological Consulting Services

Concha Marina

Este capítulo discute el conjunto de conchas recuperado en Cerro de Trincheras durante las temporadas de trabajo de campo de 1995 y 1996. Este conjunto proveyó evidencia sobre la producción de joyería en concha e incluyó piezas terminadas y concha no trabajada. Estas conchas representaron 52 géneros de conchas marinas y 69 especies. Todas de Panamic province del Golfo de California. El género más común fue *Glycymeris* seguido por *Conus*. Los artesanos de concha trinchereños hicieron mayormente cuentas, anillos, brazaletes, aros y sonajeros. La evidencia sugiere que los trinchereños se involucraron en comercio interregional pero que ellos produjeron la mayoría de los bienes para consumo local.

The excavations at Cerro de Trincheras yielded a total of 6,867 marine shell artifacts. The assemblage includes finished pieces, unworked shell, in-process pieces and workshop debris. Several areas of the site (Areas B1, B2, B6, and D) appear to have been more involved in shell jewelry manufacture than others, although evidence for manufacture is exhibited by all excavated areas of the site. The finished goods produced at Cerro de Trincheras are typical in form as compared to those found in the U.S. Southwest including bracelets, rings, tinklers, pendants, and beads. What sets Cerro de Trincheras apart from Hohokam assemblages is the relatively equal emphasis on *Conus* rings (20 percent) and *Glycymeris* bracelets (17 percent), whereas most Classic Period Hohokam sites tend to exhibit a heavier emphasis on bracelets and beads (Bradley 1996).

This report provides the preliminary results of the marine shell analysis of the entire Cerro de Trincheras excavated shell assemblage. Data recording took place by the author at INAH-Sonora in Hermosillo during the summer months of 1995 and 1996 under the direction of Elisa Villalpando, co-director of the project. Each shell artifact was measured with metric calipers, weighed on a triple beam balance scale, identified to genera and species (consistent with Keen 1971), and observations were recorded to artifact form, condition, and modification characteristics such as grinding, cutting, incising, and perforating. All data were directly entered into a computer using the Paradox data management program. The summary of these data is presented below.

Genera and Species

Of the 6,867 marine shell artifacts, 5,674 were of identifiable genera (Table 6.1). Forty-eight marine shell genera and 76 separate species were recorded for the assemblage (Table 6.2). All identified marine shell originated in the Panamic shell province, which begins at the northern extent of the Gulf of California and runs south along the Pacific coast of México. No California coastal species were present. Only one example of a freshwater mussel (unidentified genus) was retrieved during excavation.

Of the 6,867 shell artifacts, 6,241 pieces were identifiable by class. Gastropods (univalves) are the dominant shell order in the assemblage consisting of 58 percent of the identifiable portion of the assemblage. Pelecypods (bivalves) make up the remaining 42 percent of the collection.

The majority of shell belongs to the *Conus* genus (53 percent) with *Glycymeris* as the second largest category (26 percent). The next highest frequency of shell genera is *Laevicardium* (9 percent). The remaining genera assignments result in frequencies of two percent of the assemblage or less.

The extremely high frequency of *Conus* at Cerro de Trincheras is unusual when compared with nearby contemporary Hohokam assemblages in Arizona. In a paper comparing Hohokam shell artifact assemblages from the Soho, Civano, and Polvoron Phases of the Classic Period, Arthur Vokes (1992) found *Conus* made up 5 percent of the assemblage in the first two phases and almost 25 percent in the Polvoron. The Polvoron appears to be contemporary with the Cerro de Trincheras occupation (A.D. 1300-1450) and Vokes (1992) reports an increasing focus upon *Conus* at Hohokam sites through the end of the Hohokam sequence. However, there is no indication that any Hohokam assemblages emphasized *Conus* to the degree found at Cerro de Trincheras.

Another anomaly, when compared to Hohokam assemblages in the Classic Period, is the relative paucity of *Laevicardium* at Cerro de Trincheras, where it represents only nine percent of the total assemblage. For the sample of Classic Period Hohokam sites that Vokes (1992) includes in his report this species represents 31 percent of the assemblage in the Soho Phase, 48 percent in the Civano, and 30 percent during the Polvoron Phase.

The frequency of *Glycymeris* at Cerro de Trincheras appears to be somewhat more in line with the Hohokam sample. Twenty-six percent of the Cerro de Trincheras assemblage is represented by this species. Vokes (1992) reports a 28 percent frequency of *Glycymeris* for his study assemblage in the Soho Phase, which declines to 17 percent in the Polvoron.

Shell Artifact Forms

Of the 6,867 shell artifacts at Cerro de Trincheras, 4,956 were identifiable by specific artifact type. Table 6.3 presents the types identified, their counts, and absolute frequencies. Production debris represents the largest category of identified forms, constituting 35 percent of the total. Beads (22 percent), *Glycymeris* bracelets (17 percent), and *Conus* rings (20 percent), either finished or in-process, represent the remaining majority of the collection (Figure 6.1).

The portion of the assemblage not identifiable by type appears to consist primarily of production debris. Given the extremely small size of these fragments, combined with the obscuring effects of erosion, these pieces were assigned to an "unidentified fragment" class (FNI). A separate "unidentified object" class (ONI) includes 203 artifacts exhibiting

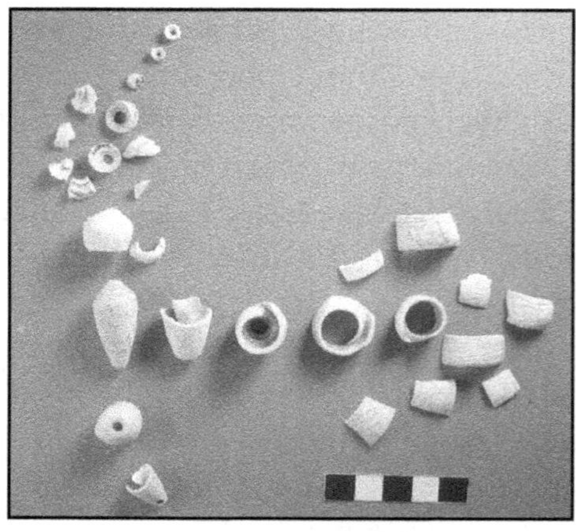

Figure 6.1. Conus bead and ring manufacturing processes.

evidence of work but too fragmentary as to allow a specific type assignment.

Beads

Shell beads (Figure 6.2) make up 22 percent (n = 1069) of the 4,956 identified objects in the assemblage (including identified workshop debris). Excluding the workshop debris, of all finished types (n = 3142), beads represent 34 percent of the assemblage. I identified several beads types including whole shell beads, disk (discoidal) beads, "saucer-shaped" beads, and cylindrical beads. Table 6.4 presents the relative frequencies of finished artifacts, excluding the production debris data.

Figure 6.2. Shell beads.

Whole Shell Beads

Whole shell beads (Figure 6.3) comprise 29 percent (n = 310) of the total shell beads (n = 1069; Table 6.4). Artisans used gastropods to produce all of the whole shell beads. *Nassarius* sp. is the most common gastropod used (33 percent), followed by *Conus* sp. (24 percent). Two different methods of manufacture were used in producing whole shell beads at Cerro de Trincheras. Of the 310 whole shell beads, The Trinchereños produced 148 (48 percent) by grinding or breaking away the apex of the univalve, often removing the interior spire of the shell. They then strung the shell bead through the apex, down through the interior channel of the shell and out through the natural shell aperture.

Of the remaining 163 whole shell beads, 160 were simply perforated by drilling, cutting, or grinding a hole into the exterior shell wall. This allowed stringing into the perforation through the shell's interior channel and out through the aperture. *Nassarius* sp. and *Columbella* sp. univalves were typically modified in this way to produce whole shell beads. The remaining three whole shell beads exhibit both the apex removal and body perforating methods, allowing either mode of suspension.

I classified whole perforated bivalve shells as pendants. Artisans perforated whole bivalve beads and pendants by simply grinding or perforating the umbo for stringing. The distinction commonly cited in the U.S. Southwest shell literature between these beads and pendants is arbitrarily based on size, which is a continuous variable. Therefore, to avoid imposing a potentially false distinction, I classified all whole perforated bivalve shells as pendants.

Figure 6.3. Whole shell bead.

Discoidal (Disk) Beads

Disk beads comprise 26 percent (n = 281) of the bead assemblage. Trincherеños manufactured disk beads by initially cutting or breaking a piece of a shell into "blanks," or small pieces of shell that are easier to manipulate. The blanks were then perforated with a small lithic drill, the edges were ground into a circular disk shape, and they finally ground and polished smooth the entire surface. These beads are flat when viewed in profile. The extensive grinding involved in producing disk beads typically obliterates diagnostic characteristics, making genus and species assignments impossible. Occasionally, however, an incompletely ground bead surface exhibits enough of the natural shell surface to allow a genus and/or species assignment. Of the 281 disk beads in the assemblage, only 83 were identified to genus: *Conus* sp. constitutes 60 percent of these and *Spondylus/Chama* sp. accounts for 21 percent (n = 17). The remaining genera assignments of disk beads include *Glycymeris, Laevicardium, Oliva,* and *Pinctada.*

Spondylus sp. and *Chama* sp., which both exhibit vibrant orange and purple coloring, appear to have been highly prized and rare in the Greater Southwest and other parts of the Americas (Safer and Gill 1982). I combined the two genera in this analysis due to the absence on the beads from Cerro de Trincheras of the diagnostic hinge markings that allow the two shell types to be distinguished (Vokes 1983). Excavators at Cerro de Trincheras recovered only 17 disk beads made of this material. Since they encountered no manufacturing waste of this shell type it is likely that *Spondylus* sp. and *Chama* sp. beads were traded into the site in finished form. *Spondylus/Chama* beads, typically 2 cm in diameter or more, tend to be larger than disk beads made from other genera, which average about 1 cm in diameter.

"Saucer-shaped" Beads

The saucer-shaped bead, is a rare type of bead in the prehispanic Southwest/Northwest that was encountered at Cerro de Trincheras. In a top-down view they appear to be disk beads, circular or oval with a central perforation. However, in profile they have a distinctively curved or "saucer-shape." This results from the use of naturally curved small univalves. These beads were not ground flat as were most gastropod disk beads.

Saucer-shaped beads occur elsewhere in the prehispanic Southwest/Northwest and are typically made from *Olivella* sp.shells. California coast tribes produced great quantities of *Olivella* saucer-shaped beads and are believed to be the source of those occurring in the Southwest/Northwest (Nelson 1991). However, of the 205 saucer-shaped beads recovered at Cerro de Trincheras, *Conus* sp. was the only identifiable genus. Numerous in-process examples of these beads were encountered at Cerro de Trincheras, which indicates local manufacture.

Cylindrical Beads/Section Beads

Cylindrical beads (Figure 6.4) make up only three percent of the bead total (n = 25). Artisans produced the majority (n = 23) from the long curling tube of sea worms from the family *Vermetidae*. Typically, a section of this tube was cut and both ends ground smooth.

Figure 6.4. Cylindrical bead.

Truncated/Choker Beads

Truncated/Choker Beads are much less common at Cerro de Trincheras than other bead forms. To manufacture these beads, artisans removed the apex, spiral, and lower end of the shell by cutting or grinding. The remaining middle section of the shell forms a barrel-shaped "truncated" bead. Excavators retrieved eleven truncated beads, five of which were made from *Olivella* sp., five from *Conus* sp., and one from an indeterminate genus. Di Peso and others (1974b) classified as truncated beads what other researchers usually considered to be *Conus* sp. rings. Investigators often make the distinction between a truncated bead and a ring arbitrarily assigned based on size. In this analysis, rather than create a separate bead category, I classified all artifacts produced from the medial section of *Conus* sp. shells as rings.

It is impossible with the available data to determine whether the Trincherenos used these *Conus* ornaments from Cerro de Trincheras as rings or beads. We found no inhumations with individuals wearing these ornaments. Therefore, although the term "ring" implies an interpretation of use, none is intended. The term is maintained only for consistency and comparative purposes with other analyses.

Cap Beads

Cap Beads make up 22 percent of the bead category with 237 examples. Artisans at Cerro de Trincheras, almost exclusively manufactured them from the top spire portion of *Conus* sp. shells. They removed the "cap" of the shell from the medial and distal portions by percussion. Then they removed the apex to form the suspension hole and finally they ground and polished the whole piece.

Bilobed Beads

Of interest to this study is that *no* bilobed beads were encountered at Cerro de Trincheras. Although they do not occur in great numbers in the Hohokam region, they do occur with some regularity at Classic Period Hohokam sites. Their absence at Cerro de Trincheras is notable.

Bead Pendants

Bead Pendants (Figures 6.5 and 6.6) are represented at Cerro de Trincheras by only two examples, both of which are *Conus*. These are classified as bead pendants due to the combination of perforation styles on a single artifact: the apex is removed and the body is perforated at one end, allowing either vertical or horizontal suspension.

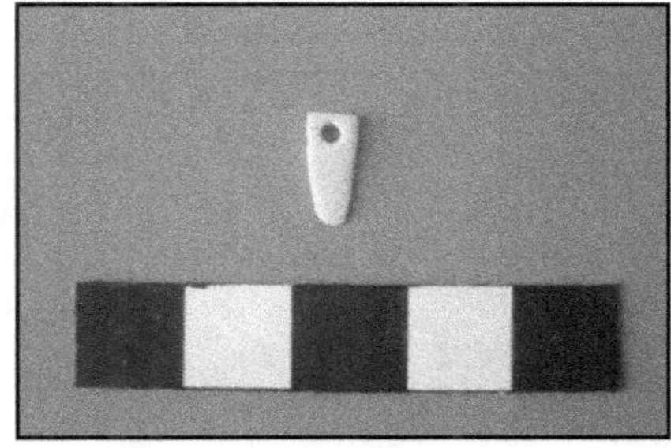

Figure 6.5. Pendant.

Figure 6.6. Pendant.

Rings

Marine shell rings provide 31 percent of the finished artifact category with 981 examples. Only 20 of these are *Glycymeris maculata*, a smaller bivalve than the more archaeologically common *Glycymeris gigantea,* which was used to make shell bracelets. Artisans produced *Glycymeris* rings using a manufacturing process quite similar to that used for producing *Glycymeris* bracelets. They first removed the central portion of the shell, leaving an exterior band which they then ground and polished into a thin ring with a roughly square or rectangular section. Nine other rings made from bivalves were not identifiable by genus, but were most likely made from *Glycymeris maculata*.

The remaining 954 rings identified by genus were made from *Conus* sp. univalves. *Conus* rings (Figures 6.7 and 6.8) were produced by removing the apex, spire, columella (central spire), and lower third of the shell. The remaining central portion of the shell forms the ring, which was then ground and polished to remove the rough edges. Nineteen examples of in-process rings were recovered, as well as large quantities of *Conus* fragments from the top and bottom of the shell, which presumably was ring-processing waste. Occasionally *Conus* rings were decorated with incised geometric designs.

Bracelets

Archaeologists recovered a total of 857 bracelet fragments during excavations at Cerro de Trincheras (Figures 6.9 and 6.10). These bracelets comprises 27 percent of the finished shell artifact assemblage. No whole bracelets were encountered. All recovered bracelet fragments were made from *Glycymeris gigantea* bivalves. There is extensive evidence for

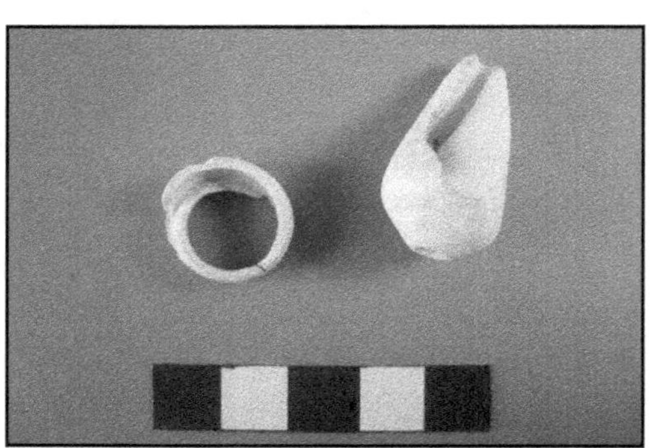

Figure 6.7. Conus *ring and whole shell.*

Figure 6.8. Conus *rings.*

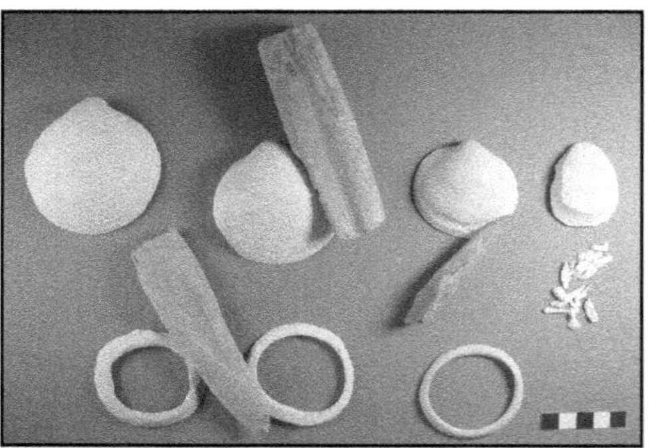

Figure 6.9. Bracelet manufacturing process.

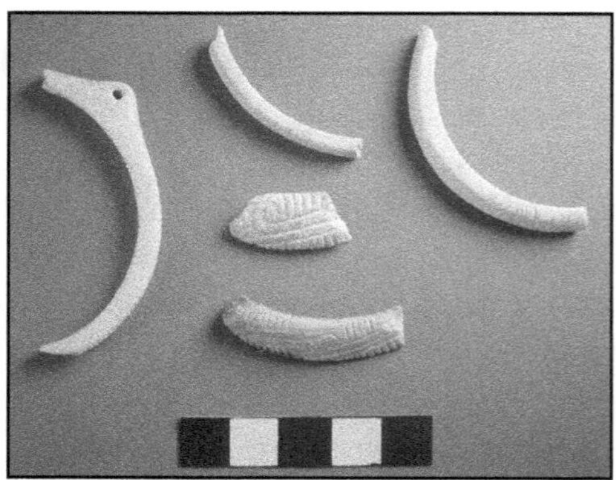

Figure 6.10. Bracelet fragments.

bracelet manufacturing at the site. We found in-process bracelets as well as characteristic bracelet manufacturing debris.

Artisans at Cerro de Trincheras used the faceted core removal technique to make bracelets. Once a bracelet is completed it is normally impossible to determine what type of core removal technique was used, as all diagnostic attributes are ground and polished away in the finishing stages. However, excavations at the site have yielded 92 cores (or tapas) with distinctive faceting and thinned edges, indicating the method of bracelet manufacture.

This method entails grinding the central exterior portion of the shell at different angles, thereby thinning the shell wall and facilitating removal of the core through percussion. Once the core is removed reaming further widens the rough interior opening of the bracelet "blank". The final stage involves grinding and polishing to finish the piece. Like *Conus* rings, artisans occasionally added incised geometric designs to the outer edge of the bracelet (Figures 6.11 and 6.12).

Figure 6.11. Incised bracelet fragments.

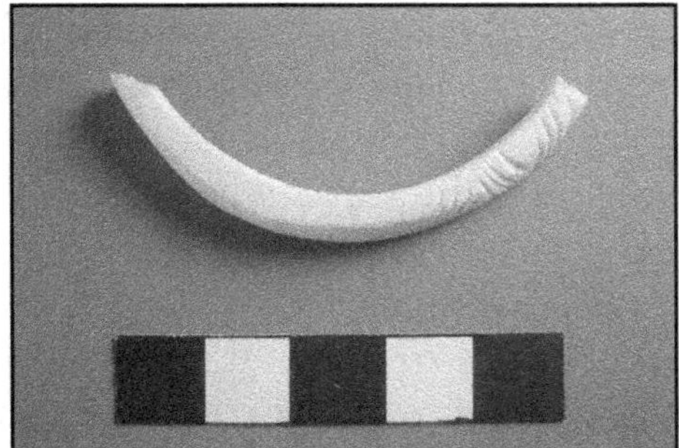

Figure 6.12. Incised bracelet fragment.

The core removed by this technique is faceted on top with walls thinning toward the edges and broken irregularly. Johnson (1960:183) records only three of these characteristic cores at the nearby Trincheras site, La Playa, and feels it indicates a "lack of popularity among resident artisans" (cited in Huckell 1979:161). The faceted core technique has also been documented by Huckell (1979) for several sites in the Papagueria: ten whole or fragmented faceted cores from AZ Y:8:3 (ASM), five at Ventana Cave, hundreds recorded for the Lost City Site, two from AZ Z:14:21 (ASM), and two from Gu Achi. There is also a single faceted core recorded for Los Muertos in the Hohokam core area, indicating that, although this technique may have been known outside the Papagueria and Trincheras areas, it did not become widespread elsewhere.

Two other core removal techniques for bracelet manufacture are recorded for the U.S. Southwest: the grinding method and the rough core method. Hohokam artisans preferred the grinding method of bracelet manufacture and entails grinding the central exterior portion of the shell down until a sufficient opening was achieved (Huckell 1979:161). Additional reaming and chipping of the edges of the opening to further widen it usually followed this thinning. Shell Town exhibited large quantities of shell dust in stratigraphic lenses encountered during excavation. These lenses are interpreted as the refuse from the grinding method of bracelet manufacture (Marmaduke and Martynec 1993). In most cases, in the absence of shell abrasion dust lenses, the use of this method must be deduced from in-process pieces with characteristic grinding patterns.

The rough core removal technique occurs at the Trincheras component of the La Playa, Sonora Site. This method entails incising a groove around the top part of the shell that is to be removed, subsequent deepening of the groove with stone flakes until the thickness of the shell is almost perforated, then knocking the core off by percussion (Huckell 1979). These cores exhibit characteristically thick edges that are fairly regular (Woodward 1936:121). No grinding is used in the removal of the core, which Johnson (1960) suggests is the preferred method of manufacture for the Trincheras tradition as a whole.

The Cerro de Trincheras data, however, do not support this generalization. None of the unfaceted and thick edged cores characteristic of the rough core removal technique, such as evidenced at La Playa, have been recovered at Cerro de Trincheras. Furthermore, we encountered no shell abrasion lenses that might indicate the use of the grinding method of core removal. This implies that there may have been a change of preferred core removal techniques through time in the Trincheras area. One hypothetical scenario could be of an earlier preference for the rough-core removal technique, for which there is much evidence at La Playa, that is subsequently replaced by a faceted core removal technique. Such a scenario is supported by the great quantities of faceted cores at Cerro de Trincheras and by a few examples from La Playa. These sites are only approximately ten km apart, which does not support an argument for a geographical preference for these two methods of core removal.

The occupation at Cerro de Trincheras has been dated as occurring from A.D. 1300 to A.D. 1450. The long series of occupations through time at La Playa, together with the undatable surface collections of the shell cores collected from the site (Johnson 1960), do not currently allow testing for the proposed temporal shift of core removal techniques. The resolution of this issue will have to await further research in the Trincheras region.

The geographic distribution of core removal techniques in shell bracelet manufacturing is important in terms of understanding of the Trincheras shell working tradition. The grinding method is arguably restricted to the Hohokam core area (Huckell 1979), whereas the rough-core and faceted core removal techniques are restricted to the Papagueria and the Trincheras areas to the south. This geographic distribution also implies a certain cultural distance between the shell working tradition of the core Hohokam area compared with those of the Papagueria and Trincheras areas. The shell data do not support arguments that the Trincheras tradition was an offshoot of the Hohokam.

The 41 in-process bracelet fragments that we collected during excavation also provide production of shell bracelets at Cerro de Trincheras. Further support is provided by the retrieval of 292 *Glycymeris gigantea* fragments of manufacturing waste. As mentioned above, 92 of these fragments are faceted cores/tapas, the central portion of the shell that craftspersons removed to form the central opening of the bracelet. The large category of small unidentified fragments (FNI) may include a significant amount of additional production debris. However, unless these fragments possessed definitive characteristics of reduction from percussion, they were assigned to the unidentified fragment category.

Pendants

Shell pendants (Figures 6.13 through 6.16) are classified as such based upon their vertical orientation when suspended. Excavations yielded 146 pendants or five percent of the finished artifact total. Of these, 122 were made from Pelecypods (bivalves), 22 from Gastropods (univalves), and two were so modified as to prevent class assignment.

Table 6.5 presents the absolute quantities and relative frequencies of shell genera and species identified for pendants. Artisans used *Glycymeris* sp. shells to make the great majority of shell pendants with 85 examples (65 percent). They used *Pinctada* sp., a nacre-

Figure 6.13. Pendants.

Figure 6.14. Pendants.

Figure 6.15. Pendants.

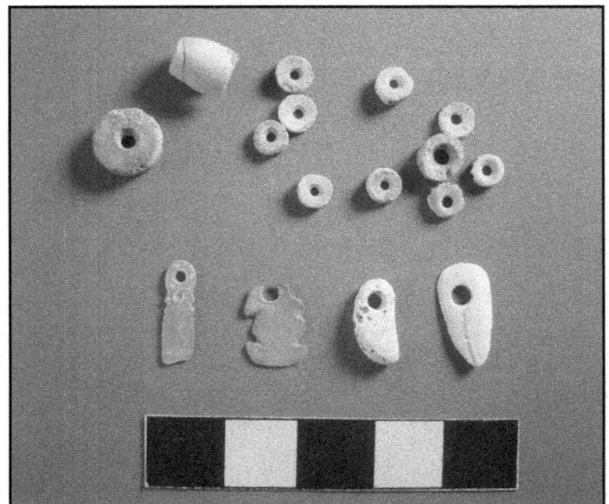
Figure 6.16. Beads and pendants.

ous pearly shell, to manufacture ten of the pendants (8 percent). *Spondylus/Chama* shells are only represented by a single identified pendant example at the site. Although *Pecten vodgesi* shells were identified in the excavated sample (n = 36), none were complete enough to confidently assign as pendants. Nelson (1991) argues the Hohokam placed a high value on *Pecten vodgesi* pendants.

Table 6.6 presents a summary of pendant types, their absolute counts, and relative frequencies. Perforated whole shells, which are otherwise unmodified, comprise the largest category of pendants with 68 examples or 52 percent of the total. Only four zoomorphic type pendants were encountered during excavation: two frogs, a Gila monster, and a turtle (Figures 6.17, 6.18, and 6.19). Crafts persons carved the frogs and turtle from *Glycymeris gigantea,* while an artisan carved the Gila monster from *Laevicardium elatum.* Reworked bracelet fragments constitute 22 percent of the pendants identified as to form with 11 examples. Trinchereños produced these pendants by perforating the umbo and grinding the broken edges smooth to form a "coat hanger" shape.

Tinklers

All the tinklers (Figure 6.20) encountered during excavation were made from *Conus* sp. univalves. Artisans manufactured tinklers by removing the apex and spire down the shoulder of the shell, along with the columella or central spire. All of the Cerro de Trincheras examples are perforated for stringing at the distal end of the aperture at the narrowest portion of the cone shell. A total of 69 tinklers, both whole and fragmented, were encountered, representing two percent of the total of finished shell artifacts. None were decorated with incising.

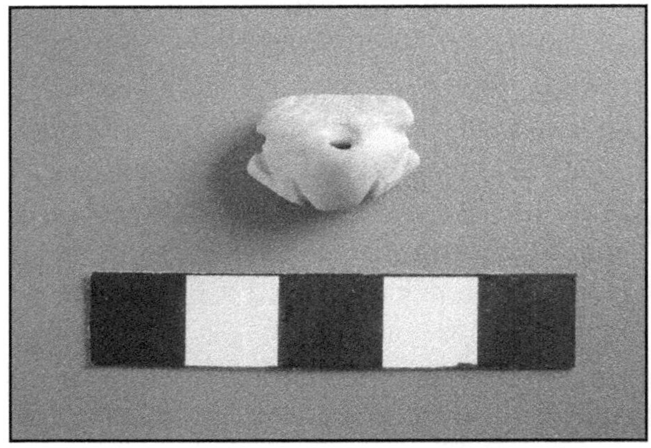

Figure 6.17. Frog zoomorphic pendant.

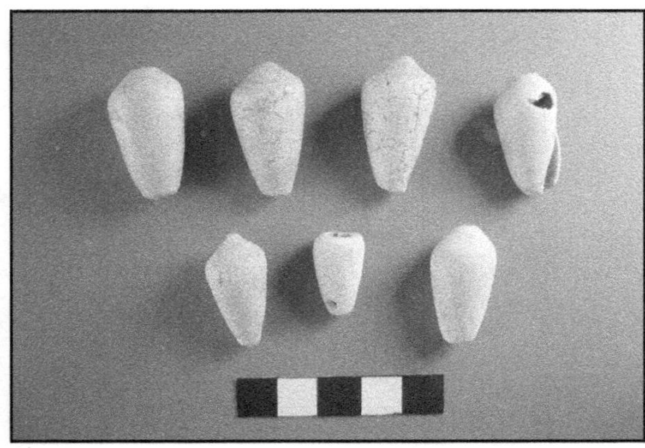

Figure 6.20. Tinklers.

Figure 6.18. Frog and sea turtle zoomorphic pendants.

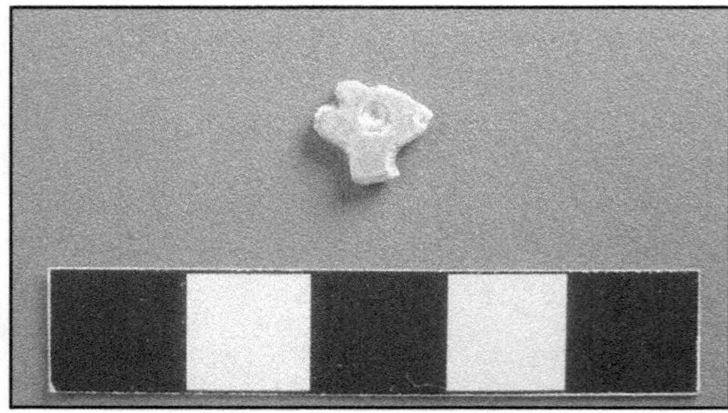

Figure 6.21. Deer zoomorphic object fragment.

Figure 6.19. Gila Monster zoomorphic pendant.

Figure 6.22. Worked shell debitage.

Other Forms

We found a carved shell zoomorphic object during excavation. This piece is a small fragment of a once larger finished piece; therefore it exhibits no evidence of perforation. An artisan carved the object from *Pinctada mazatlanica* and the field crew affectionately referred to as "Bambi" due to its likeness to a small deer head (Figure 6.21). It is possibly a pendant fragment.

I classified two objects as "ear cuffs," although their actual function is uncertain. Both are curved pieces of shell made from small gastropods, which strongly resemble ear cuffs in modern day usage.

We recovered two small pieces of shell that are squarish in shape and have beveled edges. I classified them as mosaic pieces due to their form, although no finished mosaic work was encountered.

Whole unworked shell is somewhat rare at Cerro de Trincheras with only 59 examples encountered during excavation. The largest category of whole unworked shell genera is *Conus* (34 percent; n = 20). No whole *Glycymeris gigantea* bivalves were encountered, although five *Glycymeris maculata* were recorded. Table 6.7 provides a summary of all unworked whole shells with their absolute counts and relative frequencies.

Archaeologists recovered eleven spangles during excavation at Cerro de Trincheras. Spangles resemble disk beads, but typically are long ovals in plan that were sewn to some object, such as clothing, rather than having been perforated and strung.

Evidence for Shell Ornament Production

Evidence for shell production at Cerro de Trincheras includes manufacturing debris (Figure 6.22) and in-process objects discarded prior to completion. Manufacturing debris includes the 92 discarded cores (tapas) from *Glycymeris* bracelet manufacture as well as the debitage associated with shell reduction. Ground stone and pecked stone implements (n = 16) were encountered during excavation, which are believed to be associated with shell manufacturing. Included in this assemblage are reamers, lap-stones, and grooved ground stone palettes. The ground stone analysis report (Greenwald, Chapter 5, this volume) provides more information regarding these artifacts.

In-process pieces total 328 items. Table 6.8 presents absolute quantities of each in-process artifact form and their relative frequencies. Beads are the largest category of in-process artifacts, with 241 examples. *Glycymeris* Bracelets are represented by 41 in-process examples and Conus rings with 19 examples. There are 19 unidentified in-process examples. Tinklers (n = 2), spangles (n = 4), and pendants (n = 2) make up the remainder of the in-process assemblage.

Table 6.9 indicates the intra-site distribution of in-process artifacts. Area D stands out as having the highest frequency with 33 percent (n = 117). This is not surprising given the high amount of workshop debris, discussed below, which was encountered during excavation.

Table 6.10 presents the absolute quantities of genera identified for workshop debris. There are 1,755 fragments of workshop debris in the total excavated marine shell assemblage or 35 percent of the total identified shell artifacts recovered during excavation. This category consists of characteristic manufacturing waste (DT = Deshecho de Taller) produced during the shell working process. *Conus* sp. comprises the overwhelming majority (66 percent) of this total. Shell fragments of *Glycymeris* and *Laevicardium* comprise 19 percent (n = 292) and 14 percent (n = 212) respectively of the category. I only included fragments that could be definitively identified as manufacturing waste in this category. There is a high probability that a large portion of the unidentified fragment category (FNC = Fragmento no Classificado) in this analysis is made up of manufacturing waste, but assignments to that category (DT) were made with circumspection.

Table 6.11 presents the intra-site distribution of manufacturing waste per area. Area D has the largest amount with 370 fragments, or 21 percent of the total. Several other areas of the site, Areas B1, B2, and B6, also had substantial amounts of manufacturing waste. Significantly, every area investigated by excavation yielded manufacturing waste. However, the four areas mentioned above appear to exhibit the greatest concentration of this artifact category. Therefore, it appears that although shell jewelry manufacture may have occurred across all portions of the site investigated, some areas of the site were significantly more involved in this activity than others.

Areas B1, B2, B6, and D also exhibited the greatest quantities of total shell artifacts (Table 6.12). Area D yielded 1,061 shell artifacts, or 15 percent of the site total. Area B6 yielded 1,068 shell artifacts, or16 percent of the site total. Area B1 has 986 shell artifacts, or 14 percent of the site total, while Area B2 has 822, or 12 percent of shell artifacts at the site.

It is notable that those areas listed above with the largest quantities and relative frequencies of shell artifacts also exhibit the largest quantities of shell manufacturing waste. This suggests that these were highly productive shell manufacturing loci. Furthermore, it appears that the inhabitants of these areas most likely retained control over their finished products, which is suggested by the large quantities of finished shell artifacts.

Intra-Site Distribution of Marine Shell Finished Artifacts

Tables 6.13-17 present distributional data by site area for beads, rings, bracelets, pendants, and tinklers. It is notable that for all shell artifact categories, except beads, the majority of each artifact type was retrieved from Areas B1 and B6. Both of these areas, as discussed above, exhibit large quantities of overall finished artifacts as well as large quantities of shell jewelry manufacturing debris relative to other excavated areas.

Table 6.18 details the quantity of marine shell artifacts found per feature. El Caracolito stands out as having the majority of shell in this category, with 509 shell artifacts. This feature, located in Area D, has been posited as a shell workshop due to the large quantity of shell workshop debris found within. El Caracolito yielded 147 fragments of workshop debris (DT) and 75 in-process artifacts.

El Caracolito, containing roughly a third of the shell found in Area D, exhibits a heavy emphasis on *Conus* artifacts. Although large quantities of shell working debris were located in other areas of the site, no other features exhibit as great a concentration as El Caracolito. The apparent focus on *Conus* in this workshop area is even more notable given the resemblance of that structure in plan to a *Conus* univalve in section. It is uncertain at this point whether this resemblance is deliberate or coincidental.

Marine shell artifact patterning exhibited at the site is clearly that of an extensive shell working tradition. Although shell jewelry manufacture apparently took place across the investigated portion of the site, Areas B1, B2, B6, and D were obviously much more intensively involved in this industry than were the other areas. The intra-site distribution of several shell artifact types indicates that Areas B1 and B6 retained more finished shell products than other areas of the site. The relationship between marine shell procurement, jewelry production, and distribution appears to be complex at the site.

Future work will be directed toward understanding the intra-site distribution of the different shell artifact categories and how these patterns relate to the organization of shell jewelry production at the site, as well as examining the interregional shell trade issue. The following section provides a summary of the shell data for each excavated area of Cerro de Trincheras.

Area Summary

Area A1

Area A1 is located at the crest of the cerro. This area yielded 277 pieces of shell, comprising 4 percent of the excavated site total. Shell artifacts identifiable by genera total 231, with 46 pieces not identifiable at this level of analysis. Of the identified sample there are 121 pieces of *Conus* (52 percent), compared to only 48 pieces of *Glycymeris* (21 percent). Table 6.19 provides the distribution by genus for each area of the site. Only 11 genera were identified for the Area A1 assemblage, which is much fewer than for Area B1 (see below). Of note, given the interpretation of this area as a ceremonial precinct of some sort, are the relatively low quantities of shell in Area A1 compared to several other excavated terraces at the site.

Table 6.20 presents the shell artifact types identified for each area. Artifacts classified as DT, "deshecho de taller" (workshop debris), totaled 46 pieces for Area A1 (23 percent of the identifiable assemblage from Area A1). In addition to this manufacturing debris, evidence of shell jewelry manufacture is also exhibited by six in-process pieces: one bracelet, three beads, one spangle and three unidentifiable as to the final intended form. Some level of shell working is evidenced, although at a very small scale compared to other areas of the site.

Rings and beads make up the great majority of the identified assemblage (27 percent and 30 percent respectively) in Area A1. Bracelets constitute only 13 percent of the identified sample, less than is common elsewhere at the site. Of the shell artifacts recovered from this area, three rings and two bracelets were incised with decorative designs. Only four tinklers are represented (two percent) which is notable given their general association with ritual. Whatever the special function of this area was, it appears not to have involved much use of marine shell.

Area A1 exhibits no examples of *Spondylus*, although a single fragment of *Pecten vogdesi* was recovered. Scholars argue that both of these shell types were highly valued by many American prehispanic societies including the Hohokam (e.g., Nelson 1991, Paulsen 1974). As with every example of *Pecten vogdesi* retrieved at Cerro de Trincheras, the one example found in Area A1 shows no evidence of working, nor was there enough of the fragment to determine if it had once been part of a pendant.

Overall, Area A1 shows little presence of dance regalia (tinklers) or other potential high-value shell items (*Pecten vogdesi* pendants, *Spondylus* artifacts, and incised rings and bracelets). Additionally, while evidence for shell working is present, it appears to on a small scale.

Area B1

Area B1, comprised of two residential terraces, yielded 986 pieces of shell, comprising 14 percent of the site total. Shell identified by genus for this area total 826. There are 431 pieces of *Conus* (52 percent) and 244 pieces of *Glycymeris* (30 percent; Table 6.19). The diversity of shell species represented in Area B1 is striking. There are 26 different genera identified for this area alone, making it the most diverse of all the excavated areas.

We found 736 shell artifacts in Area B1 that we could identify by artifact type. Workshop debris constitutes 26 percent (n = 193) of the identified total. Thirty-six in-process artifacts that were recovered during excavation provide additional evidence of shell jewelry manufacture in this area: 27 beads, four bracelets, one tinkler, and four in-process pieces of undetermined artifact type.

Finished rings (n = 185) and bracelets (n = 175) have nearly equal relative frequencies for the identified sample of the area (25 percent and 24 percent respectively). Beads constitute 19 percent of this sample with 138 examples. Area B1 exhibits the greatest number of recorded tinklers for the site with 16 examples. Several of these tinklers from Area B1 are identified as being in-process.

Area B1 yielded 16 incised *Glycymeris* bracelets and 12 incised *Conus* rings. Incised bracelets and rings are relatively rare across the site. If one considers the additional skill and effort required to produce these designs, as well as their potentially high aesthetic appeal, these items arguably may be classified as high-value items.

Area B1 is also notable for the relatively large quantity of both *Spondylus* (n = 5) and *Pecten vogdesi* (n = 7) artifacts found there. It is appears that Area B1 had somewhat better access to, or produced and retained more of, these items than other areas of the site. In Area B1, 16 tinklers, seven *Pecten vogdesi* and five *Spondylus* artifacts, 16 incised bracelets and 12 incised rings were encountered. Future comparison between different artifact material classes for all the excavated areas of the site should provide needed data to determine whether the inhabitants of this area were perhaps the local "elite." This area appears to be a specialized intensive shell jewelry production area, one of four such areas thus far identified at the site, and likely the locus of tinkler manufacture given the available data.

Area B2

Area B2, a residential terrace, also had a large diversity of shell genera, with 21 different genera thus far identified. A total of 822 pieces of shell were recovered from this area, constituting 12 percent of the site total. Of these, 621 were identifiable to the genus level. *Conus* comprises the majority of the identified sample, with 314 items (51 percent). *Glycymeris* is the second largest shell category, with 169 examples (27 percent). This is a departure from Area B1, where the relative frequencies between the two types are almost equal. *Laevicardium* is represented by 70 pieces (11 percent). Each of the remaining genera recorded for the area comprise three percent or less of the identified sample. One *Spondylus* artifacts and four fragments of *Pecten vodgesi* were retrieved in the excavation of Area B2.

Of the 822 pieces of shell retrieved from Area B2, 562 were identifiable by artifact type. Workshop debris constitutes 41 percent (n = 233) of the identified total. Additional evidence of shell jewelry production in this area is provided by the 26 in-process pieces retrieved during excavation. These include 18 beads, three bracelets, two rings, and three in-process pieces of undetermined artifact type.

Conus rings are the most numerous of the area's shell artifacts, with 119 examples (21 percent). Bracelets (n = 95) and beads (n = 89) were retrieved in roughly equal relative frequencies (17 percent and 16 percent, respectively). Area B2 also has several potentially high-value goods, including four tinklers, one piece of *Spondylus*, four pieces of *Pecten vogdesi*, four incised rings, two incised pendants, six incised bracelets, and two incised unidentified objects.

Area B3

Area B3, comprised of two residential terraces, yielded substantially less shell than Areas B1 and B2. Only 249 pieces of shell were recovered in Area B3, constituting only four percent of the excavated site total. Genera identifications were possible for 190 pieces of the area assemblage. A total of ten marine shell genera were identified.

Conus makes is the most common genus for this area, with 92 examples (48 percent). *Glycymeris* is represented by 61 examples (32 percent). Fifteen *Laevicardium* pieces were identified for the area (8 percent). No *Spondylus* was encountered in Area B3, although four pieces of *Pecten vogdesi* were recovered.

Area B3 yielded 249 shell artifacts, of which 170 were identifiable by artifact type. Workshop debris constitutes 45 percent of this total (n = 76), the largest category for the area. Additional evidence of shell jewelry production in this area includes nine in-process artifacts: eight beads and one bracelet.

Rings and bracelets occur in roughly equal amounts in Area B3: 25 rings (15 percent) and 24 bracelets (14 percent). Three pendants were also retrieved. One of these, made from *Pinctada mazatlanica*, a type of "mother of pearl," has a narrow elongated rectangular form with some decorative notching on the sides. A single tinkler was recovered. Four incised artifacts, three bracelets and one ring, were encountered in this area.

Area B3 is difficult to characterize. There is some evidence of shell jewelry manufacture, along with a few pieces of potentially high-value shell goods. If this terrace was a habitation locale, it appears the residents made a small amount of shell for personal use and had access to a few high-value pieces.

Area B4

Area B4, a residential terrace, yielded 478 shell artifacts during excavation (seven percent of the site total). Of these, 261 were identifiable to the genus level. Seventeen marine shell genera are represented in Area B4. *Conus* is represented with 141 examples (54 percent), *Glycymeris* with 64 (25 percent), and *Laevicardium* with 14 (five percent). Three *Spondylus* artifacts were recovered, but no *Pecten vogdesi.* Relative to other investigated areas of the site, a large number (n = 9) of *Pinctada mazatlanica* artifacts were encountered in Area B4.

There were 478 shell artifacts recovered from Area B4, 339 of which were identifiable by artifact form. Beads are the most numerous, with 116 examples (34 percent). Sixty rings (18 percent) and 32 bracelets (9 percent) were recovered. It is notable that outside of Area E, this is the only investigated area of the site that yielded no tinklers.

One incised-design bracelet was recovered in Area B4, as were four incised-design rings and four incised shell artifacts not identified by form. In addition, a fragment of what appears to be the head of a deer pendant was found. It is made from *Pinctada mazatlanica* and is unique at the site (Figure 6.21).

It is apparent that shell jewelry was produced in Area B4. One hundred and thirteen fragments of workshop debris were encountered (33 percent of the area total). In addition, 21 in-process pieces were recovered: 15 beads, two bracelets, one ring, and three in-process artifacts of indeterminate artifact type.

Area B5

Area B5, La Cancha, yielded 321 pieces of marine shell, five percent of the site's total.

Genera identifications were possible for 272 of these, with 14 genera represented. *Conus* constitutes the largest identified sample with 55 percent (n = 149) and *Glycymeris* is the second largest, with 26 percent (n = 71). *Nassarius* (n = 15, or 6 percent) and *Laevicardium* (n = 21, or 8 percent) are the next most inclusive categories. The remainder (Table 6.19) constitute two percent or less of the area sample. Both *Spondylus/Chama* (n = 3) and *Pecten vogdesi* (n = 2) were found in this area, indicating access to these high value shell types.

Beads make up the greatest proportion of those artifacts from Area B5 that could be identified by artifact type (Table 6.20), with 50 examples (22 percent). Rings and bracelets are similarly represented, with 40 (17.5 percent) and 42 (18 percent) examples, respectively. Two incised-decorated rings and three such bracelets were recovered during excavation of this area. Only one tinkler was recovered.

Although low in overall quantity (n = 92), the proportion of workshop debris in Area B5 is quite high, constituting 40 percent of the identified total. In-process artifacts were also recovered in this area, with 16 examples: 14 beads, and two bracelets. As with other areas of the site, some shell working is evident, although not at any great scale.

Given the low overall quantity of shell in this area compared with other areas of the site, remarkably large amounts of high-value goods were retrieved: three *Spondylus/Chama* and two *Pecten vogdesi* artifacts, two incised rings, and three incised bracelets. Only a single tinkler was recovered from this area. Shell jewelry manufacture is evident, although it is minor in scale compared to other areas of the site.

Area B6

Area B6, comprised of three residential terraces, stands out for the sheer quantity of shell recovered in excavation (n = 1068, or 16 percent of the site total) compared to other excavated areas of the site (Table 6.12). Of these, 990 were identifiable to the genus level, of which 20 are present (Table 6.19). *Conus* (47 percent) and *Glycymeris* (35 percent) constitute the majority of the area assemblage, with 465 and 350 pieces respectively. *Laevicardium* (9 percent) is the next greatest contributor, with 85 pieces represented. *Pecten vogdesi* and *Spondylus/Chama* are both represented in the area assemblage with eight examples of the former and a single example of the latter.

Manufacturing debris constitutes the largest category of shell artifact types in Area B6, with 315 pieces or 38 percent of the identified total for the area (Table 6.20). Further evidence for intra-area shell jewelry manufacture includes 38 in-process pieces, with 18 beads, ten bracelets, eight rings, one spangle, and two pieces of undetermined form. Apparently, more shell jewelry was produced in this area than would be expected for merely intra-household use only. This may have been a communal shell jewelry manufacturing area where numerous artisans worked. These artisans may have represented more than one household and may have produced shell jewelry for trade, an example of which may be represented by El Caracolito in Area D.

Bracelets (25 percent of the identified sample) are more prevalent in this area than rings (18 percent), which is remarkable at the site; typically rings tend to dominate the assemblage or are roughly equal in frequency to bracelets in most areas. Tinklers, represented here by 15 examples, are equaled in quantity elsewhere at the site only in Area B1. Still they account for less than two percent of the identified sample in Area B6. Significantly, the greatest number of incised artifacts recovered to date from the site were encountered in Area B6: 18 bracelets, five rings, a single "ear cuff," a pendant and two unidentified objects.

Area B6 appears to be an intensive or

extensive shell jewelry manufacturing area, one of four such areas at the site. A large variety of shell species are present, along with a relatively large quantity of shell artifacts (16 percent of the excavated site total). Large quantities of finished goods were located in this area, indicating the artisans may have maintained control of their goods. High-value shell items include eight pieces of *Pecten vogdesi* and one of *Spondylus/Chama,* 15 tinklers, and the largest quantity of incised shell bracelets found at the site (n = 18). The presence of tinklers and incised bracelets in such relatively large quantities, compared to other areas of the site, may indicate production of these artifact types in this area, or a greater access to these goods.

Area B7

Area B7, comprised of two residential terraces, yielded 651 shell artifacts, or 9 percent of the site total (Table 6.12). Of these, 578 pieces were identifiable at the genus level, of which 22 genera are represented (Table 6.19). *Conus* constitutes the majority of shell from this area with, 285 examples (49 percent). *Glycymeris* is the second largest category, with 142 examples (25 percent). *Laevicardium* makes up the next largest category (n = 50, or 9 percent). Although the area exhibits a relatively great diversity in shell genera, the majority of genera are only represented by a few pieces. The two potentially high-value shell genera, *Spondylus/ Chama* and *Pecten vogdesi* are both present in relatively high numbers compared with other areas of the site at nine and six examples respectively.

Of the 651 pieces of shell recovered in Area B7, 476 were identifiable by artifact type (Table 6.20). Evidence of shell jewelry manufacture in Area B7 includes 117 pieces of manufacturing debris, or 25 percent of all shell identified by artifact type. Additionally, 25 in-process shell artifacts were identified: 16 beads, five bracelets, two rings, and two unidentified by type. Shell jewelry production, while significant, appears not to have been as intensive or as extensive as occurred in other areas of the site. The ratio of shell debitage to finished artifacts in this area is 1:3. The large quantity of shell artifacts and the amount of manufacturing debris suggests this area may have produced more shell goods than were consumed at the household level.

Beads are the most frequent artifact types for this area, with 30 percent (n = 143) of the identified total. Rings, with 24 percent (n = 112) are the second most frequent, and bracelets (n = 76) follow with16 percent. Eight tinklers were recovered in this area, along with seven incised bracelets, six incised rings, and two unidentified incised objects.

Area B7 may be characterized as a shell jewelry manufacturing locale, although one that is neither as intensive nor extensive as the four big loci (Areas B1, B2, B6, and D) that are discussed in more detail below. It appears, however, that shell jewelry was produced in this area at a greater scale than would have been necessary for household consumption alone. Once again, it is difficult to ascertain at this stage in the analysis whether this area represents a specialized activity locus with individuals from more than one household coming to this location to craft shell jewelry or, conversely, if this represents a single household or extended family producing shell jewelry beyond their own needs, possibly for trade.

Area B7 apparently had access to potentially high-value goods. Both *Spondylus/ Chama* (n = 9) and *Pecten vogdesi* (n = 6) are represented in fairly high quantities, as are tinklers (n = 8). In addition, 15 incised shell artifacts were recovered during excavation of this area.

Area B8

Excavations in Area B8 (two elite terraces of El Mirador) recovered 411 shell artifacts, 6 percent of the site total (Table 6.12). Of these, 349 were identifiable at the genus level (Table 6.19). *Conus* constitutes the majority of the identified genera with 179 examples or 51 percent, while only 86 examples, or 25 percent, of *Glycymeris* was represented. *Laevicardium* constitutes only nine percent of the sample, with 32 pieces. No *Pecten vogdesi* shells were recovered from this area, but two *Spondylus/Chama* artifacts were recovered.

Of the 316 shell artifacts that could be identified by artifact type (Table 6.20), beads made are the majority, with 95 examples (30 percent). Rings and bracelets were represented by 74 (23 percent) and 48 (15 percent) examples, respectively. A remarkably high number of incised rings and bracelets were encountered (n = 18): 11 incised rings, six incised bracelets, and one incised but otherwise unidentifiable shell artifact. Additionally, six tinklers were recovered from this area. The artisans associated with this area apparently had access to a variety of potentially high-value shell goods: tinklers, *Spondylus/Chama* shell, and incised rings and bracelets.

Shell jewelry production is evident, with 73 pieces of production debris (23 percent) and 19 in-process pieces. The in-process pieces include 16 beads, three bracelets, and a single ring. The small quantity of production debris suggests a low level of shell jewelry production for this area, not inconsistent with one or two households producing only enough for their own use.

Area B9

Area B9 (an elite terrace of El Mirador) yielded 157 pieces of marine shell totaling only 2 percent of the site total (Table 6.12). Of these, 147 were identifiable at the genus level (Table 6.19). *Conus* is represented by 76 examples (52 percent), while *Glycymeris* is represented by only 36 examples (25 percent). The next largest category is *Laevicardium* with 10 pieces (7 percent). A single *Spondylus/Chama* artifact and two *Pecten vogdesi* artifacts were encountered in this area.

Of the 157 pieces of shell from Area B9, 126 were identifiable by artifact type (Table 6.20). Remarkably, *Conus* rings make up the largest category of finished artifacts with 30 (24 percent) examples recovered. Twenty-nine beads (23 percent) and 17 bracelet fragments (14 percent) make up the two next largest categories. Three tinklers and four spangles were recovered by excavation in this area.

Workshop debris constitutes 31 percent (n = 39) of the area total. Additional evidence for shell jewelry manufacture includes eight in-process artifacts: three beads, two spangles, two bracelets and one tinkler. This in-process tinkler is one of only two recovered from the site during excavation. A low level of shell craft production is indicated for this area, either for intra-household use and/or a very low level of trade.

The individuals associated with this area had a degree of access to potentially high-value shell goods. *Spondylus/Chama* and *Pecten* are both present, although with only three total examples. Three tinklers were also recorded, as well as two incised shell artifacts (one ring and one unidentified object). Although these quantities are small, they suggest some level of access to these goods.

Area B10

Area B10, an elite terrace of El Mirador, yielded 53 shell artifacts, constituting only one percent of the excavated site total (Table 6.12). Of these, 50 pieces were identifiable to the genus level (Table 6.19). Six genera are represented, with *Conus* constituting the majority (n = 21, or 42 percent). *Glycymeris* is represented by 16 examples (32 percent) and *Laevicardium* with eight (16 percent). No *Spondylus/Chama* or *Pecten vogdesi* shells were recovered in this area.

Of the 53 shell artifacts recovered from Area B10, 37 were identified by artifact type (Table 6.20). Rings constitute the largest category of finished goods, with seven examples (19 percent), followed by five bracelets (14 percent). Three pendants were recovered from this area. Only two beads and a single tinkler were encountered. No incised shell artifacts are present.

Production evidence includes 18 pieces of manufacturing debris (49 percent of the identified total) and a single in-process bracelet fragment. Of the potentially high-value goods identified in this study, only one tinkler is recorded for Area B10. The small quantity of shell recovered from this area, including a low quantity of production debris, suggests that only a few shell artifacts were produced in this area. Overall, Area B10 appears to have been not much involved in either the receipt or production of shell goods.

Area B11

Area B11, a residential terrace, yielded 237 pieces of shell, constituting three percent of the excavated site total (Table 6.12). Of these, 217 were identifiable among 12 different genera (Table 6.19). *Glycymeris* and *Conus* are nearly equal in their representation in this area, with 76 (35 percent) and 78 (36 percent) examples, respectively. This distribution is not typical at Cerro de Trincheras and deserves further consideration. The next largest category of genera is *Laevicardium*, with 36 examples (17 percent). No *Spondylus/Chama* was noted for this area, but one example of *Pecten vogdesi* was recovered.

Of the 237 pieces of shell recorded for Area B11, 170 were identifiable by artifact type (Table 6.20). Of the finished artifacts, bracelets were the largest category, with 43 fragments (25 percent). Rings were represented by 34 examples (20 percent) and beads by 19 (11 percent). Seven tinklers were encountered, along with ten incised bracelets and one unidentified incised shell object. Access to several of the proposed high-value goods in Area B11 is evidenced by the recovery of the seven tinklers, five incised bracelets and a single *Pecten vogdesi* fragment.

Production debris constitutes 34 percent (n = 57) of the identified sample. Shell jewelry production is also evidenced by 11 in-process pieces, including three beads, three bracelets, two rings, two pendants, and one item of unidentifiable final form. The small quantity of manufacture debris in Area B11, indicates a low level of production.

Area D: A Specialized Shell Jewelry Manufacturing Locus

We discovered a specialized shell jewelry manufacturing locale on the occupational terraces of Area D. This area of the site yielded 1061 pieces, including unmodified shell, in-process objects, finished pieces, and manufacturing debris. This assemblage constitutes 15 percent of the excavated site total, an amount exceeded only in Area B6 (Table 6.12).

Of the marine shell recovered in Area D, 702 pieces were identifiable by artifact type (Table 6.20). Of these, manufacturing debris constitutes 53 percent (n = 370). Of the finished artifacts, beads are most numerous with 170 examples (24 percent). Rings are the next largest category with 85 examples (12 percent), followed by bracelets, with 51 examples (7 percent).

Two incised bracelet fragments and four incised ring fragments were recovered from this area. Area D yielded six fragments of *Pecten vogdesi* and two pieces of *Spondylus/ Chama.* Only three tinklers were recovered, which suggests that if they were being produced in this area, most were consumed elsewhere. It seems more likely, however, that tinklers were being produced at the site, perhaps in Area B1.

El Caracolito in Area D, a circular house with either a low stone wall or wall foundation, contained 509 pieces of shell. This feature is unique for its shell items in all stages of manufacture, its total quantity of shell artifacts, as well as its large amount manufacturing debris in a single location. It is almost certainly a specialized shell jewelry manufactory. Shell artifacts classified as manufacturing debris constitute 35 percent (n = 147) of the feature total. This manufacturing locus apparently specialized almost exclusively in the production of *Conus* jewelry, which constitutes 75 percent of the identified total for the feature, including all stages of manufacture.

Significant surface grinding was performed on the *Conus* shell jewelry during manufacture, which often made species identification difficult. However, it is notable that, where identification by species was possible, 139 items in Area D were identified as *Conus ximenes.* This suggests that jewelry manufacturing focused not just on *Conus* shell products, but focused on *Conus ximenes* as the primary raw material.

It is also notable that both examples of a three-dimensional carved frog effigy pendant recovered at the site came from El Caracolito. These were carved from the umbo of *Glycymeris gigantea* bivalves. Additionally, a unique artifact form for the site, a flat frog pendant carved from a tapa of *Glycymeris gigantea*, was also recovered here (Figure 6.17). It may be significant that the only marine shell frog effigies that have been recovered from this site are both associated with this feature. The unusual architectural feature, El Caracolito, may have held some special meaning for the inhabitants of the site. This round structure, indicated by a low stone wall or wall foundation has a notable attribute. A low, stone wall base curves from the west side of the structure towards its center. Viewed in plan it resembles the section of a *Conus* shell with the "cap" (apex and spiral) removed. Given the structure's specialized function, this may be a symbolic or iconic encoding into the architectural design.

Area E

Extensive excavations in Area E (pithouse hamlet) recovered only 91 pieces of shell, or one percent of the site total (Table 6.12). The main occupation of this area, which lies on the flats behind the main *cerro*, the cremation cemetery, and a small *cerrito*, is contemporary with the occupation up on the main cerro. Area E is a small settlement with associated pithouses, middens, storage pits, hearths, interments and cremations.

Of the area assemblage, 63 pieces of shell were identifiable at the genus level (Table 6.19). *Glycymeris* constitutes 41 percent (n = 26) of the identified sample, while *Conus* constitutes 32 percent (n = 20). Only two *Laevicardium* fragments were recovered in Area E.

Of the 91 pieces recorded for Area E, only 54 were identifiable by artifact type (Table 6.20). Excavators recovered 17 bracelet fragments (31 percent of the identified artifacts) one of which exhibits decorative incising. Ten rings were recovered (19 percent), of which three are decorated with incised designs. In addition, five pendants were found (9 percent), one of which is unique at the site. It is a flat zoomorphic pendant, possibly representing a Gila Monster, made from *Laevicardium elatum* (Figure 6.19). A pendant carved to resemble a sea turtle was also recovered from this area. It is decorated by surface incising and is made from the tapa of a *Glycymeris gigantea* shell (Figure 6.18).

Evidence for shell jewelry production in Area E is represented by only 12 pieces (22 percent of the area total) classified as workshop debris. No in process pieces were recovered. The residents of Area E were apparently not as involved in shell jewelry production were the inhabitants up on the cerro. They may, however, have had some access to potentially high-value shell items, as one *Spondylus* bead and two fragments of *Pecten vogdesi* were found here.

The scale of production at Cerro de Trincheras was apparently greater than would be needed for local consumption. This indicates the potential for small-scale export to other regions. However, an important inference of this study is that Cerro de Trincheras did not export substantial quantities of marine shell artifacts to other regions in the prehispanic Southwest/Northwest.

Interregional Interaction: Casas Grandes and Cerro De Trincheras

Excavators were struck by the apparent absence of Tucson Basin or Phoenix Basin ceramic types at Cerro de Trincheras. For many years scholars have argued that Cerro de Trincheras was a southern extension of the Hohokam and was active in moving raw shell and shell goods northward to the Hohokam core area. Our investigation produced little, if any, evidence to support this scenario. To the contrary, the most common painted ceramics found at Cerro de Trincheras were Chihuahuan Polychromes, which suggests that long-distance relationships likely lay to the east with the Casas Grandes area (Chapter 3, this volume).

Given these Chihuahuan tradewares present at Cerro de Trincheras, this section reports the results of analysis to determine whether Cerro de Trincheras might have been involved in trading shell eastward to Casas Grandes. Contemporary assemblages of shell artifacts from Medio Period Paquimé (Casas Grandes) and Cerro de Trincheras possess notable similarities and differences. The similarities included several traits, distinct from prehispanic U.S. Southwest examples, including the presence of a "saucer-shaped" bead form and a resemblance between Chihuahuan Polychrome iconography (particularly Ramos Polychrome) and incised shell designs at Cerro de Trincheras.

Archaeologists traditionally interpret saucer-shaped beads, found rarely in the prehispanic U.S. Southwest, as indicating interaction with California coast groups who produced and widely traded this bead form (Jernigan 1978:37, Nelson 1991:58). California coast saucer-shaped beads, along with the examples found at U.S. Southwest sites are typically made from *Olivella* sp. gastropods (Nelson 1991:58). Nelson lists only three sites in Arizona with these saucer-shaped beads, including only six or seven examples altogether from Escalante Ruin, Los Muertos, and Babocomari Village. No saucer-shaped *Olivella* sp. specimens have been identified, however, at Cerro de Trincheras or Paquimé (Di Peso et al. 1974b).

Of the 205 saucer-shaped beads recovered from Cerro de Trincheras 130 were assigned to the *Conus* genus. While Paquimé's analyst only identified four out of 844 specimens to genus, all were assigned to *Conus* (Di Peso et al. 1974b). Neither analysis assigned any of the beads to the genus *Olivella*. Given the large quantities of the beads recovered at Paquimé, it is unclear if these four pieces are representative of the whole assemblage. During analysis 31 examples of in-process saucer-shaped beads at Cerro de Trincheras were identified, but Di Peso and others (1974b) do not note any in-process examples at Paquimé. The lack of evidence for the production of these beads at Paquimé suggests they were not made locally. It is possible, therefore, that these *Conus* saucer-shaped beads originated in the Trincheras area. Cerro de Trincheras is the only locale in either the U.S. Southwest or Northwest México to date that has yielded evidence for the production of this form. Although the overall quantities of these beads at both sites are relatively small, they serve as one possible indicator of interaction between the two areas.

In addition to the saucer-shaped bead data, incised shell designs from Cerro de Trincheras provide another line of evidence supporting possible interaction with Paquimé. Incised shell apparently enjoyed somewhat greater popularity at Cerro de Trincheras than at Paquimé, but occurs infrequently at both sites. At Cerro de Trincheras a variety of incised designs on *Glycymeris* bracelets and *Conus* rings were recorded. Most of these designs appear similar to ones used by Hohokam artisans, including geometric motifs interpreted by Haury (1976) and Jernigan (1978) as representing an idealized serpent motif. Additionally, Cerro de Trincheras yielded several incised shell designs that have not been reported from sites in the U.S. Southwest. These designs include geometric interlocking scrolls and angled lines, often with hatching, and with the design portion in relief above the background. A circle or square is integrated into the design with a small dot depression in the center, which is bracketed with a raised edge border. This incised shell style, especially the interlocking angled scrolls, is strikingly similar to several Chihuahua Polychromes, especially Ramos Polychrome (Arleyn Simon, personal communication). Shell artisans at Cerro de Trincheras would have encountered these designs on the Chihuahuan Polychrome trade wares found at the site. Apparently Paquimé did not produce or import shell goods with these designs, as none of the incised shell work found at Paquimé includes these motifs (Di Peso et al. 1974b).

Remarkable as these similarities may be, it must be emphasized that significant differences exist between the shell assemblages of these two centers. These include differences in the quantity of shell, the genera present, the sources of the marine shell, and in the types of items produced.

The major difference lies in the sheer quantity of shell. Paquimé yielded 3,907,402 individual pieces of marine shell (Di Peso et al. 1974b), compared to 6,867 pieces from Cerro de Trincheras. The vast majority of Paquimé shell (3,307,024) were *Nassarius* sp. beads that were found in three rooms of Unit 8. Excluding these beads, the shell count at Paquimé is 600,378. Di Peso also excavated a much larger portion of Casas Grandes (~ 40 percent), than has been investigated at Cerro de Trincheras (~1.5 percent). If these samples are representative, and if we extrapolate from them then the total shell artifact population at Casas Grandes would be 1,500,945 pieces, while the total at Cerro de Trincheras would be 457,800 pieces.

There are numerous problems with calculations of the total populations of shell from the Casas Grandes and Cerro de Trincheras samples. Both excavations used judgmental samples that tended to emphasize contexts that would be rich in shell and therefore both samples may over estimate the population of shell at each site. Excavation methods differed significantly between the sites both in terms of earth removal (primarily by trowel at Cerro de Trincheras, and primarily by shovel at Casas Grandes), and screening (1/4-inch at Cerro de Trincheras and 1/2-inch to 1-inch mesh at Casas Grandes). Given these differences we would expect that the Cerro de Trincheras excavations recovered a higher proportion of the shell present than did the excavations at

Casas Grandes. Thus, the calculations probably under estimate the magnitude of the difference in quantity of shell at the two sites. The approximations only serve to make gross relative comparisons between the two sites, and not to make accurate or precise estimates of the total populations of shell at either site. Raw counts overstate the differences in the quantity of shell at each site, but even if they are adjusted, the postulated difference remains on the order of three times more shell at Paquimé than at Cerro de Trincheras.

The assemblage at Paquimé includes two California coast marine shell genera: *Haliotis* sp. and *Dentallium* sp. (Di Peso et al. 1974b:401). The analysis of the Cerro de Trincheras material found no California coast specific genera, suggesting that Paquimé had a source of shells not used by the people at Cerro de Trincheras.

It is also apparent that Paquimé imported shell from farther south on the gulf coast of west México than did Cerro de Trincheras. The excavations at Paquimé recovered 1,122 examples of a rare shell type, *Persicula bandera* (Di Peso et al. 1974b:Fig.660-6). The only known natural habitat for this shell is at Banderas Bay, Jalisco (Keen 1971:635). In the Casas Grandes sample one shell in 535 was *Persicula bandera*. Applying this ratio to the Cerro de Trincheras sample, we expect to find 12 specimens of this species. Its complete absence from the Cerro de Trincheras assemblage suggests that Paquiméan shell workers obtained marine shell from yet another source not used by the people of Trincheras.

The Paquimé investigators concluded that the majority of shell found there was obtained from the coastal region around Guaymas and/or the nearby deltas of the Yaqui and Matape Rivers (Di Peso et al. 1974b:401). The site of Cerro de Trincheras is at the confluence of two possible shell routes (Villalpando 1988). The most probable route would have followed the Magdalena River to the coast at Desemboque near Puerto Lobos. The other route would have come up the Bacoachi Arroyo, which enters the Gulf of California north of Kino Bay, then heads immediately to the south of Cerro de Trincheras (Robles 1973). Although both of these potential sources are much farther north than the Guaymas area, the shell species available in this northern region of the coast match the genera found at Cerro de Trincheras. It appears that the primary sources for both sites are quite geographically distant from one another.

The different shell species assemblages from both sites also reflect the disparities in the source areas, as well as indicating possible differences in the preferred species for each tradition. Paquimé has 73 marine shell species, including 40 species not represented at Cerro de Trincheras. The 78 recorded marine shell species at Cerro de Trincheras, on the other hand, include 44 that do not occur at Paquimé.

Consideration of the various artifact forms also show marked differences between the two sites (Table 6.21). Several revisions of the data sets were necessary to provide comparable assemblages. For example, Di Peso and others (1974b) recorded as truncated beads what are commonly called *Conus* "rings" in the shell literature. For comparative purposes these items were moved into a ring category. Additionally, all unidentified fragments and objects, as well as manufacturing debris were excluded. This has little effect on the Casas Grandes data due to the negligible quantities of manufacturing debris found there.

Nassarius sp. beads constitute the overwhelming majority of the recovered Paquimé shell (n = 3,711,930) at 97.18 percent of the total assemblage (Di Peso et al. 1974b:Fig. 660-6). Three rooms in Unit 8, interpreted as storerooms, yielded 3,307,024 of these artifacts. In order to provide a basis of comparability with other shell artifact frequencies, this obvious outlier of all *Nassarius* sp. shell has also been omitted from the Paquimé inventory (Table 6.21).

The differences in artifact forms between the two sites are remarkable. Cerro de Trincheras emphasized bracelets/armlets (27 percent) much more than Paquimé (0.04 percent). *Conus* rings at Cerro de Trincheras have a significantly higher frequency (31 percent) than at Paquimé (0.36 percent). Paquimé obviously focused much more on beads (~74 percent) and tinklers (20 percent) than did Cerro de Trincheras (34 percent and two percent, respectively). If *Nassarius* sp. beads are added back into the Paquimé assemblage, the bead frequency would rise to 99.29 percent of the site's total. These differences between the sites may express the cultural differences in shell artifact form preferences (possibly tied to use and meaning), which may indicate a considerable cultural distance between the two traditions.

There is negligible manufacturing debris recorded for Paquimé, suggesting that many artifacts were imported as finished products. Bradley (1995) argues that this lack of manufacturing debris probably results from an emphasis on only slightly modified gastropod beads that would result in minimal manufacturing debris. However, there are significant quantities of shell jewelry items at Paquimé, such as bracelets, tinklers, and *Conus* shell rings that, if produced at the site, would have left significant quantities of distinctive manufacturing waste. Production of these pieces at Paquimé would also be evidenced by in-process pieces, broken or discarded prior to completion, like those recovered in such great quantities at Cerro de Trincheras. The Paquimé report (Di Peso et al. 1974b:523-525) indicates that only 20 partially worked pieces were identified by analysis. Therefore, Paquimé probably imported these goods in finished form, some of which may have originated in the Trincheras area. A reanalysis of the unidentified fragments from Paquimé for evidence of production waste would help to resolve the question of local shell craft production at the site.

Overall, the differences between the marine shell assemblages from Paquimé and Cerro de Trincheras far outweigh their similarities. Paquimé was probably acquiring shell from at least two or more sources, one of which may have been Cerro de Trincheras. Specifically, evidence suggests that Cerro de Trincheras may have traded saucer-shaped beads to Paquimé. The lack of evidence for saucer-shaped bead production at Paquimé, such as in-process pieces, indicates that these items were probably traded into the site in finished form. Cerro de Trincheras is, thus far, the only known site with evidence of the production of this bead form in the Greater Southwest, thereby making it the probable source of these beads at Paquimé.

Additional evidence for interaction lies in the resemblance of iconography on Cerro de Trincheras incised shell bracelets and rings to Chihuahuan polychrome ceramics. Other types of shell artifacts were probably also traded to Paquimé from Cerro de Trincheras, but most categories have such a broad geographic distribution that pinpointing Trincheras as the origin is not currently feasible. Recent attempts (Bradley 1996) to develop a chemical characterization sourcing method, such as one used by turquoise analysts have thus far been unsuccessful when applied to marine shell from archaeological contexts.

The nature and level of interaction between the two sites is still unclear. This initial investigation shows that some level of interaction appears to have occurred. The quantity of Paquimé shell in raw or finished form that originated from the Trincheras region is unknown. This preliminary study indicates that the quantities of shell traded were not great and that Cerro de Trincheras was not a primary marine shell source for Paquimé.

Discussion

The marine shell assemblage from Cerro de Trincheras is remarkably important and informative with regard to understanding the relationship between this site and those of the Hohokam core area and other areas in northwest México. It is quite clear that the prehistoric inhabitants of Cerro de Trincheras were indeed producing large quantities of shell artifacts. However, it is not clear that they produced these objects for export in interregional trade with other groups. Thus far, no strong trade relationship with any other group has been identified. The conclusion is that Cerro de Trincheras, although involved at some small level of interregional trade, was producing shell goods primarily for local consumption. Whether Cerro de Trincheras was procuring shell or even producing finished shell jewelry items for intra-regional trade with other Trincheras settlements in the area is still unclear.

Tables for Chapter 6

Table 6.1. Count by Genus

Genus/Genero	Quantity/Cantidad	% de Total
Acanthina	2	0
Aguadulce	1	0
Anadara	40	1
Arca	2	0
Argopecten	3	0
Atrina	2	0
Attiliosa	1	0
Bulla	1	0
Cancellaria	4	0
Cardita	2	0
Carditamera	2	0
Cerithidea	2	0
Cerithium	1	0
Chama	3	0
Chione	8	0
Columbella	84	1
Conus	3024	53
Fusinus	2	0
Glycymeris	1475	26
Hexaplex	1	0
Isognomon	1	0
Laevicardium	491	9
Leucozonia	2	0
Littorina	2	0
Lucina	1	0
Melongena	1	0
Modiolus	1	0
Murex	3	0
Muricanthus	3	0
NACREOUS	10	0
Nassarius	111	2
Nemocardium	6	0
Neorapana	1	0
Oliva	9	0
Olivella	73	1
Pecten	45	1
Phenacolepas	1	0
Pinctada	45	1
Polinices	1	0
Pteria	1	0
Spondylus/Chama	28	0
Strigilla	3	0
Terebra	6	0
Thais	4	0
Theodoxus	7	0
Trachycardium	97	2
Trivia	7	0
Turbo	1	0
Turritella	21	0
VERMETIDAE	30	1
Vermicularia	2	0
Total	5674	100

Table 6.2. Count by Genus and Species*

Genus/Genero	Species/Especie	Quantity/Cantidad	% de Total
Acanthina	sp.	2	0
Aguadulce	sp.	1	0
Anadara	sp.	23	0
Anadara	*multicostata*	16	0
Anadara	*reinharti*	1	0
Arca	sp.	1	0
Arca	*pacifica*	1	0
Argopecten	*circularis*	1	0
Argopecten	sp.	2	0
Atrina	sp.	2	0
Attiliosa	*incompta*	1	0
Bulla	*gouldiana*	1	0
Cancellaria	*obesa*	4	0
Cardita	sp.	1	0
Cardita	*radiata*	1	0
Carditamera	*gracilis*	2	0
Cerithidea	*albonodosa*	2	0
Cerithium	*malculosum*	1	0
Chama	*frondosa*	3	0
Chione	*californiesis*	1	0
Chione	*discrepans*	1	0
Chione	*fluctifraga*	2	0
Chione	sp.	1	0
Chione	*tumens*	1	0
Chione	*undatella*	2	0
Columbella	*aureomexicana*	2	0
Columbella	*fuscata*	76	1
Columbella	sp.	4	0
Columbella	*maculata*	1	0
Columbella	*strobiformis*	1	0
Conus	*californicus*	10	0
Conus	sp.	2294	40
Conus	*lucidus*	1	0
Conus	*perplexus*	20	0
Conus	*princeps*	21	0
Conus	*purpurascens*	1	0
Conus	*regularis*	1	0
Conus	*virgatus*	1	0
Conus	*ximenes*	675	12
Fusinus	*fredbakeri*	1	0
Fusinus	sp.	1	0
Glycymeris	*gigantean*	1348	24
Glycymeris	sp.	4	0
Glycymeris	*lintea*	18	0
Glycymeris	*maculata*	105	2
Hexaplex	*erythrostomus*	1	0
Isognomon	sp.	1	0
Laevicardium	*elatum*	470	8
Laevicardium	*elenense*	1	0
Laevicardium	sp.	20	0
Leucozonia	*cerata*	2	0
Littorina	*aspera*	1	0
Littorina	sp.	1	0
Lucina	*prolongata*	1	0
Melongena	*patula*	1	0
Modiolus	*modiolus*	1	0
Murex	sp.	3	0
Muricanthus	*nigritus*	3	0
NACREOUS	sp.	10	0
Nassarius	*iodes*	110	2

Table 6.2. Count by Genus and Species*, cont'd

Genus/Genero	Species/Especie	Quantity/Cantidad	% de Total
Nassarius	*versicolor*	1	0
Nemocardium	sp.	6	0
Neorapana	*tuberculata*	1	0
Oliva	*incrassata*	2	0
Oliva	sp.	6	0
Oliva	*undatella*	1	0
Olivella	*dama*	21	0
Olivella	sp.	20	0
Olivella	*intorta*	32	1
Pecten	sp.	9	0
Pecten	*vogdesi*	36	1
Phenacolepas	*malonei*	1	0
Pinctada	*mazatlanica*	45	1
Polinices	*uber*	1	0
Pteria	*sterna*	1	0
Spondylus/Chama	sp.	28	0
Strigilla	*chroma*	3	0
Terebra	*balaenorum*	1	0
Terebra	*hindsii*	4	0
Terebra	sp.	1	0
Thais	*biserialis*	2	0
Thais	sp.	2	0
Theodoxus	*luteofasciatus*	7	0
Trachycardium	*panamense*	95	2
Trachycardium	*senticosum*	1	0
Trachycardium	*trachycardium*	1	0
Trivia	sp.	2	0
Trivia	*radians*	2	0
Trivia	*solandri*	3	0
Turbo	*fluctuosus*	1	0
Turritella	*anactor*	3	0
Turritella	*gonostoma*	3	0
Turritella	sp.	3	0
Turritella	*leucostoma*	12	0
VERMETIDAE	sp.	30	1
Vermicularia	*eburnea*	2	0
	Total	5674	100

*Note: Unidentified to genus level n = 1193 (% of total [n = 6867] = 17%)

Table 6.3. Types, Counts, and Absolute Frequencies

Objeto/Object*	Quantity/Cantidad	% de Total
Anillo/Ring	981	20
Bracelete/Bracelet	857	17
Bracelete-pendiente/Bracelet-pendant	1	0
Cuenta/Bead	1069	22
Cuenta-pendiente/Bead-pendant	2	0
"Ear Cuff"	2	0
Figurilla/Figurine	2	0
Mosaic	2	0
Natural/Unmodified	59	1
Pendiente/Pendant	146	3
Deshecho de taller/Workshop debris	1755	35
"Spangle"	11	0
"Tinkler"	69	1
Subtotal	4956	100
*Note: the following were unidentified as to artifact type		
Unidentified Fragment/Fragmento no identificado	1708	25
Unidentified Worked Artifact/Objeto no identificado	203	3
Subtotal	1911	28
Total	6867	100

Table 6.4. Relative Frequencies of Finished Artifacts

Type/Tipo	Cantidad de Tipo	% de Total
Cap bead	237	22
Saucer shaped bead	205	19
Disk bead	281	26
Cylindrical bead	25	3
Truncated/choker bead	11	1
Whole shell bead	310	29
Total	1069	100

Table 6.5. Absolute Quantities and Relative Frequencies of Pendant Shell Genera and Species

Genus/Genero	Cantidad de Objeto	% de Total
Argopecten	1	1
Atrina	2	2
Cancellaria	1	1
Chama	1	1
Chione	1	1
Conus	7	5
Glycymeris	85	65
Laevicardium	7	5
NACREOUS	1	1
Oliva	1	1
Pinctada	10	8
Pteria	1	1
Spondylus/Chama	1	1
Terebra	2	2
Trachycardium	5	4
Turritella	3	2
VERMETIDAE	1	1
Subtotal	130	100
Unidentified	16	
Total Pendientes	146	100

Table 6.6. Pendant Types, Absolute Counts, and Relative Frequencies

Form/Forma	Quantity/ Cantidad	% de Total
Circular	3	2.3
Irregular	11	8.5
Natural/Unmodified	68	52.3
Oval	5	3.8
Rectangular	5	3.8
Semi-circular	2	1.5
Triangular	4	3.1
Zoomorphic	4	3.1
Reworked Bracelet	28	21.5
Subtotal	130	100.0
Indeterminate Form	16	
Total Pendientes	146	100.0

Table 6.7. Count by Genus and Species of Unworked Whole Shells

Genus/Genero	Species/Especie	Quantity/Cantidad	% de Total
Acanthina	*sp.*	1	2
Cancellaria	*obesa*	1	2
Columbella	*fuscata*	1	2
Conus	*sp.*	2	3
Conus	*ximenes*	18	31
Glycymeris	*gigantea*	3	5
Glycymeris	*maculata*	2	3
Indeterminate	*sp.*	8	14
Laevicardium	*elatum*	2	3
Lucina	*prolongata*	1	2
Nassarius	*iodes*	7	12
Nemocardium	*sp.*	1	2
Oliva	*sp.*	1	2
Olivella	*intorta*	1	2
Pecten	*sp.*	1	2
Pecten	*vogdesi*	1	2
Phenacolepas	*malonei*	1	2
Theodoxus	*luteofasciatus*	1	2
Turritella	*anactor*	1	2
Turritella	*sp.*	1	2
Turritella	*leucostoma*	4	7
Subotal		59	100
Unidentified		8	
Total		67	100

Table 6.8. Absolute Quantities of In-Process Artifact Forms and Relative Frequencies

Object/Objeto		Quantity/Cantidad	% de Total
Anillo		19	6
Bracelete		41	13
Cuenta		241	78
Pendiente		2	1
"Spangle"		4	1
"Tinkler"		2	1
	Subtotal	309	100
Unidentified objects		19	
	Total	328	100

Table 6.9. Intra-Site Distribution of In-Process Artifacts

Area	Quantity/Cantidad	% de Total
A1	8	2
B1	39	11
B2	28	8
B3	9	3
B4	26	7
B5	17	5
B6	43	12
B7	27	8
B8	21	6
B9	8	2
B10	1	0
B11	11	3
D	117	33
Total	355	100

Table 6.10. Absolute Quantities of Genera Identified for Workshop Debris

Genus/Genero	Quantity/Cantidad	% de Total
Anadara	9	1
Chione	1	0
Conus	1018	66
Glycymeris	292	19
Laevicardium	212	14
Nemocardium	1	0
Olivella	2	0
Pecten	3	0
Pinctada	10	1
Terebra	1	0
Turbo	1	0
Subtotal	1550	100
Unidentified Genera	205	
Total	1755	100

Table 6.11. Intra-Site Distribution of Manufacturing Waste per Area

Area	Quantity/Cantidad	% de Total
A1	46	3
B	1	0
B1	193	11
B2	233	13
B3	76	4
B4	113	6
B5	92	5
B6	315	18
B7	117	7
B8	73	4
B9	39	2
B10	18	1
B11	57	3
D	370	21
E	12	1
Total	1755	100

Table 6.12. Count of Shell Artifacts by Area

Area	Quantity/Cantidad	% de Total
A1	277	4
B	5	0
B1	986	14
B2	822	12
B3	249	4
B4	478	7
B5	321	5
B6	1068	16
B7	651	9
B8	411	6
B9	157	2
B10	53	1
B11	237	3
D	1061	15
E	91	1
Total	6867	100

Table 6.13. Bead Count by Area

Area	Quantity/Cantidad	% de Total
A1	60	6
B1	138	13
B2	89	8
B3	40	4
B4	116	11
B5	50	5
B6	108	10
B7	143	13
B8	95	9
B9	29	3
B10	2	0
B11	19	2
D	170	16
E	8	1
Total	1067	100

Table 6.14. Ring Count by Area

Area	Quantity/Cantidad	% de Total
A1	26	3
B1	175	20
B2	95	11
B3	24	3
B4	32	4
B5	42	5
B6	206	24
B7	76	9
B8	48	6
B9	17	2
B10	5	1
B11	43	5
D	51	6
E	17	2
Total	857	100

Table 6.15. Bracelet Count by Area

Area	Quantity/Cantidad	% de Total
A1	53	5
B	3	0
B1	185	19
B2	119	12
B3	25	3
B4	60	6
B5	40	4
B6	146	15
B7	112	11
B8	74	8
B9	30	3
B10	7	1
B11	34	3
D	85	9
E	10	1
Total	983	100

Table 6.16. Pendant Count by Area

Area	Quantity/Cantidad	% de Total
A1	4	3
B	1	1
B1	20	14
B2	19	13
B3	3	2
B4	12	8
B5	5	3
B6	21	14
B7	13	9
B8	14	10
B9	3	2
B10	3	2
B11	9	6
D	14	10
E	5	3
Total	146	100

Table 6.17. Tinkler Count by Area

Area	Quantity/Cantidad	% de Total
A1	4	6
B1	16	23
B2	4	6
B3	1	1
B5	1	1
B6	15	22
B7	8	12
B8	6	9
B9	3	4
B10	1	1
B11	7	10
D	3	4
Total	69	100

Table 6.18. Marine Shell Artifact Count by Feature

Construccion/Feature	Cantidad de artifactos de concha
Configuracion de piedras/Rock arrangement 4	52
Pithouse 2	2
La Cancha	234
El Caracol	56
Hoyo/Pit 10	10
Fogon/Hearth 1	1
Jacal 7	20
Jacal 1	20
Plataforma/Platform 3	41
Jacal 2	34
Hoyo/Pit 14	16
Estructura circular de piedra/Circular stone structure 17	9
Terraza Ancilaria/Ancillary terrace 1	4
Hoyo/Pit 1	1
Fogon/Hearth 4	1
Hoyo/Pit 2	3
Hoyo/Pit 3	1
Hoyo/Pit 4	1
Basurero/Midden 1	6
Configuracion de piedras/Rock arrangement 5	10
Hoyo/Pit 19	1
Entierro/Burial 11	3
Hoyo/Pit 20	4
Entierro/Burial 3	2
Estructura cuadrangular de piedra/Quadrangular stone structure 3	80
Hoyo/Pit 21	1
Hoyo/Pit 22	2
Hoyo/Pit 6	2
Configuracion de piedras/Rock arrangement 1	1
Ramada Posible/ Possible Ramada 1	1
Estructura cuadrangular de piedra/Quadrangular stone structure 4	59
El Caracolito	509
Hoyo/Pit 15	1
Hoyo/Pit 11	8
Fogon/Hearth 13	1
Hoyo/Pit 13	1
Fogon/Hearth 10	2
Superficie Occupacional/Occupational Surface 3	2
Entierro/Burial 2	1
Configuracion de piedras/Rock arrangement 3	1
Basurero/Midden 2	5
Hoyo/Pit 8	2
Fogon/Hearth 11	2
Pithouse 3	2
Jacal 3	14
Hoyo/Pit 16	2
Pithouse 5	22

Table 6.18. Marine Shell Artifact Count by Feature, cont'd

Construccion/Feature	Cantidad de artifactos de concha
Entierro/Burial 5	1
Estructura circular de piedra/Circular stone structure 18	46
Estructura cuadrangular de piedra/Quadrangular stone structure 1	109
Plataforma/Platform 1	55
Estructura circular de piedra/Circular stone structure 18	46
Platforma/Platform 2	96
Estructura circular de piedra/Circular stone structure 20	12
Superficie Occupacional/Occupational Surface 4	2
Entierro/Burial 6	7
Entierro/Burial 7	3
Entierro/Burial 8	1
Configuracion de piedras/Rock arrangement 6	5
Jacal 5	138
Fogon/Hearth 16	3
Elemento de acceso: Rampa/Access feature: Ramp 2	3
Estructura cuadrangular de piedra/Quadrangular stone structure 2	12
Jacal 6	25
Entierro/Burial 9	1
Estructura circular de piedra/Circular stone structure 4	9
Estructura circular de piedra/Circular stone structure 5	1
Estructura circular de piedra/Circular stone structure 7	1
Estructura circular de piedra/Circular stone structure 8	6
Estructura circular de piedra/Circular stone structure 12	1
Estructura circular de piedra/Circular stone structure 15	2
Estructura circular de piedra/Circular stone structure 22	39
Estructura circular de piedra/Circular stone structure 1	1
Estructura circular de piedra/Circular stone structure 24	2
Terrace 3	21
Terrace 11	11
Terrace 13	12
Terrace 15	1
Terrace 17	1
Terrace19	5
Total	1931

Table 6.19. Genus Count by Area

Area	Genus/Genero	Quantity/Cantidad	% de Area Total
A1	Indeterminate	46	
A1	*Anadara*	4	2
A1	*Columbella*	4	2
A1	*Conus*	121	52
A1	*Glycymeris*	48	21
A1	*Laevicardium*	29	13
A1	*Nassarius*	12	5
A1	*Olivella*	1	0
A1	*Pecten*	1	0
A1	*Pinctada*	1	0
A1	*Trachycardium*	4	2
A1	*Turritella*	2	1
A1	VERMETIDAE	4	2
A1 Subtotal Identified		231	100
A1 Subtotal All		277	
B	*Conus*	3	6
B	*Glycymeris*	1	2
B	VERMETIDAE	1	2
B Subtotal		5	100
B1	Indeterminate	160	
B1	*Carditamera*	1	0
B1	*Cerithidea*	1	0
B1	*Chione*	2	0
B1	*Columbella*	17	2
B1	*Conus*	431	52
B1	*Glycymeris*	244	30
B1	*Hexaplex*	1	0
B1	*Isognomon*	1	0
B1	*Laevicardium*	59	7
B1	*Leuconzonia*	1	0
B1	*Murex*	1	0
B1	*Muricanthus*	2	0
B1	*Nassarius*	7	1
B1	*Oliva*	1	0
B1	*Olivella*	11	1
B1	*Pecten*	8	1
B1	*Phenacolepas*	1	0
B1	*Pinctada*	8	1
B1	*Spondylus/Chama*	5	1
B1	*Strigilla*	1	0
B1	*Terebra*	3	0
B1	*Theodoxus*	3	0
B1	*Trachycardium*	12	1

Table 6.19. Genus Count by Area, cont'd

Area	Genus/Genero	Quantity/Cantidad	% de Area Total
B1	*Trivia*	1	0
B1	*Turritella*	1	0
B1	VERMETIDAE	2	0
B1	*Vermicularia*	1	0
B1 Subtotal		826	100
B1 Subtotal All		986	
B2	Indeterminate	201	
B2	*Anadara*	1	0
B2	*Argopecten*	1	0
B2	*Chione*	1	0
B2	*Columbella*	10	2
B2	*Conus*	314	51
B2	*Glycymeris*	169	27
B2	*Laevicardium*	70	11
B2	*Muricanthus*	1	0
B2	*Nassarius*	5	1
B2	*Nemocardium*	1	0
B2	*Olivella*	10	2
B2	*Pecten*	4	1
B2	*Pinctada*	8	1
B2	*Spondylus/Chama*	1	0
B2	*Strigilla*	1	0
B2	*Terebra*	1	0
B2	*Thais*	3	0
B2	*Trachycardium*	17	3
B2	*Turritella*	1	0
B2	VERMETIDAE	1	0
B2	*Vermicularia*	1	0
B2 Subtotal		621	100
B2 Subtotal All		822	
B3	Indeterminate	58	
B3	*Aguadulce*	1	1
B3	*Cancellaria*	1	1
B3	*Columbella*	2	1
B3	*Conus*	92	48
B3	*Glycymeris*	61	32
B3	*Laevicardium*	15	8
B3	*Nassarius*	4	2
B3	*Olivella*	4	2
B3	*Pecten*	4	2
B3	*Trachycardium*	6	3
B3	*Turritella*	1	1
B3 Subtotal		191	100
B3 Subtotal All		249	

Table 6.19. Genus Count by Area, cont'd

Area	Genus/Genero	Quantity/Cantidad	% de Area Total
B4	Indeterminate	217	
B4	*Anadara*	1	0
B4	*Arca*	1	0
B4	*Carditamera*	1	0
B4	*Chione*	1	0
B4	*Columbella*	4	2
B4	*Conus*	141	54
B4	*Fusinus*	2	1
B4	*Glycymeris*	64	25
B4	*Laevicardium*	14	5
B4	*Littorina*	1	0
B4	*Nassarius*	10	4
B4	*Olivella*	3	1
B4	*Pinctada*	9	3
B4	*Spondylus/Chama*	3	1
B4	*Trachycardium*	2	1
B4	*Turbo*	1	0
B4	VERMETIDAE	3	1
B4 Subtotal		261	100
B4 Subtotal All		478	
B5	Indeterminate	49	
B5	*Atrina*	1	0
B5	*Chione*	1	0
B5	*Columbella*	1	0
B5	*Conus*	149	55
B5	*Glycymeris*	71	26
B5	*Laevicardium*	21	8
B5	*Nassarius*	15	6
B5	*Olivella*	1	0
B5	*Pecten*	2	1
B5	*Pinctada*	1	0
B5	*Spondylus/Chama*	3	1
B5	*Trachycardium*	4	1
B5	*Trivia*	1	0
B5	*Turritella*	1	0
B5 Subtotal		272	100
B5 Subtotal All		321	
B6	Indeterminate	78	
B6	*Anadara*	19	2
B6	*Cerithium*	1	0
B6	*Chama*	1	0
B6	*Columbella*	5	1
B6	*Conus*	465	47
B6	*Glycymeris*	350	35
B6	*Laevicardium*	85	9

Table 6.19. Genus Count by Area, cont'd

Area	Genus/Genero	Quantity/Cantidad	% de Area Total
B6	*Littorina*	1	0
B6	NACREOUS	1	0
B6	*Nassarius*	14	1
B6	*Nemocardium*	2	0
B6	*Oliva*	3	0
B6	*Olivella*	7	1
B6	*Pecten*	8	1
B6	*Pinctada*	3	0
B6	*Spondylus/Chama*	1	0
B6	*Theodoxus*	1	0
B6	*Trachycardium*	14	1
B6	*Trivia*	1	0
B6	*Turritella*	3	0
B6	VERMETIDAE	5	1
B6 Subtotal		990	100
B6 Subtotal All		1068	
B7	Indeterminate	73	
B7	*Anadara*	5	1
B7	*Arca*	1	0
B7	*Attiliosa*	1	0
B7	*Chione*	1	0
B7	*Columbella*	14	2
B7	*Conus*	285	49
B7	*Glycymeris*	142	25
B7	*Laevicardium*	50	9
B7	*Lucina*	1	0
B7	*Murex*	2	0
B7	NACREOUS	5	1
B7	*Nassarius*	21	4
B7	*Nemocardium*	2	0
B7	*Neorapana*	1	0
B7	*Oliva*	3	1
B7	*Olivella*	8	1
B7	*Pecten*	6	1
B7	*Pinctada*	3	1
B7	*Spondylus/Chama*	9	2
B7	*Terebra*	1	0
B7	*Trachycardium*	5	1
B7	*Turritella*	7	1
B7	VERMETIDAE	5	1
B7 Subtotal		578	100
B7 Subtotal All		651	

Table 6.19. Genus Count by Area, cont'd

Area	Genus/Genero	Quantity/Cantidad	% de Area Total
B8	Indeterminate	62	
B8	*Anadara*	1	0
B8	*Argopecten*	1	0
B8	*Cardita*	1	0
B8	*Chama*	2	1
B8	*Columbella*	3	1
B8	*Conus*	179	51
B8	*Glycymeris*	86	25
B8	*Laevicardium*	32	9
B8	NACREOUS	1	0
B8	*Nassarius*	12	3
B8	*Oliva*	2	1
B8	*Olivella*	11	3
B8	*Pinctada*	2	1
B8	*Spondylus/Chama*	2	1
B8	*Theodoxus*	1	0
B8	*Trachycardium*	7	2
B8	*Trivia*	1	0
B8	*Turritella*	2	1
B8	VERMETIDAE	3	1
B8 Subtotal		349	100
B8 Subtotal All		411	
B9	Indeterminate	10	
B9	*Anadara*	2	1
B9	*Columbella*	2	1
B9	*Conus*	76	52
B9	*Glycymeris*	36	24
B9	*Laevicardium*	10	7
B9	*Nassarius*	3	2
B9	*Olivella*	5	3
B9	*Pecten*	2	1
B9	*Pinctada*	1	1
B9	*Polinices*	1	1
B9	*Spondylus/Chama*	1	1
B9	*Trachycardium*	3	2
B9	*Trivia*	1	1
B9	*Turritella*	1	1
B9	VERMETIDAE	3	2
B9 Subtotal		147	100
B9 Subtotal All		157	

Table 6.19. Genus Count by Area, cont'd

Area	Genus/Genero	Quantity/Cantidad	% de Area Total
B10	*Anadara*	2	4
B10	*Columbella*	1	2
B10	*Conus*	21	42
B10	*Glycymeris*	16	32
B10	*Laevicardium*	8	16
B10	NACREOUS	1	2
B10	*Trachycardium*	1	2
B10 Subtotal		50	100
B10 Subtotal All		53	
B11	Indeterminate	20	
B11	*Anadara*	4	2
B11	*Cerithidea*	1	0
B11	*Chione*	1	0
B11	*Conus*	76	35
B11	*Glycymeris*	78	36
B11	*Laevicardium*	36	17
B11	NACREOUS	2	1
B11	*Nassarius*	1	0
B11	*Olivella*	3	1
B11	*Pecten*	1	0
B11	*Theodoxus*	2	1
B11	*Trachycardium*	11	5
B11	*Turritella*	1	0
B11 Subtotal		217	100
B11 Subtotal All		237	
D	Indeterminate	188	
D	*Acanthina*	1	0
D	*Anadara*	1	0
D	*Atrina*	1	0
D	*Bulla*	1	0
D	*Cancellaria*	3	0
D	*Cardita*	1	0
D	*Chione*	1	0
D	*Columbella*	20	2
D	*Conus*	651	75
D	*Glycymeris*	83	10
D	*Laevicardium*	60	7
D	*Nassarius*	7	1
D	*Nemocardium*	1	0
D	*Olivella*	9	1
D	*Pecten*	6	1
D	*Pinctada*	9	1
D	*Spondylus/Chama*	2	0
D	*Strigilla*	1	0
D	*Thais*	1	0

Table 6.19. Genus Count by Area, cont'd

Area	Genus/Genero	Quantity/Cantidad	% de Area Total
D	*Trachycardium*	11	1
D	*Trivia*	2	0
D	*Turritella*	1	0
D Subtotal		873	100
D Subtotal All		1061	
E	Indeterminate	28	
E	*Acanthina*	1	2
E	*Argopecten*	1	2
E	*Columbella*	1	2
E	*Conus*	20	32
E	*Glycymeris*	26	41
E	*Laevicardium*	2	3
E	*Leucozonia*	1	2
E	*Melongena*	1	2
E	*Modiolus*	1	2
E	*Pecten*	3	5
E	*Pteria*	1	2
E	*Spondylus/Chama*	1	2
E	*Terebra*	1	2
E	VERMETIDAE	3	5
E Subtotal		63	100
E Subtotal All		91	
TOTAL		6867	

Table 6.20. Shell Artifact Types per Area

Area	A	A%	B	B%	BP	BP%	C	C%	CP	CP%	EC	EC%	F	F%	M	M%	N	N%
A1	53	27	26	13			60	30									3	2
B	3	60																
B1	185	25	175	24			138	19									9	1
B2	119	21	95	17			89	16									3	1
B3	25	15	24	14			40	24										
B4	60	18	32	9			116	34					1	0			5	1
B5	40	17	42	18			50	22									2	1
B6	146	18	206	25			108	13			1	0			1	0	19	2
B7	112	24	76	16			143	30									7	1
B8	74	23	48	15			95	30	2	1					1	0	1	0
B9	30	24	17	13			29	23									1	1
B10	7	19	5	14			2	5										
B11	34	20	43	25			19	11									1	1
D	85	12	51	7	1	0	170	24			1	0					7	1
E	10	19	17	31			8	15					1	2			1	2
TOTAL	983	20	857	17	1	0	1067	22	2	0	2	0	2	0	2	0	59	1

Area	P	P%	DT	DT%	SP	SP%	TK	TK%	Subtotal	Subtotal%	FNI	ONI	TOTAL
A1	4	2	46	23	2	1	4	2	198	100	73	6	277
B	1	20	1	20					5	100			5
B1	20	3	193	26			16	2	736	100	219	31	986
B2	19	3	233	41			4	1	562	100	229	31	822
B3	3	2	76	45	1	1	1	1	170	100	74	5	249
B4	12	4	113	33					339	100	108	31	478
B5	5	2	92	40			1	0	232	100	82	7	321
B6	21	3	315	38	1	0	15	2	833	100	212	23	1068
B7	13	3	117	25			8	2	476	100	160	15	651
B8	14	4	73	23	2	1	6	2	316	100	87	8	411
B9	3	2	39	31	4	3	3	2	126	100	28	3	157
B10	3	8	18	49	1	3	1	3	37	100	16		53
B11	9	5	57	34			7	4	170	100	56	11	237
D	14	2	370	53			3	0	702	100	334	25	1061
E	5	9	12	22					54	100	30	7	91
TOTAL	146	3	1755	35	11	0	69	1	4956	100	1708	203	6867

*Note: Artifact types are A = Anillo/Ring, B = Bracelete/Bracelet, BP = Bracelete-pendiente/Bracelet-pendant, C = Cuenta/Bead, CP = Cuenta-pendiente/Bead-pendant, EC = Ear Cuff, F = Figurilla/Figurine, M = Mosaic , n = Natural/Unmodified, P = Pendiente/Pendant , DT = Deshecho de Taller/Worked Debris, SP = Spangle , TK = Tinkler, FNI = Fragmento no identificado/ Unidentified fragment, ONI = Objeto no identificado/Unidentified worked artifact.

Table 6.21. Comparing Trincheras and Paquime Counts

Artifact form	Trincheras Quantity.	Trincheras %	Paquime Quantity.	Paquime %
Beads	1069	34.08	80292	74.64
Bracelet/Armlet	857	27.32	434	0.40
Rings	981	31.27	387	0.36
Tinklers	69	2.21	21849	20.31
Pendants	146	4.65	4231	3.94
Spangles	11	0.35	141	0.13
Strand Dividers	0	0.00	9	0.01
Containers	0	0.00	2	0.00
Disks	0	0.00	8	0.01
Trumpet/Altar Pc	0	0.00	176	0.16
Cuff	1	0.03	0	0.00
Tool	1	0.03	0	0.00
Tessarae	2	0.06	44	0.04
Total	3137	100.00	107573	100.00

Chapter 7
Miscellaneous Artifacts

Bridget M. Zavala. Universidad Juárez del Estado de Durango

Artefactos Variados

Este capítulo discute una variedad de artefactos recuperados en Cerro de Trincheras durante las temporadas de trabajo de campo de 1995 y 1996. Este conjunto incluía discos de cerámica y de piedra, cerámica y piedra trabajada, pipas, mangos de cerámica y fragmentos de figurines. Las variaciones tipológicas y espaciales de estos hallazgos permiten comprender la función de los artefactos y comportamientos de los habitantes prehispánicos de Cerro desde la producción de hilo a la creación de malacates para la producción de artefactos de concha. Zavala discute la posible naturaleza ritual de artefactos asociados con las estructuras especializadas tales como La Cancha y El Caracol.

The excavations at the site of Cerros de Trincheras (SON:F:2:1 [CR]), in Sonora, México in 1995 and 1996 have allowed us to refine much of our understanding of the Trincheras tradition. Among the archaeological materials recovered were spindle whorls, worked ceramics, stone disks, and pipes. In this report, I included information on ceramic disks, other worked ceramic artifacts, ceramic ornaments, perforated stone disks and pipes. For each material class, I first discuss the methods implemented in the excavation and analysis of these artifacts. Then, I categorize the material, discuss its spatial distribution and consider issues related to each artifact class wherever possible.

Methods

Bridget Zavala (SUNY Binghamton, 1996) and Júpiter Martínez Ramirez (INAH, Sonora, 1997) analyzed the worked ceramics and perforated stone disks in Hermosillo, Sonora. Our crew recovered 1,543 worked ceramics from Cerro de Trincheras and 479 perforated stone disks. When they were identified in the field, archaeologists bagged these artifacts separately with unique bag numbers. When analysts identified worked ceramic artifacts during the analysis of the lithic and ceramic material they bagged them with a unique bag number and set them aside for analysis.

To facilitate inter-site comparison, I based my analysis on previous studies by Di Peso (1974, 1956) and Teague (1998). In general my aim for this study was to: 1) document the variability of worked ceramic artifacts and stone disks, 2) infer details about the textile manufacture at the site of Cerro de Trincheras, 3) consider alternative uses for some of these artifacts.

For each artifact, the investigators classified the artifacts into five types: 1) perforated disks 2) disks without a perforation, 3) worked sherds (not a disk), 4) molded or bead whorls and 5) unknown. Then, recorders assigned each a specific shape. Subsequently, the analysts recorded the condition of the artifact (complete or broken) and the ceramic type it was crafted from. The archaeologists then, documented each object's weight, length or diameter, width (when appropriate). For perforated disks, the recorders also documented the type of perforation (biconical, uniconical, partial, molded, or shaft straight down). I present the results of the analysis in the sections that follow. First, I discuss perforated disks and molded spindle whorls and relate them to spindle whorls in general. Second, I discuss disks (without a perforation) at the site. Then I generally describe the worked ceramics (other than disks). Finally, I make some conclusions about worked ceramics at Cerro de Trincheras.

In order to address the question of textile production at Cerro de Trincheras, we analyzed the molded ceramic spindle whorls as well as the all perforated ceramic and stone disks. During the excavations, the archaeologists recovered 479 perforated ceramic disks, 52 of which were complete, and 50 perforated stone disks, six of which were complete. The crew also recovered 900 non-perforated ceramic disks and 155 worked ceramics that where not disks perforated or otherwise. Generally, in the Southwest/Northwest perforated ceramic disks have been interpreted as spindle whorls and non-perforated ceramic disks as spindle whorls blanks in process to production or gaming pieces.

Perforated Disks/Spindle Whorls

The general archaeological assumption is that perforated disks were used as spindle whorls. In the Northwest/Southwest this interpretation is based on ethnographic analogy and their recovery from archaeological contexts with spindles and yarn still in place (Stone and Foster 1994:201; DiPeso 1951; Kent 1983). Spindle whorls are tools used in the manufacture of yarn from fibers to help put the twist into the yarn being spun (Teague 1998). The spinner inserts a spindle through the perforation. He/she then attached fibers to the spindle shaft and spun the fibers (Kent 1983 for review of spinning process). Often spindles are made of wood and rarely recovered from archaeological contexts. Archaeologists have recovered three types of whorls in the Southwest/ Northwest, worked ceramic whorls, modeled bead whorls and stone whorls. The size and shape of the whorl as well as the fibers being spun affect the quality and thickness of the yarn being produced. Some fibers require more twist than others. This results in a clear association between the shape of the whorl and the fibers that are being spun. For example, bead whorls minimize the diameter and maximize weight allowing the spindle whorl to rotate faster. Fine yarns and yarns made of short fibers that require faster spindle whorls. These relationships between the form of the whorl and the yarn produced allows archaeologists to make some general inferences about textile manufacture from whorl attributes.

Archaeologists have recovered perforated disks made of stone, bone, antler, wood and pottery from sites all over the Southwest/ Northwest. The Seri of Sonora have perforated disks (in some cases made of Trincheras pottery) yet, the Seri do not weave or grow cotton. Bowen (1976:73) suggests that they probably did not do so in the past either. Among the Seri, these artifacts often formed a part of tops used as toys by children (Bowen 1976: 73) and were used as drill weights during shell artifact manufacture (Villalpando 1998, personal communication). It is possible that the people of Trincheras used perforated ceramic disks as spindle whorls, toys, and drill weights.

Excavators at Cerro de Trincheras found artifacts that correspond morphologically with all three of the types of whorls recovered from pre-Hispanic contexts: modeled bead whorls, worked ceramic whorls and stone whorls. Worked ceramic whorls are sherds shaped by flaking and grinding into roughly circular disks with a perforation through the middle. Worked ceramic whorls can have ground, irregular, and notched edges. Modeled bead whorls are formed by hand from clay (Stone and Foster 1994:203) with a perforation in the middle. Stone whorls are made of stone and are ground into disk-like or three-dimensional shapes with a perforation in the middle.

Perforated Disks at Cerro de Trincheras

In the section that follows, I first describe the perforated disk assemblage. Then, I describe the spatial distribution of the perforated disks at cerro de trincheras. Finally, I consider issues of textile production at Cerro de Trincheras. We collected 479 perforated sherd disks from excavation units (Table 7.1). Fifty-two of the perforated ceramic disks were complete. The excavators also located six modeled bead whorls. Three of the bead whorls we recovered were complete (Figure 7.1). Fifty stone whorls were also collected of which only six were complete. The crew most often recovered fragments of sherd and stone whorls. Stone and Foster (1994: 206) state that sherd whorls are more likely to break because of their mechanical properties. This does not appear to be the case at Cerro de Trincheras since the rate of fragmentation is almost the same for both stone and sherd whorls. The sample of bead whorls was too small to make any generalizations about fragmentation of bead whorls.

The sherd whorls, with one exception were manufactured from local plain ware ceramics (Lisa 3, Lisa 3A and Lisa Tardía). The most common ceramic type used for the production of spindle whorls is Lisa 3 (64 percent). Lisa 3 was produced by a coil and scrape method. Lisa Tardía was made with a paddle-and-anvil method characterized by a browner color, paddle and finger impressions on the interior, lower friability, and a finer external finish. Lisa 3a combines elements from both Lisa 3 and Lisa Tardía with paddle impressions as well as finger and scraping marks.

The overwhelming majority of the perforated stone disks at Cerro de Trincheras were made of phyllite (n = 26). Though the people of Trincheras made perforated disks of shale (n = 3), sandstone (n = 3), dacite (n = 1), limestone (n = 2), siltstone (n = 3), rhyolite (n = 1), trachyte (n = 1) quartzite (n = 2) and slate (n = 7).

We identified five types of perforated ceramic disks. The most common spindle whorl was Type A (n = 369) that we defined as a perforated disk with ground edges (Figure 7.2). Nineteen percent (n = 93) of the perforated disks found were Type E's. We defined Type E as a perforated roughly circular disk with no evidence of grinding on edges. Other archaeologists have interpreted Type E artifacts as spindle whorls in the process of manufacture (Stone and Foster 1994:206). Our crew found eight roughly oval perforated disks with at least one worked edge that we defined as Type I. Two types of spindle whorls had decorated edges: Type G and Type H. Type G spindle whorls have some incising on its edges (Figure 7.3). We collected four Type G spindle whorls. Type H (n = 2) refers to disks with notching all around its edges. The final spindle whorl type was a bobbin shaped perforated ceramic disk called Type D (Figure 7.4).

All the types identified for ceramic disks were also represented in the perforated stone disk assemblage with the addition of one type. As with the ceramic perforated disks the most common form was Type A (n = 27). The archae-

Table 7.1. Spindle Whorls at Cerro de Trincheras

Type	Complete n	%	Broken n	%	Total	Percentage
Sherd	53	11.09	425	88.91	478	89.51
Modeled	3	50	3	50	6	1.12
Stone	6	12	44	88	50	9.36
Total	62	22.10	472	88.39	534	100

Figure 7.1. Bead whorl.

Figure 7.3. Type G perforated ceramic disk with some edge incising.

Figure 7.2. Type A perforated ceramic disk.

Figure 7.4. Type D bobbin-shaped ceramic disk.

ologists recovered five Type D stone whorls defined as flat bobbin shaped disks not present in the ceramic assemblage. The crew also collected four Type C (tall bobbin shaped), four Type B (bead whorls) perforated disks, three Type E disks (with irregular edges) and three Type L (edges ground to a point). Two of the stone disks had some edge notching (Type G) and one had notching all around (Type H).

We recorded attributes on disk edges and perforations in order to understand the production sequence of spindle whorls at Trincheras. Artisans first, chipped the sherds to a roughly circular edge. Then they ground down the edges. On a few disks, the crafts person used incising or notching (Figure 7.3) to decorate the edge of the whorl. Finally they perforated the disks. Seventy-one (n = 340) percent of the perforated disks at the site had a bi-conical perforation. Twenty-three percent (n = 86) were only partially perforated. Five percent (n = 23) of the perforated disks had cylindrical perforations suggesting that reaming must have been implemented. The remainder (n = 29) were fragmentary leaving no clear evidence of the nature of the perforation. Artisans shaped the shaped clay into an elliptical or round shape to make modeled whorls. All must have been shaped around a central shaft as evidenced by the cylindrical perforation. None of the modeled whorls from Cerro de Trincheras had any evidence of decoration in contrast to those found in the Hohokam area sites (Stone and Foster 1994:210). Since we recovered only one stone whorl in process of production, we can say little about the production sequence of these artifacts. Phyllite, shale, sandstone, dacite, limestone, siltstone, rhyolite, and slate were presumably chipped into a circular form, perforated, and ground into a disk.

Studies have demonstrated a close association between whorl attributes and the size of the of yarn produced (Teague 1998: 47). Figure 7.5 shows the relationship between the weight and diameter of perforated disks at Cerro de Trincheras. An examination of the spindle whorls suggests the spinners at Trincheras preferred to use spindle whorls between 20 to 35 mm in diameter weighing 8-14 grams. Further the data suggests that the Trinchereños used Types A and E to spin fine fibers (more than 12,000 m/kg). Contrastingly, the stone and bead whorls were probably used to spin fine to medium fibers (between 2,000

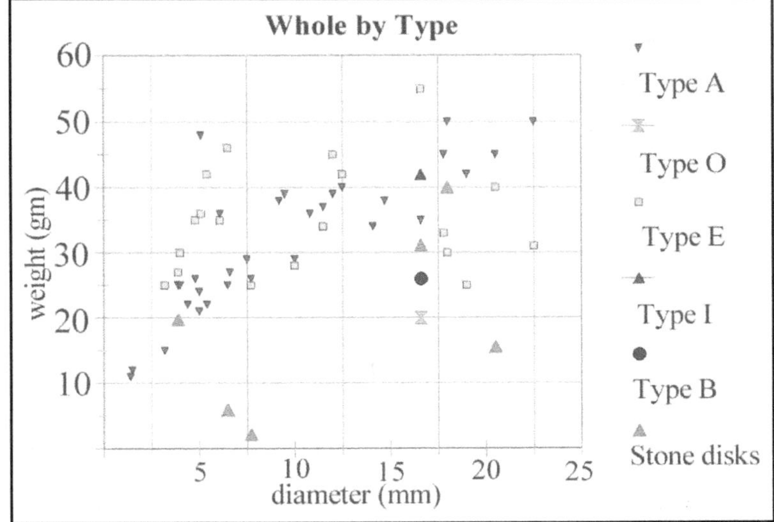

Figure 7.5. Relationship between weight and diameter of spindle whorls.

to 12,000 m/kg).

Inferring specific fiber type from whorl size is much more difficult since there is no one-to-one correspondence between whorl type and fiber type. Nevertheless, Teague (1998: 45) suggests using information on yarn weight as well as botanical data to inform inferences about fiber type. Generally, in the Northwest/ Southwest, fine yarn is produced from cotton while medium yarns are made from non-cotton fibers. At Cerro de Trincheras, only two plant species were recovered that could have served as material for yarn manufacture: cotton (*Gossypium hirsutum*) and agave (*Agave* sp.). Given data on yarn weight previously discussed it is likely the inhabitants of Cerro de Trincheras were most probably spinning yarn made of both agave and cotton but tended to spin finer yarns of cotton.

The intensity of textile production at Cerro de Trincheras could be inferred from the ratio of spindle whorls to the entire ceramic assemblage. Spindle whorls represent .05 percent of the total ceramic assemblage excavated at Cerro de Trincheras. This figure is close to the average at eleven Hohokam sites (see Stone and Foster 1994:217). Any comparisons of intensity of textile production through time are impossible at this time due to the small time span indicated by radiocarbon dates at the site.

The spatial distribution of spindle whorls at the site can be used to locate areas where textile production might have occurred (Table 7.2). Most ceramic spindle whorls were recovered from excavation areas on generally residential terraces B6 (n = 86) and B1 (n = 83). This is especially interesting since the next largest concentration of spindle whorls occurred in the pithouse hamlet, Area E (n = 64). Our crew found 58 spindle whorls in B4 (residential terrace) making it the next largest concentration of whorls at the site. Area A1

Table 7.2. Spindle Whorl Types by Excavation Area

Area	Perforated ceramic disk	Modeled bead whorl	Perforated stone disk	Total by area
A1	28	3	5	36
B1	78	0	5	83
B2	35	0	1	36
B3	26	0	5	31
B4	55	0	3	58
B5	6	1	3	10
B6	83	0	3	86
B7	28	1	7	36
B8	11	0	6	17
B9	13	0	0	13
B10	6	0	1	7
B11	23	0	2	25
D	19	1	5	25
E	64	0	0	64
Total	475	6	46	527

(cerro crest) and the residential or occupational terraces of Areas B2, B3, B7, B11 and D all had 20 to 40 spindle whorls each. Our crew recovered less than 20 spindle whorls from Areas B5 (La Cancha) and B8-10 (El Mirador). This probably indicates little textile production at these sections of the hill.

A very different pattern emerges from the spatial distribution of perforated stone disk that suggests a different function. The majority of perforated stone disks were in areas of relatively low artifact density and in areas were perforated ceramic disk were not found in abundance. The majority of perforated stone disks were recovered from excavation Area B7 (n = 10). We excavated five perforated stone disks from each A1, B3, B8, and E. Less than five were collected from excavation Areas B1 (n = 4), B2 (n = 1), B4 (n = 3), B5 (n = 2), B6 (n = 2), B9 (n = 4), B10 (n = 1), and B11 (n = 2). No perforated stone disks were found in Area D.

Most of the activities associated with perforated ceramic disks must have taken place on the terrace surfaces rather than within structures or features. Only 11 perforated sherd disks were found inside features (Table 7.3). The excavators collected three ceramic spindle whorls from the interior of El Caracol. Two perforated disks were found in each Jacal 3 (Area B4), and Quadrangular Stone Structure 1 (Area B6). The crew also collected a single perforated disk from each of the following features: in Jacal 7 (Area B1), Pithouse 2 (Area E), and Quadrangular Stone Structure 3 and Pit 3 both (Area D). Only five perforated stone disks were found in features. One was collected from La Cancha (Area B5) and another from El Caracol (Area A1). The excavators found one perforated stone disk accompanying Burial 4 (Area B4) on Platform 1 (Area B6) and in Jacal 5 (Area B7).

Summary

The analysis of the worked ceramics at Cerro the Trincheras suggests that the inhabitants were spinning fine to medium weight yarn at the site. The number of these artifacts and the Seri example suggest that perhaps these artifacts also served as drill weights for the production of shell artifacts. Future studies should involve how the distribution of perforated disks correlates with the distribution of shell good as well as lithic artifacts that may have been part of the shell manufacturing process.

The preliminary analysis shows a concentration of perforated disks on B4 that suggests that this terrace may have been a space heavily dedicated to the production of textiles or shell manufacture. Further investigations may consider why bead whorls and perforated stone disks are located in higher numbers in Area A1, an area of low artifact recovery. That in combination with the recovery of three whole perforated ceramic disks and one perforated stone disk from the interior of 'El Caracol' is especially interesting. Furthermore, the recovery of a perforated stone disk from a mortuary context could suggest that these artifacts may have been ornaments rather than spinning tools. Thus, it is possible that the differing distribution for these artifact classes could reflect restricted access to these goods or even different functions.

Ceramic Disks

The most common category of worked ceramic artifact found at Cerro de Trincheras was the ceramic disk. Ceramic disks are sherds shaped into a roughly circular shape with no evidence of perforation. Archaeologists in the Northwest/Southwest have interpreted these artifacts as gaming pieces or spindle whorl blanks. The crew recovered 900 ceramic disks from the site, 174 of which were complete. Ceramic disks

Table 7.3. Worked Ceramics and Stone in Features

Feature	Excavation area	Ceramic perforated disks	Ceramic disks	Other worked ceramics	Total
El Caracol	A1	3	11	3	17
Circular Stone Structure 1	A1	0	1	0	1
Circular Stone Structure 22	A1	0	4	1	5
Jacal 1	B1	0	2	0	2
Jacal 7	B1	1	4	15	20
Jacal 2	B2	0	1	0	2
Ancillary Terrace 1	B3	0	2	0	2
Circular Stone Structure 17	B3	0	7	0	7
Burial 4	B4	0	2	0	2
Jacal 3	B4	2	6	2	10
Pit 15	B4	0	9	1	10
Platform 3	B4	0	32	2	34
La Cancha	B5	0	7	5	12
Burial 5	B6	0	1	0	1
Circular Stone Structure 18	B6	0	11	1	12
Circular Stone Structure 19	B6	0	6	0	6
Circular Stone Structure 20	B6	0	5	1	6
Jacal 4	B6	0	4	0	4
Platform 1	B6	0	4	1	5
Platform 2	B6	0	18	10	28
Quadrangular Stone Structure 1	B6	2	3	4	9
Jacal 5	B7	0	5	3	8
Jacal 6	B9	0	4	2	6
Quadrangular Stone Structure 2	B9	0	3	1	4
Rock Arrangement 6	B11	0	1	0	1
El Caracolito	D	0	25	5	30
Quadrangular Stone Structure 3	D	1	8	0	9
Rock Arrangement 4	D	0	1	0	1
Rock Arrangement 5	D	0	1	0	1
Pit 3	D	1	1	0	2
Pit 20	D	0	5	0	5
Midden 1	E	0	1	1	2
Pithouse 2	E	1	3	0	4
Pithouse 3	E	0	3	0	3
Terrace 13	-	0	8	0	8
Total		11	209	58	279

generally fell into three morphological categories. The most common was Type F (n = 601), sherd disk with flaked edges and no evidence of grinding. Type E (n = 241) was the next most common, disk-shaped sherds with ground edges. Type I (n = 47) followed constituted by oval-shaped disks. We also collected four disks with completely notched edges (Type H) and four with some edge notching (Type G). Two disks (Type L) had edges ground to a point.

The inhabitants of Trincheras fashioned the majority of their ceramic disks from Lisa 3 ceramics (n = 500). They also made many of Lisa Tardía (n = 328) pottery. Only 63 disks were made from Lisa 3a ceramics. The remaining six disks were made from Santa Cruz Polychrome, Trincheras Purple-on-red, or an identified ceramic type.

In general, the distribution of ceramic disks mirrors general patterns of artifact density at the site. The majority of the disks originated from lower northwest sector of Area B. We collected 156 disks from B1, 149 from B4, 121 from B6, 101 from B3, and 81 from B2. The only exception was B5- La Cancha- from which the excavators collected only 12 disks. The crew excavated a high number (n = 80) from Area D. Disks were regularly found in El Mirador [B7 (n = 50), B8 (n = 32), and B9(n = 17)] but to a lesser degree. Area E (n = 37) and Area A1 (n = 29) were the areas of least concentration of disks indicating that what ever activities were associated with these disks were rarely carried out in these areas.

The crew recovered 209 ceramic disks from the interior of 35 features at the site (Table 7.3). Of those feature where disks were found most had less than or equal to 5 disks but 5 features had a large concentration of these artifacts. The excavators collected the most disks from Platform 3 in Area B4 (n = 32). 'El Caracolito' in Area D also had a high number of disks (n = 25). The third largest quantity of disks was found on Platform 2 (n = 18) in B6. Followed by 11 disks from El Caracol in A1 and 11 disks from Circular Stone Structure 18 in B6. The fact that these artifacts were found in large quantities in both El Caracol and El Caracolito, two of the specialized features at the site could suggest that the activities associated with disks may have been special and carried out on platforms, and Circular Stone Structure18 as well as the specialized features.

Stone Disks

Unlike pottery disks with perforations, stone disk were not more common than their perforated counterparts at Trincheras. The crew collected only eight stone disks during excavation only one of which as complete. Stone disks were made of dacite, chert, chalcedony, shale, and phyllite. Three were circular with ground edges (Type F). Three were disks with edges ground down to a point (Type L). One had a flat bobbin shape (Type D) and the last was a circular disk with not sign of grinding on its edges (Type E).

The distribution of stone disks was similar to that of its perforated ones. The crew recovered two stone disks from Area B7 and a single one from each A1, B2, B6, B8, B9, and E. The excavators only found two inside features, one in El Caracol and another in Circular Stone Structure 18.

Other Worked Ceramics

The crew also recovered 155 worked ceramic sherds that were not disks. These artifacts showed evidence of grinding, rounding or beveling of an edge. During analysis, these worked sherds were classified into three classes: scrapers (Type K), ornaments (Type O), and irregular shapes (Type J). Fifty ceramic scrapers were identified. All of these showed evidence of beveling of at least one edge and tended to be roughly rectangular. They ranged from 12 to 70 mm in length with a width of up to 54 mm. Eight ceramic ornaments were also collected during excavation. Ceramic ornaments were defined as small bead like or pendant shaped sherds. The crew recovered 118 worked ceramics with shapes other than disks, pendants or scrapers. The Type J worked ceramics were sometimes triangular, square, rectangular, clover shaped or too irregular to classify. All of these were drawn to scale during analysis to facilitate further classification in the future. It appears that most of these were shaped for a purpose rather than worn down during use. Most worked ceramics were made of Lisa 3 (n = 80) or Lisa Tardía (n = 67) ceramics. Only 34 of these were complete. Most of these artifacts were collected from Area B6 (n = 31), though a large number (n = 22) were also recovered from B1.

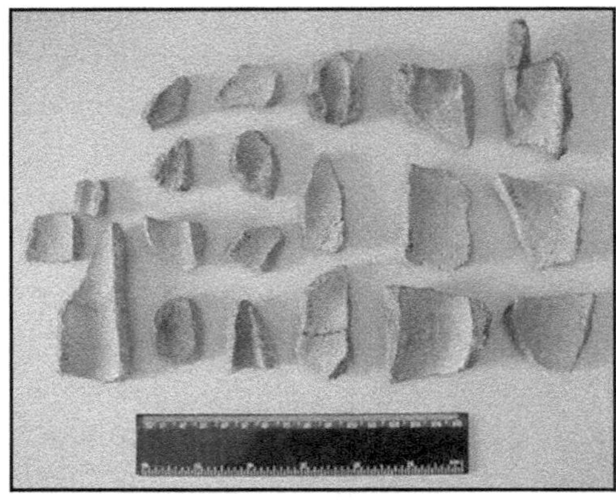

Figure 7.6. Pipes from Cerro de Trincheras.

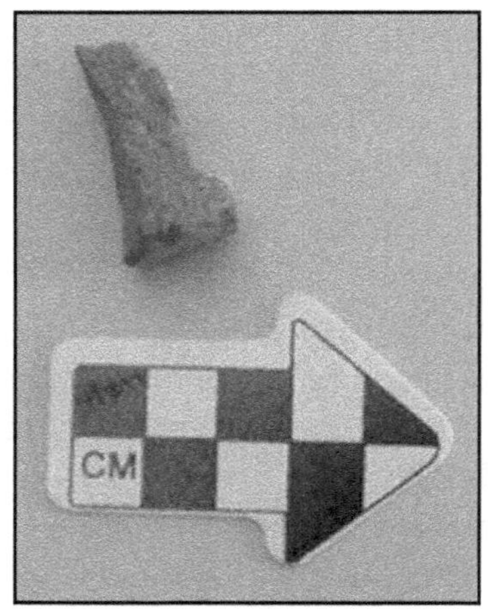

Figure 7.7. Fragment of possible ceramic spoon handle.

Other Worked Stone

In addition to the stone disks the team collected five additional modified stone artifacts during excavation. Two of these were pendants, one made of calcareous siltstone and the other of limestone. Dawn Greenwald (Chapter 5) and César Villalobos (Chapter 8) also discuss pendants. The remaining three stone artifacts were unidentifiable. Two of these were made of phyllite and one was fashioned from shale. The function of these artifacts is unknown.

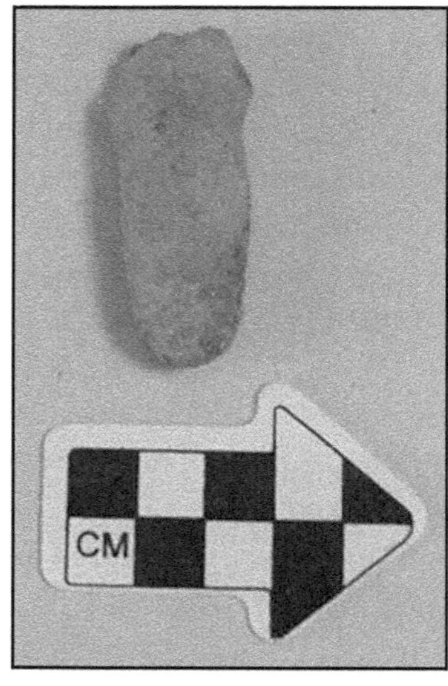

Figure 7.8. Figurine fragment.

Pipes

The crew found 19 pipe fragments at Cerros de Trincheras (Figure 7.6). All of the pipes, with the exception of one were located in Area B8. The other was found in Area B5 in La Cancha and the La Cancha pipe was the only one with any evidence of burning. All 19 fragments the pipes were made of clay and were presumably of the 'cloud blower' variety. The fragments ranged from 78 to 2 mm with a thickness of 5 to 11 mm. The interior diameter of the pipes ranged from 20 to 60 mm. The concentration of the pipes on B8 suggests that this area in 'El Mirador' may have been associated with ritual activity.

Miscellaneous Ceramic Artifacts

The crew collected five unusual ceramic artifacts at cerro de trincheras. The first was a handle possibly to a ceramic spoon (Figure 7.7), 61 mm long. The second was a figurine fragment that appears to have been the body of an anthropomorphic figure 51 mm long (Figure 7.8). The third was a piece of a possible figurine fragment that may be a piece of the face. These three artifacts were all from excavation Area B7. The fourth ceramic artifact was a fragment of a cup. Finally, a small possible ceramic lid was collected from the interior of La Cancha weighing 9 grams fashioned from Lisa 3 ceramic.

Conclusions

In this report I have studied the variation, typological and spatial, of several stone and ceramic artifact classes. I included here the results of the analysis of ceramic and stone disks, other ceramic and stone artifacts, and pipes collected during the excavation of the site of Cerro de Trincheras. I presented their morphological and spatial variability and tired to associate this with the behavior of the pre-Hispanic inhabitants of the terraced village. Where possible I considered the possible function of these artifacts.

As in other places in the Northwest/ Southwest I assumed perforated stone and ceramic disk may have been used as spindle whorls at the site. The analysis of the perforated disks suggests that the inhabitants were spinning fine to medium weight yarn at the site made of cotton or agave most of which may have taken place on B4. I also proposed an alternative function for the perforated disks as they may have also served as drill weights for the production of shell artifacts, a question worthy of future study.

I identified differences in the distribution of ceramic and perforated stone disks. While the ceramic spindle whorls were concentrated in areas of generally heavy domestic production while their stone counterparts were most common on areas of relatively low artifact domestic refuse (B7 and A1). The crew's recovery of 3 whole perforated ceramic disks and one perforated stone disk from the interior of 'El Caracol' is especially of note. It is therefore possible that the differing distribution for these artifact classes could reflect restricted access to these goods or even different functions.

The team also found a large number of ceramic and stone disks. The disks exhibited a the same range of morphological variability as perforated disks and were clustered in lower northwest sector of Area B, an area of high domestic activity. One interesting fact about these artifacts was their concentration in large quantities in both El Caracol and El Caracolito, two of the specialized features suggesting that the activities associated with disks may have been special and carried out on platforms, and Circular Stone Structure18, as well as the specialized features.

The Trincherenos also worked ceramic sherds into a variety of different shapes both through use and to use as tools. Scrapers were commonly made by beveling an edge of a sherd. In addition we also recovered pendants and sherds shaped into a wide variety of shapes. Furthermore, they also made ceramic pipes, figurines, cups and handles at the site.

Chapter 8
Ornamentos en Piedra

César Villalobos. Centro INAH Sonora
Adriana Hinojo. Centro INAH Sonora
Ricardo Amaya. Universidad de Sonora

Stone Ornaments

This chapter discusses the 276 stone ornaments recovered during the 1995 and 1996 field seasons at Cerro de Trincheras. Trinchereño artisans made a variety of stone ornaments including disk and tubular beads and pendants to hang on necklaces. Petrographic and primary material analyses show that ornaments were manufacture from stone local to the cerro, as well as green jadeite-like and blue turquoise-like stone, neither of which naturally occur in the immediate area of the site.

El presente informe forma parte de los trabajos arqueológicos realizados en las primaveras de 1995 y 1996 bajo el proyecto Cerro de Trincheras coordinado por Elisa Villalpando (Centro INAH Sonora) y Randall McGuire (SUNY-Binghamton). Los materiales se recuperaron en las excavaciones realizadas en diversas áreas del Cerro de Trincheras. El procedimiento consistió en analizar los artefactos vaciando la información obtenida en una base de datos, una vez terminada ésta se procedió a realizar las estadísticas que a continuación se presentan.

Los ornamentos en piedra (Figura 8.1) jugaron un papel importante en la época Prehispánica, en el Cerro de Trincheras predominaron las cuentas de forma circular y tabulares, y en menor proporción los pendientes (Figura 8.2 y 8.3). Llama la atención el tamaño pequeño de la mayoría de los objetos, casi el 75% de los objetos no superan 1 gramo de peso, esto tiene como consecuencia que muchas de estas cuentas son extremadamente pequeñas.

Estos artefactos fueron parte de collares y del arreglo personal así como de fino acabado en otros artefactos, sin embargo, la totalidad de los que se presentan en este análisis son objetos recuperados en contextos de relleno, es decir, ninguno proviene de contextos primarios de deposición, por lo tanto, el análisis describe su morfología, cantidad, área de distribución al interior del sitio, entre otras categorías.

Figura 8.1. Ornamentos en piedra.

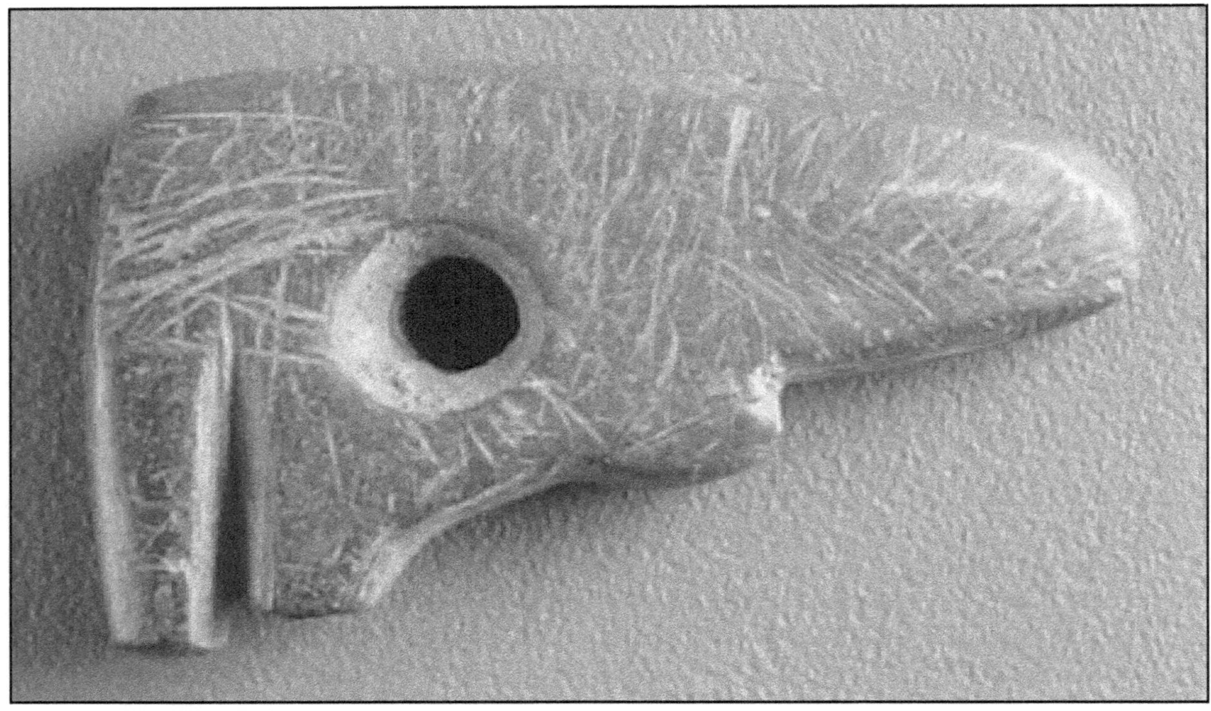

Figura 8.2. Zoomorphico pendiente riojo.

Presentamos una descripción puntual tanto de los materiales color verde y color azul, por tratarse de materiales "exóticos" (no locales) que podrían compararse con los de otras áreas.

Asimismo se pudo realizar un estudio de lá minas delgadas en el Departamento de Geología de la Universidad de Sonora con los Geólogos Ricardo Amaya y Saúl Herrera, para la descripción mineralógica de los materiales representativos analizados (previa autorización del Consejo de Arqueología).

Cabe mencionar que este análisis incluye una variedad de artefactos ornamentales, y aunque este análisis no se refiere únicamente a las cuentas, la mayor cantidad de ellas se refiere a éstas. En términos generales las cuentas se distinguen de los pendientes por la perforación central de las primeras, mientras que los pendientes, la perforación cargada a uno de sus extremos.

El análisis incluyo todos aquellos artefactos que por su apariencia fueran ornamentales, o los que por su forma se asociaran a esta función (cuentas, pendientes y otros como placas o cubos pequeños de piedra). El total de artefactos analizados suma 276 piezas, entre ellas, 224 (81.16%) están completas mientras que 52 (18.84%) se encuentran incompletas.

De estos artefactos no todos están terminados, algunos de ellos, se encuentran

Figura 8.3. Pendiente riojo.

en proceso de manufactura. En este sentido trabajamos bajo la hipótesis siguiente: si hay una producción especializada, los artefactos en "proceso" deberían estar agrupados en un área específica.

Si hay una producción y un autoconsumo, los artefactos en "proceso" y "terminados" se distribuirán de igual forma en todos los sectores. De esta forma tenemos 84 (30.8%) en proceso (Figura 8.4) y 191 (69.2%) artefactos terminados (Figura 8.5).

Estas gráficas sirven de alguna manera para proponer tentativamente que no hay un área de especialización, en todas las áreas que hay artefactos, los hay de los dos tipos, en proceso y terminados. Salta a la vista que en el área B10 se registraron 4 en proceso pero no artefactos terminados.

Respecto a la distribución espacial del total artefactos (226) las áreas en donde se localizan son A1 (7.97%), B1 (7.25%), B2 (7.25%), B3 (2.54%), B4 (5.80%), B5 (3.78%), B6 (13.77%), B7 (20.65%), B8 (11.96%), B9 (1.45%), B10 (1.45%), B11 (3.26%), D (4.35%) y E (1.45%). Siendo las áreas B5, B6, B7 y B8 las que mayor cantidad presentan (Figura 8.6).

A partir del color macroscópico se los materiales se clasificaron en 8 grandes grupos los de color café, gris, negro y rojo resaltan los de color azul y los de color verde, que por su apariencia no parecen ser de origen local (Figura 8.7). Los porcentajes de cada uno de ellos son los siguientes: Azul (1.45%), Blanco (3.99%), Café (17.3%), Gris (34.06%), Negro (13.04%), Rojo (17.75%), Rosa (0.36%) y Verde (12.35-2%). Respecto a las 4 cuentas de color azul, dos se presentan en el área B4 (50%), una en la B5 (25%) y una en la B7 (25%).

En prácticamente todos los sectores en donde hay cuentas también se presentan las de color verde (a excepción de B11) (Figura 8.8). Del total de las 33 artefactos su distribución en las áreas fue la siguiente: A (16%), B1 (12%), B2 (12%), B4 (9%), B5 (3%), B6 (9%), B7 (27%), B8 (9%), B9 (3%), B10 (3%), E (3%) y D (3%).

El peso en gramos refleja el tamaño de los artefactos, el resultado es que la mayoría

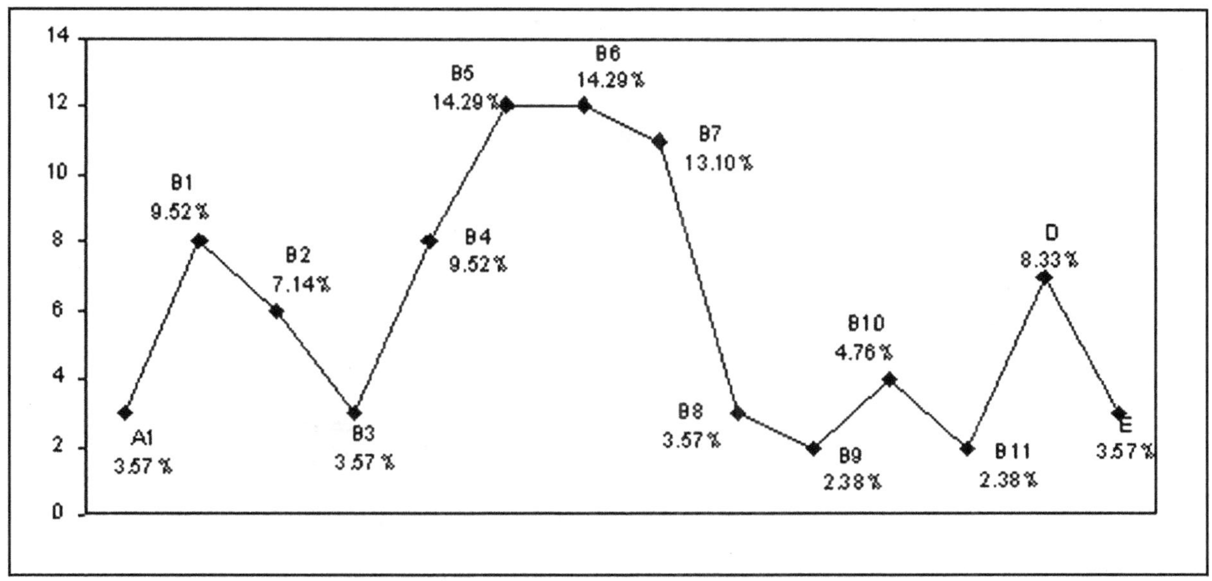

Figura 8.4. Manufactura: en proceso (muestra 84).

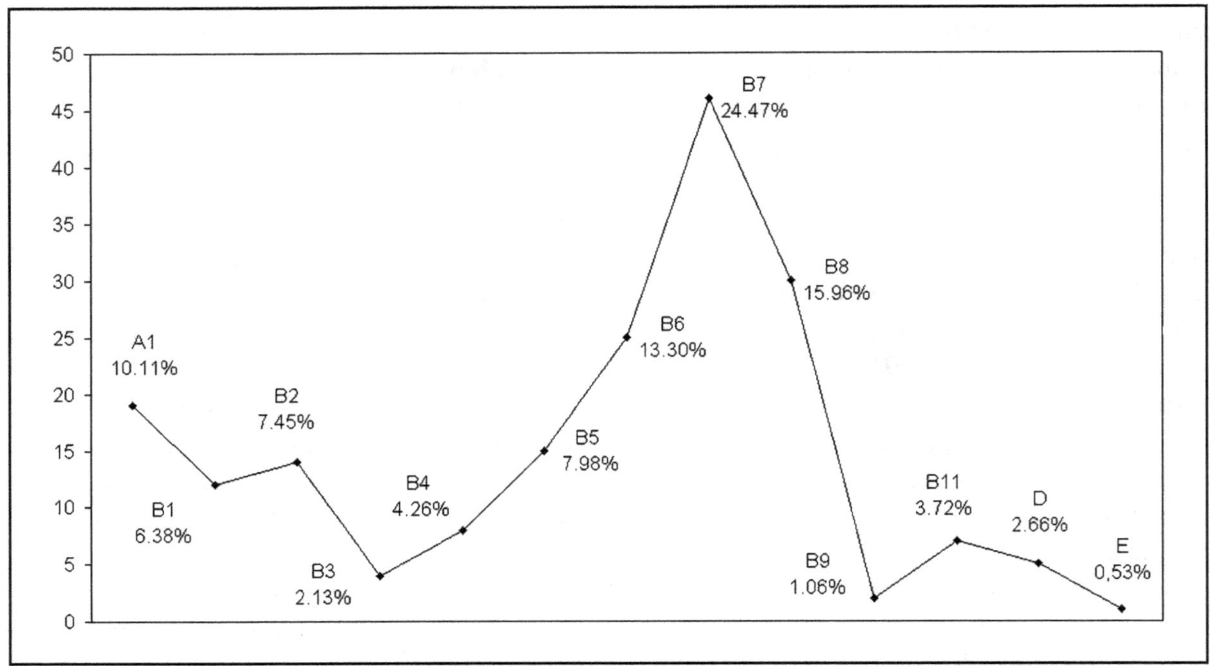

Figura 8.5. Manufactura: terminado (muestra 191).

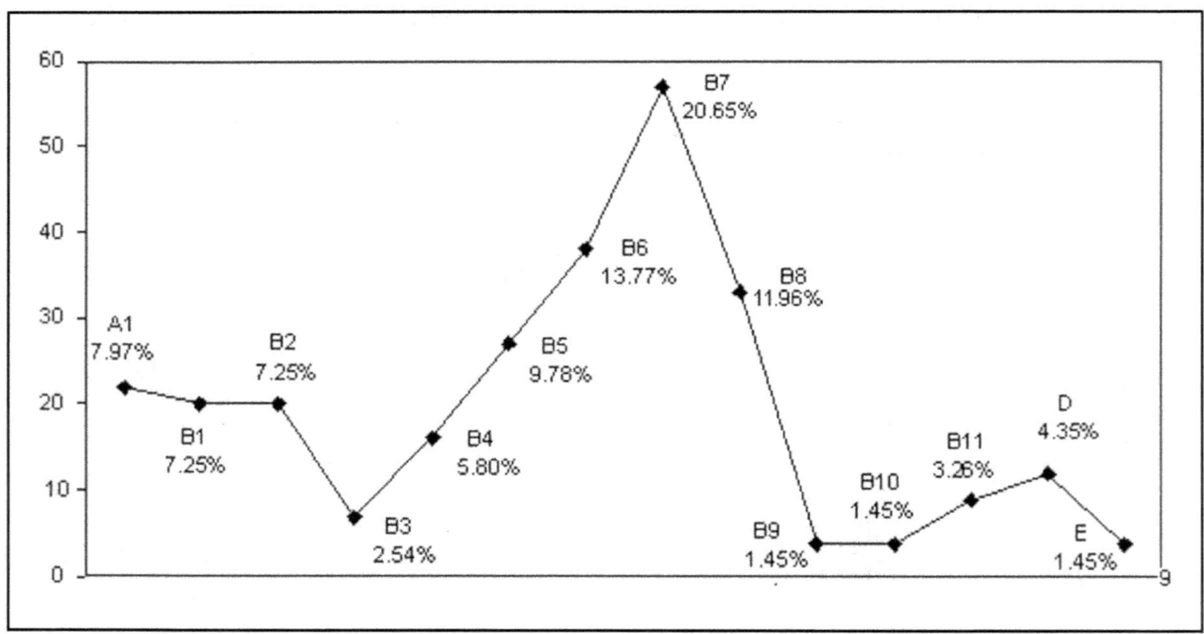

Figura 8.6. Distribución de artefactos por área.

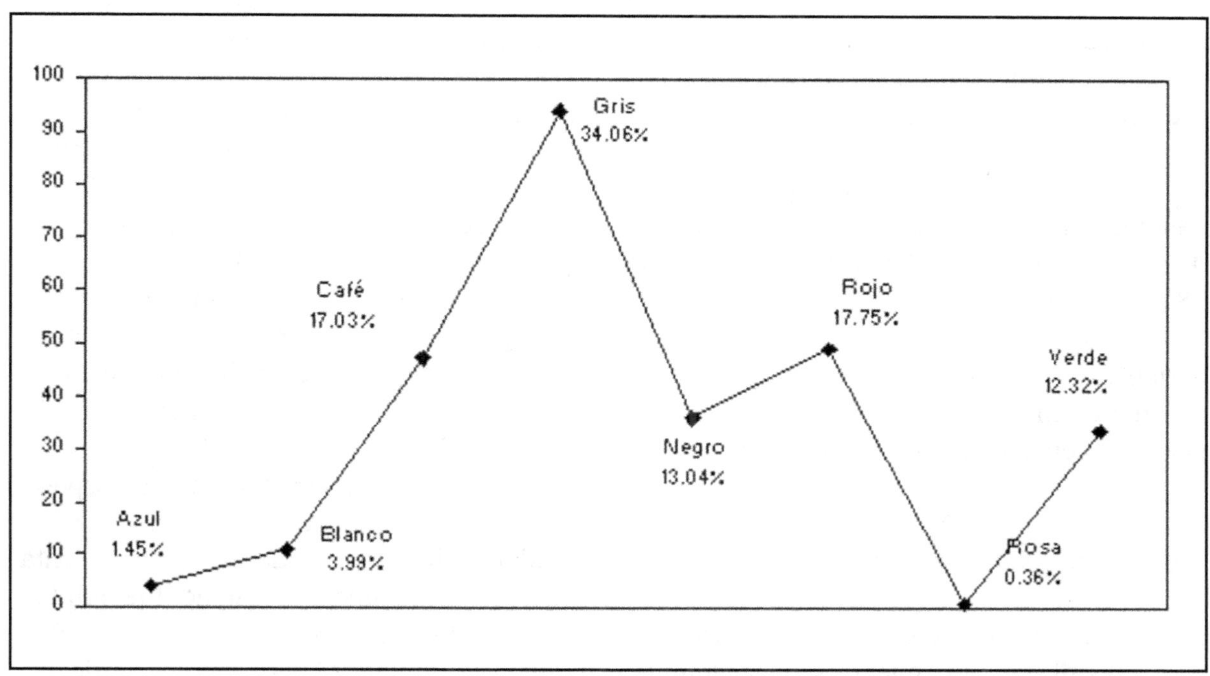

Figura 8.7. Artefactos por color.

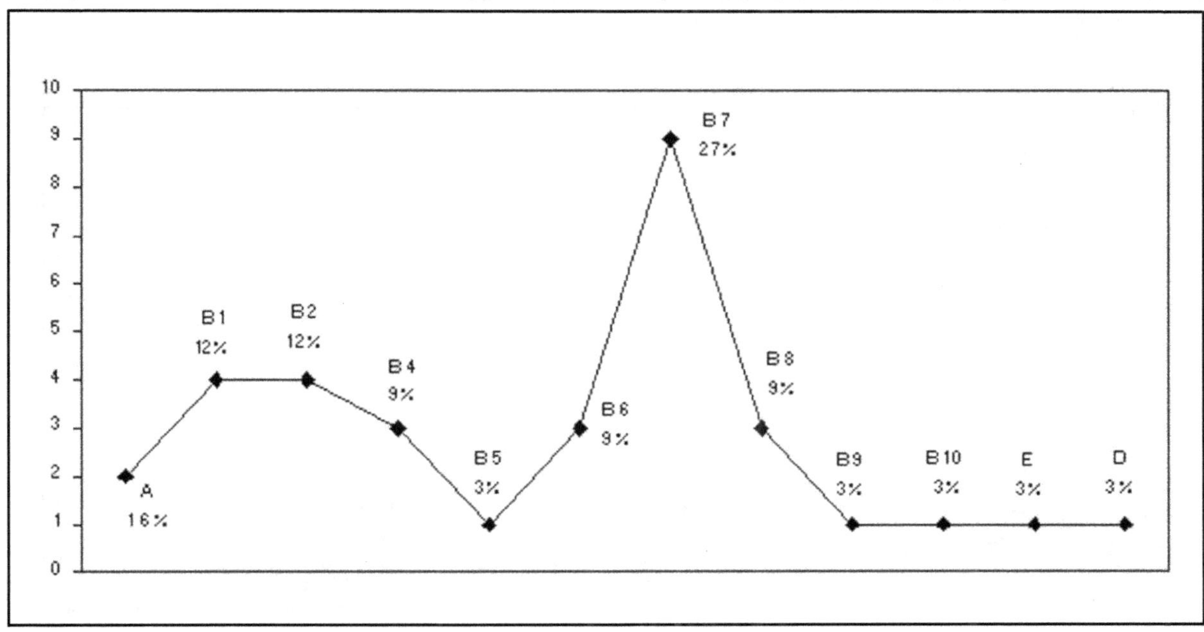

Figura 8.8. Cuentas Color Verde (muestras 33).

de las cuentas pesan menos de un gramo, y esto se traduce en que son muy pequeñas (de hecho, muchas de ellas son milimétricas) (Figura 8.9).

Las cuentas se dividieron por su forma general, encontrando dos grandes grupos, el discoidal con 248 (89.86%) y el tubular con 28 (10.14%).

De las cuentas discoidales se obtuvo una variante de 8 tipos, entre ellos el más numeroso fue el circular (81.45%) (un disco plano perforado en el centro) (Figura 8.10).

Descripción de Materiales "Exóticos"

En el caso de la piedra azul, tenemos dos pequeñas placas, una cuenta y un pendiente. Las piedras verdes son más numerosas pues de estos hay 33 artefactos. Siendo las cuentas circulares las más numerosas (19), no obstante las hay también tubulares (12) y un par de pendientes.

Descripción de las Cuentas Verdes

1. Cuenta circular (24801): color verde, menor a 1 g, diámetro 46 mm y un espesor de 30 mm, su vista en sección es rectangular horizontal, se encuentra pulida en el borde y sus caras. Área B5.
2. Cuenta circular (7762): color verde, menor a 1 g, diámetro 40 mm y un espesor de 23 mm, su vista en sección es plana, se encuentra erosionada en sus caras. Área B4.
3. Cuenta circular (11371): color verde, menor a 1 g, diámetro 50 mm y un espesor de 28 mm, su vista en sección es rectangular horizontal, una de sus caras presenta desprendimientos, no obstante fue pulida sobre éstos. Área B2.
4. Cuenta circular (23384.1): color verde, menor a 1 g, diámetro 33 mm y un espesor de 10 mm, su vista en sección es plana, se encuentra pulida en el borde. Área B7.
5. Cuenta circular (29041): color verde, menor a 1 g, diámetro 36 mm y un espesor

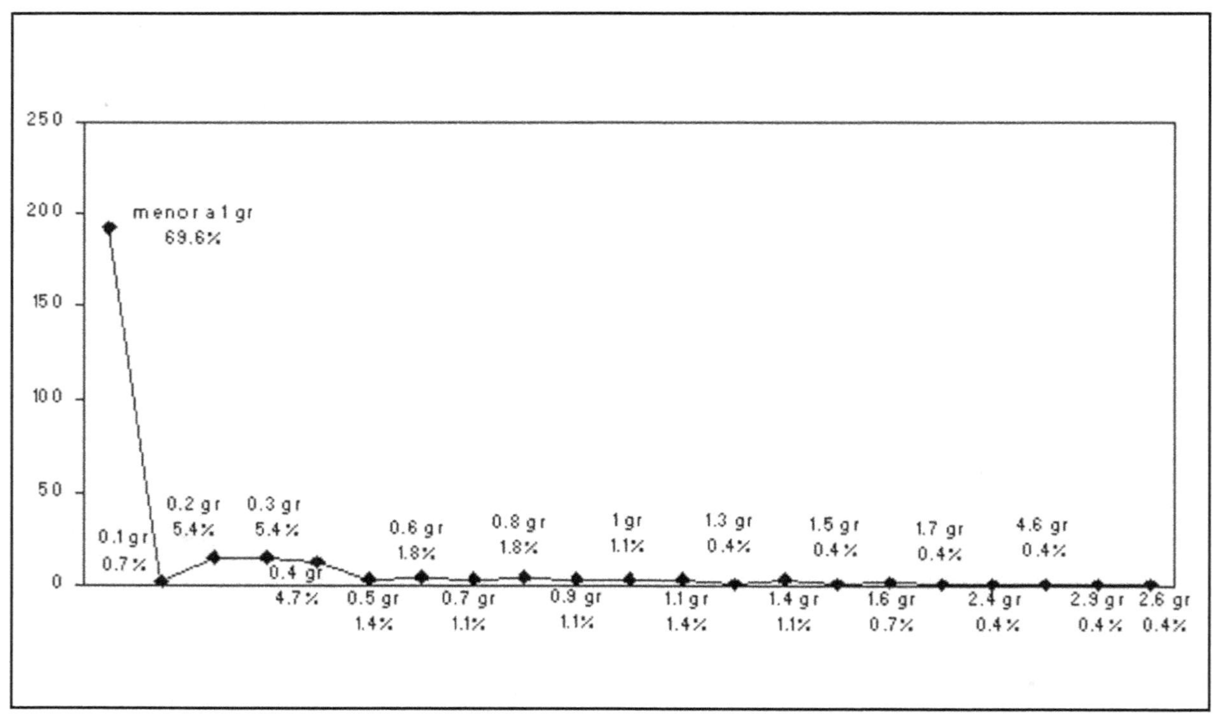

Figura 8.9. Presencia de artefactos por peso.

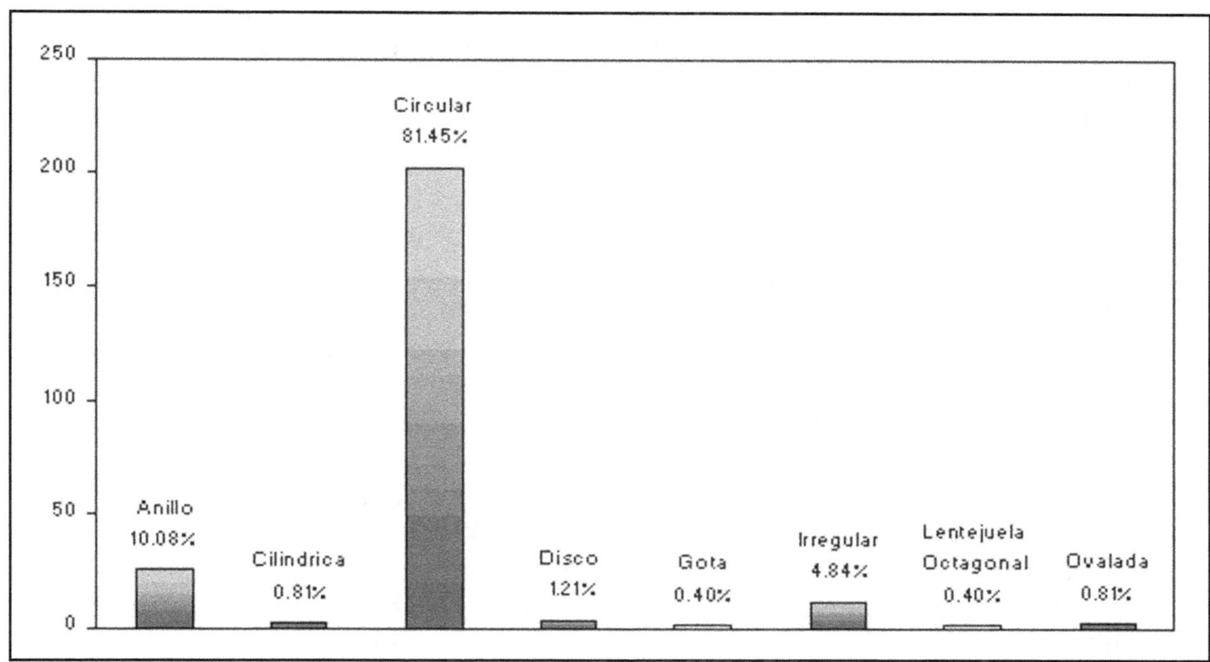

Figura 8.10. Clasificación de las cuenta discoidales.

de 13 mm, su vista en sección es plana, se encuentra pulida en el borde. Área A1.

6. Cuenta circular (29796.2): color verde, menor a 1 g, fragmento muy pequeño de una parte de la cuenta. Área B6.
7. Cuenta circular (32241): color verde, menor a 1 g, diámetro 47 mm y un espesor de 23 mm, su vista en sección es rectangular horizontal, en sus caras presenta microfracturas, sin pulir. Área B10.
8. Cuenta circular (12788): color verde, menor a 1 g, diámetro 55 mm y un espesor de 20 mm, su vista en sección es plana, una de sus caras presenta microfracturas, no obstante fue pulida sobre éstos. Área B2.
9. Cuenta circular (20805): color verde, menor a 1 g, diámetro 45 mm y un espesor de 24 mm, su vista en sección es plana, una de sus caras presenta incisiones, probablemente producto del objeto con el que fue pulido, la perforación es asimétrica, parece que no fue terminada formalmente pero presenta huellas de uso. Área B6 (Figura 8.11).
10. Cuenta circular (20769): color verde, menor a 1 g, diámetro 42 mm y un espesor de 26 mm, su vista en sección es plana, borde pulido, vista al microscopio presenta unas inclusiones negras. Área B6.
11. Cuenta circular (23494): color verde oscuro, menor a 1 g, diámetro 20 mm y un espesor de 30 mm, su vista en sección rectangular/horizontal, con el cuerpo pulido, fractura en borde. Área B7.
12. Cuenta circular (12022): color verde oscuro, menor a 1 g, diámetro 47 mm y un espesor de 22 mm, su vista en sección rectangular/horizontal, con las caras y el cuerpo pulido, vista al microscopio presenta inclusiones amarillas. Área B2.
13. Cuenta circular (8461): color verde, menor a 1 g, diámetro 60 mm y un espesor de 36 mm, su vista en sección rectangular/horizontal, con las caras y el cuerpo pulido, vista al microscopio presenta inclusiones rojo-cafetosas. Área B4.
14. Cuenta circular (28381): color verde

oscuro, menor a 1 g, diámetro 44 mm y un espesor de 25 mm, su vista en sección es plana, pulido en el borde y en las caras, vista al microscopio presenta inclusiones rojo y amarillas, a simple vista su color es negro, sin embargo, al microscopio se ve claramente que es verde oscuro además de presentar las características inclusiones y textura vidriosa de este tipo de material. Área B8.

15. Cuenta circular (17482): color verde muy claro, menor a 1 g, diámetro 55 mm y un espesor de 21 mm, su vista en sección es rectangular/horizontal, pulido en cuerpo y caras, vista al microscopio presenta inclusiones amarillas. A simple vista su color es blanco, sin embargo, al microscopio se ve claramente que se puede clasificar dentro de las piedras verdes pues presenta las características inclusiones y textura vidriosa de este tipo de material. Área B2.
16. Cuenta circular (23424.2): color verde muy claro, menor a 1 g, diámetro 54 mm y un espesor de 20 mm, su vista en sección es plana. Vista al microscopio presenta inclusiones amarillas. A simple vista su color es gris claro, casi blanco, sin embargo, al microscopio se ve claramente que se puede clasificar dentro de las piedras verdes pues presenta las características inclusiones y textura vidriosa de este tipo de material. Área B5.
17. Cuenta circular (33813): color gris claro, menor a 1 g, diámetro 71 mm y un espesor de 25 mm, su vista en sección es plana, pulido en cuerpo y caras. A simple vista su color es gris claro, sin embargo, al microscopio se ve claramente que se puede clasificar dentro de las piedras verdes pues presenta las características inclusiones y textura vidriosa de este tipo de material. Área B7.
18. Cuenta circular (12413): color verde claro, .menor a 1 g, diámetro 50 mm y un espesor de 13 mm, su vista en sección es triangular. A simple vista su color es verde claro, sin embargo, al microscopio se ve claramente que se puede clasificar dentro de las piedras verdes pues presenta las características inclusiones y textura vidriosa de este tipo de material. Área D.
19. Cuenta circular (27075): color verde oscuro, menor a 1 g, diámetro 47 mm y un espesor de 22 mm, su vista en sección es

Figura 8.11. La cuenta circular.

plana, pulido en el borde, vista al microscopio presenta inclusiones rojo, negras y amarillas, un buen ejemplo de las características de este tipo de materia prima. Área B7.

20. Cuenta tubular (28160): color verde grisáceo, .9 g, diámetro 56 mm, largo 1.24 cm, y un espesor de 56 mm. Vista en sección rectangular/vertical. Presenta pulido en cuerpo y microfracturas. En las dos caras presenta dos vetas color blanco. A simple vista su color es gris oscuro, sin embargo, al microscopio se ve claramente que se puede clasificar dentro de las piedras verdes pues presenta las características inclusiones y textura vidriosa de este tipo de material. Área B8.
21. Cuenta tubular (7831): color verde, .55 g, diámetro 30 mm, largo 64 mm, y un espesor de 30 mm. Vista en sección plana/vertical. Presenta pulido en cuerpo y caras. Microfracturas en cuerpo. Vista al microscopio presenta inclusiones rojizas-cafetosas. Área B4.
22. Cuenta tubular (30765): color verde claro, menor a 1 g, diámetro 57 mm, largo 88 mm, y un espesor de 57 mm. Vista en sección rectangular/vertical. Presenta facetado en borde sin pulimiento, microfracturas en caras. Área A1.
23. Cuenta tubular (16126): color verde, menor a 1 g, diámetro 54 mm, largo 99 mm, y un espesor de 54 mm. Vista en sección rectangular/vertical. Presenta pulido, microfracturas en caras. Vista la microscopio presenta inclusiones rojizas y amarillas. Área B1.
24. Cuenta tubular (27037): color verde claro, menor a .6 g, diámetro 60 mm, largo 1.04 cm, y un espesor de 60 mm. Vista en sección rectangular/vertical. Presenta pulido en cuerpo y bordes, microfracturas en caras. Presenta una veta blanquecina en uno de los extremos. Vista la microscopio presenta inclusiones negras, rojizas y amarillas. Área B7.
25. Cuenta tubular (23435.1): color verde claro, 1.1 g, diámetro 70 mm, largo 1.35 cm, y un espesor de 70 mm. Vista en sección rectangular/vertical. Presenta facetado longitudinal en cuerpo. Vista al microscopio presenta inclusiones rojizas y amarillas. Área B7 (Figura 8.12).
26. Cuenta tubular (23435.2): color verde oscuro, menor a 1 g, diámetro 53 mm, largo 1.23 cm, y un espesor de 53 mm. Vista en sección rectangular/vertical. Presenta pulido en cuerpo y caras. Microfracturas en cuerpo. Vista al microscopio presenta inclusiones rojizas-cafetosas. Área B7 (Figura 8.12).
27. Cuenta tubular (8779): color verde oscuro, menor a 1 g, diámetro 47 mm, largo 77 mm, y un espesor de 47 mm. Vista en sección rectangular/vertical. Presenta fractura en una cara. Vista al microscopio presenta inclusiones café-rojizas y negras. Área B1.
28. Cuenta tubular (30055): color verde, menor a 1 g, diámetro 50 mm, largo 77 mm, y un espesor de 50 mm. Vista en sección rectangular/vertical. Presenta facetado en cuerpo por desgaste. Las facetas forman cuatro caras pero sus características cilíndricas no se alteran. Área B8.

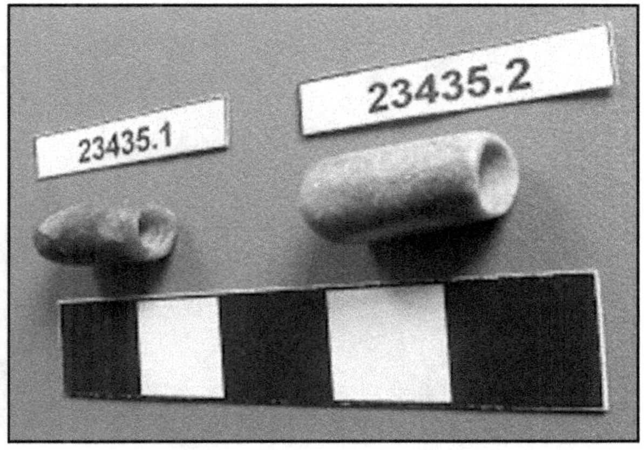

Figura 8.12. Las cuentas tubulares.

29. Cuenta tubular (32128): color verde, .6 g, diámetro 52 mm, largo 1.10 cm, y un espesor de 50 mm. Vista en sección rectangular/vertical. Presenta pulido en cuerpo y caras, vista al microscopio presenta inclusiones amarillas y rojas. Área B9.
30. Cuenta tubular (13916): color verde oscuro, menor a 1 g, diámetro 54 mm, largo 80 y un espesor de 70 mm. Vista en sección rectangular/vertical. Presenta pulido en cuerpo y caras. Microfracturas en cara. Área B1.
31. Cuenta tubular (9325): color verde, 1 g, diámetro 64 mm, largo 1.26 cm, y un espesor de 64 mm. Vista en sección rectangular/vertical. Presenta facetado en cuerpo por desgaste, se observan líneas de tallado. Área B1. (Muestra para identificación macroscópica con el inge).
32. Pendiente (30124): color verde, .3 g, forma rectangular asimétrica, largo 1.33 cm, espesor 20 mm y un ancho de 44 mm, su vista en sección es plana, presenta pulido en bordes y caras. En términos generales se puede decir que presenta "forma de colmillo". Área B8.
33. Pendiente (8961): color verde oscuro, .5 g, forma asimétrica, largo 1.36 cm, espesor 31 mm y un ancho de 86 mm, su vista en sección es plana, presenta pulido en bordes y caras. Línea grabada en canto y en una de sus caras. A simple vista parece un ave completa de perfil; sin embargo, por la posición del orificio, lo que sería el pico quedaría hacia abajo, lo que produce visualmente un parecido más cercano a un pez que a un ave. Vista al microscopio presenta inclusiones rojo-cafetosas. Área E (Figura 8.13).

Descripción de las Cuentas Azules

34. Placa (22088): color azul claro, menor a 1 g, largo 36 mm, ancho 32 mm y un espesor de 10 mm, su vista en sección es plana. Area B5.
35. Placa (23299): color azul claro, 2 g, largo 62 mm, ancho 46 mm y un espesor de 18 mm, su vista en sección es plana. Facetado por desgaste y pulido en caras. Area B7. Enviado al laboratorio de geología para su identificación mineralógica.

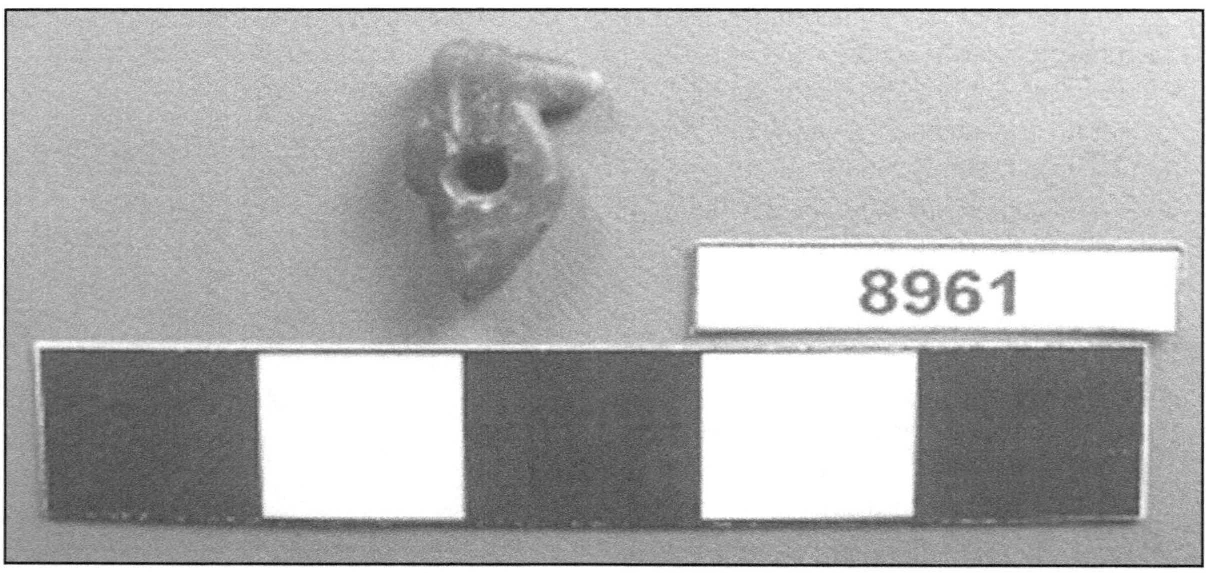

Figura 8.13. Una pendiente.

36. Pendiente (7861): color azul claro, .2 g, diámetro 56 mm y un espesor de 24 mm, su vista en sección es plana, pulido en cuerpo y caras. En una de las caras presenta un cristal de cuarzo (de la misma materia prima). Esta impureza de la materia prima se aprovechó y el grano de cuarzo quedó en el centro exacto de la composición de la pieza. Área B4 (Figura 8.14).
37. Cuenta circular (8397): color azul claro, .4g, diámetro 74 mm y un espesor de 27 mm, su vista en sección es plana. Pulido en el borde. Area B4. Enviado al laboratorio de Geología para su identificación mineralógica.

Discusión

La mayoría de las rocas resultaron ser metamórficas del tipo hornfels siendo originalmente de rocas sedimentarias, aunque hay algunas que provienen de rocas volcánicas como el basalto. La descripción morfológica y mineralógica nos indica que la mayoría de estas rocas (tanto las metamórficas como las volcánicas) podrían provenir de los alrededores del cerro debido a sus características inherentes. No obstante, se presentan dos tipos de rocas que perecen ser materiales alógenos, se trata de piedra verde y azul.

La piedra verde por su color y textura podría tratarse de jadeíta, sin embargo, el análisis de lámina delgada arrojó otros componentes que nos son los propios de esta piedra preciada en época Prehispánica, entre ellos se encuentran que la jadeíta proviene de rocas ígneas ultrabásicas, mientras que los materiales que se analizaron provienen de una roca metamórfica, preliminarmente afirmamos que los materiales verdes no son de jadeíta. En cuanto a la piedra azul, a la que coloquialmente llamamos turquesa, tampoco presenta los componentes propios de este mineral.

En los dos casos se trata de piedras cuyo color fue sumamente importante en época Prehispánica pero en ambos casos no se trata de minerales "originales". Esto es realmente sugerente debido al uso de este color culturalmente, es decir, al no provenir de un yacimiento "original," podría significar muchas cosas, pero hay que ser cautelosos al formular una interpretación preliminar.

Recordemos que de las piezas color azul sólo tenemos cuatro pequeños artefactos, de los cuales uno fue utilizado para la identificación mineralógica. Observamos al microscopio

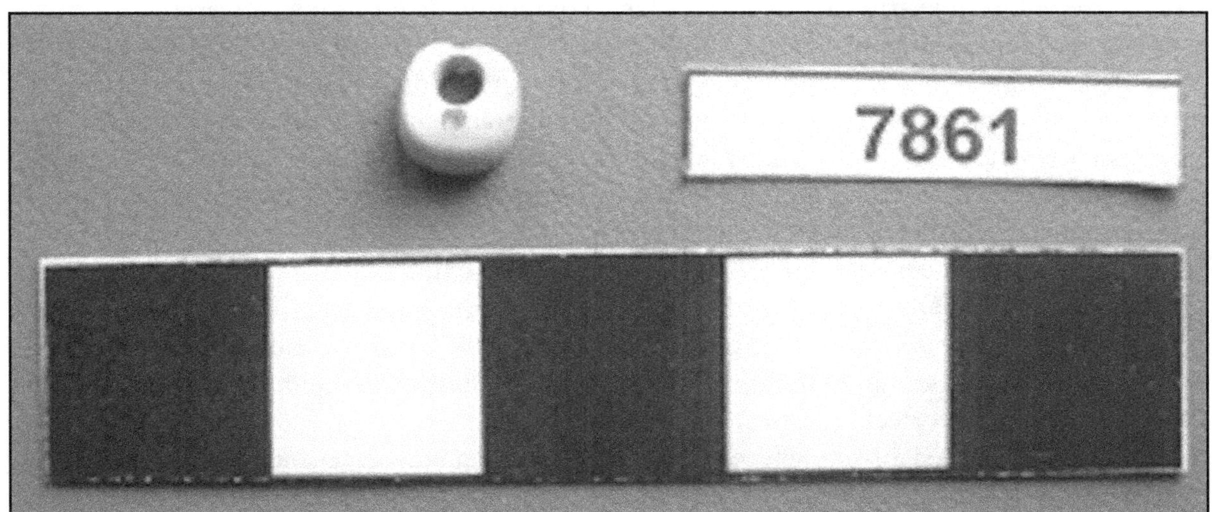

Figura 8.14. Una pendiente.

los tres restantes y parecería que poseen las mismas características que la muestra que fue analizada, dado el caso de que los artefactos color azul provinieran de la misma fuente, tendríamos que ninguno es de extracción minera, este análisis por tanto, nos habla de que en el Cerro de Trincheras hubo Turquesa Falsa .

Al decir Turquesa Falsa no utilizamos el término en su acepción peyorativa, al hacerlo, creemos importante señalar una cosa, si el azul de esta roca está dado por procesos de metamorfismo eso podría significar un cierto distanciamiento con los grupos que se dedicaban a la extracción de este material. Si no fueron minerales originales, es significativa la presencia debido a un uso cultural de esos colores, y sobre todo, a los procesos sociales que se dieron (no es lo mismo participar en una red de intercambio con *grupos mineros* que explotar rocas metamórficas color azul).

Análisis Petrográfico

Se enviaron para su análisis diferentes muestras tanto de objetos terminados como de materia prima para la identificación mineralógica al Departamento de Geología de la Universidad de Sonora con los geólogos Ricardo Amaya y Saúl Herrera. Las muestras fueron procesadas y montadas en una lámina delgada.

El primer paso consistió en seleccionar un artefacto que fuera representativo de la materia prima sobre la cual fueron realizados la mayoría de los ornamentos, se debería seleccionar uno que por sus características no afectara, ni en cualidad ni en cantidad, al resto de los artefactos pues una pequeña parte de éste sería prácticamente pulverizado, antes de enviarlos la laboratorio se realizó un registro detallado del artefacto para su correcta correlación con el grueso del material. Así mismo, seleccionamos seis muestras de probable materia prima tanto del propio Cerro de Trincheras (SON:F:10:2) como del sitio La Playa (SON:F:10:3).

Ya con la muestra en laboratorio el procedimiento consiste en hacer un corte en la roca para obtener una superficie lo más plana posible, posteriormente se coloca una pequeña capa sobre un porta objetos para que quede pegada al vidrio, inmediatamente se aplican abrasivos hasta conseguir una capa traslúcida que permita identificar los minerales presentes, finalmente se coloca un cubre objetos para que la roca quede estabilizada de manera firme entre el cubre objetos y el porta objetos. El paso final consiste en observar con el microscopio petrográfico las partículas y de ahí se obtiene la descripción. Si el microscopio está adaptado para realizar tomas fotográficas, se realizan de acuerdo a la escala pertinente; en este caso se realizaron tomas a 5X y 10X.

Para evitar confusiones en el tratamiento de las láminas, la nomenclatura para definir a los artefactos fue “Composito,” seguido por una letra correspondiente, para las materias primas fue “Lamina,” también seguido por una letra correspondiente.

Composito A: Gris Claro con Vetas Rojizas. 1 muestra

Material de grano muy fino, esencialmente compuesto de cuarzo+sericita+epidota granular. Con opacos de color café rojizo en pequeños agregados y diseminados. Se presentan zonas alargadas ricas en clorita incolora.

Composito B: Azul. 2 muestras

Material extremadamente fino (Figura 8.15). Minerales no identificables con certeza aceptable. Parece ser una mezcla de cuarzo+feldespato+epidota granular extremadamente fina.

Roca metamófica: horfnels de cuarzo-feldespato-epidota.

1) Formada por metamorfismo de contacto o hidrotermal de una roca sedimentaria de grano muy fino.

2) Formada por alteración hidrotermal de la matriz de una roca volcánica.

Composito C: Gris. 2 muestras

Material formado en su totalidad por talco (Figura 8.16). Roca metamórfica: esquisto de talco. Formada por metamorfismo dinámico e hidrotermal de rocas ígneas básicas a ultrabásicas.

Composito D: Gris claro. 1 muestra

Material constituido totalmente por talco (Figura 8.17). Roca Metamórfica: Esquisto de talco.

Formada por metamorfismo dinámico e hidrotermal de rocas ígneas básicas a ultrabásicas. Es el mismo material de la muestra C, pero parece haber sido alterado parcialmente o recristalizado.

Composito E: Verde grisáceo. 1 muestra

Material de grano muy fino en su mayor parte, con una matriz compuesta de sericita+epidota+clorita+cuarzo+opacos (Figura 8.18). Se observan cristales muy pequeños, aunque de mayor tamaño que los minerales de la matriz, de cuarzo y de feldespato alterado. Pequeños agregados de clorita verde+opacos.

Roca metamórfica: hornfels de sericita-epidota-clorita-cuarzo.

Formada por metamorfismo de contacto e hidrotermal. La roca original parece ser una roca sedimentaria de grano fino como una

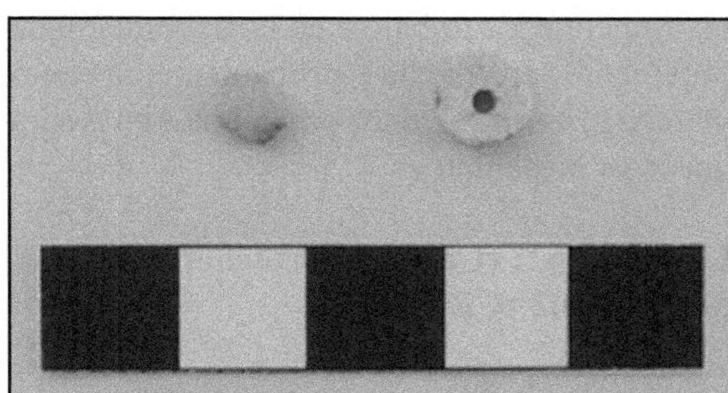

Figura 8.15. Cuenta enviada al laboratorio.

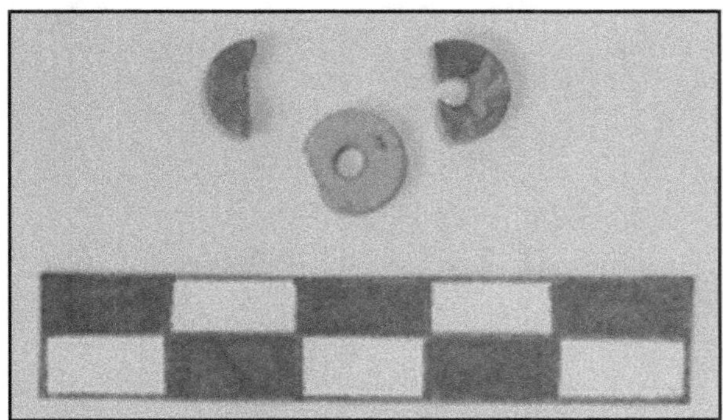

Figura 8.16. Cuenta enviada al laboratorio.

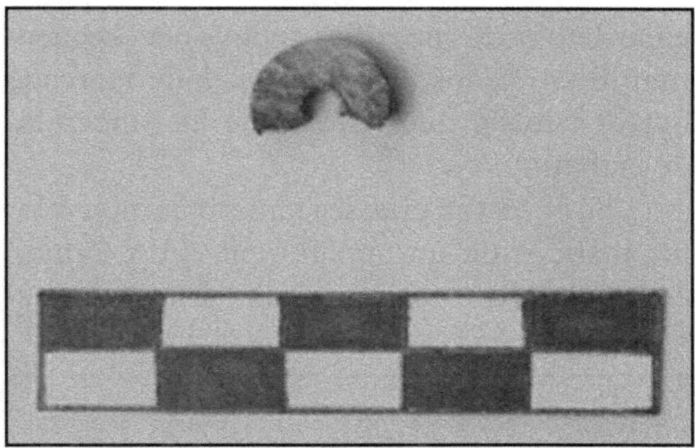

Figura 8.17. Cuenta enviada al laboratorio.

Figura 8.18. Pendiente enviado al laboratorio.

arensica fina o lutita arenosa.

Composito F: Rojas. 2 muestras

Material muy fino (Figuras 8.19). Opacos muy fino café rojizo: 60%
Cuarzo + sericita+ clorita:40%
Roca metamorfica: Hornfels de opacos-cuarzo-sericita-clorita
Imposible de determinar la roca original

Composito G: Verde claro. 2 muestras

Material de grano muy fino (Figuras 8.20).
Clorita incolora: 60%
Sericita:35%
Epidota+rutilo:5%
La epidota y el rutilo (mineral color rojizo o amarillento de muy alto relieve) se encuentran diseminados como cristales de marcado mayor tamaño que el resto de los minerales de la matriz.

Se observan grandes fantasmas minerales prismáticos de un tamaño entre 1 y 2 mm, completamente reemplazados por una mezcla de clorita incolora+sericita. Este mineral puede ser un mineral metamórfico original, posiblemente cordierita y/o andalusita. Hay otros minerales reemplazados parcialmente por epidota, los cuales pueden ser igualmente cordierita y/o andalusita.

Roca metamórfica:hornfels de clorita-sericita.

Puede ser el resultado de la alteración hidrotermal de otra roca metamórfica (hornfels de cordierita y/o andalusita) pre-existente.

Figura 8.19. Pendiente enviado al laboratorio.

Muestras de Probable Materia Prima

Enviamos así mismo muestras adicionales para identificación petrográfica de materiales comúnmente llamados esquistos provenientes del cerro El Revolcadero en el sitio La Playa (SON:F:10:3 [CR]) ubicado 8 km. al norte del Cerro de Trincheras. Así como rocas del propio Cerro de Trincheras. En los sitios referidos estos materiales fueron utilizados ya sea como instrumentos de trabajo o en la elaboración de ornamentos en concha y probablemente como materia prima de algunos ornamentos en piedra que aquí presentamos.

Lámina "A": (Cerro de Trincheras SON:F:10:2 [CR])

La muestra indica una roca de origen ígneo

Figura 8.20. Cuenta enviada al laboratorio.

extrusivo, color pardo grisáceo de textura ligeramente porfídica, por la presencia de fenocristales de plagioclasa y feldespato potásico, que están incluidos dentro de una matriz microcristalina y de composición cuarzofeldespática. El porcentaje de fenocristales (con rangos de tamaños entre fracciones de mm, hasta un máximo de 1.5 y 2.0 mm) del orden de 10 a 15% y se representan por plagioclasa (oligoclasa) y feldespato potásico (sanidina); escasos cristales de biotita, que han sido totalmente reemplazada por óxidos+sericita y oxidos de fierro. A pesar de que existen aparentes rasgos remanentes texturales que indicarían la opción de una roca piroclástica (toba), se prefiere la clasificación de una Riodacita – Cuarzolatita.

Nota: Esta muestra fue enviada al laboratorio bajo el presupuesto coloquial entre los arqueólogos que era una Latita.

Lámina "B": (La Playa SON:F:10:3 [CR])

En muestra de mano esta roca corresponde a una roca sedimentaria de color gris claro verdoso, con fracturas de color rojizo por efectos de oxidación. La textura observada en lámina delgada corresponde a una granulometría fina a muy fina, constituida por cristales subredondeados/redondeados (tamaños de fracciones de mm) de cuarzo, feldespatos y minerales opacos-óxidos, que están incluidos dentro de un cementante que contiene mezclas de material sericítico-arcilloso + clorita + calcita + minerales opacos/óxidos de fierro. La clorita, en términos generales, deriva de la transformación de biotita hidrotermal o metamórfica. Existen estructuras ovoides-lenticulares, que corresponden a concreciones rellenas de clorita y calcita + álgunos óxidos. Esta roca, originalmente sedimentaria de granulometría muy fina (lutita o arenisca muy fina), por los efectos de hidrotermalismo – metamorfismo puede ser referida como un hornfels de sericita – clorita – cuarzo.

Lámina "C": (Cerro de Trincheras SON:F:10:2 [CR])

Roca de origen ígneo volcánico, de color verde oscuro - grisáceo, presenta rasgos texturales combinados: Porfídico y volcanoclástico (tobáceo). En la lámina delgada se observan fenocristales de plagioclasa, rangos de tamaño entre fracciones de mm, hasta un máximo de 1.5 a 2 mm, que muestran un reemplazamiento variable por epidota + sericita + minerales arcillosos + óxidos de fierro. Existen fragmentos de rocas de origen volcánico y composición andesítica, con tamaños hasta 2 mm, mostrando también los efectos de alteración hidrotermal. Esta roca, de acuerdo con el contexto geológico de la región, se hace equivalente a uno de los niveles de rocas que definen a la Formación Tarahumara, que ha sido datada en el rango entre 68 y 86 Ma.

Lámina "D": (La Playa SON:F:10:3 [CR])

Esta muestra presenta rasgos texturales que identifican a una roca sedimentaria que en lámina delgada presenta una textura de granulometría muy fina, definida por microcristales subredondeados y subangulares de cuarzo + feldespatos + minerales opacos – óxidos de fierro, que están incluidos dentro de un cementante conformado por mezclas de sericita + minerales arcillosos + óxidos e fierro, que al igual que los componentes del cementante, presentan una orientación preferencial. Las características composicionales y granulométricas son muy similares a lo observado en la Lámina "B," existiendo variaciones locales en cuanto a la concentración y tamaño de los cristales de cuarzo y feldespatos. La roca se clasifica como una roca sedimentaria, del tipo de la lutita – arenisca de grano muy fino, afectada por hidrotermalismo – metamorfismo, que propicia el considerarla como un hornfels de clorita + sericita + cuarzo.

Lámina "E": (Cerro de Trincheras SON:F:10:2 [CR])

Esta roca, de color verde grisáceo, presenta evidencias de un intenso hidrotermalismo-metamorfismo, a tal grado que se han modificado las características composicionales y texturales originales de la roca. Dentro de la matriz de grano fino, constituida por abundantes microcristales de biotita y hornblenda secundaria (hidrotermal) + clorita + epidota + opacos-óxidos de fierro, existen rasgos remanentes de lo que probablemente pudieran haber correspondido a cristales de plagioclasa. Microvetilla rellena de cuarzo + epidota + clorita; lo que corrobora el efecto hidrotermal.

La roca se clasifica como una probable andesita muy afectada por hidrotermalismo – metamorfismo.

Una clasificación alterna, es la de considerarla como una roca sedimentaria de grano muy fino; aunque no se observaron microcristales de cuarzo.

Nota: Esta muestra fue enviada al laboratorio bajo el presupuesto coloquial entre los arqueólogos que era un Basalto.

Lámina "F": (La Playa SON:F:10:3 [CR])

Esta muestra, de color verde claro, corresponde a una roca de origen sedimentario de granulometría extremadamente fina. En términos comparativos, esta muestra "F," presenta características texturales y composicionales similares al Composito B, aunque con una ligera tendencia en cuanto a un mayor tamaño y en la concentración de los cristales de cuarzo y feldespatos, que definen zonas o bandas dentro del cementante constituido por abundante material arcillo-sericitico + clorita + óxidos-minerales opacos, que contiene estructuras ovoides – concreciones, rellenas por clorita y calcita, al igual que lo reportado para la muestra "B". Por lo mismo, se clasifica también, como una roca originalmente sedimentaria de grano muy fino (lutita – lodolita), afectada por procesos hidrotermales y de metamorfismo, que la transforman a un hornfels de clorita + sericita + cuarzo.

Nota: Esta muestra fue enviada al laboratorio bajo el presupuesto coloquial entre los arqueólogos que era un Esquisto verde.

Ahora bien, ¿para qué nos sirve el análisis de láminas delgadas? La riqueza de este tipo de resultados consiste en llevar a interpretaciones del pasado cultural nuestros resultados, es decir, de qué no sirve saber si la rocas tienen un alto contenido de sericita o son transformadas por hidrotermalismo, si no podemos llevar estas a interpretaciones de carácter cultural. Por ejemplo, la diferencia que implica que una roca cristalice en superficie (extrusiva) o que cristalice debajo de la superficie (intrusiva) puede significar mucho. Es sabido que las rocas extrusivas (como la andesita) puede resultar mejor material para el lasqueo, pues su propia consistencia la hace ser una roca resistente pero a la vez maleable, por el contrario, una roca intrusiva (como la diorita) podría, hasta cierto punto, tener menor densidad, eso significaría que puede romperse con mayor facilidad tanto en los lasqueos de preparación como en el uso de la herramienta en sí.

Asimismo, resulta evidente (después de los análisis presentados) que en la selección de la materia prima existe la preconcepción del producto final que quiere obtener el artesano, es decir, la mayoría de los ornamentos que analizamos fueron realizados en rocas de origen sedimentario o rocas que provienen de éstas pero que sufrieron metamorfismo, esto se traduce en que todas estas rocas son extremadamente suaves para ser trabajadas en los tamaños milimétricos en los que fueron trazadas muchas de las cuentas, por ejemplo, de todos los ornamentos (un total de 276) únicamente dos cuentas fueron realizadas en basalto fino(roca ígnea), o sea, en materiales que por sus características inherentes son duros.

Continuar con este tipo de análisis son los que nos permitirían traducir a significados culturales, y hasta detectar patrones, en el uso de ciertos materiales en el pasado. Consideramos que estas láminas que presentamos, son un aproximación que nos permiten dirigirnos hacia la resolución de preguntas concretas tales como:

¿Toda piedra azul debe ser registrada como Turquesa? ¿El uso de rocas sedimentarias significa que no hubo extracción sistemática de yacimientos para la manufactura de ornamentos en piedra? ¿Todas las piedras verdes se puede considerara jadeíta?

Pero estas preguntas no deben, y no pueden, ser formuladas de manera aislada e independiente, es decir, si una cuenta proviene de una roca volcánica no contesta nada en si misma, lo contesta en la medida que realizamos preguntas interrelacionadas, es decir, ¿cuáles son los yacimientos de la extracción de tal o cual material?, ¿cuál es su secuencia operativa desde el yacimiento hasta ser producto terminado? ¿Cómo interpretamos nuestro registro arqueológico más allá de la cuantificación?

Enfocando nuestra atención a este tipo de análisis, sin perder de vista la interpretación cultural que los arqueólogos hacemos del pasado, estaríamos en la posibilidad de empezar por responder añejas preguntas.

Chapter 9
Culturally Modified Bone

Radhika Sundararajan. Binghamton University

Huesos Modificados

Este capítulo discute los 169 artefactos de hueso culturalmente modificados recuperados en Cerro de Trincheras durante las temporadas de trabajo de campo de 1995 y 1996. Los atefactos en esta categoría incluyen elementos de punta tales como horquillas para el pelo, varios huesos trabajados y cuatro tipos de hueso mellado incluyendo escofinas. Sundararja trata estos artefactos en relación a su función en el sitio y a las prácticas estéticas y los compara con hueso animal no modificado de Cerro de Trincheras. Los excavadores recuperaron la mayoría de los huesos modificados del Locus B, el cual contenía la mayor parte de las terrazas habitacionales del sitio. Esto sugiere que los individuos viviendo en el área eran los más involcrados con la producción de huesos y uso de estos implementos. Finalmente, Sundararjan compara este conjunto con la interpretación funcional y con el contexto de otros sitios trabajados del noroeste y el sudoeste.

This work examines the modified bone assemblage from the site of Cerro de Trincheras in Sonora, México. Although the remains of culturally modified animal bones are present at most prehistoric sites, very few archaeological reports provide adequate discussions of bone tools; most of the time these artifacts are included in a site's faunal report simply as faunal remains rather than as artifacts. In this manner, they are investigated only in regard to subsistence practices.

Bone artifacts potentially provide important data for understanding prehistoric society. Bone may serve as functional items, as in the case of awls used in the manufacture of textiles and basketry. Bone may also be used as decorative pieces, as in the case of hairpins or decorated bone. Cultural preferences for portions of animal bone have both functional and aesthetic values.

Descriptive and functional analyses of culturally modified bone recovered from Cerro de Trincheras follows. This section will also discuss the available ethnographic data that can inform on the significance of artifact tool classes as well as their distribution at Cerro de Trincheras. In addition, I will make comparisons of Trincheras worked bone to the unmodified faunal remains, and assemblages from other Southwestern sites.

Bone Implements from Cerro de Trincheras

A total of 181 bones recovered from Cerro de Trincheras demonstrated some degree of cultural modifications. Twelve specimens exhibited only butchering marks and were not included as bone implements. Stahl (Chapter 11) discusses these bones in his report on the Cerro de Trincheras archaeofaunal assemblage. This report analyzes 169 artifacts (2 percent of the total animal bones recovered) that displayed considerable cultural modification, including polishing, cutting and notching.

Bone Tool Manufacturing Techniques

Di Peso et al. (1974:6) describe the five types of modifications on bone found in the Southwest. Splintering is "accomplished by smashing or battering a long bone to obtain small, narrow fragments which were further worked to complete the tool." Splitting is "done by sawing a long bone along its length." Notching is "accomplished by partially sawing through bone in a series of short cuts" Cutting or sawing is "used not only to obtain a piece of bone the desired size, but to further shape objects by cutting off irregularities along edges, parts of condyles, or the like." Abrading was done to finish the surface of the artifact. Evidence for this technique is observed "in the form of minute scratches and /or smoothed facets on the surfaces of specimens."

The first stage of bone artifact manufacture involves the cleaning and removal of any excess tissue. A thin layer of soft periosteal tissue covers fresh bone. This may be removed during food preparation through sustained boiling, by maceration in water, or by scraping with a stone flake or scraper. The latter method inflicts deep, irregularly spaced striations running longitudinally along the surface of the bone (Olsen 1979). The frequent appearance of these striae, even on unfinished bone objects, suggests that the Trinchereños prepared many bones by scraping.

Bones from prior meals, which had been tossed in the midden, could have been recovered later for use as tool material after the soft tissue had deteriorated. According to Olsen (1979), even bone and antler that was cleaned a year earlier could be worked almost as easily as fresh bone, provided that it was first hydrated by two or three days of soaking. Artisans could not, however, have easily used severely weathered bone, which cracks and peels in unpredictable ways when worked.

Olsen (1979) refers to "grooving and snapping" as a common method for cutting bone to proper dimensions. This is accomplished by incising a groove through about three-quarters of the thickness of the bone. Artisans could have done this with a stone flake or graver. After this, a quick blow of a chisel or pressure of the hands will split the bone along the groove. Marks on the freshly cut edge appear as a series of fine striations running parallel to the groove (Olsen 1979). This technique was used on many of the bone artifacts from Trincheras (n = 79). Artisans shaped awls and hairpins by longitudinal grooving.

Trinchereños used hacking as a less common method of manufacturing with bone. They often used a stone cleaver or axe to separate antler tines, likely used for the pressure flaking of flint, from the main beams. This technique produced deep V-shaped cuts and irregular breakage around the point of impact. The two antler tines recovered from Trincheras demonstrated this irregular breakage at their base. We found no evidence that Trinchereños used percussion and pressure flaking to work bone.

Once they had roughly fashioned bone into an appropriate shape, artisans used a variety of techniques to finish the artifact. Trinchereños frequently used sandstone abraders to finish artifacts and to resharpen awls and needles. Sandstone abrasion produces a wear pattern appearing as a series of very fine parallel striations that are closely spaced and barely visible to the unaided eye. These striae often zigzag back on each other as the abrader is moved back and forth. If an area is abraded for an extended period of time, the striations develop in uniform planes that form facets (Olsen 1979).

Many of the bone artifacts from Trincheras and throughout the Southwest are highly polished and lustrous. This suggests that artisans used wet leather and sandstone alternately used to burnish bone implements. Although such finely finished products appear to require considerable time and effort, Olsen (1979) notes that similar polishes have been replicated on deer metapodials in less than 20 minutes.

I used a 30x binocular microscope to observe polish or striations. Polish was located on the tips and shafts of artifacts, generally surrounding the tip but sometimes extending further up one side than the other. This pattern is interpreted as a result of wear, but the extent of the polish may cover the entire specimen as well. Teague and Crown (1983) note that polish on artifact shafts was not impervious to weathering; it could be observed in small patches where the cortical surface was intact. Thus, they suggest that, "weathering may affect polish differently due to use, which would be located on the tip, versus shaft polish which would have been acquired during manufacture" (Teague & Crown 1983:593). Although the cortical surface on much of the worked bone is heavily weathered, evidence of polish could be observed macroscopically. This could be used to support inferences about function, although the fragmentary and poor condition of the bone artifacts made this difficult at times.

Kidder (1932) notes that large quantities of unfinished or unused fragments of bone artifacts are often recovered from sites. He attributes this to the fact that the raw material for bone artifacts is readily available. It is likely that when artisans ruined artifacts during manufacture they simply discarded the damaged bone. Perhaps many of the bone artifacts from Cerro de Trincheras that demonstrated no use wear, or appear partially completed, may have been discarded in this manner.

The Cerro de Trincheras Assemblage

I identified three broad artifact classes within the Cerro de Trincheras modified bone assemblage. These are pointed implements, worked bone and notched bone. Pointed implements are those artifacts characterized by a long, tapering shaft and a pointed tip. Many of these items have round, polished edges and marks along the shaft and tip. Worked bones show evidence of cultural modification and use; these items are usually cut, polished and may have small marks suggesting they were utilized in a fashion similar to awls. These specimens are often highly fragmented. Notched bones have small lines incised into the bone surface. The category of notched bone includes four discreet types: Type A refers to those specimens that resemble 'rasps' which have been recovered from other Southwestern sites; Type B includes items that demonstrate a series of small, parallel notches that do not appear to have served a particular function; Type C includes two incised specimens which were likely decorative in nature; Type D represents incised *Lepus* (jack rabbit) dental elements.

Standard observations include presence of and degree of burning, polish, and use wear. I also noted shape, completeness of edges, degree of weathering, presence of spiral fractures, split bone shafts, or cut ends, as well as measurements of length, width and thickness. For these measurements, I only measured bones with complete dimensions. Incomplete dimensions are denoted by the letter f.

The degree of weathering refers to the condition of the cortical surface. According to Szuter (1988:387), heavily weathered bone is "flaked, eroded, root-etched, or covered with a caliche-like deposit." Heavy weathering tends to obliterate traces of wear patterns (Teague & Crown 1983). Bone that is in good condition has an intact cortical surface, and slightly weathered bone has minimal surface damage (Szuter 1988). Burned bone at Trincheras is either scorched (black or brown) or calcined (white gray, or blue-gray). The striae observed as indications of usewear are either longitudinal (down the length of shaft) or at an angle to the shaft (crosswise, or at a 45 degree angle to the shaft).

The presence of spiral fractures at one or both ends of artifacts indicate that the bone was broken while relatively fresh. At Trincheras, 18 percent (n = 31/169) of the modified bone had spiral fractures present at one or both ends. Eight of these specimens were recovered from Area 8, El Mirador. Morlan (1983), however, observed that slightly weathered bones will still exhibit the characteristic spiral breakage pattern of fresh bone when broken.

Szuter (1988) notes that Hohokam modified bone assemblages are often highly fragmented and heavily weathered; these characteristics often obscure traces of manufacturing techniques and/or use wear marks. These issues are applicable to the Cerro de Trincheras modified bone assemblage. As a result, the surface treatment of many specimens could not be determined. Of those that could be determined, 2 percent (4/169) had polish limited to the shaft, and 16.5 percent (28/169) had polish on both the shaft and tip. Five percent (8/169) showed polish restricted to the tip, which can be considered the result of use wear rather than manufacturing techniques (Szuter 1988).

During the course of their analysis, Teague and Crown (1983) realized that one way to understand the large percentage of burned artifacts in an assemblage might be to observe the location of burning on the worked bone. Burning might occur only as an end product of trash disposal. If this is true, they argue, then the patterning of burning should be random. The location of the burning should occur as often on the tip of the artifact as on the shaft or basal end. If the burning is purposive, however, then patterning should exist. The bone might be burned to make it easier to work or produce a better artifact. An observable patterning of burning may give insight into the reasons for such burning (Teague & Crown 1983:598).

Of interest in the Cerro de Trincheras assemblage are the relative frequencies of burning within artifact classes, as well as the distribution of burned artifacts at the site. Within the class of worked bone fragments (n = 70), 60 percent (n = 42) are burned to some degree. Of these burned items 60 percent (n = 25) were almost completely calcined, and the remaining 40 percent (n = 17) were almost fully scorched. In four cases, burning was limited to parts of the shaft or edges. All but three of these artifacts were excavated from Area B. The three exceptions were all calcined fragments recovered from El Caracol (A1).

Fifty-two percent of the notched bone at Cerro de Trincheras (n = 23/44) was exposed to heat. Of the five notched bones that were almost fully scorched, four were of Type A (two of these were recovered from Area A1, one from B1 and one from B9); the other was of Type B (found in B1). Of the ten mostly calcined notched bones, seven were of Type A, and three of Type B; all were found in Locus B. The next most common patterning was scorching at one end. Three specimens displayed this trend: one of Type A and two of Type B (both recovered from Area B7). No Type C or D notched bone was burned.

At Cerro de Trincheras, 6 of the 17 pointed tool portions were burned. Two were almost completely scorched, and both of these were portions of blunt awls. Two blunt awl tips and one fine point awl tip were almost completely calcined. One portion of a blunt awl was calcined just at the tip. All of these artifacts were incomplete (five out of the six were only tips, the sixth being a partial shaft and tip) and had usewear marks. One was recovered from Area A1, the rest from Area B.

Pointed Implement

Di Peso (1974:1) employs the following terminology for describing pointed bone artifacts: the butt describes "the base or blunt edge, which may be the natural articular condyle (head) and may be highly modified and shaped;" the shaft is "the central portion of the tool;" the tip is "the pointed end;" and, the shoulder refers to the area "where the butt joins the shaft and/or tip."

I could only identify five of the pointed implements in the Trincheras assemblage to genus and skeletal element. All five were *Odocoileus* (deer) metapodials. Artisans had fashioned eight implements from mammalian long bones, and two items from unidentifiable taxon and skeletal elements. Artiodactyl metapodia made good tools several reasons. There is a central groove on both the anterior and posterior surfaces of metatarsal, and the posterior surface of metacarpal elements of deer that serve to guide a graver when splitting the bone (Olsen 1979). Also, there are two metacarpal and two metatarsal elements in each deer, pronghorn, and bighorn sheep. Thus, each Artiodactyl skeleton yields four metapodia. The archaeofauna from Cerro de Trincheras indicate that the site's occupants frequently hunted deer and thus produced a readily available supply of Artiodactyl bone for bone tool manufacture.

The function of a pointed implement can be inferred by examining its functional tip. I took tip width and thickness measurements for all pointed implements recovered from Cerro de Trincheras (n = 17). Following Olsen (1979), I measured width by placing the artifact on a piece of graph paper with the marrow cavity down and measuring 5 mm from the tip. I then rotated the bone 90° and measured 5 mm from the tip to determine thickness. This method insures that measurements represent the morphology of the artifact rather than patterns of use that would be present closer to the tip. These measurements were taken in an effort to standardize measurements of bone artifacts that would facilitate comparison with other sites (Szuter 1988). However, the resulting measurements may not be related to functional requirements if the measured tools are at the ends of their use lives (Glass 1984).

Olsen (1979, 1980) uses these measurements to calculate a ratio of tip width to thickness as a possible means of distinguishing between awls and hairpins. She argues that hairpins are wider than they are thick:

> Fine-tipped awls have equal tip width and thickness, and blunt-tipped awls have a tip morphology more similar to hairpins. The latter form is obviously difficult to distinguish from hairpins on the basis of tip measurements alone, but by the use of additional criteria such as polish, manufacturing technique, and context, the distinction may sometimes be made. (Olsen 1979:355)

The ratio of tip width to thickness for the pointed implements from Cerro de Trincheras is presented in Table 9.1.

The pointed implements at Cerro de Trincheras have very similar tip morphologies. Fine tipped awls and blunt tipped awls are especially similar. This, in addition to poor preservation, renders distinction of these artifact classes difficult. In the case of this study, fine tipped awls were defined as those artifacts that have a ratio of tip width to thickness equal to or below 1.23, in addition to a round tip cross-section (n = 4). Blunt tipped awls have a width to thickness ratio between 1.21 and 1.95 (n = 7). Tip-cross section varied, but was most often lenticular (n = 6/7). Hairpins are those items with the highest tip width to thickness ratios in addition to lenticular tip cross-section (n = 4). Each of these artifact classes is treated separately below.

Table 9.1. Tip Width to Thickness Measurements for Pointed Implements

Bag Number	Tip width	Tip thickness	Cross-section	Ratio	Classification
14813	2.42	2.23	Round	1.09	Fine tipped awl
16063	3.24	2.71	Round	1.20	Fine tipped awl
11485	3.46	2.80	Round	1.23	Fine tipped awl
12497	4.50	3.51	Round	1.28	Fine tipped awl
27060	4.15	3.29	Round	1.26	Blunt tipped awl
12729	2.54	1.86	Lenticular	1.37	Blunt tipped awl
28207	3.70	2.64	Lenticular	1.40	Blunt tipped awl
8991	4.98	3.54	Lenticular	1.41	Blunt tipped awl
15915	4.31	2.87	Lenticular	1.50	Blunt tipped awl
9084	7.96	5.30	Lenticular	1.50	Blunt tipped tool
28382	4.43	2.87	Lenticular	1.54	Blunt tipped awl
27598	4.97	2.89	Lenticular	1.72	Blunt tipped awl
7281	8.99	4.61	Lenticular	1.95	Hairpin
12747	7.69	3.48	Pyramidal	2.21	Spatulate tool
30333	7.75	3.13	Lenticular	2.47	Hairpin
30280	9.03	3.26	Lenticular	2.77	Hairpin
12588	---	---	Lenticular	Shaft only	Hairpin

Awls

Awls are sharply pointed implements used prehistorically to make or enlarge small holes in a wide range of relatively soft materials (Rodgers 1987:166). This category comprises a broad range of tools with points of varying shape used for tasks such as hide piercing and basketry (Glass 1984). Artisans formed most, if not all of the awls at Cerro de Trincheras, by cutting out a long, narrow section of the diaphysis of a limb bone using the groove and snap technique. By this method, they could carefully predetermine the size and shape of the finished product.

I found it difficult to clearly define bone awls because of the wide range in manufacturing quality, the multiplicity of uses, frequent reshaping of the tips (which destroys previous wear patterns), and the blending of the awls into what are believed to be ornamental hairpins. In order to differentiate awls by function, I based classification on observable wear, sharpness and shape of the point, and overall polish in addition to any decoration (Olsen 1979). Most awls from Cerro de Trincheras can be separated into two basic functional classes: fine pointed awls (n = 4, Figure 9.1) and blunt awls (n = 7, Figure 9.2).

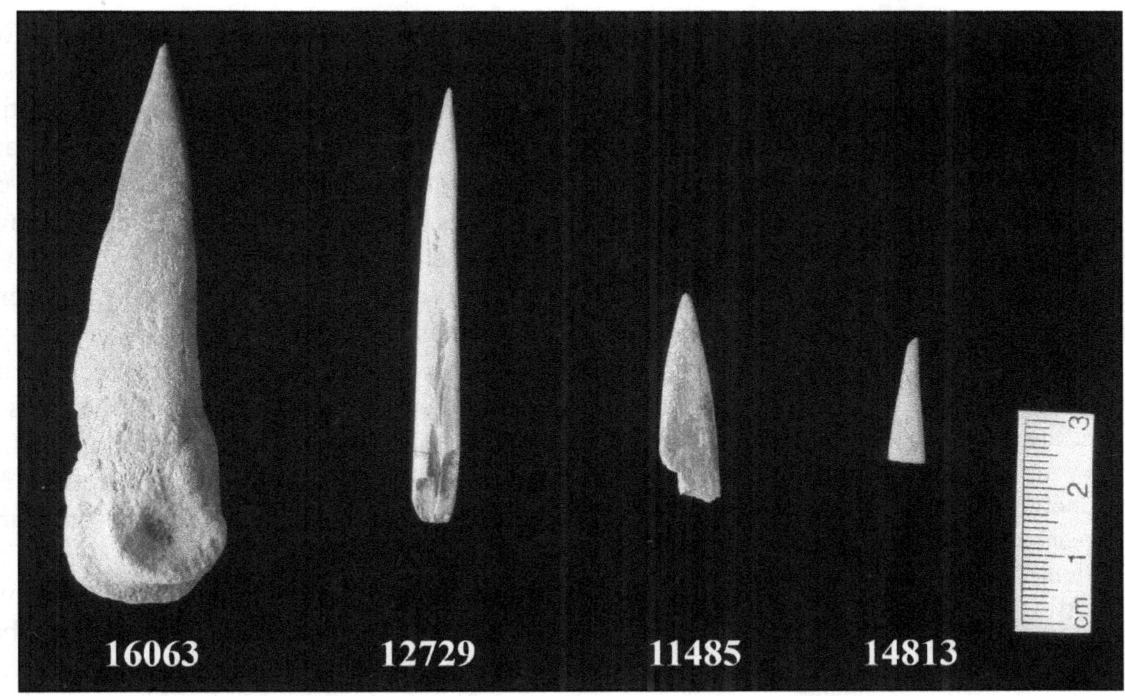

Figure 9.1. Fine point (fine coil) awls.

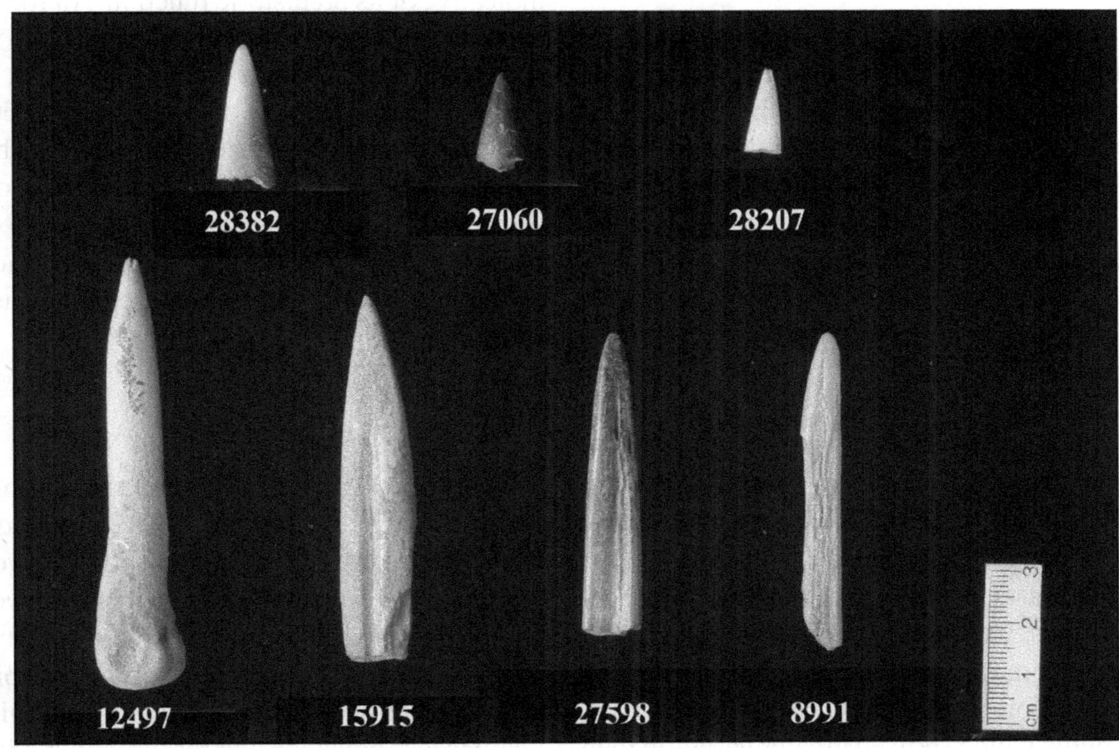

Figure 9.2. Blunt point (coarse coil) awls.

Olsen (1979) defines fine pointed awls as round in cross-section with an extremely fine point; with wear that appears as light polish and resharpening abrasion around the tip. In extreme cases, the tip may become restricted or a trough may form just above the tip. "This type of sharp, finely pointed instrument is also best suited for piercing hides" (Olsen 1979:355). Blunt awls are longer, stouter, have lenticular tips, and

> . . . are not effectively designed for either sewing or basket making. Their exact functions cannot be determined from wear patterns or ethnographic analogies. Blunt awls constitute only a very small portion of the awls. Also, blunt awls grade into hairpins in a classification of this kind. It can be difficult to devise clear demarcation between small, simply made hairpins and the more carefully produced blunt awls. (Olsen 1980:58)

By experimenting on various grades of leather, Olsen (1979) observed that larger, blunt points would not pierce the leather, despite the application of maximum hand pressure, short of breaking the tip. The blunt-tipped awls merely stretched or compacted the leather. The leather was easily pierced with the rotary motion of a fine-pointed awl. Enlargement of the perforation was then possible with a blunt-tipped awl. (Olsen 1979)

Di Peso (1956, 1974) identifies two types of awls based on tip morphology and usewear marks. These two types are coarse and fine coil awls, named for their supposed use in weaving different types of baskets.

Blunt-tipped awls, or "coarse coil basketry awls," are believed to be more generalized perforating implements, as indicated by the variation in use scratches on tips, shafts, and butts, which showed greater variation than the fine pointed awls (Di Peso 1974).

According to Di Peso et al. (1956), awls with cross-sectionally round tips were used in weaving coiled baskets. They call the fine pointed awls "fine coil basketry awls" and these awls are characterized by variable wear scratches on the tip, either at a 45-degree angle or parallel to the shaft.

I divided the awls recovered from Cerro de Trincheras into the two categories suggested by Di Peso, using both tip cross-section and tip width to thickness ratio. Of the awls at Trincheras, the two of the fine pointed (fine coil) awls had scratches near the tip that ran crosswise to the shaft. The other two had marks running at a 45-degree angle to the shaft. Two of the seven blunt pointed (coarse coil) awls had crosswise marks near the tip. Two had crosswise marks in addition to marks 45° to the shaft. Two had marks running 45° to the shaft, and one had no observable use wear marks.

The polish present on an awl may be indicative of its prehistoric function. All four of the fine pointed awls had polish restricted to the tip (two of these were only tip fragments). Of the blunt-tipped awls, two had polish restricted to the tip, three were mostly polished, one had polish restricted to the convex face and one showed no polish. The latter fragment, however, was moderately weathered and traces of use polish may have been removed as a result.

Hairpins

Teague & Crown (1983:585) describe hairpins as artifacts that are carved, drilled, or abraded from the distal end of a metapodial, were calcined, were recovered from burials, were highly polished along the shaft, or had two finished edges. The vast majority of hairpins exhibit little or no wear polish at the point. There is less breakage and resharpening of the points than on awls. Artisans most frequently

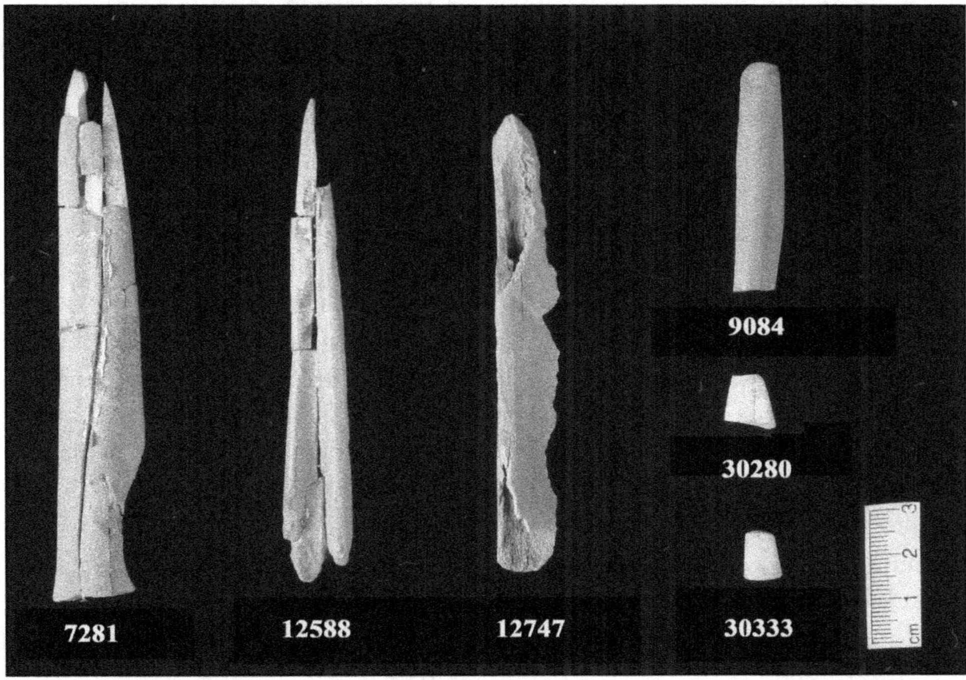

Figure 9.3. Hairpins (7281, 12588, 30280, and 30333) and other pointed implements.

used metapodial or cannon bones of artiodactyls for making hairpins (Olsen 1979).

According to Olsen (1979), the vast majority of hairpins exhibit little or no wear polish on their points. Of the artifacts from Cerro de Trincheras that resemble hairpins or portions of hairpins (n = 4, Figure 9.3), all demonstrated polish along most of the shaft. For the two artifacts that were represented by more than a tip fragment, in no case was polish limited to the tip. All of these implements have relatively blunt tips, with two (Bag Nos. 30280 and 30333, Figure 9.3) so rounded that any resemblance to a point has been lost almost completely lost.

Other Pointed Tools

A few pointed implements do not appear to fit into either an awl or hairpin category. One recovered item was pointed at one end and spatulate at the other (No. 12747, Figure 9.3). The only mention of a comparable item elsewhere in the Southwest is at Hawikuh. Hodge (1920) calls these "spatulate awls," in which one side of the tool is pointed, and the other side squared or rounded. He writes, "The usefulness of such a combination implement is manifest, since the spatulate end might be used in many cases for smoothing or rubbing where a point would not serve. . . the flat end is generally ground or worn obliquely" (Hodge 1920:99). However, the item found at Cerro de Trincheras is the only pointed implement not made from a long bone; it was fashioned from a mammalian scapular blade. The spatulate end appears delicate in comparison to the robust point at the opposite end of the tool. There is no observable use wear and slight polish visible only on the convex surface of the instrument.

Another item resembles an awl; however, judging from the deep notch present at its tip, this artifact has an extremely rounded tip, suggesting it was used extensively (No. 9084, Figure 9.3). Morphologically, this item could have been classified as a hairpin, but the use wear present at the tip implies that it was not purely an ornamental item. It is more likely functionally similar to blunt tipped awls, although its distinctive use wear suggests this item was used more harshly than the delicately tipped awls. Glass (1984) argues that extremely blunt artifacts may represent the terminal stages in the functional life of a piercing tool, after which a sharp point cannot be maintained.

Worked Bone

I could not interpret the use of these objects with any certainty. They exhibit a fair degree of cultural modification, but their high degree of fragmentation inhibits functional interpretation. Most of the fragments in the Trincheras assemblage are probably from the shaft portion of awls or hairpins rather than from the more diagnostic tip or articular end. These specimens show evidence of modification similar to that observed on pointed implements; however, they are too fragmentary to be assigned to a specific category. Most are split shafts from mammalian long bones with finished, or partly finished edges (Figures 9.4 and 9.5). However, in the absence of a functional tip or a tapered shaft, these fragments are tentatively classified simply as worked bone instead of the more specific awl or hairpin category.

Most of the pieces are either rounded (n = 29, Figure 9.4) or tabular (n = 29, Figure 9.5). A few are classified as pyramidical (n = 3), irregular (n = 2), articular ends (n = 3) or tube fragments (n = 3). This distinction is based on artifact cross section: rounded pieces are U-shaped in cross section; tabular pieces are lenticular or oval-shaped; pyramidical pieces are somewhat triangular in profile; tubular fragments have not been split down the shaft; and, irregular pieces are inconsistent in form. Very often, irregular fragments are severely weathered.

Worked bone fragments had often been polished with visible use wear. Pieces with longitudinal striae (n = 12, half of these were recovered from Areas B2 or B7) or crosswise marks (n = 21, six of these from El Mirador, B8) likely acquired these striae through use. Twenty percent (n = 14/70) of the assemblage displays two finished edges with use wear marks along both edges. These fragments were likely portions of finished and utilized tools.

In addition, there are six bone pieces

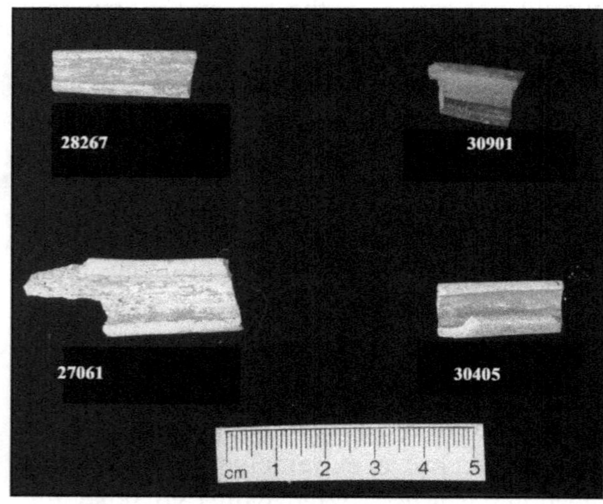

Figure 9.4. Rounded worked bone.

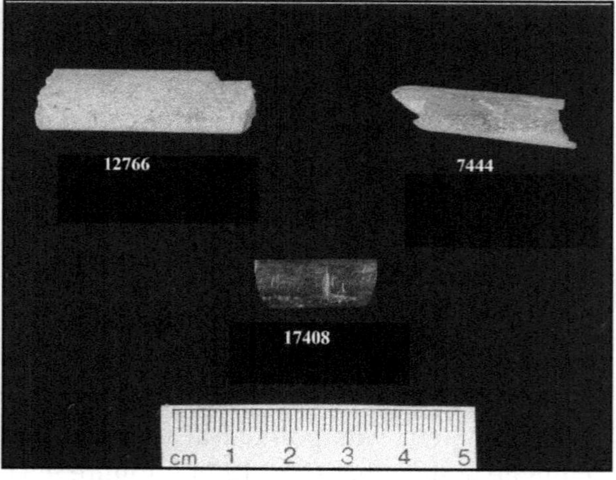

Figure 9.5. Tabular worked bone.

that have clearly been substantially worked although their use remains unclear (Figure 9.6). Specimen No. 15998 has one finely beveled and polished end, and was clearly broken on its opposite end while the bone was still relatively fresh. Specimen No. 12173 resembles a pointed implement but is so fragmented that the absence of a tip and tapering sides prevents classification beyond that of worked bone. Specimen No. 28303 is the articular end of an isolated and partly polished artiodactyl metapodial fragment. There are, however, no apparent usewear marks to help discern function. Specimen No. 12931 is a cut mammal rib that has been extensively polished. The only use wear marks are longitudinal striae that were probably created though polishing. The angled cut has formed a relatively effective edge that could have been used for a variety of purposes. Specimen No. 30326 is an artiodactyl metapodial shaft that had been cut so that one end is beveled and partially polished. It has marks running 45° to the shaft on its convex face. Morphologically this artifact could have been used as a scraper, but lacks distinctive use wear marks. Specimen No. 27511 is a partial shaft of a mammalian long bone that has been cut at one end, polished and completely lacks any use wear markings.

Notched Bone

On each notched bone I recorded the average distance between the notches and the presence of visible striations running perpendicular to the notching. The presence of striations across notches suggests that the Trinchereños used these bones by rubbing an implement over the notched areas. A majority of the notched artifacts had one notched side (n = 25) while a few had two notched sides (n = 4). Some pieces were too fragmentary to determine the number of notched sides (n = 13). The notched bone artifacts (n = 42) from Trincheras can be divided into four general types. Each type appears to have served different functions, and are treated individually below.

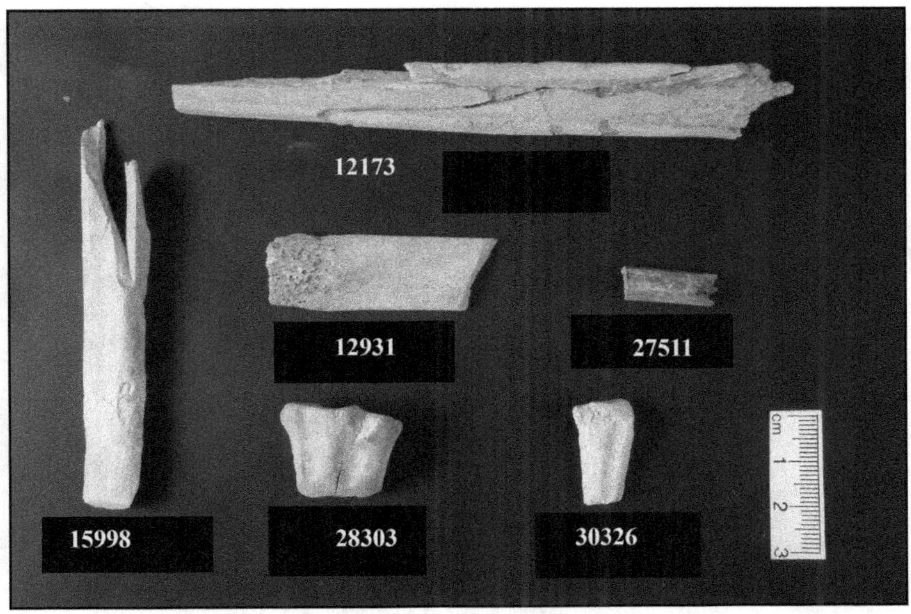

Figure 9.6. Strange worked bone.

Type A

Type A (n = 27) most likely corresponds with items described as 'rasps' from other Southwestern sites (Figure 9.7). These notched specimens, most often from scapular or rib portions, are similar to those used by present-day indigenous groups. These items create sound to accompany music when another bone is rubbed over the notches (Di Peso 1974). This group includes most of the notched bone fashioned from scapular or rib elements (n = 3 scapular, n = 1 rib, n = 22 indeterminate long bone fragments). These items are the most likely to have had striations running across their notches (n = 17 with striae, versus n = 6 without) and just one side notched (n = 22 one side, versus n = 5 that were undetermined due to extensive fragmentation). The average distance between the notches for Type A is 3.07 millimeters. Six of these items were recovered from El Mirador (B8) and two were found one each in Areas A1 and B2, for a total of eight items.

Type B

This group includes notched bone that does not appear to have functioned as rasps (n = 12, Figure 9.8). The notches are often located on the interior surface underside of the split shaft, on the side of the marrow cavity. These bones usually do not have striae across their notched areas (n = 4 with striae, versus n = 8 without), and may have two sides notched (n = 3 with one side notched, n = 1 with two sides, and n = 8 fragmentary). These items are more often made of longbone (n = 9) rather than scapular (n = 1) or rib elements (none). One artifact was fashioned from an *Odocoileus* metapodial shaft, and one specimen could not be identified to element. The average distance between the notches in this group is 2.46 mm. Areas B6, B7 and B8 each yielded two of these specimens. The notches on Type B artifacts were more likely ornamental rather than functional, as the rasps described above. To date, this type of notching has not been described elsewhere in the Southwest, and seems to be restricted to Cerro de Trincheras.

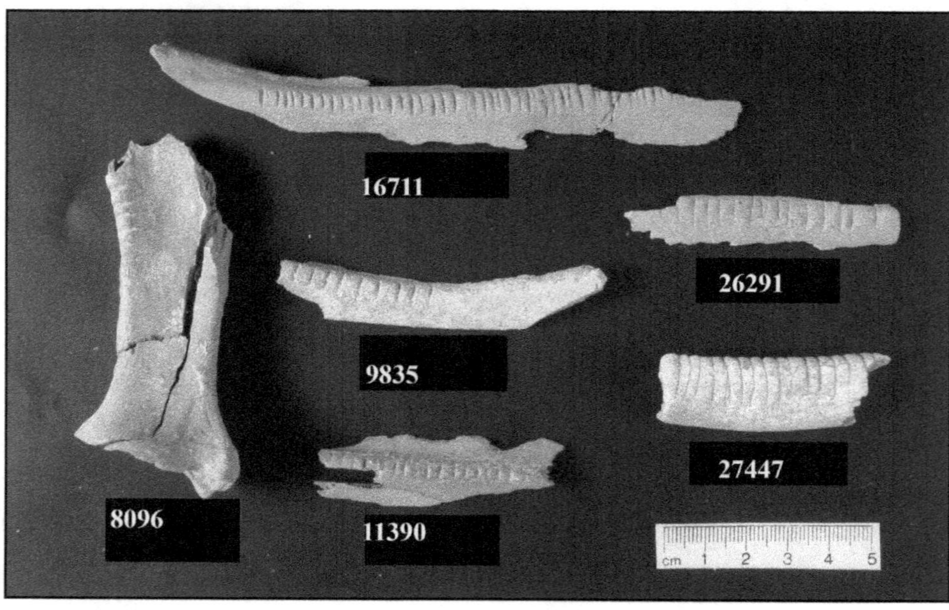

Figure 9.7. Type A notched bone.

Figure 9.8. Types B and C notched bone.

Type C

This group consists of two specimens that appear to have been incised (Nos. 8799 and 22793, Figure 9.8). These specimens were recovered from Areas B1 and B6, respectively. Specimen No. 8799 has two lines running approximately parallel to one another near the edges of the piece. It is polished and exhibits no signs of usewear. Specimen No. 22793 is a fragment of bone with a series of incised lines that appear to be part of a decoration. The bone is flat, thin, partially burned, and most likely not part of a long bone. The partial design on this fragment appears to be similar to those found on shell pendants recovered from Cerro de Trincheras. No other incised bones of this nature have been described from sites in the Southwest U.S. or in Northwest México.

Type D

Type D notched bone (n = 3) describes jack rabbit (*Lepus*) dental elements that appear to have been intentionally notched, with post-cranial notching similar to the other bones in the assemblage (Figure 9.9). These notches appear at right angles to one another, generally on the lingual border. Two of these specimens (Nos. 15571 and 15572) were recovered from Area E in relleno (fill) 32. Another was found in Area B7, Level D, Jacal 5. Specimen No. 21492, an almost complete first upper incisor, has four distinct notches. The two other specimens are upper molars, one with eight notches (No. 15572) and a smaller, fragmented tooth with two notches (No. 15571) (Stahl Chapter 11). The average distance between these notches is 1.65 millimeters.

Alternatively, these specimens may be examples of coincidentally patterned right-angle cracking of dehydrated dental enamel; however, the notches appear to be very regular and too deep to have resulted from attritional factors. Again, this type of notching has not been described in any other sites in the Southwest U.S or Northwest México.

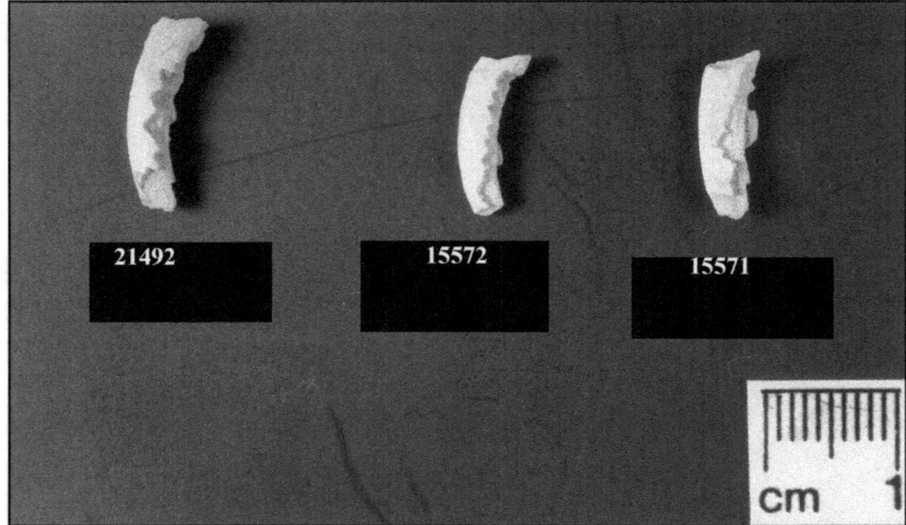

Figure 9.9. Type D notched bone.

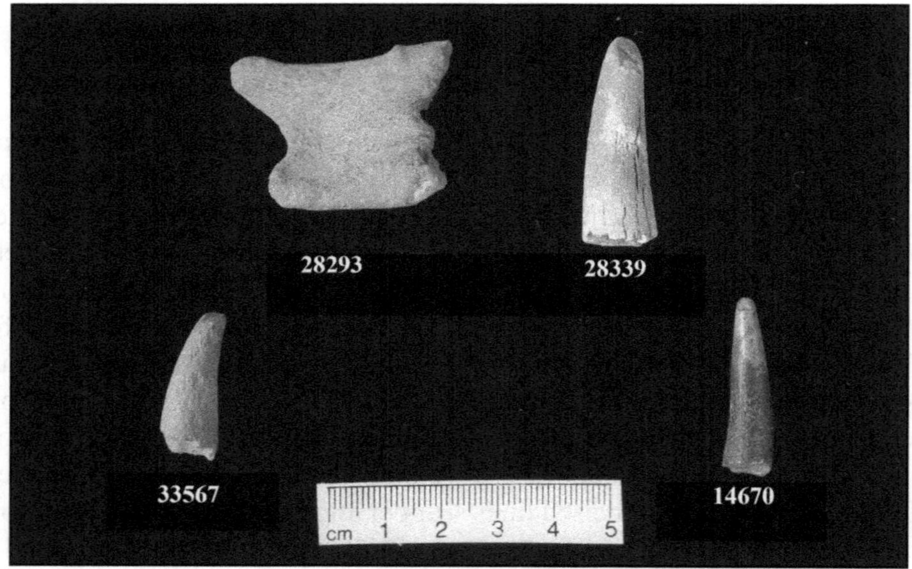

Figure 9.10. Antler.

Antler

The antler artifacts from Cerro de Trincheras (n = 4, Figure 9.10) include two artiodactyl antler tines, one probable tine fragment and a rectangular section. Two are polished, and two others are burned. The two burned specimens are from Area B8 (El Mirador). All four antler artifacts are moderately weathered.

Generally artisans chop or break a tine off of the antler beam. Only occasionally do they smooth the broken surface with an abrader. None of the antler tine artifacts have been smoothed at the base. These items were probably used in pressure flaking stone tools. Very little preparation is necessary on tine flakers. The natural points on tines require no modification prior to use, although broken tips were occasionally resharpened. Olsen (1980) indicates that wear at the tip of a tine tool is the key to their function. However, tips of antlers often acquire considerable wear prior to being shed by the deer (Olsen 1979). Antler tines may have been used in a fashion similar to awl tips (Stahl Chapter 11). The rectangular antler item (No. 28293) shows considerable wear facets and probable intentional shaping, but its function remains indeterminate.

Discussion and Concluding Statements

A number of functional inferences can be made about the modified bone assemblage from Cerro de Trincheras via analogy to available ethnographic data and comparisons to assemblages from throughout the Southwest/Northwest.

Ethnographic Data and Possible Function of Tools

The function of some classes of artifacts recovered from Trincheras can be inferred by reference to available ethnographic data. Anthropologists collected the majority of this data during the early part of this century. Other classes of tools lack any functional analogs, thus suggestions regarding function remain speculative.

Awls and Hairpins

According to Hodge (1920) and Kissel (1916), awls were used for piercing skins in order to perforate holes for the passage of the binding element during sewing. They were used also in weaving and basket making. Materials used to produce basketry were chosen carefully. According to Tanner (1976:16), the basket weaver often used wide or narrow strips, or complete elements from: Awillow, broad and narrow leafed yucca, beargrass, desert willow, bullrushes, cattail, squawbush, sages, rabbitbrush, the outer bark from several plants such as devil's claw (Martynia), and various other grasses and rushes."

Feinman (1991), however, believes that aboriginal peoples used pointed implements as ceremonial bloodletters. He argues that bone tools from Sonoran Desert sites, because of their relative infrequency, have been grouped in inclusive categories. He notes that some awls seem both too sharp and fragile to make particularly effective or long-lived utilitarian tools. Other awls recovered from Hohokam sites (e.g., Haury 1937, Tuthill 1947) are similar in form to pointed bone implements from Mesoamerica, presumed to be for bloodletting (Brasy and Stone 1986:23).

Of greater interest to Feinman are what analysts have identified as hairpins. He notes (Feinman 1991:468), citing Haury (1945) that most analysts agree they were not used as simple piercing tools:

> Namely, in a few cases from across the Southwest (Fewkes 1927, Cummings 1940, DiPeso 1956) these worked bones have been recovered in burials close to the head of the deceased. Although the so-called hairpins frequently are found in burial contexts (Haury 1945, 1976), the relatively small proportion situated above the skull would seem to cast doubt on the notion that these objects merely served to adorn the hair. Such hairpins, when recovered in burial contexts, are just as likely not to be located near the head.

He argues for a re-evaluation of hairpins as simple bone ornaments. I classified the items found at Cerro de Trincheras as hairpins based on tip and shaft morphology. These specimens have not been ornately decorated, which may serve as evidence for their non-ceremonial nature. All four hairpins at Trincheras were recovered from terraces (two from B1, one from B3 and one from B2) rather than the more ceremonial areas of the site (El Caracol or La Cancha). However, no worked bone was found in any of the burials excavated at Cerro de Trincheras.

Rasps

"Sounding rasps made of wood or bone are traditional musical instruments in the Southwest. Today, the Hopi, Zuni, Rio Grande pueblos, Navajo, Apache, Pima, Papago, Tarahumara, and other tribes still use rasps as noise-makers in ceremonies" (Hodge 1920:137). Most of the modern rasps are long wooden sticks that are stroked with deer or sheep scapulae, while the end of the rasp rests on a resonator (Olsen 1980). These instruments were stroked with another stick or bone to create a low vibrating tone. The Acoma of New Mexico call these items "scraping sticks." They consist of two parts: a stick having notches cut horizontally across its surface; and, a shorter stick or a bone that is rubbed across the notches (Densmore 1957). Archaeologically, sounding rasps have been recovered from Hohokam, Anasazi, and Mogollon sites (Tanner 1976).

Type A notched bones from Trincheras have wear marks that support the hypothesis that they were used as musical rasps. The corners of the notches are often rounded from wear and may be worn down considerably.

The Zuni also used notched sticks and knotted strings for recording the passage of time by days and noting the number of sheep owned by an individual (Hodge 1920). It is not unlikely that bones could have been similarly used in former times. An object with a small number of notches and an edge that shows no wear is likely to have been used as a tally (Hodge 1920). Some of the Type B notched bone may have served as tallies, although in many instances the notching appears more decorative than functional.

Contents of the Modified Bone in Comparison to Trincheras Faunal Assemblage

The species of animals used in the manufacture of bone tools differs proportionally from those represented amongst the unworked faunal remains. Of the identifiable elements, a majority (n = 24 of 28 identified specimens) was from artiodactyls and only four from *Lepus*. In contrast, *Lepus* dominated the total faunal assemblage and rodent remains. Szuter (1991a) cites ethnographic literature from the American Southwest and México to indicate that artiodactyl skull and lower legs were used for their bones and therefore may be differentially represented in the archaeological record. The skin and antlers from the skull were used to make headdresses while metapodial elements were used for tools (Szuter 1991a). The metapodia that are used for tools also would have been good sources of marrow even if their meat content was low (Szuter 1991a). Metapodia can be identified even when highly fragmented; however, the large quantity of long bone fragments that could not be identified, could mask the variety of elements that were used to make tools (Teague & Crown 1983:596). The bone artifacts recovered from Trincheras reflect a heavy dependence on deer. The elements used for tools were clearly selected for their shape, strength, and availability (Olsen 1979).

Cerro de Trincheras and Other Southwestern Sites

Like the Hohokam, the prehistoric people of Trincheras did not look upon bone and antler as the preferred materials for the production of artifacts. Their dependence on stone and shell did not carry over to equally useful animal bone. This was not because of the lack of raw material, as the larger animals (deer and antelope) were readily available to them. The heavy reliance on bone and the wide range of objects produced from it by the Anasazi make the dearth of bone among the Hohokam more enigmatic. I would not discount Haury's (1976) assertion of a prehistoric cultural restriction that discouraged the use of bone. Aboriginal people probably used the widely available desert hardwoods as a substitutes material for bone, particularly for the more functional types of artifacts (Haury 1976). Wood was readily available, more easily shaped and equally serviceable for the production of items like awls, skewers, picks and musical rasps (Haury 1976).

A characteristic of Hohokam sites is a high percentage of burned or heat-treated bone. Forty-four percent (n = 74/169) of the bone artifacts at Cerro de Trincheras are burned. However, only 29 percent (5/17) of the pointed implements were burned, in contrast to 50 percent of awls and tubes from Snaketown, 56 percent from Salt-Gila Aqueduct sites, and 58 percent at Las Colinas (Szuter 1988). Twenty-three percent of the total archaeofaunal assemblage is burned, but the modified bones have a higher percentage of items that have been exposed to heat.

There are a number of important differences between the Cerro de Trincheras modified bone assemblage and those recovered from Hohokam sites. Most hairpins excavated from Hohokam sites are from burial contexts (DiPeso 1956; Haury 1976), whereas none of the hairpins from Trincheras were. However, at Trincheras, all three artifacts likely to have been hairpins were recovered from terrace units in Area B.

Notched bone rasps have been recovered archaeologically from throughout the Southwest, including Hohokam, Anasazi and Mogollon sites (Tanner 1976). However, all notched bone described by DiPeso (1956, 1974) from the San Cayetano and Casas Grandes sites had only one notched ridge. The sounding rasps from Kinishiba were manufactured by cutting transverse notches into the margin of a long thin bone (Olsen 1980). Artisans made scapular rasps by separating the caudal border from the rest of the blade. They grooved and snapped along the border, or chipped away the excess blade. The bottom of each V-shaped piece is undamaged from wear, since the accompanying stick or bone rubbed against the upper surface only. (Olsen 1980). These rasps are present at Cerro de Trincheras, but the notched bone assemblage is not limited to this type.

Hohokam sites in Arizona commonly include a greater array of bone artifacts than those recovered from Trincheras. Tubes are the most numerous bone artifacts at Snaketown, yet they are completely absent from Cerro de Trincheras (Gladwin et al. 1965). "A noticeable characteristic of tubes is the smoothly worn surface on the inner margins of the lips, sometimes a distinct bevel directed toward the outer surface. The worn incised patterns provide evidence of much handling. Use by healers as sucking tubes is not improbable" (Haury 1976:304). Also absent from Trincheras are typical splinter awls, found at most Hohokam sites, and ulnar awls found by Di Peso (1956) at San Cayetano. Items described as 'skewers,' "slender, tapering bone objects pointed at both ends . . . thought to have been used as nose ornaments," with blunt point unlike awls, were missing from the Trincheras modified bone assemblage (Di Peso 1974: 46). Also absent are 'pins,' described by Di Peso (1974) as small, well finished items made from splinters. Beads were discovered at Casas Grandes that were fashioned from sawed sections of bird bones (Di Peso 1974). None were recovered from Trincheras.

However, artifacts similar to those atypical items discovered at Cerro de Trincheras have been found at other Southwestern/Northwestern sites. One pointed implement at Cerro de Trincheras (No. 9084) resembles what Di Peso (1974) calls a 'flaker' from Casas Grandes. He thought that this object was used in the manufacture of chipped stone implements. It appears to have been manufactured by sawing and splitting a long bone shaft and abrading it to a blunt tip. The condyle and cut shaft edges are ground down (Di Peso 1974).

Three spatulate tools somewhat similar to one found at Cerro de Trincheras (No. 12747) were recovered from the Tucson Basin San Xavier Bridge site. The function of these items was not determined (Ravesloot 1987), but one was recovered from an inhumation and another from a cremation.

Concluding Statements

There exists a dearth of archaeological reports that provide adequate bone tool analysis, resulting in the omission of essential data needed for a comprehensive understanding of the past. This study has attempted to provide a detailed analysis of the culturally modified bone recovered from Cerro de Trincheras during 1995 and 1996 field seasons.

For the most part, the Trincheras modified bone assemblage is very similar to other assemblages from Sonoran Desert sites. Most are burned, highly fragmented, and relatively small in number. A majority of the fragments are polished and split mammalian long bone shafts. Many with use wear suggest that they were part of an awl or other pointed implement. However, the Trincheras assemblage lacks 'distinctive' Hohokam artifacts: tubes, beads, pins, and skewers. That these were absent, simply not recovered, or did not preserve remains undetermined for the moment; however, if they do occur at Cerro de Trincheras, they do so with a frequency so low that two field seasons were insufficient to yield a single element that could readily be identified as one of these items.

There are, however, important differences between the Cerro de Trincheras assemblage and those found at other Sonoran sites. For example, the Trincheras assemblage contains a greater variety of notched bone than has been documented at other Sonoran Desert sites. However, the notched bone at Trincheras falls into three distinct categories, two of which are seemingly unrepresented elsewhere in the Southwest. Type A rasps are found elsewhere in the Southwest, for example, at San Cayetano and among modern Native American groups. Type B artifacts seem to be decorative in nature, possibly as shaft portions of awls or hairpins. However, the absence of this type of notching on any complete awls limits further development of this hypothesis. Type C incised bone and Type D notched *Lepus* teeth are specimens that appear specific to Cerro de Trincheras; there is no mention of similar artifacts among other Sonoran Desert sites.

The distribution of these unique notched bone types does not appear to correspond to specific areas of the site (El Caracol, El Mirador or La Cancha, for example). These areas often yielded very few artifacts. A majority of the modified bone at Trincheras was recovered from Locus B, which contained the majority of habitational terraces at the site. This suggests that the individuals living in this area were the most heavily involved in modified bone production and use of these implements.

Chapter 10

Environment, Farming, and Plant Resources

Suzanne K. Fish. Arizona State Museum

Botánica

Este capítulo discute las muestras de flotación y polen recuperadas en Cerro de Trincheras durante las temporadas de trabajo de campo de 1995 y 1996. Fish sitúa los hallazgos en un contexto medioambiental mayor al sitio y se focaliza en plantas desérticas recolectadas, vegetación fluvial del Río Magdalena y plantas domésticas y semillas agrícolas de campos cercanos al cerro. Comparasiones entre zonas residencial y especializada reflejan un medio ambiente altamente modificado por el hombre a través de prácticas agrícolas.

In the basin and range country of northwest Sonora, the valley of the Rio Magdalena surrounding Cerro de Trincheras is notable for its unusual breadth. Relatively large Sonoran Desert plants, the leguminous trees and columnar cacti that cover slopes and are interspersed on shrubby basin interiors, reflect the benefits of a bimodal pattern of rainfall for the desert scrub vegetation of this region. Averaging slightly less than 300 mm annually, direct rainfall is inadequate for farming without supplemental water in a climatic regime with summer temperatures routinely exceeding 38° C or 100° F (Turner and Brown 1994:191). However, summer rainfall in July and August averages more than 160 mm (Hastings 1964:145) and is comparable to high summer rainfall areas in Arizona portions of the Sonoran Desert with optimal opportunities for floodwater farming (S. Fish and Nabhan 1991). In keeping with the extensive potential for both riverine irrigation and floodwater farming on the basin floor and gentle slopes, botanical remains from Cerro de Trincheras indicate a strongly agricultural subsistence base, augmented by a wide array of gathered resources.

Sonoran Desert Agriculture at Cerro de Trincheras

Estimates for a prehispanic population at Cerro de Trincheras that may have exceeded 1000 (McGuire et al. 1999:136) place this intensively investigated hillside village in a very populous range for the Northwest/Southwest, and compare favorably with estimates by Di Peso et al. (1974a:199) and others (e.g., Cordell 1997; Lekson 1999:16; Minnis 1989) of 2500 to 5000 residents for the renowned and generally contemporary town of Casas Grandes or Paquime in northwest Chihuahua. Late prehispanic demography contrasts with a lower population in the Cerro de Trincheras vicinity during the last century. In 1931, there were 500 people in the town of Trincheras and a total of only 2000 for the surrounding municipio (Sauer and Brand 1931:91). At that time, inhabitants of the municipio were predominantly supported by non-mechanized farming. Currently, Trincheras's economy includes contributions from railroads and ranching, with less reliance on cultivation.

Former agricultural practices in the town of Trincheras provide insights into prehispanic agricultural productivity and surrounding settlement patterns that were recorded by full coverage survey. The following description is drawn from survey results (Fish and Fish 2004:53-58). More favorable conditions for traditional farming than at present, observed near the beginning of the twentieth century, are particularly relevant. Geographers Carl Sauer and Donald Brand (1931:132) attributed an accelerated decline of agriculture during the early 1900s to a catastrophic erosion cycle that began late in the preceding century with overgrazing, the drastic entrenchment of drainages, and a concomitant loss of sustained flows and divertible runoff. By 1930, high water tables and marshy stretches of river floodplain such as a cienega reported near the base of Cerro de Trincheras likewise had disappeared. Remaining sources of potential domestic water consist of favorable stretches of the river with persistent surface water, shallow and sometimes hand-dug wells near the floodplain, reservoirs on valley slope drainages, and springs in the mountains at the basin edge.

Despite decreasing flow in the Rio Magdalena over the past century due to entrenchment and upstream pumping, the placement of modern gravity canals in the area indicates both optimal locations for headings and the general extent of topographically-controlled irrigable land. These were critical parameters for farmers in the past. A large system of canals on the south side of the river presently heads 4 km upstream of Cerro de Trincheras, where bedrock beneath the channel maintains year-round surface flow even when other stretches are seasonally dry. Surrounding the off-take for this current irrigation network is a dense cluster of sites with overlapping chronological components, beginning with preceramic occupations and ending with the ruins of a pre-Revolution hacienda.

A conservative estimate of 725 hectares within the survey area is irrigated today with gravity-fed canals from the Rio Magdalena. With previously greater river volume, a topographically viable prehispanic version of this system might have extended near the foot of Cerro de Trincheras, expanding potentially irrigable land by more than 150 additional hectares. Canals heading downstream on both sides of the river today demonstrate the potential for extensive irrigation of the flat basin bottom as it widens to the west of Cerro de Trincheras. Across the river from the present town of Trincheras is its predecessor town, San Rafael, abandoned in 1927 after devastating floods (Sauer and Brand 1931:92). Here again, a clustering of successive prehispanic occupations coincides with the location of modern canals.

Diversion of tributaries and ephemeral drainages supported many floodwater or *temporal* fields around Trincheras in the early 1900s; at that time, some of these secondary drainages still carried perennial or seasonally extended flows (Sauer and Brand 1931:132). These tributaries to the Rio Magdalena originate in the mountains bordering the basin or on its broad upper slopes and drain large interior expanses. Use of these watercourses for floodwater farming has now largely ceased with a few exceptions. Near the town of Trincheras, seasonal runoff in such drainages on the south side of the river continues to be directed into reservoirs for cattle and onto floodplain-edge fields. Today it reaches these fields via siphons that channel the drainages under a railroad track that parallels the river and skirts the northern flanks of Cerro de Trincheras. The small sites of floodwater farmers who diverted the prehistorically unentrenched streams are scattered across a linear zone just uphill from the floodplain, where tributaries form alluvial fans to either side of Cerro de Trincheras (Fish and Fish 2004:Figure 3.2). Another area of limited present-day floodwater farming is the vicinity of Ejido Las Playas, on the north side of the river in the general vicinity of the modern town. Here, long shallow ditches lead storm flows from drainages onto seasonal plots.

On both sides of the Rio Magdalena, elongated zones with few sites are located between the river and its higher terrace elevations. These zones include land subject to flooding and bands of modern and, presumably, prehispanic irrigated fields. The occasional sites that could be identified within these areas often coincide suggestively with the paths of present canals. Both river flooding and modern mechanized leveling of irrigated farmland undoubtedly obscure sites and their boundaries. The twentieth century abandonment of the San Rafael town site (Sauer and Brand 1931:92) illustrates how riverine dynamics also may have shifted settlements and fields of this zone in the past.

Earlier ceramic sites predating the El Cerro phase occupation of Cerro de Trincheras are significantly less numerous than later settlements contemporary with the center, notwithstanding the fact that they represent a considerably greater time span (Fish and Fish 2004:Figure 3.1). They are distributed throughout the survey area surrounding Cerro de Trincheras and indicate reliance on both irrigation and floodwater farming. Many of the largest earlier sites were abandoned by the El Cerro phase, by approximately A.D. 1300. The increase in sites attending the relatively brief El Cerro phase interval of about 150 years registers peak population for the prehistoric sequence and probably some substantial level of population influx. A notable change at this time was an intensified use of floodwater farming zones south of the river, signaled by the appearance of many small sites to both sides of the populous center (Fish and Fish 2004:Figure 3.2). The single survey transect that crosses much of the basin along a tributary west of Cerro de Trincheras also shows expanded floodwater settlements on more distant middle and upper basin slopes.

Aggregation in the late prehispanic Southwest/Northwest frequently coincided with irrigated core areas where the intensification of agricultural production could support increasingly dense populations (Dean et al. 1994; Fish and Fish 1994). Expanded cropping on more marginal land was also associated with increasingly aggregated centers, often taking the form of vast arrays of stone features such as gravel mulches, grids, terraces, and rock piles in the U.S. Southwest. In the Cerro de Trincheras hinterland, existing canal systems may well have been extended to their maximum capacities during the El Cerro phase. More clearly documented is the intensification of floodwater techniques tapping the broad basin watersheds of the Rio Magdalena tributaries, many of which remain unentrenched and still amenable to diversion in the current era of otherwise pervasive down cutting. Although this mode of farming has largely disappeared around Trincheras today, William Doolittle (1988) describes remnant systems of productive floodwater fields still cultivated with traditional methods on the Rio Sonora to the east.

The inhabitants of Cerro de Trincheras were positioned for immediate access to productive irrigated land between their hill town and the river. On the other side of the hill, small contemporary settlements attest to the expanded cultivation of floodwater fields; Area E, the pithouse cluster at the base of the hill, may be similar to these sorts of settlements. Cerro de Trincheras residents could have readily maintained fields in both irrigated and floodwater zones.

Flotation and Pollen Results

Evidence for vegetation and use of plant resources during the occupation of Cerro de Trincheras is based on the analysis of charred macrofossils from 89 productive flotation samples and 63 separately collected charcoal samples, and the analysis of 97 pollen samples. Macrobotanical and pollen samples were examined from contexts throughout the excavated areas of the site. A majority of separately collected charcoal items and a high proportion of flotation samples (33 of 89) are from Area E at the base of the hill, the locale in which more intact structures and associated residential features were preserved.

Pollen Analytical Methods

Suzanne Fish conducted the pollen analysis. Approximately 60 cc of sediment were processed per sample. *Lycopodium* spore tracers were added to monitor extraction results. Following deflocculation in dilute hydrochloric acid, a mechanical swirl step as described by Mehringer (1967:136-137) separated the heavier sediment fraction. Samples were not screened through fine mesh, insuring maximum recovery of aggregated pollen grains. Heavy liquid flotation in zinc bromide of 2.0 density further reduced extraneous matrix material. Rinses with hydrofluoric acid, water, and absolute alcohol completed the extraction process. The extract was mounted in a glycerol medium and stained for microscope viewing.

Sample tabulation provided a standard sum of 200 noncultigen pollen grains for each sample (Table 10.1). This sum was shown to adequately register representative distributions of common pollen types from Southwestern vegetation communities (Martin 1963:30-31). Infrequent pollen types listed in the "Other" category in Table 10.1 are individually identified in Table 10.2. Percentages for types other than cultigens in Tables 10.1-10.3 were calculated on the basis of the standard sum. Cultigen pollen was tabulated in addition to the 200-grain standard sum to avoid numerical constraint on the percentages of types more directly related to natural vegetation and environment in the site vicinity. Therefore, the value for cultigens is not a percentage, but represents the number of grains encountered while completing the standard sum; cultigen values can be compared among samples on this basis. Corn and cucurbit (including squash and pumpkin) are designated cultigen categories in the Cerro de Trincheras analysis, although the possibility of the morphologically similar pollen of wild cucurbits cannot be ruled out in all cases for the latter category.

After tabulation, additional material was scanned at a lower magnification to detect rare types, particularly those with economic significance. Identifications made only in scanning are indicated in the tables. Types that occurred in aggregates of six or more pollen grains are also noted. Because such pollen clusters are less efficiently transported by wind than single grains, aggregates indicate the likelihood of a relatively immediate plant source for the pollen. Aggregates may also indicate direct introduction of pollen from the immature floral parts of a source plant, because pollen is usually dispersed as single grains at maturity rather than as clusters. The presence of aggregates thus provides evidence that may be considered in economic interpretation.

The pollen occurrences interpreted as indicating resource use at Cerro de Trincheras are summarized in Table 10.4. Pollen of domesticates is the most straightforward indication of cultural introduction, because a source in natural vegetation is not possible. Corn pollen is unequivocal in this sense. The pollen of wild gourds cannot be differentiated from that of some domesticated squash. However, cucurbit pollen is typically so rare that it is here assigned a cultural origin in every case. Several other highly probable resource types are automatically included in the table on the basis of their importance in the subsistence of indigenous peoples of the region, as well as their very limited occurrences among samples from natural vegetation. Cacti pollen is designated as a resource indication for this reason and includes three categories: prickly pear, cholla, and saguaro-type (saguaro, hedgehog, and related taxa). Sedge and cattail also receive resource designations because the pollen is seldom deposited by natural means at appreciable distances from plant sources in damp habitats.

Several pollen types representing common species of local vegetation occur in multiple samples in low percentages. An economic designation was assigned to mesquite, willow, hackberry, ocotillo, and undifferentiated species in the carrot and potato families where aggregates provided additional evidence for plant sources in the immediate environs of the site provenience. The occasional presence of aggregates is also the criterion by which a resource significance was ascribed to specific instances of grass pollen, a relatively frequent type in site samples. Unfortunately, species among potentially utilized grasses cannot be distinguished through pollen morphology. Aggregates are so numerous for *cheno-am* pollen (the morphologically indistinguishable pollen of chenopods and amaranths), on the other hand, that it is not possible to conclusively discriminate between pollen introduced with resources and pollen dispersed directly into site proveniences by the dense weeds of residential environs; undoubtedly site occupants consumed the edible seeds and greens of these weedy species. Similarly, the many instances of spiderling aggregates are not included in Table 10.4 despite possible consumption of the plant as greens because it is likely that this pollen type primarily represents local weeds.

Flotation and Charcoal Specimen Analytical Methods

Charles Miksicek analyzed the flotation samples and identified individual charcoal specimens that were recognized and collected separately during excavation. All flotation samples were processed at the Cerro de Trincheras field laboratory in Trincheras, Sonora, using the swirl and pour flotation method (Watson 1976:78-80). During analysis, each flotation sample was passed through a nested series of geological sieves with mesh sizes of 4.0, 2.0, and .5 mm. This pre-sorting removes many modern rootlets and produces subsamples with similar-sized particles that can be more effectively scanned by the analyst. Each fraction was then sorted at 7X under a binocular dissecting microscope. All charcoal fragments from the 2.0 and 4.0 mm fractions were sorted from each sample and weighted to the nearest .1 g. Charred seeds and other non-wood materials are presented in Table 10.4. A random grab sample of at least 25 wood charcoal fragments was selected for identification from each flotation sample (Table 10.5). When fewer than 25 pieces were present, all fragments large enough to manipulate were examined. Individually collected charcoal identifications are listed in Table 10.6. Charred seeds and wood charcoal fragments were identified with the aid of modern comparative material collected from Sonoran Desert vegetation in southern Arizona and standard references such as Musil (1963), Martin and Barkley (1973), and Miles (1978). Taxonomic nomenclature follows Kearney and Peebles (1960), as updated by Lehr (1978) and Lehr and Pinkava (1980, 1982).

Two terms in Table 10.4 require further explanation. Seed Density or Charred Seeds/ Liter is calculated by dividing the number of seeds or other potential food plant parts (maize cobs, squash rind fragments, cholla buds, agave remains, etc.) by the volume of the sample. Volumetrically Standardized Richness or Charred Taxa/Liter is one measure of sample diversity. Although richness values may be rather inflated for very small samples (those with soil volumes less than 1 liter) or somewhat depressed for large samples (over 8 liters), this is not a problem here because most analyzed samples came from 4 liters of soil matrix and subsampling did not occur.

Cerro de Trincheras Environment

Together, taxa identified in pollen and charred macrobotanical analyses portray a vegetation structure with dominant species much like that of today. Small tree forms and large cacti characteristic of the resource-rich, low-elevation basins of the Sonoran Desert are well represented by ironwood, paloverde, ocotillo, saguaro, organ pipe, cholla, and prickly pear. Bursera, another tree of moderate size, is currently restricted to the slopes of Cerro de Trincheras and perhaps other hills. Shrubby vegetation includes creosote bush, bursage, desert bloom, and saltbush. The latter two shrubs would have been most common in riparian-edge communities.

Riparian species are prominent in wood charcoal, with a clear emphasis on mesquite, which, a with hackberry and desert willow, would have grown along the larger tributaries as well as the river. Willow, cottonwood, cattail, and sedge pollen indicates vegetation of perennially damp habitats along the Rio Magdalena. These species also would have been associated with canals and reservoirs. Alder and walnut are riparian taxa of upper slope drainages at the basin edge.

Both pollen and charred plant remains reflect a highly modified natural environment at Cerro de Trincheras and in the surrounding landscape. Agricultural weed taxa are abundant in samples, overlapping in species composition with the weeds growing on the disturbed and organically enriched soils of residential areas. The cheno-am category is particularly prominent in Cerro de Trincheras samples.

Pollen of a set of three weedy plants occurs in elevated frequencies compared with samples from natural Sonoran Desert vegetation (Hevly et al. 1965). Spiderling, globe mallow, and Arizona poppy have been recovered in relatively high percentages from the sediments of prehistoric fields and appear to have been important elements of a weedy flora characteristically associated with Sonoran Desert agriculture in the Hohokam area (Fish 1985, 1994). The pollen of these weeds that grew in contact with crops would have been transported into residential settlements on the outer surfaces of harvests. These three taxa also would have been constituents of weedy residential vegetation.

Most of the other herbaceous species in the botanical remains from Cerro de Trincheras fit a weedy category, although many also furnish edible products and raw materials. Among these are tidestromia, wild buckwheat, Indian wheat, spurge, purslane, and species in the carrot, potato, and sunflower families.

Cerro de Trincheras Crops

Corn is widely distributed among flotation and pollen samples, appearing in the great majority of residential contexts. Its repeated occurrence as pollen, kernels, and cupules in samples from terrace occupation surfaces strongly suggests the presence of extensive domestic trash. Evidence of the additional domesticates, squash or pumpkin, beans, and cotton, is always much more infrequent than for corn in archaeological contexts due to very low pollen dispersal by plants and poorly preserved charred remains. Cucurbits are rarely recovered in open sites, but were identified in the form of charred rind fragments and pollen. Also rare and fragile, charred beans occur in a single instance. Cotton is represented by burnt seeds, recovered only in Area E with its better protected depositional contexts and large number of flotation samples. The limited record of these domesticated crops other than corn in no way implies their restricted consumption by residents of Cerro de Trincheras. Their occurrence is sufficiently infrequent among samples, however, to preclude meaningful quantitative and distributional comparisons.

Charred agave occurred in more than one third of the excavated site areas. The absence of agave pollen at Cerro de Trincheras is in keeping with the usual harvest of the plants prior to flower stalk emergence, an event that depletes stored energy and caloric value. The cultivated status of the agave remains cannot be conclusively determined by distinctive morphological criteria. Nevertheless, the varied plant parts--fibers, spines, and heart and stalk tissue--and their broad recovery implies a plentiful and convenient source that is at odds with distant natural populations in uplands at the basin edge. Agave cultivation is well documented among contemporary Hohokam to the north in southern Arizona (Fish et al. 1985, 1992). Agave plantings along terrace edges as suggested by McGuire et al. (1999) or in the narrow terraces of Area D would follow customary placements of these succulents cultivated throughout México and Central America. Large primary flakes in the Cerro de Trincheras chipped stone assemblage could have served to sever tough agave leaves at harvest, as among the Hohokam, further suggesting cultivation by hill residents (Fish et al. 2004:90-92).

Cerro de Trincheras Gathered Resources

Well-represented and widespread gathered resources include mesquite pods, cactus fruits and buds, grass seeds, and chenopods. Although small charred seeds are infrequent in terrace contexts due to generally shallow depths and poor preservation, instances of saguaro and organ pipe cactus were identified. Prickly pear is indicated by pollen. Several charred cholla buds reenforce an abundant pollen record of cholla. Charred grass remains include a bentgrass-type, panic grass, gramma grass, and native barley. Among these resources in the gathered category, cholla, panic grass, and native barley also could represent tended or cultivated plants according to Hohokam research and ethnohistoric and ethnographic practices in northwest México and the southwest United States (Bohrer 1991; Fish and Nabhan 1991). The list of resources gathered for food further includes amaranth seeds, edible parts of species in the carrot and potato families, hackberry fruits, willow (catkins), sedge seeds, and cattail shoots, roots, and the copious, edible pollen.

Wood charcoal recovered from Cerro de Trincheras monitors an unknown mix of fuel and construction uses, and possibly craft materials to a lesser extent. Tables 10.5 and 10.6 include both wood from trees and a variety of smaller woody materials including saguaro ribs, ocotillo stems, and shrubs. Woody species in Table 10.6 were individually collected when encountered in a limited number of site areas and are redundant with those recovered by flotation in Table 10.5.

Unquestionably, mesquite was the universally preferred wood. Recovered charcoal is likely to indicate fuel use in a high proportion of cases, but ethnographically mesquite is also widely used in constructing structures. The secondary prominence of paloverde is less easily interpreted. Paloverde wood has undesirable fuel qualities and probably would have been avoided if alternatives were available, yet it appears more consistently than the third most common species, ironwood. It may be that paloverde was primarily used for some architectural purpose. Cutting large-diameter pieces of dense ironwood would have been difficult, but otherwise it should have been a valued fuel.

Areal Patterns in Cerro de Trincheras Botanical Remains

As common species in Sonoran Desert weedy vegetation, chenopods and amaranths proliferate in culturally disturbed and organically enriched habitation areas. For example, modern samples from Tohono O'odham residential precincts near the Santa Cruz River at San Xavier Mission near Tucson, Arizona, contain more than 60 percent cheno-am pollen (Lytle-Webb 1978). High values for this type are typical of samples from southwestern U.S. archaeological sites. The high background levels of cheno-am pollen aggregates across Cerro de Trincheras proveniences can be largely attributed to weedy growth throughout.

Magnitudes of cheno-am pollen in archaeological sites often appear related to the magnitude of weedy plant communities dominated by these taxa, reflecting the duration, intensity, and extent of ground disturbance and other occupational impacts on vegetation of the immediate area. For example, cheno-am percentages correlated well with these variables among site types and sizes in the Tonto Basin (Fish 1995). Table 10.7 compares cheno-am frequencies among the spatially and functionally differentiated areas of Cerro de Trincheras. The generally residential terraces (Areas B1, 2, 3, 4, 6, 7, and 11), El Mirador terraces (Areas B8, 9), La Cancha (Area B5), and Area D ranged from averages of 45.8 to 66 percent. The Area E hamlet averaged somewhat less at 43.9 percent, perhaps indicating a slightly lower occupational intensity. In sharp contrast to all other areas, the Area A1 summit averaged only 17.1 percent cheno-am pollen. This dramatic difference is in keeping with much less everyday activity in this specialized precinct with restricted access perhaps in conjunction with a unique effort to keep it free of weedy growth.

Areal comparisons based on ubiquity measure values for flotation samples show little differentiation in wood selection among several area divisions of the site. Ubiquity (also called relative frequency or presence value) is defined as the percentage of samples that contain a certain taxon (Hubbard 1980) and is a comparative measure that avoids bias due to large numbers of instances concentrated in a few samples. Table 10.8 compares ubiquity measures for the most common wood taxa from four site areas with higher sample numbers, although samples from El Mirador and Area A1 are fewer and percentages are therefore more tentative. Saguaro ribs occur in low percentages in all three non-summit areas where walls and roofing of residential structures would be expected. Ocotillo stems, another less frequently preserved construction element, were identified in both ordinary residential terraces and Area E. Desert willow, in the same two areas, is also used as structural wood in Hohokam sites.

Residential Area Comparisons

Tables 10.9 and 10.10 give ubiquity values for non-wood charcoal and pollen resources, in the primarily residential hill terraces of Areas B1, 2, 3, 4, 6, 7, and 11 and in the Area E hamlet. (Results from burial samples are excluded due to their non-domestic nature.) The following comparison focuses on relatively large bodies of more ordinary residential data from the hill terraces and the settlement below; resource patterns from the public Area A1 summit and La Cancha, the elite El Mirador terraces, and Area D with its probable agricultural terraces are discussed separately. As a caveat, pollen sample numbers are low from Area E and should be treated separately.

The nature of contexts sampled at Cerro de Trincheras influences recovery patterns to a substantial degree. Houses, containing resource debris in floors, hearths, and other features, were not as well preserved or easily located on the terraces compared to the pit houses of Area E. Extramural occupational surfaces on terraces would have accumulated more dispersed residues and were subject to destructive post-depositional processes. The necessary emphasis on terrace contexts among all samples undoubtedly affects the richness and diversity of the botanical record in Table 10.9, especially in terms of fragile and vulnerable charcoal. Because of the better-protected deposits and sampling emphasis for charred remains in Area E, resource diversity is disproportionately registered there. Both pollen and charcoal techniques, however, reveal a generally similar overall diversity in resources from the domestic debris on terraces.

Pollen and charred macrobotanical analyses register an essentially overlapping suite of resources, but with distinctive ubiquity values and a few unique taxa identified by only one of the analytical techniques. Such differences are the outcome of differential pollen and charcoal residues in the archaeological record due to the particular plant parts that were utilized, depositional pathways, and preservation potential. Both techniques show highest overall ubiquities for corn or maize, establishing the centrality of agricultural production in Cerro de Trincheras subsistence.

In view of their typical rarity in both pollen and charcoal samples, it is difficult to quantitatively assess beans, cucurbits, and cotton. Agave is not represented by pollen. With these cautions, it can be noted that cucurbit pollen was recovered in both residential divisions and charred remains in Area E. Cotton seeds are restricted to Area E recovery, and primarily in one feature there (Table 10.4). Charred agave fibers appear in moderate amounts on the hill and the hamlet below, with agave spines only in Area E. These Cerro de Trincheras agave ubiquity values would be in a low-range for Hohokam sites where pervasive cultivation has been documented, but nevertheless suggest that local plants were processed on the site rather than at some distant location where natural populations could be selected.

Together pollen and flotation results emphasize the importance of cacti. High cholla pollen ubiquities pertain to the consumption of pollen-bearing buds. A few of the fragile charred buds were even preserved in both residential areas. Saguaro-type and prickly pear pollen occur in terrace and Area E samples, with saguaro and organ pipe seeds in low numbers from Area E. Fragile charred mesquite pods were preserved only on the hill, while the more hardy seeds and pollen aggregates appear in each sector. In relatively moderate ubiquity values according to one or both of the botanical techniques, evidence of chenopods or amaranths, grasses, cattail, willow, species of the potato and carrot families also spans hill terraces and the hamlet.

Common residential resources at Cerro de Trincheras have routine counterparts among

Hohokam neighbors with similar approaches to farming and gathering in low-elevation Sonoran Desert basins to the north. A few exceptions include organ pipe cactus seeds, available in geographically restricted locales within Hohokam country. Tansy mustard, with a tendency toward localized emphasis among the Hohokam (Gasser and Kwiatkowski 1991:438) is a minor resource omission at Cerro de Trincheras.

A comparison between residential terrace contexts and those of the Area E hamlet below the hill reveals a contrast that likely reflects meaningful activity patterns. Kernels make up only six percent of total instances of flotation corn remains in Area E samples, with the remainder composed of cupules, the more durable cob fragments (Table 10.4). Among less protected terrace samples, 30 percent of the corn remains are the more fragile kernels. The significantly higher proportion of kernels from terrace deposits, where they would have been more subject to damage, suggests that terrace inhabitants initially processed the crop to remove kernels at field-side or some intermediate location more often than did inhabitants of Area E. Prior shelling of the corn to remove the kernels below the hill would have been an efficient means to reduce weight for uphill transport and to avoid the accumulation of discarded husks and cobs on terrace surfaces.

Bursera was identified only once among woody remains. The small trees in this genus produce resins, bark, and even woody tissues used as aromatic substances in ethnographic and prehispanic rituals. *Copal* is the incense made from these species. The trees grow today on terraces on the rocky slopes of Cerro de Trincheras, but not on the surrounding valley floor. The single instance of bursera wood, however, is from the Area E hamlet at the bottom of the hill rather than in the uppermost specialized areas of probable ritual practice.

Specialized Areas at Cerro de Trincheras

Area D contains non-residential terraces that may have been planted in agave. The Caracolito in this area is also unusual in its architecture and abundant shell contents. Botanical remains furnish little insight into agricultural or other non-residential activities. The mix of resource evidence and its distribution among Area D proveniences parallels that on residential terraces generally, although in the low range for all taxa. This pattern likely reflects the presence of at least limited domestic residues everywhere on the site.

La Cancha, a mid-slope space for public activities, yielded minimal evidence of plant resources. Only trace amounts of cactus and corn pollen (Table 10.3) and one instance of charred grass (Table 10.4) were present in samples. Again, low-level recovery is commensurate with a widespread light scatter of domestic debris rather than domestic accumulation.

Residents of elevated status appear to have used El Mirador terraces. The Area B8 terrace likely was reserved for public observances but produced resource evidence including a few charred corn cupules, a fragment of agave stalk, and pollen of cholla, saguaro and corn. Area B9, an elite residential terrace, had a diverse pollen assemblage of cultigens and gathered resource types and charred grass stems. Area B10, a terrace serving as a highly visible performance platform, is represented by a single flotation sample containing agave stalk.

Area A1 is a formally delimited area on the hill summit with restricted access and is the location of the Caracol and other specialized structures. Pollen identified only traces of cactus types. Charred grasses and woody materials may be structural remains, again implies the absence of appreciable domestic debris. Charred fragments of agave stalk occurred on a terrace occupation surface in Area A1 and agave heart in the fill of a circular stone structure.

Although fibers and spines were recovered in residential terraces on the hill and in Area E, agave stalk and heart tissues are unique to El Mirador and the summit precinct. These parts are infrequently identified among Hohokam samples, and their patterned location at Cerro de Trincheras is unlikely to be incidental. Heart tissue may result from consumption of sweet baked food or, more speculatively, could signal fermentation for an alcoholic beverage. The significance of the stalks is more problematic. Young tender stalks are sweet and can be cooked. Stalks also represent sturdy poles that could be used for construction or crafts. At the same time, cultivated agave is almost universally harvested prior to stalk emergence because its rapid growth depletes the plant's stored carbohydrates that would otherwise constitute the edible resource. If residents cultivated the agave, the stalk entailed a specialized harvest, or it had to be imported from distant wild plants.

Conclusions

In the absence of large data sets of plant remains from the immediate region, Hohokam records offer a basis of comparison with prehistoric farmers employing much the same mix of agricultural techniques in similar Sonoran Desert basins. Because of the many Cerro de Trincheras samples from non-comparable terrace contexts, comparison is necessarily general. The substantial level of agricultural dependence, evidenced primarily by the broad distribution of corn, at Cerro de Trincheras falls within the normal range of Hohokam sites (e.g., Gasser and Kwiatkowski 1991; Gish 1991). Cultivation of cucurbits, beans, cotton, and probably agave is also shared. Wild resources reveal parallel emphases such as the heavy use of cholla and other cacti. Minor differences are exemplified by the absence of tansy mustard seeds and the related pollen, although further sampling might well encounter this taxon. The recovery of organ pipe cactus at Cerro de Trincheras, on the other hand, is a more predictable outcome of its natural distribution.

In spite of the regionally high population concentrated at Cerro de Trincheras and the prominence of the site, there is little botanical evidence that inhabitants acquired and consumed plant resources from distant zones. If they cultivated agave, as seems likely, an isolated identification of yucca is the only indication of an upland or otherwise exotic wild species. Production from irrigated and floodwater fields, along with bountiful Sonoran Desert resources, within their basin appears to have been sufficient to support the populous residents of this terraced hillside town. Overall, the botanical record from Cerro de Trincheras suggests a mosaic surrounding the hill of topographically differentiated irrigated and fields, shrubby successional vegetation, and patches of heavily utilized riparian and desert growth.

TABLES FOR CHAPTER 10

Feature Type Abbreviations:

AT = ancillary terrace
B = burial
CSS = circular stone structure
H = hearth
M = midden
n = north
OS = occupational surface
PF = platform
PH = pithouse
PP = puddling pit
PT = pit
QSS = quadrangular stone structure
RA = rock arrangement
T = terrace

Table 10.1. Sample Tabulation

	Sample Number	Bursage-type	Sunflower Family	Chenopod & Amaranth	Tidestromia	Grass Family	Spiderling-type	Globe Mallow	Arizona Poppy	Evening Primrose Family	Wild Buckwheat	Spurge-type	Potato Family	Prickly Pear	Cholla	Saguaro-type	Pea Family	Mesquite	Paloverde	Creosote Bush	Ocotillo	Pine	Oak	Willow	Indeterminate	Other	Corn (no. of grains)	Cucurbit (no. of grains)
Area A1																												
T736 CSS4, OS	24465	38.0	12.5	21.0		6.5	5.0								+							4.0	0.5		11.5	1.0		
T716 OS	27556	41.5	21.0	8.0	3.5	+	*14.0	2.0			0.5					0.5		0.5				1.5		1.0	5.5	0.5		
T736 OS	30970	44.5	17.5	13.5		2.5	11.0				0.5											4.5	+		6.0			
T736 OS	30974	29.0	18.0	26.0	0.5	4.0	4.5				2.0	1.5								1.0		2.0		1.0	9.5	1.0		
Area B1																												
T347 OS	17129	10.5	7.5	60.0		1.5	12.0						0.5		0.5				1.5			0.5			5.0	0.5	1	
T347 OS	13569	8.0	4.5	*53.0		3.0	21.0				0.5						0.5					+			9.5			
T347 terrace fill	12823	4.0	15.0	48.5		5.0	6.0	0.5	0.5		1.0				*2.0					3.0		2.0			12.5		+	
T347 J7, OS	13575	28.0	11.5	41.5	1.0	1.0	8.5	1.0			1.0						0.5		0.5			2.0			3.0	0.5		
T347 J7, OS	16116	17.5	6.0	56.0		2.5	7.5									1.0		*1.0							8.5		2	
T347 J1, OS	16855																											
T351 surface	10328	39.5	16.0	22.5	1.0	6.0					3.0								0.5			1.5			10.0			
T351 rubble from above	10329																											
T351 OS	10330	11.0	4.5	*48.5		2.5	*24.0	3.0					0.5												6.0		+	
T351 OS	10148	5.5	9.0	*57.0		1.0	6.5	1.0							2.5					4.5		3.0	1.0		9.0			
T351 OS	10788	8.0	3.5	*63.0		3.5	8.5			0.5	1.5	0.5								1.0		2.5			7.0	0.5	1	
T351 OS	12612	9.5	6.0	55.5		4.0	*16.0		0.5		1.0				*1.5							0.5	0.5	0.5	4.5			
T351 terrace fill	10331																											
T351 pre-terrace surface	10332	10.5	6.0	*47.0		1.0	21.0				1.5				*1.5					0.5		1.0			9.5	0.5	+	
Area B2																												
T370 OS	10631	8.5	4.5	*56.5		*8.5	7.5		+		0.5		1.0	1.0	1.5							1.0		0.5	8.0	1.0	*3	

Table 10.1. Sample Tabulation, cont'd

	Sample Number	Bursage-type	Sunflower Family	Chenopod & Amaranth	Tidestromia	Grass Family	Spiderling-type	Globe Mallow	Arizona Poppy	Evening Primrose Family	Wild Buckwheat	Spurge-type	Potato Family	Prickly Pear	Cholla	Saguaro-type	Pea Family	Mesquite	Paloverde	Creosote Bush	Ocotillo	Pine	Oak	Willow	Indeterminate	Other	Corn (no. of grains)	Cucurbit (no. of grains)
T370 OS	10636	3.0	6.5	*49.0		4.0	21.0	2.0			3.0		2.0			0.5		0.5				+			8.0	0.5	+	
T370 OS	10637	5.5	9.0	*50.5		3.5	*17.5		0.5						4.0	1.0	1.0					0.5	1.0		5.5	0.5	2	
T370 terrace fill	10383	6.0	1.5	59.5		1.0	*27.0	1.0																0.5	3.0	0.5		
T370 J2, floor	10922	9.5	6.0	*68.5		0.5	3.0	1.5				0.5			*7.5	0.5		0.5					0.5		1.5		+	
T370 J2, floor	11436	4.0	3.0	*71.0		2.5	9.0				2.0				6.5							+			2.0		*3	+
T370 B3, head	10899	6.5	7.0	*62.5		+	14.5	2.0														1.5		+	6.0			
T370 B3, hip	11056	3.5	2.5	*81.0		1.5	4.5	+			0.5											2.0			4.5		+	
Area B3																												
T330 OS	7033	7.0	4.5	45.5	+	1.5	*21.0	+		1.5					2.0		2.5			3.0		3.0			8.5		2	
T330 OS	8257	4.5	8.0	47.5		3.0	12.0		0.5		0.5		0.5		*10.5				2.5			1.0	+	+	9.0	0.5		
T330 OS	6871	11.0	6.5	*53.0		2.0	*16.5	2.5	1.0	2.5	1.0				1.5		1.0								1.5		*5	
T330 terrace fill	6924																											
T330 AT1, ramp	7494	9.0	3.5	*61.0		4.5	5.0	0.5			2.5	1.0	*1.0		0.5					0.5		2.0	1.0		7.5	0.5	1	
T330 CSS17, floor	6975	7.5	8.0	58.5		2.5	*14.0	1.5						0.5				0.5				1.0		0.5	5.5		+	
T330 CSS17, floor	6976	6.0	8.0	*49.0		*5.0	*8.5		0.5	0.5					*4.0	*11.0					1.0	0.5			6.0		*3	
Area B4																												
T329 OS	8335	4.5	6.5	*61.0		3.0	11.0	1.0			2.5				1.0				0.5			0.5	0.5		8.0			
T329 OS	8429	9.5	11.0	49.5		6.5	7.0	1.0	1.0		3.0	0.5								1.0		3.5			6.5			
T329 PF3, floor	7970																											
T329, J3, floor	7975	22.5	10.0	31.5		3.5	*16.0	1.5	+			0.5			4.0	1.0		2.0			+	2.0		+	3.0	2.5	1	
T329 J3, floor	7989	8.0	4.0	47.5		4.5	17.0	3.5			2.0				3.0			*6.0				0.5			1.5	2.5	*6	
T329 J3, floor	7991	11.0	7.5	39.5		1.0	*26.0			1.0			*4.5		*1.0										7.5	1.0	*2	

Table 10.1. Sample Tabulation, cont'd

	Sample Number	Bursage-type	Sunflower Family	Chenopod & Amaranth	Tidestromia	Grass Family	Spiderling-type	Globe Mallow	Arizona Poppy	Evening Primrose Family	Wild Buckwheat	Spurge-type	Potato Family	Prickly Pear	Cholla	Saguaro-type	Pea Family	Mesquite	Paloverde	Creosote Bush	Ocotillo	Pine	Oak	Willow	Indeterminate	Other	Corn (no. of grains)	Cucurbit (no. of grains)
Area B5																												
La Cancha, OS	20201	12.5	6.5	*52.0		3.0	13.5	3.5	2.0		0.5											1.0			5.5			
La Cancha, OS	20205	17.0	3.5	*43.0		1.0	*21.0		3.5						+						0.5	1.0		0.5	8.5	0.5		
La Cancha, OS	20348	15.0	9.0	49.5		1.5	14.5	2.5	2.0													1.0		0.5	4.5			
La Cancha, OS	20444	13.5	2.0	*51.5		2.5	*14.0	1.5	1.0		1.0	1.0				0.5						3.0	1.5		7.0			
La Cancha, OS	20445	16.0	4.5	*56.0	0.5	3.0	8.5															2.0			9.5		+	
La Cancha, OS	24671	24.0	8.0	*39.5		5.5	6.0	0.5			7.5								0.5	0.5		1.5	+		6.5			
La Cancha, OS	24672	21.0	2.5	*45.5		3.0	10.5	2.5																2.0	12.0	0.5		
La Cancha, OS	24673	18.5	5.0	53.0		4.5	9.5	0.5			0.5							+	0.5			+	0.5		7.5			
La Cancha, OS	24907	14.0	6.5	*49.0	0.5	4.0	8.5	0.5			2.0	2.0	1.0				1.5			2.5		2.5			5.5			
Area B6																												
T576 OS	20831																											
T576 OS	20860	4.5	6.5	*66.0		1.5	7.0		0.5						1.5	*2.0		*6.0				0.5			0.5	3.5	*5	1
T576 J4, floor	20861	1.5	2.0	*69.5		*9.0	*3.5	0.5	1.0	0.5				*3.0	*4.5			0.5			*2.0				2.5		*8	
T576 PT17	22889	6.0	0.5	*71.5	1.0		9.5	0.5						0.5	*2.0					0.5		0.5		*1.5	3.0	3.0	1	
T594 QSS1, floor	28815	6.5	+	*61.5		*2.5	*22.5		0.5	+				0.5	3.5	*1.0						+			1.5		*2	
T594 QSS1, floor	29804	3.0	3.5	62.0		3.0	*21.0		2.0	1.0					*1.0							1.0		*1.5	1.0		1	
T593 PF2	31866	5.5	1.0	*64.5	*1.0	0.5	*16.0		3.0		3.5				2.0		0.5	1.0							1.5		*7	
T593 CSS19	31982	8.0	1.5	*69.0		1.0	*13.5		0.5						*4.0							0.5			2.0		1	
Area B7																												
T211 OS	23098	12.5	6.0	48.5	0.5	1.5	18.0				3.0					1.0						2.0	0.5		6.0	0.5	+	
T211 OS	23125	7.0	4.0	63.0		3.5	6.5	1.0		0.5	2.0		0.5	1.0	1.5				1.0	+					8.5			
T211 OS	23419	5.5	2.5	57.5		2.0	14.0		0.5						*2.0			*4.0				2.0		1.0	8.0	1.0	2	

Table 10.1. Sample Tabulation, cont'd

	Sample Number	Bursage-type	Sunflower Family	Chenopod & Amaranth	Tidestromia	Grass Family	Spiderling-type	Globe Mallow	Arizona Poppy	Evening Primrose Family	Wild Buckwheat	Spurge-type	Potato Family	Prickly Pear	Cholla	Saguaro-type	Pea Family	Mesquite	Paloverde	Creosote Bush	Ocotillo	Pine	Oak	Willow	Indeterminate	Other	Corn (no. of grains)	Cucurbit (no. of grains)
Area B8																												
T280 OS	28126	13.0	8.5	*54.0	0.5	2.5	7.5				3.0	0.5										1.0	0.5		8.5	0.5		
T280 OS	30051	16.5	6.0	*54.0		2.0	9.0	+			0.5				7.5			0.5				1.5		1.0	1.5	1.0		
T280 OS	30089	22.5	3.0	*48.0		3.5	12.0					1.0				0.5	1.0					2.5			6.0			
T280 OS	30105	18.0	7.5	*47.5	+	4.5	3.0	2.5	1.0		1.5				1.0				0.5	1.0		2.0		0.5	9.5		1	
Area B9																												
T277 OS	30425	14.5	7.0	*53.0		3.5	4.0	2.0		0.5	1.0		4*		1.5				+		*2.5	2.0			4.5		1	
T277 J6, floor	32144	21.0	5.5	*42.5	*3.0	2.0	8.5	0.5		1.0	2.0		1.5		10.0			*0.5					+		1.5	0.5	*7	1
Area B11																												
T553 OS	32902	9.0	14.5	57.5		1.5	6.5								2.0	1.0						0.5			7.5		+	
Area D																												
T3 OS	15016																											
T9 OS	9525	8.0	6.5	55.5		2.5	*14.0	1.0		0.5			1.0										0.5	1.0	9.0	0.5	+	
T11 OS	14953	6.5	13.0	48.0		0.5	*22.0		0.5		0.5				0.5				1.0	0.5		3.0			4.0			
T13N OS	17089	8.0	3.5	58.5	0.5	2.0	10.5				4.5				+				0.5			2.0		1.0	8.5	0.5		
T15N OS	14957	13.0	6.5	*68.0		2.5					8.0											+			2.0			
T17N OS	14984	10.5	7.0	57.5		1.5	8.5	0.5	0.5		7.0		0.5						2.0			1.0			3.5			
T19N OS	14986	14.5	4.0	*63.0		3.5	6.0		0.5		2.5					0.5	0.5		+	0.5		2.0			3.0			
RA4, platform surface	10456	16.0	8.5	47.0		4.0	13.0															0.5			11.0			
RA4, platform	10454																											
RA5, platform surface	10474	45.0	28.5	11.5		3.0	2.0	2.0			2.5	0.5	1.0								0.5	+	1.0		2.5			
RA5, platform surface	10723	36.5	19.5	31.0	1.0	1.5	4.0												0.5			1.0			5.0			

Table 10.1. Sample Tabulation, cont'd

	Sample Number	Bursage-type	Sunflower Family	Chenopod & Amaranth	Tidestromia	Grass Family	Spiderling-type	Globe Mallow	Arizona Poppy	Evening Primrose Family	Wild Buckwheat	Spurge-type	Potato Family	Prickly Pear	Cholla	Saguaro-type	Pea Family	Mesquite	Paloverde	Creosote Bush	Ocotillo	Pine	Oak	Willow	Indeterminate	Other	Corn (no. of grains)	Cucurbit (no. of grains)
B11, head	11729																											
QSS3, floor	14050	9.5	7.0	54.5	*3.5	0.5	11.5				3.0						0.5					1.5	0.5		8.0			
QSS3, floor	14969	13.0	5.0	*60.0	2.0	2.5	7.5	1.0			1.0								0.5			1.0			6.5		2	
QSS4, floor	15398	7.5	8.0	*59.0		2.0	*19.0								*2.0			*2.0							0.5			
QSS4, floor	15399	12.0	4.5	62.5	0.5	*4.0	9.0			0.5					+	*3.0							1.0		3.0		1	
El Caracolito, floor	15940																											
Area E																												
Modern Surface	9627	48.0	19.5	16.5		4.5					3.5	1.0								1.0		0.5		0.5	2.5	2.5		
PH2, floor	12360	31.0	6.0	*46.0		3.0	3.0	1.0		+	+				*6.0							+			4.0		*9	
PH2, floor	12361	22.5	9.0	38.5			+	2.0	0.5	1.5	2.0		*2.5	0.5	+	*1.0					*3.0			*4.0	0.5	1.5	2	
PH2, floor	16096	27.0	3.5	34.0		2.5	13.5			2.0	1.5				*45.0					0.5		3.0			8.0		*1	
PT1	11009	20.0	7.5	*56.5		0.5	*5.0	+							*3.5			*5.0							2.0		1	
PT2	11835	3.5	1.5	*62.0			*8.0								*8.0	*2.0									4.0		*4	3*
PH1, floor	16325	26.5	5.0	34.5		6.5	9.5							2.5	2.0			*2.5		0.5		2.0			4.5	4.0	2	
PH1, floor	16326	5.0	3.5	*46.0			2.0				7.0							1.0	1.0		*5.0	1.0	2.0		8.0	0.5	1	
PP2	11313																											
PH9, entry	13478	18.5	2.5	*52.5		4.0	*19.0					1.0			0.5	+									1.5	0.5	+	

Table 10.1. Sample Tabulation, cont'd

	Sample Number	Bursage-type	Sunflower Family	Chenopod & Amaranth	Tidestromia	Grass Family	Spiderling-type	Globe Mallow	Arizona Poppy	Evening Primrose Family	Wild Buckwheat	Spurge-type	Potato Family	Prickly Pear	Cholla	Saguaro-type	Pea Family	Mesquite	Paloverde	Creosote Bush	Ocotillo	Pine	Oak	Willow	Indeterminate	Other	Corn (no. of grains)	Cucurbit (no. of grains)
OS2	14901	36.5	5.0	32.0		4.0	15.5			1.0	2.5				1.0				1.0			1.0			0.5			
B2, head	15384	14.5	7.0	48.5		2.5	13.0	1.5	1.0		1.0											3.0			8.0		1	
B2, hip	15383	19.5	7.5	43.0	0.5	2.0	8.5	3.0		0.5					1.5			0.5				3.5		0.5	9.5		+	
PP1	16341	21.0	13.5	36.5		6.5	4.0	2.0		0.5								+		1.0		4.5	1.0	2.5	5.0	2.0		

Percentages of noncultigen pollen types are calculated on the basis of a 200-grain standard sum of all noncultigen pollen.

Values for cultigen pollen types (Zea and Cucurbita) are expressed as the number of pollen grains encountered in tabulation.

* Indicates a pollen type occurring in aggregates of 6 or more pollen grains.

+ Indicates a pollen type observed only in scanning of additional material after tabulation of the 200-grain standard sum.

Table 10.2. Pollen Sample Taxa by Area

	Sample #	Pollen Taxa
Area A1		
T736 CSS4 OS	24465	1.0 Mormon Tea
T716 OS	27556	0.5 Buckthorn Family
T736 OS	30974	0.5 Hackberry; 0.5 Mormon Tea
Area B1		
T347 OS	17129	0.5 Alder
T347 J7 OS	13575	0.5 Mimosa
T351 OS	10788	0.5 Rose Family
T351 pre-terrace surface	10332	0.5 Alder
Area B2		
T370 OS	10631	1.0 Rose Family
T370 OS	10636	0.5 Sedge
T370 OS	10637	0.5 Carrot Family
T370 terrace fill	10383	0.5 Purslane
Area B3		
T330 OS	8257	0.5 Purslane
T330 ramp	7494	0.5 Lily Family
Area B4		
T329 J3 floor	7975	2.5 Sedge
T329 J3 floor	7989	2.0* Carrot Family, 0.5 Ash
T329 J3 floor	7991	0.5 Mint Family; 0.5 Walnut
Area B5		
La Cancha OS	20205	0.5 Mormon Tea
La Cancha OS	24672	0.5 Ash
Area B6		
T576 OS	20860	1.5 Lily Family, 2.0 Cattail
T576 PT17	22889	3.0 Cattail
Area B7		
T211 OS	23098	0.5 Rose Family
T211 OS	23419	0.5 Dandelion-type, 0.5 Indian Wheat
Area B8		
T280 OS	28126	0.5 Alder
T280 OS	30051	0.5 Mormon Tea, 0.5 Lily Family
Area B9		
T277 J6 floor	32144	0.5* Hackberry
Area D		
T9 OS	9525	0.5 Sedge
T13N OS	17089	0.5 Dandelion-type
Area E		
Modern surface	9627	2.0 Indian Wheat, 0.5 Alder
PH2 floor	12361	1.5* Carrot Family
PH1 floor	16325	3.5* Hackberry, 0.5 Rose Family
PH1 floor	16326	0.5 Mormon Tea
PH9 entry	13478	0.5 Buckthorn Family
PP1	16341	2.0 Cattail

* Indicates a pollen type occurring in aggregates of 6 or more pollen grains.

Table 10.3. Economic Pollen Types

	Sample Number	Grass Family	Potato Family	Prickly Pear	Cholla	Saguaro-type	Mesquite	Ocotillo	Willow	Cattail	Sedge Family	Hackberry	Carrot Family	Corn (no. of grains)	Cucurbit (no. of grains)
Area A1															
T736,CSSS4,OS	24465				+										
T716, OS	27556					0.5									
Area B1															
T347, OS	17129				0.5									1	
T347, terrace fill	12823				*2.0									+	
T347, J&, OS	16116					1.0	*1.0							2	
T351, OS	10330													+	
T351, OS	10148				2.5										
T351, OS	10788													1	
T351, OS	12612				*1.5										
T351, pre-terrace surface	10332				*1.5									+	
Area B2															
T370, OS	10631	*8.5		1.0	1.5									*3	
T370, OS	10636					0.5					0.5			+	
T370, OS	10637				4.0	1.0								2	
T370, J2, floor	10922				*7.5	0.5								+	
T370, J2, floor	11436				6.5									*3	+
T370, B3, hip	11056													+	
Area B3															
T330, OS	7033				2.0									2	
T330, OS	8257				*10.5										
T330, OS	6871				1.5									*5	
T330, AT1, ramp	7494		*1.0		0.5									1	
T330, CSS17, floor	6975			0.5										+	
T330, CSS17, floor	6976	*5.0			*4.0	*11.0								*3	
Area B4															
T329, OS	8335				1.0									1	
T329, PF3, floor	7970				4.0	1.0					2.5				
T329, J3, floor	7975				4.0	1.0					2.5			1	
T329, J3, floor	7989				3.0		*6.0						*2.0	*6	
T329. B4	7992		*4.5		*1.0									*2	
Area B5															
La Cancha, OS	20205				+										
La Cancha, OS	20444					0.5									
La Cancha, OS	20445													+	

Table 10.3. Economic Pollen Types, cont'd

	Sample Number	Grass Family	Potato Family	Prickly Pear	Cholla	Saguaro-type	Mesquite	Ocotillo	Willow	Cattail	Sedge Family	Hackberry	Carrot Family	Corn (no. of grains)	Cucurbit (no. of grains)
Area B6															
T576, OS	20860				1.5	*2.0	*6.0			2.0				*5	1
T576, OS	20861	*9.0		*3.0	*4.5			*2.0						*8	
T576, PT17	22889				0.5	*2.0			*1.5	3.0				1	
T594, QSS1, floor	28815	*2.5		0.5	3.5	*1.0								*2	
T594, QSS1, floor	29804				*1.0				*1.5					1	
T593, PF2	31866				2.0									*7	
T593, CSS19	31982				*4.0									1	
Area B7															
T211, OS	23098					1.0								+	
T211, OS	23125				1.0	1.5									
T211, OS	23419				*2.0		*4.0							2	
Area B8															
T280, OS	30051				7.5										
T280, OS	30089					0.5									
T280, OS	30105				1.0									1	
Area B9															
T277, OS	30425		*4.0		1.5			*2.5						1	
T277, J6, floor	32144				10.0		*0.5					*0.5		*7	1
Area B11															
T553, OS	32902				2.0	1.0								+	
Area D															
T9, OS	9525										0.5			+	
T11, OS	14953				0.5										
T13N, OS	17089				+										
T19N, OS	14986					0.5									
QSS3, floor	14969													2	
OSS4, floor	15398				*2.0		*2.0								
QSS4, floor	15399	*4.0			+	*3.0								1	
Area E															
PH2, floor	12360				*6.0									*9	
PH2, floor	12361	*11.0	*2.5	0.5	+	*1.0		*3.0	*4.0				*1.5	*2	
PH2, floor	16096				*4.5									*1	
PT1	11009				*3.5									1	*3
PT2	11835	*11.0			*8.0	*2.0								*4	
PH1, floor	16325			2.5	2.0		*2.5					*3.5		2	

Table 10.3. Economic Pollen Types, cont'd

	Sample Number	Grass Family	Potato Family	Prickly Pear	Cholla	Saguaro-type	Mesquite	Ocotillo	Willow	Cattail	Sedge Family	Hackberry	Carrot Family	Corn (no. of grains)	Cucurbit (no. of grains)
PH1, floor	16326	*18.0						*5.0						1	
PH9, entry	13478				0.5	+								+	
OS2	14901				1.0										
B2, head	15384													1	
B2, hip	15383				1.5									+	
PP1	16341									2.0					

Percentages of noncultigen pollen types are calculated on the basis of a 200-grain standard sum of all noncultigen pollen.

Values for cultigen pollen types (Zea and Cucurbita) are expressed as the number of pollen grains encountered in tabulation.

* Indicates a pollen type occurring in aggregates of 6 or more pollen grains.

+ Indicates a pollen type observed only in scanning of additional material after tabulation of the 200-grain standard sum.

Table 10.4. Seed and Other Wood Data

	Sample Number	Maize Cupule	Maize Kernel	Agave Fiber	Agave Spine	Agave Heart	Agave Stalk	Unknown Seed Frags.	Grass Stem	Unknown Vesicular Mat.	Mesquite Seed	Other	Richness	Density
Area A1														
T731 CSS4 feature fill	23651					1		2	2			Grama Grass 39, Native Barley 1	1.00	10.75
T736 CSS4 OS	24464												0.00	0.00
T736 CSS4 cultural fill	21628												0.00	0.00
T736 CSS5 feature fill	24002											Grama Grass 1	0.25	0.25
T791 CSS7 feature fill	24255												0.00	0.00
T791 CSS8 feature fill	24372											Bursage 1	0.25	0.25
El Carocol cultural fill	21626												0.00	0.00
T716 OS	27617						1	1			1		0.75	0.75
Area B1														
T347 cultural fill	12824		1					1				Amaranth 2	0.75	1.00
T347 wall	13718											Chenopodium 1	0.25	0.25
T351 cultural fill	8996		6					1					0.50	1.75
T352 cultural fill	11674		1										0.25	0.25
Area B2														
T370 J2 feature fill	10916												0.00	0.00
T370 wall fall	8757									2			0.25	0.50
T370 cultural fill	10627									1	1	Cholla Bud 1	0.75	0.75
Area B3														
T330 cultural fill	6729												0.00	0.00
Area B4														
T329 PF3 cultural fill	7947												0.00	0.00
T329 H14 feature fill	7738												0.00	0.00
T329 J3 cultural fill	7997		15					2			2	Mesquite Pod 2, Carrot Family 1	1.00	5.00
T329 PT16 cultural fill	17184		20					2					0.50	5.50
T329 wall fall	7914							1					0.25	0.25
Area B5														
La Cancha cultural fill	26630											Bentgrass-type 1	0.25	0.25
Area B6														
T576 OS4 feature fill	29995							2		3		Cholla Bud 2	0.75	1.75
T576 H15 feature fill	22299							1					0.25	0.25
T576 PT17 cultural fill	22882	1						4	1		2	Mesquite Pod 1, Panic Grass 1	1.00	2.00
T576 PT17 feature fill	22910	3						2	1		1	Cholla Bud 1	1.00	1.75

	Sample Number	Maize Cupule	Maize Kernel	Agave Fiber	Agave Spine	Agave Heart	Agave Stalk	Unknown Seed Frags.	Grass Stem	Unknown Vesicular Mat.	Mesquite Seed	Other	Richness	Density
Table 10.4. Seed and Other Wood Data, cont'd														
T576 cultural fill	22781	1											0.25	0.25
T576 CSS18 cultural fill	26122							1					0.25	0.25
T594 CSS18 feature fill	26480	1											0.25	0.25
T594 QSS1 feature fill	29947							3				Panic Grass 1	0.50	1.00
T594 QSS1 feature fill	29948	3						1					0.50	1.00
T594 PF1 feature fill	28615		1					1					0.50	1.00
T593 PF2 feature fill	31749											Cholla Bud 1	0.25	0.25
Area B7														
T210 J5 feature fill	21441							2		1			0.50	0.75
T210 J5 feature fill	23140		1					2		1			0.75	1.00
T210 J5 feature fill	23173	2		1				2					0.75	1.25
T210 H16 feature fill	21224												0.00	0.00
T211 cultural fill	21117							1				Bean 1, Panic Grass 2, Chenopodium 1	1.00	1.25
T211 cultural fill	21196	1		1				2		1			1.00	1.25
T211 cultural fill	21478												0.00	0.00
T211 cultural fill	23379	1						1				Chenopodium 1	0.75	0.75
T211 cultural fill	27039								1			Chenopodium 1	0.25	0.25
Area B8														
T280 cultural fill	27492							1		1			0.50	0.50
T280 cultural fill	28305	2											0.25	0.50
T280 cultural fill	28349							1					0.25	0.25
T280 cultural fill	28489												0.00	0.00
T280 cultural fill	30052	1					1						0.50	0.50
Area B9														
T277 cultural fill	32001							1	3				0.25	0.25
Area B10														
T226 cultural fill	32428						1						0.25	0.25
Area B11														
T554 cultural fill	32772										1		0.25	0.25
Area D														
RA5 feature fill	10713							2					0.25	0.50
QSS3 feature fill	14968								2			Chenopodium 1	0.25	0.25

Table 10.4. Seed and Other Wood Data, cont'd

	Sample Number	Maize Cupule	Maize Kernel	Agave Fiber	Agave Spine	Agave Heart	Agave Stalk	Unknown Seed Frags.	Grass Stem	Unknown Vesicular Mat.	Mesquite Seed	Other	Richness	Density
El Caracolito feature fill	15939							1				Poppy 1	0.50	0.50
N94 E56 feature fill	14098	2											0.25	0.50
T13 cultural fill	17088												0.00	0.00
T17 cultural fill	14983												0.00	0.00
Area E														
H12 feature fill	15419							3				Panic Grass 1, Chenopodium 2	0.75	1.50
H12 feature fill	16066								1			Bentgrass-type 3	0.25	0.75
PH2 feature fill	12358	1							3				0.25	0.25
H1 feature fill	9607	1								1			0.50	0.50
PT 10 feature fill	9655												0.00	0.00
PT1 feature fill	9805	1						5			1		0.75	1.75
PT2 feature fill	11189	5						4	4			Cholla Bud 1	0.75	2.50
PT2 feature fill	11181	2						1	3			Cotton 4, Squash Rind 2	1.00	2.25
PT2 feature fill	11836	2		2				3	2			Cotton 2, Squash Rind 3	1.00	2.50
PT2 feature fill	11840							3					0.25	0.75
PT2 feature fill	11850	3		2				9	2				0.75	3.50
PT2 feature fill	11865	10	1	2				6	9			Cotton 2, Saguaro 4, Chenopodium 2	1.50	6.75
PT3 feature fill	11020	3						4					0.50	1.75
PT4 feature fill	11029	2						4	1				0.75	1.50
PH1 feature fill	15566	2											0.25	0.50
PH1 feature fill	15574	5						2	2			Saguaro 1	0.75	2.00
PH1 feature fill	16310	5						1	1			Cotton? 1, Organ Pipe 1,	0.75	1.75
M1 feature fill	13079	5	1					2	2		1		0.75	2.25
M1 feature fill	13105	6		2				2	4		1		1.00	2.75
PT8 feature fill	14176							1					0.25	0.25
H6 feature fill	14259	23	1					1					0.50	6.25
PT12 feature fill	16350							1					0.25	0.25
PT11 feature fill	14420	3						3					0.50	1.50
PT13 feature fill	11932							1					0.00	0.00
H8 feature fill	14341	8	1					2					0.50	2.75
H9 feature fill	15404	1										Columnar Seed Coat 1	0.50	0.50
RA3 feature fill	15412	1						1	1				0.50	0.50
H7 feature fill	15555											Bursage 2	0.25	0.50
M2 feature fill	16018	4	1					1			1	Panic Grass 1	1.00	2.00
M2 feature fill	16398	2						2					0.50	1.00
H11 feature fill	16355												0.00	0.00

Table 10.4. Seed and Other Wood Data, cont'd														
	Sample Number	Maize Cupule	Maize Kernel	Agave Fiber	Agave Spine	Agave Heart	Agave Stalk	Unknown Seed Frags.	Grass Stem	Unknown Vesicular Mat.	Mesquite Seed	Other	Richness	Density
PH13 feature fill	16327	5	1		1			3				Columar Seed Coat 1	1.00	2.75
H2 feature fill	16393				1								0.25	0.25

Table 10.5. Flotation Wood Charcoal Data

	Sample Number	Weight of Charred Frags (gms)	Mesquite	Desert Willow	Cottonwood	Willow	Ironwood	Palo Verde	Saguaro	Desert Broom	Salt Bush-type	Unknown Legume	Unknown Charcoal Type A	Creosote	Bursera	Cholla	Ocotillo	Indeterminate
Area A1																		
T731 CSS4 feature fill	23651	1.6	1					32										1
T736 CSS4 floor	24464	0.1	5					3										2
T736 CSS4 cultural fill	21628	0.1	5															1
T736 CSS5 feature fill	24002	0.1																2
T791 CSS7 feature fill	24255	0.0																
T791 CSS8 feature fill	24372	0.0																
El Caracol cultural fill	21626	0.0																
T716 OS	27617	0.7	30															
Area B1																		
T347 cultural fill	12824	1.1	17				5	5										1
T347 wall	13718	0.7	16				1	9										2
T351 cultural fill	8996	0.3	18				2	4	1		1	1		1				1
T351 cultural fill	11674	0.1	7					2										2
Area B2																		
T370 J2 feature fill	10916	0.9	20					7										1
T370 wall fall	8757	2.3	26															
T370 cultural fill	10627	0.6	21					4										3
Area B3																		
T330 cultural fill	6729	0.1	2															
Area B4																		
T329 PF3 cultural fill	7947	0.2	10				1	2										1
T329 H14 feature fill	7738	0.1	2															
T329 J3 cultural fill	7997	0.2	5															
T329 PT16 cultural fill	17184	0.3	20	1				5										
T329 wall fall	7914	0.4	19				1	6				1						2
Area B5																		
La Cancha cultural fill	26630	0.1	10					1										3
Area B6																		
T576 OS4 feature fill	29995	2.0	5				2	4	17				3					2
T576 H15 feature fill	22299	0.7	24				2	1	1				1					1

Table 10.5. Flotation Wood Charcoal Data, cont'd

	Sample Number	Weight of Charred Frags (gms)	Mesquite	Desert Willow	Cottonwood	Willow	Ironwood	Palo Verde	Saguaro	Desert Broom	Salt Bush-type	Unknown Legume	Unknown Charcoal Type A	Creosote	Bursera	Cholla	Ocotillo	Indeterminate
T576 PT17 cultural fill	22882	0.3	17							1				1				7
T576 PT17 feature fill	22910	0.8	24				1	6			1						1	4
T576 cultural fill	22781	4.4	25	1			2	2	1				1					
T576 CSS18 cultural fill	26122	0.2	5	1				4										3
T594 CSS18 feature fill	26480	0.6	23	2			2	2					1					
T594 QSS1 feature fill	29947	0.7	27				1	2										2
T594 QSS1 feature fill	29948	0.8	29	2			1	9	1				1					6
T594 PF1 feature fill	28615	2.0	20		1		5	4			2							4
T593 PF2 feature fill	31749	0.4	21	1			8	5					1					1
Area B7																		
T210 J5 feature fill	21441	0.2	31					1										
T210 J5 feature fill	23140	0.2	31					1						1				1
T210 J5 feature fill	23173	0.3	31															2
T210 H16 feature fill	21224	0.5	26					7		1								
T211 cultural fill	21117	0.3	15	1			1	7			1		1	1				5
T211 cultural fill	21196	0.2	14				1	1					1					4
T211 cultural fill	21478	0.1	10					1										3
T211 cultural fill	23379	0.1	14										1					4
T211 cultural fill	27039	0.1	13				1	3										1
Area B8																		
T280 cultural fill	27492	0.2	17															4
T280 cultural fill	28305	1.7	25					4										1
T280 cultural fill	28349	0.1	11															4
T280 cultural fill	28489	0.1	3															
T280 cultural fill	30052	0.2	27					2	1									2
Area B9																		
T277 cultural fill	32001	24.7	12				16	1					1					1
Area B10																		
T226 cultural fill	32428	0.2	18															3
Area B11																		
T554 cultural fill	32772	0.6	21					5						3				

Table 10.5. Flotation Wood Charcoal Data, cont'd

	Sample Number	Weight of Charred Frags (gms)	Mesquite	Desert Willow	Cottonwood	Willow	Ironwood	Palo Verde	Saguaro	Desert Broom	Salt Bush-type	Unknown Legume	Unknown Charcoal Type A	Creosote	Bursera	Cholla	Ocotillo	Indeterminate
Area D																		
RA5 feature fill	10713	0.1																1
QSS3 feature fill	14968	0.3	14				1	5										3
El Caracolito feature fill	15939	0.2	11						1					1				5
N94 E56 feature fill	14098	0.3	21					4	2									3
T13 cultural fill	17088	0.2	5				5											4
T17 cultural fill	14983	0.1	3															
Area E																		
H12 feature fill	15419	0.6	10				13	1		1				1				2
H12 feature fill	16066	0.9	5				10	11										
PH2 feature fill	12358	0.2	3				6	8			1							3
H1 feature fill	9607	1.0	11					9	5	1								2
PT10 feature fill	9655	0.1	4															
PT1 feature fill	9805	0.6	14				4	9										3
PT2 feature fill	11180	1.8	11				6	7			1				5			1
PT2 feature fill	11181	1.4	8				12	7									1	
PT2 feature fill	11836	5.3	10				6	11										
PT2 feature fill	11840	1.0	17				7	4										1
PT2 feature fill	11850	1.3	4	1			4	15	2							1		2
PT2 feature fill	11865	2.8	14				9	9										
PT3 feature fill	11020	3.4	15				6	5				1						1
PT4 feature fill	11029	0.9	16				6	6										1
PH1 feature fill	15566	0.6	19				5	4	1	1			1					4
PH1 feature fill	15574	1.4	17				4	4	5									1
PH1 feature fill	16310	1.2	16				7	4										
M1 feature fill	13079	3.4	14				4	8				1						
M1 feature fill	13105	8.2	4	2	1		12	8			1							
PT6 feature fill	14176	0.7		7			11	8										
H6 feature fill	14259	1.9	9			1	1	2	15									
PT12 feature fill	16350	1.9	7				3	18										
PT11 feature fill	14420	6.7	7				16	4										
PT13 feature fill	11932	4.7	4				3	20										2
H8 feature fill	14341	12.9	11				16	1										
H9 feature fill	15404	37.4	6	1							21							

Table 10.5. Flotation Wood Charcoal Data, cont'd

	Sample Number	Weight of Charred Frags (gms)	Mesquite	Desert Willow	Cottonwood	Willow	Ironwood	Palo Verde	Saguaro	Desert Broom	Salt Bush-type	Unknown Legume	Unknown Charcoal Type A	Creosote	Bursera	Cholla	Ocotillo	Indeterminate
RA3 feature fill	15412	20.0	27															2
H7 feature fill	15555	39.2	10				6	12										
M2 feature fill	16018	0.4	14				7	8										2
M2 feature fill	16398	0.1	4				3											1
H11 feature fill	16355	1.1	17				4	6										
PH3 feature fill	16327	2.2	10				12	5										
H2 feature fill	16393	8.0	12				15											1

Table 10.6. Individually Collected Charred Macrofossil Identifications

Provenience	Sample #	Weight (g)	Identification (# of fragments)
Area B1			
T347 RA4 cultural fill	14809	12.4	Mesquite 11, Palo Verde 1
T347 cultural fill	12841	1.5	Mesquite 4, Ironwood 2, Palo Verde 1
T347 wall fall	13915	15.0	Mesquite 11
T347 wall fall	14694	61.3	Mesquite 14
T347 cultural fill	15062	10.1	Mesquite 12, Unknown Vesicular Material 1
T351 cultural fill	12154	3.0	Mesquite 5, Palo Verde 1, Unknown A, Creosote 1
T351 cultural fill	12166	6.0	Mesquite 8
T351 cultural fill	12985	23.8	Mesuite 19, Palo Verde 3, Saguaro 2, Unknown Legume 1
Area B2			
T370 J2 feature fill	12032	0.2	Mesquite 1
T370 B3 feature fill	11059	0.1	Palo Verde 1
T370 wall fall	8758	4.5	Mesquite 10
T370 cultural fill	10682	2.7	Mesquite 4, Palo Verde 5
T370 cultural fill	10917	9.3	Mesquite 8, Palo Verde 2, Unknown Legume 1
T370 cultural fill	12041	0.6	Mesquite 1
Area B4			
T329 PF3 cultural fill	7977	1.5	Mesquite 4, Palo Verde 1
T329 J3 feature fill	17177	0.2	Mesquite 5, Maize Kernels 4
T329 cultural fill	8158	1.0	Mesquite 6, Palo Verde 2
T329 cultural fill	8159	0.2	Ironwood 1, Palo Verde 1, Creosote 1
T329 cultural fill	8164	2.1	Mesquite 5, Ironwood 1
T329 cultural fill	8183	2.7	Mesquite 7, Ironwood 2, Palo Verde 1
Area E			
PH2 feature fill	16039	6.8	Mesquite 1, Ironwood 9, Palo Verde 3
H12 feature fill	16357	10.2	Mesquite 4, Ironwood 6, Palo Verde 2, Mesquite Seed 1
H1 cultural fill	9608	2.3	Saguaro 2, Desert Broom 2
PT1 feature fill	11007	5.2	Ironwood 1
H3 cultural fill	10963	0.1	Ironwood 1
PT1 feature fill	10993	5.8	Mesquite 1, Ironwood 6, Palo Verde 4
H4 feature fill	10984	0.1	Palo Verde 1
PT1 feature fill	10998	5.4	Mesquite 5, Ironwood 2, Saltbush 1
PT2 feature fill	11178	17.0	Mesquite 1
PT2 feature fill	11837	7.0	Ironwood 3
PT2 feature fill	15428	?	Ironwood 3
PT3 feature fill	11021	5.6	Ironwood 2
PT3 feature fill	11022	7.5	Mesquite 2, Ironwood 2, Palo Verde 4

Table 10.6. Individually Collected Charred Macrofossil Identifications, cont'd

Provenience	Sample #	Weight (g)	Identification (# of fragments)
PT3 feature fill	11026	16.2	Ironwood 4, Palo Verde 1
PT4 feature fill	11030	4.5	Mesquite 2
PT4 feature fill	11037	5.0	Mesquite 3, Ironwood 3
PT5 feature fill	11052	1.6	Mesquite 2, Ironwood 1, Unknown Legume 1
PH1 feature fill	15570	29.8	Mesquite 4, Ironwood 6
PH1 feature fill	16311	11.3	Mesquite 6, Ironwood 4, Palo Verde 1
PT6 feature fill	14177	0.6	Desert Willow 1, Ironwood 1
H6 feature fill	13623	3.7	Mesquite 1, Saguaro 9, Bursage 1
PT12 feature fill	16351	12.5	Mesquite 3, Ironwood 1, Palo Verde 11, Unknown Legume 1
PR1 feature fill	14294	8.6	Mesquite 1, Ironwood 9, Palo Verde 1
PR1 feature fill	14296	29.1	Ironwood 10, Palo Verde 1
PT11 feature fill	12324	1.6	Mesquite 1
PT11 feature fill	12329	1.9	Mesquite 1
H13 feature fill	11919	6.7	Mesquite 11, Palo Verde 1
PT13 feature fill	11933	3.2	Mesquite 4, Ironwood 3, Palo Verde 2
PT13 feature fill	14909	8.7	Ironwood 1
H10 feature fill	11989	0.4	Mesquite 1
H10 feature fill	14873	1.9	Mesquite 12, Palo Verde 1
B2 feature fill	14335	6.1	Mesquite 3, Ironwood 5, Palo Verde 4
B2 feature fill	15385	4.3	Ironwood 2, Palo Verde 1
H8 feature fill	14348	3.0	Mesquite 1, Ironwood 6, Palo Verde 3
H9 feature fill	15380	14.6	Mesquite 2, Palo Verde 9
H9 feature fill	15403	150.5	Mesquite 12, Palo Verde 1, Saltbush 8
RA3 feature fill	14948	12.0	Mesquite 11, Palo Verde 1
PT7 feature fill	15544	28.4	Mesquite 11, Ironwood 4, Palo Verde 1
H7 feature fill	15552	254.1	Mesquite 12, Ironwood 20, Palo Verde 14
M2 feature fill	16019	1.1	Mesquite 5, Ironwood 1, Palo Verde 1
PT8 feature fill	16012	7.3	Mesquite 3, Ironwood 6, Palo Verde 2
PH3 feature fill	16331	81.7	Mesquite 10, Ironwood 8, Palo Verde 8, Unknown Legume 1
H2 feature fill	16395	16.4	Mesquite 2, Ironwood 11
N130E154	9816	?	Mesquite 7

Table 10.7. Percentages of Cheno-am Pollen from Cerro de Trincheras Site Areas

	Range Residential Terraces	Average Residential Terraces	Average Area E	Average Area D	Average La Cancha	Avg. (Area B8) El Mirador	Avg. (Area B9) El Mirador	Avg. (Area A1) Summit
Sample (n)	39.0	39.0	10.0	13.0	9.0	4.0	2.0	4.0
% Cheno-am	45.8-66.0	55.0	43.9	52.0	48.8	50.9	47.8	17.1

Excludes modern surface and burial samples.

Residential terraces = Areas B1, 2, 3, 4, 6, 7, 11.

Table 10.8. Ubiquity Values for Wood Flotation Categories from Cerro de Trincheras Site Areas

	Sample (N)	Mesquite	Ironwood	Paloverde	Saguaro	Desert Willow	Ocotillo	Bursera
Residential Terraces	34	100	50	79	15	21	3	3
Area E	48	98	60	58	10	8	2	2
El Mirador								
Areas B8, 9,10	7	100	14	43	14	0	0	0
Area A1								
Summit	8	50	0	25	0	0	0	0

Ubiquity = % flotation samples containing a wood category.

Residential terraces = Areas B1, 2, 3, 4, 6, 7, 11.

Table 10.9. Ubiquity Values for Seed and Other Non-wood Categories from Residential Areas

	Residential terraces (n = 34)	Area E (n = 33)
Maize cupule	24	70
Maize kernel	21	18
Bean	3	0
Squash rind	0	6
Cotton seed	0	12
Mesquite seed	15	12
Mesquite pod	6	0
Cholla bud	12	3
Saguaro seed	0	6
Organ Pipe seed	0	3
Chenopod seed	12	6
Amaranth seed	3	0
Carrott family seed	3	0
Panic Grass	9	3
Bentgrass-type	0	3
Agave fiber	6	12
Agave spine	0	6

Ubiquity = % of total flotation samples containing a seed or non-wood category.

Residential Terraces = Areas B1, 2, 3, 4, 6, 7, 11.

Table 10.10. Values for Economic Pollen Types from Residential Areas

	Corn	Cucurbit	Mesquite	Cholla	Prickly Pear	Saguaro-type	Grass Family	Potato Family	Carrot Family	Ocotillo	Hackberry	Cattail	Sedge	Willow
Residential Terraces (n = 39)	77	5	8	74	10	33	10	5	3	3	0	5	8	5
Area E (n = 10)	80	10	10	80	20	30	30	10	10	20	10	10	0	10

Ubiquity = % of total pollen samples containing an economic pollen type.

Residential Terraces = Areas B1, 2, 3, 4, 6, 7, 11.

Excludes modern surface and burial samples.

Chapter 11
Archaeofaunal Remains

Peter W. Stahl. Binghamton University

Fauna

El equipo de trabajo de campo recuperó un total de 8,009 restos de arqueofauna en Cerro de Trincheras durante las temporadas de trabajo de campo de 1995 y 1996, a través de clasificación manual, cribación y recuperación por flotación. Este capítulo provee una descripción de la base de datos de especímenes y análogos contmporáneos, y una discusión combinando formación y preservación. Los resultados de los análisis muestran qué fragmentos de hueso de indeterminados mamíferos dominan el arreglo. Esos especímenes que podrían ser identificados, son típicos de paisajes áridos y revelan un conjunto característicamente bajo en riqueza y dominado por unos pocos taxa claves que fueron posiblemente de alguna importancia prehistorica, especialmente liebres, conejos de cola blanca y algunas especies de venado. El resto de las aves, mamíferos carnívoros y taxa asociados con medios acuáticos están presentes aunque fueron ocasionalmente recuprados. Varios roedores de menor tamaño también están presentes, muchos de los cuales son de tipo intrusivo. Los análisis muestran que este conjunto no difiere de manera significativa de la mayoría de los conjuntos de arqueofauna de Hohokam.

Excavators retrieved 8099 non-shell archaeofaunal specimens via handsorting, backscreening with standard mesh apertures, and flotation recovery during the 1995 and 1996 excavation seasons at Cerro de Trincheras. The archaeofaunal materials were shipped in their original field specimen bags from Trincheras, via Tucson to Binghamton, New York where they were temporarily curated prior to and during analysis. All specimens were removed, examined, and repacked according to their unique proveniences. As most of the sample consisted of small fragments, the majority of specimens were visually inspected with the aid of an illuminated lense and 64 power zoom microscope. The fragile character of most remains prohibited the use of extensive cleaning other than with fine-point dental picks and soft brushes. Standard observations included: element, portion, side, fusion/age, qualitative observations (articulation, abrasion, chewing/puncturing, digestion, rodent gnawing, intrusive appearance, weathering, cut marks, polishing and modifications, with number, orientation and further description where appropriate), degree and orientation of heat treatment, weight (to .01 g) and quantity. All observations were entered, along with provenience information, into a computer database (Paradox Ver. 3.5). Cultural modification of bone remains is only briefly mentioned in the following sections as it is treated separately in greater detail by Radhika Sundararajan (Chapter 9).

Zoological identifications were facilitated through comparison with three collections. During both excavation seasons, I collected representative faunal specimens from on and around the site through trapping, solicitation, and surface pick up. Collected specimens were processed in the field and returned to the United States in anticipation of analysis. The bulk of the comparisons were facilitated through use of comparative skeletal materials housed in the Archaeological Analytical Research Facility at Binghamton University. Further identifications were undertaken using the extensive reference collections of the Departments of Ornithology and Mammology at the American Museum of Natural History, New York.

A numerical summary of zoological identifications within the recovered faunal sample is presented in Table 11.1. The table presents the assemblage in taxonomic sequence, accompanied by the total number of recovered specimens. Also included, where appropriate, are Minimum Number of Individuals (MNI) and Minimum Number of Elements (MNE) statistics for positive identifications at the level of zoological Family and lower. Both MNI and MNE estimations are minimum figures derived for the site as a whole. MNE statistics are based upon eight arbitrary body segments: (1) head and neck; (2) thorax; (3) scapula and proximal humerus; distal humerus and proximal ulna/radius; (5) distal ulna/radius and manus; (6) pelvis and proximal femur; (7) distal femur and proximal tibia; and (8) distal tibia, lower leg and pes. These can be compared with comparable statistics provided below in the description of the archaeofaunal database, in which maximum figures are estimated for each taxon through separation by excavation unit.

A subsequent section of this report contains an assessment of assemblage formation, which examines assemblage survivorship and discusses various factors of assemblage accumulation and attrition. A final discussion section concludes with inter- and intra-assemblage comparison, and suggested inferences regarding environmental and subsistence reconstruction.

Description of the Archaeofaunal Data Base and Contemporary Faunal Analogs

The degree to which archaeofaunal remains could be zoologically identified is severely hampered by extreme fragmentation, a point that is returned to in a separate section. The entire sample of 8009 remains weighs only 4288.05 g; therefore, average specimen weight is less than 2 g. Moreover, the majority of specimens (n = 4934, 61.6 percent) weigh less than 1 g. Not surprisingly, almost one quarter of the entire sample (n = 1963, 24.5 percent) remains unidentifiable to the level of zoological class (Table 11.2).

The total weight of the indeterminate category is 115.46 g (mean = .59 g), and consists mainly of tiny fragments too small to reliably assign to zoological class. Almost one half of the indeterminate subsample derives from surficial levels (n = 883, 45 percent), and a significant portion was recovered in flotation fraction (n = 368, 18.7 percent). Within the subsample of indeterminate fragments, five pieces are culturally modified. Three longbone fragments and two indeterminate fragments appear to have been polished; and one of the polished indeterminate fragments is the tip portion of a possible awl.

With the exception of one surficial fragment associated with Platform 3 in Area B4, which appears to be the calcined and fragmented dactyla of a tiny crustacean (order: Decapoda; e.g., crab, shrimps, lobsters), the remainder of the examined material consists of vertebrate remains. The vertebrate archaeofaunal component is detailed below, in taxonomic order. Each section describes the surviving elements along with their corresponding portion and descriptive statistics. Number of Identified Specimens (NISP) is provided for all zoological categories. MNI and MNE statistics are included for all identifications at the level of zoological Family and lower. In all cases, MNI and MNE statistics are maximum estimations as they are derived by separating identifications according to excavation unit (unit and level). Brief identifications and natural histories of potential contemporary faunal analogs are provided in the appropriate sections.

Class: Osteichthyes

Three tiny vertebrae from some sort of small bony fish were recovered through water flotation of sediments in Area B2. One complete vertebra, weighing less than .01 g was associated with sediments at 25 to 45 cm in depth. Two complete vertebrae, weighing a combined total of less than .01 g were recovered from inside an *olla* associated with a concentration of domestic materials in Jacal 2.

Class: Amphibia

A total of 14 amphibian remains (Table 11.3) are identified in the Cerro de Trincheras archaeofaunal sample; all but two fragments deriving from surficial or immediately subsurficial contexts. Total weight of this small sample is 2.6 g. All remains are identified as frogs and toads (order: Anuran), the only members of this class that are found in contemporary desert environs. The relatively high survivorship of distal humeri, along with a proximal ulna fragment and almost complete urostyles is suggestive of a density-dependant survivorship.

The standard osteological criteria used to distinguish toads (family: Bufonidae) from frogs (family: Ranidae) involve edentulous mandibles and articular aspects of the vertebral column (Tihen 1962:158), usually rendering the sure identification of fragmented post-cranial elements difficult. Nevertheless, through consultation with a range of *bufonid* and *ranid* skeletons and the aid of illustrated guides (e.g., Tihen 1962; Olsen 1968), a few tentative identifications below the level of family are suggested. The almost complete sacrum of a large *Bufo* sp. was recovered from surficial contexts in Area B1, along with unidentified urostylar, tibial, and humeral anuran fragments, suggesting intrusive death. Two other pelvic and one atlas fragment are also identified as bufonid. From the surviving evidence, it would be difficult to attempt further zoological resolution, certainly as a number of *bufonids* range into the area today (Table 11.4). One large, almost complete vertebra compares quite favorably with specimens of *Rana catesbeiana*. If this identification is accurate, it could have implications for nearby watered conditions. Although the bullfrog ranges into the northern deserts of México (Flore-Villela 1993), it demands nearby sources of permanent water, and can be found in desert oases, irrigated farmlands and marshes (Stebbins 1985: 93).

Class: Reptilia

A total of 170 reptilian remains, comprising a cumulative weight of 122.69 g are identified in the sample (Table 11.5). The majority of reptilian remains not identified below the level of zoological class consist of fragmented vertebrae, lacking the diagnostic articulations necessary for more exacting identification. In general, these are tiny fragments weighing a total of only .26 g. Approximately one third of the subsample was recovered in flotation fraction.

The bulk of the Trincheras reptilian sample is comprised of turtle and/or tortoise (order: Chelonia) remains, which overwhelmingly survives in the form of distinctly identifiable carapace and plastron fragments. Unfortunately, 87 fragments with a cumulative weight not exceeding 83.83 g (mean = .96 g) lack any diagnostic features that would facilitate a more accurate identification than the ordinal level. Four chelonid remains, three of which are complete, are identified as *Terrapene* (box turtles). Two specimens from the same context in Area B8 are complete and paired xiphiplastron elements, whereas one complete marginal element and one unspecified carapace fragment which compares well with *Terrapene* are derived from adjoining levels in Area B1. Two forms of this genus currently inhabit the Sonoran desert of northwestern México (Flore-Villela 1993). The endemic spotted box turtle (*Terrapene nelsoni*) occurs in disjunct populations throughout southern Sonora and adjoining regions to the south (Ernst and Barbour 1989:198). A more likely analog is the non-endemic desert box turtle (*Terrapene ornata luteola*) that ranges throughout larger areas of southwestern North America and adjacent areas of México (Ernst and Barbour 1989:196; Stebbins 1985:103). An inhabitant of open areas, the desert box turtle is tolerant of desertic conditions where it forages diurnally for a chiefly carnivorous diet (Ernst and Barbour 1989:197). A complete nuchal element was identified as *Gopherus*, in association with four complete marginal elements from Area B8 that compare well with members of this genus. One fragmented marginal and one fragmented costal element from different contexts in Area B11 also compare favorably with this taxon. Currently the only species of the genus that inhabits the Sonoran desert is the desert tortoise (*Gopherus agassizii*), a non-endemic form that ranges throughout the American west, Sonora, and adjacent portions of Baja and Sinaloa. This terrestrial desert species requires burrowing substrates, and is often found in desert oases, washes and rocky slopes with suitable substrates, often in association with creosote and thornscrub (Ernst and Barbour 1989:273; Stebbins 1985:104).

Sixteen fragments weighing less than .5 g are identified as some form of small lizard (suborder: Sauria). Approximately one third of this subsample is identified from flotation fraction, with one unidentifiable Saurian tooth recovered from the contents of an *olla* in Area B2. A complete maxilla with dentition compares favorably with corresponding elements of Collared lizard (*Crotaphytus* spp.). Currently, two forms of the genus are recognized as ranging into the Sonoran deserts (Flores-Villela 1993); however, subspecies of the desert collared lizard (*Crotaphytus insularis*) appear to range southward into extreme western Arizona and Baja California (Stebbins 1985: Map 80). The common collared lizard (*Crotaphytus collaris*) is a rock-dwelling species, perfectly suited for the terrain of Cerro de Trincheras, where it readily frequents the rocky outcrops and boulders strewn throughout the site. The complete frontal bone of a horned lizard (*Phrynosoma* spp.) is readily identified from deposits recovered in Area B6. Currently, many members of this genus are found as endemic and non-endemic forms throughout the Sonoran region of México (Flores-Villela 1993). Two species in particular, the desert horned lizard (*Phrynosoma platyrhinos*) and the regal horned lizard (*Phrynosoma solare*) are potential analogs. Both forms can inhabit rocky areas within arid, desertic environments associated with cactus, mesquite and creosote, where they forage principally for ants (Stebbins 1985:140; 142). The fragmented mandible of some form of skink is identified. Flores-Villela (1993:27-28) lists one endemic and two non-endemic species of *Eumeces* spp. as inhabiting Sonora; whereas Stebbins (1985:Map 107) traces only the mountain skink (*Eumeces callicephalus*) as ranging to the west of the general area. Although found in upland oak and pine habitats in rocky area of the United States, Mexican forms range to near sea level (Stebbins 1985:148).

Nine vertebral and rib fragments, and 30

complete vertebrae weighing a total of 4.49 g (mean = .12 g) are identified as the remains of snakes. With few exceptions, these are most likely associated with small taxa. Some vertebrae have a decidedly intrusive appearance, whereas in some areas of the site, sets of vertebrae recovered from the same context appear to be from the same animal thereby suggesting the possibility of non-cultural origin. These points are returned to below.

Class: Aves

The Sonoran desert is characterized by a taxonomically rich avifauna of resident and migrant species (Table 11.4) however, only 69 identifiably avian remains, weighing a total of 23.57 g were recovered during excavations at Cerro de Trincheras (Table 11.6). A significant portion of the indeterminate avian component consists of possible shell fragments. All of these remains were recovered from surficial deposits and likely represent the non-archaeological residues of local nesting birds. With the exception of four fragments, the non-shell component is derived from small to medium-sized birds, no larger than a pigeon. Virtually the entire subsample of indeterminate avian remains is surficial in origin, and represents a relatively comprehensive cross-section of avian skeletal fragments. Some of the remains appear to be noticeably weathered, with one localized concentration of bones with markedly intrusive or recent appearance. These points are returned to below.

A fragmented distal ulna with shaft portion of a relatively large bird was recovered from sub-surface context in Area B9. Tentatively identified as some form of medium-sized duck, it compares most favorably with consulted skeletons of mallards (*Anas platyrhynchos* [Spanish: *Pato de Collar*, *Pato Real*]). Nevertheless, this area of the Sonoran desert is a popular winter home to a large assortment of migrant waterfowl (Table 11.4), especially ducks, all of which require some form of water source like marshes or arable fields and irrigation ditches (Howell and Webb 1995:159-165).

The distal ulna and shaft portion of a large bird, recovered in archaeological context from Area E, compares best with skeletal material from some form of vulture (Spanish: *Buitre*, *Aura*), especially *Cathartes* sp. Although two genera of vultures appear as year-round residents throughout large tracts of México and North America, the black vulture (*Coragyps atratus*) has suffered recent population decrease and localized extirpation, and is an uncommon local resident in southern Arizona (Howell and Webb 1995:174; Peterson 1990:182). The turkey vulture (*Cathartes aura*) is quite common to the area, and resident flocks use the summit of the site as a communal roost, from which individuals soar in search of prey.

The distal end of a humerus from subsurface context in area B6 is identified as a fragment of hawk (*Buteo* spp. [Spanish: *Aguililla*]) red-tailed hawks (*Buteo jamaicensis* [Spanish: *Aguililla Colirroja*]) are year-round breeding residents of the area, where they are commonly seen perching on fence posts and high places, or soaring in search of prey. The similar-sized ferruginous hawk (*Buteo regalis* [Spanish: *Aguililla Real*]) is a winter visitor to the area (Howell and Webb 1995:203-204).

The complete phalanx of a large bird tentatively identified as some form of quail (Phasianid [Spanish: *Codorniz*]) was recovered in Area B2 from a deposit of packed earth. A number of smaller quails are year-round residents in this area of the Sonoran desert (Table 11.4). All forms inhabit desert scrub with patches of cover and agricultural fields (Howell and Webb 1995:229-234).

Surficial contexts in Areas B2 and B8 yielded the distal humerus and ulna of some sort of pigeon and/or dove (Spanish: *Tórtola*, *Paloma*), many species of which are locally available to the area in the form of resident breeding populations (Table 11.4).

The remains of a young parrot were recovered from Level 2 of Area B1, Unit N97 E86. Over the years, archaeologists and zoologists have considered a range of taxa, restricted to *Ara* spp. and *Rhyncopsitta pachyrhynchus*, in the study of psittacid remains from the prehistoric southwest (e.g., Creel and McKusick 1994; Hargrave 1970; Minnis et al. 1993; Olsen 1967). Two species of Mexican macaws, the military macaw (*Ara militaris* [Spanish: *Guacamaya Verde*]), and the scarlet macaw (*Ara macao* [Spanish: *Guacamaya Roja*]) have been reported in numerous excavations throughout the greater Southwest. Whereas the larger scarlet macaw is currently a resident of humid forests to the south, the smaller military macaw ranges as far as southern Sonora, yet remains locally restricted in forests and foothills of the Sierra Madre Occidental to the south of Cerro de Trincheras (Howell and Webb 1995:337). The thick-billed parrot (*Rhyncopsitta pachyrhynchus* [Spanish: *Cotorra-serrana Occidental*]), ranges farther north in the forests of the Sierra Madres, with former range extensions as far north as southeastern Arizona (Howell and Webb 1995:338; Olsen 1967:59). All of the Trincheras remains are appendicular elements, including portions of the major elements of one left wing, and fragments of the lower portions of both legs. One unidentified longbone shaft from a medium-sized bird derives from the same context and may be a part of the same individual. Due to the specifics of diagnostic criteria, and the kinds of bones surviving in archaeological context at Cerro de Trincheras, overall size differences are the only major criteria for distinguishing amongst psittacids (Olsen 1967:58). However, as the remains are those of a juvenile individual, a number of skeletons were consulted for comparison, including both macaws, the thick-billed parrot, and a comprehensive collection of skeletons from small-bodied Amazons (Spanish: *Loro*) of the genus *Amazona*, whose distributions range throughout southern México. On the basis of size-comparisons, it is very unlikely that the Trincheras parrot is a macaw. There is little overlap in the general size of smaller adult thick-billed parrots and either of the substantially larger adult macaws. The archaeological specimen is too well ossified to be considered a nestling macaw. On the other hand, there is very little size overlap between the larger thick-billed parrot, when compared to all but one species of the smaller Amazons. The sub-adult archaeological specimen compares favorably in form and size with mature adult Amazon skeletons, and therefore is best considered a juvenile thick-billed parrot.

A complete right tarsometatarsus was recovered from Area B9 in archaeological context and compares well with a larger cuculid, most likely the greater roadrunner (*Geococcyx californianus* [Spanish: *Churea, Correcaminos Mayor*]). Currently, this terrestrial resident of the northern Mexican deserts is a common sight in open and semi-open areas supporting nearby cover (Howell and Webb 1995:350).

The right humeral shaft of an unidentified medium-bodied bird, recovered from surficial contexts in area B1 possibly derives from a larger corvid, most likely a raven (Spanish: *Cuervo*) of the genus *Corvus*. Currently, two forms of raven, the smaller Chihuahuan raven (*Corvus cryptoleucus* [Spanish: *Cuervo Llanero*]) and the larger northern or common raven (*Corvus corax* [Spanish: *Cuervo Grande*]), are conspicuous denizons of open and semi-open areas with adequate nearby nesting sites (Howell and Webb 1995:546-548).

Class: Mamalia

The bulk of the Cerro de Trincheras archaeofaunal sample is comprised of indeterminate mammalian remains (n = 4565, 57 percent).

Due to extensive fragmentation, a rough estimation of original body size could not be assigned to a large portion of this subsample (n = 2019, 44.2 percent), which consists mainly of long bone and indeterminate fragments (Table 11.7). Additionally, the majority of polished and/or otherwise modified remains are fashioned from mammalian elements (n = 131/181, 72.4 percent). Most often, the cultural modification of these pieces tends to obliterate any osteologically diagnostic criteria, thereby obscuring further identification. A later section considers cultural modification as a factor in overall assemblage attrition. All of the modified and/or polished pieces in the indeterminate mammal category (n = 33, 18.2 percent) are fashioned from unspecified longbone and indeterminate fragments. Recognizable elaboration, beyond simple polishing, includes typical marginal notching (n = 11), a few possible bone awl points (n = 6), and one striated and one decorated piece. The remaining subsample of indeterminate mammalian remains are assigned to rough body size estimations and described in separate sections below.

Indeterminate Small Mammal Remains

A total of 126 indeterminate mammalian fragments are considered as having possibly originated from small mammalian taxa, generally no larger than 300 mm in total length, or roughly the size of a common wood rat. These remains are listed in Table 11.8 and weigh only 2.53 g, mean = .02 g). Roughly one third of this subsample (n = 40) derives from flotation fraction. Eleven fragments have a markedly intrusive appearance, nine of which are cranial fragments concentrated in surficial contexts of El Caracol (Area A1). An associated cranial fragment in the same context appears to have been partially digested and regurgitated, possibly by some form of raptor. These and related points are returned to below.

Indeterminate Medium Mammal Remains

A significant number of indeterminate remains derive from some medium mammalian taxa (n = 1024, 247.63 g, mean = .24 g), generally no larger than a medium-bodied carnivore with body lengths not exceeding a maximum of 1000 mm (Table 11.9). All of the modified and/or polished pieces in the indeterminate medium mammal category (n = 30, 16.6 percent) are fashioned from unspecified longbone and indeterminate fragments. Recognizable elaboration, beyond simple polishing, consists of typical marginal notching on two indeterminate longbone elements. Based upon appearance, seven of the fragments are likely intrusive. All derive from surficial deposits. Rodent gnawing is observed on one indeterminate long bone fragment, and a complete phalanx appears to have been digested. Both derive from surficial contexts, whereas the shaft of a mammal rib from below surface appears to have been chewed by a carnivore.

Indeterminate Large Mammal Remains

A restricted range of skeletal fragments derive from some indeterminate large mammalian taxa (n = 1396, 1762.16 g, mean = 1.26 g), defined as larger than a medium-bodied carnivore with body lengths exceeding 1000 mm (Table 11.10). These consist primarily of indeterminate long bone shaft splinters and fragments of axial elements, particularly ribs and vertebrae. Two indeterminate longbone fragments bear two visible cut marks each, and are oriented transversely to the length of the shaft. A significant portion (n = 81, 44.6 percent) of these remains are culturally modified to varying degrees, through polishing and/or some other form of modification. These included possible bone awls (n = 11), points (n = 5), and needles (n = 1), with two fragments showing simple multiple striations. The majority (n = 26) are decorated with multiple notching, ranging from two to as many as 42 notches. The larger overall fragment size is a potentially a surviving window through which to identify further attritional agency, as many of the indeterminate large remains bear evidence of weathering (n = 189), carnivore tooth marks (n = 2), rodent gnawing (n = 3), and abrasion (n = 4). These, and related points are returned to in a separate section.

Lagomorpha Remains

The mammalian order that includes hares and rabbits is represented in the Cerro de Trincheras archaeofaunal sample by 424 bone fragments (294.4 g). Only five fragments within this subsample are unidentified lower than the level of family (Leporidae: rabbit/hare). These include one unspecified alveolar fragment, one upper molar fragment, one phalangeal fragment, one metapodial shaft from a large individual, and one complete phalanx from a small individual. The remainder of the subsample is discussed below.

A total of 53 bone fragments (16.76 g, mean = .32 g) comprise the subsample of cottontail specimens in the recovered deposits (Table 11.11). These remains are identified only to the level of genus as two sympatric species currently occupy the northern Sonoran desert of México. Both taxa exhibit significant overlap in body size, and osteological criteria used in species identification are restricted to specific aspects of cranial morphology, involving relative size differences. The eastern cottontail (*Sylvilagus floridanus* [Spanish: *Conejo Castellano*]) tends to be associated with the vegetational cover of mountainous regions where it inhabits grasses, mesquite, chaparral and woodlands, and can also frequent cultivated fields (Ceballos González and Galindo Leal 1984:137; Hoffmeister 1986:127). The desert cottontail (*Sylvilagus audubonii* [Spanish: *Conejo Serrano*]) ranges widely but generally inhabits thickets and scrubs of lower elevation grasslands and deserts, seeking refuge in abandoned burrows and rocky crags (Ceballos González and Galindo Leal 1984:140; Hoffmeister 1986:137). desert cottontails are quite common, especially in the irrigated croplands to the north of the site, and I suspect that the majority of small leporid archaeofaunal specimens derive from this taxon. Although locally hunted today in Trincheras, all consumption of lagomorphs tends to be at least seasonally avoided for fear of ingesting intestinal parasites.

The *Sylvilagus* archaeofaunal specimens are distributed throughout all but one of the excavation areas at the site. They tend to be found as isolated specimens within excavation units, hence the relatively high MNI and MNE when considering the relatively low NISP figure. With few exceptions these specimens derive from shallow deposits within 10 cm of the surface. Ten specimens appear with weathering, whereas one calcaneum may have been partially digested.

The greatest number of archaeofaunal specimens identified to one genus consist of jack rabbit remains (n = 366, 277.17 g, mean = .76 g), and are listed in Table 11.12. As in the case of cottontails, two sympatric species of *Lepus* currently inhabit the area. Reliable osteological criteria used to distinguish between the two forms consist of relative size differences in cranial morphology as well as shape and size attributes in upper incisor cross-sections (Hoffmeister 1986:144). The kinds of elements represented in the sample, coupled with extreme fragmentation, inhibit higher resolution identification beyond the level of genus. Currently, two species of jack rabbits inhabit the Sonoran desert of northern México. The black-tailed jack rabbit (*Lepus californicus* [Spanish: *Liebre de Cola Negra*]) occupies low elevation desert and open-scrub forest with suitable forage, and is particularly attracted to range and croplands. The larger antelope jack rabbit (*Lepus alleni* [Spanish: *Liebre*]) is commonly observed in the area today; an inhabitant of relatively drier desertic conditions associated with creosote, mesquite and sparse grass cover (Hoffmeister 1986:139-146).

Jack rabbit remains are the single most abundant of any recovered and identified taxon at Cerro de Trincheras. As with cottontails, *Lepus* spp. specimens are distributed throughout all excavation areas at the site, but tend to be less isolated within excavation units; however, MNI and MNE estimations remain high in comparison to the relatively low NISP figure. Unlike cottontail remains, almost one half of the jack rabbit subassemblage was recovered from feature fill and stratigraphic levels below 10 cm from surface (n = 176, 47 percent). Seven specimens indicate substantial weathering, two specimens display glossy intrusive appearance, and one distal tibia and shaft portion survives with tooth puncture marks. Approximately 10 percent of the subsample (n = 40) appears to have been heat-treated to varying degrees.

The larger jack rabbit specimens also exhibit a minor degree of cultural modification in the form of polishing and possible notching of dental elements. Five specimens, including one glenoid portion of a scapula, two humeri, one metatarsus, and one tibial fragment appear to have been artificially polished. Three dental elements may have been intentionally notched, much in the same way as post-cranial notching. These appear as right-angle excisions, generally on the lingual borders of one almost complete first upper incisor (4 notches), one upper molar (8 notches), and one smaller fragmented upper molar (2 notches) specimen. Whether or not these are examples of intentional cultural modification or simply coincidentally patterned right-angled cracking of dehydrated dental enamel, remains open to speculation.

Rodent Remains

The remains of varyingly sized rodents are quite numerous in the archaeofaunal assemblage (n = 584, 7.3 percent of the entire sample). Finer resolution identification of smaller-sized rodent taxa is based principally on molar cusp morphology; therefore, a large portion of the rodent subsample, which consists either of non-dental and non-tooth bearing elements, or isolated fragments not directly associated with highly diagnostic materials, is identified at the ordinal and occasionally familial level. Ordinal-level identifications are assigned arbitrary size designations where possible or appropriate. Two specimens, one an ulnar fragment from an unidentified large sized rodent, the other a humeral shaft of a medium sized rodent compare well with rodent elements but could not be identified further. Twelve specimens, mostly fragmented incisors could be readily identified as rodent; however, the extent of fragmentation inhibits assignation of an arbitrary body size.

A total of eight specimens (2.15 g, mean = .27 g) are identified as the remains of some indeterminate large rodent, using the live body dimensions of a rock squirrel (*Spermophilus variegatus*) as a guide. I suspect that the majority, if not all, of these specimens are originally from this taxon. The subsample includes: one anterior fragment of a lower incisor; one scapular blade fragment; one sacrum; four complete metatarsi; and one complete first phalanx. With the exception of the scapular fragment and phalanx, all specimens derive from excavation contexts below 10 cm depth.

A larger sample of archaeofaunal specimens (n = 108, 10.58 g, mean = .1 g) are identified as originating from indeterminate medium-sized rodents (Table 11.13), using the live body dimensions of rodent taxa like the smaller ground squirrels (e.g., *Ammospermophilis* spp.) and wood rats (*Neotoma albigula*) as a rough guide. Over one quarter of this subsample derives from surficial deposits at the site. One surficial specimen is possibly calcined, otherwise many of the indeterminate medium-sized rodent bones exhibit qualities suggestive of intrusive accumulation. These include a number with the characteristic intrusive sheen, and a few which appear to have been chewed and possibly partially digested. In particular, two specific contexts in Area A1, associated with El Caracol, yielded concentrations of specimens which accounted for nearly one half (n = 49) of the subsample. In both contexts, the molar-bearing remains of woodrat (*Neotoma*) are identified, and it is likely that these indeterminately identified bones derive from this taxon. One of these contexts may represent the remains of a disintegrated pellet or possible scat. These, and related topics dealing with assemblage formation and attrition are discussed in a separate section below.

The bulk of indeterminate rodent specimens (n = 275, 7.23 g, mean = .026 g) derive from small-bodied taxa, comparable in size to the typical field mouse, which comprise the majority of rodents, including all taxa within the families Geomyidae, Heteromyidae and Muridae (Table 11.14).

Almost one third of the subsample was recovered in flotation fraction, with over 53 per cent associated with surficial contexts. Flotation fraction from within and around an *olla* in Jacal 2 (Area B2), yielded diagnostic elements in addition to a number of indeterminate small rodent specimens. These include the striated upper incisors of either *Reithrodontomys* or *Perognathus*, and identifiable molars of *Peromyscus eremicus*. Along with the remains of a small lizard, these may be suggestive of post-discard accumulation, incidental to the small fish vertebrae found within the *olla*. As with the indeterminate medium rodent specimens, many appear with surfaces typical of intrusive bones; whereas a few may have been partially digested. Two of these contexts may represent the remains of a disintegrated pellet or possible scat. A third, consists of complete and articulated calcaneum and astragalus. Some of the contexts from which the indeterminate small rodent remains derive yield concentrations of specimens, and most of these contain diagnostic remains from virtually the entire set of small rodents. These, and related topics dealing with assemblage formation and attrition are further discussed in a separate section below.

A total of 88 specimens (51.18 g, mean = .58 g) are varyingly identified as squirrel (family: Sciuridae) remains (Table 11.15). Identification to the familial level and lower is based upon the recovery of diagnostic dental material. Post-cranial materials are also assessed on the basis of close contextual associations with highly diagnostic specimens. Although genus and species level identifications are generally based on surviving dental material, along with standard craniometric criteria (e.g., Hoffmeister 1986), these criteria are often hindered in the archaeological record by variable fragmentation, which in turn dictates the zoological precision to which specimens can be identified. These criteria are less important for the identification of large sciurid taxa (defined as *Spermophilus variegatus*), but are of crucial importance for identifying the many smaller sciurid taxa, due to the great degree of size overlap between implicated taxa, principally *Ammospermophilus harrisii* and *Spermophilus tereticaudus*. For these reasons, specimens that could not be identified below the level of zoological family, were grouped, where possible, into arbitrary size categories.

A total of 42, principally post-cranial specimens, are identified to the level of family. Most are from sub-surficial archaeological contexts, and only one distal tibia fragment from surficial contexts displays the fresh sheen of intrusive material. The most likely candidates include Harris' antelope squirrel (*Ammospermophilus harrisii* [Spanish: *Ardilla*]) and the round-tailed ground squirrel (*Spermophilus tereticaudus*), although the former is the only relevant taxon identified in the Cerro de Trincheras archaeofaunal sample. Harris' antelope squirrel is a very common inhabitant on and around the site, preferring rocky areas and slopes that support vegetational thickets (Hoffmeister 1986:172). The round-tailed ground squirrel constructs colonial burrows in sandy soils that support creosote bush (Hoffmeister 1986:184). Identification to genus and species is based upon published craniometric data in Hoffmeister (1986). The majority of these specimens (total n = 14) are cranial and/or tooth-bearing elements, along with closely associated post-cranial materials. I suspect that most, if not all of the medium-bodied sciurid specimens are remains of *Ammospermophilus*, a ubiquitous denizen of the site today. Larger sciurid specimens (n = 33) are identified as the remains of the larger-bodied rock squirrel (*Spermophilus variegatus* [Spanish: *Ardillón*, *Techalote*]) whose burrows and nests are plentiful on the rocky slopes of the site, where they are frequently observed scurrying in search of favored foods including cactus fruits, agave blooms, ephedra seeds, and cultivated crops (Ceballos Gonzlez and Glaindo Leal 1984:154; Hoffmeister 1986:176). Many of the recovered *Spermophilus* specimens are found concentrated in specific contextual associations, and at times with an intrusive surficial appearance. Many of these and the smaller sciurid specimens in the assemblage are also relatively complete. These and other aspects of assemblage formation are discussed in a separate section below.

Various identified non-sciurd rodent specimens were recovered during the Cerro de Trincheras excavations. This subsample of 91 specimens (6.0 g, mean = .07g) pertains to three rodent families: Geomyidae (pocket gophers), Heteromyidae (pocket mice), and Muridae (mice and rats). All specimens are identified on the basis of dental or tooth-bearing elements (Table 11.16).

The right mandible of Bottas pocket gopher (*Thomomys bottae* [Spanish: *Tuza*]) was recovered from the surface of an excavation unit in Area A1. This taxon is ubiquitous throughout areas supporting sufficient herbaceous forage and soil conditions conducive to tunneling. A solitary animal, which normally spends most of its life in extensive burrow systems, the pocket gopher is commonly seen in the area today when it surfaces to eject backdirt. Although a diurnal species, gopher remains are commonly encountered in owl pellets, suggesting a certain degree of surficial nocturnal foraging (e.g., Hoffmeister 1986:225). The surficial context and intrusive sheen of the Cerro de Trincheras specimen suggests non-archaeological accumulation, a point that is expanded upon below.

As many as 25 specimens of Heteromyid rodents are identified, the majority pertaining to some species of pocket mouse (*Perognathus* spp. [Spanish: *Ratón*]), which is represented in the immediate area by at least four specific forms (Table 11.4). In general, these taxa include small-bodied nocturnal mice which subsist mainly on seeds, but whose omnivorous diets enable them to inhabit a variety of habitats supporting xerophytic cover. In particular, the rock pocket mouse (*Perognathus intermedius*) is restricted to rocky environs (Hoffmeister 1986:246-298). Nine upper incisors, including two premaxilla fragments with teeth are tentatively identified either as specimens of *Perognathus*, or of harvest mouse (*Reithrodontomys* spp. [Spanish: *Ratón*]), both murid genera of similarly-sized mice. Either genus is characterized by grooved incisors. At least two species of *Reithrodontomys* currently inhabit the area (Table 11.4), and are found throughout a wide range of habitats in México and the American Southwest that support adequate cover and seeds for their mostly granivorous diet (Ceballos González and Galindo Leal 1984:183; Hoffmeister 1986:325). Many of the Heteromyid remains are identified from flotation fraction and from surficial contexts. As earlier stated, one specimen was recovered through flotation from the contents of an *olla*. At least two specimens have an intrusive appearance, and I suspect that most if not all are non-cultural accumulations.

Ten specimens are identified as *Peromyscus*, and although at least four species of this genus currently range into the northern Sonoran desert of México (Table 11.4), I strongly suspect that they all derive from the cactus mouse (*P. eremicus* [Spanish: *Ratón*]). The majority of these specimens compare well with dental materials of this species. In particular, Hoffmeister (1986: Fig 5.179, 336) indicates the lack of a mesoloph in the upper first and second molars of the cactus mouse, when compared to most other members of the genus. A comparison of various species of *Peromyscus* in my collections, corroborates a similar absence of mesolophid structures in the lower first and second molars of this taxon when compared to at least two other species. Furthermore, during two brief visits to the site in 1995 and 1996, I trapped numerous cactus mice in and around the rocky fissures of Cerro de Trincheras. This species is adapted to desertic conditions and can be found in a variety of habitats that support the necessary vegetation for its principally herbaceous diet (Hoffmeister 1986:337). The identified specimens tend to be found as isolated remains throughout various contexts within the site, including one lower first molar recovered in the heavy fraction of the floated olla contents in Area B2.

Five maxillae and mandibles with teeth represent at least two individuals from closely associated contexts in Area A1, most likely the hispid cotton rat (*Sigmodon hispidus* [Spanish: *Rata Algodonera*]). This medium-sized murid ranges throughout the Sonoran and Chihuahuan deserts of México where it occupies a wide variety of habitats, including rocky areas that support sufficient vegetative cover (Ceballos González and Galindo Leal 1984:212). The intrusive appearance of at least one of these specimens, along with their primarily surficial contexts suggest that they may not be archaeological.

Wood rats (*Neotoma* spp. [Spanish: *Rata*]), are represented in the Cerro de Trincheras assemblage by 46 specimens. At least three species of *Neotoma* currently range into the Sonoran desert of México (Table 11.4). One maxilla with teeth compares well with published diagnostic dental descriptions (Hoffmeister 1986: 402, Fig 5.220) and comparative material collected in the Trincheras town site of the white-throated wood rat (*Neotoma albigula*). This taxon lives in a wide array of habitats but frequents cholla, cactus and rocky areas where it forages and constructs its nests (Hoffmeister 1986:406-407). Most of the specimens were recovered in concentrations of skeletal material from contiguous excavation units in Area A1, especially in association with El Caracol. This, and the intrusive appearance of many of the cranial and mandibular elements suggests that the wood rat remains were accumulated by some non-cultural agency such as raptors, which are the principal predators of this taxon.

Carnivore Remains

A relatively small quantity (n = 39, 110.99 g, mean = 2.85 g) of carnivore specimens are identified in the Cerros de Trincheras archaeofaunal assemblage (Table 11.17). Less than one quarter could not be identified to a lower zoological category than class. With the exception of one fragmented radius, all derive from a medium-sized carnivore, defined as roughly the size of an average domestic dog. Most of these specimens are highly fragmented and/or derive from elements with overall poor diagnostic acuity, and tend to be spatially associated with specimens identified to taxonomic categories lower than the level of class.

Almost one half of the carnivore specimens are further identified as some sort of canid (dogs and foxes). At least three separate canid taxa, in addition to domestic varieties, currently range into the Sonoran desert of northern México (Table 11.4). One proximal metatarsal digit, identified as the remains of a larger *Canis* spp. compares well with that of a coyote (*Canis latrans*), an omnivorous generalist that presently ranges widely throughout various habitats in North and Central America (Ceballos González and Galindo Leal 1984:228, Hoffmeister 1986:461). A right maxilla with teeth is tentatively identified as that of a domestic dog (*Canis familiaris*). The specimen was recovered in Area E, and associated with fill from Pithouse 3, which also yielded one half of an atlas vertebra, and the root of a canine tooth. All these materials pertain to a very young individual. Other canid materials are identified for relatively medium and small taxa. The latter could include kit fox (*C. macrotis* [Spanish: *Zorra*]), a small canid of desert scrub and grassland, which feeds on small prey items similar to many of the identified taxa in the Cerro de Trincheras archaeofaunal assemblage (Hoffmeister 1986:471). The larger gray fox (*Urocyon cinereoargenteus* [Spanish: *Zorra Gris*]) shares this catholic diet, and accordingly ranges throughout a wide variety of habitats within the western hemisphere. In Arizona, it has been observed to inhabit unoccupied badger holes (Hoffmeister 1986:475). Gray fox is occasionally observed in and around the site environs, where a relatively complete and articulated skeleton was collected from the surface in 1995.

At least four specimens are identified as the remains of coati (*Nasua nasua* [Spanish: *Coatí*]), a larger procyonid that principally inhabits woodland areas, especially in the mountains to the west of the Sonoran deserts of northern México. Usually found near water sources, they are known to traverse desert scrub, as they forage crepuscularly for a highly omnivorous diet under vegetation, in trees, and under rocks (Ceballos González and Galindo Leal 1984:235, Hoffmeister 1986:488).

Over one quarter of the carnivore specimens are identified as badger (*Taxidea taxus* [Spanish: *Hurón, Tlalcoyote*]) remains. The temporary burrows of these powerful diggers are presently found on the site of Cerro de Trincheras. Their varied diet includes smaller prey items like those that are identified in the archaeofaunal assemblage. They are in turn preyed upon by golden eagles and coyotes (Ceballos González and Galindo Leal 1984:240, Hoffmeister 1986:498).

The complete left third metatarsal digit of a large feline was recovered from archaeological levels in Platform 2 (Area B6). The metatarsus is comparable to both jaguar (*Felis onca*) and mountain lion or puma (*F. concolor*) elements in the collections of the AMNH, but compares best with that of Puma, which ranges widely throughout various habitats in the western hemisphere, and over all of México. Dietary preferences include reptiles, and medium to large-bodied mammals, especially deer (Ceballos González and Galindo Leal 1984:248, Hoffmeister 1986:521).

Perissodactyl (Odd-toed Ungulate) Remains

Two large, and almost complete thoracic vertebrae, along with an unidentified epiphyseal fragment from a large mammal, were uncovered in the terraces of Area B11 on the eastern flanks of the northern slope of Cerro de Trincheras. The vertebral specimens are remains of a horse or possibly a mule (*Equus* spp.), which were excavated in Circular Stone Structure 25, and represent a recent, non-archaeological intrusion.

Artiodactyl (Even-toed Ungulate) Remains

A total of 175 specimens (825.94 g = 4.7 g) are identified as the remains of even-toed ungulates, likely representing individuals from no more than two genera of deer (Table 11.18). Twenty-four specimens are identified only to the level of order, and a further three are identified as deer (family: Cervidae), although I suspect that they are all probably fragments deriving from some species of *Odocoileus*. With the exception of two obviously intrusive domestic cattle (*Bos* sp.) specimens in areas A1 and B6, the remainder of the sample is either identified as, or compares well with native deer. Currently, two species range into the Sonoran desert of northern México, the shite-tailed deer (*Odocoileus virginianus* [Spanish: *Venado Cola Blanca*]), and mule deer (*Odocoileus hemionus* [Spanish: *Venado*]). Both species prefer herbaceous browse, require a certain degree of vegetative cover, and although found primarily in woodland communities, can frequent desert scrub. Where both species are occur together, the white-tailed deer tends to be found at higher elevations (Hoffmeister 1986:538).

One third (n = 58) of the artiodactyl subsample derives from surficial contexts, with six surficial specimens displaying weathering damage and a further two appearing somewhat abraded. Two specimens have visible carnivore chewing/puncture marks and an additional two display damage from rodent gnawing. Indeed, with the exception of the smaller, structurally dense carpal/tarsal elements, virtually the entire subsample consists of fragments. There is no question that much of this fragmentation is a factor of human agency, as 24 of the specimens display human modification. In particular, distal portions of deer metapodia appear modified and/or polished (n = 16), having in some cases been fashioned into awls, along with one scraper, and one metatarsus with as many as 12 surficial notches. Notching, however, appears most commonly on scapular fragments (n = 4), having been elaborated with as few as five and as many as 17 distinct notches. Antler tines are also modified and/or polished with at least two suggestive of awl tips. These artifacts are described in a separate study of modified bone remains (Sundararajan Chapter 9).

Archaeofaunal Assemblage Formation

Assemblage Preservation

An overwhelming impression of bone preservation in the Cerro de Trincheras archaeofaunal assemblage is one of small particle size, high fragmentation and isolated survivorship in dispersed contexts throughout the site. The average weight of each fragment in the entire sample is less than 2 g (mean = 1.87 g). Almost one quarter (n = 1963, 24.5 percent) of the assemblage is not reliably identifiable to the level of zoological class, whereas an overwhelming majority of the specimens (n = 6595, 82.3 percent) remain unidentifed above the level of zoological order. Small particle size is guided to some extent by the small body size that characterizes a high proportion of the potentially available faunal taxa; however, intense fragmentation is likely the main cause. A small fraction (n = 409, 5.1 percent) of the entire assemblage consists of complete or almost complete skeletal elements, and these are generally associated with specific taxa; a point which is explored in greater detail below. Furthermore, these small and fragmented specimens tend to appear isolated in scattered deposits throughout the site excavations. This is clearly illustrated in the wide discrepancies between minimum MNI estimations computed for the entire assemblage (Table 11.1) and maximum MNI estimations that treat excavation units as separate depositional events. An average of less than seven bone specimens (mean = 6.6) were recovered from each excavation unit; a number that drops further (mean = 4.6) when discrete levels are taken into account. The following discussion further explores these main themes through a detailed account of intra-taxon variability in assemblage preservation, and a consideration of some of the factors involved in assemblage attrition and accumulation.

Skeletal Representation

Skeletal representation amongst the lower vertebrates, suggests the possibility that smaller taxa tend to be represented by a more comprehensive degree of skeletal completeness. The small subsample of amphibian remains derives entirely from post-cranial elements. Although dominated by humeral fragments from as many as three different individuals, the remainder of the specimens from this small sample is associated with elements distributed from throughout the appendicular skeleton (Table 11.3). Reptilian remains are numerically dominated by durable and identifiable carapace and plastron fragments from relatively larger turtles and tortoises. For similar reasons, the subsample of identified snake remains is dominated by highly diagnostic (to the level of Sub Order) vertebral specimens. Otherwise, the remains of small lizards (Sauria, *Crotaphytus*, *Phrynosoma*, Scincidae, and likely most indeterminate Reptilia) tend to be represented by a relatively even distribution of cranial, vertebral, and limb elements.

All evidence suggests that the remains of the young parrot (*Rhyncopsitta*) derive from one individual. Otherwise, with the exclusion of eggshell fragments, the remaining avian subsample appears to be dominated by pectoral elements, and to a lesser extent the lower pelvic limb and phalangeal elements from a variety of birds. The identified remains of larger avian taxa are virtually all based on wing elements (Table 11.5).

I suggest that this tentative pattern of relatively comprehensive skeletal representation amongst smaller-bodied taxa, in contrast to their larger counterparts, is further revealed in a detailed examination of mammalian taxa. I compiled and statistically compared four lists of surviving bone specimens and their respective portions for the obviously non-intrusive (e.g., *Equus*, *Bos* are excluded) mammalian faunas by zoological order. They consist of: 1. Lagomorpha, including rabbit (Table 11.11) and jack rabbit (Table 11.12) specimens; 2. Rodentia, including all variously-sized and identified examples (Tables 11.13-16); 3. Carnivora (Table 11.17); and, 4. Artiodactyla, excluding *Bos* specimens (Table 11.18). Standard t-tests suggest that overall skeletal representation within Rodentia, is statistically no different from skeletal representation within Lagomorpha, yet is statistically different from representation within both Carnivora and Artiodactyla. Skeletal representation within Lagomorpha, Carnivora, and Artiodactyla are statistically no different from each other. Order: Rodentia, of course, includes all of the small-bodied mammals at the site, as well as the medium-bodied *Spermophilus variegatus*; however, it is demonstrated below that a finer-grained differentiation can be established within the rodent subsample. The Carnivora subsample is relatively small and does include some medium-sized taxa; otherwise, the overall pattern suggests that relatively diminutive taxa that are smaller than a jack rabbit in dimension, survive differently than their larger-bodied carnivore and ungulate counterparts at the site.

The frequencies of differential skeletal representation are portrayed for each Order in

Table 11.19. For ease of illustration, specimens and their respective portions are displayed as arbitrary body segments. Rodents are dominated by cranial and dental specimens. The latter are particularly important for purposes of identification. Rabbits tend to be represented by bones of the extremities and of the upper pelvic girdle; nevertheless, skeletal representation within both orders tends to be relatively more even than representation for their larger-bodied counterparts. Carnivores are dominated by cranial and dental fragments as well as specimens from the upper pelvic girdle. Artiodactyla specimens, virtually all from white-tailed deer, overwhelmingly consist of bones of the extremities and cranial/dental specimens.

In order to complete the overall picture of mammalian assemblage representation, I also plotted the indeterminate mammalian specimens (Tables 11.13-16) by element (Table 11.20). Comparisons using t-test statistics do not suggest any statistically significant differences between the subsamples. Here, mammal remains consist of specimens so highly fragmented that they could not be reliably assigned to any arbitrary size category. Not surprisingly, the majority of these specimens include indeterminate (to element) fragments. Large and medium indeterminate mammal specimens are dominated by longbone and indeterminate (to element) fragments. Small indeterminate mammal specimens are also dominated by longbone and indeterminate (to element) fragments as well as vertebral fragments. Although it cannot be statistically demonstrated, the subsample of small indeterminate mammal remains includes more skeletal categories, which tends to even out the degree of skeletal representation in contrast to the larger indeterminate mammal remains (Table 11.20).

Up to now I have suggested that small-bodied taxa, especially rodents, and probably frog/toads and small lizards are represented in the Cerro de Trincheras assemblage by an overall greater degree of skeletal representation. This is further corroborated through examining body representation within the entire rodent subsample (Table 11.21). Small and medium-sized rodents include all taxa smaller than or equal to the bodily dimensions (HB < 200 mm) of medium-sized ground squirrels (e.g., *Ammospermophilus harrisii*, *Spermophilus tereticaudus*) or wood rat (e.g., *Neotoma albigula*). The large-sized rodent category probably consists exclusively of one taxon (*Spermophilus variegatus*) that can be arbitrarily considered a medium-sized mammal (HB > 250 mm). Although, rodent taxa as a whole survive differently from larger-bodied carnivores and ungulates, t-test comparisons suggest that skeletal survivorship is statistically different between small and medium rodents on the one hand, and the larger-bodied rodents on the other. The larger rodent specimens are dominated by cranial and dental material, virtually all of which is definitely identified as *S. variegatus*. Based on Table 11.21, I suggest that the smaller rodents again are more evenly represented in terms of skeletal portions than their larger-bodied counterparts. Subsequent sections continue to explore this, and related themes, as they contribute to an understanding of archaeofaunal assemblage formation at Cerro de Trincheras.

Element Completeness

Although the archaeofaunal assemblage is highly fragmented, a very small portion survives relatively complete (n = 409, 5.1 percent). Table 11.22 shows a subsample of 397 relatively intact elements that are minimally identified to the level of zoological order or suborder. The sample excludes the intact remains of *Equus*, an obvious recent intrusion. The sample includes discrete skeletal elements that are recorded either as complete or almost complete; that is, with only minimal subsequent structural damage and therefore likely deposited intact at the time of accumulation. Over one half (n = 209, 52.6 percent) of the relatively complete elements are identifiable rodent remains. Further broken down by size categories (Table 11.22), it is clear that the majority (n = 184, 46.3 percent) consist of smaller-bodied rodents. Together with the frog/toads, small lizards, and snakes, a majority of relatively complete elements in the assemblage derive from markedly smaller-sized taxa (n = 227, 57.2 percent). Lagomorph remains also significantly contribute to this category (n = 77, 19.4 percent), with the majority of the relatively complete elements recorded for the larger-bodied *Lepus*, a point that will be returned to below. The relatively intact elements from small and medium-sized taxa derive from all portions of the skeleton.

Only ten (2.5 percent) carnivore elements are complete, including: four intact phalangeal elements from medium-sized canids; one mandible of the medium-sized *Nasus nasua*, one mandible and three post-cranial elements of *Taxidea taxus*; and one metatarsus of the large-bodied *Felis concolor*. All of the intact artiodactyl elements (n = 29, 7.3 percent) consist of *Odocoileus* spp. carpal/tarsal or phalangeal elements, and therefore derive exclusively from the distal appendages. It appears that the smaller-bodied taxa, principally the smallest taxa in the archaeofaunal assemblage contribute the most relatively intact elements to an otherwise highly fragmented assemblage. Also, unlike their larger-bodied counterparts these elements are not restricted to specific areas of the skeleton, but represent all areas of the skeletal bauplan.

Spatial Concentration

Despite the size and prehistoric significance of Cerro de Trincheras, and the magnitude of recent excavations at the site, the number of specimens in the recovered archaeofaunal collection is relatively small. Furthermore, the bulk of the assemblage is characterized by small particle size, which is likely a factor of high fragmentation. As earlier mentioned, these small and fragmented specimens appear isolated in scattered deposits throughout the site excavations, a point clearly illustrated when comparing the minimum MNI estimations computed for the entire assemblage (Table 11.1) with their maximum MNI counterparts which arbitrarily treat excavation units as separate depositional events. On average, less than seven bone specimens (mean = 6.6) were recovered from each excavation unit.

Nevertheless, all specimens do not appear randomly isolated, as certain patterns in the spatial survivorship of archaeofaunal specimens can be suggested. In particular, spatial concentration of bone survivorship appears to be governed, to some extent, by body size. Table 11.23 illustrates the degree to which archaeofaunal specimens from potentially similar taxa appear associated in the same spatial provenience. The data are tabulated according to the number of occasions that specimens identified to zoological order and suborder occur in isolated (1) contexts, and in increasingly higher concentrations of like material (2-5 or more). Table 11.24 shows the same data for proveniences from which two or more related items were recovered. Clearly, rodents and lagomorphs dominate the number of archaeological occurrences in which two or more like specimens were recovered per provenience. Although the bulk of relatively identifiable (minimally to order) specimens appear either in isolation or with unidentifiable fragments, rodent, and to a lesser extent lagomorph, specimens tend to appear spatially concentrated in more excavated proveniences. This is certainly the case when compared with survivorship of larger-bodied mammalian taxa (Table 11.25). Moreover, a finer-grained breakdown of this spatial survivorship clearly suggests that a greater proportion of small and medium rodents appear in spatial concentrations throughout the site than their larger-bodied counterparts (Table 11.26). This is further examined in a subsequent section of this report.

Density-mediated Survivorship

It appears that the relative structural density of different skeletal elements has varyingly mediated the survivorship of bone material in the Cerro de Trincheras assemblage. I computed separate statistical correlations between published density figures for *Odocoileus* (Lyman 1984), *Lepus*, and *Sylvilagus* (Pavao 1996), with recovered archaeofaunal specimens, using both 'traditional' and maximum density values for the surviving element portions (Lyman 1994:257). Table 11.27 lists the ranked frequencies of skeletal portions for which corresponding volume density figures are available. Identifiable shaft portions are divided between their respective proximal and distal counterparts. Note that all structural density values are measured from mandibular and post-cranial elements scan sites; therefore, appraisals of density-mediated attrition do not include individual dental or cranial elements.

Skeletal survivorship of all identifiably cervid material in the archaeofaunal assemblage is clearly mediated by structural density, whether assessed on the basis of `traditional' ($rs = .56$, $P = .0019$) or maximum ($rs = .62$, $P < .001$) density values. The reason for this relationship is rather obvious. The skeletal profile is dominated by structurally dense skeletal portions that are also highly diagnostic for purposes of zoological identification. In particular, these include proximal and distal metapodia fragments, larger tarsal, and phalangeal elements. As noted above, all of the intact artiodactyla elements consist of either carpal/tarsal or phalangeal elements from *Odocoileus* spp. It is also important to point out here that the overwhelming majority of identifiably cervid tools and/or otherwise culturally modified bone implements consists of worked metapodial shafts, with or without their respective ends. Otherwise, the remaining examples of worked bone consist of modified and polished antler fragments, and scapular specimens. Virtually all of the latter exhibit notching along the dorsal border of the scapular spine.

Leporid skeletal survivorship at Cerro de Trincheras is variable. The remains of *Lepus* do not appear to have been mediated by structural density, whether assessed on the basis of 'traditional' ($rs = .18$, $P = .392$) or maximum ($rs = .17$, $P = .407$) density values. With the exception of the patella, all skeletal portions available in the analysis are represented at the site. Many of the most frequently recovered specimens are those of the relatively lower density portions of the foot, which also appear in the subsample as relatively complete elements. As with the cervid remains, it is again interesting to note that a few examples of the three most frequently represented element portions dominate the number of culturally modified bone implements of this taxon. Conversely, the remains of the smaller *Sylvilagus* appear to have been mediated by structural density, whether assessed on the basis of 'traditional' ($rs = .45$, $P = .045$), or maximum ($rs = .46$, $P = .031$) values. Structurally dense portions of the mandible, pelvis, humerus, and femur dominate the small subsample; however, over one half of the density values used to assess this aspect of assemblage survivorship are absent. These, and related issues are further examined below in discussion of assemblage accumulation and attrition.

Summary

I suggest a number of trends in the survivorship of archaeofaunal materials at the site of

Cerro de Trincheras. I suspect that these are largely governed by differences in relative body size, best considered along a continuum from small (e.g., TL < 300 mm, or squirrel/wood rat size and smaller) through medium (e.g., TL< 1000 mm, or medium carnivore size) to large (e.g., TL > 1000 mm) taxa. Against an overall backdrop of small particle size, high fragmentation, and spatially isolated survivorship, the smallest taxa tend to survive with a relatively greater degree of skeletal representation, and a greater proportion of relatively complete skeletal elements. At the other end of the continuum, skeletal representation of larger taxa is dominated by a more restricted range of skeletal elements, most of which are fragmented. Complete elements consist almost exclusively of durable and non-muscle bearing carpal/tarsal and phalangeal bones. Statistical comparisons with reliable data suggest that large deer skeletal specimens tend to survive because they are structurally dense, whereas medium-sized jack rabbit specimens do not. The smaller skeletal remains of *Sylvilagus*, however, appear to follow a pattern of density-mediated survivorship. These patterns are discussed below in an assessment of factors potentially responsible for archaeofaunal assemblage accumulation and attrition.

Archaeofaunal Assemblage Accumulation and Attrition

In this section, I examine various kinds of evidence used to implicate variables that potentially contributed to archaeofaunal assemblage formation, particularly during and after the prehistoric occupation of Cerro de Trincheras. These include: (1) attritional factors implicated in the subtraction of archaeofaunal specimens subsequent to assemblage accumulation; and, (2) cultural and non-cultural factors implicated in the accumulation of archaeofaunal specimens during prehistoric occupation and after prehistoric abandonment.

Each subsample of archaeofaunal specimens from the separate excavation units at the site is dominated by specimens that are either indeterminately identified to class and/or identified as indeterminate mammal. Figures 11.1 and 11.2 illustrate the relationship between sample size and diversity measures for all categories of identified archaeofaunal specimens (excluding indeterminate and indeterminate mammal categories) by excavation unit (Kintigh 1992). The overall impression suggests an assemblage characterized by relatively low richness and minimum evenness; however, these two characteristics vary spatially across the site. This variability is explored below as an aid for understanding factors that contributed to assemblage formation.

Recovery Bias

The bulk of the Cerro de Trincheras archaeofaunal assemblage was recovered with the use of 1/4-inch aperture screening. This standardized recovery technique was opportunistically facilitated by handsorting during excavation. Flotation recovery was employed in a variety of contexts during both excavation seasons; however, this report includes only those materials retrieved and sorted during the 1995 season, including proveniences in Areas B1, B2, B3, D, and E.

Recovery loss through the use of standard 1/4-inch mesh screen is negligible for the larger mammalian taxa identified in the assemblage, yet becomes important for medium-sized and smaller mammals. The majority of skeletal elements for both species of lagomorphs should be fairly well represented; however, many from the smaller taxa will be missed with 1/4-inch screen aperture. Medium-sized rodents like *Sigmodon, Neotoma,* and the smaller sciurids are large enough for commonly diagnostic skeletal elements like crania and mandibles, as

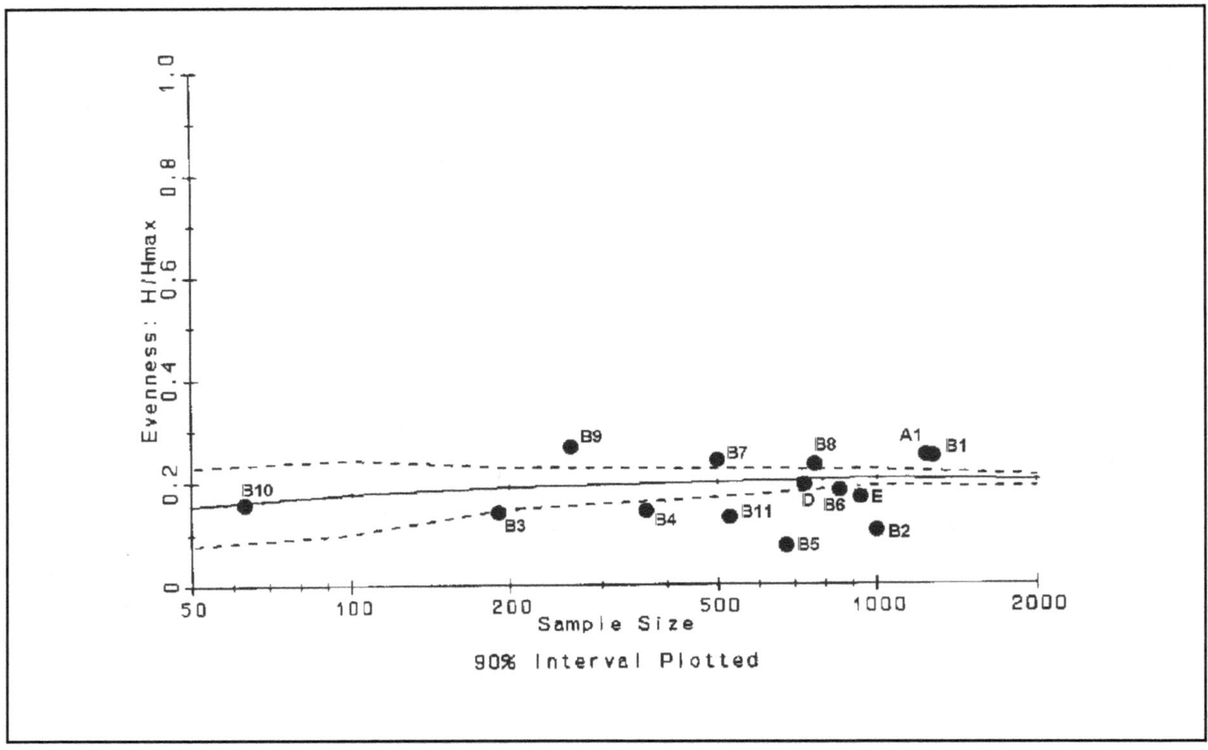

Figure 11.1. Evenness and richness of identified specimen categories by excavation area.

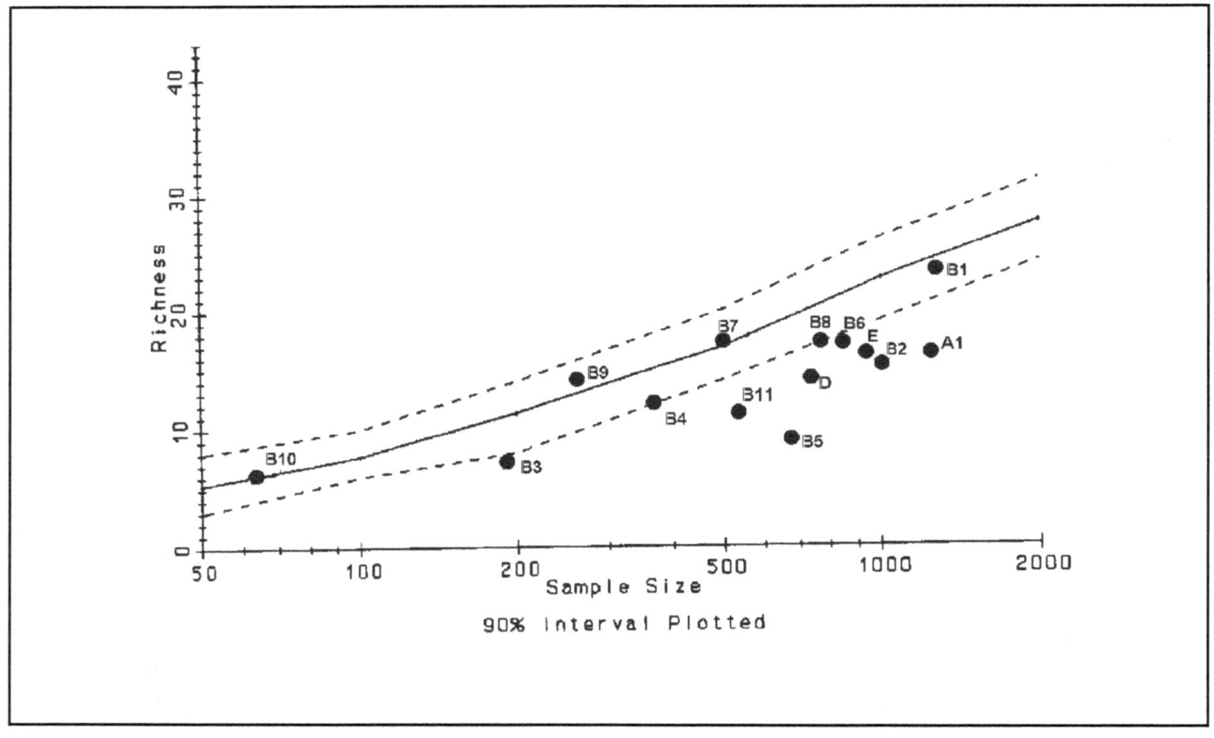

Figure 11.2. Richness of identified specimen categories by excavation area.

well as pelves, femora, scapulae, and humeri to be recovered. With the exception of crania, most skeletal elements from the smallest taxa, especially the majority of rodents, are usually lost (Shaffer 1992:131). Despite a dramatic improvement in overall skeletal representation for these smaller taxa with the use of smaller aperture mesh, significant losses are still recorded (Shaffer and Sanchez 1994:527).

The most commonly recovered medium-sized rodent specimens generally include diagnostic cranial and dental fragments, femora, tibia, mandibles, humeri, pelves, vertebrae, and scapulae (Tables 11.13 and 11.15). The small rodents are strongly represented by diagnostic tooth-bearing elements of the head, in addition to the longest appendicular elements, including femora, humeri, and tibae (Tables 11.14 and 11.16). It is likely that the overall skeletal representation of these small mammalian taxa, as well as many of the diminutive amphibians, reptiles, and birds, is underrepresented through recovery bias using standard 1/4-inch aperture mesh. It is also possible that the density-mediated skeletal representation of the smaller lagomorph taxon may be the patterned outcome of bone loss through 1/4-inch screening. This may be reflected in the relative underrepresentation of smaller, low-density elements from the manus and pes that are poorly represented in the *Sylvilagus* skeletal profiles when compared with their larger counterparts for *Lepus* (Tables 11.11, 11.12, and 11.26).

The potential effect of element loss through recovery bias on taxon representation, is illustrated in the contents of flotation fraction. A total of 1168 specimens were examined from 81 floated contexts in the 1995 excavations. Typically, the bulk (n = 960) of this special subsample is too small to be reliably identified to zoological class; however, flotation fraction usually recovers many of the taxa normally lost through screen mesh with as little as 1/8-inch aperture. Approximately one half of the unidentified mammalian specimens (n = 84), are probably from some form of small mammal (n = 41, 49 percent). Rodent remains dominate the identified bone matertial in flotation fraction. All of these specimens (n = 103) derive from small-bodied taxa, including diagnostic material of Heteromyids and Murids. A significant portion of the smaller reptile component, especially specimens of lizards and snakes, is also identified in flotation fraction. Representation of larger taxa like leporids (n = 4) is not significantly improved through flotation recovery. Perhaps more importantly, 39 of the 81 flotation samples recovered the remains of small rodents, and 12 of 81 recovered specimens of small reptiles. Three of the five floated contexts are characterized by relatively minimal evenness of identified specimens (Figure 11.1), and I suspect that this is related to an increased relative domination by smaller rodent specimens. Moreover, I further suspect that an intensive recovery strategy from all of the site contexts would likely reveal a background 'rain' of smaller rodents and reptiles.

Weathering

The most obvious examples of weathering damage, generally in the form of bleaching and exfoliation, were recorded during analysis. This subsample is relatively small (n = 383) as it includes only the most conspicuously weathered specimens. Almost one half of the subsample (n = 163, 42.6 percent) predictably derives from contexts within 10 cm of present surface levels. Spatial distributions for obviously weathered specimens are listed by excavation area in Table 11.28. Clearly, the bulk of weathered remains appears concentrated in principally five of the 14 excavation areas. A total of 315 (82.2 percent) obviously weathered specimens were recovered from deposits in Areas A1, B5, B6, B11, and E. Considered by taxon, these obviously weathered specimens are comprised of indeterminate mammal (n = 311, 81.2 percent), followed by *Odocoileus* (n = 17, 4.4 percent) and indeterminate to class (n = 12, 3.1 percent) fragments. A further breakdown of the weathered indeterminate mammal specimens includes a considerable portion of large mammal specimens (n = 190, 61.1 percent) with a further 99 (31.8 percent) so extensively fragmented that they could not be estimated to relative body size. An overwhelming portion (n = 366, 84.4 percent) of these weathered mammalian fragments was recovered from deposits in the same five excavation units. Four of the five deposits exhibit significantly minimal evenness of identified materials, whereas all five are significantly low in corresponding richness (Figure 11.1).

I suggest that weathering and possibly resultant fragmentation was particularly severe within deposits represented by a specific set of Excavation Areas. Area B5, B6, and B11 are the lowest elevation terrace units excavated at the site. Area E, of course, is an extensive exposure directly at the base of a small cerro to the south of the site. Area A1 represents the Caracol at the site's eastern summit. All areas commonly share an increased lateral exposure of surface area. Experimental studies in the Sonoran desert of Arizona reveal the rapid and extensive onset of bleaching and exfoliation of exposed skeletal materials in open-air settings (Galloway 1997); these are the most likely areas within the sample of excavated deposits to experience a differentially greater amount of weathering.

I suspect that the greatest degree of in situ weathering damage to bone occurred in and around those areas of the site with decreased topographical gradient and increased level surface area. These same five units contain 63.8 percent of the total indeterminate large mammal bone specimens. In contrast, indeterminate medium mammal bone is fairly evenly distributed across the deposits represented in all of the excavation units, as only Area E yields over 10 percent of these specimens. indeterminate (to class) specimens are concentrated in Areas B2, B1, A1, D, E, B7, B8, and B3; however, the corresponding numbers for five of these units are inflated as a factor of flotation recovery. A perusal of *Odocoileus* skeletal representation suggests that specimens recovered from these excavation areas are dominated by elements and portions of high structural density, particularly from the lower appendages. These typically include metapodia, phalanges, carpal/tarsals, as well as isolated dental elements. Subsequent sections further explore other possible reasons for this apparent density-mediated survivorship.

Non-human Attritional Variables

A few (n = 29), relatively rare examples of non-human bone modification are represented in the Cerro de Trincheras assemblage; however, considering the diminutive overall particle size of the average specimen, this is not surprising. Examples are recorded from specimens recovered in nine of the 14 excavation units, which suggests that non-human attrition took place throughout the site. The most frequently recorded modifications include chewing and/or tooth puncture marks, possible gastric etching from partial digestion, and visible rodent gnawing.

Chewing/puncture marks (n = 8) are generally restricted to longbone shafts of mammals, although one rib and one scapular glenoid specimen of indeterminate mammal taxa, are recorded with carnivore imprints. In two cases, identified mammalian taxa with chewing/puncture modification include specimens from one *Odocoileus* metapodial shaft and one *Lepus* distal tibial shaft.

Evidence for possible gastric modification of partially digested materials (n = 14) is restricted to smaller taxa, either small or medium-sized rodents, and in one case, a possible *Sylvilagus* calcaneum fragment. Two examples are recorded from Area D, and all the rest are recovered from deposits located in Area A1. At least three concentrations of gastric damaged bone specimens are located in the highest precincts of Area A1, and could represent the regurgitated meals of a raptor. The archaeofaunal subsample from Area A1 is the only spatial sample on the site that is both significantly low in richness and maximal in evenness (Figure 11.1). The majority of identified archaeofaunal categories in this area are from small taxa, particularly rodents. These and other lines of evidence are returned to below in a discussion of assemblage accumulation.

Evidence for rodent gnawing (n = 7) is generally found in terrace units (B1, B4, B6, B7) with one example from Area E. Each of the terrace fragments occurs on mammalian longbone specimens; three examples from indeterminate large mammals, one from an indeterminate medium mammal, and one from the proximal portion of an *Odocoileus* metatarsus. The Area E example is located on an indeterminate fragment of an unidentified mammal.

Cultural Attritional Variables

Evidence of cut marks on specimens is very rare (n = 3), undoubtedly due to the overall small average particle size within the archaeofaunal assemblage. These marks are restricted to mammalian elements recovered from terrace excavation units. One large mammalian longbone in Area B2 has two transverse marks on what appears to be a distal shaft portion. Another large mammalian longbone in Area B5 also appears with two transverse cut marks, and an indeterminate fragment from a large mammal bone from Area B10 has one possible cut mark.

A relatively large number of bones within the Cerro de Trincheras archaeofaunal assemblage (n = 1868, 23.3 percent) appear to have been subjected to various degrees of heat treatment. Arbitrary stages of heat treatment, based on surface coloration are recorded where appropriate, following Gilchrist and Mytum (1986:32). Pale brown to reddish brown coloration, representing low fire temperatures (200°-300°C) is recorded for 75 (4 percent) of the heat-treated bone. Dark brown to blackish coloration, representing moderate fire temperature (300°-400° C) is recorded for 209 (11.2 percent) of the heat-treated bone. Dark blue-grey to light grey coloration, representing high fire temperature (400°-500° C) is recorded for 429 (23 percent) of the heat-treated bone. The majority of the heat-treated specimens (n = 1155, 61.8 percent) appears to have been calcined (pinkish-grey to white, 500°+). It is, however, often difficult to visually separate calcined from bleached bone, and it is cautioned that somewhat over one half of the calcined specimens are found in surficial contexts. Nevertheless, with the exception of Area B5, surprisingly few of these calcined specimens were recovered in spatially level areas, where it is suspected that bone specimens were subjected to the greatest degree of sub aerial weathering. The overwhelming majority of calcined fragments (n = 993, 86 percent) are found in terrace units.

Virtually all of the heat-treated bone (n = 1747, 93.5 percent) consists of some indeterminate (to class), and a relatively large amount of indeterminate mammal fragments. Within the subsample of heat treated indeterminate mammal bone (n = 1467), 688 specimens are only identified as indeterminate mammal bone, whereas 563 and 210 derive from large and medium mammalian taxa respectively; only six specimens could be identified as small mammalian taxa. This might suggest that heat treatment, whether for food consumption, tool manufacture, or post-consumption discard acted as an attritional variable in the destruction of skeletal portion from large and medium-sized mammals. This is corroborated to some extent by the heat-treated specimens of *Odocoileus* and Artiodactyla that survive in sufficient condition for identification. This small subset of 38 specimens is almost completely comprised of element portions with relatively high structural density, including metapodia and phalanges, as well as antlers and teeth. Heat treatment of surviving leporid specimens (n = 51) appears to be particularly concentrated on the appendages, especially the lower limbs and manus/pes.

A detailed analysis of cultural modification is considered by Radhika Sundararajan in her separate study of modified animal bone from Cerro de Trincheras (Chapter 9). The total of 181 archaeofaunal specimens that appear variably polished and/or otherwise modified are examined here only as potential variables in assemblage formation. Modified bone is often heat treated (n = 86, 47.5 percent), mainly at lower firing temperatures (e.g., < 400° C). The entire subset of modified bone is restricted to indeterminate (n = 5), and principally mammalian (n = 176) specimens. The majority of examples appear to have been modified and/or fragmented so extensively that they could not be identified lower then the level of zoological Class. A total of 144 specimens are identified only as "mammal", 111 (77.1 percent) of which are classed as large and medium examples. The majority of these specimens (n = 119, 82.6 percent) include indeterminate longbone fragments. Identifiable mammalian taxa whose bone remains are modified, include only *Lepus* and *Odocoileus* (including examples of indeterminate Artiodactyla). Eight lagomorph specimens include possible notching of three *Lepus* teeth, two polished distal humeri, and one polished example each of a scapula, tibia, and metapodium. The 24 modified Artiodactyla specimens are represented only by durable elements and/or respective portions of metapodia (n = 16), scapulae (n = 4), and antlers (n = 3). The majority are awls fashioned from metapodia and antlers, in addition to a metapodial rasp, and the typical notching of scapular spines and borders.

It may be significant that the majority of modified archaeofaunal specimens are spatially concentrated within the terrace excavation units at Cerro de Trincheras. Of the 181 modified specimens, 159 (87.9 percent) were recovered from deposits in the sloping terrace units (Table 11.29), where the overwhelming majority of calcined bone, consisting of medium to large-bodied mammals is located. This is also the only area from which bones with cut marks were recovered. A small portion (n = 26, 14.4 percent) of the modified bone elements is found within special construction features throughout the site, but mainly in these terrace units. This might suggest that terrace areas were more heavily involved in bone tool manufacture/use/discard than areas adjoining the site; however, it is also possible that more tools were once discarded in the lower level areas but were subsequently destroyed beyond recognition (e.g., weathering).

Finally, there is some evidence to suggest that one of the lower and more level terrace areas, Area B5, may have been subject to at least some attrition from heavy machinery. Over 95 percent of the bone specimens recovered in this area are not identifiable to any category lower than the level of zoological class. For the relative size of the archaeofaunal subsample recovered in this excavation area, it is characteristically low in richness and exhibits minimal evenness of identified specimen categories. Relative frequencies are dominated by as few as 12 *Lepus* specimens, and a further six *Ammospermophilus* specimens which may be intrusive. The increased accessibility of these lower units to various disturbance mechanisms further underscores the greater potential that steeper terrace locations have for overall specimen preservation.

Assemblage Accumulation

Much of the archaeofaunal assemblage from Cerro de Trincheras had certainly accumulated after and before the Cerro reverted to a locally significant habitat for vertebrate predator and prey alike. However, the recovered deposits are undoubtedly also the partial accumulations of non-human factors. Today, circling buzzards are only the most conspicuous of a host of predators inhabiting the Cerro. Numerous raptors use its higher precincts as convenient roosts from which to soar above the adjacent agricultural fields in search of prey, whereas various resident and non-resident terrestrial carnivores roam its flanks in pursuit of a broad menu of prey items that inhabit the protective crags of its rocky terraces.

In general, what can be identified in the Cerro de Trincheras archaeofaunal assemblage suggests the accumulation of a relatively limited range of faunas, which tend to be dominated by a few taxonomic categories (Figure 11.1). Some of these categories appear in virtually every excavated context at the site: *Lepus* and *Odocoileus* in each of the 14 areas; some form of rodent and turtle specimen in all but one area; and, *Sylvilagus* remains in all but two areas. However, for each taxa, respective concentrations of bone specimens indicate patterned variation across the excavation units.

Rodent remains are found in 175 excavation units across the site. In 64 (36.6 percent) of these contexts, their identifiable remains are found in concentrations of two or more, and I suspect that this figure would increase dramatically with the inclusion of flotation fraction from the 1996 excavation season. It is important to note some high concentrations of rodent remains, particularly in Area A1. Over forty percent of the excavated units at this eastern summit of the site contain rodent bone concentrations, especially within El Caracol, which yielded as many as 81 identifiable rodent bones. High concentrations of rodent material were recovered from five relatively contiguous units. Many of these specimens are characterized by the glossy surface appearance typical of recent intrusive material, and at least three caudal vertebrae from one animal were recovered articulated. Spatially associated and highly diagnostic dental elements suggest that many of the larger specimens are likely the remains of *Neotoma*, and that some of the smaller specimens are likely the remains of Heteromyids, especially *Perognathus*, as well as *Sigmodon*. The vertebral remains of small snakes are also particularly abundant in surficial contexts from Area A1, especially within El Caracol. Some of these specimens, including one urostyle of a small anuran, display the glossy surface appearance typical of recent intrusive material. On the basis of their recovered condition and context (e.g., Stahl 1996), I strongly suspect that many, if not most, of the bone specimens in this high elevation precinct are the remains of prey items introduced by roosting raptors from the adjacent fields below.

Identifiable Heteromyid and *Neotoma* dental elements are implicated in spatial concentrations across the site; however, it is interesting to note that no *Peromyscus* remains are found in Area A1. Some examples were recovered from deposits in the relatively open Areas D and E; however, most were recovered from rocky terrace units. Many of these diminutive rodents live in the site's rocky crags today, and the possibility of intrusion through non-predator-related death cannot be ruled out. The floated contents of a globular *olla* retrieved from the domestic fill of Jacal 2 (Area B2) contain the remains of *Peromy-*

scus, a Heteromyid rodent, small lizard, and two tiny fish vertebrae. Due to a concentration of small rodent bones in and under the *olla*, I suspect that the rodent remains are likely post-depositional intrusions, whereas the fish vertebrae represent the prehistoric contents of the pot. Three isolated contexts across the site yielded concentrations of larger-bodied rodent bone, much of which was relatively complete. These include concentrations of *Spermophilus variegatus* bone in fill from Area B1, and two contexts with the relatively complete remains of *Ammospermophilus harrisii* in Areas B5 and E. Both taxa are common inhabitants of the site today.

Leporid bone specimens were recovered from more excavation units across the site than any other identifiable taxon. Of the 276 units with leporid bone specimens, 74 (26.8 percent) have concentrations of two or more bones, the highest including 15 specimens in Area E. With the exception of some significant surficial concentrations in Area A1, *Sylvilagus* specimens are usually found as isolated bones in terrace contexts. *Sylvilagus* is an important menu item for a variety of raptors and terrestrial carnivores, and I suspect that the surficial, weathered specimens in Area A1 are the remains of a recent meal. On the other hand, *Lepus* specimens are found in greater concentrations of two or more bones (61/250, 24.4 percent), and are abundantly represented in every excavation area. I suspect that the relatively isolated occurrences and the possible predator-related concentrations of *Sylvilagus* specimens probably explain why they display density-mediated survivorship on the site. This would be consistent with the density-dependent survivorship of Artiodactyla remains that are found in 134 excavation unit contexts, but with only 19 (14.1 percent) yielding concentrations of two or more specimens. One buried context in Area B1 contributed as many as 16 weathered fragments, possibly from the peduncle and tines of a cervid antler. Turtle remains, representing at least two taxa (*Terrapene* and *Gopherus*) are restricted to only 53 excavation units, virtually all of which are located on the sloping terraces. Only 15 (28 percent) of these contexts yielded concentrations of two or more Chelonid specimens, usually carapace and/or plastron fragments.

Some of the recovered archaeofaunal materials are obviously recent intrusive accumulations, and were omitted from most of the analyses. Two almost complete thoracic vertebrae of some kind of horse or burro (*Equus* spp.) were identified in deposits recovered from Area B11, and are associated with a fairly recent burial intrusion. Two isolated specimens of Domestic Cattle (*Bos* spp.) are identified on the Cerro. A buried distal metapodium with surviving shaft portion was uncovered in deposits at the Cerro summit in Area A1, and surficial contexts in Area B6 yielded the unfused first phalanx of an immature cow. Finally, various egg shell specimens were collected in surficial contexts from the high terraces of Areas B7, 8, and 9. They likely represent the unsuccessful reproductive ventures of local nesting birds on the site.

Summary and Discussion

Some general characteristics of the excavated Cerro de Trincheras archaeofaunal sample include small particle size, high fragmentation, and isolated recovery from spatially dispersed deposits throughout the site. These interrelated characteristics of assemblage survivorship are likely implicated, along with varying body size, in a differentially patterned history of assemblage accumulation and attrition. Bone accumulations of relatively diminutive taxa, especially small and medium-sized rodents, and presumably also amphibians, lizards, and snakes are probably intrusive to the prehistoric cultural deposits. These accumulations are generally characterized by relatively comprehensive skeletal representation, element completeness, and spatial concentration. I suspect that many specimens from the smallest taxa were likely lost during recovery; otherwise their appearance would have been akin to a pervasive background 'rain' of faunal specimens. Furthermore, rare cases of gastric damage, articulated elements, and intrusive appearance lend credence to the suggestion that many, if not most, of the archaeologically visible small taxon specimen concentrations can be attributed to predation and/or non-predator-related in situ death.

The survivorship of *Lepus* specimens are not significantly correlated with structural bone density; however, those of *Sylvilagus* are. The density-dependent survivorship of smaller rabbit remains may be due to recovery loss, however, in at least one specific context they likely represent the remains of an unknown raptor's meal. The relatively isolated spatial survivorship of *Sylvilagus* bones is more like the survivorship of *Odocoileus* specimens, which is significantly density mediated and spatially dispersed in various contexts throughout the site. With the exception of the special concentration of *Rhyncopsitta* bones, this also characterizes the survivorship of most larger bird and carnivore remains in the assemblage. Accumulations of larger animals generally include skeletal representation restricted to certain portions of the skeleton, higher fragmentation, and spatially isolated survivorship. The rare examples of complete elements, especially from *Odocoileus,* usually include durable bones of the distal appendages. Attritional factors are many in the Sonoran desert. Significant numbers of weathered bone from larger taxa were recovered in excavation units with gentler topographical gradients and increased surface exposure. Rare evidence of rodent gnawing on large mammal bones is restricted to terrace units, which are currently inhabited by larger sciurids like *Spermophilus variegatus.* Prehistoric cultural consumption and discard are also likely factors in the prehistoric attrition of bones from larger mammalian taxa on these terrace units. The few examples of cut marked bones, and the highest concentrations of heat-treated and culturally modified specimens were recovered from deposits in terrace excavation units.

Multiple lines of evidence lead me to believe that the majority of small-bodied taxa recovered during excavations at Cerro de Trincheras are intrusive to the prehistoric cultural deposits. These include all, or certainly most, of the smaller rodents (e.g., *Thomomys, Reithrodontomys/Perognathus, Perognathus, Peromyscus, Sigmodon, Neotoma*), and probably some of the medium-sized taxa as well (e.g., specific concentrations of *Sylvilagus, Ammospermophilus, Spermophilus*). I suspect that we could add most of the small reptiles and amphibians to this list as well. I suggest that all or most of the *Lepus, Odocoileus* and turtle or tortoise remains are prehistoric cultural accumulations, and were introduced up on to the site from the surrounding plains and/or nearby hills. To this list, I would add probably all or most of the relatively isolated mammalian carnivore and bird remains. The specimen concentrations of *Rhyncopsitta pachyrhyncus* are likely a unique context, possibly representing the (unsuccessful) care of a young parrot. Similarily, if the identification of a possible domestic dog (*Canis familiaris*) is valid, then this would also suggest the presence of at least one kind of animal domesticate on the site.

The Cerro de Trincheras archaeofaunal assemblage is dominated by indeterminate mammalian bone fragments. Those specimens that could be further identified are typical of local arid landscapes, and reveal an assemblage characteristically low in richness and dominated by a few key taxa that were likely of prehistoric significance, especially jack rabbits, cottontails, and some species of deer. The remains of birds and mammalian carnivores are present, although sporadically recovered from deposits throughout the site. Many smaller rodents are represented in the assemblage, but certainly most of the smaller specimens are intrusive. In most respects, the Cerro de Trincheras archaeofaunal assemblage does not differ significantly from the majority of studied Hohokam archaeofaunal assemblages (Gasser and Kwiatkowski 1991:444; Greene and Mathews 1976; Szuter 1991a:70).

The actual degree to which the prehistoric inhabitants of the northern Sonoran deserts of México culturally modified their landscape for subsistence pursuits is difficult to infer from this small archaeofaunal sample alone. Nevertheless, certain patterns are broadly similar to Szuter's (1991b) interesting implications of agriculturally induced landscape modifications by Hohokam desert horticulturalists for prehistoric faunal exploitation. The overall frequencies of small and medium-sized rodent taxa in the assemblage are quite high, a factor that I suspect is indeed associated with aspects of landscape alteration. However, if my suspicion that most, if not all, of the smaller and certainly some of the larger rodent remains are not prehistoric cultural accumulations is valid, then this implication is not necessarily associated with a prehistoric landscape alteration.

Dietary inferences drawn from the Cerro de Trincheras assemblage, like all its contemporaneous counterparts across the international border, suggest a heavy reliance on medium-sized game animals, especially lagomorphs and likely some of the larger rodents. Cottontails are certainly far less frequent than jack rabbits in the assemblage. The "lagomorph index" (Szuter and Bayham 1989) at the site is 12.6, or well below the maximum suggested ratio for larger village sites that are expected to impact local surroundings more profoundly than their smaller farmstead counterparts (Szuter 1991b:285). The obviously greater importance of jack rabbits may indeed reflect a significant degree of land clearance below the site for farming activities, a scenario that is also apparent in the contemporary agricultural fields surrounding the modern town of Trincheras. On the other hand, the corresponding "artiodactyl index" is a relatively low 29.5, more typical of upland sites less committed to farming activities (Szuter and Bayham 1989:91). Whether or not these indices represent inferential evidence for substantial landscape modification as a factor of prehistoric horticulture, it is important to caution that the respective NISP values of Lagomorpha and Artiodactyla used in their calculations are variably mediated by structural density. The relatively high frequencies of *Lepus* are as likely to be affected by a lack of density-dependent survivorship as the relatively low frequencies of *Odocoileus* are affected by density-dependent survivorship. The exact mechanisms for this variable survivorship may always remain equivocal; however, prehistoric cultural consumption and discard are strongly implicated in the survivorship of larger artiodactyl remains.

There are some water-associated taxa identified in the assemblage. For example, if the tentative identification of *Rana catesbeiana* is at all valid, this would suggest some watered conditions in the local vicinity. Similar inferences might also be drawn from the identification of *Terrapene* elements, as this taxon's activity is controlled to a large extent by the availability of water (Ernst and Barbour 1989:197). The remains of some kind of duck might also be suggestive of watered environments; however, the area is today visited by a broad variety of non-resident birds, including many migrant waterfowl (Table 11.4). Certainly, their remains are not uncommon, having been identified in other contemporaneous prehistoric contexts from south-central Arizona (Szuter 1991a:72).

In at least one excavated context, the vertebral remains of a small, unidentified fish were recovered from the contents of an *olla* associated with a domestic construction.

As a final thought, many of the archaeological inferences suggested herein remain inconclusive. A certain degree of equifinality is typical of all interpretations based on the analysis of recovered archaeofaunal assemblages. Some of the suggested inferences await corroboration or refutation from additional types of archaeological evidence at the site. Comparison with similar assemblages from the northern Sonoran desert of México would be beneficial; however, this must await further study. This initial impression of the zooarchaeological record from Cerro de Trincheras represents the first of its kind, and hopefully can be used as a standard for future comparisons.

TABLES FOR CHAPTER 11

Table 11.1. Numerical Summary of Recovered Archaeofaunal Materials

Taxon/Category	Total Number Recovered	MNI	MNE
Indeterminate	1963		
Decapoda Indet.	1		
Osteichthyes Indet.	3		
Anura Indet.	9		
Bufo spp.	2	1	1
cf. *Bufo* spp.	2		
cf. *Rana catesbiaena*	1	1	1
Reptilia Indet	12		
cf. Reptilia	1		
Chelonia Indet.	82		
Chelonia Indet?	1		
cf. Chelonia Indet.	4		
Terrapene spp.	3	1	1
cf. *Terrapene* spp.	1		
Gopherus spp.	1	1	1
cf. *Gopherus* spp.	6		
Sauria Indet.	16		
cf. *Crotaphytus* spp.	1	1	1
Phrynosoma spp.	1	1	1
Scincidae	2	1	1
Serpentes Indet.	39		
Aves Indet.	48		
cf. Aves	2		
Anatinae	1	1	1
cf. *Cathartes* spp.	1	1	1
Buteo spp.	1	1	1
cf. Phasianidae	1	1	1
Columbidae	1	1	1
cf. Columbidae	1	1	1
cf. *Rhyncopsitta pachyrhynchus*	11	1	1
cf. *Geococcyx californianus*	1	1	1
cf. Corvidae	1	1	1
Mamalia Indet.	4565		
Leporidae	5	1	2
Sylvilagus spp.	45	5	20
cf. *Sylvilagus* spp.	8		
Lepus spp.	324	18	81
cf. *Lepus* spp.	42		
Rodentia Indet.	403		
cf. Rodentia Indet.	2		
Sciuridae	39	3	13
cf. Sciuridae	3		
Ammospermophilus spp.	4	2	2

Table 11.1. Numerical Summary of Recovered Archaeofaunal Materials, cont'd

Taxon/Category		Total Number Recovered	MNI	MNE
Mamalia (cont.)	cf. *Ammospermophilus* spp.	3		
	Ammospermophilus harrisi	2		
	cf. *Ammospermophilus harrisii*	4		
	Spermophilus variegatus	20	3	9
	Spermophilus cf. variegatus	1		
	cf. *Spermophilus variegatus*	12		
	Thomomys bottae	1	1	1
	Heteromyidae	3	1	1
	Reithrodontomys/Perognathus	9	2	6
	Perognathus spp.	10		
	cf. *Perognathus* spp.	3	4	4
	Peromyscus spp.	2		
	Peromyscus eremicus	4		
	Peromyscus cf. *eremicus*	4		
	Sigmodon spp.	5	2	2
	Neotoma spp.	46	9	9
	Neotoma cf. *albigula*	1		
	cf. *Neotoma* spp.	3		
	Carnivora Indet.	7		
	cf. Carnivora Indet.	1		
	Canidae	8	2	3
	cf. Canidae	2		
	Canis spp.	5	2	3
	Canis cf. *familiaris*	1	1	1
	Nasua spp.	2	1	2
	Nasua nasua	1		
	cf. *Nasua* spp.	1		
	Taxidea spp.	4	1	4
	Taxidea taxus	3		
	cf. *Taxidea* spp.	1		
	cf. *Taxidea taxus*	2		
	Felis concolor	1	1	1
	Equus spp.	2	1	1
	Artiodactyla Indet.	19		
	Artiodactyla Indet?	5		
	Cervidae	3	1	2
	Odocoileus spp.	106	5	12
	cf. *Odocoileus* spp.	40		
	Bos spp.	1	1	1
	cf. *Bos* spp.	1	1	1
	Total	8009		

Table 11.2. Indeterminate Remains

Element	Portion	Quantity
Cranial	Fragment	7
Tooth	Fragment	4
Vertebra	Fragment	1
Caudal Vertebra	Fragment	1
Longbone	Complete	1
	Shaft	12
	Fragment	71
Phalanx	Fragment	1
Shell?	Fragment	2
Indeterminate	Fragment	1839
Total		1963

Table 11.3. Amphibian Remains

Taxon	Element	NISP	MNI	MNE
Anura	Humerus Distal	4		
	Humerus Shaft	1		
	Ulna Proximal	1		
	Tibia Almost Complete	1		
	Urostyle Almost Complete	2		
cf. *Bufo*	Atlas Fragment	1	1	1
	Ischium Complete	1	1	1
Bufo	Acetabulum (ilium)	1	1	1
	Sacrum Almost Complete	1	1	1
cf. *Rana catesbeiana*	Vertebra Almost Complete	1	1	1
Totals		14	5	5

Table 11.4. Resident and Migrant Native Vertebrate Faunas with Potential Contemporary Range Extensions into the Northern Portions of the Sonoran Desert in México (compiled from Hoffmeister 1986; Howell and Webb: 1995; Peterson 1990; Stebbins 1985)

		Amphibia	
Anura			
	Pelobatidae	*Scaphiophus couchii*	Couch Spadefoot
		Scaphiophus hammondi	Western Spadefoot
		Scaphiophus multiplicatus	Southern Spadefoot
	Bufonidae	*Bufo alvarius*	Sonoran Desert Toad
		Bufo punctatus	Red-spotted Toad
		Bufo cognatus	Great Plains Toad
		Bufo retiformia	Sonoran Green Toad
	Hylidae	*Pternhyla fodiens*	Northern Casque-headed Frog
	Ranidae	*Rana yavapaiensis*	Lowland Leopard Frog
		Rana catesbeiana	Bullfrog
	Mycrohylidae	*Gastrophryne olivacea*	Sinaloan Narrow-mouthed Toad
		Reptilia	
Chelonia			
	Kinosternidae	*Kinosternon flavescens*	Yellow Mud Turtle
		Kinosternon sonoriense	Sonoran Mud Turtle
	Emydidae	*Terrapene ornata*	Desert Box Turtle
	Testudinidae	*Gopherus agassizii*	Desert Tortoise
	Gekkonidae	*Coleonyx variegatus*	Desert Banded Gecko
	Iguanidae	*Dipsosaurus dorsalis*	Desert Iguana
		Sauromalus obesus	Common Chuckwalla
		Holbrookia maculata	Lesser Earless Lizard
		Cophosaurus texanus	Greater Earless Lizard
		Callisaurus draconoides	Zebra-tailed Lizard
		Crotaphytus collaris	Sonoran Collared Lizard
		Gambelia wislizenii	Large-spotted Leopard Lizard
		Sceloporus magister	Sonoran Spiny Lizard
		Uta stansburiana	Side-blotched Lizard
		Urosaurus graciosus	Arizona Brush Lizard
		Urosaurus ornatus	Tree Lizard
		Phrynosoma platyrhinos	Desert Horned Lizard
		Phrynosoma solare	Regal Horned Lizard
	Scincidae	*Eumeces callicephalus*	Mountain Skink
	Teiidae	*Cnemidophorus burti*	Giant Spotted Whiptail
		Cnemidophorus sonorae	Sonoran Spotted Whiptail
		Cnemidophorus tigris	Painted Desert Whiptail
	Helodermatidae	*Heloderma suspectum*	Gila Monster
	Leptotyphlopidae	*Leptotyphlops humilis*	Western Blind Snake
	Boidae	*Lichanura trivirgata*	Mexican Rosy Boa
	Colubridae	*Phyllorhynchus decurtatus*	Spotted Leaf-nosed Snake
		Phyllorhynchus browni	Pima Leaf-nosed Snake
		Masticophis flagellum	Sonoran Coachwhip
		Masticophis bilineatus	Sonoran Mountain Whipsnake
		Salvadora hexalepis	Desert Patch-Nosed Snake
		Arizona elegans	Arizona Glossy Snake
		Pituophis melanoleucus	Sonoran Gopher Snake
		Lampropeltis getulus	Black King Snake
		Rhinocheilus lecontei	Long-nosed Snake

Table 11.4. Resident and Migrant Native Vertebrate Faunas with Potential Contemporary Range Extensions into the Northern Portions of the Sonoran Desert in México, cont'd

	Thamnophis cyrtopsis	Black-necked Garter Snake	
	Thamnophis marcianus	Checkered Garter Snake	
	Sonora semiannulata	Ground Snake	
	Chionactis palarostris	Sonoran Shovel-nosed Snake	
	Chilomeniscus cinctus	Banded Sand Snake	
	Trimorphodon biscutatus	Sonoran Lyre Snake	
	Hypsiglena torquate	Night Snake	
Elapidae	*Micruroides euryxanthus*	Western Coral Snake	
Viperidae	*Crotalus atrox*	Western Diamondback Rattlesnake	
	Crotalus cerastes	Sidewinder	
	Crotalus molossus	Black-tailed Rattlesnake	
	Crotalus tigris	Tiger Rattlesnake	
	Crotalus scutulatus	Mojave Rattlesnake	
	Aves (B=Breeding; W=Winter; R=Resident)		
Podicepedidae	*Podilymbus podiceps*	Pied-Billed Grebe	B
	Podiceps nigricolis	Eared Grebe	W
	Aechmophorus occidentalis	Western Grebe	W
Threskiornithidae	*Botaurus lentiginosus*	American Bittern	W
	Nycticorax nicticorax	Black-crowned Night Heron	W
Ardeidae	*Ardea herodias*	Great Blue Heron	W
	Casmerodius albus	Great Egret	W
Anatidae	*Chen caerulescens*	Snow Goose	W
	Branta canadensis	Canada Goose	W
	Anas crecca	Green-winged Teal	W
	Anas paltyrhynchos	Mallard	W
	Anas acuta	Northern Pintail	W
	Anas cyanoptera	Cinnamon Teal	
	Anas clypeata	Northern Shoveler	W
	Anas strepera	Gadwall	W
	Anas americana	American Widgeon	W
	Aythya valisineria	Canvasback	W
	Aythya affinis	Lesser Scaup	W
	Bucephala albeola	Bufflehead	W
	Mergus merganser	Common Merganser	W
	Oxyura jamaicensis	Ruddy Duck	W
Cathartidae	*Cathartes aura*	Turkey Vulture	R
Accipitridae	*Circus cyaneus*	Northern Harrier	W
	Accipiter striatus	Sharp-shinned Hawk	W
	Accipiter cooperi	Cooper's Hawk	
	Buteo jamaicensis	Red-tailed Hawk	R
	Buteo regalis	Ferruginous Hawk	W
	Aquila chrysaeotus	Golden Eagle	R
	Polyborus plancus	Crested Caracara	R
Falconidae	*Falco sparverius*	American Kestrel	R
	Falco mexicanus	Prairie Falcon	
Phasianidae	*Meleagris gallopavo*	Wild Turkey	R
	Cyrtonyx montezumae	Montezuma Quail	R
	Callipepla squamata	Scaled Quail	R
	Callipepla gambeli	Gambel's Quail	R

Table 11.4. Resident and Migrant Native Vertebrate Faunas with Potential Contemporary Range Extensions into the Northern Portions of the Sonoran Desert in México, cont'd

Rallidae	*Rallus limicola*	Virginia Rail	W
	Porzama carolina	Sora Rail	W
	Gallinula chloropus	Common Moorehen	R
	Fulica americana	American Coot	R
Charadriidae	*Charadrius vociferus*	Killdeer	R
Scolopacidae	*Tringa melanoleuca*	Greater Yellowlegs	W
	Actitis macularia	Spotted Sandpiper	W
	Calidris minutilla	Least Sandpiper	W
	Limnodromus scolopaceus	Long-billed Dowitcher	W
	Gallingo gallingo	Common Snipe	W
Laridae	*Larus delawarensis*	Ring-billed Gull	W
Columbidae	*Columba fasciata*	Band-tailed Pigeon	R
	Zenaida asiatica	White-winged Dove	R
	Zenaida macroura	Mourning Dove	B
	Columbina inca	Inca Dove	R
	Columbina passerina	Common Ground-Dove	R
Cuculidae	*Coccyzcus americanus*	Yellow-billed Cuckoo	B
	Geococcyx californicus	Greater Roadrunner	R
Strigidae	*Tyto alba*	Barn Owl	R
	Otus flammeolus	Flammulated Owl	B
	Otus kennicottii	Western Screech-owl	R
	Bubo virginianus	Great Horned Owl	R
	Glaucidium gnoma	Northern Pygmy Owl	R
	Micrathene whitneyi	Elf Owl	B
	Athene cunicularia	Burrowing Owl	R
	Strix occidentalis	Spotted Owl	R
	Asio flammeus	Short-eared Owl	W
Caprimulgidae	*Chordeiles acutipennis*	Lesser Nighthawk	B
	Chordeiles minor	Common Nighthawk	B
	Phalaenoptilus nuttallii	Common Poorwill	W
	Caprimulgua vociferus	Whip-poor-will	B
Apodidae	*Aeronautes saxatalis*	White-throated Swift	R
Trochilidae	*Archilocus alexandri*	Black-chinned Hummingbird	B
	Calypte anna	Anna's Hummingbird	B
	Calypte costae	Costa's Hummingbird	B
Alcedinidae	*Ceryle alcyon*	Belted Kingfisher	W
Picidae	*Melanerpes formicivorus*	Acorn Woodpecker	R
	Melanerpes uropygialis	Gila Woodpecker	R
	Sphyrapicus nuchalis	Red-naped Sapsucker	W
	Sphyrapicus thryoideus	Williamson's Sapsucker	W
	Picoides scalaris	Ladder-backed Woodpecker	R
	Picoides villosus	Hairy Woodpecker	R
	Colaptes auratus	Northern Flicker	R
Tyrannidae	*Contopus sordidulus*	Western Wood-Peewee	B
	Empidonax wrightii	Gray Flycatcher	W
	Empidonax hammondi	Hammond's Flycatcher	W
	Empidonax oberholseri	Dusky Flyctcher	W

Table 11.4. Resident and Migrant Native Vertebrate Faunas with Potential Contemporary Range Extensions into the Northern Portions of the Sonoran Desert in México, cont'd

Tyrannidae (cont'd)	*Empidonax occidentalis*	Cordilleran Flycatcher	W
	Sayornis nigricans	Black Phoebe	
	Sayornis saya	Say's Phoebe	R
	Pyrocephalus rubinus	Vermillion Flycatcher	R
	Myiarchus cinerascens	Ash-throated Flycatcher	R
	Tyrannus vociferans	Cassin's Kingbird	B
	Tyrannus verticalis	Western Kingbird	B
Alaudidae	*Eremophilia alpestris*	Horned Lark	R
Hirundinidae	*Progne subis*	Purple Martin	B
	Tachycineta bicolor	Tree Swallow	W
	Tachycineta thalassina	Violet-green Swallow	B
	Stegidopteryx serripennis	N. Rough-winged Swallow	B
	Hirunda pyrrhonota	Cliff Swallow	B
	Hirunda rustica	Barn Swallow	B
Corvidae	*Cyanocitta stelleri*	Steller's Jay	R
	Aphelocoma coerulescens	Scrub Jay	R
	Aphelocoma ultramarina	Gray-brested Jay	R
	Corvus cryptoleucus	Chihuahuan Raven	R
	Corvus corax	Common Raven	R
Paridae	*Auriparus flaviceps*	Verdin	R
Aegithalidae	*Psaltriparus minimus*	Bushtit	R
Sittidae	*Sitta carolinensis*	White-breasted Nuthatch	R
	Sitta pygmaea	Pygmy Nutchatch	R
Certhidae	*Campylorhynchus brunnneicapillus*	Cactus Wren	R
	Salpinctes obsoletus	Rock Wren	R
	Catherpes mexicanus	Canyon Wren	R
	Thryomanes bewickii	Bewick's Wren	
	Troglodytes aedon	House Wren	
	Cistothorus palustris	Marsh Wren	W
Muscicapidae	*Regulus calendula*	Ruby-crowned Kinglet	W
	Polioptila caerulea	Blue-gray Gnatcatcher	R
	Polioptila melanura	Black-tailed Gnatcatcher	R
	Sialia sialis	Eastern Bluebird	R
	Sialia mexicana	Western Bluebird	W
	Sialia currucoides	Mountain Bluebird	W
	Myadestes townsendi	Townsend's Solitaire	W
	Catharus guttatus	Hermit Thrush	W
	Turdus migratorius	American Robin	
Mimidae	*Mimus polyglottos*	Northern Mockingbird	R
	Oreoscoptes montanus	Sage Thrasher	W
	Toxostoma bendirei	Bendire's Thrasher	
	Toxostoma curvirostre	Curve-Billed Thrasher	R
	Toxostoma crissale	Crissal Thrasher	R
Motacillidae	*Anthus rubescens*	American Pipit	W
	Anthus spragueii	Sprague's Pipit	W

Table 11.4. Resident and Migrant Native Vertebrate Faunas with Potential Contemporary Range Extensions into the Northern Portions of the Sonoran Desert in México, cont'd

Bombycillidae	*Bombycilla cedrorum*	Cedar Waxwing	W
Ptilogonatidae	*Phainopepla nitens*	Phainopepla	R
Laniidae	*Lanius ludovicianus*	Loggerhead Shrike	R
Vireonidae	*Vireo bellii*	Vell's Vireo	B
	Vireo vicinor	Gray Vireo	W
	Vireo huttoni	Hutton's Vireo	R
	Vireo gilvus	Warbling Vireo	B
Emberiidae	*Vermivora celata*	Orange-crowned Warbler	W
	Vermivora luciae	Lucy's Warbler	B
	Dendroica petechia	Yellow Warbler	B
	Dendroica coronata	Yellow-rumped Warbler	
	Dendroica townsendi	Townsend's Warbler	W
	Dendroica graciae	Grace's Warbler	B
	Geothlypis trichas	Common Yellowthroat	R
	Cardellina rubrifrons	Red-faced Warbler	B
	Myioborus picta	Painted Redstart	R
	Icteria virens	Yellow-breasted Chat	B
	Peudramus taeniatus	Olive Warbler	R
	Piranga flava	Hepatic Tanager	R
	Piranga rubra	Summer Tanager	B
	Cardinalis cardinalis	Northern Cardinal	R
	Cardinalis sinuatus	Pyrrhuloxia	R
	Pheucticus melanocephalus	Black-headed Grosbeak	B
	Guiraca caerulea	Blue Grosbeak	
	Passerina amoena	Lazuli Bunting	B
	Passerina versicolor	Varied Bunting	B
	Piplio chlorurus	Green-tailed Towhee	W
	Piplio erythrophthalmus	Rufous-sided Towhee	
	Piplio fuscus	Canyon Towhee	R
	Aimophilia cassinii	Cassin's Sparrow	W
	Aimophilia ruficeps	Rufous-crowned Sparrow	R
	Spizella passerina	Chipping Sparrow	
	Spizella breweri	Brewer's Sparrow	W
	Spizella atrogularis	Black-chinned Sparrow	W
	Pooecetes gramineus	Vesper Sparrow	W
	Chondestes grammacus	Lark Sparrow	
	Amphispiza bilineata	Black-throated Sparrow	R
	Amphispiza belli	Sage Sparrow	W
	Calamospiza melanocorys	Lark Bunting	W
	Passerculus sandwichensis	Savannah Sparrow	W
	Ammodramus bairdii	Baird's Sparrow	W
	Ammodramus savannarum	Grashopper Sparrow	R
	Passerella iliaca	Fox Sparrow	W
	Melospiza lincolnii	Lincoln's Sparrow	W
	Zonotrichia leucophrys	White-crowned Sparrow	W
	Junco hyemalis	Dark-eyed Junco	W

Table 11.4. Resident and Migrant Native Vertebrate Faunas with Potential Contemporary Range Extensions into the Northern Portions of the Sonoran Desert in México, cont'd

	Emberiidae (cont'd)	*Calcarius lapponicus*	Chestnut-collared Longspur	W
		Agelaius phoeniceus	Red-winged Blackbird	B
		Sternella magna	Eastern Meadowlark	R
		Sternella neglecta	Western Meadowlark	W
		Xanthocephalus xanthocephalus	Yellow-headed Blackbird	W
		Euphagus carolinus	Brewer's Blackbird	W
		Quiscalus mexicanus	Great-tailed Grackle	R
		Molothrus aeneus	Brown-headed Cowbird	
		Icterus cucullatus	Hooded Oriole	R
		Icterus galbula	Northern Oriole	
		Icterus parisorum	Scott's Oriole	R
	Fringillidae	*Carpodacus cassinii*	Cassin's Finch	R
		Carpodacus mexicanus	House Finch	R
		Loxia curvirostra	Red Crossbill	R
		Cardeulis pinus	Pine Siskin	
		Cardeulis psaltria	Lesser Goldfinch	R
		Cardeulis lawrencei	Lawrence's Goldfinch	W
		Cardeulis tristis	American Goldfinch	W
		Coccothraustes vespertina	Evening Frossbeak	
		Mammalia		
Insectivora				
	Soricidae	*Notiosorex crawfordi*	Desert Shrew	
Chiroptera				
	Mormoopidae	*Mormoops megalophylla*	Ghost-faced Bat	
	Phyllostomidae	*Macrotus californicus*	California Leaf nosed Bat	
		Choeronycteris mexicana	Long-tongued Bat	
		Leptonycteris sanborni	Sanborn's Long-Nosed Nat	
	Vespertilionidae	*Myotis yumanensis*	Yuma Myotis	
		Myotis velifer	Cave Myotis	
		Myotis thysanodes	Fronged Myotis	
		Mytois californicus	California Myotis	
		Pipistrellus hesperus	Western Pipistrelle	
		Eptesicus fuscus	Big Brown Bat	
		Lasiurus ega	Southern Yellow Bat	
		Lasiurus cinereus	Hoary Bat	
		Plecotus townsendii	Townsend's Big-Eared Bat	
		Antrozous pallidus	Pallid Bat	
	Molossidae	*Tadarida brasiliensis*	American Free-tailed Bat	
		Tadarida femorosacca	Pocketed Free-tailed Bat	
		Tadarida macrotis	Big Free-tailed Bat	
		Eumops perotis	Western Mastiff Bat	
		Eumpos underwoodi	Underwood's Mastiff Bat	

Table 11.4. Resident and Migrant Native Vertebrate Faunas with Potential Contemporary Range Extensions into the Northern Portions of the Sonoran Desert in México, cont'd

	Leporidae	*Sylvilagus floridanus*	Eastern Cottontail
		Sylvilagus audubonii	Desert Cottontail
		Lepus californicus	Black-tailed Jack Rabbit
		Lepus alleni	Antelope Jack Rabbit
Rodentia			
	Sciuridae		
		Ammospermophilus harrisii	Harris' Antelope Squirrel
		Spermophilus variegatus	Rock Squirrel
		Spermophilus tereticaudus	Round-tailed Ground Squirrel
	Geomyidae	*Thomomys bottae*	Botta's Pocket Gopher
	Heteromyidae	*Perognathus amplus*	Arizona Pocket Mouse
		Perognathus intermedius	Rock Pocket Mouse
		Perognathus penicillatus	Desert Pocket Mouse
		Perognathus baileyi	Bailey's Pocket Mouse
		Dipodomys spectabilis	Banner-tailed Kangaroo Rat
		Dipidomys merriami	Merriam's Kangaroo Rat

Table 11.5. Reptilian Remains

Taxon	Element	NISP	MNI	MNE
cf. Reptilia	Phalanx Complete	1		
Reptilia	Vertebra Almost Complete	1		
	Vertebra Fragment	7		
	Caudal Vert. Almost Complete	1		
	Rib Complete	1		
	Rib Proximal	1		
	Ilium Fragment	1		
Chelonia?	Marginal Fragment	1		
cf. Chelonia	Vertebra Almost Complete	1		
	Plastron Fragment	2		
	Carapace Fragment	1		
Chelonia	Vertebra Fragment	1		
	Carapace Fragment	43		
	Costal Fragment	10		
	Hypolastron Fragment	1		
	Neural Fragment	1		
	Nuchal Fragment	1		
	Marginal Complete	4		
	Marginal Fragment	11		
	Marginal Almost Complete	2		
	Plastron Fragment	6		
	Scapulo-coracoid Fragment	1		
	Phalanx Complete	1		
cf. *Terrapene*	Marginal Complete	1		
Terrapene	Xiphiplastron Complete	2	1	1
	Carapace Fragment	1	1	1
cf. *Gopherus*	Marginal Complete	4		
	Marginal Almost Complete	1	1	1
	Costal Almost Complete	1	1	1
Gopherus	Nuchal Complete	1	1	1
Sauria	Cranial Fragment	1		
	Tooth Complete	1		
	Maxilla Fragment	1		
	Vertebra Complete	4		

Table 11.5. Reptilian Remains, cont'd

Taxon	Element	NISP	MNI	MNE
Sauria (cont'd)	Vertebra Almost Complete	2		
	Vertebra Fragment	1		
	Rib Proximal	1		
	Pelvis Fragment	1		
	Tibia Complete	1		
	Longbone Shaft	3		
cf. *Crotaphytus*	Maxilla Complete	1	1	1
Phrynosoma	Frontal Complete	1	1	1
Scincidae	Mandible Fragment	2	1	1
Serpentes	Vertebra Complete	30		
	Vertebra Almost Complete	2		
	Vertebra Fragment	4		
	Rib Proximal	3		
		170	8	8

Table 11.6. Avian Remains

Taxon	Element	NISP	MNI	MNE
cf. Aves	Scapula Blade	1		
	Humerus Distal	1		
Aves	Shell Fragment	18		
	Maxilla Complete	1		
	Vertebra Complete	3		
	Vertebra Almost Complete	1		
	Synsacrum Fragment	1		
	Coracoid Proximal	1		
	Coracoid Distal	2		
	Scapula Blade	1		
	Humerus Proximal	1		
	Humerus Distal	4		

Table 11.6. Avian Remains, cont'd

Taxon	Element	NISP	MNI	MNE
	Ulna Proximal	1		
	Ulna Shaft	1		
	Ulna Distal	2		
	Radius Distal	2		
	Tibiotarsus Proximal	1		
	Tibiotarsus Distal	2		
	Tarsometatarsus Shaft	1		
	Longbone Shaft	3		
	4th Phalanx Complete	1		
	Phalanx Complete	1		
Anatinae	Ulna Distal	1	1	1
cf. *Cathartes*	Ulna Proximal	1	1	1
Buteo	Humerus Distal	1	1	1
cf. Phasianidae	Phalanx Complete	1	1	1
cf. Columbidae	Ulna Distal	1	1	1
Columbidae	Humerus Distal	1	1	1
cf. *Rhyncopsitta*	Coracoid Proximal	1	1	1
	Scapula Complete	1		
	Humerus Distal	1		
	Radius Proximal	1		
	Ulna Proximal	1		
	Carpometacarpus	1		
	Femur Distal	2		
	Tibiotarsus Proximal	2		
	Tarsometatarsus Complete	1		
cf. *Geococcyx*	Tarsometatarsus Complete	1	1	1
cf. Corvidae	Humerus Shaft	1	1	1
		69	9	9

Table 11.7. Indeterminate Mammal Remains

Element	Portion	Quantity
Cranial	Fragment	84
Alveolus	Fragment	1
Tooth	Fragment	18
Vertebra	Almost Complete	1
	Centrum Fragment	1
	Fragment	3
Rib	Fragment	46
Tibia	Shaft Fragment	1
Longbone	Fragment	453
Indeterminate	Fragment	1411
Total		2019

Table 11.8. Indeterminate Small Mammal Remains

Element	Portion	Quantity
Cranial	Fragment	11
Mandible	Fragment	1
Alveolar	Fragment	1
Tooth	Fragment	7
Vertebra	Fragment	4
Vertebral Centrum	Fragment	2
	Epiphysis	1
Caudal Vertebra	Complete	13
	Almost Complete	1
	Fragment	2
Rib	Proximal	1
	Fragment	1
Acetabulum	Fragment	2
Longbone	Shaft	16
	Fragment	32

Table 11.8. Indeterminate Small Mammal Remains, cont'd		
Element	Portion	Quantity
Metapodium	Complete	1
	Distal	1
	Fragment	1
Phalanx	Almost Complete	1
	Distal	1
Third Phalanx	Almost Complete	1
Indeterminate	Fragment	24
Articular Condyle	Fragment	1
Total		126

Table 11.9. Indeterminate Medium Mammal Remains		
Element	Portion	Quantity
Cranium	Fragment	12
Alveolar	Fragment	6
Thoracic Vertebra	Almost Complete	1
Vertebra	Centrum	6
	Fragment	4
Caudal Vertebra	Complete	4
	Almost Complete	1
	Fragment	1
Rib	Complete	2
	Proximal	3
	Shaft	5
	Fragment	10
Sternum	Complete	1
Scapula	Blade Fragment	5
Ulna	Shaft Fragment	1
Acetabulum	Fragment	1
Ischium	Fragment	1
Femur	Proximal	2

Table 11.9. Indeterminate Medium Mammal Remains, cont'd

Element	Portion	Quantity
Tibia	Shaft Fragment	1
Longbone	Shaft Fragment	22
	Epiphyseal Fragment	5
	Indeterminate	866
Metapodium	Distal	1
Phalanx	Complete	1
	Shaft	2
Indeterminate	Fragment	60
Total		1024

Table 11.10. Indeterminate Large Mammal Remains

Element	Portion	Quantity
Cranium	Fragment	20
Alveolus	Fragment	2
Tooth	Fragment	11
Thoracic Vertebra	Spine	1
Vertebra	Fragment	20
Rib	Proximal	4
	Shaft	14
	Fragment	61
Scapula	Proximal	1
	Spine	1
	Blade	4
Longbone	Shaft	10
	Fragment	852
Indeterminate	Fragment	395
Total		1396

Table 11.11. Cottontail Remains				
Taxon	Element	NISP	MNI	MNE
cf. Sylvilagus	Vertebra	2	2	2
	Acetabulum	1	1	1
	Femur	3	2	2
	Calcaneum	1	1	1
	Phalanx	1	1	1
Sylvilagus	Premaxilla with Teeth	2	2	2
	Maxilla with Teeth	1		
	Palate	1		
	Squamosal	1	1	1
	Mandible	5	4	4
	Scapula	5	5	5
	Humerus	7	5	7
	Metacarpus	1	1	1
	Pelvis	4	3	4
	Femur	5	5	5
	Tibia	5	4	5
	Calcaneum	3	3	3
	Metatarsus	1	1	1
	Phalange	4	3	4
Total		53	44	49

Table 11.12. Jack Rabbit Remains

Identification	Element	NISP	MNE	MNI
cf. Lepus	Maxilla	1	1	1
	Mandible	3	3	2
	Tooth	1	1	1
	Tympanic Bulla	1		
	Vertebra Fragment	1	1	1
	Thoracic Vertebra	1	1	1
	Lumbar Vertebra	2	2	1
	Rib	1		
	Pelvis Fragment	2	2	2
	Scapula Fragment	8	8	7
	Humerus	2	2	1
	Ulna	1	1	1
	Radius	1	1	1
	Femur	3	3	3
	Tibia	6	6	6
	Metapodium	2	2	2
	Phalanx	6	6	5
Lepus	Mandible	17	17	11
	Premaxilla	1	1	1
	Maxilla	1	1	1
	Upper Incisor	1	1	1
	Upper Molar	10	5	3
	Lower Premolar	2	2	2
	Cranial Fragment	1	1	1
	Zygoma	1	1	1
	Tympanic Bulla	2	1	1
	Occipital Fragment	2	2	2
	Atlas	1	1	1
	Axis	3	2	1
	Cervical Vertebra	1	1	1
	Thoracic Vertebra	6	6	3

Table 11.12. Jack Rabbit Remains, cont'd

Identification	Element	NISP	MNE	MNI
Lepus	Lumbar Vertebra	4	4	2
	Sacrum	2	2	2
	Scapula	35	34	30
	Humerus	35	25	34
	Ulna	15	15	11
	Radius	16	16	14
	Metacarpus	14	14	10
	Pelvis Fragments	11	11	11
	Femur	14	14	14
	Tibia	29	28	27
	Astragalus	12	11	11
	Calcaneum	17	17	17
	Cuboid	1	1	1
	Navicular	4	4	4
	Metapodial Fragment	9	6	1
	Metatarsus	28	22	17
	Phalanx	29	21	15
Total		366	327	282

Table 11.13. Indeterminate Medium Rodent Remains

Element	Portion	Quantity
Premaxilla	Fragment with Incisor	2
Maxilla	Fragment	1
Jugal	Fragment	1
Tympanic Bulla	Complete	3
Basioccipital	Complete	1
Mandible	Fragment	7
Upper Incisor	Complete	1
	Fragment	2
Lower Incisor	Fragment	4
Atlas	Complete	1
Axis	Complete	2
	Almost Complete	1
Cervical Vertebra	Complete	1
Thoracic Vertebra	Complete	12
	Almost Complete	2
Lumbar Vertebra	Complete	1
	Almost Complete	1
First Sacral Vertebra	Complete	1
Caudal Vertebra	Complete	7
	Almost Complete	1
Vertebra	Complete	1
	Fragment	1
Humerus	Distal	3
	Proximal	2
Ulna	Proximal	3
Radius	Complete	1
	Distal	1
	Shaft	1
Pelvis	Fragment	5

Table 11.13. Indeterminate Medium Rodent Remains, cont'd		
Element	Portion	Quantity
Femur	Proximal	9
	Shaft	8
	Distal	5
Tibia	Proximal	3
	Distal	1
Fibula	Shaft	1
Calcaneum	Complete	1
Astragalus	Complete	2
	Fragment	1
Metapodium	Complete	2
	Proximal	1
Phalanx	Complete	3
	Proximal	1
Total		108

Table 11.14. Indeterminate Small Rodent Remains

Element	Portion	Quantity
Cranium	Fragment	1
Premaxilla	Fragment with Incisor	1
Maxilla	Fragment with Molars	1
	Fragment	10
Alveolus	Fragment	1
Interparietal	Complete	1
Tympanic Bulla	Complete	1
	Almost Complete	2
	Fragment	1
Mandible	Almost Complete	1
	Fragment	15
Incisor	Fragment	2
Upper Incisor	Complete	3
	Almost Complete	1
	Fragment	8
Lower Incisor	Complete	1
	Almost Complete	5
	Fragment	17
Atlas	Complete	2
	Fragment	1
Thoracic Vertebra	Complete	5
	Almost Complete	3
	Fragment	2
Lumbar	Complete	3
Sacrum	Complete	3
	Almost Complete	2
Caudal Vertebra	Complete	3
Vertebra	Fragment	2
Rib	Proximal	3
Scapula	Complete	1
	Fragment	7

Table 11.14. Indeterminate Small Rodent Remains, cont'd

Element	Portion	Quantity
Humerus	Almost Complete	2
	Proximal	1
	Distal	3
	Shaft	25
Ulna	Proximal	6
	Distal	1
Radius	Proximal	1
Pelvis	Complete	1
	Almost Complete	5
	Fragment	16
Femur	Complete	3
	Proximal	19
	Distal	3
	Shaft	7
Tibia	Complete	2
	Almost Complete	3
	Proximal	3
	Distal	2
	Shaft	15
Calcaneum	Complete	10
	Almost Complete	1
	Fragment	2
Astragalus	Complete	2
Metatarsus	Complete	3
	Proximal	1
Metapodial	Complete	9
	Proximal	5
	Distal	6
Phalanx	Complete	7
	Proximal	2
Total		275

Table 11.15. Sciurid (Squirrel) Remains				
Identification	Element	NISP	MNI	MNE
Sciuridae	Atlas	1		1
	Femur	1	1	1
	Tibia	1	1	1
Sciuridae (Small)	Maxilla with Teeth	1	1	1
	Molar	1	1	1
Sciuridae (Medium)	Mandible	4	3	3
	Lower Incisor	1		1
	Atlas	1	1	1
	Axis	1	1	1
	Cervical Vertebra	2	2	2
	Thoracic Vertebra	1		
	Lumbar Vertebra	2	2	2
	Caudal Vertebra	1	1	1
	Scapula	4	4	4
	Humerus	2	2	2
	Ulna	1	1	1
	Pelvis	6	2	3
	Femur	2	2	2
	Tibia	6	5	6
cf. Sciuridae	Thoracic Vertebra	2	1	2
	Humerus	1	1	1
Ammospermophilus	Cranial	1	1	1
	Mandible	1		
	Pelvis	1		1
	Femur	1		
cf. Ammospermophilus	Mandible	3	2	2
Ammospermophilus harrisi	Cranium	2	2	2

Table 11.15. Sciurid (Squirrel) Remains, cont'd				
Identification	Element	NISP	MNI	MNE
cf. Ammospermophilus harrisii	Atlas	1		
	Humerus	2		2
	Femur	1		1
Spermophilus variegatus	Premaxilla with Incisor	1		
	Maxilla with Teeth	2		
	Mandible	5	3	4
	Cranial	4	3	3
	Atlas	1		1
	Cervical Vertebra	1		1
	Scapula	1		1
	Humerus	2	1	2
	Femur	2	2	2
	Tibia	1	1	1
cf. Spermophilus variegatus	Mandible	1	1	1
	Atlas	2		2
	Thoracic Vertebra	2	1	2
	Scapula	1		1
	Humerus	1	1	1
	Pelvis	2	2	2
	Femur	3	2	3
Spermophilus cf. variegatus	Radius	1	1	1
Total		88	55	74

Table 11.16. Identified Non-Sciurid Rodent Remains

Identification	Element	NISP	MNI	MNE
Thomomys bottae	Mandible with Teeth	1	1	1
Heteromyidae	Mandible with Teeth	2	2	2
	4th Upper Molar	1	1	1
Reithrodontomys/Perognathus	Premaxilla with Teeth	2	2	2
	Upper Incisor	7	2	2
Perognathus	Rostrum	1	1	1
	Mandible with Teeth	9	8	8
cf. Perognathus	Upper Incisor	2	1	1
	1st Lower Molar	1		
Peromyscus	2nd Upper Molar	1	1	1
	Mandible with Teeth	1	1	1
Peromyscus eremicus	Maxilla with Teeth	1	1	1
	Mandible with Teeth	3	3	3
Peromyscus cf. eremicus	Mandible with Teeth	3	3	3
	1st Lower Molar	1	1	1
Sigmodon	Maxilla with Teeth	3	2	2
	Mandible with Teeth	2	2	2
Neotoma	Maxilla with Teeth	14	8	8
	2nd Upper Molar	1	1	1
	Molar Fragments	18	1	1
	Mandible with Teeth	10	8	8
	1st Lower Molar	2	1	1
	2nd Lower Molar	1		
Neotoma cf. albigula	Maxilla with Teeth	1	1	1
cf. Neotoma	Mandible	3		
Total		91	52	52

Table 11.17. Carnivore Remains

Identification	Element	NISP	MNI	MNE
Carnivora (Medium)	Canine	2		
	Atlas	1		
	Ulna	1		
	Femur	2		
	1st Phalanx	1		
cf. Carnivora (Small)	Radius	1		
Canidae	Tibia	1	1	1
	Phalanx	2		
Canidae (Medium)	Maxilla	1	1	1
	Humerus	1	1	1
	Tibia	1	1	1
	Femur	1	1	1
cf. Canidae (Medium)	Phalanx	2	2	2
Canidae (Small)	Femur	1	1	1
Canis spp. (Large)	Lower 3rd Incisor	1	1	1
	Femur	3	3	3
	Metatarsus	1	1	1
Canis cf. familiaris	Maxilla with Teeth	1	1	1
Nasua	Humerus	1	1	1
	Ulna	1	1	1
Nasua nasua	Mandible with Teeth	1	1	1
cf. Nasua	Femur	1	1	1
Taxidea	Maxilla with Teeth	1	1	1
	Ulna	1	1	1
	Radius	1	1	1
	Acetabulum	1	1	1

Table 11.17. Carnivore Remains, cont'd

Identification	Element	NISP	MNI	MNE
Taxidea taxus	Mandible with Teeth	1	1	1
	Humerus	1	1	1
	Radius	1	1	1
cf. Taxidea taxus	Maxilla	1	1	1
	Squamosal	1	1	1
	Femur	1	1	1
Felis concolor	3rd Metatarsus	1	1	1
Total		39	29	29

Table 11.18. Ungulate (Artiodactyla) Remains

Identification	Element	NISP	MNI	MNE
Artiodactyla	Antler	4		
	Molar	7		
	Metapodium	3		
Artiodactyla?	Antler?	4		
Artiodactyla (Large)	Antler	1		
	Molar	3		
	Metatarsus	1		
Artiodactyla? (Large)	Antler	1		
Cervidae	Rib	1	1	1
	Metapodium	2	2	2
Odocoileus	Antler	2	2	2
	Temporal/Petrous	1	1	1
	Upper Molar	1	1	1
	Mandible	2	2	2
	Lower 3rd Premolar	1	1	1
	Lower Molar	2	2	2

Table 11.18. Ungulate (Artiodactyla) Remains, cont'd

Identification	Element	NISP	MNI	MNE
Odocoileus	Atlas	1		1
	Lumbar Vertebra	3		1
	Scapula	3	3	3
	Humerus	2	2	2
	Radius	2	2	2
	Pisiform	1	1	1
	Magnum	2	2	2
	Cuneiform	1	1	1
	Sesamoid	1	1	1
	Metacarpus	7	6	6
	1st Phalanx	12	10	8
	2nd Phalanx	9	5	6
	3rd Phalanx	2	1	1
	Pelvis	4	4	4
	Femur	1	1	1
	Patella	1	1	1
	Tibia	3	3	3
	Astragalus	3	3	3
	Calcaneum	2	2	2
	Lateral Malleolus	2	2	2
	Naviculo-cuboid	3	3	3
	Metatarsus	10	9	9
	Metapodium	22	21	21
cf. Odocoileus	Antler	17	1	1
	Molar	2	2	2
	Temporal/Petrous	1	1	1
	Sphenoid	1	1	1
	Scapula	2	1	1
	Metatarsus	3	3	3
	Sesamoid	1	1	1

Table 11.18. Ungulate (Artiodactyla) Remains, cont'd

Identification	Element	NISP	MNI	MNE
cf. Odocoileus	Pelvis	1	1	1
	Femur	2	2	2
	Astragalus	2	2	2
	Metapodium	8	6	6
Bos	Metapodium	1	1	1
cf. Bos	1st Phalanx	1		
Total		175	117	118

Table 11.19. Body Part Representation of Mammalian Orders

	Rodentia	Carnivora	Artiodactyla	Lagomorpha
Head	223	9	57	58
Vert./Rib	76	1	6	24
Upper Fore	60	3	7	92
Lower Fore	17	6	2	33
Upper Hind	93	10	8	37
Lower Hind	38	2	4	40
Manus/Pes	45	6	93	108

Table 11.20. Body Part Representation of Indeterminate Mammalian Remains

	Mammal	L. Mammal	M. Mammal	S. Mammal
Cranial	85	22	18	1
Vertebral	5	30	17	30
Longbone	453	862	893	49
Indeterminate	1411	395	60	24
Rib	46	79	20	2
Tibia	1	0	1	0
Tooth	18	11	0	7
Scapular	0	6	5	0
Pelvis	0	0	2	2
Femur	0	0	2	0
Metapodial	0	0	1	3
Phalanx	0	0	3	3
Sternum	0	0	1	0
Ulna	0	0	1	0
Mandible	0	0	0	1

Table 11.21. Body Part Representation, Order: Rodentia

	Small Rodents	Medium Rodents	Large Rodents
Head	72	36	14
Vert./Rib	29	42	6
Upper Fore	39	15	6
Lower Fore	8	7	2
Upper Hind	54	38	7
Lower Hind	25	11	1
Manus/Pes	48	11	5

Table 11.22. Complete and Almost Complete Elements Order and Sub Order (n = 397)

Small Rodentia	103
Medium Rodentia	81
Lagomorpha	77
Serpentes	32
Artiodactyla	29
Large Rodentia	25
Chelonia	18
Aves	11
Carnivora	10
Sauria	8
Anura	3

Table 11.23. Frequency of Occurrence in Spatial Contexts, Orders and Sub Orders (Percent in italics)

Taxon	1	2	3	4	5+
Anura	11 *1.5*		1 *2.8*		
Chelonia	42 *5.9*	8 *7.1*	6 *16.7*	1 *5.9*	2 *6.4*
Sauria	9 *1.3*	3 *2.6*		1 *5.9*	
Serpentes	21 *3.0*	1 *0.9*			3 *9.7*
Aves	30 *4.2*	3 *2.6*	2 *5.5*	1 *5.9*	
Lagomorpha	244 *34.3*	45 *39.8*	4 *1.1*	6 *35.3*	8 *25.8*
Small Rodentia	112 *15.8*	33 *29.2*	16 *44.4*	4 *23.5*	10 *32.3*
Medium Rodentia	45 *6.3*	7 *6.2*	2 *5.5*	2 *11.8*	5 *16.1*
Large Rodentia	41 *5.8*	3 *2.6*	2 *5.5*	1 *5.9*	1 *3.2*
Artiodactyla	123 *17.3*	7 *6.2*	3 *8.3*	1 *5.9*	2 *6.4*
Carnivora	33 *4.6*	3 *2.6*			
Totals	711 *100*	113 *99.8*	36 *99.8*	17 *100*	31 *99.9*

Table 11.24. Specimens Identified to Order/Sub Order, Frequency of Occurrence in Spatial Contexts (>2/context)

	2	3	4	5+
Rodentia	43	20	6	15
Lagomorpha	45	4	6	8
Artiodactyla	7	3	1	2
Serpentes	1			3
Chelonia	8	6	1	2
Aves	3	2	1	
Carnivora		3		
Sauria	3		1	
Anura	1			

Table 11.25. Concentration of Mammalian Specimens Identified to Order, Frequency of Occurrence in Spatial Contexts

	1	2	3	4	5+
Rodentia	198	43	20	7	16
Lagomorpha	244	45	4	6	8
Artiodactyla	123	7	3	1	2
Carnivora	33	3	0	0	0

Table 11.26. Concentration of Rodent Specimens by Size, Frequency of Occurrence in Spatial Contexts

	1	2	3	4	5+
Small	112	33	16	4	10
Medium	45	7	2	2	5
Large	41	3	2	1	1

Table 11.27. Ranked Frequency of Skeletal Portions

Skeletal Portion	*Cervidae*	*Skeletal Portion*	*Lepus*	*Skeletal Portion*	*Sylvilagus*
Proximal Femur	0	Patella	0	Proximal Radius	0
Cervical Vertebra	0	Atlas	1.0	Distal Radius	0
Proximal Radius	0	Rib	1.0	Lumbar Vertebra	0
Sternum	0	Distal Radius	2.0	Sacrum	0
Axis	0	Proximal Humerus	2.0	Proximal Ulna	1.0
Thoracic Vertebra	0	Sacrum	2.0	Distal Ulna	0
Proximal Humerus	0	Axis	3.0	Astragalus	0
Sacrum	0	Distal Ulna	3.5	Rib	0
Atlas	1.0	Lumbar Vertebra	6.0	Axis	0
Rib	1.0	Proximal Femur	7.0	Atlas	0
Proximal Tibia	1.0	Distal Femur	9.0	Patella	0
Patella	1.0	Proximal Ulna	11.5	Sternum	0
Lumbar Vertebra	1.0	Astragalus	12.0	Distal Metatarsus	1.0
Distal Radius	2.0	Pelvis	13.0	Proximal Tibia	1.5
Distal Humerus	2.0	Proximal Tibia	14.0	Proximal Phalange	2.0
Mandible	2.0	Proximal Radius	15.0	Prox. Metatarsus	2.0
Calcaneum	2.0	Calcaneum	17.0	Proximal Humerus	2.0
Distal Tibia	2.0	Mandible	20.0	Distal Phalange	3.0
3rd Phalanx	2.0	Distal Tibia	21.0	Distal Tibia	3.5
Naviculo-cuboid	3.0	Proximal Phalange	22.0	Proximal Femur	3.5
Distal Femur	3.0	Distal Metatarsus	22.0	Calcaneum	4.0
Scapula	4.0	Distal Phalange	29.0	Distal Femur	4.5
Pelvis	4.0	Prox. Metatarsus	34.0	Proximal Humerus	5.0
Astragalus	5.0	Distal Humerus	35.0	Scapula	5.0
2nd Phalanx	9.0	Scapula	43.0	Pelvis	5.0
1st Phalanx	12.0			Mandible	5.0
Prox. Metatarsus	26.0				
Distal Metatarsus	28.0				
Total	111.0		346.0		43.0

Table 11.28. Concentrations of Weathered Specimens in Excavation Units

Area	N	%
A1	110	*28.7*
B1	20	*5.2*
B2	2	*0.5*
B3	1	*0.3*
B4	10	*2.6*
B5	40	*10.4*
B6	32	*8.4*
B7	8	*2.1*
B8	21	*5.5*
B9	3	*0.8*
B10	2	*0.5*
B11	81	*21.0*
D	1	*0.3*
E	52	*13.6*
Total	383	*99.9*

Table 11.29. Frequency of Modified Bone by Excavation Area

Area	*Qty.*
A1	12
B1	25
B2	50
B3	8
B4	6
B5	3
B6	8
B7	13
B8	25
B9	13
B10	2
B11	6
D	5
E	5
Total	159

Chapter 12

El Tratamiento Mortuorio

Elisa Villalpando. Centro INAH Sonora

Mortuary

This chapter discusses human remains encountered during the 1995 and 1996 field seasons at Cerro de Trincheras. Out of respect for indigenous peoples in the Southwest/ Northwest the project research design did not call for the excavation of burials, however, ten inhumations representing 11 individuals (5 children, 2 sub-adult, and 4 adults) and one cremation were encountered despite efforts of avoidance. Nine of the burials were primary inhumations and only two contained offerings. Overall mortuary practices recorded at Cerro de Trincheras paralleled those seen among the Sedentary Period Hohokam with the cremation of the vast majority of individuals and few scattered inhumations in domestic spaces..

Introducción

Este apartado se ha elaborado a partir de las notas de campo de quienes excavaron las inhumaciones y cremaciones de Cerro de Trincheras, además de los análisis realizados por las Antropólogas Físicas Lorrie Lincoln-Babb, Penny Minturn y la Dra. Ethne Barnes, quienes revisaron los elementos excavados en el Laboratorio de Arqueología del Centro INAH Sonora, en años posteriores al trabajo de campo. De manera particular, el análisis dental fue elaborado por Lincoln-Babb en 1997 y consistió en la observación y registro de patologías dentales que incluyeron caries, lasqueo, e hypoplasia del esmalte; rasgos relacionados con las coronas dentales se registraron cuando fue posible. El análisis osteopatológico fue realizado por Barnes en junio de 2004, también en el Centro INAH Sonora.

Es pertinente señalar que antes de iniciar las excavaciones de Cerro de Trincheras fuimos informados localmente, que el área comprendida entre la ladera sur del cerro y el primer cerrito donde se encuentran los petrograbados, era una localidad en donde había muchos huesos quemados y donde en tiempos anteriores a nuestro proyecto, habían excavado ollas con cremaciones. Por ese motivo, uno de los acuerdos que tomamos en reunión realizada en la ciudad de Caborca, Sonora, entre el Comité de Preservación de la Nación Tohono O'odham y los directores del proyecto, fue no perturbar esa área; sin embargo, en apego a la normatividad federal que señala la Ley de Monumentos y Zonas Arqueológicos, Artísticos e Históricos, y a la aprobación del proyecto presentado ante el Consejo de Arqueología, dentro de las áreas excavadas se recuperaron 10 inhumaciones y 1 cremación, las que serán descritas a continuación.

Entierro 1

Se trató de una cremación localizada en el Área E al estar excavando los cuadrantes de una unidad. Inicialmente se encontró una concentración de tiestos que a mayor profundidad parecían estar incrustados dentro de un cráneo que estaba hacia arriba. Los fragmentos del cráneo eran extremadamente pequeños, pertenecientes posiblemente a un infante o un niño. No se encontraron otros huesos dentro del cuadrante excavado y el cráneo no parecía estar quemado, pero si estaba en un estado avanzado de desintegración, por lo que no podía moverse. La matríz alrededor de la cremación era de color café grisácea ligera a oscura. En toda esta unidad hubo muchas evidencias de áreas quemadas y ceniza. Este cráneo no se removió.

Entierro 2

Es un entierro localizado en el Área E, con una longitud máxima de .55 m, ancho máximo de .42 m (Figura 12.1). Se encontró un metate sobre el cráneo. Se tomaron muestras para fechamiento radiométrico bajo el metate y sobre el cráneo.

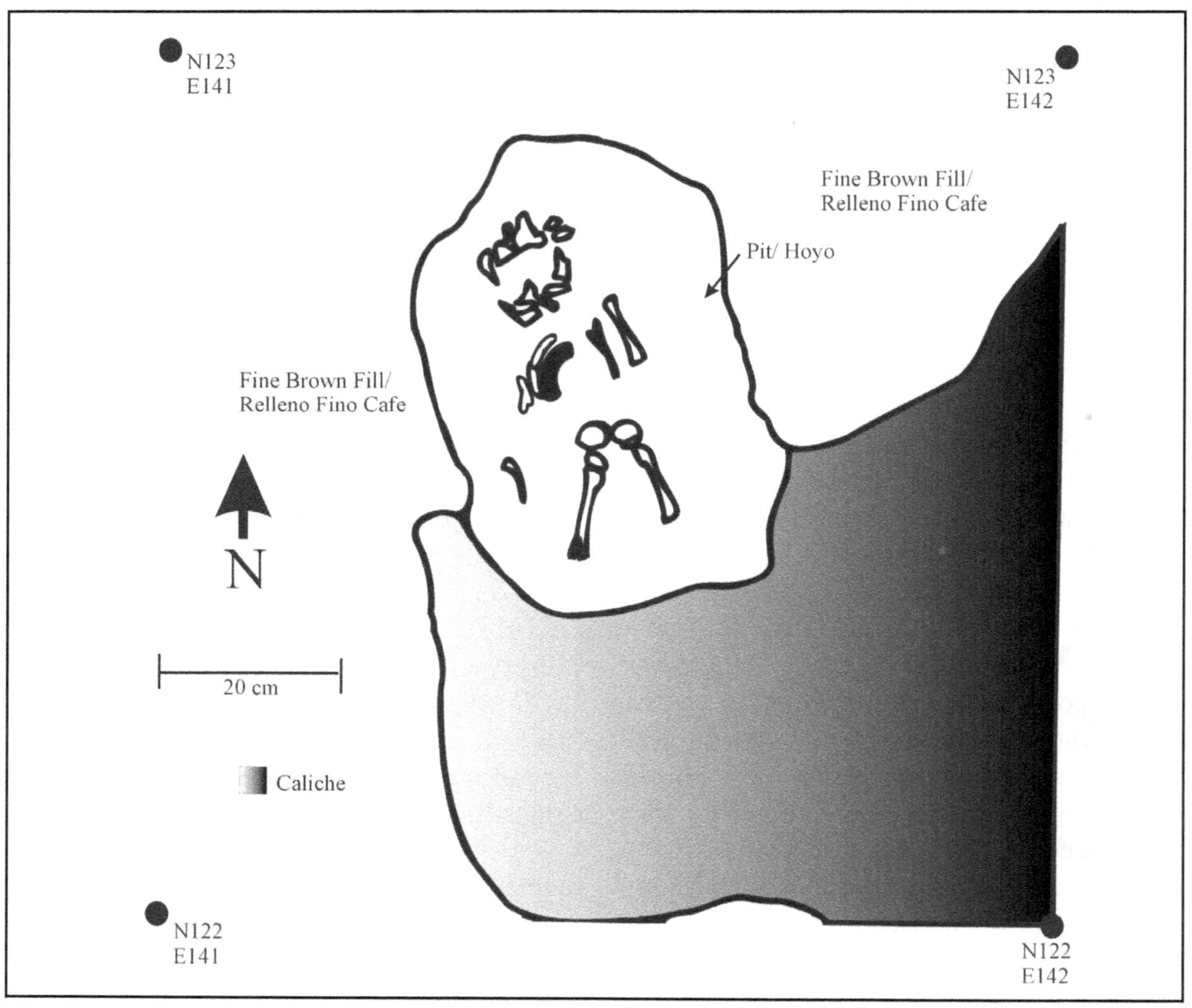

Figura 12.1. Entierro 2.

Se trata de un entierro infantil en posición decúbito dorsal extendido; el cráneo estuvo hecho pedazos y la constitución era extremadamente delgada. El cuerpo descansaba sobre una depresión de la superficie de adobe con revoque; las rocas sobre el entierro estaban quebradas y quemadas y había mucho carbón, pero no abajo del cuerpo. Se encontraron algunos tiestos cerámicos en las inmediaciones del cráneo así como una concha pequeña; alrededor del cuerpo se recuperaron varias lascas. Algunos dientes se localizaron aunque no estuvo claro si ya habían hecho erupción.

El análisis en laboratorio revela que se trata de un infante entre 3 y 6 meses, determinada la edad por el grado de desarrollo de las seis coronas dentales no permanentes asociadas. La preservación de los huesos y de los dientes es de regular a buena. Las coronas de los dientes identificados fueron los primeros molares mandibulares y maxilares, un incisivo maxilar central y un canino derecho mandibular. Sólo el incisivo central demostró una raíz de desarrollo. El canino derecho mandibular y el primer molar estuvieron in situ en un fragmento de mandíbula. El resto de los dientes se perdió. No se encontraron patologías dentales de desarrollo.

Entierro 3

Esta inhumación se recuperó del Área B2 (Figura 12.2); tuvo 1.20 m de largo y ancho máximo se identificó como de un adulto, masculino, con una edad entre 40-45 años (Lincoln-Babb, n.d. and Minturn 1995) o 45-50 años (Ethne Barnes n.d.: comunicación personal).

Se trata de un entierro semiflexionado, en posición decúbito dorsal. Las piernas se encontraron flexionadas con las rodillas más altas que el nivel del cráneo y ligeramente desplazadas hacia el costado izquierdo. La porción frontal del cráneo se encontró severamente dañada y sólo dos o tres dientes estaban en su ubicación original, la cavidad nasal totalmente destruida. Algunos de los dientes se encontraron en el área del estómago.

El cuerpo fue depositado ligeramente sentado y los brazos presentaban posturas diferentes. El brazo izquierdo se encontraba extendido y descansando pegado al costado izquierdo y al dorso, con la mano bajo o pegada a la pierna. El brazo derecho estaba flexionado desde el codo hacia abajo y descansando a la altura del esternón, con la mano a la altura del cuello. Muchos de los huesos de la mano estaban entre las costillas.

En campo se pudo apreciar que aparentemente este individuo sufría de una enfermedad que le impedía moverse con facilidad, ya que la sección baja de la espina dorsal, desde las costillas flotantes hasta la cavidad pélvica, estaba completamente fusionada. Las vértebras estaban fusionadas por lo que pudieron levan-

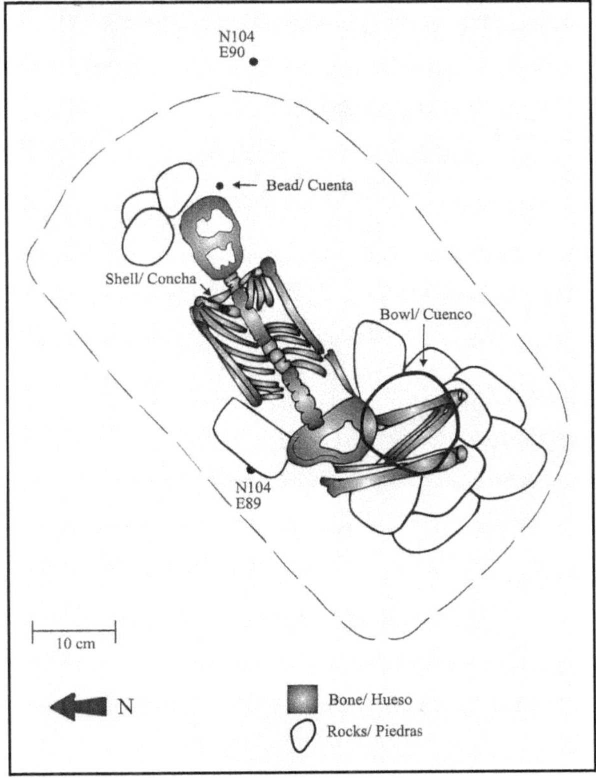

Figura 12.2. Entierro 3.

tarse en una sola pieza.

Las ofrendas funerarias fueron un pendiente de concha localizado a la altura del esternón, una cuenta de piedra verde localizada arriba del cráneo y un cuenco de cerámica a la altura de las rodillas.

El análisis osteopatológico realizado por Barnes señala que el cráneo pudo ser parcialmente reconstruido presentando forma de ovoide a redondeado, el rango dentro de braquicéfalos, con un índice craneal de 84.48 y alisamiento vertical del occipital. La edad fue calculada sobre la symphysis pública, el sexo determinado por lo robusto de los huesos, arco púbico estrecho y abertura ciática. Las variantes de desarrollo incluyen coalisión bilateral no ósea del tercer metatarsal cuneiforme, y apertura bilateral timpánica pequeña. Severa espondilitis anquilosa con fusión patológica de la espina, costillas y junturas sacro-iliacas, osteoporosis, severa enfermedad degenerativa de las suturas en ambas caderas, huesos púbicos de cuerpo rugoso y crestas iliacas. Evidencia de sobre uso de los hombros y acuclillamiento en el tobillo izquierdo.

El análisis dental realizado en laboratorio por Lincoln-Babb señala que la preservación de los dientes fue regular, y sólo se recuperaron 8 ejemplares. Los maxilares incluyeron el canino superior izquierdo, el primer y segundo premolar de ambos lados y el segundo molar izquierdo. Un primer y tercer molar inferiores con una morfología inusual estuvieron presentes. El desgaste dental fue considerable como moderado con algo de exposición de la dentina y alisado de las coronas. Además de exhibir la mayor cantidad de dentina que ningún otro diente, los premolares izquierdos también comparten lesiones de caries interproximales en sus uniones del esmalte. Otras patologías observadas fueron lasqueo del esmalte para el primer molar inferior e hipercementosis de la raíz para el segundo molar superior.

Entierro 4

Este elemento fue un entierro secundario en el Área B4; el largo y ancho máximo fue de 40 cm y la profundidad máxima de 25 cm (Figura 12.3). Estuvo posiblemente asociado al Jacal 3 y 20 cm más profundo que éste, ya que fue localizado al oeste del hoyo de poste del extremo oeste de este elemento. La Terraza Ancilar 1 del Área B3 se encontró directamente atrás o al sur de este entierro, por lo que se consideró que podían haber estado asociados.

El cuerpo no estaba articulado ni estuvo completo. El cráneo había perdido la mandíbula y sólo se encontraron 2 vértebras lumbares, 2 costillas, 1 fémur, los huesos de los brazos, pero ninguno de las manos. La posición de los huesos en relación a las rocas de los alrededores y entre sí, sugiere que no se trata de un entierro primario, sino de una deposición posterior. No se encontró ninguna ofrenda. Se tomó muestra de flotación a 85 cm de profundidad.

Fue identificado como infantil de 8-9 años de edad, con base en el desarrollo dental (Ethne Barnes n.d.: comunicación personal), subadulto de 12-15 años (Lincoln-Babb, n.d.).

La preservación dental fue moderada: tres dientes y dos fragmentos de coronas de la dentición permanente estuvieron presentes. Entre los dientes presentes se incluyen el segundo premolar del maxilar derecho y el segundo molar y la corona de desarrollo de un tercer molar maxilar. Los fragmentos de corona fueron de un primer molar y un premolar. Una lesión por caries sobre el segundo molar fue la única patología dental observada. Esta pequeña área fue localizada sobre la superficie oclusal del diente.

Entierro 5

Localizado en el Área B6, en la T593; tuvo un largo máximo de 97 cm y ancho máximo de 50 cm. Se trata de un entierro primario en posición

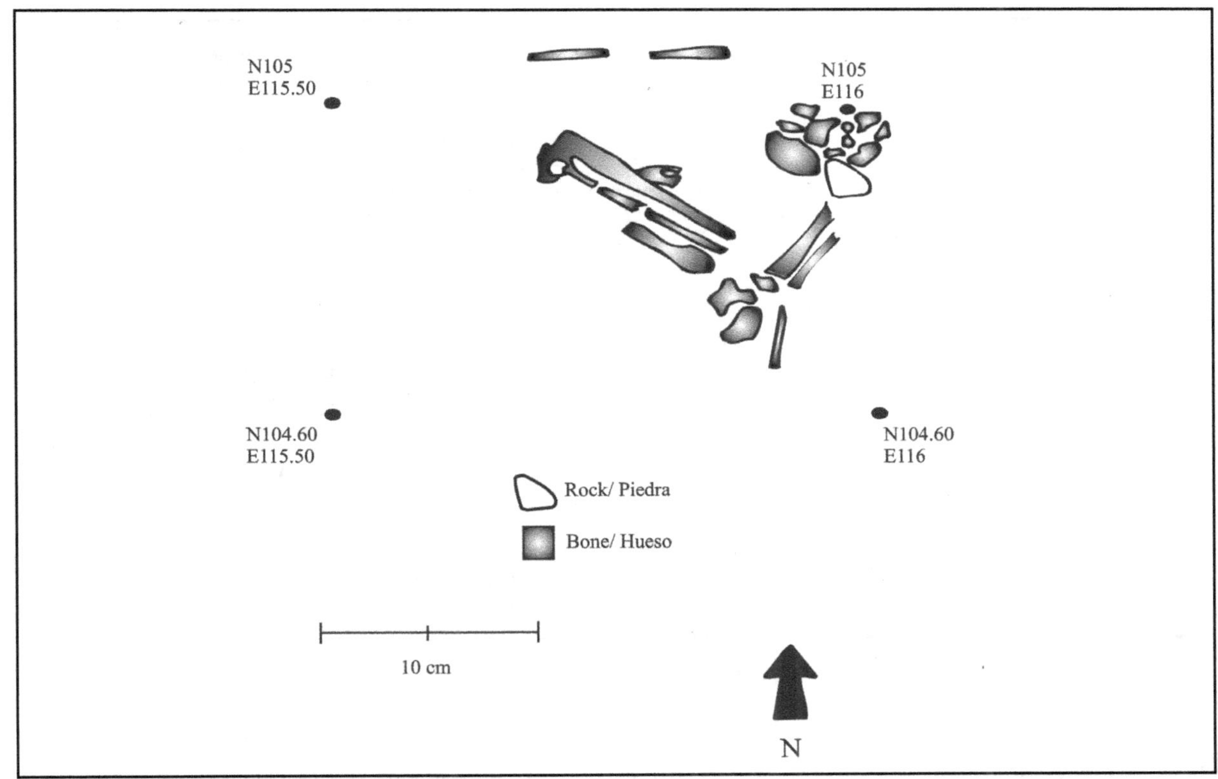

Figura 12.3. Entierro 4.

extendida ventral, con una orientación aproximada en eje este-oeste, depositado intencionalmente debajo de una capa de piedras y tierra en el interior de la Estructura Cuadrangular 1, después de que fue abandonada.

Los huesos largos y las costillas de este individuo masculino adulto se observaron en un buen estado de conservación; sin embargo no se encontró el cráneo ni un fémur, posiblemente por estar más cerca de la superficie. El área pélvica creó un cambio en la textura del suelo, formando una zona más compacta y más dura. No hubo restos dentales de este individuo.

Entierro 6

Se localizó en el Área B6, T593; el área del entierro tuvo un largo máximo de 82 cm, ancho máximo de 56 cm y profundidad máxima de 14 cm (Figura 12.4). Es un entierro primario de dos infantes dispuestos frente a frente, uno de ellos de 4-5 años y el otro de 6-7 años. Estaban dispuestos en una orientación este-oeste, una cabeza hacia el este y otra al oeste.

El mejor conservado fue el del lado norte, cuya posición fue extendido lateral izquierdo y orientación suroeste-noroeste, con las extremidades inferiores más arriba que la cabeza. Los brazos estuvieron arriba y sobre el pecho. El cráneo estuvo bastante fracturado pero completo.

El segundo individuo estaba en malas condiciones de preservación con orientación del cuerpo noroeste-suroeste. Lo mejor conservado fue el cráneo y algunas costillas. La posición probablemente era extendido lateral derecho, con la cabeza hacia el oeste.

Ambos individuos presentaban algunos huesos sin posición anatómica, lo que parece ser una alteración debido a un movimiento de

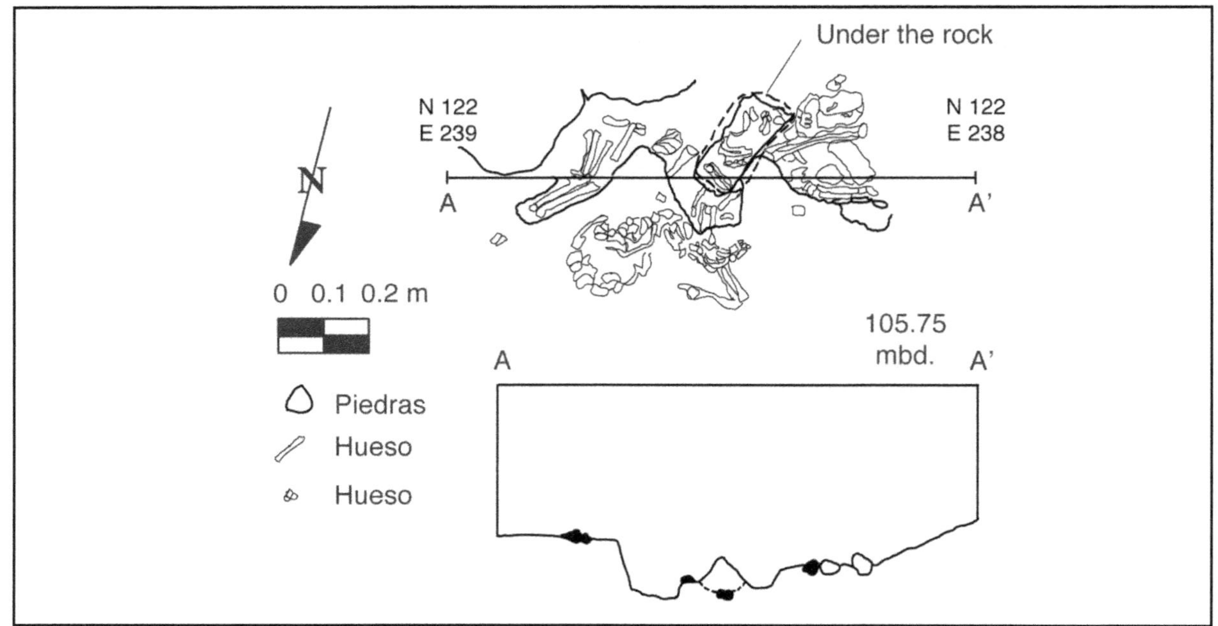

Figura 12.4. Entierro 6.

derrumbe que cambió la posición de algunos de los huesos. Ambos individuos parecen haber sido depositados de manera simultánea; el relleno usado para cubrir los cuerpos fue una tierra arcillo-limosa de color rojizo con piedras medianas y pequeñas. El entierro fue sobre la capa de derrumbe y el evento de deposición parecería haber tenido lugar posteriormente al abandono y derrumbe de la Estructura Circular de Piedra 20 del Área B6, lo que parecería ser una constante de uso de círculos de piedra como lugar de entierros post-ocupación.

El análisis de laboratorio reportó que en el infante de 4-6 años, la preservación de los restos dentales fue buena. Cuatro dientes no permanentes estuvieron presentes incluyendo el incisivo central derecho maxilar, ambos caninos superiores y el primer y segundo molares inferiores izquierdos. También estuvieron presentes seis dientes permanentes en diferentes etapas de desarrollo: el primer molar superior izquierdo, los primeros molares inferiores, el segundo molar derecho y tres premolares. No se presentaron patologías para este infante.

Los restos dentales del segundo individuo estuvieron pobremente preservados. Están presentes trece dientes no permanentes y 14 permanentes; los no permanentes incluyeron los cuatro caninos y el primer y segundo molares de ambas arcadas. También estuvo presente el incisivo central superior izquierdo. Los dientes permanentes fueron el incisivo central superior e inferior y los primeros molares, el canino derecho superior y el segundo molar izquierdo, así como el incisivo lateral izquierdo inferior, ambos primeros premolares y el segundo premolar izquierdo y el morar. Tampoco se observaron patologías en ninguno de los dientes.

Entierro 7

Se localizó en el Área B6, en la T593; las dimensiones máximas de largo y ancho fueron 54 y 38 cm (Figura 12.5), respectivamente, así como 21 cm de profundidad. Se trata de un entierro infantil primario, en posición fetal, decúbito lateral izquierdo, flexionado, orientación norte-sur. La cabeza se encontraba

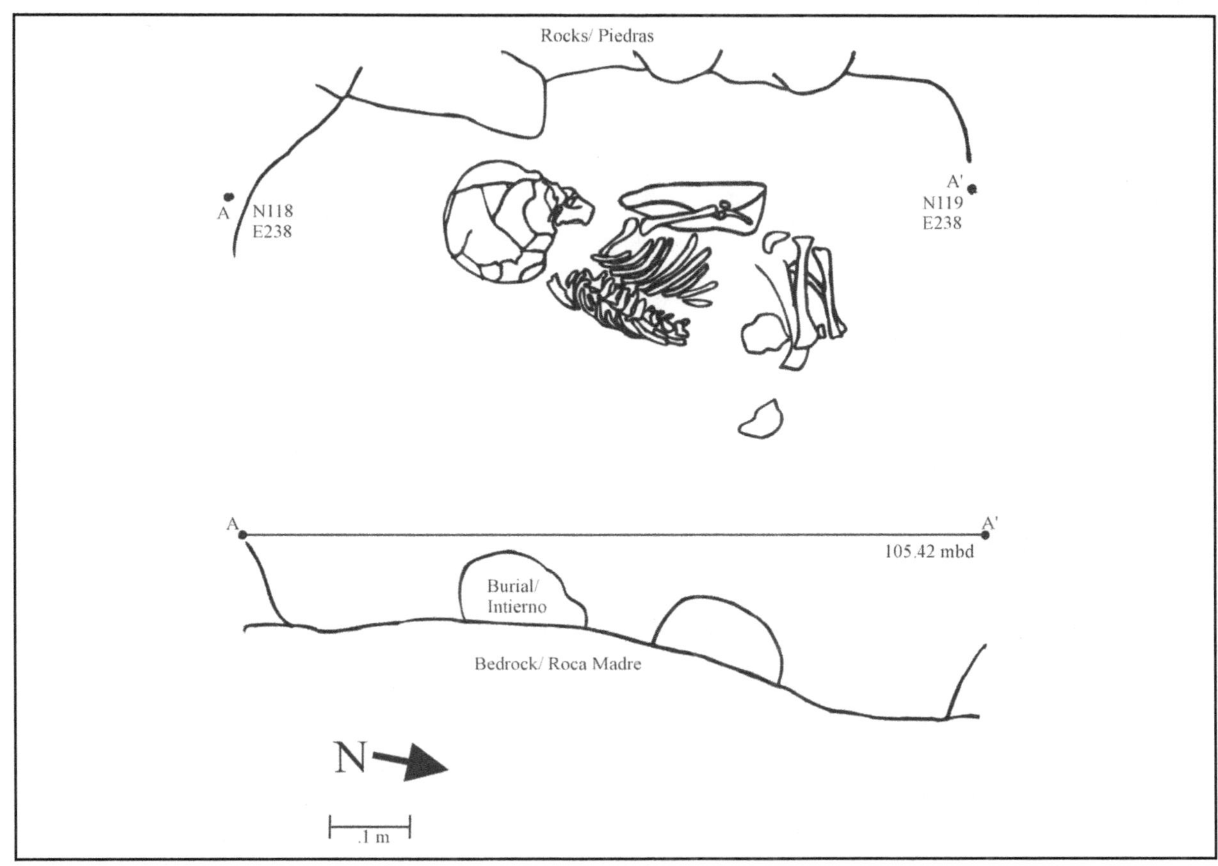

Figura 12.5. Entierro 7.

orientada hacia el sur. En general los huesos presentaron un buen estado de conservación.

Se localizó sobre el relleno de la terraza que consistió en una tierra gris clara con pequeñas piedras. Tuvo el brazo derecho sobre una piedra sin alteración cultural y dos piezas de desecho de talla, una debajo de las vértebras lumbares y la otra sobre el estómago.

En laboratorio se asignó una edad de 30-36 meses, con base en el desarrollo dental (Ethne Barnes n.d.: comunicación personal). Presentó gran osículo en lamba y un defecto de desarrollo algo extraño: la tercera y cuarta vértebra torácica en bloque y la tercera hemivértebra torácica derecha, resultado del cambio hemimetamere durante el desarrollo en la etapa embriomática.

De acuerdo con el análisis dental de Lincoln-Babb se calculó una edad de 4-6 años, encontrando que la preservación de los dientes es buena. Estuvieron presentes doce dientes no permanentes, el primer y segundo molares y los caninos izquierdos tanto maxilares como mandibulares, el incisivo lateral izquierdo superior y el incisivo central izquierdo inferior. Las coronas de los primeros molares permanentes se observaron en sus criptas dentro del hueso. No se observaron patologías dentales de este individuo.

Entierro 8

Localizado en el Área B6, en la T594. Es un entierro semiflexionado lateral derecho que se encontró en una pobre condición de preservación, con un largo máximo de 1.04 m, un ancho máximo de .34 m y una profundidad máxima de .14 m (Figura 12.6).

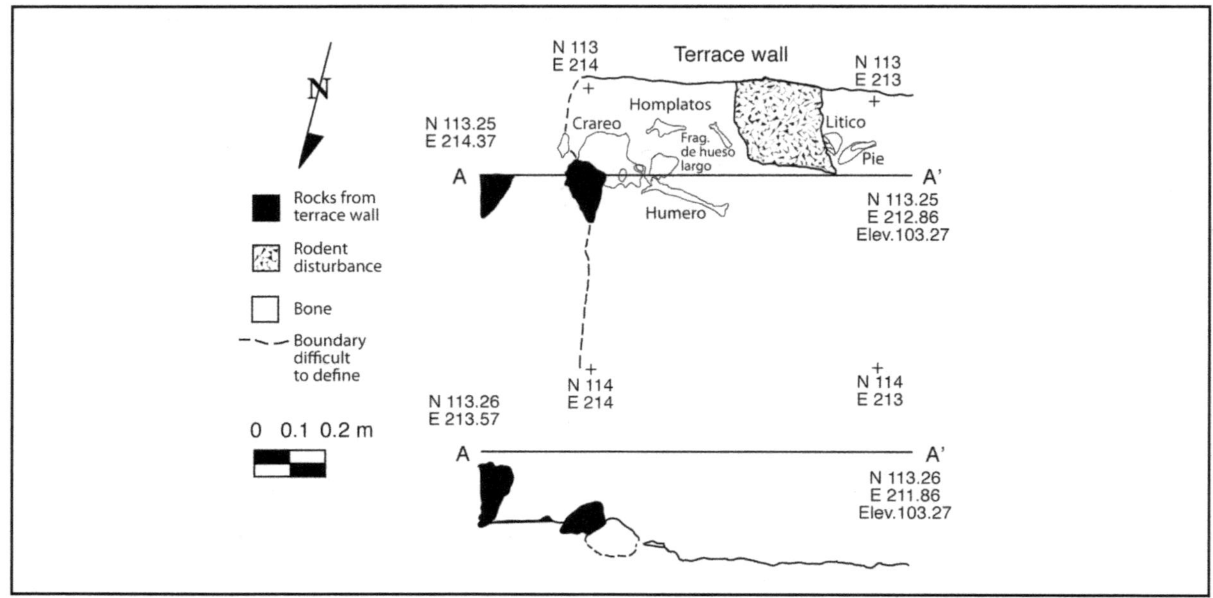

Figura 12.6. Entierro 8.

El cráneo estaba aplastado bajo el relleno de la Estructura Circular de Piedra 18; hubo algunos huesos sobre la superficie de ese derrumbe, pequeños fragmentos que estuvieron extremadamente intemperizados. Se recuperaron inicialmente las vértebras cervicales, huesos de los hombros, húmero, un metacarpal y parte del frente. La mayoría de los otros huesos estaban dispersos y perturbados por madrigueras de roedor que intruyeron cortando la porción media del cuerpo. Algunos de los huesos pudieron haber sido removidos de la posición original.

Un limo rojizo que se deslavó hacia la Estructura Cuadrangular de Piedra 1 después de la ocupación y por su ocurrencia sobre la superficie, o justo bajo la misma, parecería indicar que el cuerpo se depositó sobre la superficie. Hubo algunas rocas sobre y alrededor del área de los huesos, que pudieron haber estado apiladas sobre el cuerpo.

Se colocó dentro de la Estructura Cuadrangular de Piedra 1, un cuarto circular que se abre en la T594, pegado al muro de T576. Es un evento post-ocupacional claramente por encima del nivel del suelo, e intrusivo al estrato de color rojizo que está arriba de los sedimentos de acumulación de agua sobre el nivel del piso.

Posteriormente a la excavación total del elemento, se encontraron huesos adicionales que parecían pertenecer al mismo individuo, tanto por las condiciones semejantes de preservación, proximidad al entierro, presencia de actividad de roedores y la no duplicación de los huesos recuperados. Estos últimos fueron un radio, una ulna, metacarpales, una costilla, una clavícula y dos vértebras.

La identificación del individuo en laboratorio, según Barnes, es un adulto masculino de edad entre 30-40 años. La edad con base en el desgaste dental y el sexo determinado por la robustez de los huesos. Os acromion del lado derecho, desconocido del lado izquierdo. Evidencia de uso repetitivo de jalado o de rotación hacia adentro del brazo derecho (desconocido para el lado izquierdo) y de flexión en el antebrazo izquierdo (igualmente desconocido para el lado derecho).

Para Lincoln-Babb este individuo debió tener una edad entre 40-45 años. La preservación dental es mediana. La cantidad de hueso

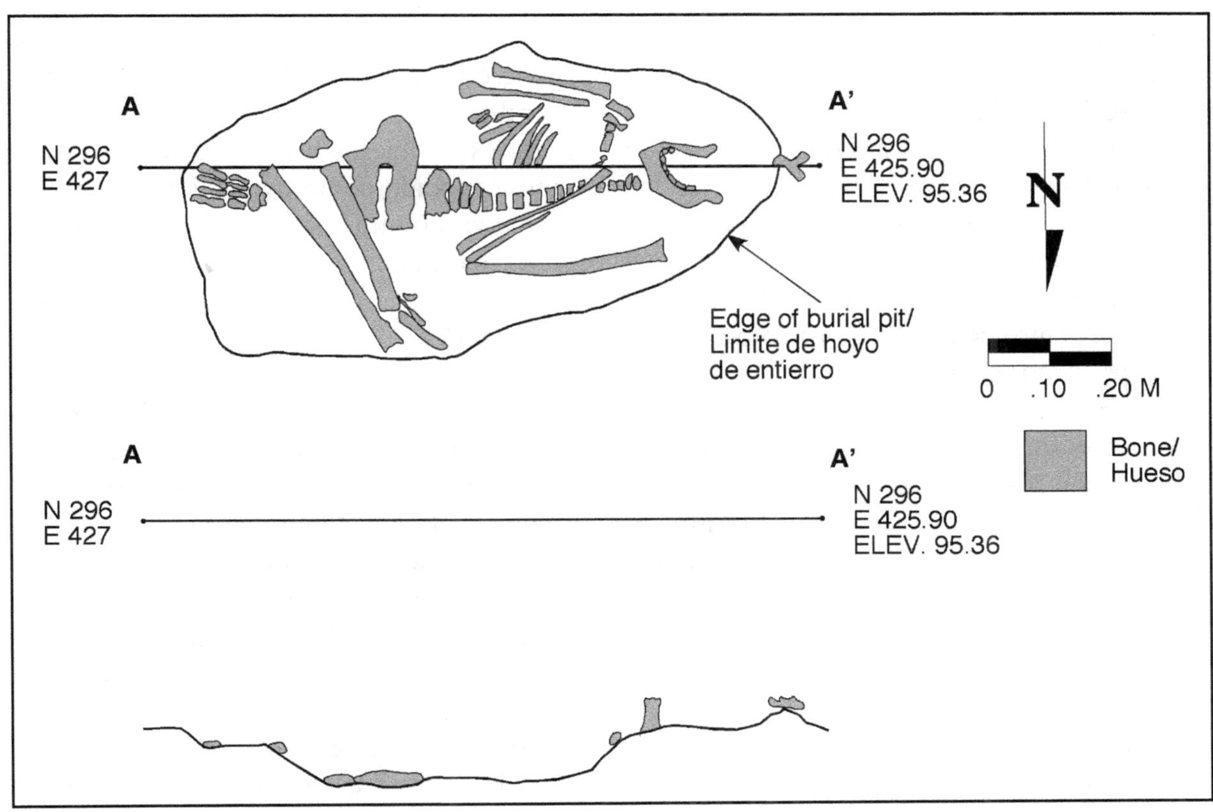

Figura 12.7. Entierro 9.

alveolar presente estuvo limitada a una sección de la mandíbula derecha. También estuvieron presentes 20 dientes permanentes y la dentición maxilar fue completa con excepción del incisivo lateral derecho y los molares segundo y tercero. Los mandibulares que estuvieron presentes fueron el segundo y tercer molar izquierdo, los incisivos laterales y del lado derecho, el canino derecho, los premolares y el primer y tercer molar. De la pequeña porción de hueso mandibular que estuvo presente fue posible determinar que el segundo molar derecho tuvo una pérdida antemortem. En relación al desgaste dental, los molares estuvieron seriamente desgastados y exhibían cantidades sustanciales de dentina; el resto de los dientes tenían superficies oclusales ligeramente desgastadas con cantidades moderadas de dentina.

Lincoln-Babb observó algunas patologías. Dos dientes estuvieron severamente dañados por caries, el segundo premolar derecho inferior y el primer molar. La pérdida del segundo molar posiblemente ocurrió por caries. El alveolo de este molar estaba en proceso de recuperación de un absceso muy destructivo. Dos dientes mostraron hypoplasia del esmalte en sus superficies: el canino derecho inferior y el incisivo lateral superior izquierdo. Tres dientes tuvieron superficies oclusales lasqueadas, los dos primeros molares superiores y el incisivo lateral izquierdo.

Entierro 9

Recuperado en el Área B9, T277; largo máximo 47 cm, ancho máximo 58 cm, profundidad máxima 16 cm. Es un entierro primario flexionado asociado con el derrumbe del muro que atraviesa a 3 metros de norte a sur el muro principal de la T277 (Figura 12.7). Se localizó en excelente condición, recuperándose casi todos los huesos con excepción del cráneo; su orientación fue hacia el oeste. Es un entierro flexionado decúbito dorsal izquierdo. La fosa en la cual se depositó el entierro no tiene una forma muy definida. Parece que ambas rodillas y el cráneo estuvieron expuestos, lo cual explicaría su ausencia. Se localizó un pedazo de cerámica dentro de la pelvis, así como huesos de un pequeño roedor.

Para Barnes se trata de un adolescente masculino de entre 14 y 15 años, la edad inferida con base en el desarrollo dental y las fusiones de la epífisis, el sexo determinado por el arco púbico angosto y el agujero ciático de la pelvis, así como los grandes dientes. Los incisivos centrales inferiores apretados y el incisivo central izquierdo muestran unas ranuras verticales profundas. Las variantes de desarrollo incluyen un esternón Tipo II con una gran abertura séptica, facetas transicionales de la primera lumbar y el pie derecho con polidactilia (seis dedos). Se desconoce para el pie izquierdo. El quinto metatarsal derecho anormalmente ancho con dos cabezas articuladas para los dos conjuntos de falanges que están desaparecidas. El quinto metatarsal también tiene facetas articulares con el cuarto metatarsal a lo largo del eje que no está presente sobre el cuarto metatarsal del pie izquierdo, con pérdida del quinto metatarsal.

Para Lincoln-Babb se trata de un subadulto masculino de 16-18 años. La preservación de la mandíbula fue excelente y los 15 dientes estuvieron presentes. No se recuperó hueso maxilar. Todos los dientes mandibulares de la dentición permanente estuvieron presentes; sin embargo, los terceros molares no habían erupcionado aunque estaban visibles dentro del hueso alveolar. También estaba presente el incisivo central izquierdo superior. El desgaste dental fue mínimo con muy pocos puntos de dentina observables sobre las superficies oclusales.

Ligeros a moderados depósitos de sarro estuvieron presentes en las superficies labiales de los dientes delanteros. Los segundos molares inferiores exhibieron bandas de esmalte decolorado, conocido como hypocalcificación. No se observaron otras patologías como caries o enfermedades peridontales.

Entierro 10

Estuvo ubicado en el Área B11, T556, cercano al muro de la T554. Largo máximo 65 cm y ancho máximo 55 cm, con una profundidad máxima de 44 cm (Figura 12.8).

Este entierro apareció en el relleno de la terraza y se reportó como un infante en una posición que no pudo ser definida con exactitud; es primario con una alteración de las extremidades inferiores. El cráneo apareció orientado hacia el oeste, con la cara girada hacia el sur. Las vértebras cervicales y las costillas presentaron clara posición anatómica, pero en dirección hacia el este, por lo que se considera que estaba flexionado lateral derecho. Las extremidades inferiores probablemente fueron removidas o alteradas por un evento muy posterior al enterramiento.

El análisis de laboratorio reporta una edad de 18-24 meses (Ethne Barnes n.d.: comunicación personal) con base en el desarrollo dental. Squamosa occipital de la parte posterior del cráneo muestra una depresión de 18 x 19 mm que parece ser una fractura sanada que no intruyó hacia adentro.

Lincoln-Babb consideró que se trata de un individuo entre 4 y 6 años de edad, con una excelente preservación de los restos dentales. Estuvieron presentes 16 dientes no permanentes y 5 permanentes en varias etapas de desarrollo. Los diez mandibulares de la dentición no permanente estuvieron in situ en la mandíbula; los incisivos lateral y central maxilares izquierdos, caninos y los primeros y segundos molares estuvieron también posicio-

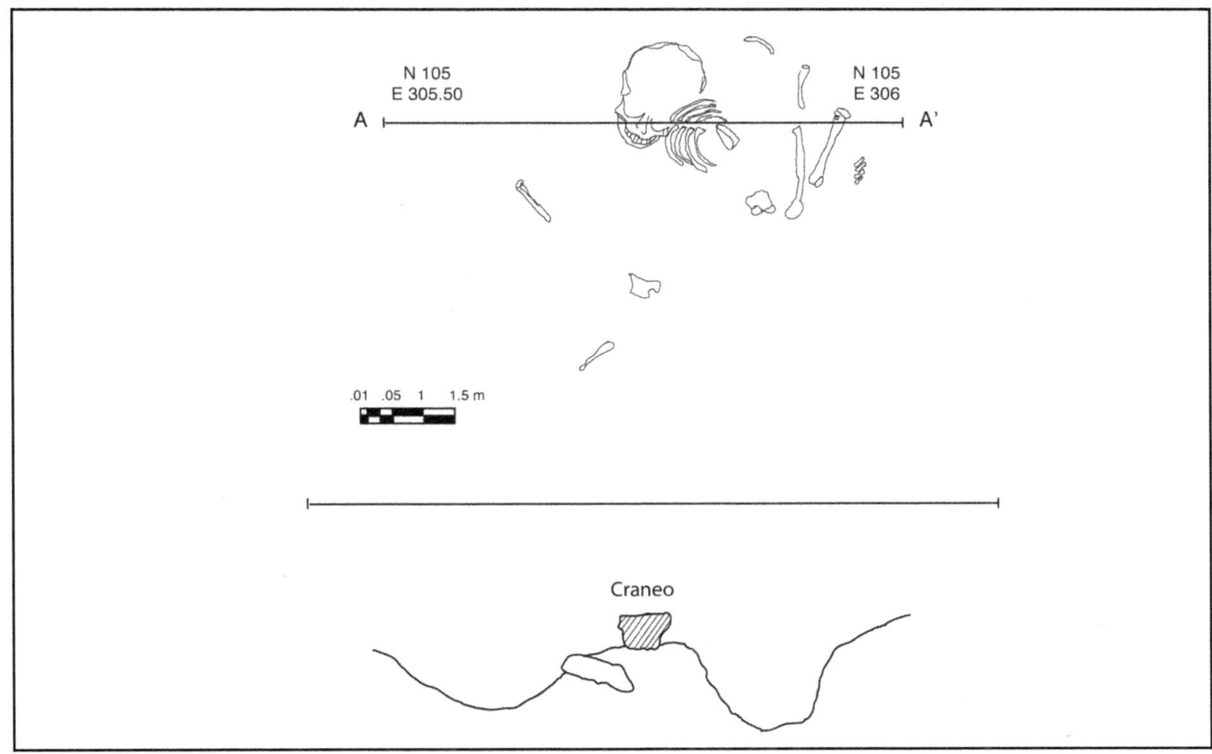

Figura 12.8. Entierro 10.

nados con su alveolo. El primer molar derecho fue el único presente del maxilar derecho. Los dientes permanentes observados incluyeron el primer molar derecho superior (haciendo erupción) y el antimere de este diente y las coronas parciales de los incisivos superiores izquierdos central y lateral, así como el canino derecho. No tuvo ninguna patología.

Entierro 11

Este elemento fue recuperado del Área D; tuvo un largo máximo de 96 cm, ancho máximo de 60 cm y profundidad máxima de 20 cm (Figura 12.9). Se trata de un entierro de adulto del que no se pudo determinar la edad; sólo hubo fragmento de cráneo y otros huesos.

Fue una inhumación semiflexionada, los huesos estuvieron en muy mal estado de conservación tanto por haber estado demasiado cerca de la superficie, como porque una madriguera de roedor pasó a través de todo el cuerpo. Se recuperaron sólo fragmentos de cráneo, húmero, costillas tibia y fíbula. Por la colocación de los huesos es posible saber que estaba descansando lateral, con las rodillas flexionadas y los brazos rectos al lado.

El único artefacto claramente asociado fue un anillo de Conus encontrado cerca de donde debió estar la mano derecha. Hubo también un tiesto entre los huesos, que se recolectó como ofrenda.

El cuerpo no se encontró en una fosa definida claramente; pudo haber sido puesto en un relleno de terraza cubierto con rocas de gran tamaño.

Esta inhumación está adyacente hacia el oeste del Hoyo 20. Está directamente al este de lo que parece ser un cuarto rectangular de la T11. Está también en seguida de lo que parece ser la entrada de este cuarto a la T9.

No hubo restos dentales de este individuo.

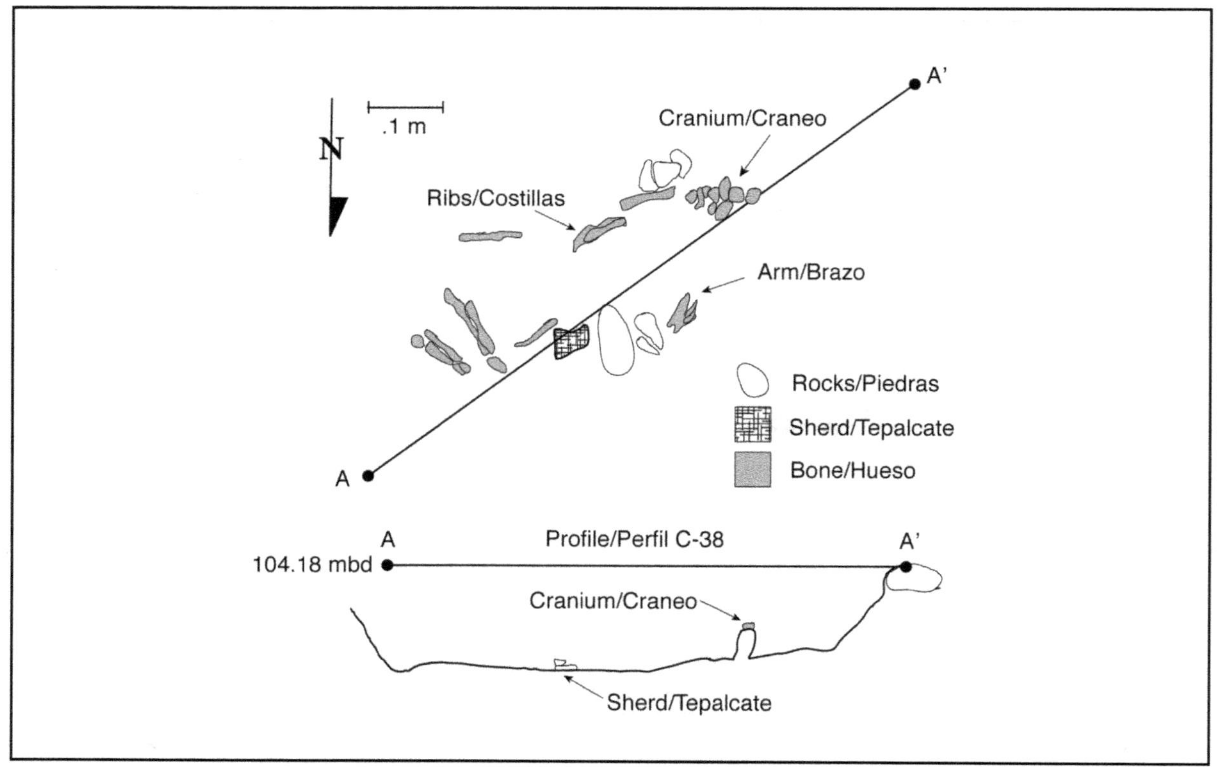

Figura 12.9. Entierro 11.

Comentarios

Si bien una muestra de sólo 11 entierros no es muy amplia, como puede apreciarse en la tabla anterior, algunas consideraciones son pertinentes respecto a las características de estas inhumaciones. En primer lugar, debemos destacar que la cremación (Entierro 1) se presentó en el Área E, que es la localidad al sur del conjunto de cerros en la parte posterior del cerro principal. Es un área donde se identificaron casas en foso y se ha propuesto que se trataría de una aldea contemporánea con la ocupación principal de Cerro de Trincheras, que en relación con el tratamiento funerario, habrían practicado la cremación de sus muertos.

La mayoría de los entierros recuperados en las dos temporadas de campo son entierros primarios, sólo uno de ellos fue secundario. El sexo sólo pudo ser identificado en cuatro de las inhumaciones como masculino, especialmente por encontrarse en condiciones de alteración significativa los huesos que harían posible esta identificación. En relación a la edad, cuatro de ellos fueron de adulto, dos de sub-adulto y seis infantiles menores de 7 años (uno de ellos la cremación); esto es así debido a que el Entierro 6 fue una inhumación doble.

Respecto a la orientación del cuerpo, seis estuvieron este-oeste, cuatro con el cráneo hacia el oeste y dos hacia el este; en dos inhumaciones la orientación del cuerpo fue norte-sur, uno noreste-suroeste, uno suroeste-noroeste y uno noroeste-suroeste. En seis de ellos estuvo el cráneo hacia el oeste y en cuatro hacia el este, uno más lo tuvo hacia el norte. En ocho de las inhumaciones fue posible realizar análisis dental y sólo en el Entierro 3 fue posible hacer una medición del rango craneal, quedando dentro del los índices de braquicéfalo.

Respecto a la forma del enterramiento, tres de ellos fueron extendidos, mientras que 7 estuvieron flexionados o semiflexionados, mostrando una preferencia por esta manera de disposición del cuerpo.

Es significativo también que la mayoría de las inhumaciones estuvieron en las proximidades de los derrumbes de los muros, lo que coincidiría con lo que se ha reportado en tiempos históricos dentro de los grupos Tohono O'odham, quienes utilizaron las laderas de los cerros para disponer de los cuerpos cubriéndolos con las rocas de las inmediaciones. Este parece haber sido el tratamiento mortuorio de la mayoría de las inhumaciones, ya que los cuerpos aparecieron en las inmediaciones de los muros de las terrazas o dentro de los muros derrumbados de los cuartos adosados.

Solamente dos inhumaciones presentaron materiales asociados claramente como ofrendas, los entierros 3 y 11, en posición flexionado y semiflexionado respectivamente. El entierro 3 tuvo asociado un pendiente de concha localizado a la altura del esternón, una cuenta de piedra verde localizada arriba del cráneo y una vasija cerámica Trincheras Lisa 3 a la altura de las rodillas. Esto último es importante por el hecho que habíamos propuesto que las inhumaciones podrían haber ocurrido posteriores a la ocupación del sitio; sin embargo, la identificación de la cerámica como Trincheras Lisa 3, le asignaría una contemporaneidad con dicha ocupación.

Es interesante también, que a pesar de la enorme cantidad de ornamentos en concha recuperados del sitio, sólo dos de las inhumaciones tuvieron una clara asociación. Esto nos permite considerar que no estaba relacionada al tratamiento mortuorio, sino que era parte del adorno personal de los habitantes del cerro. Las excavaciones de Cerro de Trincheras produjeron más de 6,800 especimenes de sólo un 1.5 por ciento del sitio excavado (Vargas Chapter 6), por lo que una manufactura intensiva de ornamentos en pelecípodos y gasterópodos se ha evidenciado en el sitio, incluyendo cantidades sustanciales de desecho de manufactura, ornamentos en proceso y adornos terminados (Vargas 1997) que debieron formar parte de eventos especiales practicados en este centro regional. Es importante destacar también que la asociación de un fragmento de Conus con el Entierro 11, permitió en campo identificarlo como anillo, ya que se encontró cerca de los huesos de la mano derecha y no como en San Cayetano Tumacacori donde algunos ornamentos en este gasterópodo estuvieron como cuentas alrededor del cuello de ciertos personajes. El pendiente de concha nacarado asociado al Entierro 3, seguramente colgaba suspendido como adorno frontal, mientras que la cuenta de piedra verde, posiblemente fue un adorno del pelo de ese hombre.

En los últimos años se han recuperado más de 250 inhumaciones del sitio La Playa, a 10 kilómetros al norte de Cerro de Trincheras, en las márgenes del Arroyo Boquillas. Si bien la disposición de los cuerpos ha sido muy variada, destacan los entierros flexionados y semiflexionados en correspondencia con las Fases San Pedro y Ciénega del periodo de Agricultura Temprana (1600 a.C.-circa 200 d.C.). Es interesante que los habitantes de Cerro de Trincheras continuaron sepultando a sus muertos en estas mismas posiciones, marcándonos una continuidad cultural en el tratamiento mortuorio de estos grupos del desierto sonorense.

En el desierto de Sonora la cremación como práctica mortuoria está asociada con las comunidades agricultoras del periodo cerámico, del siglo III en adelante. En el caso de Cerro de Trincheras, parecería que ambas prácticas son contemporáneas, tal vez reflejando diferencias de estatus dentro de la sociedad o a algún otro factor que no queda claro en nuestras apreciaciones. La disposición de los muertos bajo los derrumbes de muros de terrazas y otros elementos arquitectónicos, inicialmente nos había llevado a suponer que estos entierros habrían sido realizados después del siglo XIV, cuando ya el cerro se habría abandonado. Sin embargo, la presencia de un cuerpo de olla identificada como Trincheras Lisa 3, asociada al Entierro 3, nos marcaría la contemporaneidad con la ocupación del cerro, lo que nos podría llevar a suponer el abandono de ciertas áreas dentro del asentamiento en aquellas unidades domésticas donde hubiera ocurrido un deceso, o la reutilización de vasijas de la antigua ocupación, cuando el sitio ya había sido abandonado.

Chapter 13
Área A1, Plaza de El Caracol

Emiliano Gallaga Murrieta. Centro INAH Sonora

Area A1

Area A1 is located on the eastern saddle of the cerro crest and encompasses the Plaza de Caracol. The Plaza consisted of several architectural features that include the spiral-walled El Caracol and 20 circular stone structures. Archaeological investigation included the excavation of El Caracol and 16 of the circular stone structures and the stripping of a portion of the plaza surface. The paucity of domestic artifacts recovered from A1 indicates that this locus was not intensively inhabited. Alternatively, architectural survey, excavations and stripping within Area A1 suggest female gendered ritual purposes for the Plaza that were characterized by privacy and intimacy. This chapter discusses Area A1 investigations and the results of that work.

Introducción

El sitio Cerro de Trincheras se encuentra dividido en cinco áreas de investigación que están directamente relacionadas con la superficie que ocupa el cerro. En este caso se describirá el Área A, la cual se ubica en la porción superior del cerro. Esta área se comenzó a trabajar en la segunda temporada de campo, a principios del mes de febrero de 1996 y culminó a finales del mes de abril del mismo año. Debido a las limitantes de tiempo y a que el área es de grandes dimensiones, sólo se escogió una porción de está, a la que se le denominó Área A1. Al finalizar la temporada de excavación terminó denominándose Plaza de El Caracol.

El área escogida se localiza en una de las porciones planas de la cresta superior del cerro. Viendo al sitio de norte a sur se ubica en el lado este del cerro; el área se localiza entre la cima o pico en de medio y el pico de la porción este.

La Plaza de El Caracol cuenta con una vegetación catalogada como Arizona Uplands (Dimmitt 2000). Está es una asociación de especies arbustivas con una altura aproximada de .5 m hasta 5 m de altura; se caracteriza por el predominio de especies con hojas compuestas, pequeñas y perennes en algunos y caediza en otros. Estos arbustos comparten el espacio asociándose con especies de cactáceas, principalmente de los géneros *Opuntia* y *Carnegiea*.

En nuestra área contamos con una gran cantidad de arbustos donde predominan los del tipo *Larrea tridentata* (hediondilla o gobernadora) y *Ambrosia dumosa* (ambrosia); algunos arboles en el que predominan el *Cercidium microphillum* (palo verde), y algunos ejemplares de *Fouuieria splendens* (ocotillo), *Olneya tesota* (palo fierro) y *Prosopis juliflora* (mezquite). También se localizan cactáceas como el *Carnegiea gigantea* (sahuaro), *Ferocactus* sp. (biznaga), *Opuntia* sp. (cholla) (Figura 13.1) (Lehr 1978).

En cuanto a la fauna, el sitio cuenta con una gran diversidad aunque en el Área A1 sólo se identificaron los siguientes, en el genero de insectos, al *Escorpión* (alacran), *Scolopendra heros* (ciempiés), *Taeneopoda eques* (chapulin), y varios tipos de arañas y chanates. Dentro de los mamíferos identificamos *Citellus variegatus* (ardilla), *Netoma albigula* (rata de campo), *Uma notata* (cachora) y *Crotalus atrox* (víbora de cascabel). Como aves se identificaron al *Geococcyx californianu*s (correcaminos), *Bubo virginianus* (búho), codorniz y zopilote (Howell and Webb 1995).

Debido a que esta área se localiza en la porción superior del cerro donde corren fuertes vientos y carece de una gran cobertura de flora, se encuentran superficies muy erosionadas donde predominan los suelos de tipo regosol que se caracterizan por ser de colores cafés claros y con un escaso contenido de materia orgánica. Por lo general son de poca profundidad (entre 0 y 30 cm) y en bastantes porciones es posible apreciar la roca madre, que en este caso es de origen volcánico.

En lo que respecta a los rasgos arqueológicos, mencionaremos a manera introductoria que nuestra área presenta una superficie nivelada por un sistema de terrazas ubicadas a los lados del cerro (Figura 13.2). El área cuenta con 12 terrazas que son las siguientes: en la porción norte la T791 (43 m de largo, .60 m de alta), T711 (26 m de largo, 1.17 m de alta) y T709 (40 m de largo, 1.20 m de alta); en la porción sur contamos con la T715 (60 m de largo, 1.10 de alta), T740 (29 m de largo, 1.30 de alta), T716 (62 m de largo, .78 m de alta)

Figura 13.1. Área A1.

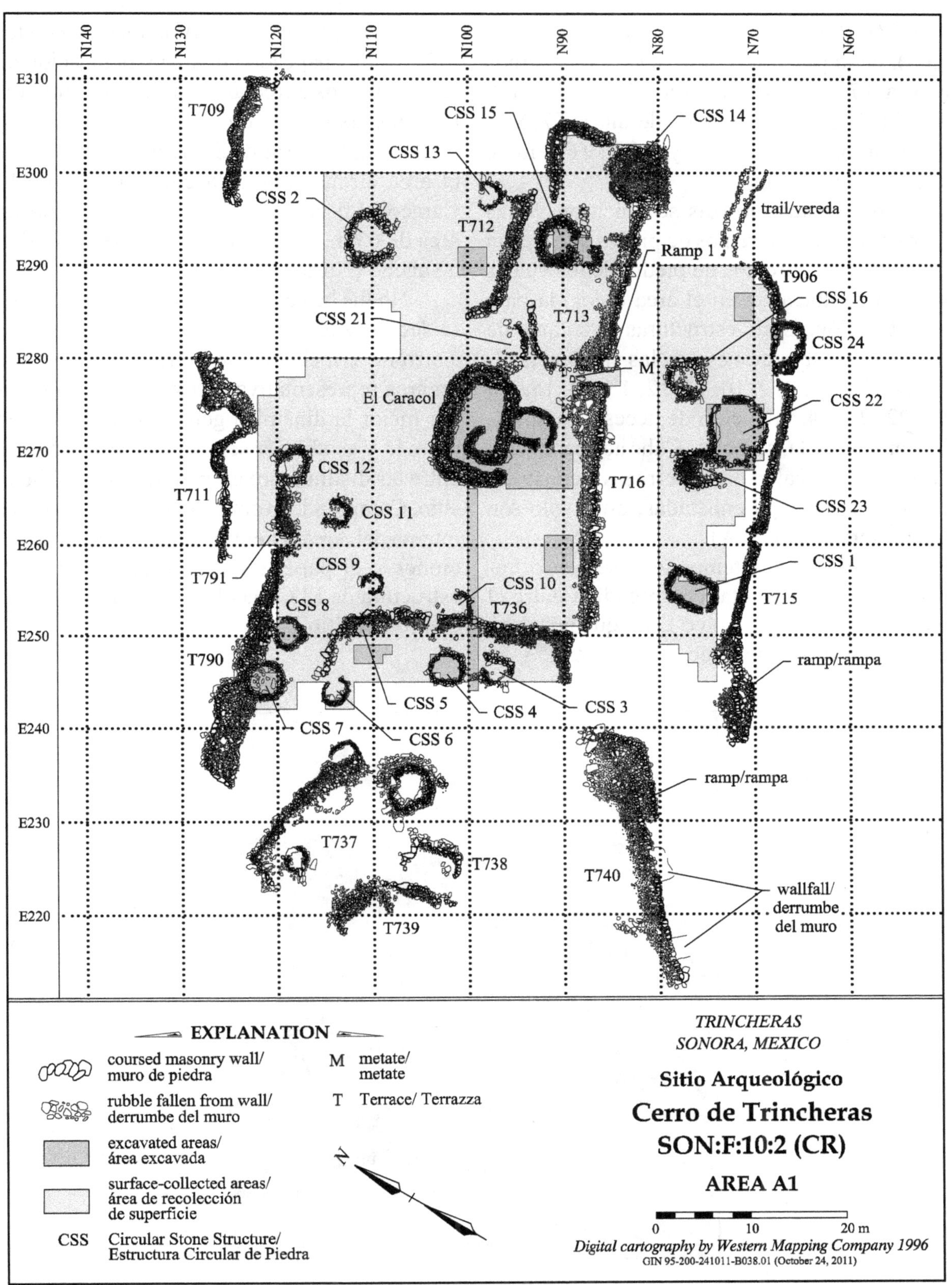

Figura 13.2. Mapa de Área A1.

y la T712 (16 m de largo, .95 de alta) (Figura 13.3); en la porción central del área contamos con la T736 (26 m de largo, .72 m de alta), T737 (51 m de largo, 1.12 de alta), T738 (5 m de largo, .85 m de alta) y la T739 (15 m de largo, .55 m de alta).

Sobre estas terrazas se ubicaron varias construcciones o círculos de piedra que dieron un total de 27 círculos de piedra de los cuales sólo 23 se ubicaban en el área escogida para investigación. Estas estructuras circulares de piedra o construcciones son las siguientes: 1, 2, 3, 4, 5, 6, 7, 8, 9, 10, 11, 12, 13, 14, 15, 16, 21, 22, 23, 24, elemento de acceso: rampa 1, El Caracol y El Caracol A. Cabe aclarar que en el Área A se localizan más terrazas y construcciones que las aquí enlistadas; éstas sólo son las comprendidas en A1.

Al inicio de la temporada, se penso trabajar la superficie total comprendida entre el pico de en Medio y el pico Este, que nos daba un área de 105 m de largo (Este a Oeste) y 50 m de ancho (Norte a Sur). Al comenzar con los trabajos de chapeado del área y planeación de la retícula nos percatamos de que era un área bastante extensa para cubrirla en tan poco tiempo por lo que se decidió trabajar solamente el área circundante a la construcción de El Caracol. Lo cual nos dio como resultado un área de 63 m de largo (Este a Oeste) por 40 m de ancho (Norte a Sur).

No fue hasta la segunda temporada en que se decidió excavar la porción superior del sitio Cerro de Trincheras. Se pretendió contar con un área representativa de ésta, para comprender mejor la dinámica general del sitio como un todo y establecer semejanzas y diferencias entre las distintas áreas en las que se dividió el sitio. Comprender o entender mejor la dinámica interna del Área A1 entre las distintas construcciones y el papel que pudo haber tenido la estructura de El Caracol en la dinámica social dentro del sitio.

Figura 13.3. Vista de Área A1 de abajo, el lado sur del cerro.

Métodos

Dentro de las primeras actividades que se realizaron fue la del reconocimiento de la zona para establecer los accesos o la ruta de acenso más factible; decidir la extensión del área de investigación y familiarizarse con ésta. Posteriormente se realizo un registro fotográfico de cómo se encontró el área antes de cual¬quier intervención. Como en todo proyecto, el proceso de la investigación varió a lo largo de la temporada. En un principio se estableció una metodología de trabajo en la que se planteaba realizar excavaciones extensivas a lo largo de todo el sitio, incluyendo el Área A1. Al percatarnos de lo extensivo de la misma y del tiem¬po con el que contábamos, se tomo la decisión de reducir el área de investigación, realizar una recolección de superficie de manera extensiva en toda el área establecida y delimitar algunas zonas de excavación en áreas que se considaran relevantes para la comprensión del sitio. Como por ejemplo el interior de algunas construcciones, los rellenos de las terrazas o posibles áreas de actividad.

Otra de las razones por las que se cambio la metodología inicial, fue que al realizar la limpieza de yerbas y arbustos, se percato el grado de erosión que sufre el área y de la perturbación, tanto animal como humana, de los contextos arqueológicos. De igual manera se noto la cercanía de la roca madre (de origen volcánico) a la superficie. Lo que nos sugería la falta de rellenos o capas dentro de las cuales pudieran contener tanto materiales como información de las actividades realizadas. Por lo que se optó por la recolección de superficie extensiva por considerar que podría brindarnos más información, a nivel general, que la de realizar excavaciones extensivas.

En general, la metodología de trabajo consistió en cinco actividades principales que fueron: A) limpieza y reticulación del área; B) calas de aproximación, recolección de superficie y excavación; C) mapeo; D) rellenado de áreas de excavación, restauración y conservación del área (actividades que describiremos más adelante). Vale la pena aclarar que estas actividades no se realizaron una detrás de la otra sino que en varias ocasiones se alternaron o se realizaron al mismo momento, dependiendo de las características del área y de las necesidades que fueron surgiendo. Estas cinco actividades se describirán en detalle. Para realizar este trabajo fueron asignados dos arqueólogos: una de nacionalidad estadounidense Debora Langer, estudiante de arqueología de la Universidad de Binghamton, NY como ayudante de excavación; y un Mexicano, Emiliano Gallaga M., pasante de arqueología de la Escuela Nacional de Antropología e Historia (E.N.A.H) de México como jefe de excavación. Por otro lado fueron contratados cuatro trabajadores de la población local como apoyo logístico. Este equipo consistente en seis personas laboró en el área de principios del mes de febrero a finales de abril (con excepción de Debora L. quien al final de la temporada fue transferida a otra área). También se contó con la participación, durante una parte de la temporada, de la pasante de arqueología Elizabeth Bagwell, quien desempeño actividades diversas como excavación y dibujo.

Limpieza y Reticulación del Área

Una de las primeras actividades que se realizaron en el Área A1 fue la de limpieza del área, la cual consistió en chapearla o deshierbarla, actividad que consumió cerca de dos semanas. Como se mencionó anteriormente, se pensaba trabajar en una área más grande. En este sentido, no sólo se chapeó el área delimitada, sino unos 5 m de más por lado o en algunos casos la terraza inferior. Esto se realizó con el fin de tener una mejor visión o comprensión del área a trabajar y poder liberar las paredes o muros de las terrazas que a las que posteriormente se les reintegrarían las porciones colapsadas.

Para esta etapa del proyecto se utilizaron machetes, pinzas para podar, hacha, una sierra y una pinza de perico para cortar raíces o ramas. Esta etapa fue realizada por los cuatro trabajadores contratados y supervisada por los arqueólogos. Cabe aclarar que en este proceso se respetaron todos los árboles de gran tamaño como fueron el palo verde y el palo fierro; solamente se podaron aquellos que impedían la visibilidad del teodolito durante el establecimiento de la retícula.

De igual manera, mientras se realizaba el chapeado del área, se estableció la retícula de excavación. Dicha actividad estuvo a cargo de John McGregor y auxiliado por los arqueólogos antes mencionados. La base de la retícula se estableció, en un principio, en el centro de nuestra área original. Que fue en la porción más elevada del área, de la cual se podía cubrir toda el área propuesta originalmente. Posteriormente al cambiar las dimensiones de nuestra área sólo se retículo la porción Oeste sin necesidad de cambiar nuestra base (Figura 13.2).

Debido a las dimensiones de nuestra área (60 m de largo por 40 m de ancho) y de las condiciones del terreno, la retícula se basó en rectángulos de 5 m de ancho (Norte a Sur) por 10 m (Este a Oeste). Para esta actividad se utilizó un teodolito láser, un mazo, varillas de metal, spray de color amarillo y cinta de plástico de diversos colores para marcar los puntos en la superficie. Es importante recalcar que una vez concluida la limpieza del área fue posible identificar más elementos arquitectónicos de los que se tenía conocimiento como es el caso de algunos círculos de piedra, terrazas chicas que se encontraban colapsadas o cubiertas de maleza, accesos, caminos o veredas que se encontraban escondidos por la vegetación.

Calas de Aproximación y Recolección de Superficie

Una vez limpiada el área y establecida la retícula se realizo una primera cala de aproximación para tener una mejor idea del relleno y conocer las capas existentes. En un principio se pensó realizar la cala "cortando" el área de Oeste a Este, pero debido a los resultados obtenidos sólo se realizó del borde Oeste de la retícula hasta la pared Oeste de El Caracol. Contó con una dimensión de 1 m de ancho por 22.70 m de largo (Figura 13.2) ubicada en los cuadros N 99-100, E 244-266.

De esta primera etapa de la cala se identificaron tres capas estratigráficas de tipo natural (Harris 1989) las cuales describiremos a continuación:

> Capa 1. Superficie, compuesta de material orgánico y de material arqueológico.
>
> Capa 2. Compuesta de tierra café amarillento claro (10YR 5/4, yellowish brown), muy fina y en algunas porciones se encontraba mezclada con piedra chica (del tamaño de un limón) y mediana (del tamaño de una toronja); también contó con material arqueológico.
>
> Capa 3. - Roca madre; aparecía por lo general a escasos 5 a 10 cm de profundidad y en algunos casos 20 a 25 cm (Figura 13.4). No presentó material arqueológico.

De esta manera inferimos que la formación de contextos es la siguiente: primero contamos con la capa 3 (roca madre) a la cual se le añade una segunda capa (2), la cual un pequeño porcentaje puede ser por deposición natural pero consideramos que la gran mayoría es depositada artificialmente, es decir es acarreada por los grupos humanos para rellenar las terrazas creadas para nivelar la superficie. Posiblemente, debido al alto grado de erosión,

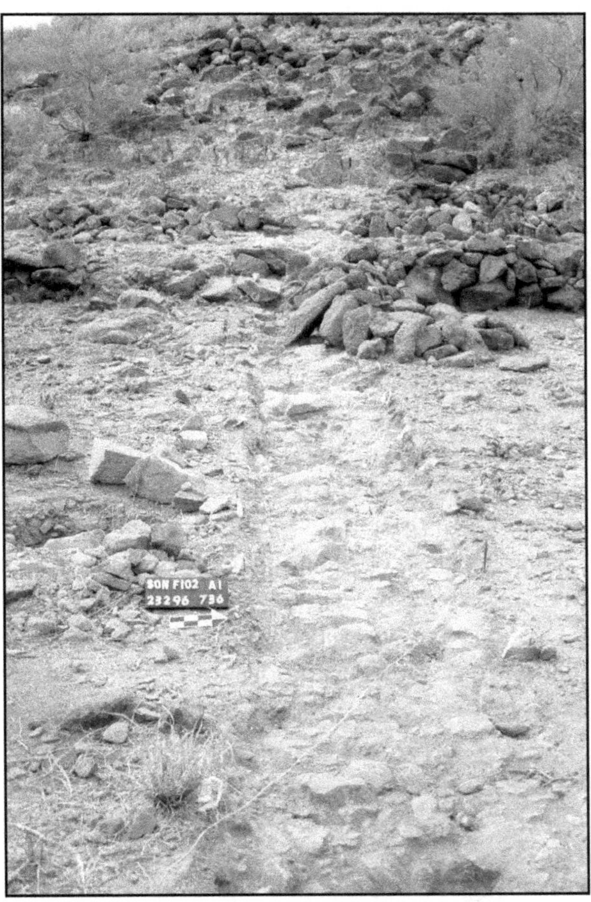

Figura 13.4. Cala de aproximación.

la porción última de esta deposición artificial o cultural ya no existe por lo que la última capa identificada en este proceso es la 1, que es producto de la deposición natural por la acción del tiempo y de la descomposición del detritus natural.

Con estos resultados se tomó la decisión de no continuar con la cala y no realizar más calas a lo largo y ancho del área, por lo que se comenzó con la recolección de superficie la cual se realizó en unidades de un metro cuadrado. Como nuestra retícula estaba basada en cuadros de 5 por 10 m, se tuvo que elabororar un sistema que nos diera las unidades por metro cuadrado. Este sistema consistió en una serie de retículas móviles de 4 m cuadrados c/u, elaborada con cuerda a manera de "red;" esta se ponía en el área a muestrear y se movía hacia otra área una vez concluida la anterior. La recolección se realizó por líneas de norte a sur, comenzando por la esquina suroeste hasta el extremo opuesto (este).

La metodología utilizada fue la siguiente: Se establecían las retículas móviles en la línea en cuestión, y se estableció que cada trabajador se haría cargo de un metro cuadrado a la vez de tal manera que éste recolectaba el material arqueológico que se observaba fácilmente. Posteriormente con una brocha se limpiaba toda la superficie de la unidad (detritus natural y material cultural). El mismo trabajador realizaba el cribado para posteriormente realizar la recolección del material rescatado en las cribas.Despues, una vez llenadas las carretillas de tierra se procedía a depositarlas en un área previamente establecida para tal efecto.

Desde el principio de la temporada se establecieron cuatro criterios generales de clasificación del material que fueron cerámica, lítica, concha y hueso y de manera especifica cerámica decorada e instrumentos líticos. Además cada unidad contaba con un registro de bolsa para cada tipo de material localizado, el cual varió de cero a seis bolsas distintas de material. A mediados de la temporada se terminó la recolección en la superficie establecida y se decidió expandir el área de trabajo hacia la porción Sur, sobre la terraza inferior T715 (Figura 13.2). Esto significo volver a chapear, reticular y realizar la recolección de superficie, con la misma metodología mencionada anteriormente.

De esta manera se logró cubrir, a final de la temporada, un total de 2,192 m^2 de un total de 2,500 m^2 aproximadamente. La diferencia existente en los metros cuadrados se debió al hecho de que en algunas ocasiones las áreas de recolección se localizaban sobre muros de estructuras, de terrazas y/o áreas erosionadas que no contenían material cultural y en algunos casos ni tierra, solamente la roca madre.

Para esta etapa de la investigación se utilizaron cucharillas, brochas, cubetas de metal, recogedores, una barreta, clavos, un mazo, cinta de plástico, dos cintas métricas (una de 30 m y otra de 50 m), dos brújulas, una escoba, una caja de herramientas, dos cribas, dos carretillas y cuatro "retículas móviles."

Excavación

A pesar de que en un principio se había considerado que no se realzarían excavaciones extensivas y solamente se excavaría en algunas áreas relevantes de esta área, al final de la temporada se lograron liberar 257 m^2, lo que representó cerca del 10 por ciento del total del área. De estos, 161 m^2 corresponden al interior de construcciones y los restantes 96 m^2 a espacios al aire libre de las terrazas (Figura 13.5). Las construcciones liberadas fueron escogidas de manera arbitraria, dependiendo de las condiciones de preservación en la que se localizaban y la importancia social que aparentemente pudieron haber desempeñado.

En el caso del resto de las áreas (al aire libre) liberadas, fueron igualmente designadas arbitrariamente por el estado de conservación y aparente no perturbación, tanto humana como animal. Así como en áreas en las que se localizaron un mayor número de materiales en superficie y en las que aparentemente se contaba con un mínimo de 10 cm de espesor de la superficie a la roca madre. Estas áreas de sondeo se realizaron para permitirnos tener una mejor idea de la formación de los contextos de estas terrazas, patrón de construcción de las mismas y de la posible utilización de los espacios.

Figura 13.5. Excavación del Plaza de El Caracol.

En este sentido se excavaron 15 m^2 de la T736; 60 m^2 de la T716; 9 m^2 de la T712 y 12 m^2 de la T715, llegando hasta la roca madre. En lo que respecta a estas áreas, presentaron una estratigrafía muy homogénea. Las capas localizadas fueron similares a las tres capas descritas para la cala 1 (Harris 1989).

Volviendo a las construcciones, se excavaron un total de 13 de 23, que fueron las siguientes: 1, 2, 4, 5, 7, 8, 14, 15, 15.A, 22, 24, El Caracol y El Caracol A que es el cuarto que se anexa a la construcción de El Caracol (Figura 13.2). Todas éstas se localizan a lo largo y ancho del área de investigación.

Sólo mencionaremos a manera general que el comportamiento de los contextos arqueológicos de las construcciones fue similar en la mayoría de ellas, donde sólo se localizaron las tres capas descritas anteriormente que fueron Capa 1 (superficie), Capa 2 (tierra café claro con piedras de diversos tamaños) y la Capa 3 (roca madre), la cual se localizó en promedio entre los 10 y los 15 cm de profundidad. El patrón anterior no se localizó en las construcciones 4, 24, El Caracol y en El Caracol A. En estas estructuras se identificaron cuatro capas, en las que se localizó una superficie apisonada entre la Capa 1 (superficie) y la Capa 2 (relleno prehispánico). Pero debido a los materiales asociados a ella, se descartó que pudiera ser contemporánea con las construcciones. Los material asociados fueron vidrio obscuro (posiblemente de cerveza) y huesos largos de vaca.

En lo que se refiere al color de las capas, es interesante mencionar que en el sitio Cerro de Trincheras, se ha establecido un patrón interpretativo de ocupación. En el cual se determina el contexto o grado de ocupación de un área apartir del color del suelo. De esta manera se estableció que cuando los suelos son de tonalidades obscuras es indicativo de una extensa o amplia actividad; si por el contrario los suelos son bastante claros se establece que no hubo una gran actividad en estas áreas. Las tonalidades obscuras están identificadas como ceniza mezclada con las áreas de ocupación. De esta manera el color de las capas identificadas nos sugiere que el lapso de ocupación o uso de la mayoría de las construcciones del Área A1 fue relativamente corto.

En el transcurso de la excavación también se sacaron diversas muestras como es el caso de polen y flotación, las cuales se obtuvieron debajo de fragmentos de cerámica de gran tamaño o de una "olla parcial." Pero la gran mayoría de las muestras se sacaron de manera arbitraria de alguna porción del área excavada y sin distinción de cada una de las construcciones. Las muestras se obtuvieron con el fin de determinar posibles actividades que pudieran haberse realizado en el interior de las construcciones, de ser posible los paleoambientes, así como los alimentos consumidos o materiales orgánicos presentes. En caso de muestras de fechamiento, no se pudieron obtener muestras de C-14 porque desgraciadamente no se localizaron fogones, áreas de cocción o trozos significativos de carbón.

En el caso de las áreas de sondeo al aire libre también se obtuvieron muestras de polen y flotación para contrastar los resultados obtenidos con los de las construcciones y poder determinar, si es posible, qué actividades se realizaban en el interior de las mismas y cuáles afuera. Cabe mencionar que tanto la recolección de superficie como la excavación no se realizaron una detrás de la otra, sino que se estuvo alternando, según las circunstancias surgidas en el transcurso del proyecto.

Para esta etapa de la investigación se utilizaron cuatro cucharillas, dos palas, dos picoletas, un pico, ocho brochas, cuatro cubetas de metal, cuatro recogedores, una barreta, clavos, un mazo, cinta de plástico, dos cintas métricas (una de 30 m y otra de 50 m), dos brújulas, una escoba, una caja de herramientas, dos cribas, dos carretillas, un pizarrón para registro fotográfico y una cámara (Figura 13.6).

Mapeo del Área

Esta actividad se realizó a lo largo de toda la temporada, la cual tuvo el fin de mapear toda el área de investigación y áreas circundantes con el fin de poder contar con una mejor idea del contexto urbanístico, la relación existente entre las terrazas y las construcciones localizadas en esta porción del Área A, y para posteriormente comparar esta área con el resto del sitio.

La metodología utilizada fue la siguiente: primero se realizó de manera independiente el dibujo, tanto en planta como en corte (cuando se trató de una construcción excavada), de cada una de las construcciones a una escala general de 1/20 dentro de las hojas de registro de construcciones. Éste, consistió en dibujar cada una de las piedras que conponían la construcción, tratando de esta manera de mostrar más detalladamente la forma de la estructura, la relación de los espació interiores, accesos y orientación.

De igual forma, si en el interior o en el exterior circundante a la construcción era localizado algún material o elemento cultural (metates, manos, lítica, cerámica o concha), se dibujaban en la posición exacta en la que se encontraban. En esta primera etapa los dibujos fueron realizados en campo, la mitad de ellos, por la pasante de arqueología Elizabeth Bagwell y el resto de ellos por el pasante de arqueología Emiliano Gallaga.

En una segunda etapa se dibujaron en campo, a la misma escala de 1/20, cada una de las terrazas que fueron enlistadas anteriormente, al igual que los accesos y caminos

Figura 13.6. Plaza de El Caracol excavada.

identificados en el área. Estos dibujos fueron realizados por Elizabeth Bagwell y Emiliano Gallaga. Al igual que en las construcciones, los dibujos se realizaron de la misma manera, tratando de ser lo más fiel a la realidad, mostrando todos los detalles posibles. Posteriormente en laboratorio se integraron todos los dibujos en uno general a escala de 1/20 (Figura 13.2) el cual fue realizado por John McGregor. Este mapa se le redujo cerca del 75 por ciento para poder trabajar sobre el.

Para esta actividad se utilizaron los siguientes materials: papel milimétrico, lapiceros, goma de agua, dos brújulas y escalímetros.

Rellenado de Áreas de Excavación

Desde el inicio se había contemplado realizar esta actividad por lo que se estableció un área para depositar la tierra proveniente, tanto de la recolección de superficie como la de excavación. Esta área se escogió de manera arbitraria en alguna porción del área de investigación que careciera de materiales (en superficie), que se encontrara totalmente erosionada o en grados muy avanzados. Y que de igual manera fuera de fácil acceso desde todas las direcciones del área. (Figura 13.2). También se consideró desde un principio dividir el material de excavación en tierra y piedra para poder facilitar su traslado a la hora de rellenar las áreas. Por lo general esta actividad se realizó al final de la temporada. Primero se rellenaron las áreas liberadas con piedras y posteriormente se cubrían con tierra hasta dejarlas a un nivel un poco superior que el resto de la superficie, ya que de esa manera damos un margen para la filtración de la tierra al interior del relleno.

Vale la pena mencionar que en algunas ocasiones se alternó esta actividad con la de excavación. Ya que cada vez que se concluía totalmente la investigación (excavación, obtención de muestras, dibujo y fotografía), tanto de una área al aire libre como de una construcción, se procedía a rellenar con material procedente de alguna otra área en proceso de excavación o de recolección de superficie, que previamente hubiera sido cribado. Para esta etapa sólo se utilizaron dos palas, un pico, cuatro cubetas de metal y dos carretillas.

Restauración y Conservación

Debido a las características de este proyecto y las características propias del sitio, podemos mencionar que es la primera ocasión en la que se realizan actividades de restauración en construcciones Prehispánicas dentro del estado de Sonora, lo cual es de entrada, relevante.

Para realizar esta actividad nos apoyamos en la Ley Orgánica del Instituto National de Antropología e Historia (INAH) (1995) donde en su artículo segundo menciona ". . . son objetivos generales del Instituto Nacional de Antropología e Historia la investigación científica sobre antropología e historia relacionada principalmente con la población del país y con la conservación y restauración del patrimonio cultural arqueológico e histórico . . . ." Para nuestro caso concreto, nos interesa la fracción IX que menciona entre los objetivos de INAH el ". . . identificar, investigar, recuperar, proteger, restaurar, rehabilitar, vigilar y custodiar en los términos prescritos por la Ley Federal sobre Monumentos y Zonas Arqueológicos . . ." (1995). Esta ley menciona en el capitulo primero, articulo segundo que ". . . es de utilidad pública, la investigación, protección, conservación, restauración y recuperación de los monumentos arqueológicos . . . ."

En cuanto al concepto de restauración, entendemos como una operación especial de conservación, que se realiza físicamente sobre el objeto cultural, destinada a salvaguardarlo, mantenerlo y prolongar su permanencia para trasmitirlo al futuro (Díaz-Berrio 1976:4-5). Para el caso específico de las construcciones del sitio Cerro de Trincheras, la restauración que se aplicó por considerarla la más adecuada fue la de restitución de material. En algunos casos también se utilizo lo que se denomina como "anastilosis" (entiéndase la reintegración de todas aquellas piedras que a la hora de liberar las estructuras, presentaron evidencia de mostrar su posición original en el muro).

Esta actividad se realizo contemplando los lineamientos establecidos internacionalmente, sobre todo en la Carta de Venecia (1931), entre los que cabe destacar los siguientes:

-Utilización del material proveniente de la excavación y/o del área de investigación.

-Realización de un registro fotográfico (y dibujo si es necesario) de cada uno de los procesos de la restauración.

-La reintegración de material se realizó hasta donde la evidencia material nos lo permitió.

-La restauración es de carácter reversible; no se utilizaron cementantes o consolidantes.

-Se utilizo el mismo sistema constructivo empleado por los antiguos habitantes del sitio.

Como ya se mencionó, una vez desmontada el área de investigación nos percatamos de la presencia de más elementos constructivos, su estado de conservación y el grado de destrucción en el que se encontraban. Al igual que en la mayoría de los sitios arqueológicos, el sitio Cerro de Trincheras no estuvo exento de la destrucción tanto de carácter natural como de la del humano. Por esto se consideró que la restauración del Área A1 era de vital importancia para una buena interpretación del sitio. Por otro lado, para un buen desarrollo de la investigación del área, la realización de esta actividad fue vital ya que desde un principio se

Figura 13.7. El Carcol antes de restaurar.

planeo la liberación de varias construcciones, las cuales se encontraban con un alto grado de destrucción o de muros colapsados que impedían trabajar tanto en el interior como en el exterior de las mismas. En este sentido, la restauración o restitución de materiales de las distintas construcciones se llevo a cabo desde un principio de la temporada. Para este efecto se destinó un día a la semana, en este caso los sábados, para realizar la restauración de las construcciones.

La metodología utilizada fue la siguiente: una vez limpiadas las construcciones y de conocer el grado de destrucción o deterioro, se realizaba un registro fotográfico de cómo se encontraba la estructura (Figura 13.7). Posteriormente se liberaba la estructura de las piedras caídas y se restituían en la porción faltante del muro o en caso de ser un muro colapsado se desmontaba la porción colapsada hasta localizar el muro original. Luego se volvía a levantar el muro hasta donde nos lo permitía la evidencia material, sigiendo el mismo patrón de construcción. Una vez concluida esta fase se volvía a sacar un registro fotográfico con lo cual es posible apreciar los resultados (Figura 13.8).

Este mismo procedimiento se siguió no sólo para las construcciones sino para todos los elementos constructivos como los muros de las terrazas. Cabe aclarar que se logró terminar la restauración del área de investigación pero por falta de tiempo no se pudo concluir la restauración en otras áreas en las que ya se había terminado de limpiar. De alguna manera representaba un trabajo extra no contemplado en el proyecto original pero que facilitaría la comprensión, tanto del sistema constructivo como de la distribución urbana del Área A.

Por otro lado, podemos concluir que con esta actividad se cumplen los objetivos de conservar y preservar el sitio para las futuras generaciones. Así como, de alguna manera devolverle al sitio su volumen material y visual, lo cual nos permitió apreciar la planeación arquitectónica del espacio, la utilización de los materiales y la distribución de los elementos entre las distintas áreas.

Figura 13.8. El Caracol después de restaurar.

También, gracias a la restauración de los elementos arquitectónicos descritos anteriormente, nos pudimos percatar y conocer el sistema constructivo de las construcciones, terrazas, accesos y veredas, los cuales describiremos brevemente.

A manera muy general, en el caso de las construcciones, se limpia el área escogida y sin realizar cimentaciones (posiblemente por localizarse muy cerca de la superficie la roca madre), se levantan los muros con piedra volcánica sin carear. Los muros cuentan con un grosor aproximado de 30 cm hasta 1 m (dependiendo el tipo de construcción). Por lo general las caras de los muros se realizan con piedras de gran tamaño tratando de usar la cara más plana al exterior. El espacio interno se rellena con piedras de menor tamaño y piedra chica para rellenar los huecos y darle consistencia al muro. En el interior de los muros se localizó muy poca tierra que consideramos es producto de la deposición temporal y que nos indica que no se utilizó tierra como aglutinante.

En el caso de la altura de las construcciones, fue difícil determinar una altura específica ya que la evidencia localizada variaba dependiendo del grado de destrucción de las construcciones. En los círculos de piedra contamos desde 30 cm hasta 1 m de altura. Consideramos que el techo de estas estructuras era de material perecedero, similares a lo que se conoce como ramadas. No se localizaron huellas de postes pero cabe mencionar que las superficies se localizaban muy erosionadas y la roca madre muy cerca de la superficie por lo que no se descarta la posibilidad de que si hayan utilizado postes como soportes.

En el caso de las terrazas, las cuales se utilizan para nivelar la superficie, el sistema constructivo es muy similar al anterior. Salvo la diferencia de que, por lo general, se realizan dos muros con piedra gruesa: uno cuya cara da al interior del cerro y otra al exterior que es la que se observa. El interior se rellena con piedra chica y mediana, no se usa tierra como aglutinante. Dentro del Área A1 se localizaron algunos posibles ejemplos de este tipo en las T740 y T791 aunque la mayoría fueron un sólo muro exterior de piedra grande y rellenado con piedra mediana, chica y nivelado con tierra, que en algunas porciones por acción de la erosión ya no existe. También nos percatamos que los muros se sitúan cerca de afloramiento abruptos de la roca madre para evitar rellenar una gran área. En los accesos o esquinas sólo se limitan a poner piedras de gran tamaño en las que recae el peso y la tensión de los muros.

En lo que respecta a las veredas o caminos localizados, los trinchereños sólo se limitaron a "clarear" o limpiar la superficie, tanto de hierbas como de piedras por la que se trazaba el camin, por lo que de alguna manera es fácil percibirlos una vez limpiada la superficie.

Para la realización de las actividades de restauración, sólo se utilizaron cuatro cubetas de metal, una barreta y la participación de todos los integrantes del equipo.

Por otro lado, con la aplicación de la restauración nos fue posible realizar algunos conceptos de "Arqueología Experimental" que nos permitió realizar algunos cálculos de cuánto tiempo y con cuántos hombres es posible realizar ciertas construcciones o terrazas. De esta manera calculamos que, por ejemplo, para la realización de una terraza de entre 80 cm a un metro de altura por 10 m de largo, teniendo el material a la mano se logra realizar de dos a tres días trabajando ocho horas diarias con cuatro hombres. Sin más instrumentos que las manos, posiblemente algún palo que pudiera fungir como palanca, "cubetas" o algún recipiente para acarrear piedras chicas y tierra para el relleno. Hay que mencionar que el material utilizado en la elaboración de estos elementos arquitectónicos es 100 por ciento local y que en la mayoría de las veces no se requiere de salirse más allá del área circundante escogida para su construcción, para su obtención. Aunque sabemos que de igual manera representa tiempo y trabajo, el cual no se esta contemplando en el calculo anterior.

De cualquier forma, lo anterior nos estaría indicando que en realidad no se requiere de la participación de un gran número de gentes para realizar este tipo de construcciones, pero muy al contrario, sí de una razón ideológica o social para realizarla. En este caso nos estaría indicando la presencia o surgimiento de un grupo o elite que comienzan a dirigir las fuerzas del grupo social, en las que se percibe la utilización de un concepto de urbanización.

Materiales Localizados

En comparación con otras áreas de excavación dentro del sitio, el Área A1 no fue muy productiva. Esto fue debido posiblemente al gran grado de erosión existente en el área, a la perturbación humana y animal de los contextos, y al corto periodo de ocupación del área en tiempos prehispánicos (apreciaciones preliminares).

En lo que respecta a los materiales recuperados en la recolección de superficie, se presentaron en su gran mayoría material cerámico y lítico.

Dentro de los materiales cerámicos, la gran mayoría corresponden a tipos monócromos principalmente Lisa 3 y Tardía. Tambien hay un gran número de tiestos del tipo Rojo Tardío. En lo que respecta a las lozas decoradas, se lograron identificar algunos tiestos en los que sobresalen los Santa Cruz Policromo y los punzonados. El tamaño de los tiestos localizados fue por lo general de pequeñas dimensiones (2 cm^2).

En el caso del material lítico, también se localizó en pequeñas dimensiones, predominando las lascas tanto de materiales locales (basaltos, riolitas, etc) como foráneos, principalmente el de un material color verde que se asume es de origen foráneo al sitio por no localizarse en las inmediaciones de éste. Creemos que su lugar de origen es en las inmediaciones del rancho El Ocuca a unos 25 km norte del sitio Cerro de Trincheras. Aunque escasos, se localizaron algunos instrumentos líticos como machacadores o percutores, raspadores, manos, metates, algunos discos de piedra y varios fragmentos de punta.

En lo que respecta al material marino se localizaron varios fragmentos de pequeñas dimensiones de concha, en el que se dividieron en concha sin trabajar y trabajada en forma de anillos, cuentas y brazaletes.

En el área también se localizaron varios fragmentos de hueso, la mayoría pertenecientes a animales y que en algunos casos consideramos que son producto de los depredadores que habitan en el sitio (sobre todo los de menor tamaño).

Dentro de estos materiales se lograron recuperar algunos fragmentos de punzones que al parecer son de hueso pero que aún no sabemos a que tipo pertenecen.

Es importante recalcar que se localizaron un número considerable de fragmentos de metates y manos lo cual es bastante relevante ya que se consideraba que en esta área no se localizarían este tipo de artefactos por considerarla un área en la que no se practicaban actividades cotidianas. Aunque cabe aclarar que falta ver el análisis de los metates para determinar para que tipo de materiales o actividades fueron utilizados.

En el caso de los materiales procedentes de la excavación, podemos mencionar que no hubo una gran diferencia entre la diversidad de elementos recuperados, si acaso solamente en mayor cantidad pero no en variedad.

Para el caso específico de la cerámica, consideramos que el sólo hecho de localizar un mayor número de fragmentos de lozas monócromas o de uso común nos indica que en esta área se practicaban más actividades cotidianas de las que originalmente creíamos.

Un material interesante que se localizó en excavación, fueron pequeños trozos de "bajareque." Esto nos indica que algunas porciones de las construcciones fueron realizadas mediante este sistema constructivo y/o que el área pudo contener más estructuras que las que hemos identificado hasta el momento. Sin embargo, al ser construidas mediante materiales perecederos ya no es posible identificarlas.

Por otro lado, fue bastante notoria la diferencia en cantidades de material recuperado en áreas al aire libre que de áreas al interior de las construcciones. Por lo general, el material proveniente de las áreas al aire libre fue mucho mayor que el de las construcciones en el que salvo raras excepciones se recupero muy poco material. Lo anterior es un dato significativo para establecer patrones de actividad o de vida. Esta información nos permite esbozar la idea de que en los círculos de piedra o en el interior de las construcciones, por lo menos en lo que respecta al Área A1, no se están utilizando para realizar actividades cotidianas como la elaboración, preparación o consumo de alimentos, talleres o áreas de trabajo, tanto de concha, de lítica o cerámica, sino solamente para dormir o actividades que no dejan rastros materiales o que en estos momentos del análisis no son perceptibles (apreciación personal). Por lo tanto, suponemos que estas actividades se están realizando en los espacios abiertos como lo muestran por ejemplo la cantidad de pequeñas lascas de diverso material lítico localizadas al exterior de las construcciones.

Descripción de Elementos del Área A1

Dentro de el Área A1 se identificaron 24 elementos constructivos, de los cuales 19 se identificaron como "círculos de piedra," dos estructuras rectangulares (catalogados como círculos de piedra), una rampa de acceso y una estructura ceremonial (El Caracol y El Caracol A). A continuación daremos una descripción más detallada de los primeros 22 de los elementos localizados en esta área. El Caracol y El Caracol A se describirán por separado.

Estructura Circular de Piedra 1

Número en campo: C-139.
Ubicación: N 74- 80, E 252-257.
Elevación: 105.27-105.81 mbd
Forma y Tamaño: Rectangular; 4.35 x 2.30 m, altura 54 cm.
Acceso: Esquina SO, 50 cm de ancho.
Orientación: Norte- Sur.
Muros: De piedra, 50 cm de espesor y 85 cm de altura (aprox).
Techo: Posiblemente de material perecedero (ramada); no se localizó evidencia.
Piso: No se localizó apisonado.
Relleno: Muy poco relleno de tierra. La roca madre se localizó a escasos 10 cm.
Materiales: Muy poco material asociado, algunas lascas y pocos tepalcates monocromos.
Comentarios: Esta estructura se localiza en la T715, en su extremo Oeste. Se localiza ligeramente aislada de las demás estructuras de esta terraza.

Estructura Circular de Piedra 2

Número en Campo: C-7.
Ubicación: N 107-113,E 289.50-297
Elevación: 99.69-100.62 mbd
Forma y Tamaño: Circular; 3.30 x 3.37 m, altura 93 cm.
Acceso: Porción Sur, un metro de ancho.
Orientación: Norte-Sur.
Muros: De piedra, un metro de ancho y 93 cm de alto (aprox).
Techo: Sin evidencia, posiblemente de material perecedero (ramada).
Piso: No se localizó apisonado.

Relleno: Muy poco. Roca madre a escasos 5 cm.
Materiales: Muy pocos materiales asociados.
Comentarios: La estructura se localiza en la T712, en su porción NE. Se localiza aislada de las demás estructuras.

Estructura Circular de Piedra 3

Número en Campo: C-121.
Ubicación: N95-100, E 244-250.
Elevación: 100.51-101-11 mbd.
Forma y Tamaño: Circular; 3.90 x 3.30 m, altura 60 cm.
Acceso: Al Norte, 50 cm de ancho.
Orientación: Norte- Sur.
Muros: De piedra, 50 cm de ancho por 30 cm de alto.
Techo: Sin evidencia, posiblemente de material perecedero (ramada).
Piso: No se localizó apisonado.
Relleno: No se excavó.
Materiales: Muy pocos materiales asociados.
Comentarios: La estructura se encontró muy deteriorada. Se localiza en la T736, junto a la estructura 4.

Estructura Circular de Piedra 4

Número en Campo: C-122.
Ubicación: N 100-105, E 244-250.
Elevación: 99.48-100.28 mbd.
Forma y Tamaño: Circular; 4.10 x 4.00 m, altura 80 cm.
Acceso: Al Norte, 30 cm de ancho.
Orientación: Norte-Sur.
Muros: De piedra, 70 cm de ancho x 70 de alto.
Techo: Sin evidencia, posiblemente de material perecedero (ramada).
Piso: Se localizó un apisonado.
Relleno: De tierra fina y piedra de tamaño mediano.
Materiales: Se localizó una gran cantidad de material, principalmente cerámica monocroma y restos de huesos largos.
Comentarios: Se localizó una concentración de cenizas en la porción central pero asociada con materiales modernos. Posiblemente se encuentre asociada con la Estructura 3.

Estructura Circular de Piedra 5

Número en Campo: C-123.
Ubicación: N108-113, E 249-253.
Elevación: 100.96-102.06 mbd
Forma y Tamaño: Circular; 3.80 x 2.40 m, altura 50 cm.
Acceso: Al Oeste, 1.30 m de ancho.
Orientación: Este-Oeste.
Muros: De piedra, 65 cm de ancho x 60 cm de alto.
Techo: Sin evidencia, posiblemente de material perecedero (ramada).
Piso: No se localizó apisonado.
Relleno: De tierra fina. Muy poco. Roca madre a 10 cm.
Materiales: Muy pocos materiales asociados. Algunas cuentas de piedra de muy pequeño tamaño.
Comentarios: La estructura se localizó muy deteriorada. Esta ubicada en la T736 en la esquina NE.

Estructura Circular de Piedra 6

Número en Campo: C-124.
Ubicación: N 112-116, E 242-246.
Elevación: 99.05-99.40 mbd.
Forma y Tamaño: Circular; 3,20 x 2.80 m, altura 70 cm.
Acceso: Al Este, un metro de ancho.
Orientación: Este-Oeste.
Muros: De piedra, 60 cm de ancho x 70 cm de alto.
Techo: Sin evidencia, posiblemente de material perecedero.

Piso: No se localizó apisonado.
Relleno: No se excavó.
Materiales: Pocos materiales asociados.
Comentarios: Se localiza en la T736, en la esquina NO. Ligeramente asilada.

Estructura Circular de Piedra 7

Número en Campo: C-125.
Ubicación: N118-124, E 242-248.
Elevación: 101.13-102.95 mbd
Forma y Tamaño: Circular; 4.80 x 4.40 m, altura 1.10 cm.
Acceso: Al NE, 50 cm de ancho.
Orientación: Este-Oeste.
Muros: De piedra, 80 cm de ancho por 1.10 de alto.
Techo: Sin evidencia, posiblemente de material perecedero.
Piso: No se localizó apisonado.
Relleno: De tierra fina y piedra, muy poco. Roca madre a 10 cm.
Materiales: Gran cantidad de materiales asociados. Principalmente cerámica monócroma y lascas.
Comentarios: La estructura se localiza en la T791, en el extremo Oeste. Se localizó en buen estado. Posiblemente relacionada con la Estructura 8.

Estructura Circular de Piedra 8

Número en campo: C-126.
Ubicación: N116-121, E 248-252.
Elevación: 102.17-102.82 mbd
Forma y Tamaño: Circular; 4 x 3.70 m, altura 80 cm.
Acceso: Al NE, un metro de ancho.
Orientación: NE-SO.
Muros: De piedra, 80 cm de ancho x 80 cm de alto.
Techo: Sin evidencia, posiblemente de material perecedero.
Piso: No se localizó apisonado.
Relleno: De tierra fina y piedra, muy poco. Roca madre a 10 cm.
Materiales: Algunos materiales asociados como cerámica monócroma y lascas.
Comentarios: La estructura se localizó en la T791, en su porción central. Posiblemente asociada con la Estructura 7.

Estructura Circular de Piedra 9 (Figura 13.9)

Número en Campo: C-127.
Ubicación: N 108-112, E 254-258
Elevación: 101.63-102.13 mbd
Forma y Tamaño: Circular, 2.90 x 2.60 m, altura 60 cm.
Acceso: Al NO, 70 cm de ancho.
Orientación: NO-SE.
Muros: De piedra, 60 cm de ancho x 70 cm de alto.
Techo: Sin evidencia, posiblemente de material perecedero.
Piso: No se localizó apisonado.
Relleno: No se excavó.
Materiales: Muy pocos materiales asociados.
Comentarios: La estructura se localiza en la T716, cerca de la esquina NE de la T736. Se encuentra ligeramente aislada de las demás estructuras.

Estructura Circular de Piedra 10 (Figura 13.10)

Número en Campo: C-128.
Ubicación: N95-105, E 251-255.
Elevación: 100.80-101-70 mbd.
Forma y Tamaño: Circular, 3.70 x 3.40 m, altura 85 cm.
Acceso: Al Norte, un metro de ancho.
Orientación: Norte- Sur.
Muros: De piedra, 60 cm de ancho x 85 cm de alto.
Techo: Sin evidencia, posiblemente de material perecedero.

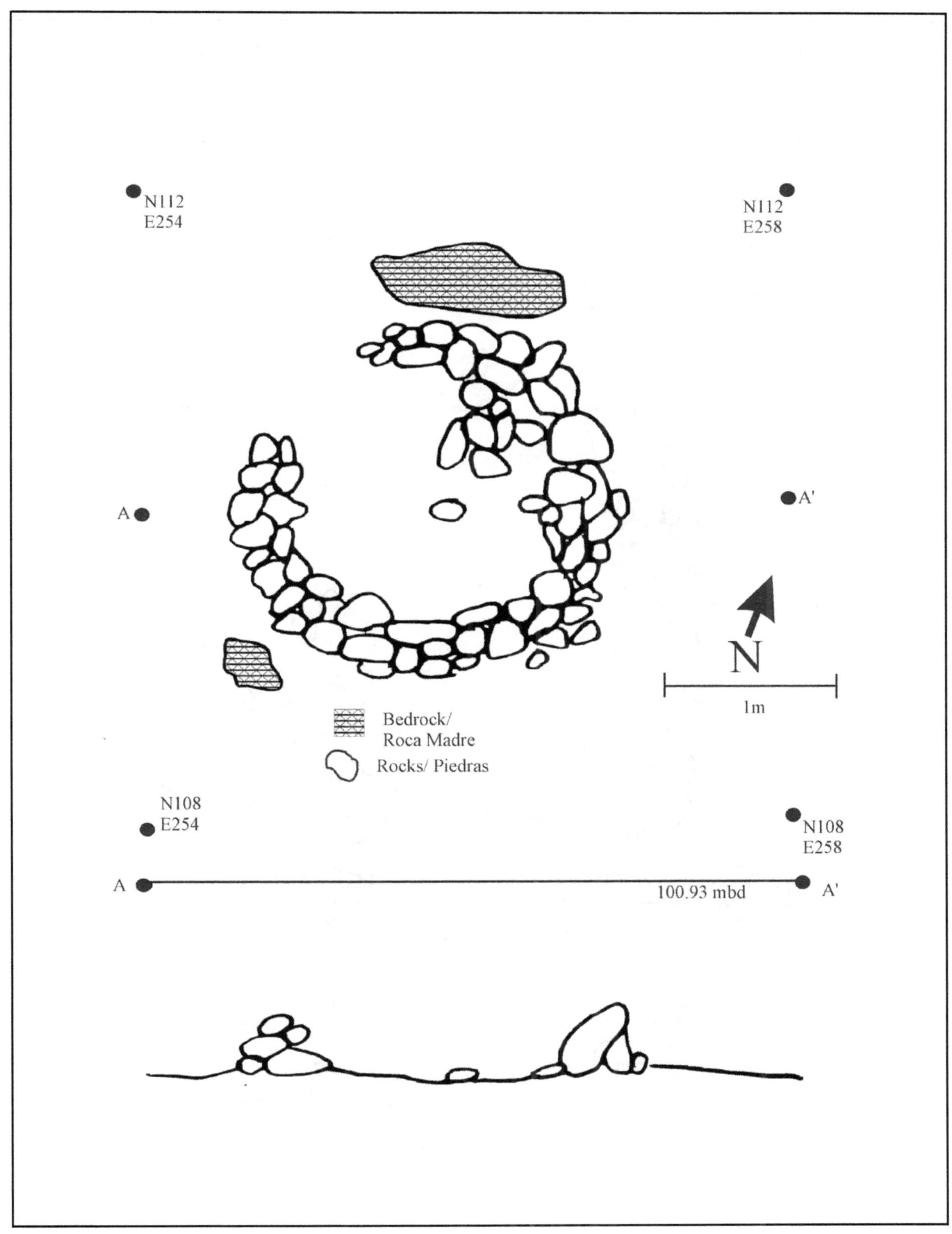

Figura 13.9. Mapa Estructura Circular de Piedra 9.

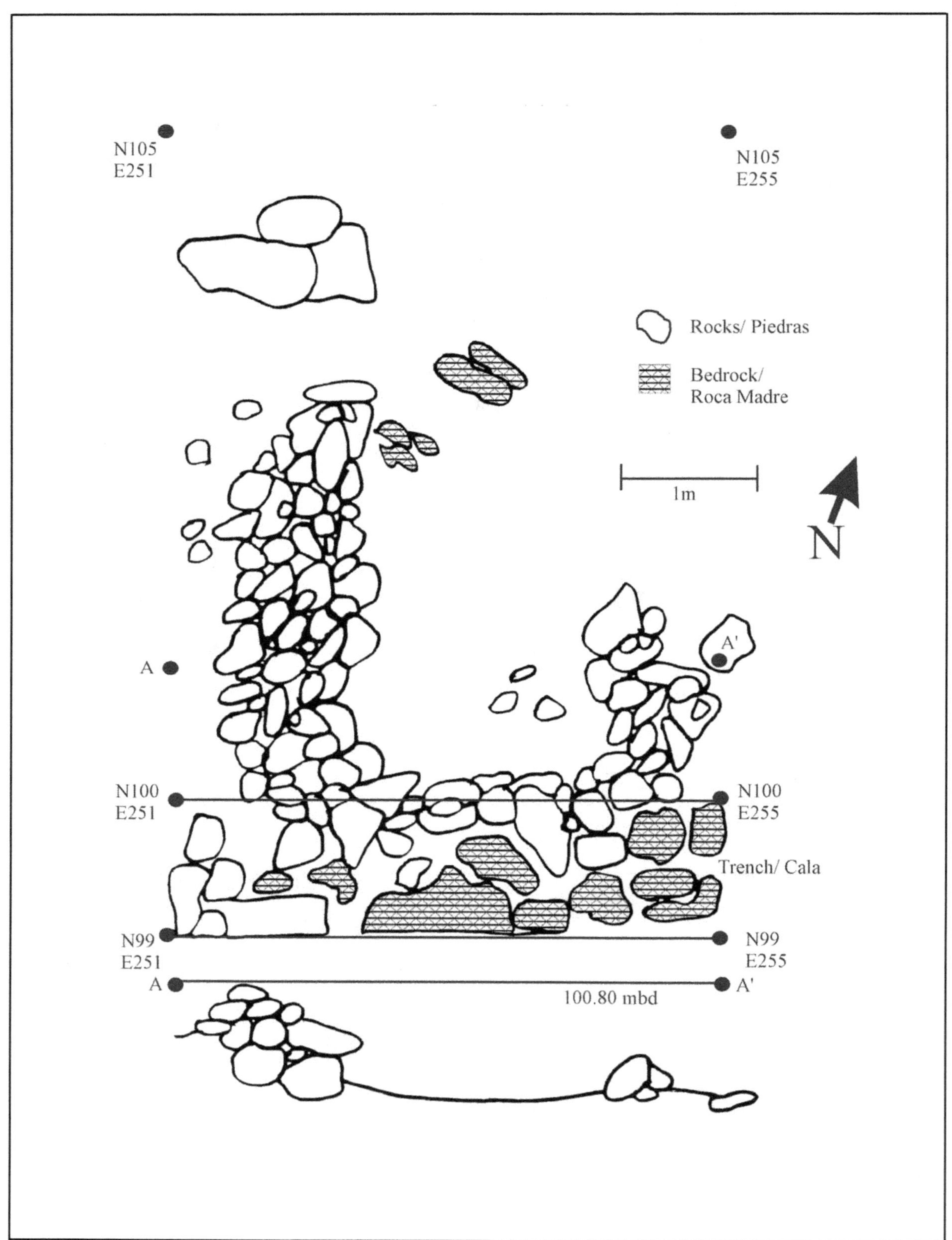

Figura 13.10. Mapa Estructura Circular de Piedra 10.

Piso: No se localizó apisonado.
Relleno: No se excavó.
Materiales: Muy pocos materiales asociados.
Comentarios: Esta estructura se encuentra sobre la T716, pero su muro Oeste es la T736. Es la única estructura en lo que se podría considerar la Plaza de El Caracol. Por su posición, a un lado del acceso hacia el interior de la T736, podría considerársele una estructura de control de acceso.

Estructura Circular de Piedra 11 (Figura 13.11)

Número en Campo: C-129.
Ubicación: N111-115, E 261-265.
Elevación: 101.97-102.57 mbd.
Forma y Tamaño: Circular, 3.50 x 2.70 m, altura 65 cm.
Acceso: Al Norte, 1.70 cm de ancho.
Orientación: Norte-Sur.
Muros: De piedra, 150 cm de ancho x 65 cm de alto.
Techo: Sin evidencia, posiblemente de material perecedero.
Piso: No se localizó apisonado.
Relleno: No se excavó.
Materiales: Muy pocos materiales asociados.
Comentarios: La estructura se localiza en la T719, en su extremo Este. Muy deteriorada.

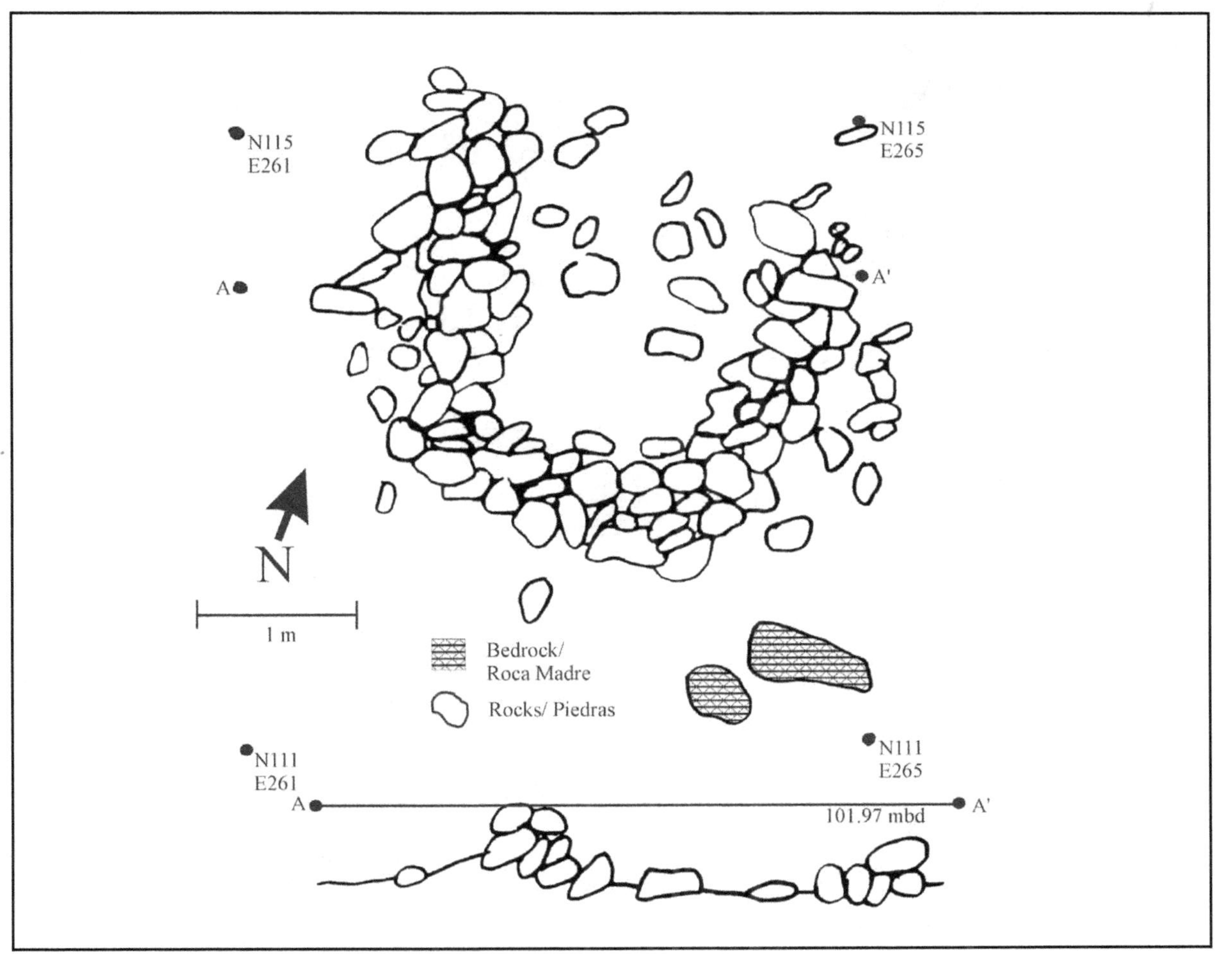

Figura 13.11. Mapa Estructura Circular de Piedra 11.

Estructura Circular de Piedra 12 (Figura 13.12)

Número en Campo: C-130.
Ubicación: N 115-120, E 266-271.
Elevación: 102.38-103.39 mbd
Forma y Tamaño: Circular, 4.10 x 3.20 m, 110 cm de alto.
Acceso: Al NO, 130 cm de ancho.
Orientación: NO-SE.
Muros: De piedra, 180 cm de ancho x 110 cm de alto.
Techo: Sin evidencia, posiblemente de material perecedero.
Piso: No se localizó apisonado.
Relleno: No se excavó.
Materiales: Muy pocos materiales asociados.
Comentarios: La estructura se localiza sobre la T791, en su extremo Este. Aunque su acceso es por la terraza inferior (T711). Se encuentra aislada de las demás estructuras.

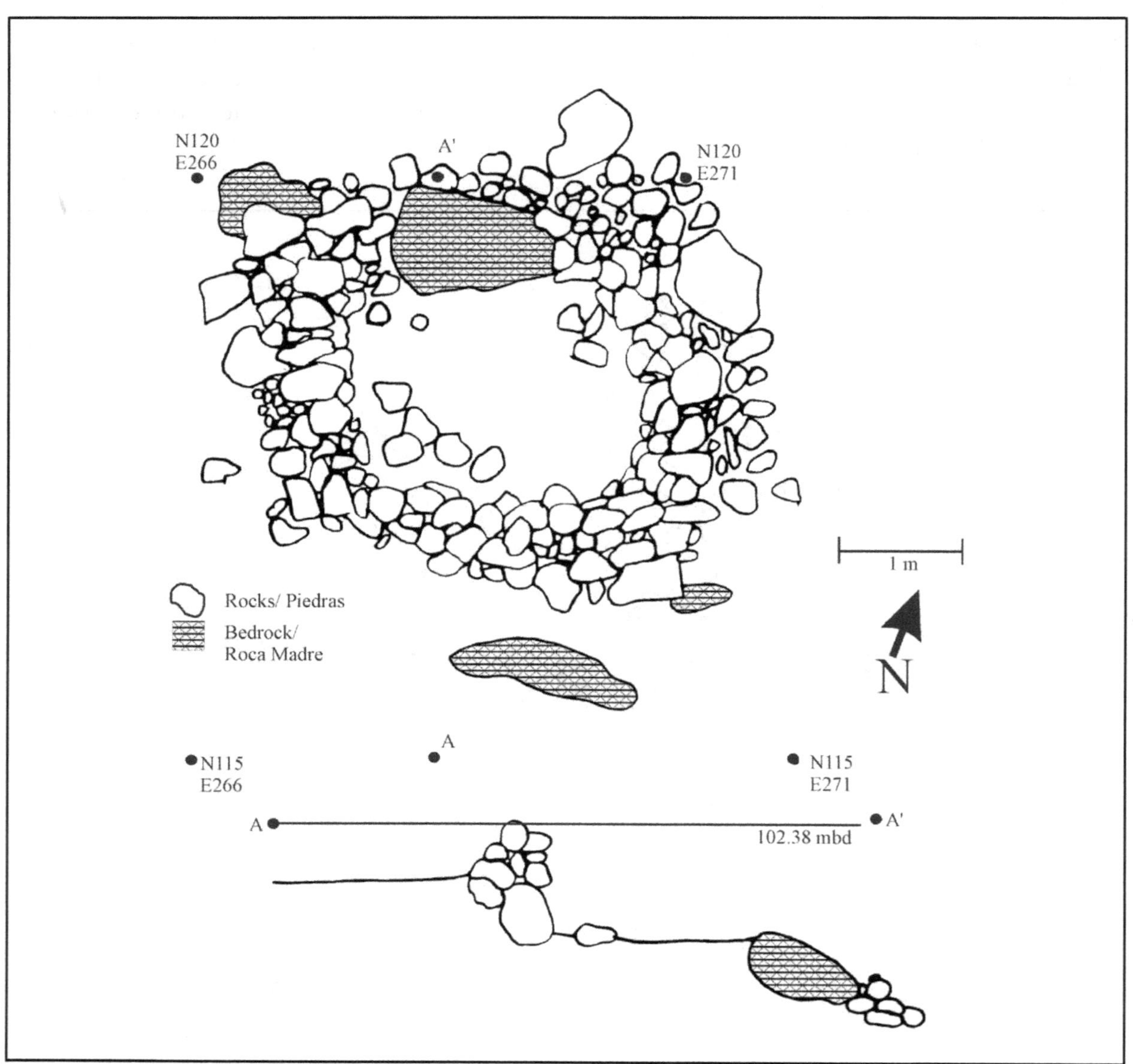

Figura 13.12. Mapa Estructura Circular de Piedra 12.

Estructura Circular de Piedra 13 (Figura 13.13)

Número en Campo: C-132.
Ubicación: N 95-100, E 295-300.
Elevación: 99.79-100.39 mbd.
Forma y Tamaño: Circular, 3.30 x 3 m, 70 cm de altura.
Acceso: Al Norte, 160 cm de ancho.
Orientación: Norte-Sur.
Muros: De piedra, 80 cm de ancho x 70 cm de alto.
Techo: Sin evidencia, posiblemente de material perecedero.
Piso: No se localizó apisonado.
Relleno: No se excavó.
Materiales: Muy pocos materiales asociados.
Comentarios: La estructura se localiza en la T712, en su extremo Este. Se localiza completamente aislada de las demás estructuras y en muy mal estado de conservación. Pos su posición, en la porción más alta del área, podría fungir como posta de control del extremo Este del área hacia el interior de la Plaza.

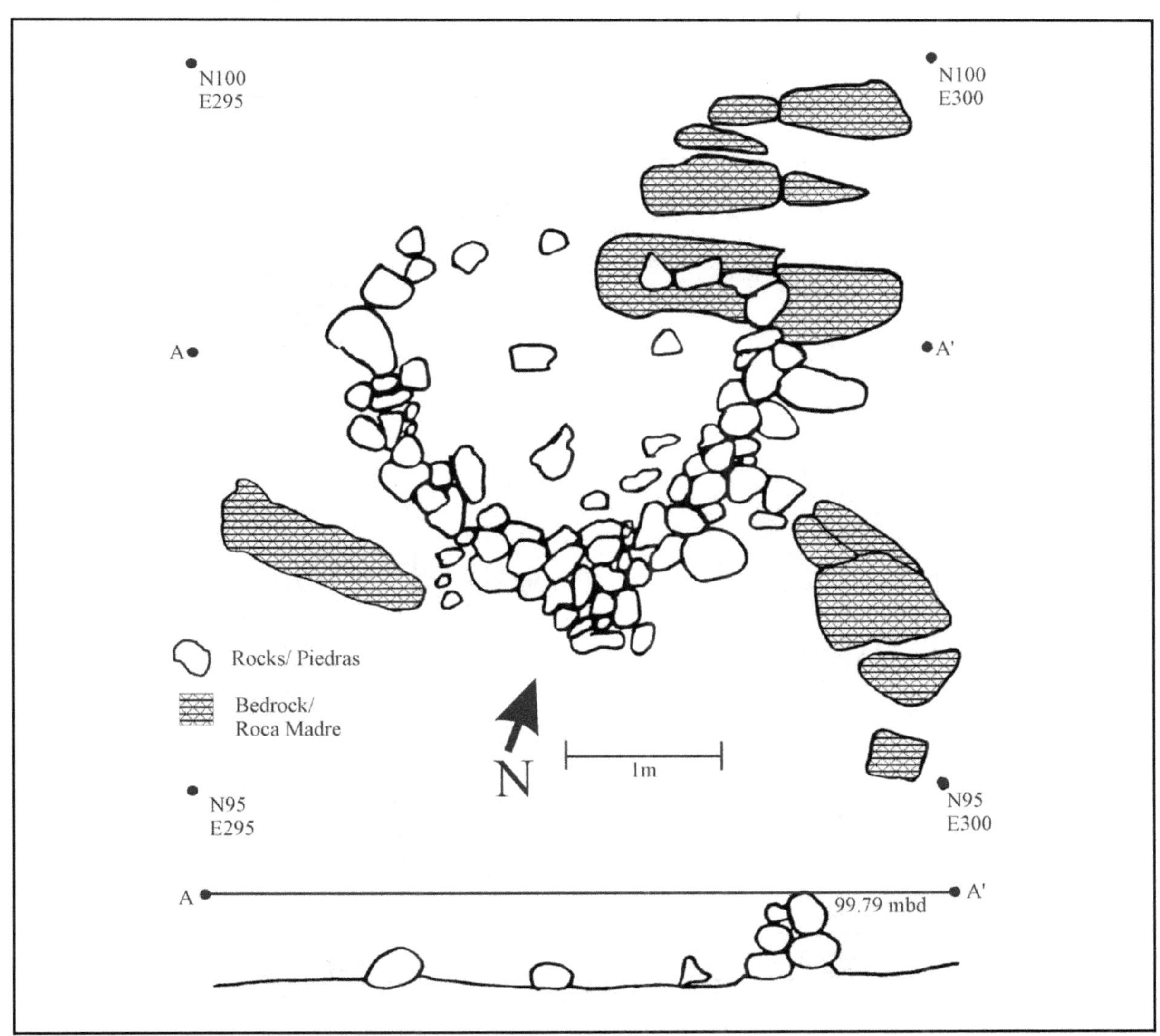

Figura 13.13. Mapa Estructura Circular de Piedra 13.

Estructura Circular de Piedra 14 (Figura 13.14)

Número en Campo: C-133.
Ubicación: N 79-85, E 296-303.
Elevación: 102.92-103.45 mbd.
Forma y Tamaño: Circular, 6.20 x 5.60 m, 60 cm de alto.
Acceso: Al NO, un metro de ancho.
Orientación: NO-SE.
Muros: De piedra, 30 cm de ancho x 60 cm de alto.
Techo: Sin evidencia.
Piso: No se localizó apisonado.
Relleno: Muy poca tierra, principalmente piedra chica y mediana. Muy erozionada y saqueada.
Materiales: Gran cantidad de materiales asociados. Tiestos monócromos de gran tamaño, lascas, machacadores y dos manos.
Comentarios: La estructura se localiza en la T716, en la esquina Este. Pos su posición, a un lado de los accesos del extremo Este, podría ser una posta de control. Por los materiales asociados nos permiten inferir que también se podrian elaborar alimentos.

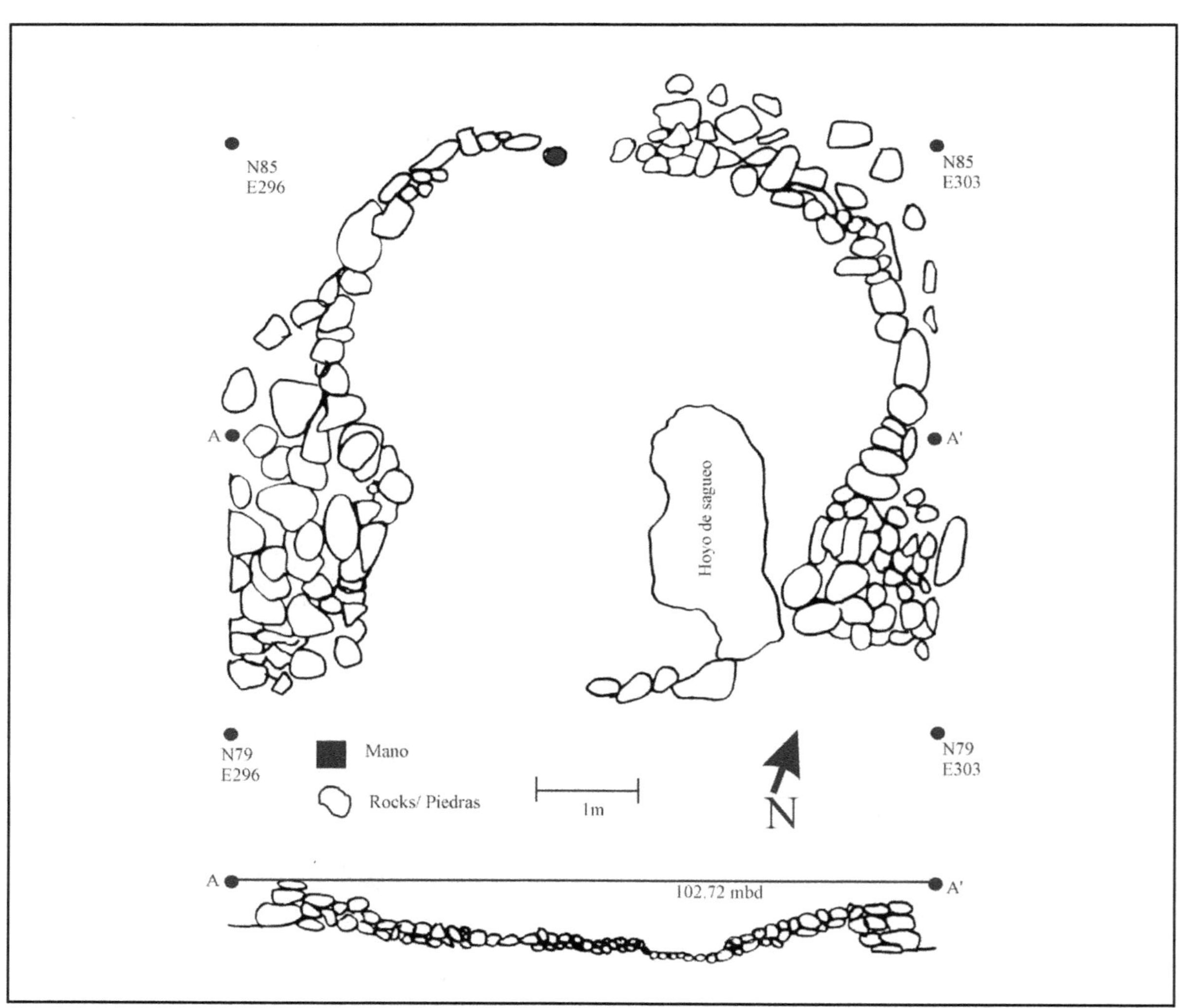

Figura 13.14. Mapa Estructura Circular de Piedra 14.

Estructura Circular de Piedra 15 (Compuesta de dos estructuras)

Primera Estructura 15 (level 3 heading)
Número en Campo: C-134.
Ubicación: N 88-93, E 290-295.
Elevación: 101.83-102-05 mbd.
Forma y Tamaño: Circular, 3.20 x 2.60 m, 90 cm de altura.
Acceso: Al SE, 50 cm de ancho.
Orientación: NO-SE.
Muros: De piedra, 70 cm de ancho x 90 cm de alto.
Techo: Sin evidencia, posiblemente de material perecedero.
Piso: No se localizó apisonado.
Relleno: De tierra fina y piedra, muy poco. Roca madre a 10 cm.
Materiales: Presentó una gran cantidad de materiales. Principalmente cerámica monócroma y lascas.
Comentarios: La estructura se localiza en la T716, en su porción Este. Es una de las estructuras mejor conservadas del área.

Segunda Estructura 15.A

Número en Campo: C-134.1.
Ubicación: N 86-88, E 289-292.
Elevación: 102.57-102.82 mbd..
Forma y Tamaño: Circular, 1.15 x .95 m, 20 cm de altura.
Acceso: Al Norte, un metro de ancho.
Orientación: Norte-Sur.
Muros: De piedra, 60 cm de ancho x 20 cm de alto.
Techo: Sin evidencia, posiblemente de material perecedero.
Piso: No se localizó apisonado.
Relleno: De tierra y piedra, muy poco. Roca madre a 5 cm.
Materiales: Presentó algunos materiales. Cerámica monócromo y lascas.
Comentarios: La estructura se localizó en la T716, en su porción Este. Muy deteriorada. Estrechamente relacionada con la 15 (C-134).

Estructura Circular de Piedra 16 (Figura 13.15)

Número en Campo: C-135.
Ubicación: N 75-80, E 275-280.
Elevación: 105-105.29 mbd.
Forma y Tamaño: Circular, 4.20 x 4 m, 80 cm de altura.
Acceso: Al SO, 50 cm de ancho.
Orientación: NE-SO.
Muros: De piedra, 40 cm de ancho por 80 cm de alto.
Techo: Sin evidencia, posiblemente de material perecedero.
Piso: No se localizó apisonado.
Relleno: No se excavó.
Materiales: Muy pocos materiales asociados.
Comentarios: Se localiza en la T715, en su porción central. Se encuentra asociada con las estructuras 22 y 23.

Estructura Circular de Piedra 21 (Figura 13.16)

Número en Campo: C-136.
Ubicación: N 93-97, E 280-283.
Elevación: 101.79-101.89 mbd.
Forma y Tamaño: Circular, 3.70 x 3 m, 55 cm de altura.
Acceso: Al Sur, 50 cm de ancho.
Orientación: Norte-Sur.
Muros: De piedra, 30 cm de ancho x 55 cm de alto.
Techo: Sin evidencia, posiblemente de material perecedero.
Piso: No se localizó apisonado.
Relleno: No se excavó.
Materiales: Muy pocos materiales asociados.
Comentarios: La estructura se localiza en la T116, en su porción central. Se local-

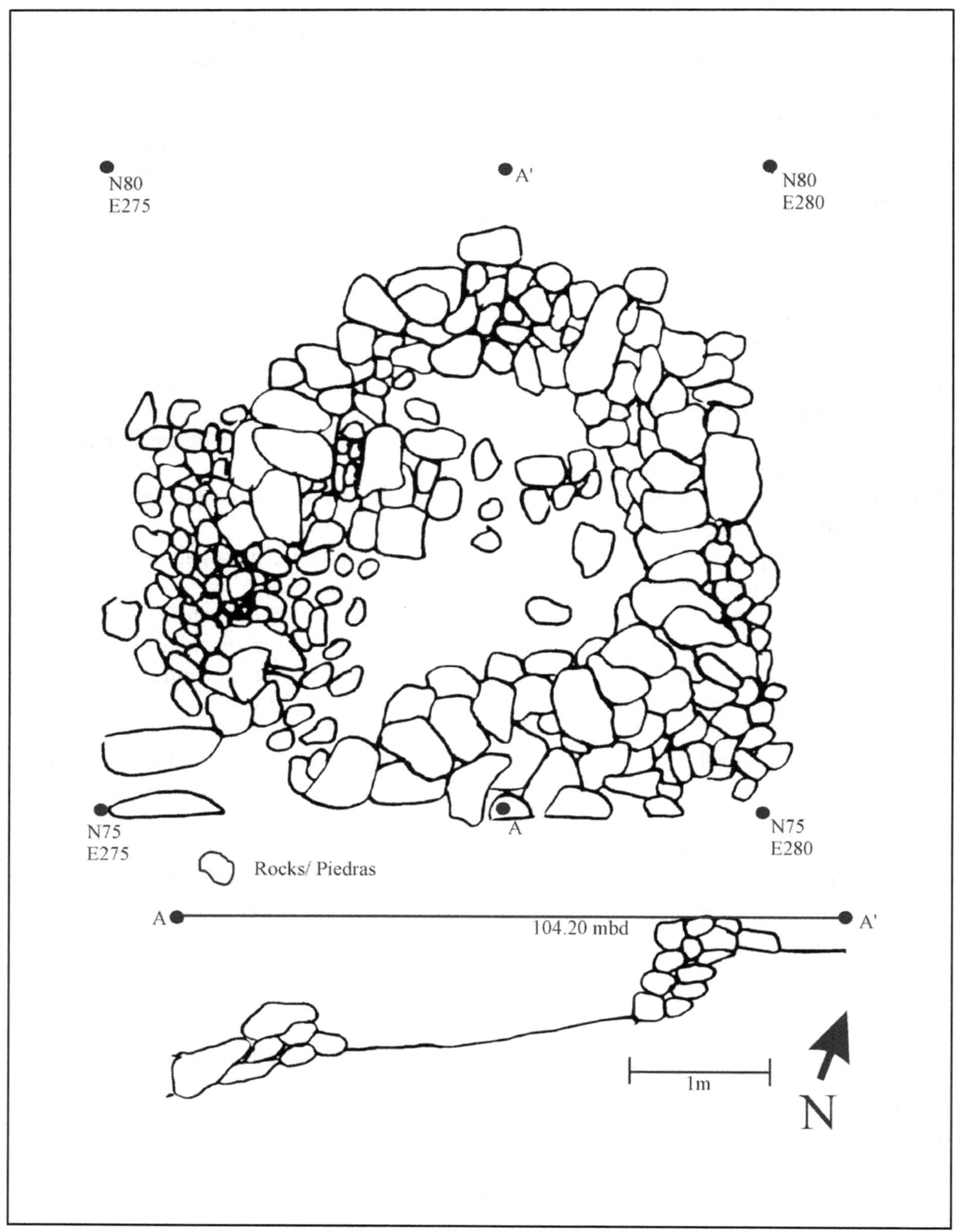

Figura 13.15. Mapa Estructura Circular de Piedra 16.

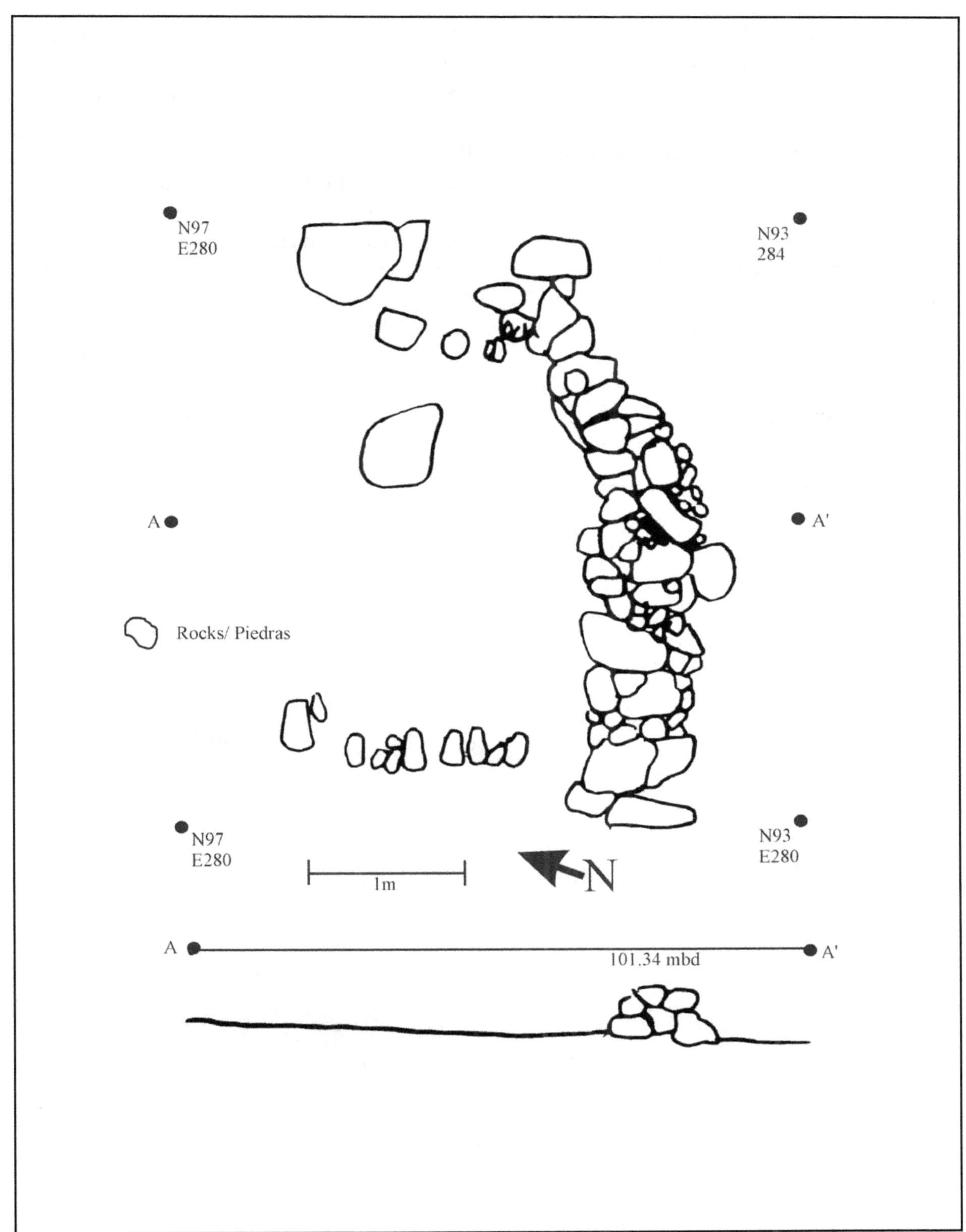

Figura 13.16. Mapa Estructura Circular de Piedra 21.

izó muy deteriorada. Su muro Oeste esta formado con el muro Este de El Caracol. Posiblemente relacionada con El Caracol.

Estructura Circular de Piedra 22 (Figura 13.17)

Número en Campo: C-137.
Ubicación: N 68-74, E 298-276.
Elevación: 105.83-106.08 mbd.
Forma y Tamaño: Rectangular, 6.40 x 5.20 m, 30 cm de altura.
Acceso: Al parecer se localiza en la esquina NE, 130 cm de ancho.
Orientación: Este-Oste.
Muros: De piedra, 90 cm de ancho x 30 cm de alto.
Techo: Sin evidencia, posiblemente de material perecedero.
Piso: No se localizó apisonado.
Relleno: De tierra muy fina y piedras. Roca madre a 10-15 cm.
Materiales: Gran cantidad de materiales. Lo más sobresalientes es la ubicación de un metate.
Comentarios: La estructura se localiza en la T715, en su porción central. Se considero a esta estructura como una unidad habitacional. Esta relacionada con las Estructuras 23 y 16.

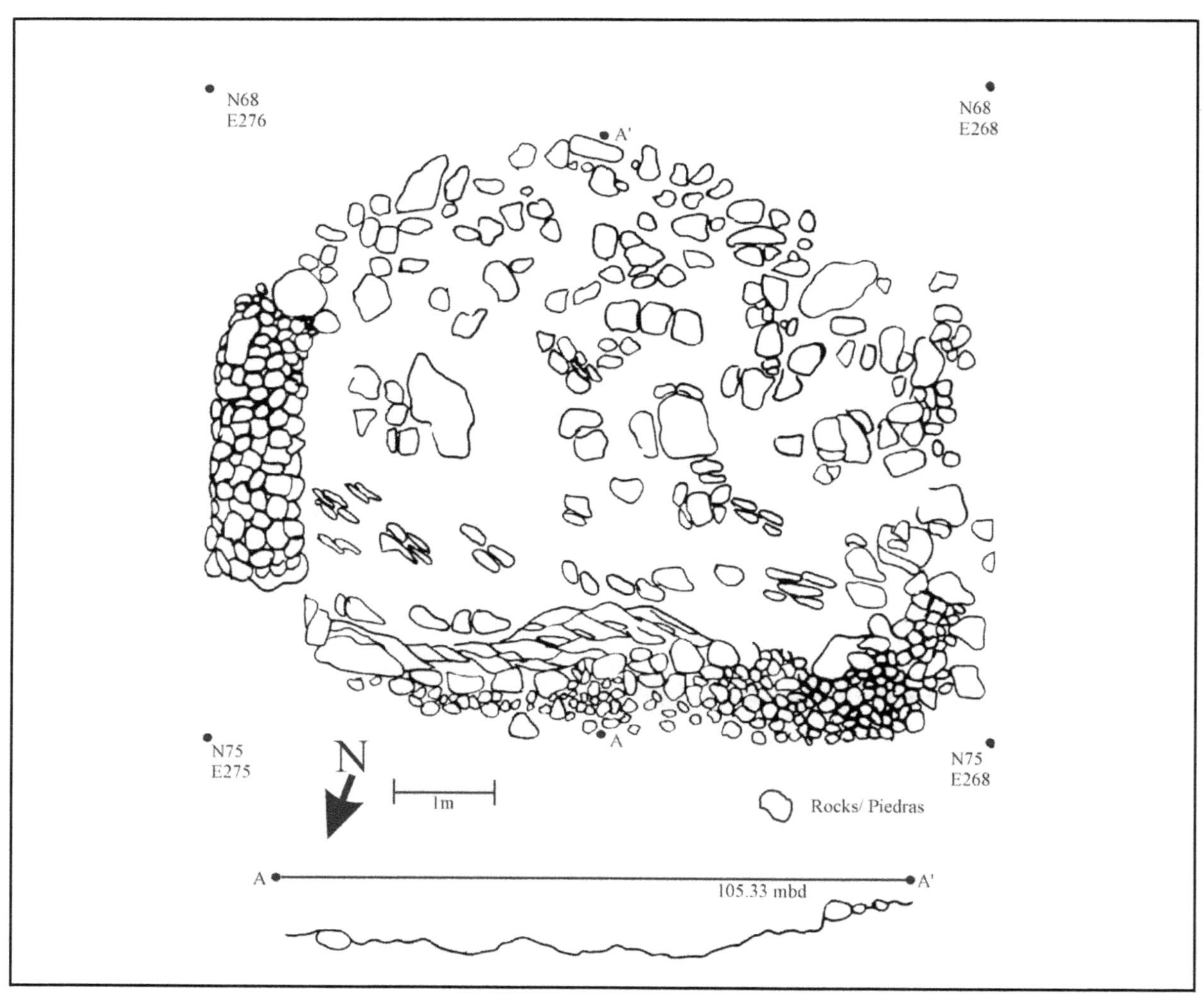

Figura 13.17. Mapa Estructura Circular de Piedra 22.

Estructura Circular de Piedra 23 (Figura 13.18)

Número en Campo: C-138.
Ubicación: N 73-79, E 266-270.
Elevación: 105.57-105.62 mbd.
Forma y Tamaño: Circular, 4.50 x 4.10 m, 40 cm de alto.
Acceso: Al SE, 50 cm de ancho.
Orientación: NO-SE.
Muros: De piedra, el muro N es de 2.50 m de ancho mientras que los demás son de 60 cm de ancho. En general tienen 40 cm de altura.
Techo: Sin evidencia, posiblemente de material perecedero.
Piso: no se localizó apisonado.
Relleno: No se excavó.
Materiales: Muy pocos materiales.
Comentarios: Esta estructura se localiza en la T715, en su porción central. Relacionada con la Estructura 22. Su uso es indeterminado, ya que sólo presenta 1 m^2 de espacio.

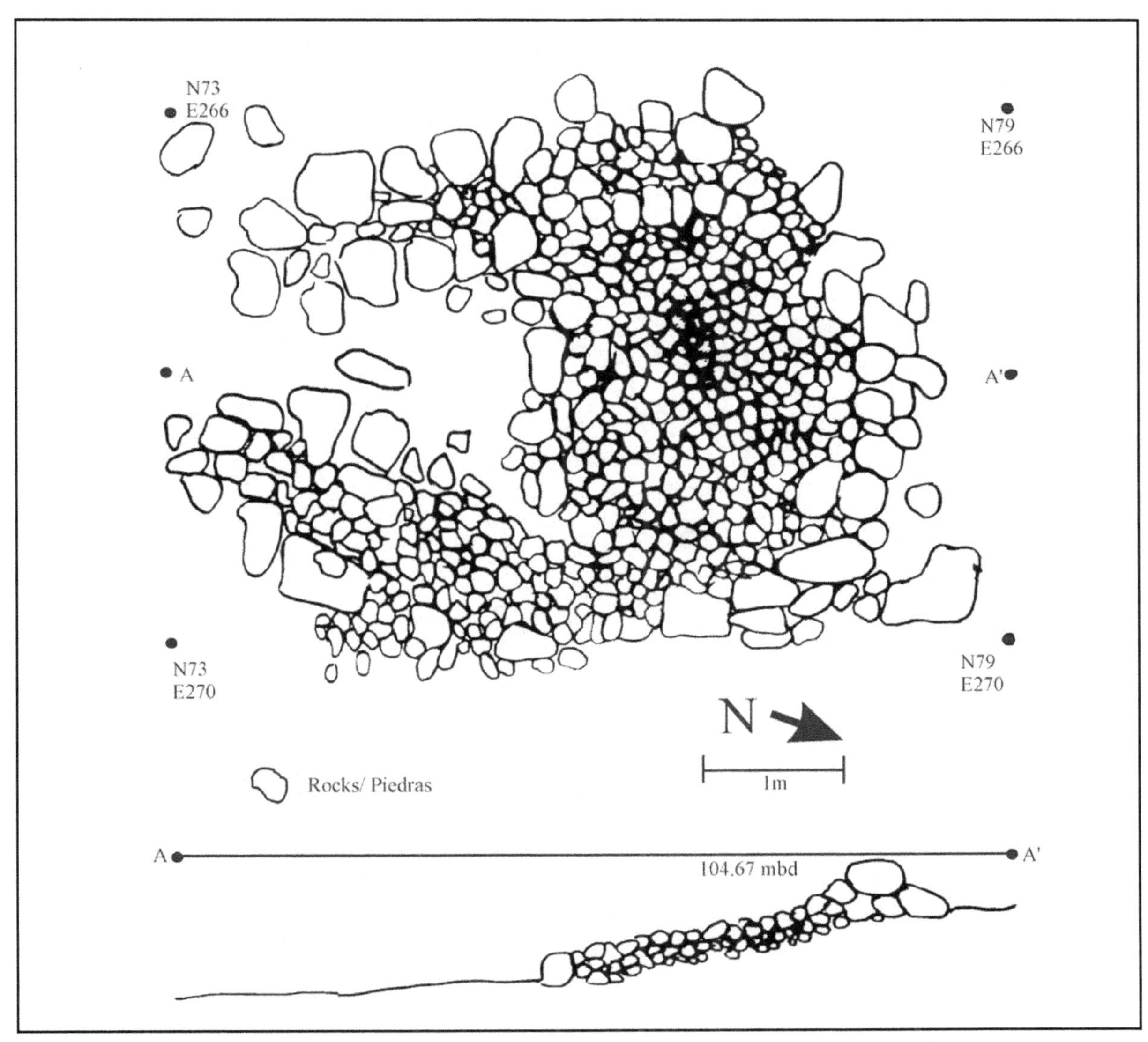

Figura 13.18. Mapa Estructura Circular de Piedra 23.

Estructura Circular de Piedra 24

Número en Campo: C-140.
Ubicación: N 64-69, E 278-284.
Elevación: 106.73-107.03 mbd.
Forma y Tamaño: Circular, 2.80 x 2.60 m, 30 cm de altura.
Acceso: En la esquina NO, 50 cm de ancho.
Orientación: Este-Oeste.
Muros: De piedra, 80 cm de ancho por 30 cm de alto.
Techo: Sin evidencia, posiblemente de material perecedero.
Piso: Se localizó un apisonado a escasos 5-8 cm.
Relleno: De tierra fina y piedra. Roca madre a 30 cm.
Materiales: Presentó gran cantidad de materiales. Principalmente cerámica monócroma y lascas.
Comentarios: Esta estructura se localiza en la T715, en su porción Este. Se encuentra asociada con uno de los accesos de la porción inferior Sur hacia el interior. Por su posición podría fungir como una posta de control.

Elemento de Acceso: Rampa 1 (Figura 13.19)

Número en campo: C-131.
Ubicación: N 85-90, E 276-280.
Elevación: 101.92-102.63 mbd.
Forma y Tamaño: Rectangular, 3.50 x 1.70 m.

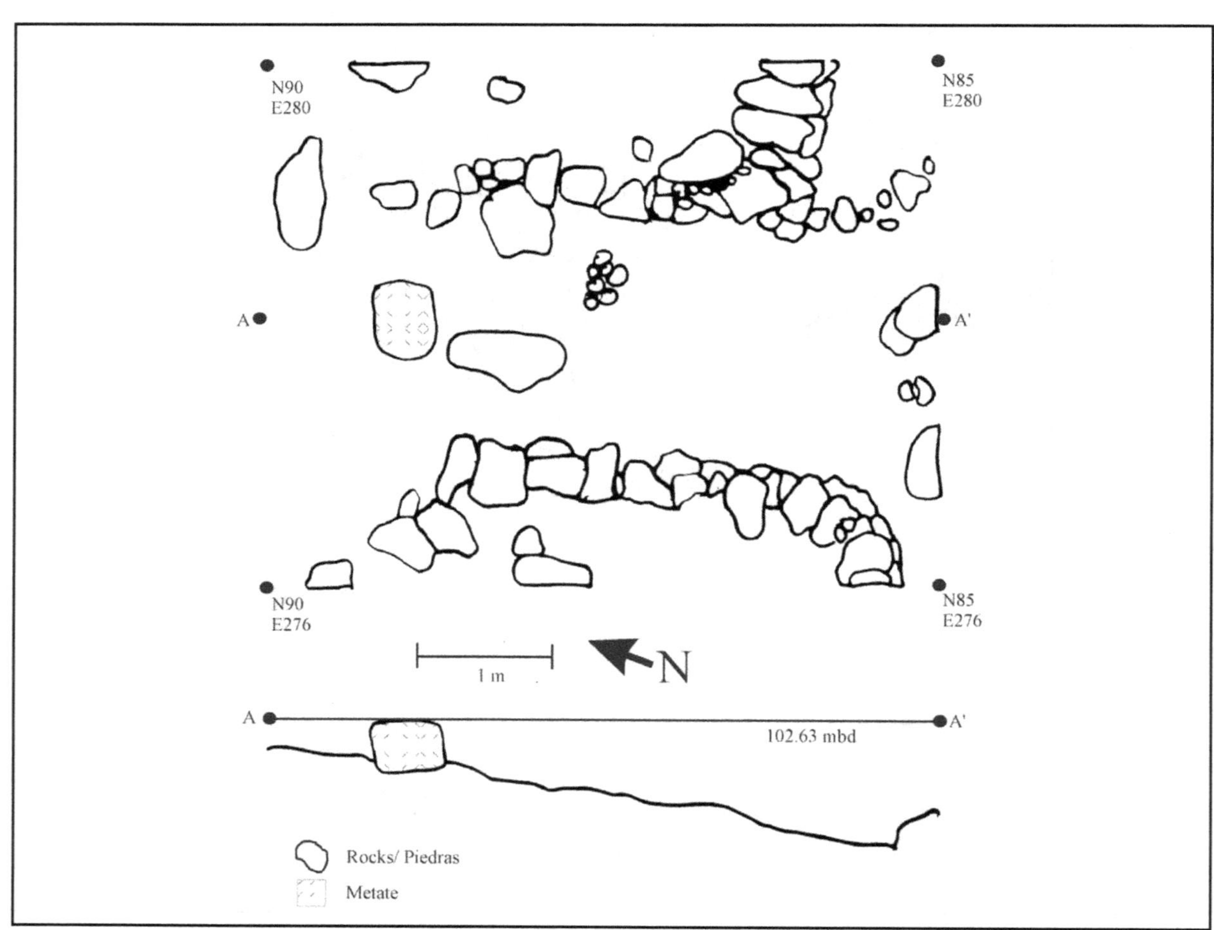

Figura 13.19. Mapa Elemento de Acceso: Rampa 1.

Orientación: NO-SE.
Piso: Formado de tierra con piedras, es posible apreciar la roca madre.
Relleno: No se excavó.
Materiales: Presentó un metate de grandes dimensiones (70 x 50 x 40) en su porción central, se desconoce el motivo.
Comentarios: Este elemento forma parte de la T716. Ubicado en la porción central. Es el único acceso entre la T716 y la terraza inferior T715.

Construcción de El Caracol

El Caracol es una de las estructuras o construcciones que más han llamado la atención de los estudiosos e investigadores (Bowen 1976; Braniff 1992; Doolittle 1984; Ekholm 1939, 1940, 1947; Hamilton 1883; Hayden 1956; Hinton 1955; Huntington 1912, 1914; Lumholtz 1912; Manje 1954; McGee 1895, 1896, 1898; Sauer y Brand 1931; Villalpando 1985) y a la que se le han atribuido infinidad de funciones en las que resalta la de un fuerte para la defensa del sitio (Hamilton 1883) o la de una mera descripción a manera de corrales Figura 13.20). Por otro lado, se desconoce hasta el momento la existencia de alguna otro estructura similar para el resto del estado de Sonora y en especial para los sitios de la cultura Trincheras.

Como una primera actividad se realizo un registro fotográfico de cómo se localizó El Caracol antes de cualquier intervención (Figura 13.21). Posteriormente se realizo la limpieza o chapeo del área lo que nos permitió conocer el estado real de conservación de la estructura y el de su destrucción; de igual manera se volvió a realizar un registro fotográfico (Figura 13.22).

Desde el inicio del proyecto se contemplo la excavación de la estructura, por lo que para realizar esta actividad se tuvo que realizar la restauración del inmueble, que como ya se mencionó anteriormente, fue por medio de la restitución de material y en algunos casos aplicar de una manera un poco ortodoxa la anastilosis de muros colapsados (Figura 13.23, Figura 13.24).

De igual manera se restauró la construcción adosada a El Caracol, la cual se a denominado El Caracol A. Realizando la restauración de El Caracol nos pudimos percatar que la construcción adosada (El Caracol A) en realidad se construyó en el mismo momento que El Caracol (Figura 13.25). Un dato interesante localizado durante el proceso de restauración fue que en el desmonte de los muros colapsados se rescataron varios fragmentos de metates muy gastados que provenían del interior de los muros. Lo anterior nos estaría indicando que la construcción de El Caracol correspondería a una fase tardía del sitio.

Por otro lado, con la realización de esta actividad en la que más de un 40 por ciento de la estructura tuvo que ser sometida a restauración, nos permitió realizar algunas aproximaciones en cuanto al requerido para levantar una construcción como ésta. Concluimos que se necesitarían cuatro hombres, trabajando ocho horas diarias durante una semana, para tener la estructura de piedra sin contar con la elaboración del techo. Vale la pena mencionar que para estos cálculos nos basamos en el supuesto de que la superficie se localizara ya nivelada y se contara con los materiales a la mano.

Una vez concluido el proceso de restauración, se procedió a realizar la recolección de superficie para lo cual se utilizo la retícula general y la metodología aplicada para el resto del área. El interior del caracol representó una superficie de 33 m^2, sin incluir los 9 m^2 de El Caracol A. Finalizada esta actividad se procedió a la excavación de la estructura, actividad que se dividió en dos etapas: una al exterior y otra al interior. La primera de ellas fue una superficie de 32 m^2 localizada en las inmediaciones de las entradas tanto de El Caracol como

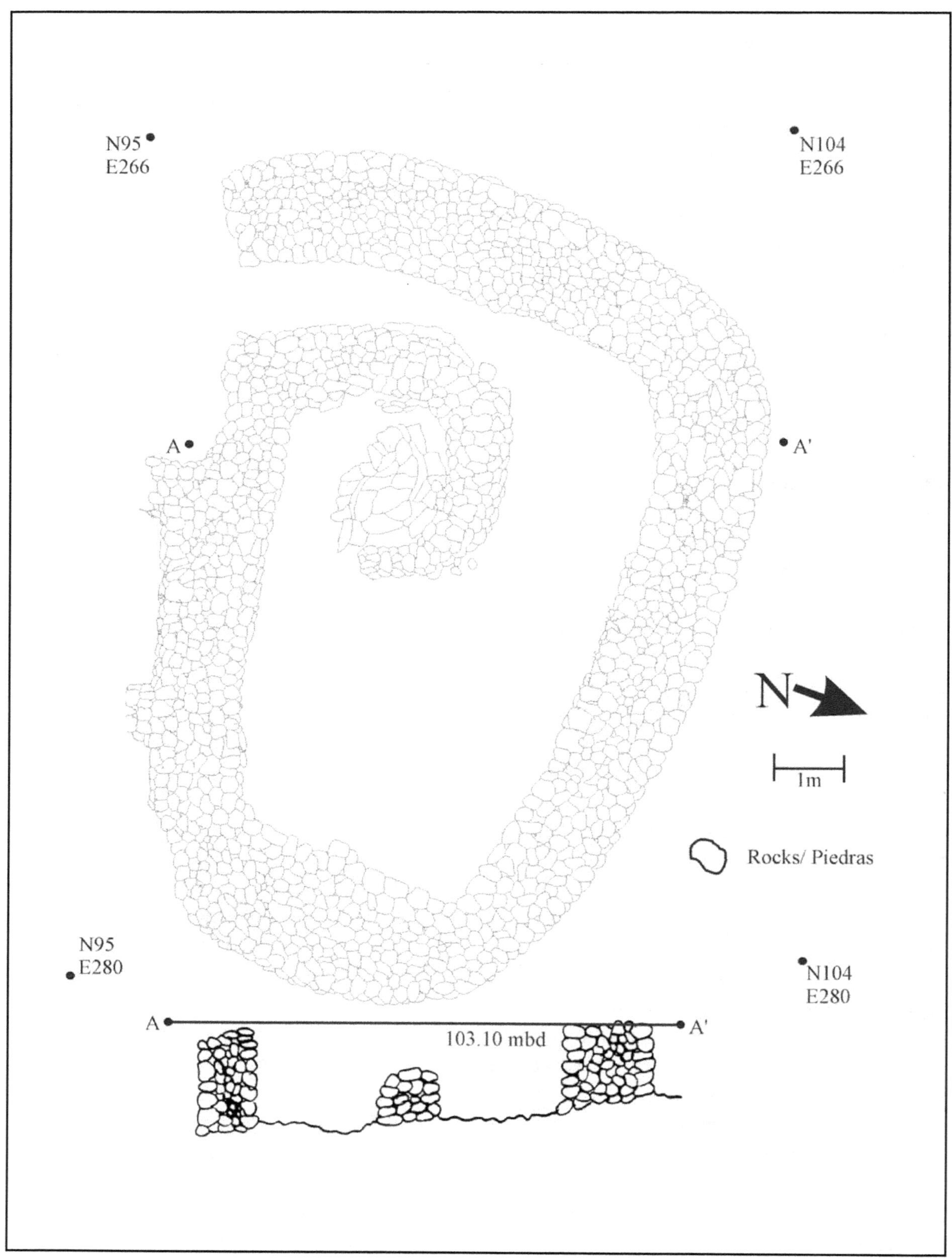

Figura 13.20. Mapa El Caracol.

Figura 13.21. El Caracol antes de excavación.

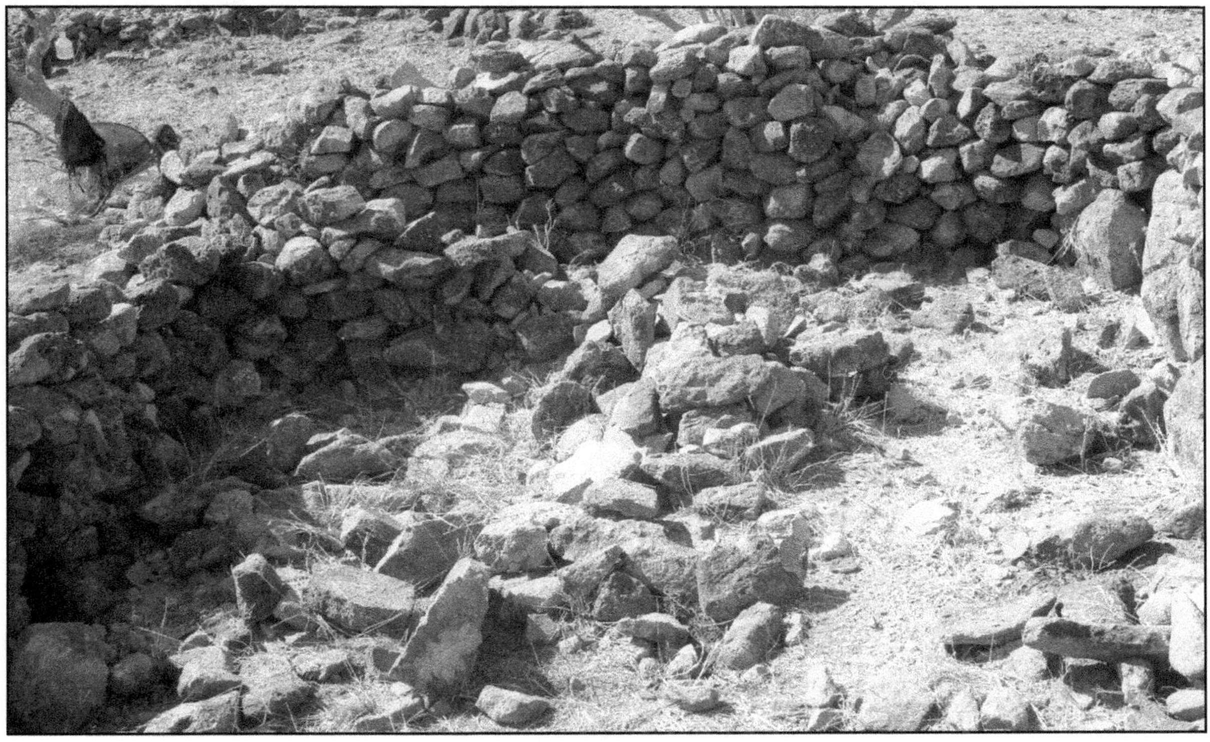

Figura 13.22. Interior de El Caracol antes de excavación.

Figura 13.23. El muro interior norte sin restaurar.

Figura 13.24. El interior del muro de la cara exterior.

Figura 13.25. El derrumbe donde la base de la equina funciona como soporte tanto para el muro de El Caracol como para la El Caracol A.

de El Caracol A (Figura 13.2). Esta actividad tuvo el objetivo de tratar de localizar restos de actividades realizadas en el exterior inmediato de estas construcciones o de localizar un apisonado producto de la entrada y salida de las mismas, lo cual no fue posible.

Una vez concluída esta primera fase, mencionaremos que la estratigrafía localizada fue similar a la del resto de las áreas excavadas. Presentando solamente tres capas, estas ya fueron descritas y no presentaron ninguna característica distinta o digna de contarse. Posteriormente se procedió a realizar la segunda fase de excavación, pero esta vez en el interior de El Caracol, en la que hay que mencionar la existencia de por lo menos dos hoyos de saqueo. Al termino de está, se estableció que el patrón estratigráfico identificado en el exterior no se cumplió para el interior. El interior de El Caracol presentó una estratigrafía más compleja con cuatro niveles o capas que se describen a continuación.

Capa 1. Superficie, compuesta por detritus natural y un poco de tierra café amarillenta clara (10YR 5/4 yellowish Brown). También se localizó material arqueológico.

Capa 2. Capa A (como se denominó en campo), compuesta de Tierra café amarillenta clara (10YR 5/4 yellowish brown), muy fina y con algunas piedras chicas. En esta capa se localizó un especie de apisonado que posiblemente sea contemporáneo con el sitio pero en algunas porciones del interior de la capa se localizaron materiales modernos como fragmentos de vidrio de refresco y/o cerveza mezclados con material Prehispánico pero que consideramos que son producto del saqueo que ha sufrido el sitio.

Capa 3. Capa B (como se denominó en campo), compuesta de tierra café grisácea oscuro (10YR 4/2 dark grayish brown), fina y con algunas piedras chicas. Se localizó material arqueológico.

Capa 4. Roca madre; la cual se localizó a escasos 20 cm - 30 cm. Sin materiales arqueológicos.

Como ya se había mencionado, dentro del Proyecto se había establecido que la coloración de las capas estratigráficas nos indican períodos o grados de ocupación de las áreas. De esta manera el descubrir una coloración distinta a la del resto de las áreas, particularmente el de la capa 3, nos indica que la construcción de El Caracol tuvo mucho más actividad o fue usada por más tiempo que el resto de las demás estructuras del área. Y que su construcción es anterior al resto de las construcciones. En este caso, consideramos que la formación de los contextos se dio de la siguiente manera: primero contamos con la Capa 4 (roca madre) a la cual se le añade un deposito artificial o cultural por medio de acarreo de tierra para nivelar la superficie. Esta capa viene siendo la capa 3. Esta actividad es posterior a la construcción de El Caracol ya que sus "muros" se localizaron en contacto con la Capa 4 o roca madre. Debido a la coloración de esta capa inferimos que se realizaron varias actividades en su interior o una ocupación prolongada.

Posteriormente viene una tercera capa que es la 2, la cual consideramos que es de carácter cultural, es decir se vuelve a acarrear tierra y se nivela la superficie. Por la coloración de esta, consideramos que no se ocupó la estructura por un período largo sino por el contrario muy corto, al que le sobreviene el abandono. Para finalizar contamos con la última capa (1), que es la que hemos denominado "superficie" en la que se mezclan deposición natural, detritus natural y materiales arqueológicos y modernos.

Por otro lado, finalizada la excavación hasta la roca madre, no se localizaron indicios o huellas de postes por lo que consideramos que el techo de esta estructura pudo consistir en una especie de ramada, aunque cabe la posibilidad de que por encontrarse muy cerca de la superficie la roca madre no existan este tipo de evidencias. También es posible que los postes utilizados hayan sido de un grosor relativamente pequeño, o que la perturbación humana haya destruido las evidencias. A estas conclusiones añadimos que en la región se carece de árboles de gran tamaño que les permita realizar techumbres más elaboradas. Sin embargo, podemos contar con dos posibles respuestas:

1). Hasta el momento de realizar este informe, carecemos de información paleoambiental que nos indique el tipo de ambiente que predomino en la época en la que el sitio Cerro de Trincheras fue ocupado durante el período Prehispánico. Sabemos que en las inmediaciones del cerro se localizaba una laguna producto de las crecidas del río Magdalena pero desconocemos el tipo de flora que pudo haber coexistido, por lo que no se descarta la existencia de árboles de considerable tamaño.

2). Por medio de resultados preliminares de los análisis de polen y flotación, sabemos de la existencia del cultivo de algún tipo de agave. Al momento de florecer, este cuenta con un "tallo" de gran tamaño, dureza y de un grosor considerable (entre 8 y 12 cm de diámetro) el cual, por analogías etnohistóricas, sabemos que sus tallos son utilizados para la elaboración de techos. Por esto consideramos que en algún momento pudieron hechar mano de este recurso; más sin embargo, debemos mencionar que hasta el momento no se ha localizado alguna evidencia que confirme esta idea.

Una vez concluída la excavación de la estructura de El Caracol, se realizó la excavación de El Caracol A en la que se localizaron las mismas capas estratigráficas que en El Caracol. Esto nos refuerza la idea de contemporaneidad entre las dos construcciones, esbozada durante el proceso de restauración de estas.

También se identificaron dos elementos nuevos que son el El Caracol B que es una porción de la roca madre localizada en el interior de El Caracol en su porción Este. Nos percatamos que se encontraba tallada una vez concluída la liberación del área. Esta porción de la roca es un pequeño afloramiento, el cual sobresalía de la superficie y, al parecer, se comenzó a trabajar la cara O por medio de percusión directa. No presenta alguna figura, diseño o forma, solamente la percusión de la superficie (Figura 13.26).

El segundo elemento es el El Caracol C que es una piedra tallada a manera de petroglifo, que se localiza en el interior de El Caracol A, en la esquina noroeste y que su porción derecha forma parte de la base del muro. El tallado corresponde solamente a tres líneas paralelas que corren de arriba a abajo y una línea vertical en la que se unen las dos primeras líneas paralelas del lado izquierdo y en la que al parecer se une la tercera línea, pero esta porción de la roca esta fragmentada (Figura 13.27).

Por otro lado, en la porción exterior del muro Este de El Caracol, se percibió una estructura bastante deteriorada. Se percibe un semicírculo, que aparentemente también se localiza adosado a El Caracol, pero no se logró determinar si esa parte del muro (Figura 13.2), formó parte de la construcción (21) o fue producto del colapsamiento de esa porción del muro de El Caracol. Al no lograrse discernir esta disyuntiva, se opto por describirla como una construcción independiente a El Caracol.

En lo que respecta a los materiales recuperados no varió significativamente con los parámetros generales del área y podemos mencionar que se siguió cumpliendo la constante de que el material proveniente de áreas al aire libre es mayor que la del interior de las construcciones. Un rasgo significativo fue el hecho de que para el interior de El Caracol se recuperaron 11 discos cerámicos y uno de piedra representando un número bastante alto para lo que fue el promedio general del Área A.

Figura 13.26. Roca madre y El Caracol B depues de excavación.

De igual manera se localizaron 10 cuentas de concha, ocho cuentas de piedra, dos metates, dos manos, varios fragmentos de piedras pulidas, tres tiestos punzonados y un sólo tiesto Ramos Policromo (el cual es el único fragmento localizado de este tipo en toda el Área A). Todos estos elementos fueron los más significativos pero cabe aclarar que se recuperaron muchos más, además de que en esta relación no se encuentran diferenciados por capas.

Lo anterior nos indica que la construcción de El Caracol contó con mucha más actividad que el resto de las construcciones del Área A1, además de una ocupación más prolongada. A su vez, el hecho de localizar un gran número de materiales de uso común como son los tipos cerámicos Lisa 3 o Tardía, así como metates y manos nos indican la realización de actividades cotidianas, tanto en esta área como en el interior de El Caracol. Claro está que cabe la posibilidad de que dichos materiales se hayan utilizado para fines rituales o ceremoniales.

Otro dato relevante es el hecho de que tomando la orientación actual, la estructura de El Caracol se encuentra perfectamente orien-

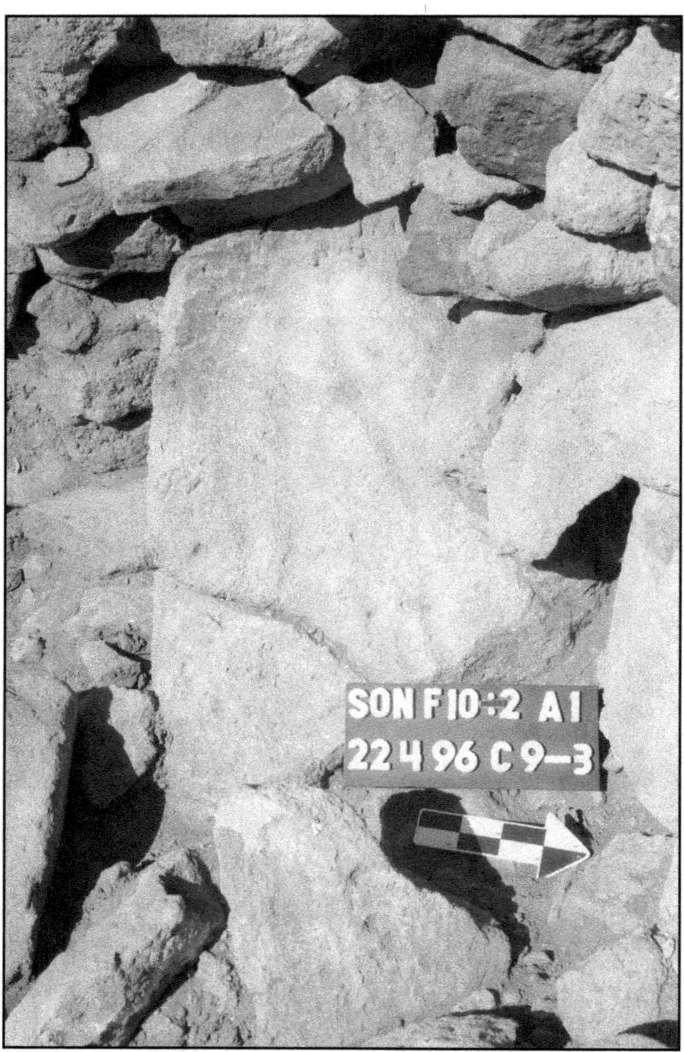

Figura 13.27. Piedra Tallada, El Caracol C.

tada hacia el Este, si acaso uno o dos grados de error, tomando como punto de referencia al elemento El Caracol B (el cual ya fue descrito con anterioridad). Por esto descartamos una relación entre el transcurso del sol y este element, dato que da soporte a la idea de que se trata de una construcción de carácter ceremonial.

Distribución de Construcciones y sus Relaciones

A lo largo del texto hemos hecho hincapié de que el área presenta una planificación bastante sencilla pero que denota un grado de desarrollo más allá de un simple grupo de agricultores incipientes. Para poderla entender comenzaremos con dar una relación de los distintos elementos constructivos con los que cuenta el área y su posible relación entre sí.

Comenzaremos con la ladera Norte del cerro en la que contamos con tres terrazas, de las cuales la T709 se localiza fuera del área de investigación y en la que no se trabajo. Así, contamos con la primera terraza que es la T711 de 26 m de largo y aproximadamente 1 m de alto. Su porción Oeste culmina en una vereda que es la que comunica las terrazas inferiores con el Área A1 por este lado del sitio. En su porción Este la terraza presenta una forma cuadrada bastante rara y que desconocemos el porque posteriormente culmina en un afloramiento rocoso (el mapa no cuenta con esta descripción geográfica); no se localizaron estructuras en su superficie pero si algunos materiales.

Le sigue la T791, la cual cuenta con 43 m de largo y de 80 cm de alto en su porción Este a 1.50 m en la porción Oeste. Presentó, en su extremo Este, el único acceso que comunica la terraza inferior con lo que posteriormente se denominaría Plaza del El Caracol. Este acceso es de 80 cm aproximadamente, y contó con algunas piedras que facilitan el acceso a manera de escalones (sin llegar a serlos). En la superficie de esta terraza se localizaron cinco construcciones o círculos de piedra que son las siguientes: 7, 8, 9, 11 y 12, los cuales presentaron un promedio de 2 a 3 m de diámetro y varios grados de deterioro. De éstas solamente la 12 presenta su acceso por la T711, las demás construcciones tienen sus accesos una vez dentro de la Plaza.

En la porción Centro-Oeste contamos con cuatro terrazas (T736, T737, T738, T739) de las cuales sólo la primera de ellas forma parte de la Plaza de El Caracol. Está (T736) corre de Norte a Sur y cuenta con 26 m de largo y aproximadamente un metro de alto. En su porción central presenta un acceso de un metro de ancho, el cual es el único acceso hacia las terrazas superiores. Vale la pena mencionar que se localiza un círculo de piedra adosado al muro de esta terraza (la 10), muy cerca del acceso, pero que se localiza en la superficie de la plaza de El Caracol. En la superficie de esta terraza se identificaron cuatro círculos de piedra de no más de 3 m de diámetro (c/u), que son las siguientes: 3, 4, 5 y la 6. Como dato interesante debemos mencionar que una quinta construcción, que es en realidad un circulo de piedra, se encuentra adosada al muro de la T737 pegada al acceso hacia esta terraza (Figura 13.2), pero como se localizó fuera del área inmediata de investigación no se le otorgo un número de construcción.

Posteriormente le sigue la T737 de 51 m de largo y una altura variable de un metro en su porción Sur y de más de dos metros en su porción Norte. La forma de esta terraza es semicircular, siguiendo la forma del basamento o afloramiento rocoso. Al igual que la terraza anterior presenta un único acceso en su porción central, el cual nos permite acceder a las terrazas superiores. Dentro de esta terraza identificamos tres círculos de piedra, dos de ellos de tamaño pequeño y uno de tamaño mediano, de más de 3 m de diámetro y con muros de cerca de 1 m de alto. A estos elementos constructivos no se les dio número de construcción por encontrarse fuera del área de investigación. Por la porción Sur de esta terraza contamos con la T738 de tan sólo 5 m de largo por 80 cm de alto y en la cual no se localizó ninguna construcción. Arriba de esta se localiza la T739 de 15 m de largo y de altura variable ya que no se logro restaurar. Sin embargo parece ser que en su porción central cuenta con un acceso, lo cual nos muestra un patrón de construcción y de una restricción de acceso.

Finalmente, por la ladera Sur del cerro, contamos con cuatro terrazas (T715, T740, T716 y la T712). La primera de ellas (T715) cuenta con una longitud de más de 60 m de largo y una altura variable de uno a 1.50 m. Esta terraza cuenta con dos accesos hacia el interior de esta terraza: uno al Oeste y otro al Este. El acceso Oeste es la culminación de una vereda o camino proveniente de otras áreas "habitacionales" ubicadas en la porción central de la ladera Sur del sitio. El acceso del lado Este presenta una vereda hacia la porción inferior del cerro y también se comunica con el acceso anterior.

En la porción terminal de esta terraza, por su lado Este (Figura 13.2), se identificó el comienzo de otra vereda que comunica hacia otra área "habitacional" ubicada en la porción Este del sitio. De esta manera tenemos que de esta terraza parten "caminos" o veredas con las distintas áreas de ocupación en la porción superior del cerro; hasta aquí el acceso entre estas áreas es relativamente libre.

Es importante mencionar que al igual que en la mayoría de las demás terrazas se localizó una construcción (24) cercana a uno de los accesos, curiosamente con el que comunica con la porción inferior del sitio.

Dentro de esta terraza se identificaron cinco construcciónes de las cuales tres son círculos de piedra, la 16, 23 y la 24; las otras dos son estructuras rectangulares (22 y 1). La 22 se localizó muy erosionada y sólo se conserva el muro Este, mientras que de los otros sólo se identifican alineamientos de piedra. A diferencia de las demás construcciones, en el interior de ésta se localizó un metate. Lo anterior nos estaría indicando que se trata, posiblemente, de un área de preparación de alimentos, aunque no se localizaron restos de fogón o de otro tipo de evidencias que nos confirmen esta idea. La segunda estructura rectangular es la 1, ubicada en la porción Oeste de la terraza. Esta se localizó en mejor estado de preservación que la anterior pero no presentó gran evidencia de materiales.

Posteriormente se localiza la T740 que se ubica en la porción Oeste del área de investigación, con una longitud de más de 29 m de largo y una altura que va de un metro, en su porción Oeste, a cerca de tres metros en la esquina Este. No presenta entrada o acceso como las anteriores terrazas. Para acceder a su interior es por medio de la T736 ó desde la plaza de El Caracol, de donde en la esquina suroeste sale una vereda que comunica con está. En esta terraza se identificó un segundo muro de contención, de cerca de 2 m de grosor, que comienza en la porción Este de la terraza, dobla la esquina y se pierde a los 8 m. Esta obra incompleta nos sugiere un proceso de expansión de la superficie de la terraza que sugiere el momento de abandono y/o el colapsamiento social del sitio. En la superficie de esta terraza no se identificó ninguna construcción salvo una posible alineación de piedras de gran tamaño en forma semicircular.

Posteriormente contamos con la T716, de cerca de 62 m de longitud por 1 m de altura aproximadamente. Esta terraza delimita la Plaza de El Caracol por su lado Sur, y cuenta con sólo un acceso de cerca de un metro en la porción central. Este nos lleva muy cerca de la estructura de El Caracol sin dar libre acceso hacia la Plaza ya que por un lado hay que flanquear la construcción 21 y por el otro lado un "acceso delimitado" por la construcción El Caracol A y unas piedras de gran tamaño (cuyo propósito desconocemos). A un lado del acceso, por la porción Este, se identifica un alineamiento de piedras que puede ser la continuación de la esquina o del patrón que ya se había percibido anteriormente, en la que se localiza una construcción cerca de cada uno de los accesos a manera de "posta." Flanqueando este acceso se localizó un metate en un piedra de grandes dimensiones (50 cm X 40 cm X 60 cm), del que desconocemos su uso o el porque se localiza en la entrada (Figura 13.2).

Sobre esta terraza se identificaron siete construcciones de las cuales dos de ellas son El Caracol y el cuarto pegado a éste. La 10 que se localiza pegada al muro de la T736 (cerca del acceso); la 21 es la construcción que se decidió que no pertenece a El Caracol; y los círculos de piedra 1 y 1.1 de pequeñas dimensiones (cerca de un metro cuadrado de área) que consideramos pudieron haber fungido como área de almacenamiento. La 14 se localizó en malas condiciones en la esquina Este de la T716 que curiosamente flanquea la entrada de un acceso lateral cuya vereda comunica con otra área en la porción Este de del Área A con la Plaza de El Caracol.

Finalmente contamos con la T712, con una longitud de 16 m y aproximadamente 80 cm de altura. Por su ubicación no presenta "accesos" como tal. En su superficie se identificaron dos círculos de piedra, trece de pequeñas dimensiones y dos de gran tamaño. En esta porción del área no se lograron identificar accesos o barreras arquitectónicas, pero es el punto de mayor altura dentro de esta área por lo que si uno se encuentra ubicado en el otro extremo, no es posible percibir que es lo que sucede dentro de la Plaza de El Caracol.

De esta manera tenemos que la Plaza de El Caracol se encuentra delimitada por la T791, en su extremo Norte, con sólo un acceso. La T736 en su extremo Oeste cuenta con sólo un accesomientras que la T716 en su extremo Sur también cuentacon sólo un acceso. Finalmente, el extremo Este que se encuentra limitado por un muro en la porción sur, y cuenta con un acceso. La porción central, por ser el punto más alto del área se consideró como una barrera natural. De tal manera contamos con un área de cerca de 390 m^2 de espacio libre para realizar diversas actividades, y cuya superficie debió haberse encontrado mejor nivelada que en la actualidad.

Otro aspecto interesante es que cualquier actividad que se realice al interior de la Plaza no se aprecia si uno se encuentra afuera de los límites descritos anteriormente, salvo aquellos ubicados en el extremo Oeste que se encuentran en la base del pico central. Por otro lado, desde esta área es posible apreciar la actividad de la mayoría del sitio.

En cuanto a los accesos, es posible apreciar que, se encuentran bastante limitados y, por lo tanto, podemos inferir que también bastante restringidos. Ademas el hecho de localizar un patrón, en el sentido de que en la mayoría de los accesos se localiza una construcción muy cerca de ellos, podría interpretarse como especies de "postas" o de controladores de acceso.

Conclusiones

Desde el principio del proyecto se considero a el Área A del Cerro de Trincheras como un área especial dentro de la distribución social del sitio. Simplemente, el hecho de localizarse en la porción superior implica status y un mayor esfuerzo a la hora de la construcción de los distintos elementos constructivos, así como la realización de las distintas actividades que pudieron llevarse a cabo.

Como se mencionó desde uninicio, se contempló la exploración de una porción de esta área para poder determinar mejor el desarrollo cultural del sitio (y todo lo que ello implica) y poder comparar esta área con las demás y determinar diferencias y semejanzas a nivel social y material. El área explorada se escogió de manera arbitraria por localizarse en ella la estructura de El Caracol, y de esta manera poder determinar su importancia dentro del sitio.

En el transcurso de la temporada de campo y de todas las actividades que se llevaron a cabo, nos pudimos percatar que esta área se trataba de algo más que una simple área de ocupación o habitacional. Lo anterior fue de suma importancia para la comprensión social del sitio ya que pasó de ser un grupo de agricultores incipientes, con caza- recolección, a un grupo más complejo socialmente en el que se comenzaba a establecer una estratificación social y elaboración de estructuras ceremoniales.

Una vez concluida la temporada de campo, se le denominó a esta área la Plaza de El Caracol por considerar que cuenta con los elementos arquitectónicos descritos anteriormente y en el que El Caracol jugó un papel relevante. Es a su alrededor que se realiza la plaza donde se localiza perfectamente delimitado, con accesos bastante restringidos, los cuales pudieron haber estado controlados.

Cronológicamente, carecemos de marcadores confiables como carbono 14 o pruebas arqueomagnéticas. Como se mencionó anteriormente, no se localizó ningún fogón o algún fragmento considerable de carbón para tal efecto, por lo que la temporalidad de esta área es por correlación cerámica, evidencias arqueológicas y comparación con otras áreas dentro del sitio. De la misma manera, el análisis estratigráfico de las distintas áreas excavadas y del análisis de los elementos constructivos del área, podemos inferir que su proceso de desarrollo del área fue la siguiente.

Primera Fase. Antes que ningún otro elemento, se edifico la estructura de El Caracol. Lo anterior se basa en el hecho de que los muros de El Caracol desplantan desde la roca madre y no de los suelos nivelados de las terrazas. Además de que se contó con una capa más antigua que el resto de las demás estructuras que parece indicarnos que se usó por una temporada relativamente larga. Por otro lado, la evidencia sugiere que esta estructura se edificó en un área relativamente nivelada de manera natural y no por la acción del hombre.

En este periodo de tiempo pudieron haberse realizando actividades ceremoniales, pero desconocemos si el Área A se encontraba habitada, y si este era el caso por sector social.

Segunda Fase. Se realizo la construcción de las distintas terrazas con las cuales se nivela una gran extensión de terreno que dio forma a la Plaza. La edificación de las terrazas no sólo sirvieron para nivelar el terreno, sino para delimitar, restringir y controlar el acceso a la plaza. Al juzgar por las evidencias arqueológicas, estos elementos constructivos se realizaron en un sólo momento constructivo.

Tercera Fase. Se realizo la construcción de los círculos de piedra y de las demás áreas de “habitación”. Por la evidencia arqueológica y los análisis estratigráficos, consideramos que esta fase no debió haber durado mucho, ya que no presento evidencia de ello.

Cuarta Fase. Abandono del sitio. Podemos mencionar que al momento de esta actividad, el área se encontraba en proceso de expansión o por lo menos es lo que se infiere por la ampliación inconclusa de la T740.

De acuerdo a lo anterior, sin contar con la ocupación temprana de El Caracol, tenemos que es un área que se ocupo relativamente durante muy poco tiempo. Lo anterior se refleja en la cantidad de materiales localizados a lo largo de la temporada, que en comparación con otras áreas, ubicadas en la porción media y baja del sitio Cerro de Trincheras, fueron cantidades mucho menores.

Por otro lado, se esperaba identificar mediante el análisis de los materiales una diferenciación social, pero no fue así. Esto se desea las cantidades localizadas asi como la calidad de los materiales, los cuales no se diferenciaban del resto de las áreas. Podríamos mencionar que en algunos casos se localizaron menos materiales de carácter suntuoso que en otras áreas en las que no se esperaba localizar dichos materiales.

Dentro del tipo de materiales a los que nos referimos se encuentran restos de lozas decoradas o de origen foráneo y concha trabajada (y sin trabajar) que son de los materiales considerados como marcadores sociales o los que podrían fungir como tales. Vale la pena mencionar que en el Área A si se localizaron restos de estos materiales pero no en las cantidades que esperábamos encontrar. De hecho se localizaron muy pequeñas cantidades que sólo nos permiten inferir su presencia en el área. Esta ausencia puede deberse a múltiples factores como al corto periodo ocupacional del área, el no haber excavado contextos de deposición de materiales de desecho, la recolección de material por parte de otros grupos humanos posterior al abandono del sitio (tanto Prehispánica como moderna) y la erosión del área.

El análisis de la distribución de los materiales dentro del Área A nos indicó que los espacios, comprendidos en el interior de las construcciones soló se utilizaron para realizar actividades que difícilmente dejaron rastros materiales. La estructura de El Caracol y la 22 presentaron un mayor número de materiales al resto de las demás y pueden ser consideradas como excepción. Por otro lado, la evidencia material nos permite inferir que en los espacios abiertos se están realizando la mayoría de las actividades como preparación de alimentos, consumo de los mismos, áreas de trabajo y socialización.

De tal manera concluimos que el área de La Plaza de El Caracol fue un espacio restringido en el cual se pudieron haber llevado a cabo ceremonias y/o festividades. También actividades como la planeación urbana se dieron alrededor de la construcción de El Caracol, área que fue utilizada durante la última fase de ocupación del sitio y por un período de tiempo muy corto, posiblemente menos de 50 años. Esté fue suficiente para dejar la evidencia material de que el desarrollo social del sitio Cerro de Trincheras había comenzado un proceso de distinción social y de distribución de los espacios que hasta el momento no tiene paralelo en ningún sitio de la Tradición Trincheras en la región.

Para finalizar, el análisis de los patrones constructivos y de los elementos de construcción no presentan ninguna evidencia de alguna influencia exterior o de la participación de algún otro grupo cultural, sino todo lo contrario. La evidencia material sugiere un desarrollo local, acoplado a las características físicas y a los materiales que ofrece el sitio. Vale la pena mencionar que en ningún momento se localizó alguna evidencia de construcciones realizadas en adobe o de "tierra," que sería un indicador de alguna "influencia" de grupos humanos de la región de Chihuahua o del suroeste de los Estados Unidos.

www.ingramcontent.com/pod-product-compliance
Lightning Source LLC
Chambersburg PA
CBHW052149280326
41926CB00110B/4390

9781889747897